OOIS'94

OOIS'94

1994 International Conference on
Object Oriented Information Systems
19–21 December 1994, London

Proceedings

Edited by

D. Patel, Y. Sun and S. Patel
South Bank University, London, UK

Presented by

Sponsored by

SOUTH BANK UNIVERSITY
·LONDON·

Springer-Verlag
London Berlin Heidelberg New York
Paris Tokyo Hong Kong
Barcelona Budapest

Dilip Patel, Yuan Sun, Shushma Patel

School of Computing, Information Systems and Mathematics,
South Bank University,
103 Borough Road,
London, SE1 0AA

ISBN-13: 978-3-540-19927-4   e-ISBN-13: 978-1-4471-3016-1
DOI: 10.1007/978-1-4471-3016-1

Typesetting: Camera ready by authors

34/3830–543210 Printed on acid-free paper

Contents

KNOWLEDGEBASES

SOFTWARE DEVELOPMENT

INTERFACE DESIGN

OBJECT DATABASES

DISTRIBUTED DATABASE SYSTEMS

OBJECT-ORIENTED DATABASES AND APPLICATIONS

Programme Committee

General Chairman

Misbah Deen UK

Programme Co-Chairmen

Keith Jeffery   UK   **Dilip Patel**   UK

Members

Motoei Azuma	Japan	**Michele Missikoff**	Italy
Terry Baylis	UK	**Maria Orlowka**	Australia
Elisa Bertino	Italy	**Mike Papazoglou**	Australia
Jim Bieman	USA	**Norman Paton**	UK
Chris Clare	UK	**Colette Rolland**	France
Klaus Dittrich	Switzerland	**Felix Saltor**	Spain
Jane Grimson	Ireland	**Tony Stockman**	UK
Peter Gray	UK	**Yuan Sun**	UK
Alan Hayes	UK	**Yannis Vassiliou**	Greece
Guo-Jie Li	China	**Robin Whitty**	UK
Gillian Lovegrove	UK	**Roberto Zicari**	Germany

Organising Committee

Chairman

Yuan Sun, South Bank University, UK

Members

Antoinette Dixon	SBU, UK	**Shushma Patel**	SBU, UK
Delores Broni	SBU, UK	**George Ubakanma**	SBU, UK
Francis Nwofor	SBU, UK		

Additional Referees

M. Bush, D. Dalcher, Q. C. Dang, G. Elliott, Y. Guo, N. Hillary, M. Hooper, J. Jones, P. Kumari, D. Langley, R. McNaughton, F. Nwofor, S. Patel, S. Polovina, P. Schleifer, D. Webster, S. Windmill

PREFACE

This volume contains the papers presented at the International Conference on Object Oriented Information Systems OOIS'94, held at South Bank University, London, December 19 - 21, 1994.

In response to our call for papers, a total 85 papers from 24 different countries were submitted. Each paper was evaluated by at least two Program Committee members and an additional reviewer. Together, we selected 41 papers for presentation at the conference and inclusion in the Proceedings. Also included are the keynote addresses by *Peter Gray* and *Michael Jackson*. The other submissions were recommended for presentation in the poster sessions.

Peter Gray, our invited speaker, evaluates the problems of object-oriented systems and data independence by looking at how object oriented database applications are failing to perceive its benefits, and instead rely too much on encapsulation. He suggests alternative kinds of object storage to preserve data independence.

The second invited speaker, *Michael Jackson* describes a way of solving problems, by focusing directly on the problems themselves, their components and structures and on the relationships between the problem and the solution method. He discusses a particular view of the role of object-orientation in software development.

The papers included in the proceedings consisted of various aspects of object-oriented modelling concepts, object-oriented databases and their applications. Eleven papers were accepted in the modelling sessions, these address the different issues of modelling aspects in the object environment. *Darlington and Guo* present the logical formalism of the actor-based concurrent object-oriented computation in terms of the deduction in linear logic. This work explores the importance of logic and other formal notations from the aspects of logical semantics. The systems development process point of view is addressed by *Moynihan,* who evaluates the relative effectiveness of functional-decomposition and object-orientation as paradigms for client/developer communications. He concludes that the functional-decomposition is superior to the object-model on several important attributes.

There were four sessions on databases; they discuss the problems of different aspects of databases, *viz.* in distributed environment; active and temporal environments; knowledgebased environment and applications. *Murphy and Grimson* describe the formal model of a multi-database dictionary by using Z notation. They discuss the issues involved in schema evolution for federated databases, new types of user privileges and their meanings, and the characterisation of legacy systems along three related dimensions. *Conrad, Gogolla and Herzig* explore the problems associated with specification and derived data by employing a designer language for specifying structure and behaviour of objects in information systems.

The papers in the hypermedia session deal directly with compound documents. *Pinon, Richez and Flory* describe a support system for the co-operative edition of multimedia documents with regards to high level submitted document processing by applying the constraints to quality assurance.

Acknowledgements

During the eighteen months of preparation, from the first call for papers through to the setting up of the committees, the acceptance of papers and the organisation, there was an increasing load put on all the people involved. Many people contributed towards the success of OOIS'94. We would like to acknowledge everyone concerned for their help, advice, co-operation and hard work. We would like to thank the Head of the School for Computing, Information Systems and Mathematics, Terry Baylis for his support and encouragement which enabled us to organise the conference. We express our deepest gratitude to Misbah Deen and Keith Jeffery for all their guidance and advice throughout the preparation. Our special thanks go to Gillian Lovegrove, Tony Stockman, Jane Grimson, Chris Clare and Robin Whitty, without whose tireless efforts this conference would have been impossible.

All the programme committee members deserve our thanks for the extraordinary work they did in the refereeing and selection of papers. The research students and staff from the Centre for Information and Office Systems deserve a special thanks for all the work they did behind the scenes and for being available whenever required. Akmal Chaudhri and Fintan Culwin are acknowledged for their assistance in publicising the conference. Our gratitude goes to the organising committee.

We would like to acknowledge the support from DATA ACCESS and particularly South Bank University.

Last but not least we would like to thank Springer-Verlag for their efficient help in the preparation of these proceedings.

Dilip Patel
Co-chairman of the Program Committee

Yuan Sun
Chairman of the Organising Committee

Shushma Patel
Co-ordinator of the Conference

London, October 1994

KEYNOTE ADDRESSES

Object-Oriented Systems and Data Independence

Peter M.D. Gray and Graham J.L. Kemp

Department of Computing Science, University of Aberdeen, King's College,
Aberdeen, Scotland, AB9 2UE

Abstract. We discuss the important database theme of Data Independence and how object oriented database applications are failing to perceive its benefits, and instead put too much reliance on encapsulation. The P/FDM object-oriented database is based on the functional data model and has a modular design based on data independence, which allows alternative kinds of object storage to be used. In this work, a relational database management system has been used to provide object storage, and we describe how the data access routines have been implemented. The principal query language used with P/FDM is Daplex, which is normally translated to Prolog, including calls to the basic data access routines. The query is optimised to minimise the expected number of calls. This gives very general method execution and pattern matching search. However, much better performance can be achieved for simpler data-intensive Daplex queries against a relational storage module by translating these to a single SQL statement, which is possible because of data independence.

1 Introduction

The well known "Third Generation Database System Manifesto" [20] demands that object-oriented database systems, if they wish to be truly advanced database systems, must maintain the major contributions of second generation systems. This is particularly true of data independence. Data independence originally came out of the ANSI-SPARC three layer model [1]. It demanded that database systems be constructed so that they provided both logical and physical data independence. Logical data independence provides that the conceptual schema must be able to *evolve* without changing external application programs. Only view definitions and mappings may need changing, for example to replace access to a stored field by access to a derived field calculated from others in the revised schema. One should also be able to change constraints in the conceptual schema without needing to recompile the external schemas [4]. In this paper we are mainly concerned with physical data independence which provides something different. It allows one to substitute a *different physical storage schema* for an existing one, and to reload the data into the new form of storage, without any change either to the conceptual schema or application programs. In general, this is done in order to change access paths or to install new indexes or to re-cluster information in order to overcome performance degradation as the database evolves. Much of this is done in modern relational systems, and some of it can be done without dumping and reloading the data, which is obviously an undesirable process.

The Third Generation Manifesto demands that "essentially all programatic access to a database should be through a non-procedural high level access language". The reason for this is to make it possible to have physical data independence. If, instead, the programmer builds into their program a sequence of explicit pointer dereferences to follow a navigation path, and one wishes to reorganise the physical storage, then it is almost impossible to find all the pointer dereferences in application code and change them! This, indeed was the main reason why people moved away from Codasyl and network databases, even though it was hard to achieve similar performance with relational systems. The driving force was the need to enforce data independence so as to cope with schema evolution!

One crucial component was a query optimiser. This made it possible for an inexpert user to write complicated queries over sets and relationships and have it run as fast as if coded by an expert programmer who was familiar with all the alternative paths through the data. Furthermore, if the storage schema changed, then the optimiser would generate new code to match it. The optimiser could do this because it was a privileged component of the system and could see details of the storage schema, and also statistics on cardinalities of object classes and the nature of indexes which were no concern of the end user. Thus data independence made possible the use of optimisers which, in turn, made it possible for general users to write far more complex queries.

2   C++ Lacks Data Independence

Let us now look at one of the best known object-oriented languages C++, which also has a number of object-oriented database vendors supporting it. The first thing to realise is that these databases are much more concerned with evolution of program code than with evolution of databases and schema. Thus the earliest databases to appear were aimed at providers of program support environments for C and C++. Many of the "objects" they were designed to hold were actually pieces of program source code or else maintenance data or references to related versions. The facilities were to do with maintaining and extending the collection of methods around classes, and with using inheritance and specialisation facilities of object-oriented programming in order to save rewriting code. Thus a lot of effort was devoted to providing persistence for the code and little attention was given to schema evolution. Early implementations took the approach of adding extra methods to selected classes that would write instances to disc on commitment and read them back transparently on pointer dereference. This was a convenience to the programmer, but it meant that there was no distinction between the conceptual schema and the storage schema! Thus the programmer still used the standard C++ syntax for operations on objects with their array and record and bitstring components, regardless of whether they were long term persistent. Instead of dealing with higher-level concepts such as entities and relationships the programmer is down at the level of operations on intimate details of record structures. Under such circumstances, it is not easy to change the storage schema independent of application code.

When object-oriented people are questioned about this, they usually express surprise that anything is amiss, and say that it can all be dealt with by using encapsulation! This, we believe, is a serious misconception. It is true that method code has to access objects in other classes by a uniform "message send" syntax which hides the nature of the storage, as one would expect with an Abstract Data Type. However, methods defined on the object class itself can see the internal structure of the object in detail and are coded up accordingly. These methods are not part of any storage schema – they are almost invariably part of the application code. If one considers any one object class implementation, then indeed it is possible to change the internal storage definition (e.g. from an array to a linked list or ordered collection) and to rewrite the class methods so that the program as a whole runs as before without changes to any other classes. However, this is not data independence! In order to have real data independence one needs to restructure the code as an integrated collection of abstract data types which faithfully represent some higher level data model, and which all change in a consistent way. Usually there is a consistent mapping from the collection of classes so that each one is mapped to the storage schema in the same way. For example, objects may all be represented as compact records, or they may all be held as associations between object identifier, function name and data value, or in some other way. In more advanced systems classes may be partitioned between different storage schemas, so that one collection is mapped one way and another collection is mapped another way; this is the scheme we use in P/FDM as described below. The crucial point is that the mapping is consistent over a collection of classes, instead of being done in an *ad hoc* fashion by the programmer so that even a privileged central management system cannot easily change it!

Much of this may seem foreign to the normal object-oriented programmer who does not have long-term persistent data. They may have fixed tables of data that are read in from sequential files, with additional data read in from menus and dialogue boxes. Their program may then create instances of many and complex classes, but these are all forgotten when the program finishes. In such a case it is easy just to use the encapsulation facilities of the classes in order to change the representation of an individual class as explained above; there is little advantage in full data independence. A more common thing is to read in structured data from a text file with a parser, and to build recursive tree structures. Once again there is no need for data independence if results are just output as a text file. The real advantage of data independence only comes when one has to selectively update a very large file. This is the case when one has to parse many megabytes of text files, taking a long time, and possibly causing thrashing of virtual memory storing the objects. Worse still, one may only access or update selectively very few of the created objects, before writing the entire file out again. Smalltalk systems partly got over this by allowing one to store a saved state of the virtual memory at the end of each session, which saves recreating it from an updated file. However, this reduces one to a single user database, since there is no way to merge two saved states created by independent users.

3 Query Optimisation

The use of declarative high-level query languages is only slowly being accepted by object database vendors. The ODMG-93 standard [3] proposes an object query language, OQL, where variables range over object identifiers, and which can return results as a bag of newly created objects. For example:

```
select couple(student:x.name, professor:z.name)
from   x in Students
       y in x.takes
       z in y.taught_by
where  z.rank = "full professor"
```

Here x ranges over a named class of student objects, whilst y ranges over a subset of course objects related to x and z ranges over a subset of professor objects related to y. The result objects are constructed by the two-place constructor "couple" and thus belong to class "couple". There is also an existential quantifier. For example the last line of the query above could be replaced by:

```
where  z.rank = "full professor" and
       exists p in x.takes: p.title = "Calculus"
```

This would select students who took calculus courses and also took courses (possibly calculus) given by full professors. One of the stated assumptions is that "OQL can be easily optimized by virtue of its declarative nature"!

The context in which OQL is to be used is not clear. Presumably it can be used stand-alone, but it seems more likely that it is intended for use embedded in C++ code, just in the way that extended SQL dialects get embedded in C. Several examples are given in which bags of objects are assigned as results to C++ variables, while input to the query is taken from C++ variables with their names distinguished by a dollar prefix. Presumably the intention is to get some kind of local query optimisation in the case of computation of a bag over a number of large sets. However, there is no concept of global query optimisation. The programmer is quite free to mix OQL with other pieces of C++ code which use explicit paths in a fashion that prevents data independence. This is very different from relational systems where the only way to access tuples or update the database is through SQL callouts. The programmer may build any fancy data structures they please to hold intermediate results, but the only way of making these persistent, or to access related components, is to call out to SQL. This indeed is what [20] advocates in order to achieve data independence.

The big problem with query optimisation for OODB applications is that much of the time it is not "query-only". Instead there is a mix of updates with data access. Now, any kind of update changes the state of the database and thus destroys the referential transparency of set expressions referring to the data. Evaluating the same expression before and after the update can produce different results. Thus it is not possible to adopt the strategy used in the ASTRID project [8], where pieces of relational algebra representing subqueries are combined together to allow overall optimisation of a large relational algebra expression through the use of rewrite rules. This can give very significant performance gains through eliminating repeated evaluation of common sub-expressions. A similar technique is used by Jiao *et al.* [12] to expand method code used to compute derived values where the methods are called from within a query in our P/FDM database. However, none of this is useful if between each expression or method call there are a number of updates, or else assignments that may side-effect parameter values.

There is a further problem with query optimisation in object-oriented systems which is to do with strong encapsulation of methods. The system referred to above [12] relies on the optimiser as a privileged component of the system being able to "reveal" method definitions. This is not usually possible with a piece of compiled C++, although source-level debuggers are able to do it. There is also a difference of philosophy between systems following the ANSI-SPARC architecture [1] in having a conceptual schema, and standard object-oriented encapsulation. The difference is that encapsulation is about hiding methods so completely that details of other methods called and object classes accessed or updated during method execution are not available to an optimiser, whereas databases are about sharing rather than hiding, so that the conceptual schema reveals all the properties and relationships of stored objects. In consequence, alternative paths can be explored and the side-effects of updates foreseen. A further complication with optimisation in object-oriented systems is that they are far more cpu-bound than database systems. Early SQL optimisers could make the assumption that most time was spent in disc access or in processing large sets, and this could then be estimated by various models. In object-oriented systems not only are methods encapsulated but the mean time (and variance) in execution is unknown and needs to be allowed for. This again makes it difficult to do global query optimisation.

There are signs that object database vendors are beginning to recognise the need for conceptual data models and data independence. The ODMG-93 standard includes a classical data description language, ODL, which describes the object types and property types and relationship types at a fairly high level, together with keys which guarantee unique external identifiers (see Sect. 5) for persistent objects. They wish to use this for the classic purpose of integrating schemas from various sources, and it is intended to map easily across to the STEP/EXPRESS standard and the new ANSI SQL3 standard. They also say that it aids portability by allowing applications "to run with minimal modification on a variety of ODBMS's" or even to run with a mixed language implementation. This is indeed one of the main advantages of data independence. However, they have only gone part of the way. Instead of forcing data independence through the use of a standard data manipulation language (which is the SQL approach), they allow a variety of manipulation languages (or just API) depending on the host language. Encouragingly, they state that their ODL/manipulation language combination "does not address the clustering or memory management issues associated with the stored physical representation of objects or access structures like indices used to accelerate physical retrieval". They then admit that "In an ideal world these would be transparent to the programmer. In the real world they are not"! Thus the programmer is allowed an additional set of constructs called "physical pragmas" to give hints to the storage manager.

Here once again we see the Jekyll-and-Hyde nature of C++! The language is an awkward compromise between high-level concepts and low-level performance tricks. Where Smalltalk chooses to do things cleanly and in a high-level way with a garbage-collector, C++ takes a short cut to do without. Increased performance is purchased at the risk of some very nasty bugs. There is a genuine tension here which is caused by customer demand for instant interactive feedback and very good real time performance. Some applications demand that one should almost cache the entire database in main memory and use pointer-swizzling techniques [21] for ultra-fast navigation. This almost certainly means that one is dealing with a single-user database, or else one has to lock large numbers of objects over long transactions. The approach of Stonebraker *et al.* [20] is to say that performance is all dictated by how the buffer pool is handled, and whether it is held on the client (possibly in screen format) or held on the server. They regard this as a matter for a special purpose DBMS implementation, but see no need to compromise with data independence. Certainly, once an object-oriented system starts to access a database through a client-server architecture, there is no excuse for not using a high level query and update language, and Stonebraker *et al.* [20] cite evidence that working at a lower level is actually less efficient.

4 Integrity Constraints in Methods

There is another way in which classic object-oriented encapsulation does not make good use of a conceptual schema. This concerns the enforcement of integrity constraints. Since an object can only be updated through its methods, it follows that the programmer must put validation checks directly in their source code. This has all sorts of snags, which are well known from the early database systems. Firstly a programmer may forget to make the check. Secondly different programmers may enforce the check in different ways, making it hard to maintain and update if the constraint has to change. Finally, there is the issue of redundant code which is copied many times in different methods. A much better solution, as advocated by Nijssen [17] is to move constraints from application programs into the compiled schema, so that they can be enforced centrally. In SQL systems this is done by storing triggered procedures with the database module. This fits well with a relational architecture but is not so suitable for object-orientation.

A better solution for object-oriented systems is that given in [6] and [2]. Here, the Colan language is used to express semantic constraints declaratively against a semantic data model as defined below. Constraints can contain a mixture of existential, universal and even numerical quantifiers over members of stored object classes. Examples from [6] are:

```
exist at most 3 r in research_assistant of lecturer.
```

```
forall l in lecturer
  forall r in research_assistant of l
    research_interests of l = research_interests of tutor of r
```

These are semantic integrity constraints that restrict the state of objects depending on their own properties and the properties of related objects. They act as invariants that have to be true in both old and new states. The constraint applies not only to lecturers, but to all specialisations of class lecturer; it is inherited in a way that cannot be overridden. Instead of relying on the programmer, triggers are automatically code-generated from the declarative definitions such as those above and attached to the class descriptors of all relevant classes. Thus one has to trap updates not just to lecturers, but to persons who are their research assistants or tutors. Updates to other properties and other classes are not affected, but a single update may trigger checks on more than one constraint. The crucial point is that the constraint can be selectively removed by sending a message to the constraint object, which can remove fragments of code without recompilation. This overcomes the three objections given above to having validation hand-coded into methods by programmers. However, it is only possible because our system is written using a semantic data model which enforces data independence and maintains a conceptual schema.

It is interesting to compare the Colan approach with that of ODE, an object database implemented in C++ [11]. They have proposed a language CIAO++ which expresses constraints with quantifiers, but using C++ syntax for record selection and boolean expressions. They do indeed generate triggers from this through a C++ precompiler. Since they do not use an incremental compiler with garbage collection, they cannot selectively remove constraints except by recompiling. They do have interesting proposals for constraint transformation and optimisation. However, the difficulties of using C++ show up in the way that they have to check every constraint at the end of any object state change, even though an understanding of the semantics of the update would allow one to eliminate many of the checks at compile time.

5 P/FDM - Combining Object-orientation with Data Independence

We shall now describe P/FDM [9], an object-oriented database whose architecture is based on data independence, and look at the advantages that this brings.

P/FDM was originally based on Shipman's functional data model FDM [19], and uses an extended version of his functional data language Daplex.

The basic concepts in the P/FDM database are entities and functions. Entities are used to represent conceptual objects, while functions represent the properties of an object. Functions are used to model both scalar attributes and relationships, and may be single-valued or multi-valued. Entity classes can be arranged in subtype-hierarchies, with subclasses inheriting the properties of their superclass, as well as having their own specialised properties.

Since Shipman's model incorporated subtype inheritance and had functions that return references to entities, it was natural to implement it by assigning unique object identifiers to entity instances, which lasted unchanged as long as they existed. The storage location and format of an object might change over its lifetime. Its schema might evolve to include (or lose) properties and relationships, but its object identifier would never change.

In order to generalise FDM to be behaviourally object-oriented, we treat Daplex functions that derive data from object properties and relationships as methods and store them in the database with the class descriptor, so that they can be shared. Since we have a Prolog implementation it is convenient to hold these methods as source text and to consult them incrementally. We also have action methods [13], which allow one to change the state of objects through operations defined at conceptual schema level. These methods and operations are all parametrised in terms of object identifiers, and although they can call out to foreign code in C or Fortran for computation, there is no way to access the internal state of objects except by primitive operations on the data model which ensures data independence.

Another part of the data model concerns constraints on entity classes, which we can now generate from Colan descriptions. However, there are a number of structural constraints enforced by the data model implementation. An important one is a uniqueness constraint that allows us to identify an entity instance by a combination of one or more property values, which together formed a printable external identifier (or key). No two instances of the same class (or its subclasses) can share the same combination of values. The external identifier can also include the external identifiers of other entities related through single-valued relationships, and so some objects can be identified purely through knowledge of related objects, and not through any properties of their own.

Given this simple idea, we were able to write a bulk load utility [18] that takes data in the form of external identifiers of entities together with property values and relationship values, and uses it to add properties and relationships and extra relationship instances to existing entity instances by cross-relating them to other instances, loaded in the same run or previously. This has been invaluable, and since it is written in terms of conceptual schema primitives it works regardless of the kind of storage schema used. As an aside, it is surprising that the object database vendors do not provide it. It may be that they are more interested in persistent storage of procedures and their class descriptors, and assume that most objects will be created by running programs rather than coming in from external data and external databases. They also have the problem that the notion of external identifier is foreign to object-oriented programmers, who are used to creating objects without regard to their long-term persistence. However, external identifiers are now included in the ODMG-93 data language, but are not mandatory.

We should note that objects loaded into the database storage all use the internal object identifier that does not change, as does all query evaluation and method calls. The external identifier can actually change its value by having a property updated (provided uniqueness is preserved), unlike the prime key of a relational tuple. For example an object for a woman can change their surname property on getting married, but continue to be related to their parents through their unchanged internal object identifier. This shows one important difference between an object data model and the relational data model.

6 Storage Modules

The use of internal object identifiers allows us to store objects in a variety of ways, following the principle of physical data independence. We first implemented an extensible hash table which related an object identifier and a function name to its value or list of values (which may of course be object identifiers). This storage lacks the clustering property of B-tree or other object stores, but it has the vital associative property of relating so-called soft object identifiers, which cannot change, to locations on disc that vary in order to allow adaptation and reorganisation. It is also beautifully easy to add new properties and relationships, classes and subclasses, and new object instances, so that the schema can evolve. Deletion is equally simple, except that one has to avoid breaking referential integrity. In order to do this, we maintain an inverse of each declared relationship function, so that we keep lists of all objects referring to an object and can remove all cross-references before object deletion. Where an object uses the identifier of another object as part of its key, we delete the whole object and so on in cascade fashion. This is in order never to have null fields in keys, and it also implements some of part-whole relationship semantics, in that deleting a top level object representing the whole also deletes all of its parts.

A separate hash table is used to relate external identifiers to object identifiers. The maintenance of this table together with relationship inverses allows us to explore alternative navigation paths, which is done by our high level Daplex optimiser, written using Prolog for pattern matching [12]. The optimiser has a simple model of the storage which allows it to estimate the number of hash table accesses in order to try and minimise them.

Another form of storage that we use represents entities as Prolog term structures in main memory. This is a more clustered form of storage, and it uses Prolog's own hash tables for access. We use it for temporary storage of small numbers of objects in design transactions. These objects can contain object identifiers of objects in hash-table storage but there are no pointers in the reverse direction, since the objects are temporary. If such an identifier is found and followed to get its value then this is transparently brought in from disc, as in commercial ODBMS. However, the cacheing of objects brought in from disc relies currently on the Unix operating system rather than a special buffer pool, but this could be changed without difficulty. Temporary storage is used to capitalise on Prolog's ability to backtrack and to build alternative object networks until one is found that satisfies some goal or some set of design constraints. We can then commit this set of objects to persistent storage by copying them across at the end of a transaction [5].

More recently, we have developed ways to use a relational database (SYBASE) for object storage. Again, queries against this kind of storage look exactly like queries against other modules. Basically, we use one relational table for each entity class but we allocate an object identifier to each tuple to store in one column. Also, the values of some attributes may be object identifiers instead of being foreign keys as in the relational data model. We are able, nevertheless to make use of indexes on object identifier columns to give fast access. Thus we use a relational storage model, which has advantages of compatibility with external data and of handling very large volumes of data, but we do not use a relational data model!

The most interesting thing about the relational storage has been our adaptation of the optimiser. We started by using the Prolog code that works for hash table or main memory storage, and just changed the primitive routines so that they sent simple SQL queries to get related objects. However, this was a slow strategy for data intensive queries, so we then wrote a piece of Prolog that could recognise certain common kinds of Daplex query and turned them into a larger piece of SQL to be executed on the server. Effectively we were using special knowledge about the storage schema to pass more selection information to the SQL optimiser to apply at source, instead of waiting to filter returned data values. We were also avoiding the overheads on many penny packets. Where the code was more complex, particularly if it called out to a method stored in the database, the Prolog pre-optimiser would fail to recognise it, and the query would just be translated in the normal way, so we could still execute it. We shall now explore this way of using relational storage in more detail.

7 Mapping FDM onto Relational Tables

The Daplex language provides data definition statements for describing data according to the functional data model. Entity classes and functions are declared in a schema, and in P/FDM each section of schema has a header line stating what kind of storage module is used to store the data values described by the declarations. When a schema relating to data stored in a relational storage module is read in, the P/FDM system checks that the declarations are consistent with the FDM-relational mapping described below.

Each object class is stored in a table which has as its name the class name. In this table, each row represents an object instance, and each column stores the value of a single-valued function on the object, where the name of the column is also the name of the function. A vital point is that we add an additional column, called *oid*, which is used to store the object identifier, used internally to identify each instance. Thus it is necessary to reload existing relational data and to assign oid values, however, the original tables can be presented as views if necessary.

Consider the following Daplex data declaration statements which introduce a new entity class called *person* and two single-valued attributes (Fig. 1 shows the schema diagram corresponding to the declarations and queries given in this paper, and Fig. 2 shows the corresponding relational tables):

```
declare person ->> entity
declare forename(person) -> string
declare surname(person) -> string
```

In the corresponding relational module, we would have a table called person with three fields – *oid, forename* and *surname.*

Subclass-superclass relationships can also be modelled. For each subclass in a relational module, another table (or view) stores the values of single-valued attributes defined only on the subclass. Each row represents a subclass instance. Each subclass table also has an oid column, and the values stored in this column are a subset of the oid values in the superclass table. The following Daplex declaration introduces the class *student* as a subclass of *person*, and *undergrad* as a subclass of *student*. The *student* subclass has two specialised properties representing a student's year of study and faculty.

```
declare student ->> person
declare undergrad ->> student
declare year(student) -> integer
declare faculty(student) -> string
```

For these declarations, we would have a table called *student* with three fields – *oid, year* and *faculty*, and a table called *undergrad* with an *oid* field. If John Brown is a student, then there would be a row in the student table with oid value matching the oid value in the person table for John Brown. Additionally, if John Brown is an undergraduate, then there will also be an entry in the undergrad table with this oid value.

The values of single-valued relationships are stored in entity tables. Suppose we have classes called *course* and *section* which are related by a single-valued relationship called *has_course* defined on section.

```
declare has_course(section) -> course
```

In the *section* table, we will have a column called *has_course* and for each instance of section the object identifier of the related course will be stored in this field. This column can also be used to find the inverse of the *has_course* relationship (called *has_course_inv*). Given an instance of the class course, the sections of that

14

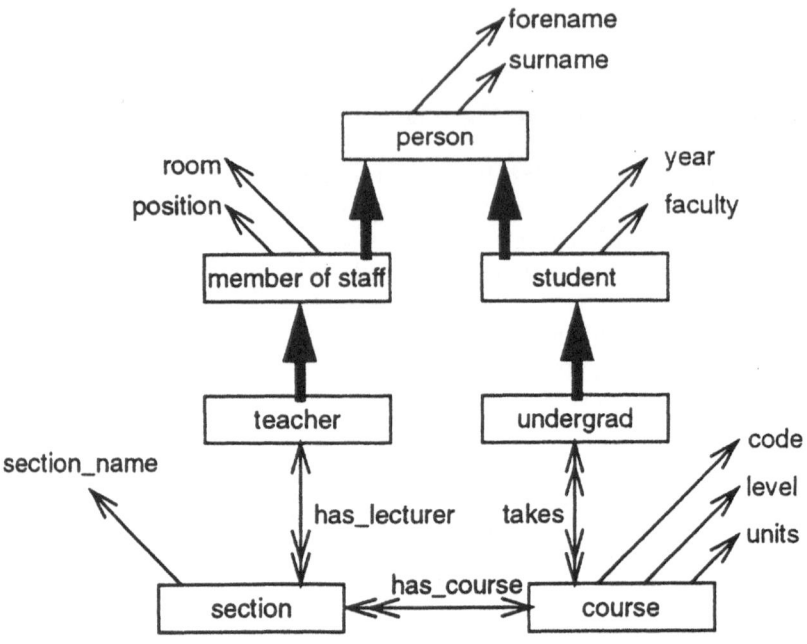

Fig. 1. Schema diagram. Object classes are represented by rectangular boxes. Labelled arrows represent relationships between objects. Thick arrows point from subclasses to their superclass.

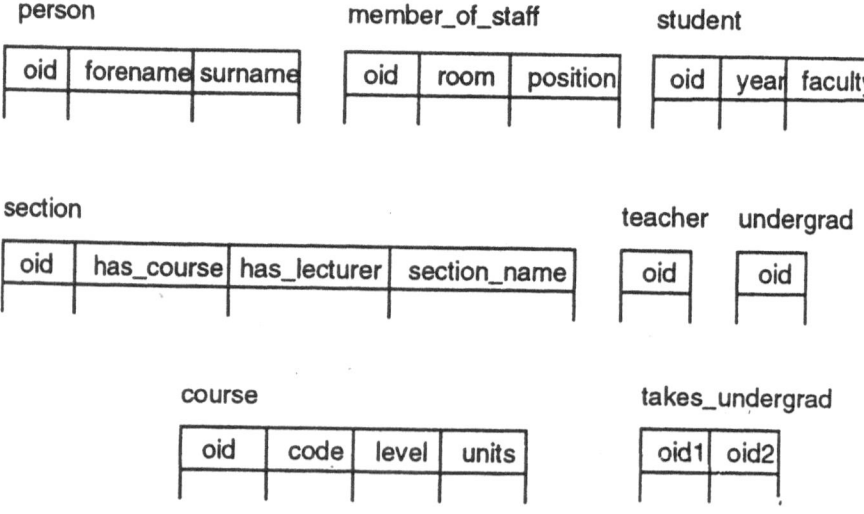

Fig. 2. Relational database tables corresponding to the schema shown in Fig. 1

course are those instances in the section table with the object identifier of the given course in the *has_course* column.

Many-to-many relationships are supported in P/FDM, and are modelled by multi-valued functions. Since a set of values cannot be stored in a field of a relational table, additional binary tables are used to model these. For example, there is a multi-valued relationship, called *takes*, relating undergraduates to the courses they take – each undergraduate can take many courses and each course can be taken by many undergraduates. This relationship is declared in Daplex as follows ("->>" indicates that this is a multi-valued function):

```
declare takes(undergrad) ->> course
```

To model this in a relational module, we introduce a binary table called *takes_undergrad* (this table name being composed from the function name and the argument type). The first column of this table is the object identifier of an undergraduate and the second stores the object identifier of one of the courses taken by that student. This table can also be used to find the inverse of this relationship.

8 Accessing Relational Storage Modules via P/FDM Primitives

The P/FDM database provides a small set of primitive routines implemented by Prolog predicates for performing data access and update. For data retrieval the two routines used are *getentity* and *getfnval* ("get-function-value"), which retrieve object identifiers and function values. When one of these predicates is called, the system identifies which kind of module must be accessed to retrieve the requested item. Below, we describe the operation of each of these predicates for a relational module. These routines have been implemented using the ProDBI interface [16].

getentity(ClassName, Oid)

The predicate getentity has as its arguments a class name and the object identifier (*Oid*) of an instance of that class. In all calls the class name must be given. If *Oid* is an uninstantiated Prolog variable, then the result of the call will be to instantiate it to the object identifier of an instance of the given class. On backtracking, *Oid* will be instantiated to the object identifiers of all other instances of that class. For a relational module, this predicate retrieves values from the oid column of the table called *ClassName*. The ProDBI interface allows successive tuples to be retrieved from the relational database on backtracking, thus all values in the oid column are retrieved in turn.

After we have retrieved an instance of a class, we usually want to access its properties (scalar attributes and/or relationships). Therefore, an additional action of the getentity routine is to retrieve the entire tuple and cache it in main memory so that an object's properties can be accessed without further calls to the database server.

If *Oid* is already instantiated when getentity is called, then getentity is used to test whether the given object belongs to the given class. This is most useful for testing subclass membership. When used in this way, the getentity routine first looks for the given instance in the cache, and only if it is not in the cache is the external relational database accessed.

getentity(ClassName, Key, Oid)

The second form of getentity takes as an argument a list containing the external key values of a particular object instance. For example, suppose the attributes *forename* and *surname* form the external key of the class *person*. Then we can retrieve the object identifier of the person called John Brown with the call:

```
getentity(person,['John','Brown'],Oid)
```

This query is answered by retrieving the oid value from the tuple in the person table with 'John' in the forename field and 'Brown' in the surname field. Note that ProDBI will use an index on the table if one exists to locate tuples that have a field with a known value.

As explained earlier, as well as scalar values, keys can include relationships. Suppose the external keys of classes *course* and *section* are declared as follows:

```
key_of course is code
key_of section is key_of(has_course), section_name
```

The external key of a section consists of the the section code and the key of the related course, which is that course's code. The following call will retrieve the object identifier of section a2 in course CS_4002:

```
getentity(section,['CS_4002','a2'],Oid)
```

To answer this query, the system first finds the object identifier of that tuple in the course table which has CS_4002 as its code. Then it finds the oid value from the tuple in the section table which has the object identifier (not the key!) of course CS_4002 in its *has_course* field and the value a2 in its *section_name* field.

Subclasses inherit the key of their superclass. For example,

```
getentity(student,['John','Brown'],Oid)
```

will first find the oid in the person table for the tuple with values 'John' and 'Brown' in the forename and surname fields, then test that there is a corresponding entry in the student table.

getfnval(Function, [Argument], Result)

A function name, representing an attribute or relationship, and an argument to which that function will be applied are given in a call to getfnval. The argument is given in a Prolog list because P/FDM supports multi-argument functions (not discussed in this paper).

Suppose getfnval is called with the function *forename* and the object identifier of a person as the argument. The result is found by retrieving the value in the *forename* field of the tuple in the person table with the given object identifier.

If *Result* is instantiated in the call, then getfnval is used as a test. For single-valued functions, getfnval first checks whether the tuple corresponding to the given argument is in the main memory cache. If it is, then the function value is immediately retrieved from that cached tuple. Otherwise, the database server is accessed via the ProDBI interface, and the entire tuple containing the requested value is retrieved and cached so that related attributes are available without requiring further database access.

Suppose in the above call, a student object identifier is given as an argument instead of a person object identifier. The forename function is not defined directly on *student*, but is inherited from the *person* superclass. In this case, the value of the inherited function would be retrieved from the corresponding entry in the *person* table (using the same oid value).

In addition to scalar attributes, getfnval is used to retrieve the values of relationship attributes. Consider the *has_course* relationship between *section* and *course*, shown in Fig. 1. This relationship is stored in the *section* table. The call

```
getfnval(has_course, [SectionOid] ,CourseOid)
```

will succeed where *CourseOid* matches the value in the *has_course* field of the tuple which has the given section identifier in the *oid* field. Values for the inverse relationship *has_course_inv* are found in a similar way. The call

```
getfnval(has_course_inv, [CourseOid] ,SectionOid)
```

will succeed where *SectionOid* matches the value in the *oid* field of a tuple which has the given course identifier in the *has_course* field. This inverse relationship is multi-valued, and the identifiers of all sections in the given course are found by backtracking.

A multi-valued function, such as that modelling the relationship between undergraduates and the courses they take is answered similarly by accessing the oids in the binary table *takes_undergrad* in Fig. 2.

9   Using Daplex to Access Data in a Relational Module

Data in P/FDM is accessed using the Daplex query language. Queries expressed in this high-level language are translated to Prolog for execution. This is done by first translating the query into a "list comprehension" (or "set expression") (see Sect. 10), and then optimising this before generating Prolog code to answer the query. This code includes calls to the P/FDM primitive routines (getentity and getfnval for data access), as well as ordinary Prolog goals. The translation process is outlined in Fig. 3.

Originally the P/FDM system had two kinds of storage module: main memory modules storing data in Prolog clauses, and hash file modules providing persistence. We have now developed a third kind using relational storage. Within a session, several different kinds of module can be open concurrently, but users access these in the same way, via the primitive routines. Daplex can also be used to query relational modules. Moreover, a single query can make reference to object classes stored in several different kinds of database module. This is because the database primitives that queries are translated into are independent of how the data they are to access is stored. It is only when these predicates are called that the system checks the actual argument types and the database meta-data [7] to identify what kind of storage module is to be accessed, and performs the necessary retrieval operation.

In the rest of this paper, we consider processing queries which only require access to relational modules. Such queries can be answered by translating these to Prolog, with calls to the basic access routines described in Sect. 2.2. Each of these calls may require the relational database to be accessed using the ProDBI interface. ProDBI itself works by sending SQL queries to the relational database server, since it doesn't have low-level access to SYBASE tables. Thus, a Daplex query is broken down into many small SQL queries, each answering only a small part of the original query. It is clear that the SQL server could often employ a more efficient query evaluation strategy if it were given the entire query at once, rather than being asked to answer sub-parts of the original query.

This drawback is illustrated by the following Daplex example, which finds the surnames of all people with forename "John".

```
for each p in person such that forename(p) = "John"
print(surname(p));
```

Translating this to Prolog with calls to P/FDM primitives, we have

```
getentity(person,P),
getfnval(forename,[P],'John'),
getfnval(surname,[P],S),
write(S),nl,
fail;
true.
```

Significantly, to answer this query, all tuples in the person table must be retrieved from the database server in turn, and for each tuple the value of the forename field is tested in Prolog. It would be better to give the constraint on the forename to the relational database server, thus letting the server filter the results to be returned. This query is equivalent to a single SQL statement:

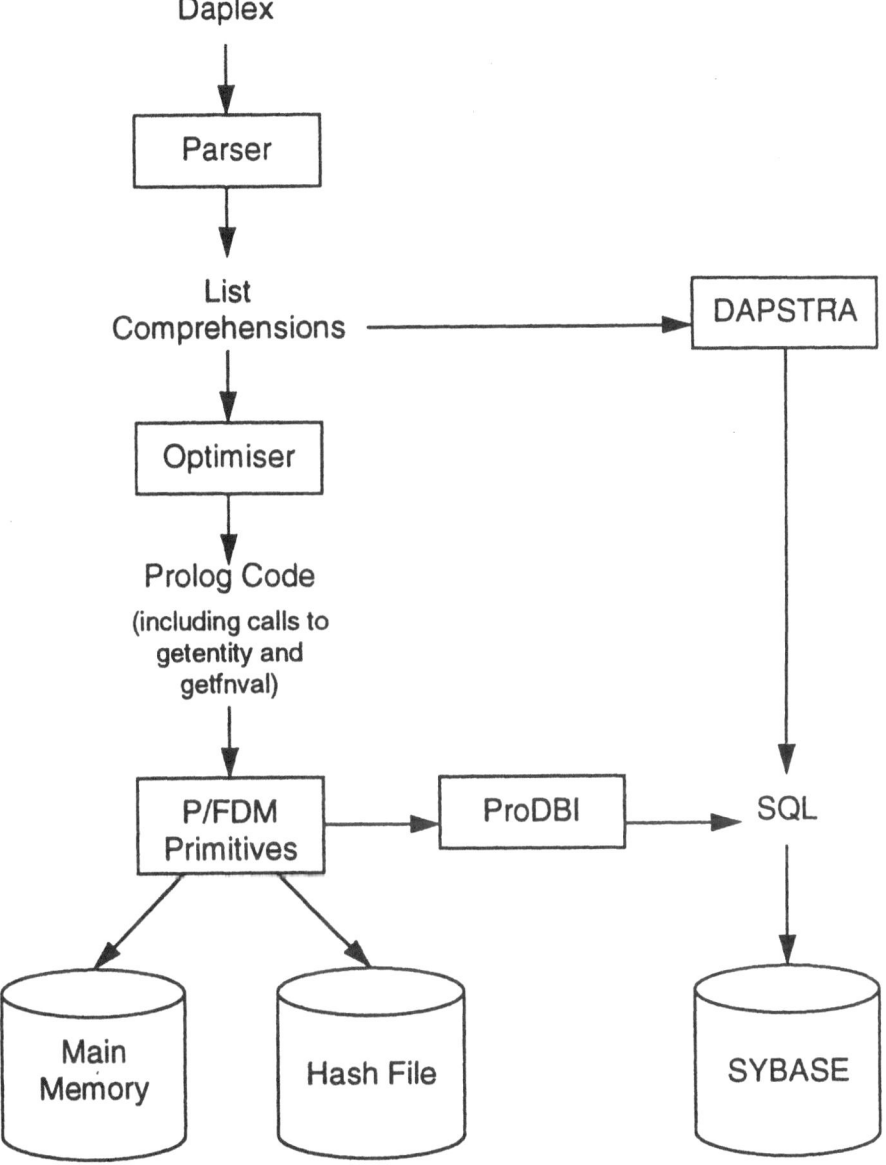

Fig. 3. Processing Daplex queries. Following the route on the left, any list comprehension can be translated to Prolog code accessing any kind of storage module. List comprehensions for simple Daplex queries against a relational module can be translated directly to SQL by the DAPSTRA program.

```
SELECT    surname
FROM      person
WHERE     forename = "John"
```

If the Daplex query could be translated to an SQL query string, then this could be passed to a relational database server. The server could then find answers to the query and return only this data to the P/FDM system, reducing the amount of data transferred from the server, and performing tests on the data values as early as possible (i.e. on the SQL server). Additionally, if the relational table has an index on the forename column (even where this is not a unique identifier), then this can be used by the database server to improve performance further. This can be done by translating the list comprehensions into single SQL statements. A program called DAPSTRA (DAPlex-to-Sql TRAnslator) [14] has been written in Prolog to perform this translation, and is described in the next section.

10   Translating List Comprehensions to SQL Using DAPSTRA

When a Daplex query is parsed, it is converted to Prolog terms containing the essential elements of the query, but in a simple form. These are equivalent to a list comprehension. For example, the query from the last section can be written as a list comprehension as follows:

[s | p ← person; f ← forename(p); f = "John"; s ← surname(p)]

The variables whose values are to be printed are listed on the left of the vertical bar. The expressions on the right of the vertical bar are called *qualifiers*, and are either *filters* or *generators*. Each generator introduces one new variable, representing a scalar value or object instance drawn from the list given by the expression. At present, the expressions in generators which DAPSTRA can deal with are for class enumeration, function evaluation (i.e. accessing a stored attribute or relationship), class conversion (regarding an instance of one class as an instance of another in the same class hierarchy) and aggregate functions (like 'maximum'). Filters specify conditions that variables must satisfy. Filters that can be handled by DAPSTRA at present are comparisons, existentially quantified sub-expressions, conjunctions and disjunctions.

DAPSTRA processes the qualifiers one-at-a-time, and, as processing proceeds, two Prolog data structures are constructed. The first of these is a symbol table which contains term structures recording the variable name, table name, table identifier and column name of each variable in the list comprehension. If a variable is used as a join value between tables, then there will be more than one entry for this variable in the symbol table. The second data structure is a term representing the eventual SQL query, and this term contains three lists – a "select-list", a "from-list" and a "where-list", corresponding to the main clauses in an SQL "select" statement. The symbol table and the three query lists are implemented as incomplete lists. Each generator adds to the symbol table and/or one or more of the query lists, and each filter adds to the "where-list". When all qualifiers have been processed, the symbol table and query lists are used to generate the SQL query text.

Once the SQL text has been generated, it can be run by passing it to the database server using a routine provided by the ProDBI interface. A Prolog variable can be bound to the results retrieved and then further processing can be carried out in Prolog. Alternatively, if query just requires values to be printed then this can be done via a C interface routine without going back into Prolog.

The following example shows nested for-loops in Daplex. This query prints the course code of each second level course, together with the name of each section in that course and the surname of the teacher giving that section.

```
for each c in course such that level(c) = 2
  for each s in has_course_inv(c)
print(code(c), section_name(s), surname(has_lecturer(s)));
```

The list comprehension for this query is:

$$[\text{ d, e, g } | \text{ a} \leftarrow \text{course; b} \leftarrow \text{level(a); b} = 2; \text{c} \leftarrow \text{has\_course\_inv(a);}$$
$$\text{d} \leftarrow \text{code(a); e} \leftarrow \text{section\_name(c); f} \leftarrow \text{has\_lecturer(c);}$$
$$\text{g} \leftarrow \text{surname(f)]}$$

This is translated to the following piece of SQL:

```
SELECT  t1.code, t2.section_name, t3.surname
FROM    course t1, section t2, person t3
WHERE   t1.level = 2 AND t2.has_course = t1.oid AND
        t2.has_lecturer = t3.oid
```

DAPSTRA can also deal with existentially quantified sub-queries. For example, the following piece of Daplex prints the codes of all courses which have some section taught by a senior lecturer:

```
for each c in course such that
  some t in has_lecturer(has_course_inv(c)) has
    position(t) = "SL"
print(code(c));
```

The list comprehension for this is:

$$[\text{ code } | \text{ c} \leftarrow \text{course; code} \leftarrow \text{code(course);}$$
$$\text{some([t } | \text{ s} \leftarrow \text{has\_course\_inv(c); t} \leftarrow \text{has\_lecturer(s);}$$
$$\text{p} \leftarrow \text{position(t); p} = \text{"SL"])]}$$

The SQL statement generated by the DAPSTRA program contains the keyword "EXISTS", followed by a sub-query. This subquery refers to the "global" table t1.

```
SELECT   t1.code
FROM     course t1
WHERE    EXISTS (SELECT  t2.has_lecturer
                 FROM    section t2, member_of_staff t3
                 WHERE   t2.has_course = t1.oid AND
                         t2.has_lecturer = t3.oid AND
                         t3.position = 'SL')
```

Attribute *position* is not stored in the teacher table, but has to be retrieved from the corresponding tuple in the member_of_staff table. Therefore, a join is performed between the section and member_of_staff tables in the sub-query, and the teacher table does not feature in the SQL query.

11   Conclusions

We have seen the advantages of taking a high-level semantic view of database operations in place of the low-level performance-driven view that is common with C++. We have used the principle of data independence to structure our system and this has allowed us to perform high-level global query optimisation in a manner that takes account of the storage schema but hides these details from the application programmer.

Our main application has been the storage of protein structure data [10] [15]. This requires one to perform complex queries that combine 3-D geometric computation, using stored methods, with navigation through a large number of objects of different types. We could have written our system concentrating on C++ class coding for speed, and then hand-writing application code in C++ using these classes in an efficient way for each application. However, this would then have made it very hard for biochemists to use the system. Furthermore, we would have a collection of application code such that, if we wished to expand or change our internal storage representation, it would be a nightmare to find and change systematically all of the object access code. In fact, many scientific programmers start by choosing a simple array representation that outgrows its usefulness and makes it very hard to evolve new classes and new types of data. By contrast, our system has stood the test of time and evolution and transportation to different systems.

The crucial idea is not to depend blindly on encapsulation in object-oriented programming, but to adapt a good high level data model together with the principle of data independence so that one is working with a coordinated collection of Abstract Data Types that do the conceptual to storage schema mapping. The ODMG-93 standard is moving in this direction through the use of an object query language and keys, but we believe that it has more to learn about data models for schema evolution and data independence.

12   Acknowledgements

We are grateful to the EC Bridge program grant BIOT CT91 0271 for supporting part of this work. Some of this material is taken from an earlier paper [14] published in the proceedings of BNCOD12 by Springer-Verlag.

References

1. ANSI: Interim Report of the ANSI/X3/SPARC Study Group on Data Base Management Systems. ACM SIGFIDET **7** (1975) 3–139
2. Bassiliades, N. and Gray, P.M.D.: Colan: A Functional Constraint Language and its Implementation. Data and Knowledge Engineering (to appear).
3. Cattell, R.G.G. (ed.): The Object Database Standard ODMG-93 (Release 1.1). Morgan Kaufmann (1994)
4. Elmasri, R. and Navathe, S.B.: Fundamentals of Database Systems (2nd edition). Benjamin/Cummings (1994)
5. Embury, S.M.: Constraint-based Updates in a Functional Data Model Database, Ph.D. Thesis, University of Aberdeen (1994)
6. Embury, S.M., Gray, P.M.D. and Bassiliades, N.D.: Constraint Maintenance Using Generated Methods in the P/FDM Object-Oriented Database. In Paton, N.W. and Williams, M.H. (eds) Proc. of 1st Int. Workshop on Rules in Database Systems (RIDS '93), Springer-Verlag (1993) 364–381
7. Embury, S.M., Jiao, Z. and Gray, P.M.D.: Using Prolog to Provide Access to Metadata in an Object-Oriented Database. In Proc. of The Practical Application of Prolog, London, 1st-3rd April (1992)
8. Gray, P.M.D.: Logic, Algebra and Databases. Ellis-Horwood (1984)
9. Gray, P.M.D., Kulkarni, K.G. and Paton, N.W.: Object-oriented databases: A semantic data model approach. Prentice Hall International (UK) Ltd., Hemel Hempstead (1992)
10. Gray, P.M.D., Paton, N.W., Kemp, G.J.L. and Fothergill, J.E.. An object-oriented database for protein structure analysis. Protein Engineering **3** (1990) 235–243
11. Jagadish, H.V. and Qian, X.: Integrity Maintenance in an Object-Oriented Database. Proc. 18th VLDB Conference (Vancouver), Morgan Kaufmann (1992) 469–479
12. Jiao, Z. and Gray, P.M.D.: Optimisation of methods in a navigational query language. In Delobel, C., Kifer, M. and Masunaga, Y. (eds.) Proc. 2nd International Conference on Deductive and Object-Oriented Databases, Springer-Verlag (1991) 22–42
13. Kemp, G.J.L.: Protein modelling: a design application of an object-oriented database. In Gero, J.S. (ed.) Artificial intelligence in design '91, Butterworth-Heinmann Ltd., (1991) 387–406
14. Kemp, G.J.L., Iriarte, J.J. and Gray, P.M.D.: Efficient Access to FDM Objects Stored in a Relational Database. In Bowers, D.S. (ed.) Directions in Databases: Proceedings of the Twelfth British National Conference on Databases (BNCOD 12), Springer-Verlag, New York, (1994) 170–186
15. Kemp, G.J.L., Jiao, Z., Gray, P.M.D. and Fothergill, J.E.: Combining Computation with Database Access in Biomolecular Computing. In Litwin, W. and Risch, T. (eds.) Applications of Databases: Proceedings of the First International Conference, ADB-94, Springer-Verlag, New York, (1994) 317–335

16. Keylink Computers Limited: ProDBI Quintus/Sybase Interface V3.0B User Manual (1992)
17. Nijssen, G.M.: Modelling in data base management systems. In Samet, P.A. (ed.) Proc. Euro. IFIP 79, North-Holland (1979) 39–52
18. Paton, N.W. and Gray, P.M.D.: Identification of database objects by key. In K. Dittrich (ed.), Advances in Object-Oriented Database Systems - Proc. OODBS-II, Springer-Verlag (1988) 280–285
19. Shipman D.W.: The Functional Data Model and the Data Language DAPLEX. ACM Transactions on Database Systems 6 (1981) 140–173
20. Stonebraker, M.L., Rowe, L.A., Lindsay, B., Gray, J., Carey, M., Brodie, M.L., Bernstein, P. and Beech, D.: Third-Generation Database System Manifesto. In Meersman, R.A., Kent, W. and Khosla, S. (eds.) Proc. DS-4: Object-Oriented Databases: Analysis, Design and Construction. Elsevier (1991) 495–511
21. White, S.J. and DeWitt, D.J.: A Performance Study of Alternative Object Faulting and Pointer Swizzling Strategies. Proc. 17th VLDB Confce. (Vancouver) (1992)

Problems, Descriptions, and Objects

Michael Jackson

Software Development Consultant
101 Hamilton Terrace
London NW8 9QX
Tel: 0171 286 1814 Fax: 0171 266 2645
E-mail: jacksonma@attmail.com or mj@doc.ic.ac.uk

ABSTRACT: The business of software development is solving problems. Following Polya, we can increase our ability to solve problems by focusing directly on problems themselves, on their parts and structures, and on the relationship between problem and solution method. This leads to an emphasis on describing the world outside the computer, and reasoning about it explicitly; to an approach to problem complexity and decomposition; and to a particular view of the proper role of object-orientation in software development.

1. Problems and Solutions

Software development projects, in my view, are concerned to solve engineering problems. Software developers make machines that are to be installed in the world, and are to make a difference in the world by interacting with it. For example, a word-processing system is a machine installed in an office, just like a typewriter, but much more powerful and versatile. As software developers we don't construct the physical fabric of the machine; we only describe the properties and behaviour of the machine we want. We present our descriptions to a general-purpose computer, which then magically takes on the properties and behaviour of the machine we have described. It is in this way that a software development problem is an engineering problem - the problem of creating a useful machine to fit some purpose.

People who are interested in the social, economic, ethical, and political aspects of software development - especially of the development of administrative or information systems - sometimes disagree with this view. Software systems, they say, are situated in a human context, and their specifications emerge and evolve by processes of continual negotiation and adaptation among all the interested parties. There is no succession of well-defined problems for the software developer to solve: the primary development activity is ongoing social interaction. Of course there is truth in this view for some developments in some situations. But at the end of the day, even in those situations, there are programs to be created: that is, there are machines to be built, and engineering problems to be solved.

But although we are engineers we are not, for the most part, like other engineers. Most of the established branches of engineering - civil, automobile, electrical, chemical, aeronautical - are specialisations. Automobile engineers don't turn their hands to designing bridges or chemical plants. Software engineers, in contrast, are usually generalists rather than specialists. Except for courses in compiler construction and in operating systems their education is in general principles and techniques rather than in specific problem areas. And most software development practitioners would think of themselves, with some justification, as being equally able to work in one problem area as in another.

This difference is of great importance. An automobile designer does not begin by trying to discover what the problem is. The problem is, as always, to design a particular kind of car. Both the purpose and the nature of each kind of car are very well understood.

The designer of a family saloon car need not consider whether the car should be able to fly; or to carry five-ton loads; or should incorporate a crane for lifting steel girders. Nor need the designer consider whether the car should have wheels or tracks; whether the driver should sit at the front or at the back; whether it should be driven by steam or nuclear power. Both the problem and its solution are very tightly constrained, and the work of the automobile engineer - except for the most brilliantly revolutionary designers - is to make very small perturbations within the given constraints.

In bespoke software development, except for a few specialised areas, the situation is quite different. Every problem, and every solution, is new. The freedom of the software developer is several orders of magnitude greater than the freedom of the automobile engineer. This is why *analysis*, and *requirements,* and *specifications*, loom so large on the software development landscape. A large part of our effort must almost always be devoted to determining what the problem is, and to devising a new solution - because it is always a new problem.

Faced with these demands, we have traditionally paid most of our attention to solutions, and little or no attention to problems. Partly, this is because of the seductive attraction of computer programming. Many developers are programmers at heart, whatever their job titles may be; their happiest hours are those spent devising how their machines should work. Those who claim to be entirely concerned with their customer's problem often try to express that problem in a data flow diagram, or some other representation of the internal behaviour of their planned machine. As a representation of the problem they offer a design for a solution. More damagingly, even resolute methodologists find it hard to pay serious attention to problems. Ralph Johnson, a leading proponent of the use of patterns in object-oriented development, says [Johnson 94]:

> "We have a tendency to focus on the solution, in large part because it is easier to notice a pattern in the systems that we build than it is to see the pattern in the problems we are solving that lead to the patterns in our solutions to them."

Of course it is easier to notice a pattern in the solutions. The solutions are set in the context of a programming language and environment that provide a rich structure and vocabulary for talking about solutions: procedures and functions and parameters and invocations; pipes and streams and processes; objects and methods and classes and instance variables. By contrast, a typical problem is set in a context that offers no such help. In the absence of a suitable vocabulary it is a daunting task to try to speak of problems. Solutions are easier. The sixpence is sought, as ever, under the street light.

2. Problem Frames: Polya

But a good starting point for talking about problems is readily available. Polya shows the way in his monograph *How to Solve It* [Polya 57]. There he expounds the work of the Greek mathematicians, especially Pappus, in the field of heuristics - techniques for finding solutions to problems for which no algorithmic method is known.

The Greeks classified simple mathematical problems into *problems to prove,* and *problems to find.* For example, the problem 'Show that if the sides of a quadrilateral are equal its diagonals bisect each other' is a problem to prove; while the problem 'Given three lengths *a, b,* and *c,* find a triangle whose sides are of those lengths' is a problem to find. The different kinds of problem can be recognised by their principal parts and the associated solution task. A problem to find always has:
- the *unknown:* here, a triangle;
- the *data*: here, the three lengths;
- the *condition:* here, that the triangle's sides should be equal to the given three lengths.

The *solution task* in a problem to find is always to find or construct the *unknown* so that it bears the relation to the *data* that is expressed by the *condition*.

Polya gives a number of heuristics for solving problems to find. For example:
    Check that you are using all the data.
    Check that you are using all the condition.
    Split the condition into parts.
    Think of a familiar problem having a similar unknown.

These heuristics can offer useful advice for solving all problems of the class because - and only because - they are expressed in terms of the problem alone. That is, they are expressed in terms of what Polya calls the *principal parts* of the problem, not parts or aspects of any putative solution.

The assemblage of principal parts and solution task that characterises a problem class merits a name. I call it a *problem frame*. I think of it as a kind of structure or jig into which a problem may be fitted so that it can be worked on. By fitting a problem into a problem frame we should be classifying it precisely enough to be able to select an appropriate method for its solution. The key requirement for a good problem frame is that it should be precise enough to give a really good grip on any problem that fits it. And the key requirement for a good method is that it should be associated with, and exploit, a sufficiently precise problem frame.

Polya writes of two problem frames for small mathematical problems. For software development, very many more will evidently be needed. Attempts to find a single general problem frame and an associated method that will work well for all software development problems are doomed to failure. They lead to the discredited and vapid emptiness of top-down decomposition, with its vacuous problem frame. The problem is characterised as - well, a problem. The method is to break it down to sub-problems that are themselves - well, problems; to break these sub-problems down to sub-sub-problems; and to continue until no further decomposition is necessary. The fact that this prescription fits every imaginable problem is the clearest possible symptom of its lack of efficacy.

3.   Software Development Problem Frames and Methods

A useful problem frame must fit its problems tightly. So a symptom of its utility will be that it excludes most problems and fits only relatively few. Here are three examples: the JSD Information System Frame, the Simple Control System Frame, and the Workpieces Frame.

The JSD Information System Frame may be suitable for an information system to be used in a commercial organisation. It has these principal parts:
- The *System*. This is the machine we must build.
- The *Real World*. This is the world about which information is required. It is dynamic, but autonomous. That is, events and state changes take place, but they are to be regarded as spontaneous and unexplained.
- The *Information Outputs*. These are the reports and displays containing the required information.
- The *Information Requests*. These are query transactions and requests for various kinds of information outputs.
- The *Information Function*. This is a relationship between the *Real World* and the *Information Outputs*.

The solution task is to construct the *System* so that it produces the *Information Outputs* in their correct relationship to the *Real World*, in response to the *Information Requests* and to events and states of the *Real World*.

The Simple Control System Frame might be suitable for controlling a device such as a Washing Machine. It has these principal parts:
- The *Controller*. This is the machine we must build.
- The *Controlled Domain*. This is the domain to be controlled. It is dynamic and both active and reactive. That is, some events and state changes occur spontaneously, without external stimulus; and there are also events that are externally controlled and cause the domain to respond by internal events and predictable internal state changes.
- The *Desired Behaviour*. This is the desired relationship among the various events and state changes of the *Controlled Domain*.

The solution task is to construct the *Controller* so that it brings about the *Desired Behaviour* in the *Controlled Domain*.

Finally, the Workpieces Frame might be suitable for a very small and simple CASE tool. It has these principal parts:
- The *Tool*. This is the machine we must build.
- The *Workpieces*. These are the objects that the users of the *Tool* create and work on, with the help of the *Tool*. They are intangible graphical or textual objects, realised entirely within the *Tool*. They are dynamic but inert: that is, their states can change, but only in response to externally controlled events.
- The *Operation Requests*. These are the users' requests for operations - such as graphic or text object creation and editing - to be performed by the *Tool*. They occur autonomously.
- The *Operation Properties*. These are desired relationships between the occurrences of the *Operation Requests* and the states of the *Workpieces*.

The solution task is to construct the *Tool* so that it responds to *Operation Requests* by operating on the *Workpieces* in accordance with the *Operation Properties*.

These three problem frames - the JSD Information System Frame, the Simple Control System Frame, and the Workpieces Frame - are significantly different. Most notably, they differ in the characteristics of those principal parts that could be said to reflect their central subject matter. In the JSD Frame, the *Real World* is active and autonomous; in the Control Frame, the *Controlled Domain* is both active and reactive; in the Workpieces Frame, the *Workpieces* are inert.

These differences, and others also, are reflected in the different methods that may be associated with each frame. The JSD method [Jackson 83, Cameron 89] may be understood as a method for solving JSD Information System problems. JSD exploits the dynamic and autonomous nature of the *Real World* by using concurrent simple sequential processes to represent the subject matter about which the *Information Outputs* must be produced. Events are regarded as primary, and states as secondary: states are defined in terms of event histories.

For Simple Control System problems a candidate method is a simplified version of the method described by Parnas and Madey [Parnas 91] and incorporated into the Core method [Faulk 92]. A central theme in this method is a distinction that is missing from JSD (and is not needed in problems that fit the JSD Information System frame). Two descriptions are made of the *Controlled Domain*: one to capture those *natural* properties that it possesses regardless of the behaviour of the Machine; and another to capture the *Desired Behaviour* - those properties with which the Machine is required to endow it. Parnas and Madey represent both sets of properties as relations over variables of the *Controlled Domain*. They call the first relation NAT, and the second REQ.

For a Workpieces problem it would be appropriate to use a method based on abstract data types, such as Larch [Guttag 85] or VDM [Jones 90] or Z [Wordsworth 92]. The definition of the type is, in effect, a description of the *Workpieces*. The operations to be performed by the *Tool* in response to the *Operation Requests* are the operations of the type. In a model-based method such as VDM or Z, the description of the model state is, of course, the description of the *Workpieces* viewed as a data structure.

The accounts given here of the different problem frames and the different associated methods are hugely simplified. This simplification is partly just a matter of the brevity of presentation in this paper. But it is much more fundamental than that. A problem frame must be simple, and the associated methods must be simple too. It is only by stripping away the tangles of complications that surround realistic problems that we can see a basis for classifying them and devising powerful methods. A method is powerful only to the extent that it exploits the particular properties of the class of problem being solved. The resulting simplification and lack of realism is a central theme in dealing with complexity. I shall return to this theme later in the paper.

4.   Describing the World

If we mean to think seriously about software development problems we must focus our attention initially on everything except the machine we will ultimately build. The *System,* the *Controller,* and the *Tool* each constitute only one principal part among several in the problem frame, and initially they are the least interesting. Our customer's requirement lies elsewhere, in the world outside the machine: that is, in the other principal parts of the frame. The machine we build will - if we are successful - satisfy the requirement; but it does not itself embody that requirement. Our primary concern is with understanding and describing what we may call the *application domain* and the *requirement:* in JSD, the *Real World* and the *Information Outputs, Requests,* and *Function;* in a Simple Control problem, the *Controlled Domain* and the *Desired Behaviour;* in a Workpieces problem, the *Workpieces* themselves and the *Operation Requests* and *Properties.*

Explicit description of the application domain is unnecessary in the small mathematical problems that Polya discusses. For those problems, the application domain is formal, and is already well known to the problem solver. When the *data* in a problem to find is a triangle, we do not expect to devote serious effort to understanding and describing the mathematical notion of a triangle. We already know what it is, and we already know its essential properties: that the sum of its interior angles is equal to two right angles; that its area is one half of the height multiplied by the base; that the length of each side is less than the sum of the two other sides; and so on. When the *unknown* is a prime number, we already know what a prime number is.

This convenient, but atypical, property is shared by the integer and integer array problems that provide so much material for the exposition of certain formal styles of program development. Those styles, and their expositors, are sometimes criticised on the ground that their techniques do not scale up: they deal in small and simple problems when real problems are large and complex. But a far more serious criticism is that they have taught generations of software developers that problem capture is a trivial task: one need scarcely do more than mention the problem before setting about its solution. Rather like the prison inmate who need only shout out 'joke number 43' to make his fellow inmates laugh.

On the contrary. In most real problems description of the application domain should consume a very large part of the total effort. The context of the problem is in the application domain, not in the machine. But immediately, this raises a severe difficulty. The application domain is almost always informal. This has several consequences.

The first consequence is that generalisation and classification is always imperfect, and always vulnerable to the production of new evidence, new counterexamples, and new objections. Everyone knows that the meaning of terms such as 'customer' and 'employee' varies from department to department within the same organisation. The meaning of 'motor vehicle' depends on whether you are talking to a lawyer, a manufacturer, a licensing authority, or the AA. There is no simple general definition under which all the meanings can be precisely subsumed.

Another consequence is that reasoning in the application domain is inherently unreliable. We may formalise our premises, and reason with correct logic to a conclusion. Yet we may still find that our conclusion is false when translated back into statements about the domain. The inevitable imprecision of our original formalisation introduces an error term - analogous, if you like, to the arithmetic error introduced when reals are represented by integers - that can vitiate the reasoning.

Another consequence is that we need a much richer and more varied repertoire of languages and notations than is needed for describing machines. The task of describing a machine - that is, of writing a program - is greatly helped by the freedom to decide that the machine should embody a simple and consistent phenomenology. So good programming languages are concisely definable, and exhibit such properties as syntactic and semantic consistency, or referential transparency. But in describing the world outside the machine we have no such freedom. We must describe the world - at least approximately - as it really is. We will certainly impose some degree of systematic consistency on our descriptions: even natural languages do that. But we are not free to sweep away the variety of the world by treating everything as a sequential process, or as a relation, or even as an object.

5. Description Types and Structures

To deal with this richness we must pay a lot of attention to the technology of description. That means that we must be aware of how descriptions are related to the subject matter they describe, of the different kinds of description that may be needed, of the properties and dimensions of each description, and of the many different structures by which descriptions may be usefully related to one another.

The basis of the relationship between a description and what it describes is the designation. A *designation* singles out certain phenomena of interest. It gives an (ineluctably) informal explanation of how the phenomena may be recognised in the application domain, and it gives a formal term - such as a predicate - by which the phenomena will be referred. For example, in the designation:

"The human genetic mother of x is m ≋ Mother(x,m)"

the designated phenomenon is the relationship of genetic motherhood between two people; it will be denoted in descriptions by using the predicate Mother (x,m). Designations form the bridge between the formal descriptions we produce in software development and the informal real world. Without explicit designations it is impossible to determine with any confidence whether a description of the world is true or false. To quote John von Neumann: There is no point in being precise if you don't know what you are talking about.

A *definition* gives a formal definition of a term that may be used by other descriptions. For example, the definition:

"Child(x,y) $\triangleq$ Mother(y,x) v Father(y,x)"

defines the term "Child(x,y)" to mean exactly the same as "Mother(y,x) or Father(y,x)". A definition can not be true or false: it can only be well-formed or not well-formed, and useful or not useful. It conveys no information whatsoever about the application domain or the machine.

A *refutable description* describes some part of the world, saying something about it that could - in principle - be refuted or disproved. Whether it could in practice be disproved is another matter: the important thing is that it could make sense to disprove it, as it can't make sense to disprove a definition. For example, here's a tiny refutable description:

$$\forall\ m,x\ \bullet\text{Mother}(x,m)\ \rightarrow\neg\text{Mother}(m,x)$$

Whatever m and x you choose, if m is the human genetic mother of x, then x is not the human genetic mother of m. To refute it you would have to find a pair of mutual genetic mothers. Inconceivable. But not nonsensical.

Because there are many parts and aspects of the world to be described, it will always be necessary to build quite elaborate structures of designations, definitions, and refutable descriptions. Determining how to separate the whole description into a number of partial descriptions - that is, how to separate concerns - is a central development activity. At a certain scale, separation is prescribed by the chosen method: JSD enjoins the developer to separate the description of the *Real World* from the description of the *Information Function*; and Parnas and Madey enjoin a separation of the NAT and REQ relations. At a larger scale, separation will be guided by the treatment of complexity, in which several methods and frames are deployed on one problem.

6. The Machine and the World

The requirement is in the application domain, but its satisfaction is to be achieved by the machine. The transition from one to the other depends on a relationship between the two. Two aspects of the relationship are of special importance for descriptive technique: interaction, and modelling.

The machine interacts with its physical environment. This means that some phenomena - events and states - are common to the machine and the environment. These common phenomena constitute what we may call the specification interface. I picture it like this:

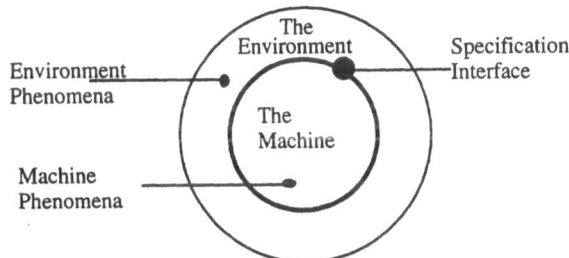

Problems and requirements are to be expressed solely in terms of the environment phenomena. Programs are to be expressed solely in terms of the machine phenomena. The bridge between them is formed by specifications, which are expressed in terms of the phenomena common to the environment and the machine.

A specification is both a restricted kind of requirement, and a restricted kind of program. Programs in general may be expressed partly in terms of phenomena that are private to the machine and not visible at the interface. Programs that refer to private machine phenomena are not specifications. (Or they are very bad specifications that may be said to exhibit implementation bias [Jones 90].) Similarly, requirements in general may be expressed partly in terms of phenomena that are private to the environment and are not shared with the machine. They, too, are not specifications: they do not give enough information for the construction of a program.

This distinction among requirements, specifications, and programs is of great significance. In a trivial problem we may write the program text directly: no sane software developer would progress from requirement through specification to program to construct the 'Hallo World' program. For a slightly less trivial problem we may content ourselves with developing a specification and progressing from there to a program. This is the danger zone for more demanding problems. The specification is a requirement - that is, it is expressed in terms of environment phenomena. So it is easy to suppose that it is the customer's requirement, ignoring the virtual certainty that the customer's requirement is not confined to the part of the environment that interfaces directly with the machine.

This is the source of some of the failures in which a system fails to achieve the required effects in the application domain. Avionics system failures furnish some notable and tragic examples. In one system a plane overshot the runway on landing in rain because the thrust reversers could not be turned on. The wheels were aquaplaning on the wet runway, and an interlock prevented engagement of the thrust reversers when the landing wheels were not turning.

Even in a context in which it is proper to confine attention to the shared phenomena there is a further danger. One may easily suppose that an interface can be equally well described from either side. But it is not so. On the machine side we can manage very well with descriptive techniques that abstract from causality and from the distinction between what is true and what we would like to be true. The causal properties of the machine are well understood in terms of the programming language, especially if it is an imperative programming language. Also, we know that we are always constructing the machine *de novo*: a general-purpose computer left alone will do nothing, it will exhibit only a null behaviour. It is therefore fully adequate to describe behaviour from the point of view of what we may call the idiot observer: in CSP terms [Hoare 85], the trace semantics is enough. The effect of behaviour outside the bounds of the specification is, naturally enough, undefined.

But as a description of the environment this conceptual parsimony is harmful. We need to know whether the precondition on an operation specification means that the environment will never, because of its internal properties, try to execute the operation when the precondition is false; or that the environment must be externally constrained to ensure the same restriction; or that the machine itself will frustrate any attempt to flout the restriction.

Another source of much confusion is the use of modelling. Modelling is an important technique in a number of methods. For example, the JSD method prescribes that the foundation of the *System* should be a model of the *Real World*: that is, that the concurrent sequential processes observable in the *Real World* should be simulated by processes within the *System*. This notion of modelling gives rise to a kind of reuse of descriptions. The same refutable description can be truthfully applied both to the *Real World* and to the *System*, by using two different sets of designations.

If there is no explicit recognition of the role of designations in a development that uses modelling in this kind of way, there will always be uncertainty about whether a particular description is intended to describe the machine or the application domain. This uncertainty is particularly noticeable in data modelling methods, and also in model-oriented methods such as VDM and Z. The reader of an Entity-Relation diagram is never sure whether the diagram describes the database or the real world. The reader of a Z operation schema is never sure whether the schema is describing the changes of state within the machine, or the effects of the operation in the world outside the machine.

One might ask: If the machine is a simulation of the world, then surely the same description applies to both. Does it matter which is being described? Of course it does matter. The simulation is only a partial simulation, and the refutable description that applies to both is only a partial description of each. Both the machine and the real world have properties that do not enter into the modelling. A database, for example, is far from a complete model of the application domain: the domain has many features that are not modelled in the database, including a range of possible causal relations among events. Symmetrically, the database has features, such as record deletion, and null values in records, that are peculiar to the machine and are not models of anything in the domain. There are therefore at least three descriptions of interest: the shared description; a description peculiar to the machine; and a description peculiar to the application domain. We must always know which of the three we are writing or reading.

7. Complexity and Problem Decomposition

The problem frames and associated methods briefly discussed earlier were all simple; certainly too simple for most realistic problems. This simplicity is an essential characteristic, because the central purpose of a problem frame is to define a class of problem for which a reliable solution method is known. The problem frame is purged of the realistic complexities that may - almost certainly will - make an otherwise simple problem difficult.

Given a repertoire of such problem frames, the complexity of realistic problems may be handled by decomposing them into simple problems. This is not the unguided decomposition of top-down functional decomposition. It differs in three important ways:
- The choice of 'subproblems' is restricted to those for which a problem frame and associated method are known. This means that the decomposition is a decomposition of a problem that you *don't* know how to solve into problems that you *do* know how to solve. (A decomposition into problems that you still don't know how to solve may make matters worse rather than better.)
- The decomposition is into *heterogeneous* subproblems. There is no *a priori* reason to decompose into several instances of one problem frame in the style of a homogeneous top-down decomposition into several procedures or into several processes. On the contrary, different aspects of a realistic problem are likely to conform to several different problem frames.
- The resulting structure of subproblems is essentially a parallel, not a hierarchical structure. The principal parts of the different problem frames overlap. In particular, they will be concerned with different views and groupings of overlapping phenomena of the problem domain. Although hierarchical relationships may sometimes be found, they will be the exception rather than the rule.

8. Objects and Problems

Object-oriented methods, especially object-oriented analysis, are an important field of application of these ideas about problems and descriptions.

The distinction between problems and solutions has not always been fully recognised in object-oriented methods. It is always tempting to fall into the traditional software trap of treating every new technique as a panacea, capable of curing all ills, and into the related trap of treating each new programming language as a language for describing problems and problem domains. In their time Fortran and COBOL were touted as problem description languages. We should avoid making the same mistake with object-oriented languages.

A salutary paper by HØydalsvik and Sindre [HØydalsvik 93] makes a number of important points. It should be compulsory reading for all students of object-orientation. The authors say:
> "An object-oriented representation might be good for some kinds of [domain] knowledge, but less suitable for other kinds of domain knowledge. Since an analysis specification has to contain many different kinds of knowledge, OOA [Object-Oriented Analysis] will only present a partial solution...."

"The main motivation for choosing OOA _ is clearly target-orientation - the analysis technique is chosen to fit in with the following design technique rather than the problem at hand."

They give two examples of domain knowledge that is hard to capture in terms of objects. Global rules, such as 'Product A should never be cheaper than product B'; and the dynamics of high-level tasks involving operations from several objects. In both cases, the granularity of an object-oriented description makes it difficult to reference all the relevant phenomena in a single description of sufficient span.

But even where there are no problems of granularity, the phenomenological assumptions built into the most commonly used object-oriented approaches may be very ill-suited to the realities of an application domain. The inadequacy of single inheritance is well-known: that particular shoe pinches almost every wearer. In principle, if we regard a class as a collection of properties, we should be prepared to contemplate any combination whatsoever of classes whatsoever. McAllester and Zabih's notion of Boolean classes [McAllester 86] is very attractive: discrete properties are defined in base classes, and the classes actually used in a description are drawn from the unrestricted powerset of those base classes. There is a connection here with the unrestricted composition of problem frames to capture a particular complex problem.

The presumption that classification is static is at least as arbitrarily restrictive as the presumption of single inheritance. There are remarkably few examples of static classification in realistic domains. As Hendler [Hendler 86] pointed out in motivating his work on Enhancements, undergraduates become graduates, and graduates become PhDs. We may also observe that pupils become teachers, warehouses become apartment buildings, caterpillars become butterflies, cotton mills become offices, and employees become pensioners. Real-world individuals not only partake freely of the properties of many classes; they also take on and shed those properties over time with at least equal freedom.

It seems to me that there are two important - but so far somewhat neglected - challenges now facing those who advocate object-oriented approaches to software development. First, to understand and exploit the true strengths of object orientation while recognising its limitations. It may, perhaps, be said that those aspects of object-orientation - classification and inheritance - that now receive most attention in tutorials and in method advocacy are its weakest aspects for describing the real worlds in which problems and requirements are found.

The second challenge, I believe, is to develop the work on patterns, and the closely related work on frameworks, that is now beginning to emerge. This work, developed in the right direction, promises to explore object-orientation in a very fruitful way, by focusing - as I believe we must - on the nature and structure of complexity, analysing some of the problems - at least in the programming context - that it is our business to solve. A new book [Gamma 94] on patterns in object-orientation ends with a provocative quotation from the software developer's favourite architect, Christopher Alexander [Alexander 79]:

"It is possible to make buildings by stringing together patterns, in a rather loose way. A building made like this is an assembly of patterns. It is not dense. It is not profound. But it is also possible to put patterns together in such a way that many patterns overlap in the same physical space: the building is very dense; it has many meanings captured in a small space; and through this density it becomes profound."

References

[Alexander 79] Christopher Alexander; The Timeless Way of Building; Oxford University Press, 1979.

[Cameron 89] J R Cameron; JSP & JSD: The Jackson Approach to Software Development; IEEE Computer Society Press, 2nd Edition 1989.

[Faulk 92] Stuart Faulk, John Brackett, Paul Ward, and James Kirby, Jr; The Core Method for Real-Time Requirements; IEEE Software Volume 9 Number 5 pages 22-33, September 1992.

[Gamma 94] Erich Gamma, Richard Helm, Ralph Johnson, John Vlissides; Design Patterns: Elements of Reusable Object-Oriented Software; Addison-Wesley 1994.

[Guttag 85] John V Guttag, James J Horning, and Jeannette M Wing; The Larch Family of Specification Languages; IEEE Software Volume 2 Number 5 pages 24-36, September 1985.

[Hendler 86] James Hendler; Enhancement for Multiple Inheritance; SIGPLAN Notices Volume 21 Number 10 pages 98-106, October 1986.

[Hoare 85] C A R Hoare; Communicating Sequential Processes; Prentice-Hall International, 1985.

[HØydalsvik 93] Geir Magne HØydalsvik and Guttorm Sindre; On the Purpose of Object-Oriented Analysis; with a discussion by Dave Thomas, Adele Goldberg, James Coplien, Peter Coad and Geir Magne HØydalsvik ; in Proceedings of OOPSLA '93, ACM Sigplan Notices Volume 28 Number 10 pages 240-258, October 1993.

[Jackson 83] M A Jackson; System Development; Prentice-Hall International, 1983.

[Johnson 94] Ralph E Johnson; Why a Conference on Pattern Languages? ACM SE Notes, Volume 19 Number 1, pages 50-52, January 1994.

[Jones 90] Cliff Jones; Systematic Software Development Using VDM; Prentice-Hall International, 2nd Edition 1990.

[McAllester 86] David McAllester and Ramin Zabih; Boolean Classes; in OOPSLA '86 Conference Proceedings: SIGPLAN Notices Volume 21 Number 11 pages 417-423, November 1986.

[Parnas 91] D L Parnas and J Madey; Functional Documentation for Computer Systems Engineering (Version 2); CRL Report 237, McMaster University, Hamilton Ontario, Canada, 1991.

[Polya 57] G Polya; How To Solve It; Princeton University Press, 2nd Edition 1957.

[Wordsworth 92] J B Wordsworth; Software Development with Z: A Practical Approach to Formal Methods in Software Engineering; Addison-Wesley, 1992.

MODELLING

Formalising Actors in Linear Logic

John Darlington   Yi-ke Guo
Department of Computing
Imperial College
180 Queen's Gate, London SW7 2BZ, U.K.
E-mail: jd, yg@doc.ic.ac.uk

Abstract

We present a logical formalism of the actor-based concurrent object oriented computation in terms of the deduction in *linear logic*. By encoding messages and objects in the actor model as formulae of linear logic, the distributed state of the actor computation, regarded as a configuration, can be represented as a multiset of object formulae and message formulae. Methods are encoded as a special form of logical implication describing the effect of the communication between objects and messages. With this logical encoding, actor based concurrent computation can be fully modelled as a deduction procedure in linear logic. In the paper, we provide a detailed mapping of the actor model into the logical system. It is shown that, with such a mapping, the logical semantics of actors can be developed.

1   Introduction

Concurrent interaction between objects is an intrinsic feature of object oriented systems. However, this feature has not been formally studied since there seems to exist no agreement on a semantic foundation for concurrent objects. The actor model proposed in [AH88] is perhaps the most well known approach so far to provide such a foundation based on a very flexible communication mechanism. In the model, concurrent computation is characterised as a communicating interaction between messages and objects. Concurrent agents, or processes, are represented as *actors* carrying the actions in response to processing communications. Methods are used to describe the effect of these communication events with respect to an object class. Although the actor model has been intensively studied and used as a general framework for modelling concurrent objects, its underlying logical structure has not been fully explored. This is partly because that logic systems developed so far mainly describe unchanging mathematical structures such as sets, functions. These logics are weak to deal with interaction and change which are central to the concurrent objects (actors). It becomes clear that a logic system modelling concurrent objects should support the reasoning about actions and change.

In [Mes89], Meseguer proposed a logic system, called *rewriting logic*, as a uniform concurrent computation model. In [MW91], Meseguer applied in the logic to establish a framework for modelling concurrent object oriented systems by formalising the actor model as a concurrent rewriting system. In the logic, an object is represented as a term

$$\langle O : C \mid a_1 : v_1, \ldots, a_n : v_n \rangle$$

where O is the object's name, C is its class, the a_i are the names of the object's attributes and v_i are their values. Each configuration is represented as a multiset of objects and messages specifying certain actions on their destination object. Such a multiset is formed in terms of an ACI constructor regarded as parallel composition. The multiset structure of the configuration allows the concurrent application of rewriting rules. Intuitively, applying a rule is caused by a communication event when messages meet the objects to which they are sent. The system evolves by concurrent rewriting (modulo ACI) of the configuration by means of rewrite rules specific to each particular system. By taking rewriting as the basic entities, rewriting logic provides a means to specify action and change. Rewriting of objects gives a precise logical understanding of the notion of "become" in the actor model which is about the change object states. However, rewriting logic lacks rich structures such as quantification mechanism which are crucial for modelling some basic features of the actor model such as asynchronous communication, local states and acquaintances.

In this paper, we present a new semantic model for actors in terms of linear logic. We show that the messages and the objects in an actor system can be uniformly represented as formulae of linear logic. The configurations of the computation can be represented as a multiset of interacting object formulae and message formulae. Methods are modeled as a special form of logical implication describing the effect of communication events between objects and messages. Concurrent computation is modelled as a concurrent transition system by applying methods. Such a transition system precisely corresponds to a deduction procedure in linear logic where linear modus ponens forms a uniform rule for modelling communication. It is shown that the new framework provides a general and powerful foundation for investigating actor-based concurrent computation.

The paper is organised as follows. The actor model is discussed in section 2 by presenting an actor-based concurrent object oriented language. In section 3, we present a lineal logic model of concurrent computation. Linear logic is introduced by emphasising its deduction structure and its use of modelling concurrent computation. A linear logic process calculus is presented as a meta language for describing the computational behaviour of the actor model. The logical meaning of the concurrent actor computation can be formalised by encoding systematically the actor language in the linear logic process calculus. As presented in section 4, the linear logic encoding provides a precise mathematical understanding of the concurrent behaviours in the actor model. The related work and future research will be discussed in the conclusion.

2 The Actor Model

The main feature of object based concurrent computation can be characterised by identifying processes with objects, inter-process communication with interactions between objects. The naturalness of concurrent objects comes from our intuitive understanding of ordinary objects and their interactions in the real world. In this sense, presenting or formalising concurrent objects and their interactions, i.e. concurrent object-oriented programming, should be conceived as modelling the properties of concurrency in the world. This idea can be traced back to the design of the Simula language in the later 60's, and has been comprehensively elaborated by the recent development of the actor-based concurrent computation models.

In the actor model, actors are concurrent communicating agents which carry out their actions in response to processing communications. All actors have names as their own unique mail addresses (or called *mailboxes*), and have their local states. The mail address may be communicated to other actors just as any other ordinary messages. Thus, mail addresses of actors provide a simple mechanism for dynamically reconfiguratting an actor system. The only way to affect the behaviour of an actor is to send it a message. An actor can only refer to its *acquaintances*, i.e., the information it was created knowning about, those it learned about from messages it received, and those it created. An actor can only send messages to acquaintance actors and only creat actors whose acquaintances are a subset of its own acquaintances. Upon receiving a message, an actor carries out the actions specified by the message. The actions an actor may perform include:

- send communications to itself or to other actors

- creat new actors

- change its own states or behaviours

Changing the behaviours of an actor can be realised by designating a replacement actor to serve the subsequent messages received at the mail address. Replacement implements the change of states and behaviours of an actor while preserving the "referencial transparency" of the identifier which always denotes that object. In the actor model, computation state, which is called the configuration, is presented by a set of messages and a set of actors. Interactions between messages and actors, and actions actors taken in response to the receiving of messages take place concurrently. The behaviours of sending messages to other actors or creating more new actors will spawn more concurrency. Moreover, the interaction between messages and actors are nondeterministic: an actor may interact with different messages depending on the arrival order of messages towards the actor. Such a nondeterminism is referred as *arrival nondeterminism*.

We present as following a simple actor-based concurrent object oriented language based on the Act3 system presented in [AH88].

$< class\_definition >$	$::=$	**class** $< class\_name >$ **with** $< variables >:< methods >$
$< method >$	$::=$	$\{< messages\_pattern >=>< actions >\}$
$< message\_pattern >$	$::=$	$message\_name(variables)$
$< action >$	$::=$	**send**$(< mail\_address >, < messages >)$
	$\mid$	**become**$(< class\_name >, < arguments >)$
	$\mid$	**let** $< bindings >$ **do** $< actions >$
	$\mid$	**if** $< constraint >$ **then** $< actions >$ **else** $< actions >$
$< message >$	$::=$	$message\_name(arguments)$
$< binging >$	$::=$	$< variable >:=< class\_name > (< arguments >)$
$< constraint >$	$::=$	$boolean\ expression$

An actor class is defined by its name, parameter variables representing the local states (acquaintances) of an actor and the definition of methods specifying the actions that an actor may take upon the receiving of various messages. Actions are presented as the four commands. The send command takes two arguments, its mailing address which is the name of the target actor, and the sending message. The result of the command it to send the message to the target actor named by the mailing address. The become command specifies the change of the behaviour of the computing actor. It can be regarded as rewriting, i.e. replacing the actor with either an actor (with the same name) of other class or its own new version with the local states changed. The conditional statement is used to state the alternative actions with respect to a conditional. A let command binds the names of newly created actors in the body of the command.

The following example is a well known example of modelling bank accounts (quoted from [MW91]). A bank account has a balance attribute and may receive messages for crediting or debiting an account or transferring funds between two accounts.

> $class$ $Account$ **with** x
> $\{crediting(val) \Rightarrow$ **become** $Account(x + val),$
> $\quad debiting(val) \Rightarrow$ **if** $val \leq x$ **then become**$(Account, x\text{-}val)$
> $\quad\quad\quad\quad\quad\quad\quad\quad\quad$ **else become**$(Account, x)$
> $\quad trans(val, B) \Rightarrow$ **if** $val \leq x$
> $\quad\quad\quad\quad$ **then** **become**$(Account, x\text{-}val),$**send**$(B, crediting\ (val))$
> $\quad\quad\quad\quad\quad\quad$ **else** **become**$(Account, x)$
> $\}$

An instance actor of the class $Account$ can be created by the let statement:

> **let** $A =$ **new** $Account(v)$ **do** ....

where v states the initial balance of the created account A. An instance actor (object) of the class $Account$ has a state variable x presenting its balance. The actor handles three messages $crediting, debiting$ and $trans$. A message $crediting(val)$ takes an argument val representing the amount of money paid to the account. When the account receives the message, its recent state is changed in terms of the $become$ command, by adding the credited money to the account. On the contrast, when the account received the message $debiting(val)$, its recent state is changed by reducing the debited money val from the account. The message $trans$ takes two arguments val, representing the money to be transformed and the mail address B indicating the other account where the money is going to be transferred. When the account receives the account $trans(val, B)$, its recent account is modified by reducing the transferring money and the money is credited to the account B by sending it a message $crediting(val)$.

Although the language is declarative, a concise representation of its computational model is not trivial. In fact, actor based computation is always specified in terms of *transition systems* modelling the evolution of the configurations in the style of Plotkin's *structured operational semantics*. However, such a formalism leaves many important mechanisms of the model unspecified. For example, the asynchronous communication protocol and the arrival nondeterminism of the message—actor interaction can not be directly modelled by using the transition system. It becomes even more hard to conceive some advanced features of the model from the transitional representation. For example, the mobility of communication for the dynamic reconfiguration of the communication structure realised by communicating mail addresses can not be explicitly reflected by transition systems. The notions of local state and acquaintance are also presented informally in the transition systems. All these indicate the necessity of a mathematical meta language to describe the sophisticated concurrent behaviours of the actor based computation. Process calculus, such as π-calculus, may be employed. However, these calculus are generally based on some kinds of synchronous communication mechanism. This fact results in the difficulty for a straightforward encoding of the actor model based on asynchronous communication.

In the next section, we present a fragment of linear logic as a logical meta language for modelling a wide range of concurrent computation models. In particular, we will show that the logic system provide a formalism of the actor model where the operational semantics are precisely captured by the deduction system of the logic.

3 A Linear Logic Model of Concurrency

Linear logic was proposed by Girard as a logic for modelling computational systems [Gir87]. In linear logic, the structural rules for weakening and contraction are dropped. Therefore, it is not possible to copy or discard arbitrary formulae during a deduction. Logical formulae become resources which may be consumed by deduction. This property makes the logic ideal for specifying computational systems, and particularly concurrent computation. In the appendix, we present linear logic by its sequent system where —o is adopted as a basic logical operation rather than a derived operation. A comprehensive description of linear logic can be found in [Gir87].

Using linear logic as the logic foundation of concurrent programming stems from the concurrent computational interpretation of linear deduction. Consider the sequent $\Gamma \vdash \Delta$ as consuming the resource of Γ to meet the requirement of Δ. A linear proof becomes a *resource construction/consumption* procedure where the root of the proof tree describes the initial state of a computation which proceeds by expanding the frontier of the partially constructed tree. The collection of leaves presents the current state of the computation. Due to the duality of the logic, we need only consider the assumption part Γ of a sequent $\Gamma \vdash \Delta$ which is viewed as a multiset of resources. These resources may be transformed into new resources by applying the inference rules (left-rules). The formulae in Γ can be regarded as concurrent processes. Logic operators (connectives and quantifiers) become combinators of the processes. Regarding each sequent as a state of the computation, the operational semantics of these combinators are provided by identifying state transitions of the computation with the inferences of the logic. The proof tree as a whole records the history of computation.

Thus, we can select an appropriate fragment of the logic as a process calculus. From a logical point of view, any statement of the calculus is a logical formula, whereas, from a computational point of view, a formula is a process. The concurrent computation of the language is modelled by deduction in the logic. The following analogies arise:

Logic		Computation
Formula	$\Longleftrightarrow$	Process
Sequent	$\Longleftrightarrow$	Configuration
Deduction	$\Longleftrightarrow$	Concurrent Computation

Following this principle of "formulae as processes, proofs as computations", basic constructions for concurrent computation can be straightforwardly related to an operational interpretation of linear deduction. A detailed description can be found in [Guo93].

We will now present a logical process calculus as a meta language for the operational behaviour of the actor model. The calculus is based on the intuitionistic linear logic [Abr90] and is a subsystem of the CDC calculus proposed as a uniform model for declarative concurrent programming [Guo93]. We first present the syntax of the language.

Let A, x, t, c be the syntactical variables ranging over agents, channel symbols, terms and conditional expressions respectively. The language has the following syntax:

$$
\begin{array}{lll}
A \triangleq & 1 & \text{unit} \\
\mid & x(t) & \text{atomic communication} \\
\mid & !c \multimap A & \text{condition} \\
\mid & \forall \bar{x}.\, m \multimap A & \text{communicating method} \\
\mid & A \otimes A & \text{parallel composition} \\
\mid & A \& A & \text{choice} \\
\mid & \exists x.A & \text{hiding} \\
\mid & !A & \text{storing}
\end{array}
$$

where the syntactical variable m ranges over a set of *receivers* defined as

$$
\begin{array}{lll}
m \triangleq & x(t) & \text{single receiver} \\
\mid & m \otimes m & \text{multiple receiver}
\end{array}
$$

A condition c in an implication $!c \multimap A$ is generally a preinterpreted formula. We assume that a built-in theory to define the meaning of the symbols justifying its truth.

Communicating methods are generally of the form

$$
(\forall \bar{x}.p_1(\overline{x_1}) \otimes \ldots \otimes p_n(\overline{x_n}) \multimap A).
$$

They are also called *multiheaded clauses* and the atomic propositions $p_i(\overline{x_i})$ are called the *heads* of the clause. When a clause has only one head, we call it *single-headed*. Computation is to take these methods as rewriting rules to reduce a multiset of formulae into a store of atomic communications. Each application of a method forms a *multiset rewriting step*.

The concurrency of the computation is reflected by using the multiplicative conjunction $\otimes$ as an operator for parallel composition. Its deduction rule

$$\frac{\Gamma, A, B \vdash \Delta}{\Gamma, A \otimes B \vdash \Delta}$$

can be understood as decomposing the resource $A \otimes B$ into the resources A and B in the context Γ.

Consider the deduction rule ($\& \vdash$):

$$(\& \vdash 1) \quad \frac{\Gamma, A \vdash \Delta}{\Gamma, A \& B \vdash \Delta} \quad (\& \vdash 2) \quad \frac{\Gamma, B \vdash \Delta}{\Gamma, A \& B \vdash \Delta}$$

The deduction can be regarded as choosing one of the component of $A \& B$ to verify the sequent within the context Γ. Since computation is to search for a successful proof, the choice may be influenced by other formulae in Γ (i.e. the environment). This corresponds to the "external choice" in concurrent programming [BG90]. Thus, don't care non-determinism (committed-choice), for which the arrival nondeterminism is a special case, can be uniformly modelled in terms of additive conjunction.

Communication between processes is realised by passing messages, as outlined in the following deduction:

$$\frac{\dfrac{\Gamma, B, A[t_1/y] \vdash \Delta}{\Gamma, B, x(t_1), x(t_1) \multimap A[t_1/y] \vdash \Delta} \; (\multimap \vdash)}{\dfrac{\Gamma, B, x(t_1), \forall y.\, x(y) \multimap A \vdash \Delta}{\Gamma, B \otimes x(t_1), \forall y.\, x(y) \multimap A \vdash \Delta} \; (\otimes \vdash)} \; (\forall \vdash)$$

The formula $x(t_1)$ can be understood as the sending of a message t_1 via a channel x. Thus, the formula $B \otimes x(t_1)$ sends the message $x(t_1)$ and then behaves like B. The formula $\forall y.\, x(y) \multimap A$ receives the message $x(t_1)$ and behaves like $A[t_1/x]$. In general, synchronisation between processes in the calculus is modelled by linear modus ponens. Consider the following deduction rule for linear implication:

$$\frac{\Gamma_1 \vdash A, \Delta_1 \qquad \Gamma_2, B \vdash \Delta_2}{\Gamma_1, \Gamma_2, A \multimap B \vdash \Delta_1, \Delta_2}$$

A special case of the inference rule is that the succedent of the lower sequent (the global requirement of computation) isn't split during deduction. That is:

$$\frac{\Gamma_1 \vdash A \qquad \Gamma_2, B \vdash \Delta}{\Gamma_1, \Gamma_2, A \multimap B \vdash \Delta}$$

The deduction step can be interpreted as transforming the current state, represented as $\Gamma_1, \Gamma_2, A \multimap B \vdash \Delta$, to the state $\Gamma_2, B \vdash \Delta$ whenever the local requirement condition A is met by a part of the environment Γ_1 (i.e. $\Gamma_1 \vdash A$) [1]. Then the deduction, called *linear modus ponens*, can be presented as:

$$\frac{\Gamma_2, B \vdash \Delta}{\Gamma_1, \Gamma_2, A \multimap B \vdash \Delta} \qquad \text{if } \Gamma_1 \vdash A$$

---

[1] The interpretation imposes a sequentiality of verifying the left branch first.

With this interpretation, linear modus ponens forms a uniform synchronisation mechanism where the implication $A \multimap B$ can be regarded as a process which will become B whenever the environment contains enough resources to meet the synchronisation condition (local requirement) represented by the premise A. Synchronisation is logically modelled as verifying the entailment between the resource Γ_1 and the local requirement A. In the case of communication, the local requirement A can be regarded as a *message pattern* waiting for matching the corresponding messages (Γ_1). Thus, linear modus ponens provides a concise means to model asynchronous communication.

The condition c in a formula $!c \multimap A$ states the synchronization condition between the environment and A. A can proceed only when c is justified with respect to recently received messages. The effect can be written as $\vdash_S c$ where S denotes the built-in theory asserting the truth of the formula c (Thus, the theory should be represented in classical logic). The modality $!$ allows the formula c to be accepted by the built-in theory in classical logic.

Variables local to a process can be introduced via existential quantification, because an existentially quantified variable can not be free outside the scope of $\exists$.

$$\frac{\Gamma, A}{\Gamma, \exists x.A} \quad x \text{ is not free in } \Gamma$$

The following derived rule, called CD because it combines contraction and dereliction, indicates that $!A$ can be understood as storing the process A:

$$\frac{!A, A, \Delta \vdash \Gamma}{!A, \Delta \vdash \Gamma} \text{ CD} - \text{Rule}$$

The inference is read as "making a copy of A and putting it into the environment". In the calculus, we use $!$ to store resources.

The operational model of the calculus is given as a special form of deduction in linear logic. It can be presented as a transition system where a configuration Γ is a multiset of agents. We use Con to denote the set of all configurations. A derivation relation $\overset{c}{\to} \subseteq Con \times Con$ represents the transition between configurations, where $\vartheta(\Gamma)$ denotes the free variables in the agents Γ.

The rules of the transition system are defined as follows:

$$\Gamma, 1 \overset{c}{\to} \Gamma,$$

$$\Gamma, A \otimes B \overset{c}{\to} \Gamma, A, B$$

$$\Gamma, A \& B \overset{c}{\to} \Gamma, A$$

$$\Gamma, A \& B \overset{c}{\to} \Gamma, B$$

$$\Gamma, !c \multimap A \overset{c}{\to} \Gamma, A \qquad \text{if } \vdash_S c$$

$$\Gamma, x_1(t_1), x_2(t_2), \ldots, x_n(t_n), (\forall \bar{y}. \otimes_{i=1}^{n} x_i(y_i) \multimap A) \overset{c}{\to} \Gamma.A[t_i/y_i]$$

$$\Gamma.\exists x.A \xrightarrow{c} \Gamma.A \qquad\qquad x \notin \vartheta(\Gamma)$$

$$\Gamma,!A \xrightarrow{c} \Gamma, A, !A$$

For any initial formula A, the initial configuration is $\Gamma_0 : \{A\}$. The computation transforms the initial configuration into a simpler system Γ_n such that no more communication is possible. The transition rules are deduction steps in linear logic. As proved in [DG92], the transition system realizes a special form of proofs in linear logic. The computation is complete in the sense that it constructs a proof that is canonical for all possible deduction of A. The soundness and completeness results can be summarised in the following theorem where we use $\vdash_{\mathcal{L}}$ to denote the provability in linear logic[2]. The theorem is a special case of the soundness and completeness of the CDC calculus [Guo93].

Theorem 3.1 *For any agent A, a term t and $x \in \vartheta(A)$, $A \vdash_{\mathcal{L}} x(t)$ iff there exists a derivation $\Gamma_0 : \{A\} \xrightarrow{c}{}^* \Gamma_n$ such that $\Gamma_n \vdash_{\mathcal{L}} x(t)$*

4 Modelling the Actor Model in Linear Logic

In this section, we present a logical formalism of the actor model by encoding the computational behaviour of its entities into linear logic formulae. The following analogies show the intuition underlying our encoding scheme.

Actor	$\Longleftrightarrow$	Formula
Message	$\Longleftrightarrow$	Formula
Configuration	$\Longleftrightarrow$	Multiset of formulae
Mail Addresses	$\Longleftrightarrow$	(Global) Channels
Local Attributes	$\Longleftrightarrow$	(Local) Channels

The linear logic formula for a class A is of the following general form:

$$! \,\forall\, name.\ v \ \ A\,(name, v) \multimap (\exists x.\ x(v) \otimes$$
$$!(\ \&_i \ \forall\ adr_i.name\,(message\_name_i, adr_i) \multimap$$
$$\exists\ name_i,\ v_i.(\,adr_i(m_i) \otimes B_i(name_i, v_i) \otimes A_i(name, newbehaviour)\,))$$

The formula states that the class name A is encoded as a channel variable. An actor of the class is generated by sending an identifier, say a, together with its initial local state v to the global class channel A. After its creation, an actor a is represented as a formula:

$$\exists\ x.\ x(v) \otimes !(\ \&_i \ \forall\ adr_i.a\,(message\_name_i, adr_i) \multimap$$
$$\exists name_i.(\,adr_i(m_i) \otimes B_i(name_i, v_i) \otimes D_i(a, newbehaviour)))$$

Where the existential quantified variable x models the local state of the actor and the formula

$$!(\forall\ adr_i.\ a\,(message\_name, adr_i) \multimap$$
$$\exists name_i.\ (adri(m_i) \otimes B_i(name_i, v_i) \otimes D_i(a, newstate)))$$

---

[2]More precisely, we assume linear logic integrated with a built-in theory for justifying conditions.

encodes a set of methods waiting on its name channel a for the messages having the pattern $(message\_name_i, adr_i)$ where $message_i$ specifies a particular task and adr_i are the identifiers of actors(mail addresses) to which the actor a may send messages. When the actor receives a message, a method will be activated to send a new message m_i to an actor adr_i, to create a new actor of the class B_i with the identifier $name_i$ and the initial state v_i by sending them to the corresponding class channel B_i and to change its own behaviour by sending its own name a together with the new state to the channel of the replacement class [3]. In the following, we present a systematic encoding of the model by defining a complete compilation scheme translating a program in the actor language defined in section 2 into linear logic formulæ.

Class as Reusable Implication: First of all, a class definition is translated into a reusable linear implication. The class name becomes a channel waiting for the message carrying the name of an instance actor of the class and its initial state. Thus, creating an actor is modelled, by the translation function $\mathcal{C}_o[\![\,]\!]$, as sending a message, consisting of the mail address of the creating actor and its initial local states to the class channel.

$$\mathcal{C}_o[\![Class_1, Class_2]\!]$$
$$= \mathcal{C}_o[\![Class_1]\!] \otimes \mathcal{C}_o[\![Class_2]\!]$$
$$\mathcal{C}_o[\![\text{class } A \text{ with } X \text{ \{methods\}}]\!]$$
$$= !\forall a, v_1, \ldots, v_n.A(a, v_1, \ldots, v_n) \multimap \exists X. \otimes_i x_i(v_i) \otimes !(\mathcal{C}_m[\![\text{methods}]\!]^{a,X}))$$

where $X = \{x_1, \ldots, x_n\}$ and $\otimes_i x_i(v_i) = x_1(v_1) \otimes \ldots \otimes x_n(v_n)$.

In the translation, the local attributes of an actor are encoded as existential quantified variables. As we presented before, existential quantification provides a logical account to the notion of locality. Thus, local attributes of an actor are its local channels. The formula $x_i(v_i)$ instantiates the initial value v_i of the local states to the corresponding local channel x_i.

Methods as the Sum of Linear Implications: In the actor language, a method presents the action that an actor may take upon the receiving of messages. At one instance, an actor receives the message which reach it first. Such an *arrival nondeterminism* can be modelled as a form of *committed choice* in terms of the additive conjunction operator. The following translation of methods of the actor a with local channels X, presented as the function $\mathcal{C}_m[\![\,]\!]^{a,X}$, maps the set of methods of a into an additive conjunction of linear implications.

$$\mathcal{C}_m[\![method_1, \ldots, method_n]\!]^{a,X}$$
$$= \mathcal{C}_m[\![method_1]\!]^{a,X} \&, \ldots, \& \mathcal{C}_m[\![method_n]\!]^{a,X}$$
$$\mathcal{C}_m[\![\langle message\_pattern \rangle => \langle actions \rangle]\!]^{a,X}$$
$$= \forall Y.\mathcal{C}_{me}[\![message\_pattern]\!]^a \multimap \mathcal{C}_a[\![actions]\!]^{a,X}$$

where Y are variables in the head of a method.

---

[3] As the special case, the replacement class can be the original class of a, i.e. $D_i = A$. Thus, the effect of the replacement is to changes the local state of a.

The function $\mathcal{C}_{me}[\![\,]\!]^a$ maps a message pattern with respect to the actor a into an atomic formula:

$$\mathcal{C}_{me}[\![message\_name(y_1, \ldots, y_m)]\!]^a$$
$$= a(message_name, y_1, \ldots, y_m)$$

Thus, with the translation, a method of the actor a with the local channels X:

$$message\_name(y_1, ..., y_n) \Rightarrow actions$$

is translated into an universally quantified implication:

$$\forall y_1, \ldots, y_n.a(message\_name, y_1, \ldots, y_n) \multimap \mathcal{C}_a[\![actions]\!]^{a,X}$$

which models the behaviour of waiting the message $(message\_name, y_1, \ldots, y_n)$ on the mail address a and carrying on the action when the message arrived with all variables y_i instantiated according to the content of the message. The function $\mathcal{C}_a[\![\,]\!]^{a,X}$ maps a set of actions the actor a may take to a multiplicative conjunction of action formulae. The multiplicative conjunction models the parallel composition of all component actions in the method.

$$\mathcal{C}_a[\![action, \ldots, action]\!]^{a,X}$$
$$= \mathcal{C}_a[\![action]\!]^{a,X} \otimes, \ldots, \otimes \mathcal{C}_a[\![action]\!]^{a,X}$$

Each individual action of an actor a with local channels X is translated by the function $\mathcal{C}_a[\![\,]\!]^{a,X}$. First of all, the command of sending a message $message\_name(args)$ to the actor with the mail address adr is translated as a message $(name, agrs)$ put on the channel adr. That is,

$$\mathcal{C}_a[\![send(adr, message\_name(args))]\!]^{a,X}$$
$$= adr(message\_name, args)$$

The **become** command $become(D, args)$ specifying the replacement of the behaviour of the actor a by creating a new actor of a foreign class D (i.e. $D \neq A$) with the state $args$ and the mail address a. Since a class name is modelled as a global channel, as we presented before, the command is encoded as sending a message $(a, args)$ to the class channel D. That is,

$$\mathcal{C}_a[\![become(D, args)]\!]^{a,X}$$
$$= D(a, args)$$

When the class of the replacement actor is the original class of the actor a (i.e. $D = A$), the **become** command changes only the local states of the actor. The translation can be simplified as:

$$\mathcal{C}_a[\![become(A, args)]\!]^{a,X}$$
$$= \forall u_1 \ldots u_n.x_1(u_1) \otimes \ldots \otimes x_n(u_n) \multimap x_1(arg_1[u_i/x_i]) \otimes \ldots \otimes x_n(arg_n[u_i/x_i])$$

where $\{x_1, \ldots, x_n\} = X$.

The encoding of the let...do command is straightforward.

$$C_a[\![\text{let } x := D(args) \text{ do } \langle actions \rangle]\!]^{a,X}$$
$$= D(x, args) \otimes C_a[\![\langle actions \rangle]\!]^{a,X}$$

That is, the behaviour of binding a newly created actor of the class D with the mail address x, which will be referred in the actions within its scope, is modelled as sending the mail address x and the initial states $args$ to the class channel D in concurrent with taking the actions.

The conditional statement is translated into an additive conjunction of two implications modelling the alternative choice determined by the truth of the condition.

$$C_a[\![\text{if } \langle conditional \rangle \text{ then } \langle actions_1 \rangle \text{ else } \langle actions_2 \rangle]\!]^{a,X}$$
$$= (C_c[\![conditional]\!] \Rightarrow C_a[\![\langle actions_1 \rangle]\!]^{a,X})$$
$$\&(\neg C_c[\![conditional]\!] \Rightarrow C_a[\![\langle actions_2 \rangle]\!]^{a,X})$$

Note that the intuitionistic implication, rather than the linear implication is used. This is because the condition is not proved by the linear sequent calculus rather by the built-in system justifying the truth of the condition following the predefined interpretation of the symbols in the condition. We use the function $C_c[\![\,]\!]$ to denote the fixed interpretation. As we presented before, such a preinterpreted condition can be viewed as a reusable formula. By the logical equivalence: $!c \multimap A \equiv c \Rightarrow A$, we use intuitionistic implication to model the conditional statement.

In order to access the local state of an actor a with the local channels $x_1, \ldots, x_n$, we always add the following formula as a built-in component into the additive conjunction of implications translating the methods.

$$\forall u_1, \ldots, u_n. \, a(read, u_1, \ldots, u_n)$$
$$\multimap \forall s_1, \ldots, s_n.(\, x_1(s_1) \otimes \ldots \otimes \, x_n(s_n)$$
$$\multimap x_1(s_1) \otimes \ldots \otimes x_n(s_n) \otimes u_1(s_1) \otimes \ldots \otimes u_n(s_n) \,)$$

With this added formula, the local state of an actor can be read and copied to the channel $u_1, \ldots, u_n$. Thus, the formula can be regarded as the translation of a *system methods* implementing the *local_state* function returning the local state of an actor in a configuration [AH88].

By the translation, the *Account* class, presented in section 2, can be encoded systematically into the following formula:

$$! \, (\forall A. \, Account(A, v)$$
$$\multimap \exists bal. \, (\, bal(v) \otimes$$
$$! \, (\forall val. \, A(crediting, val)$$
$$\multimap \forall n.(bal(n) \multimap bal(n + val) \,)$$
$$\& \quad \forall val. \, A(debiting, val)$$
$$\multimap \forall n.(bal(n) \multimap (val \leq n \Rightarrow bal(n \text{-} val) \,) \,)$$
$$\& \quad \forall val. \, A(trans, val, B)$$
$$\multimap \forall n.(bal(n) \multimap (val \leq n \Rightarrow$$
$$(bal(n \text{-} val) \otimes B(credit, val)))$$
$$\& \quad \forall x. \, A(read, x)$$
$$\multimap \forall n.(bal(n) \multimap (bal(n) \otimes x(n)))))$$

This formula defines the account class as a reusable linear implication. To open an account, an actor can be created by sending the name of the actor, together with the initial value of the account, to the global channel *Account*. The name itself is also a channel. When an account is opened, its balance attribute is initialised to the initial value and then the account is ready to receive messages on its name channel. The modality ! prefix to the inner "committed-choice" implications models the idea of " always" i.e. the effect of recursion. Messages are parametrised by the message names *crediting, debiting, trans, balance*. On receiving the *crediting* message, the actor adds the value *val* to its balance n. This is done by reading its current balance via the local private channel *bal*. By the feature of linear modus ponens, reading the private channel will consume the current value so that the addition can be done by just sending a message $val + n$ to the channel *bal*. This is a way to logically model an updating action, as the special case of the become command. The *debiting* case is similar. In the case of *trans*, the message contains the name of the account where the money is to be transferred. After retrieving the current balance from the private store and checking that there is enough money for the transfer, the transferred money is subtracted from the current balance of A and is credited to account B by concurrently sending a message $B(credit, val)$ to the environment. Note that the notion of attribute is realised as a local private channel introduced by existential quantification. Thus, each invocation for opening an account will give a new private channel *bal* as its own attribute which is logically updatable. This encoded formula illustrates a purely logical definition of a class of actors. It provides not only of a succinct declarative reading of the class but also, and even more importantly, a deductive interpretation of its concurrent computation. With the encoding, a configuration of the actor model can be encoded as a multiplicative conjunction of logical formulae logical formulae. The concurrent computation in the actor model is fully mapped to the transition system of the logic process calculus presented in section 3. Since the transition system realises a special class of linear proofs, actor-based concurrent computation is modelled as the deduction in linear logic. Following the theorem 3.1, the logical meaning of the actor model can be established by the following corollary which is proved in the forthcoming report [DG94]:

Corollary 4.0.1 *Suppose P is a program in the actor language consisting of a set of class definitions and A is a defined class. Let a be the identifier of an actor of the class A, $V : v_1, \ldots v_n$ is a sequence of values stating the initial state of a, $X : x_1, \ldots x_n$ is a sequence of variables and m is the initial message sent to a, Then, for a set of values $t_1, \ldots, t_n$*

$$\mathcal{C}_o[\![P]\!] \otimes \mathcal{C}_a[\![\text{let } a = A(V) \text{ do send}(a, m)]\!] \otimes a(read, X) \vdash_{\mathcal{L}} \otimes_i x_i(t_i) \otimes \top$$

iff there is a transition derivation :

$$G_0 : \{a(V), m\} \xrightarrow{*} G_n$$

such that local_state$(G_n, a) = t_1, \ldots, t_n$, where $\otimes_i x_i(t_i) = x_1(t_1) \otimes \ldots \otimes x_n(t_n)$ and the function local_state(G, a) returns the local state of a in the configuration G.

5 Conclusion

In this paper, we present a linear logic formalisation of the actor model. Based on the logic formalism, the concurrent computational behaviours of the model are precisely modelled as deductions in the logic. The formalism therefore establishs a logical semantics to the actor model. This work is related to some recent research work on the theoretical foundation of object-based concurrency. An interesting approach is to use algebraic process calculi for modelling concurrent objects. Since these calculi are normally of some synchronous mechanism as its underlying communication protocol, encoding the actor model in these calculi become complicated. In [HT91], Honda et.al proposed an asynchronous process calculus to model concurrent objects. As we shown in [Guo93], the calculus can be fully captured by our logical system. Thus, the linear logic model seems to be more general. Indeed, due to its richer structure and its naturalness to reason about change and interaction, linear logic constitutes an ideal meta logic for studying the properties of concurrent objects. In [KY94], Kobayashi and Yonezawa proposed a type system for actor-based concurrent object oriented programming through an encoding of an actor language into a typed logic programming based on an amalgamation of linear logic and typed λ-calculus. Due to the complicated structure of the underlying logic, it is not easy to explore the semantic properties by the encoding. We have shown that the pure linear logic provides an elegant mathematical foundation for the actor model. The relationship with Meseguer's work on the rewriting logic based concurrent object oriented programming is obvious. The key idea underlying our approach is to use linear modus ponens to model concurrent rewriting where the concurrency is inherited in the proof structure of the logic. The main advantage of the linear logic approach is that the quantification mechanism provides a simple solution of modelling communication and local state, which are the key issues of the actor model.

6 Acknowledgements

We would like to thank all the people in the Advanced Languages and Architectures Section in the Department of Computing at Imperial College who provide a stimulating working environment. This work was supported by a U.K. SERC research grant "Definitional Constraint Programming: A Foundation for Logically Correct Concurrent Systems".

References

[Abr90] Samson Abramsky. Computational Interpretation of Linear Logic. Technical report, Dept. of Computing, Imperial College, Oct. 1990.

[AH88] Gul Agha and Carl Hewitt. Concurrent Programming Using Actors. In A.Yonezawa and M. Tokoro, editors, *Object-Orientde Concurrent Programming*, pages 37–54. The MIT Press, 1988.

[BG90]   Gerard Boudol and G.Berry. The chemical abstract machine. In *Proc. of the 17th Annual ACM symposium on Principle of Programming Languages.* ACM, 1990.

[DG92]   J. Darlington and Y. Guo. Definitional constraint programming for parallel computing: An introduction. In *Proc. of the ICOT workshop on Future Direction of Parallel Programming and Architecture*, June 1992. ICOT TM-1185.

[DG94]   John Darlington and Yike Guo. Towards a logical theory of object-based concurrency. Technical report, Imperial College, May 1994.

[Gir87] Jean-Yves Girard. Linear logic. *Theoretical Computer Science*, 50(1), 1987.

[Guo93] Yike Guo. *Definitional Constraint Programming.* PhD thesis, Dept. of Computing, Imperial College, December 1993.

[HT91]   K. Honda and M. Tokoro. On Asynchronous Communication Semantics. In *Proc. of ECOOP'91 Workshop*, LNCS 612, pages 21– 51, 1991.

[KY94]   Naoki Kobayashi and Akinori Yonezawa. Type-theoretic foundations for concurrent object. Technical report, Dept of Information Science, 1994.

[Mes89] Jose Meseguer. General logics. Technical Report SRI-CSL-89-5, SRI International, March 1989.

[MW91]   Jose Meseguer and Timothy Winkler. Parallel programming in maude. Technical Report SRI-CSL-91-08, SRI International, November 1991.

A   Linear Logic

Linear logic is presented in Figure 3 in the form of a Gentzen-style sequent calculus. Since the structural rules for weakening and contraction are abolished in linear logic, a collection of formulae in a deduction should be regarded as a multiset rather than a set. The feature of resource-consciousness results from the linearity of the proofs which requires that each assumption must be used exactly once. For a sequent $\Gamma_1..\Gamma_n \vdash \Delta_1..\Delta_m$ the assumptions Γ_i can be viewed as resources and the conclusions Δ_j as requirements that have to be met by spending the given resources.

The linearity necessitates two different versions of conjunction: the *multiplicative conjunction* (tensor, $\otimes$) and the *additive conjunction* (with, &). If the multiplicative conjunction $\otimes$ is used in an assumption Γ_i of a sequent, then this reflects the fact that both components of the conjunction must make contributions to the proof derivation within the same environment. On the other hand, the use of the additive conjunction & reflects the fact that once the formula is used in the proof, either the first or the second component must be chosen for the further derivation. Dually, two versions of disjunction are required. The *multiplicative disjunction* (par, @) causes the splitting of its environment, whereas *additive disjunction* (plus, $\oplus$) causes the environment to be copied for the derivation of both components.

Another important connective is *linear implication* ($\multimap$), which can be used to localize inference. It can be derived by the logical equivalence $A \multimap B = A^\perp @ B$ where $A^\perp$ is the linear negation of A. Each sequent $\Gamma_1..\Gamma_n \vdash \Delta_1..\Delta_m$ has the intended meaning that $\otimes_{i=1}^n \Gamma_i \multimap @_{j=1}^m \Delta_j$ is valid.

The "of course" modality (!) is introduced to allow a controlled form of weakening and contraction in the language. Its dual (?) is called "why not".

Due to the symmetry of linear logic, the same multiset of formulae can be treated either as assumptions, using conjunction, or as consequences, using disjunction. Here, we concentrate on the interpretation of formulae as resources and there only deal with the rules for the left-hand side of sequents.

For a comprehensive description of linear logic see [Gir87].

Axiom:

$$(\text{Id}) \quad \overline{A \vdash A}$$

Cut :

$$\frac{\Gamma_1 \vdash G, \Delta_1 \qquad \Gamma_2, G \vdash \Delta_2}{\Gamma_1, \Gamma_2 \vdash \Delta_1, \Delta_2}$$

Structure Rule:

$$(\text{Exchange Left}) \quad \frac{\Gamma_1, A, B, \Gamma_2 \vdash \Delta}{\Gamma_1, B, A, \Gamma_2 \vdash \Delta} \qquad (\text{Exchange Right}) \quad \frac{\Gamma \vdash \Delta_1, A, B, \Delta_2}{\Gamma \vdash \Delta_1, B, A, \Delta_2}$$

Logic Rules :

$$(1 \vdash) \quad \frac{\Gamma \vdash \Delta}{\Gamma, 1 \vdash \Delta} \qquad\qquad (\vdash 1) \quad \overline{\vdash 1}$$

$$(0 \vdash) \quad \overline{\Gamma, 0 \vdash \Delta} \qquad\qquad (\vdash \top) \quad \overline{\Gamma \vdash \top, \Delta}$$

$$(\bot \vdash) \quad \overline{\bot \vdash} \qquad\qquad (\vdash \bot) \quad \frac{\Gamma \vdash \Delta}{\Gamma \vdash \bot, \Delta}$$

$$(^{\bot} \vdash) \quad \frac{\Gamma \vdash A, \Delta}{\Gamma, A^{\bot} \vdash \Delta} \qquad\qquad (\vdash^{\bot}) \quad \frac{\Gamma, A \vdash \Delta}{\Gamma \vdash A^{\bot}, \Delta}$$

$$(\otimes \vdash) \quad \frac{\Gamma, A, B \vdash \Delta}{\Gamma, A \otimes B \vdash \Delta} \qquad\qquad (\vdash \otimes) \quad \frac{\Gamma_1 \vdash A, \Delta_1 \qquad \Gamma_2 \vdash B, \Delta_2}{\Gamma_1, \Gamma_2 \vdash A \otimes B, \Delta_1, \Delta_2}$$

$$(\& \vdash) \quad \frac{\Gamma, A \vdash \Delta}{\Gamma, A \& B \vdash \Delta}, \frac{\Gamma, B \vdash \Delta}{\Gamma, A \& B \vdash \Delta} \qquad (\vdash \&) \quad \frac{\Gamma \vdash A, \Delta \qquad \Gamma \vdash B, \Delta}{\Gamma \vdash A \& B, \Delta}$$

$$(@ \vdash) \quad \frac{\Gamma_1, A \vdash \Delta_1, \qquad \Gamma_2, B \vdash \Delta_2}{\Gamma_1, \Gamma_2, A @ B \vdash \Delta_1, \Delta_2} \qquad (\vdash @) \quad \frac{\Gamma \vdash A, B, \Delta}{\Gamma \vdash A @ B, \Delta}$$

$$(\oplus \vdash) \quad \frac{\Gamma, A \vdash \Delta \qquad \Gamma, B \vdash \Delta}{\Gamma, A \oplus B \vdash \Delta} \qquad (\vdash \oplus) \quad \frac{\Gamma \vdash A, \Delta}{\Gamma \vdash A \oplus B, \Delta} \frac{\Gamma \vdash B, \Delta}{\Gamma \vdash A \oplus B, \Delta}$$

$$(\multimap \vdash) \quad \frac{\Gamma_1 \vdash A, \Delta_1 \qquad \Gamma_2, B \vdash \Delta_2}{\Gamma_1, \Gamma_2, A \multimap B \vdash \Delta_1, \Delta_2} \qquad (\vdash \multimap) \quad \frac{\Gamma, A \vdash B, \Delta}{\Gamma \vdash A \multimap B, \Delta}$$

$$(\text{Contraction } !) \quad \frac{\Gamma, !A, !A \vdash \Delta}{\Gamma, !A \vdash \Delta} \qquad (\text{Contraction } ?) \quad \frac{\Gamma \vdash ?A, ?A, \Delta}{\Gamma \vdash ?A, \Delta}$$

$$(\text{Weakening } !) \quad \frac{\Gamma \vdash \Delta}{\Gamma, !A \vdash \Delta} \qquad (\text{Weakening } ?) \quad \frac{\Gamma \vdash \Delta}{\Gamma \vdash ?A, \Delta}$$

$$(\text{Promotion } ?) \quad \frac{!\Gamma, A \vdash ?\Delta}{!\Gamma, ?A \vdash ?\Delta} \qquad (\text{Promotion } !) \quad \frac{!\Gamma \vdash A, ?\Delta}{!\Gamma \vdash !A, ?\Delta}$$

$$(\text{Dereliction } !) \quad \frac{\Gamma, A \vdash \Delta}{\Gamma, !A \vdash \Delta} \qquad (\text{Dereliction } ?) \quad \frac{\Gamma \vdash A, \Delta}{\Gamma \vdash ?A, \Delta}$$

$$(\exists \vdash *) \quad \frac{\Gamma, A \vdash \Delta}{\Gamma, \exists x. A \vdash \Delta} \qquad (\vdash \exists) \quad \frac{\Gamma \vdash A[t/x], \Delta}{\Gamma \vdash \exists x. A, \Delta}$$

$$(\forall \vdash) \quad \frac{\Gamma, A[t/x] \vdash \Delta}{\Gamma, \forall x. A \vdash \Delta} \qquad (\vdash \forall *) \quad \frac{\Gamma \vdash A, \Delta}{\Gamma \vdash \forall x. A \vdash \Delta}$$

* x is not free in lower sequent.

Figure 1: Linear Logic

Objects versus Functions in User-Validation of Requirements: Which Paradigm Works Best?

Tony Moynihan

School of Computer Applications
Dublin City University
Dublin 9
Ireland

E-Mail: Tony.Moynihan@compapp.dcu.ie   Fax: +353 1 7045442

Abstract:

This paper describes an experiment to evaluate the relative effectiveness of functional-decomposition and object-orientation as paradigms for client/developer communication in the early stages of the system development process. The subjects were twenty executives attending a management development program. The experimental task required the subjects to comment critically on the content and format of two analyses of equivalent content. The first analysis took the form of a functional-decomposition. The second analysis took the form of an object-model. The results suggest that functional-decomposition is the more effective of the two paradigms as a vehicle for early client/developer communication. Also, the subjects judged the functional-decomposition to be superior to the object-model on a number of important attributes.

Keywords:

Object-orientation, functional-decomposition, user-validation, information requirements determination

1. Introduction

The Object-Oriented approach is well established in programming. Recently, its application has been extended to include systems analysis and design (see, for example, Coad and Yourdon, 1991 and Rumbaugh et al.,1991). Simultaneously, approaches to software development which emphasise functional decomposition are increasingly seen to be 'old fashioned.'

One of the major 'selling-features' of the O-O approach is its use of a uniform set of concepts across the development process , thus supporting verification, traceability and re-use. Presumably, to obtain the full benefits of this uniformity of representation , the O-O approach should be used from the very start of the development process i.e for requirements elicitation and validation. But SHOULD it ? How effective is the O-O paradigm as the main vehicle of communication between the typical 'customer' and the developer? Are object-oriented descriptions more (or less) effective as a basis for user-validation than are descriptions based on traditional functional decomposition? The experiment described below was designed to help answer these questions.

The subjects were twenty business managers attending a part-time graduate program at the Irish Management Institute. The scenario painted for the subjects was one in which two (ficticious) computer consultants had been asked to independently report on how IT systems could help run the 'Happy Hours Health-Farm' , also ficticious! The consultants' preliminary analyses of the health farm were given to the subjects. One analysis was structured as a functional-decomposition. The other as an object-model. The contents of the two 'analyses' were equivalent, although this fact was not made explicit to the subjects.

Subjects were asked to critique the content of each of the two analyses. Subjects were also asked to record their opinions on the relative merits of the two paradigms. The 'effectiveness' of the two paradigms in communicating system functionality was inferred from the 'quality' of the subjects' critiques and from the opinions they expressed about each paradigm.

2. Previous related research

'Representation research' , as it has been described, has a long and rich tradition, with its roots in experimental psychology (e.g. Parker and Bass, 1975) and in semiotics, the 'science of signs and symbols' (e.g. Andersen, 1990.)

Abstract representations of real-world phenomena play a central role in software engineering. For this reason, representation research has been an active topic in software engineering for many years. Much of this work has been experimental, and has been designed to compare the 'effectiveness in-use' of alternative software-engineering representation schemas.

For example, in the domain of data-modelling, Juhn and Naumann (1985) compared four different data-structure representations for ease-of-understanding and 'usability.' The representations compared were the E-R model, the LDS model, the DAD model and the RDM model. The subjects were second year MBA students who were enrolled in a systems analysis and design course. They were given two experimental tasks. The first task required the subjects to interpret a given data-model. The second task required subjects to construct a data-model for a problem described in natural-language.

It was found that subjects could more accurately interpret relationships and cardinality constraints when these were expressed in the graphical E-R and LDS notation. Subjects performed best on identifier interpretation when using the relational RDM notation. On the data-model construction task, subjects performed better with the graphical E-R and LDS notation. The overall conclusion reached was that non-expert users are likely to be both more comfortable and more productive with graphical, semantic data-models like the E-R model.

Larsen and Naumann (1992) conducted an experiment to compare the utility of abstract and concrete representations in the systems analysis process. Subjects were students who had completed a graduate level course in systems analysis. Subjects worked in pairs, one playing the role of a systems analyst, the other the role of a user. The user-analyst pairs were given the task of validating an imperfect data-flow-diagram for a hypothetical system requested by the 'user.' The 'analyst' had the job of interviewing the 'user' to confirm that the proposed system met his/her requirements.

Half the pairs were given a 'physical' data-flow-diagram (i.e. a DFD containing explicit implementation details and other references to concrete real-world objects.) The other half were given a logical data-flow-diagram for the same underlying system (i.e. a DFD from which implementation details and concrete references were excluded.) It was found that user-analyst pairs who used the 'concrete' DFD discovered more anomalies (omissions, inconsistencies etc.) than did pairs using the logical DFD. The researchers generalised from these findings to conclude that concrete representations are probably more effective as a basis for user-analyst communication than are abstract representations.

Loy and Stapp (1993) conducted an experiment to compare the utility of data-flow diagrams (DFDs) and N-Squared charts for requirements specification and validation. An N-Squared chart is a more structured, matrix-like alternative to a DFD. The subjects , who were adults with a wide variety of education and work-experience, were unfamiliar with both techniques. They were first given training in the use of each. They were then given two small-scale tasks : one task involved interpreting either a DFD or an equivalent N-Squared chart; the second task involved building either a DFD or an equivalent N-Squared chart from a natural-language description. For the small-scale systems used in the experiment, DFDs seemed to provide a better basis for the interpretation task and N-Squared charts seemed to provide a better basis for the construction task. The researchers saw some evidence to suggest that for complex or large-scale systems, an N-Squared chart would be more effective than a DFD because of the former's tighter structure.

I hope the present paper will make a contribution to this field by extending it to include a comparison of the effectiveness of the functional and object-oriented paradigms in the communication of system functionality to users.

3. The 'Scenario' painted for the subjects

The first step was to choose a suitable application domain as a vehicle for the experiment. An application domain which was very unfamiliar to the subjects would clearly be' a bad choice. Subjects would have no basis on which to identify missing features or other anomalies in the experimental materials. An application domain which was very familiar to the subjects would also be a bad choice. A subject might not mention an apparent oversight in the material on the assumption that it was so obvious a point that it had been deliberately excluded.

Guided by these considerations, the application domain chosen was the management of operations in a fictitious organisation called the 'Happy Hours Health-Farm.' Obviously, few subjects were likely to have experienced a stay at a health-farm. But I felt most would be familiar with the broad theme, if only through novels and films.

I created a 'story-line' involving two computer consultants, Gerry Kelly and Liam Ryan. In the story-line, Gerry and Liam have each been asked by health-farm management to independently give a view on how IT systems could support health-farm operations. Both have made initial visits to the health-farm and have completed their preliminary analyses. These 'analyses' , Kelly's in the form of a functional-decomposition and Ryan's in the form of an object-model, were the basis for the experimental task.

4. The experimental materials

When constructing the consultants' 'analyses', I kept in mind the need for the content of the two analyses to be 'equivalent' , in the sense that the substantive content of either should be derivable from the content of the other. This point is central to the logic of our experiment ; the goal was to compare the effectiveness of the two paradigms as information presentation styles in the user-validation process. Thus equivalence of content of the two 'analyses' was obviously essential.

A second concern was the need for the two analyses to be at the same level of abstraction. Barros(1992) makes the point that user-oriented system specifications typically contain a mixture of user-goals (the 'why'), the functions to be provided (the 'what'), and implementation structures (the 'how'). Given the goal of the experiment, I chose to restrict the analyses to the functional level of abstraction (the 'what').

My next task was to choose exemplars of the two paradigms. In other words, to select the specific representation schemes to be used in the experiment. For the O-O paradigm, I chose Rumbaugh's Object Model Notation (Rumbaugh et al.,1991) , as it appears to have achieved a significant level of industry acceptance. The notation supports Generalisation (Inheritance) , Aggregation, Class Attributes/ Operations and various types of Class Association.

Functional-Decomposition is a universally used, well understood paradigm. Many schemas for presenting a functional decomposition have been proposed over the years. These differ only in minor points of layout. The schema I chose is that suggested in Martin(1982).

The 'analyses' which I constructed, one for each 'consultant', are shown in appendices 2 and 3. In each case, I prefaced the analysis with context-setting comments and explanation. With a view to achieving equivalence of content of the two analyses, I excluded class attributes and class associations from the O-O analysis. Given that the analyses are ostensibly 'first-cut' attempts by the two consultants, this restriction is probably not unrealistic.

Having constructed the two analyses, I next created 'An Extract from the Health-Farm Prospectus.' This is shown in appendix 1. As will be seen later, this 'extract' was given to the subjects and was described as a source of background information on the health-farm.

Many of the 'facts' provided in the extract were reflected in the consultants' analyses. However, the extract was 'seeded' with a number of **additional** 'facts' of potential relevance, which I deliberately omitted from the consultants' analyses. The frequency with which the subjects detected these apparent 'oversights' in the consultants' analyses was one of the dependent variables in the experiment. Five such 'seeds' were deliberately sown :

> (i) The existence of a golf-course, horse-riding school, indoor swimming pool and hydro-massage tanks for use by guests;
> (ii) The employment by the health-farm of psychologists, therapists and beauty experts;
> (iii) The organisation of activities such as music-recitals, painting sessions and mini-bus excursions;
> (iv) The availability for hire by guests of specialist equipment such as ultra-sound deep-tissue massage canopies.
> (v) The concept of a personalised 'inner-health' programme for each guest.

Finally, I designed a simple questionnaire to capture the subjects' views on the relative merits of the two 'styles' of presentation (see appendix 5).

5. The subjects

The subjects were twenty middle and senior managers from a variety of Irish organisations. All were students on a part-time executive masters program in organisational science at the Irish Management Institute. Their mean age was about 35 years. None were information systems specialists. Their course included no technical material on IS.

6. The procedure

The instructions given to the subjects appear in appendix 4.

Each subject was given a sealed envelope containing :

> (i) The Instructions
> (ii) The 'Extract' from the 'Happy Hours' Health-Farm Prospectus
> (iii) Gerry Kelly's Report

(iv) Liam Ryan's Report

(v) The questionnaire on the two styles of analysis

Subjects were first asked to read the ' extract' from the health-farm 'prospectus'. This extract was described as a source of some information about the health-farm and its operations. The subjects were next asked to take one of the two consultants' analyses and to study it (Kelly's if the subject's age was an even number of years, Ryan's if otherwise.) They were then asked to record on a blank sheet of paper what they saw to be the strengths and weaknesses of the **content** (not the **style**) of the analysis. Although some examples of things that could constitute strengths/weaknesses in an analysis were given to the subjects, (e.g. omissions, inconsistencies, narrowness of perspective etc.), no firm guidelines on approaching the task were offered in the instructions. It was hoped this 'open-endedness' would result in a richer set of responses than would be obtained by tightly structuring the task.

Subjects were next asked to repeat the above task on the second of the two reports. The instructions emphasised that subjects were to treat the two reports **independently**. In particular, they were asked **not** to re-read the first report, or to add to their comments on it.

Finally, subjects were asked to record their opinions on the relative merits of the two different styles of analysis on the questionnaire.

7. The results

The goal of the experiment was to compare the effectiveness of Object-Orientation and Functional-Decomposition as paradigms for communicating system functionality to users. The notion of 'effectiveness' was operationalised in terms of subjects' task-performance and in terms of subjects' opinions on the two 'styles' of analysis.

7.1 Subjects' task-performance

A subject's task-performance was measured in two ways :

(i) by the number of 'seeds' the subject mentioned as being missing from the analysis. It will be recalled that a 'seed' is a potentially important 'fact' planted in the prospectus extract and deliberately omitted from the consultants' analyses. Five 'seeds' were sown.

(ii) by the 'quality' of the subject's critique of the **content** of the analysis. I did not define 'quality' in advance of running the experiment. I decided to adopt an inductive approach by letting the data 'speak for itself.'

Table 1 contains a breakdown of the twenty subjects by number of missing 'seeds' identified. There is no evidence in Table 1 to suggest that seed detection rate differed across the two analyses.

	Detected No Seeds	Detected One Seed	Detected Two or More Seeds	Total
Functional Decomposition	12	3	5	20
Object-Model	15	3	2	20

Table 1 :   Numbers of subjects detecting missing 'seeds'

Subjects' comments on the **content** of each analysis fell into one of two categories. The first category contained references to apparent omissions in the analysis (other than the 'seeds'). Examples of comments in this category include :

> "The purchasing activity is totally missing."

> "What about stock control for the kitchens and bars?"

> "Scheduling of maintenance must be important"

The second category contained comments of a more strategic nature. Comments in this category related to the perspective taken in the analysis, to the relative emphasis given to the different components in the analysis, or to the priorities implied by the analysis. Examples of comments include :

> "Surely the priority should be on urgent financial reporting systems?"

> "The goal seems to be to maximise the use of IT. Its a bit mindless."

> "Should be more emphasis on measuring the cost-effectiveness of people and facilities."

> "Emphasis on **systems** to schedule appointments etc. doesn't square with the personal attention promised in the prospectus."

Tables 2 and 3 below give breakdowns of the twenty subjects by the numbers of comments made in each of these two categories for each of the two analyses.

	Identified None	Identified One or Two	Identified Three or More	Total
Functional Decomposition	6	9	5	20
Object-Model	6	11	3	20

Table 2 : Numbers of subjects identifying missing/needed extra features

	Made no Comments	Made one or More Comments	Total
Functional Decomposition	9	11	20
Object-Model	15	5	20

Table 3 : Numbers of subjects making comment on overall perspective/balance/priority

There is no evidence in Table 2 to suggest that either representation was more successful than the other in terms of the frequency of comments elicited about missing/needed extra features. But what of the **substance** of these comments? For example, did the object-model elicit more 'object oriented' comments than did the functional-decomposition? A content analysis of the comments showed that this was not the case. No systematic differences in the focus of comments relating to missing / needed extra features were found.

Regarding subjects' comments in the second category, Table 3 suggests that the functional-decomposition was far more effective than the object-model in eliciting comments of a strategic nature ($p < .05$ on Fisher's Exact Test.) Again, a content analysis revealed no differences in focus between the 'strategic' comments elicited by the object-model and those elicited by the functional-decomposition.

7.2 Subjects' opinions on the two 'styles' of analysis

Subjects' opinions on the relative merits of the two **styles** of analysis were obtained by means of the post-experiment questionnaire. Twelve subjects said they preferred the functional-decomposition. Eight subjects said they preferred the object-model. A content analysis of the completed questionnaires showed that most of the subjects drew from the same set of six broad criteria in comparing the two analyses. In Table 4 below, I have expressed these criteria in the form of the six desireable attributes that the subjects believed an analysis style should display. The table shows the numbers of subjects making positive and negative comments about each of the two styles on each of the six attributes.

		Making Positive Comment	Making Negative Comment	Making No Comment	Total
The notation and concepts are easy to understand	Functional-Decomposition	15	1	4	20
	Object-Model	5	11	4	20
It helps the reader to detect incompleteness and internal inconsistency	Functional-Decomposition	4	0	16	20
	Object-Model	1	2	17	20
It provokes the reader to make comments and ask questions	Functional-Decomposition	8	0	12	20
	Object-Model	0	1	19	20
It gives the reader a holistic understanding of the application domain	Functional-Decomposition	6	0	14	20
	Object-Model	2	6	12	20
It helps the reader to evaluate likely implementation benefits and priorities	Functional-Decomposition	9	0	11	20
	Object-Model	0	7	13	20
It helps the reader to visualise an implementation of the system	Functional-Decomposition	3	6	11	20
	Object-Model	6	5	9	20

Table 4 : Numbers of subjects making positive and negative comment on the **style** of each analysis

Table 4 shows that the subjects found the functional-decomposition easier to understand than the object-model (p<.05 on Fisher's Exact Test). Many said that functional-decomposition was a familiar and intuitively obvious concept, but found the concept of an object-model to be new and somewhat inscrutable. Interestingly, this 'novelty' does not appear to have detracted from the subjects' performance in detecting missing 'seeds' and other features in the object-model (see tables 1 and 2).

The second attribute on which the subjects judged the two analysis styles was the extent to which each helped the subject to detect incompleteness and internal inconsistency in the analysis. Table 4 provides no significant evidence of an overall preference either way on this attribute. This finding is consistent with the absence of any statistically significant difference between the subjects' 'seed' detection rates on the two analyses.

The third attribute was the extent to which the style 'provoked' the subjects to ask questions or make comments about the content of the analysis. Table 4 shows that the functional-decomposition was seen by the subjects to be the more effective in this regard (p<.05 on Fisher's Exact Test). As one subject put it : "Gerry's analysis is nice and open and warm. It invites comment. But Liam's is tight and closed and clinical. It's hard to get excited about it."

On the fourth attribute, the extent to which the subjects believed the analysis gave a complete and integrated (as opposed to a partial and fragmented) perspective of the business, there is significant evidence that the subjects thought the functional-decomposition to be the more effective (p<.05 on Fisher's Exact Test). This finding must be interpreted with care. Factually, the content of the two analyses was identical. So, it seems that the functional-decomposition gave the subjects a stronger **perception** of 'wholeness' than did the object-model.

The fifth attribute was the extent to which the analysis helped the subjects to anticipate possible implementation benefits and priorities. Overall, they clearly felt that the functional-decomposition was the more effective in this respect (p<.05 on Fisher's Exact Test). This finding, and the two findings immediately above, are consistent with the earlier finding that subjects made more comments of a 'strategic' nature about the content of the functional-decomposition than about that of the object-model.

The sixth attribute which the subjects used for comparison purposes was the extent to which the analysis helped them to visualise, in concrete terms, a possible implementation of the system. There is no statistically significant evidence in table 4 to suggest that the subjects believed one analysis to predominate over the other in this respect.

8. Conclusions

Regarding task performance, there is no evidence that subjects' rates of detection of missing 'seeds' differed across the two analyses. Nor is there evidence to suggest that either analysis was more successful than the other in eliciting criticisms and suggestions of a **detailed** nature. However, the functional-decomposition was by far the more successful in eliciting comments of a more **strategic** nature about the business and its needs, and about apparent 'mis-matches' between these needs and the content of the analysis.

Overall, subjects said that, compared with the object-model, the functional-decomposition was :

- easier to understand;
- provoked them to ask more questions and to make more comments;
- gave them a more holistic understanding of the business;
- better helped them to evaluate likely implementation benefits and priorities.

Obviously, the findings of an experiment such as this can be subject to many threats to validity. In this particular case, threats could include the artificiality of the experimental task, possible deficiencies in the operationalisation of the two paradigms, and defects in the experimental materials.

On the assumption that the findings have some external validity, what are the implications for research and practice? It seems that a raw object-model, as used in this experiment, may not be a suitable vehicle for communication between client and developer at the earliest stages of system development. It appears that an 'old-fashioned' functional-decomposition may be more effective. Why might this be the case? Perhaps the answer to this question lies in a comment made by one of the subjects: "The object-model is flat and inanimate. It reflects no sense of purpose or priority. Two organisations could have the same object-model but be facing totally different problems and pressures. The functional-decomposition leaps off the page. You can see inside the analyst's head. You can see the connection with real problems. The whole thing is linked to overall goals."

So, how do we imbue an object-model with a sense of 'purpose'? Or should we even try? The answer does not lie in applying layering, or some other structuring mechanism, to the raw object-model. The need to structure large or complex object-models to improve user-comprehension is well accepted, and a number of structuring principles have been proposed (eg. Coad's(1991) five-layer abstraction.) But these structuring principles do not seem to address the issues raised by this experiment.

Today, object-orientation is 'delivering' many benefits in the later stages of the system development process. Functional-decomposition also has its strengths, particularly as a vehicle for communication between the client and the developer. The challenge seems to be to create a synthesis of the two paradigms, incorporating the strengths of both, for use at the all-important 'front-end' of the development process.

References

(Andersen,1990): Andersen, P.B. 'A Theory of Computer Semiotics,' Cambridge University Press, 1990.

(Barros,1992): Barros, P.A. 'The nature of bias and defects in the software specification process', CS-TR-2822, Computer Science Technical Report Series, Univ. of Maryland, 1992.

(Coad et al.,1991): Coad, P. and E.Yourdon, 'Object-Oriented Analysis', New-Jersey : Yourdon Press, 1991.

(Parker et al.,1975): Parker, J.F and D.Bass., 'Pictures versus words as Stimuli in Paired-Associate Transfer,' American Journal of Psychology, Vol.88, 1975, pp. 635-642.

(Sung et al.,1985): Sung H. Yung and J. D. Naumann,'The Effectiveness of Data Representation Characteristics on User Validation', Proceedings of 5th. Int. Conf. on Information Systems, Indianapolis : Univ. of Indiana, 1985.

(Larsen et al.,1992): Larsen T.J. and J.D. Naumann, 'An Experimental Comparison of Abstract and Concrete Representations in Systems Analysis', Information and Management, 22(1992), pp. 29-40.

(Loy et al.,1993): Loy P. and Y. Stapp, 'DFDs vs. N-Squared Charts', Software Engineering Notes, Vol.18, No.3, July 1993, pp.16-17.

(Martin,1992): Martin J. 'Strategic Data Modelling', New Jersey : Prentice-Hall, 1992.

(Rumbaugh et al.,1991): Rumbaugh J. et al, 'Object-Oriented Modelling and Design', New-Jersey: Prentice-Hall, 1991.

"We offer guests a one-week regime of controlled-diet, exercise programmes, massage and other forms of 'pampering.' We pride ourselves on the individual treatment given to each guest, on our extensive range of expertise in health and medical matters, and on our facilities and beautiful grounds.

You really WILL get individual attention : 280 staff and a maximum of 120 guests ensures this. For example, you will have your very own Personal Support Team of experienced medical and keep-fit experts, who will closely monitor your requirements and progress throughout your stay.

On arrival, you will be given a thorough health-and-fitness checkup. The findings of this checkup form the basis for your individual exercise, diet and 'Inner-Health' programme. This latter could include your participation in meditation sessions, one-to-one individual counselling with a staff pychologist or therapist, and your participation in a selection of 'relaxation' activities such as painting or scheduled music recitals. Or perhaps a consultation with one of our resident beauty experts?

In addition to our saunas, jacuzzies and heated indoor swimming pool, you can experience one of our hydro-massage tanks.This is the latest in skin and muscle- tone technology. Or maybe you would like to workout on an exercise machine in one of our two superbly equipped gyms?

AND not to forget your creature comforts! Our bedrooms are furnished and decorated to the highest standards. Every room is en-suite. You are welcome to borrow massage pads , infra-red lamps and other items of health equipment free-of-charge for the duration of your stay.

We also have a wide range of specialist health-care equipment which we can install for your private use in your bedroom. For example, we have just acquired six ultra-sound deep-tissue massage canopies. The canopy can be fitted over your bed and it bathes you in penetrating and refreshing silent sound while you sleep. We must made an extra charge for items such as these.

It's not ALL indoors at the 'Happy-Hours' Health Farm! Why not take horse-riding lessons at our riding-school? Or play our nine-hole course course?
Or walk or jog on one of our many well-marked hill trails?
We are located in a beautiful part of County Wicklow. Why not book for one of our full-day or half-day mini-bus excursions?"

Appendix 1 : An Extract from the Health-Farm Prospectus

Gerry Kelly's introduction

I am an independent computer consultant. Two weeks ago, the managing director of the Happy Hours Health Farm in County Wicklow asked me to spend a few hours looking over the operation. I did so, and found that the business makes almost no use of computers.

The MD then asked me to outline my views on how IT could most help support day-to-day business operations. I reflected on this question over a day or so.

I first broke the overall task of operating the business into seven broad sub-tasks or functions that seemed to me to make sense : Resource Scheduling, Resource Allocation, Formulation of Guest Personal Health Programmes, Storage/Retrieval of Guest Records, Equipment Maintenance and Inventories, External Reporting, and Accounting/Payroll.

Under each of these broad headings, I then tried to identify specific sub-functions that are **important** to the business and that are **probably** good candidates for IT support. These are labelled 1.1, 1.2, 1.3 etc. in the diagram attached. For example, under the broad heading of Resource Allocation, one of the sub-functions I identified was 'Assign Doctors, Nurses and Physiotherapists to Guest Health-Checkups.' It seems to me that this task is an ideal one for computer-support.

The results of my analysis are attached.

I must emphasise that this is a **first-cut, preliminary analysis**, based on a very brief initial visit to the health-farm.

Appendix 2a : Gerry Kelly's Introduction

1. **Resource Scheduling**
   1.1 Schedule On-Arrival, Mid-Course and On-departure Guest Health-Checkups
   1.2 Process Guest Bookings for Saunas, Sunbeds and Exercise Machines
   1.3 Produce Weekly Duty Roster for every Bedroom Cleaner, Laboratory Technician and Keep-Fit Facility Attendant

2. **Resource Allocation**
   2.1 Assign Doctors, Nurses and Physiotherapists to Guest Health-Checkups
   2.2 Assign Doctors, Nurses and Physiotherapists to Guest Personal Support Teams (one of each to a team)
   2.3 Assign Bedrooms to Guests and Employees

3. **Formulate Guest Personal Health Programmes**
   3.1 Formulate Guest Personal Menus
   3.2 Formulate Guest Personal Exercise Programmes

4. **Store/Retrieve Guest Records**
   4.1 Guest Personal Details
   4.2 Guest Health-Checkup Results
   4.3 Guest Personal Support-Team Reports
   4.4 Guest Personal Health Programme Details
   4.5 Guest Keep-Fit Facility Usage Details
       (details of usage for each guest)

5. **Equipment Maintenance and Inventories**
   5.1 Keep the Problem/Incident Log for each Sauna, Sunbed and Exercise Machine
   5.2 Keep Maintenance Log for each Sauna, Sunbed and Exercise Machine
   5.3 Keep Guest Bedroom Equipment List (shows equipment in each guest bedroom eg. infrared lamps, massage pads.)

6. **External Reporting**
   6.1 Produce Health-Checkup Reports for Guests' General Practicioners (these are based on the guests' health-checkup results)

7. **Accounting and Payroll**
   7.1 Guest Accounting
       7.1.1 Make Guest Reservations
       7.1.2 Maintain Guest Accounts (including Billing)
   7.2 Payroll and Employee Records Administration

Appendix 2b : Gerry Kelly's Analysis

I work for Reliable Systems Limited as a Project Leader. Part of my job is to scope out possible assignments for new clients. I was asked to visit the Happy Hours Health Farm by my boss and to do a preliminary analysis of the business. My first-cut analysis is shown in figure 3b attached.

I'd better explain this diagram! Figure 3b shows the most important categories of 'objects' that I identified during my visit. An 'object' is a physical or conceptual thing that a business needs to keep information about or which it must 'process' in some way. For example, in the case of Happy Hours, the object-categories I found included guests, guest-health-checkups, guest keep-fit facilities, bedrooms, employees etc.

Some object-categories can be broken down into sub-categories. For example, figure 3b shows that a guest-health-checkup can be an 'on-arrival' checkup, a 'mid-course' checkup or a 'final' checkup. The little pyramid with the words 'is-a' beside it shows a breakdown of an object-category into sub-categories. The category 'bedroom' is another example of this ; a bedroom can be a guest-bedroom or can be an employee-bedroom .

Some objects are 'built' from one or more other objects. For example, the diagram shows that a guest-personal-support-team consists of one doctor, one nurse and one physiotherapist. Another example of this is a guest-personal-health-program, which consists of a guest-personal-menu and a guest-personal-exercise-programme.

Inside the box for each object-category , I show the functions involving that object-category that I think could usefully be supported by IT. For example, regarding guests, I have proposed the functions : keep-guest-personal-details, make-guest-reservations, keep-guest-accounts and issue-guest-bills.

Where an object-category is broken down into sub-categories, and where the function applies to ALL the sub-categories, I show the function just once, in the general-category. For example, the function 'schedule-a-checkup' applies to 'on-arrival' checkups, 'mid-course' checkups and 'final' checkups. So I show this function only once, in the general category 'guest-health-checkup.' This is to avoid repetition and improve clarity.

When an object-category is broken down into sub-categories, and where the function does NOT apply to all sub-categories, the function is shown only in the sub-categories to which it DOES apply. For example, the function 'keep-bedroom-equipment-list' applies only to a guest-bedroom, not to an employee-bedroom, hence its location on the diagram. On the other hand, 'assign-a-bedroom' applies equally to guest-bedrooms and employee-bedrooms. The function 'produce-weekly-duty-roster' is another example of this. It applies only to laboratory technicians, keep-fit facility attendants and bedroom cleaners.

Figure 3b is my best-shot , given the limited time I spent with the client. This diagram shows the Objects and Functions that I think are the most important from the point of view of running the business, and which are good candidates for computer-systems.

Appendix 3a : Liam Ryan's Introduction

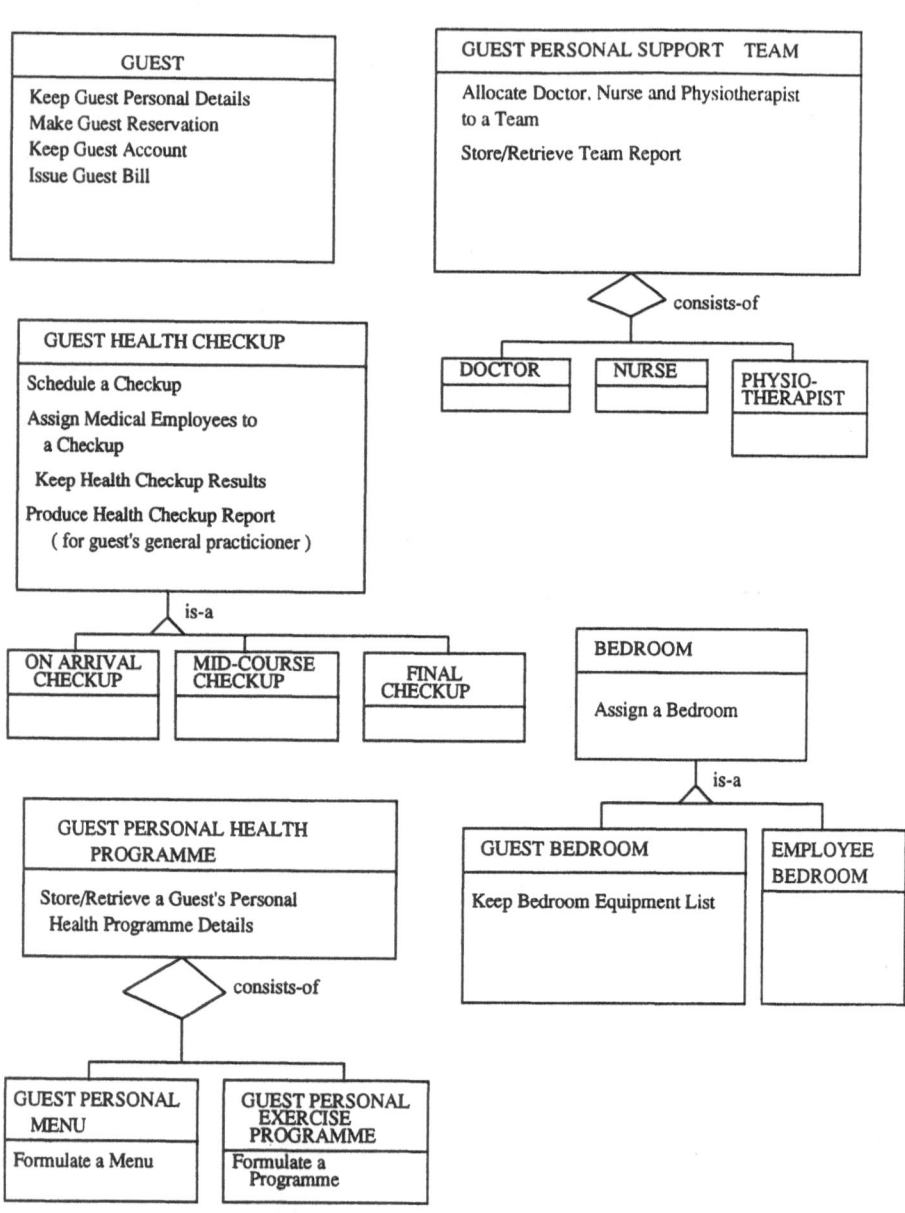

Appendix 3b : Liam Ryan's Analysis (part 1)

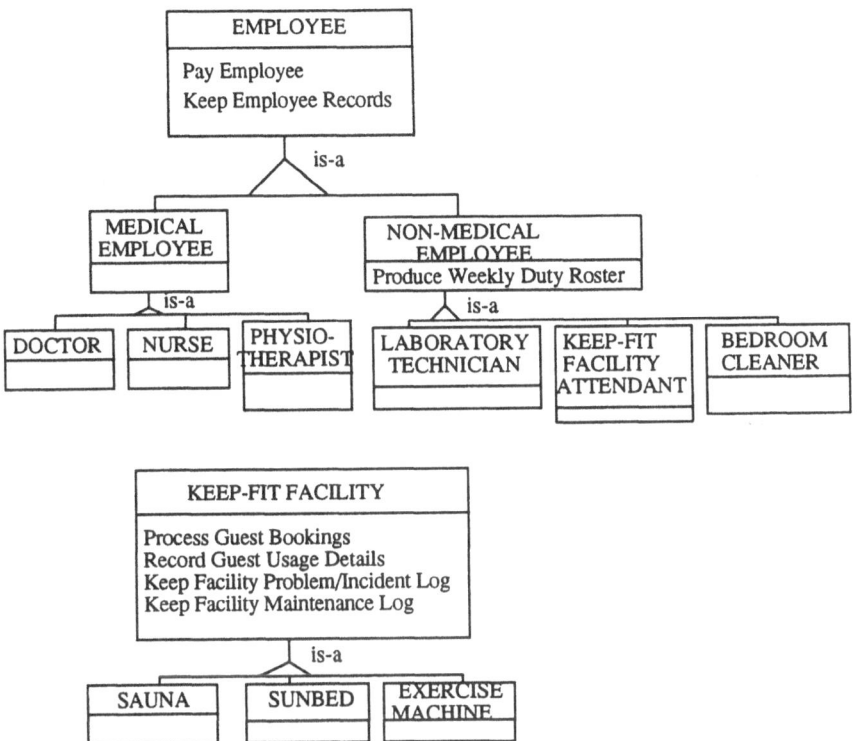

Appendix 3b : Liam Ryan's Analysis (part 2)

INSTRUCTIONS

First of all, thanks for helping out with this experiment!!   The purpose is to compare the effectiveness of different ways of presenting information about IT systems.

In this envelope, you will find :

(a) An extract from the current brochure for the Happy Hours Health-Farm in County Wicklow.

(b) Two brief analyses of Happy Hours, one by Gerry Kelly and one by Liam Ryan. Both these gentlemen are IT consultants. The management of Happy Hours asked each to independently look at Happy Hour's operations to identify opportunities for applying IT.

(c) A short questionnaire which I would like you to complete (but not yet).

The Steps to Follow :

1. Read the extract from the health-farm's brochure. This will give you some feeling for what the business does and how it works.

2. If your age in years is an **even number**, start with Gerry Kelly's analysis. If your age is an **odd number**, start with Liam Ryan's analysis.

3. Start on your first analysis (as explained in 2.). Try to identify the strengths and weaknesses in the content of the analysis, as you see it. Write your points on the blank pages attached to the analysis.

It's hard to list in advance examples of the sorts of things that could constitute strengths in first-cut brief analyses such as these. You will have to decide for yourself. It's much easier to think of examples of possible weaknesses e.g. serious omissions, internal inconsistencies, too narrow a perspective taken, consultant bias etc. Keep in mind the purpose of each analysis : to identify important aspects of the business that could probably benefit from IT support.

I know you have never run a health-farm!   Don't hesitate to use your imagination. Anyway, do your best!

4. When you have finished commenting on the first analysis, do exactly the same with the second. You may find yourself repeating some points you made earlier about the first analysis. But please make them again. **Don't omit a point on the basis that you have already made it about the first analysis. Treat each analysis independently. In particular, don't go back and add new comments to the first analysis!!**

5. When you have finished commenting on the second analysis, fill in the little questionnaire. This deals with your views on the relative merits of the different **styles** of presentation used in the two analyses.

6. Put everything back in the big envelope and return it to me.

Appendix 4 : Participant's Instructions

Which Analysis did you do first? Gerry's / Liam's (tick)

What do you **most like** about the way Gerry **presented** his
Analysis (using functions, sub-functions etc.) ?

And what do you **least like** about the way Gerry **presented** his analysis?

What do you **most like** about the way Liam **presented** his analysis (using objects etc) ?

And what did you **least like** about the way Liam **presented** his analysis?

Which of the two analysis formats do you prefer?
 Gerry's / Liam's (tick)

Why?

Roughly, how long did you spend doing the experiment?

Any Comments on the experiment?

Appendix 5 : The questions on the post-experiment questionnaire

M - An Object-Oriented Model and Method Base System for Discrete Optimization Problems

Peter Becker

Wilhelm-Schickard-Institut für Informatik,
Universität Tübingen
Sand 13, 72076 Tübingen, Germany
E-mail: becker@informatik.uni-tuebingen.de   Fax: +49 7071 / 295958

ABSTRACT. *In this article, I present the object-oriented model and method base system M. Aim of M is to provide models of optimization problems, solution algorithms, and algorithmic meta knowledge in an integrated way. This article gives a survey of M and presents especially the different concepts of user support.*

KEY WORDS: *Model Base System, Method Base System*

1. Introduction

Methods for discrete optimization play an important role in the area of control and optimization of industrial processes. Due to the fact that most of discrete problems are NP-complete, which is especially true for discrete optimization problems, a lot of specialized methods have been developed for them, which differ with respect to algorithmic properties, see e.g., [10,12]. For this reason, a user is not always able to select the algorithm that fits his needs best.

Because of the above mentioned difficulties, I propose a model and method base approach to support unexperienced users in the solution of discrete optimization problems. Analogous to a data base, a *model and method base* is defined as a software system consisting of a *model and method base system* , a set of *models*, and a set of *methods*.

A *model* or *problem class* is defined as an abstract problem specification independent of dimensions and values. In *M*, a model is a class that defines the attributes that problem instances may have, the integrity constraints that the instances have to fulfill, and the available methods. A *problem* is an instance of a model. The problem seen as an *M* object is a device to represent a real world problem, which can be solved by the associated methods. A *method* is a representation of an algorithm suitable to solve problems or to perform other operations on objects. In the following, I simply use *method base system* instead of model and method base system.

1.1. Requirements to a Method Base System

The most important tasks of a method base system are:
(1) to provide and administer discrete structures
(2) to offer facilities for the definition of models
(3) to offer facilities for the integration of methods
(4) to offer facilities for the representation of algorithmic meta knowledge
(5) to provide application interfaces

Item (1) means that the method base system is able to create and administer various discrete structures. The structures we need in the context of discrete optimization are typical discrete mathematical structures like graphs or posets. These structures are necessary for the definition of problems. As an example, take a precedence constraint hamilton path problem. For the defintion of the precedences, we may use a partial order.

Item (2) means that the method base system has to offer facilities for the definition of new problem classes. Another important aspect, within the context of user support, is the representation of specialized relationships between different models, for instance, relaxation relationships or special case relationships.

To solve or work on problems, algorithms are needed, which may be available in different forms, for instance as software library, as source code, or as commercial software package. Therefore, a method base system should offer a flexible interface for the integration of software as methods.

Item (4) is concerned with the task of selecting one or more methods out of a predefined set of solution algorithms. Therefore, a method base system should have facilities for the specification of algorithmic meta knowledge that allows the automatic selection of methods based on user's preferences. This may lead to an automatic problem solving mechanism.

Item (5) is concerned with the integration of a method base in applications. As with databases, it should be possible to integrate the whole functionality of a method base in arbitrary applications. I call such systems *embeddable* .

1.2. Characterization of M

In the following, the object-oriented method base system M is presented, which fulfills the above mentioned requirements. Aim of M is to provide models, solution algorithms, and algorithmic meta knowledge in an integrated way. M is based on the object-oriented paradigm. It offers various integration facilities to use as methods different forms of software residing in a computer network. A *method base language (MeBaL)* represents the interface between application programs and the method base system. Models, problems, and meta knowledge can be formulated by using *MeBaL*. To avoid the inefficient reimplementation of discrete structures by the method base language, M offers a concept for the easy integration of exisiting data type implementations.

M can be seen as a toolbox for the construction of a method base. In this context, the above defined terms model, problem, and method are analogous to the terms class, instance, and message in the object-oriented paradigm. The only difference is, that in M methods are also represented by objects. In this way, we get a natural modelling of discrete optimization problems. M serves in particular as an integration tool. By the means of M, it should become possible to offer software available in a computer network to the user in a consistent way as models and associated methods. For that, emphasis is put on the models resp. the problems. These will be worked on by the user with the facilities offered by M. By assigning methods to models we get a much better structuring than separating methods and data, such that the user himself is responsible for bringing them together to solve his problems.

1.3. Related Work

In the area of model management, similar approaches to M exist for linear programming problems, see [5, 4, 18]. The crucial difference between these systems and M is that the former ones are limited to one paradigm, whereas M is a meta system for nearly any paradigm used in discrete problem solving. In particular, these systems do not have extensive functionalities for the easy integration of algorithms and data types. Moreover, there do not exist concepts for representing algorithmic meta knowledge or the selection of adequate algorithms.

M's data model is comparable to data models of object-oriented database systems (OODBS), cf. [8, 4]. OODBSs put emphasis on the administration of complex structured objects. The methods defined for these objects usually do not have the complexity of algorithms used in discrete optimization. Methods of object-oriented databases are typically used for simple queries, the computation of active values, or simple update operations. The definition of these methods is usually done by the means of a query language or a special compiler, if the OODBS is embedded in an object-oriented programming language. In contrast to that, it is the task of a method base system to use virtually any software as a method: software, that neither has been written in a special language nor with a special compiler. In most cases, even the source code of the methods is unknown. Moreover, it should be possible to use external software for the implementation of complex types.

1.4. Knapsack Problems

In this article we use knapsack problems to demonstrate the various facilities of *M*. This subsection gives a short description of this problem type.

The *0-1*, or *binary, knapsack problem* is as follows: Given are a knapsack capacity *c* and a set of *n* objects. Each object has a weight w_i and a profit p_i. The task is to select a subset *A* of the objects, such that the overall weight is less than or equal to the knapsack capacity *c* and the overall profit is maximal. Formally we have:

$$\text{maximize } \Sigma_{i=1}^{n} p_i \ x_i$$

subject to:

$$\Sigma_{i=1}^{n} w_i \ x_i \leq c$$

$$x_i \in \{0,1\}$$

with $x_i = 1$, if and only if the knapsack contains object *i*.

The knapsack problem is NP-complete, but there exists a fully polynomial approximation scheme. Various algorithms based on different algorithmic paradigms have been developed to solve knapsack problems. A survey of different types of knapsack problems with associated algorithms can be found in [10]. In [6], these algorithms have been analyzed, and in particular powerful criterions for the algorithm selection are given.

The concepts of *M* are especially validated by knapsack problems and precedence constraint hamilton path problems [7]. Moreover, a lot of other models and methods have been integrated in method bases realized with *M*. For instance, we used *M* as an implementation platform for the administration and efficient retrieval of binary trees, cf. [1]. Thereby, the concepts underlying *M* were shown to be general enough to model even problems in other areas than discrete optimization.

The rest of the paper is structured in the following way: in Section 2 I shortly present the data model of *M*. Section 3 presents *MeBaL*, the method base language that is used to define operations and queries on a method base. Section 4 presents the different concepts of user support, and in Section 5 I give a glimpse of *M*'s implementation.

2. Data Model

Here, I just give a short description of the data model because the emphasis of this paper is put on the user support. The core of *M*'s data model is comparable to data models of object-oriented data base systems, cf. [8, 4].

M offers various *atomic types*. Atomic types are sets of values that are immutable, which means that the state of the elements cannot be changed. Each atomic type has a unique syntactical representation in the method base language *MeBaL*. We have the following atomic types (syntactical representation in parantheses): Real (`1.23` or `1.23e-45`), Integer (`123`), Boolean (`true` or `false`), String (`"this is a string"`), List (`[1,true,"string"]`), and Lambda Expression (`'($object.size > 100)`).

Lists can be nested and may comprise heterogenous elements as shown in the example. *Lambda expressions* in *M* are similar to lambda expressions in LISP. They represent the definition of a function. This function is not evaluated immediately but in specific situations or on demand. Lambda expressions are typically used in *M* to define rules, integrity constraints, or simple methods. In this way, we are able use the definition of a function like any other atomic value. In the following sections, we will see a lot of examples for using lambda expressions.

Beside these predefined atomic types, other atomic types can be defined. For instance, it is possible to define a data type `v3` that represents the points of the three dimensional real space. If we represent the points by lists of reals having the length three, v3 ([2.4,4.3,0.0]) would be a legal syntactical representation for an element of this type. The actual representation and available methods are defined by an object of type *class*, which is associated to the data type. Classes are explained below.

Beside atomic objects, we have mutable objects. Each *mutable object* of a method base has a *unique object identifier* (*oid*), for instance _738510687_992659, which implements a surrogate concept and serves as a logical pointer to the associated object. Syntactically the oid consists of two positive integers with leading underscores. Moreover, a *unique alias* (*identifier*) may be given to an object, thereby it is easier to reference an object. Internally the method base system uses only the object identifiers.

An object may be a class, a problem, a method, or any other instance of predefined or user defined classes. *Classes* can be seen as factories for instances (resp. objects) and are objects too. For the objects they create, classes possess construction plans that contain information about the attributes an object can have and the methods that are applicable to an object. *Instances* or *objects* are created by sending a constructor message to a class. A *problem class* or *model* is a factory for *problems*. In this sense, a model is the abstract definition of a specific problem and achieves model/data independence, cf. [18, 19]. New models are created by sending a constructor message to a special class named problemclasses. After doing this, attributes and methods can be defined for the instances of the new model by the means of special messages.

A *method* is implemented by a function of a dynamic library, by a function written in the method base language, or by an external program. It is represented by objects of the class *methods* or derived subclasses, which provide the attributes necessary for the communication between the method and the method base. By that, definition of methods using standard software is easy. For example, a method xshow for the graphical representation of partial orders has been realized using the public domain graph editor EDGE [16].

3. The Method Base Language

Operations on the method base are formulated in a *method base language*, called *MeBaL*. This method base language can either be used by a user via one of the interactive user interfaces or by any application via calls to library functions that realize a compiler/interpreter interface to *MeBaL*. In the following, I show the usage of *MeBaL* by some examples.

Here is a simple example of the interactive definition and solution of a knapsack problem in *MeBaL* (example 2.2 of [12]). User input is typeset in boldface:

```
M> kp.create_instance(alias:"mt2_2")
_744451004_304678
M+> mt2_2.capacity  <-  50
void
M+> mt2_2.profit  <-  [70,20,39,37,7,5,10]
void
M+> mt2_2.weight  <-  [31,10,20,19,4,3,6]
void
M+> mt2_2.brabo
_744451603_371556
M+> mt2_2.solution_set
[1,4]
M+> mt2_2.solution_val
107
M+> ct
M>
```

First, an instance of the problemclass kp is created. This is done by sending the message create_instance with the parameter alias to the object kp. The new problem gets the alias mt2_2 and has the oid _744451004_304678, which is the return value of this statement. The plus sign in the prompt indicates that a transaction is active. It has been started automatically by the last operation. In the next three statements, its input data is assigned, where profits and weights are represented as integer lists. The value void, which is returned by the assignment statements, identifies the *null value*. If no error occurs, assignments will always return void. In the fifth statement, the method brabo is called to solve the knapsack problem. The result of this method call is another object, a so-called *method call buffer*. This buffer contains the input and output data of the method, which runs in parallel to the method's base server process. The method call buffer is a device to query or control the status of a *running method*. After the method has terminated successfully, we are able to take a look at the solution values: brabo decided to take the items 1 and 4 into the knapsack. This results in a profit of 107. The command ct commits the transaction and the new defined object is saved to disk.

The right side of an assignment as well as the parameter values may consist of an arbitrary expression. In the following statement the profit list assigned to problem kp100 is created by calling a random generator method:

```
M> kp100.profit <- random_uniform_discrete.call(
     samplesize:100, lower:1, upper:1000)
```

The next example shows a part of a model definition and demonstrates the usage of lambda expressions. The following lines create the model kp that is the model for knapsack problems and define the attribute profit as a list consisting of positive integers. The constraint is represented by a lambda expression. This expression will be evaluated whenever an assignment to profit is made. If this evaluation yields false, the assignment will be rejected.

```
M> problemclasses.create_instance(alias:"kp")
_738510687_992659
M+> kp.define_attr(
      name: "profit",
      constraint: '( $profit.type = LIST and
            (forall p in $profit : $p.type = INTEGER and $p > 0) )
void
```

Names that begin with a dollar sign represent *variables*. For the evaluation of a constraint, the new attribute value will be assigned to a variable having the attribute's name (here profit). In the same way as shown above, other model attributes can be defined.

As a last example, we take a look at the definiton of a method that sorts the items of a knapsack problem decreasingly by profit per weight. For knapsack problems, this makes sense because most of the existing methods to solve a knapsack problem assume to get the weight and profit values in this form (only the commands are shown).

```
kp_methods.create_instance(alias: "kp_sort");
kp_sort.comment <- "Sorts items with respect to profit per weight";
kp_sort.classmethod( class: kp, name: "sort" );
kp_sort.methodtype <- METHOD_TYPE_LAMBDA;
kp_sort.prog <- '(
  $object._ppw <-
    ($object.profit)
      *pjoin
    ($object.weight)
      %transform
    '($item.first / $item.second);
  $object._perm <-
    $object._ppw.sortperm(compare: '($litem > $ritem) );
  $object._profit <-
    $object.profit.permute(permutation: $object._perm);
  $object._weight <-
    $object.weight.permute(permutation: $object._perm);
  return void )
```

As in the first example, we create the new object by sending the constructor message to a class (kp_methods). By the means of the message `classmethod`, we assign the new method to the model kp under the name `sort`. By assigning the constant value `METHOD_TYPE_LAMBDA` (constants are specified in upper case letters) to the attribute `methodtype`, we specify that the executable part of the method will be defined by a lambda expression. This definition is done by assigning the lambda expression to the attribute `prog`. This completes the method definition.

`kp_sort` performs the sorting of items in four steps. First, it computes the profit per weight values by using the `*pjoin` operator to join the profit and weight lists. The variable `object` will always be bound to the object that has called the method. The result of the join operation is a list of pairs having the profit as first and the weight of an item as second component. These pairs are then transformed into the profit per weight value by using the `%transform` operator. The list with these values is stored in the attribute _ppw of the problem. We do this because these values may be considered for the evaluation of method's performance. Then, we compute the permutation that sorts the list decreasingly by using the method `sortperm`. The permutation returned by this method is stored in the attribute _perm. We will need it later for the retransformation of a solution set. Thereafter, we permute the profit and weight lists and store the results in additional attributes. These values will be used in further solution steps by the various solvers.

The operators `*pjoin` and `%transform`, used in this example, are not predefined in *MeBaL*. Instead, we have the opportunity to define new operators for data types. If such a selfdefined operator is used, a message will be sent to one of the involved operators. For the specification of such user defined operators, *M* offers a system object (ops) with specialized messages.

Besides the functionalities presented here, the language offers the usual control structures (if, case, different loop constructs). In the next section, examples for the application of these control structures are given.

4. User Support and Automatic Selection of Methods

4.1. Weak User Support

The easiest way to support users is to present information or problem knowledge about a given problem in textual form. To achieve this, there exist some dedicated predefined methods. For instance, one has methods to list the attribute descriptions of a model or to build a survey of the existing methods of an object.

A more advanced textual support is given by documentation objects. These are specialized objects for containing model or method descriptions. Documentation objects are similar structured as manual pages. On demand, a method can be started that transforms the documentation object into a viewable form, for instance a postscript file, which can be viewed on the user's screen by the means of another method.

The development of dedicated methods to advice users gives another opportunity of support. Such methods may analyze the state of a given problem to give hints to the user. As an example, I show parts of an advice method for knapsack problems.

```
kp_advice.prog <- '(
    if isvoid $object.capacity or
       isvoid $object.profit or
       isvoid $object.weight
    then
       return "There are some input tags of the model \\
               which are not still initialized. \\
               Assign values to these input tags."
    fi;
    . . .
```

```
if isvoid $object._solution_set then
   return
   (
   $object.list_methods
      *select '($item.second.kp_methodtype = "solver")
       %transform '( [$item.first,$item.second.comment] )
   ).aggr(init: "use one of the following solvers:\\n",
          prog: '( $aggr + $item.first +
                   "\\t" $item.second + "\\n") )
fi;
 . . .
);
```

The method given above checks the single attributes of a problem, thereby it is possible to detect whether the problem has been formulated correctly, or which method should be started next. In this case, it is useful if a dedicated class has been created for the methods relevant to knapsack problems. In this way, specialized attributes can be given to knapsack methods, for instance the attribute kp_methodtype that indicates whether the method is a solver (by the attribute value "solver"). It is easy to write a statement that produces a table of the existing solvers, as shown in the second if statement.

list_methods is a method that is available by default for all objects. It gives the the names and object identifiers of all methods available for an object in a list of pairs. By the means of the attribute kp_methodtype, the solvers can simply be choosen with the *select operator. After that, the second component is substituted by the method's comment, and the aggr (aggregate) method converts the list in table format.

Moreover, it is possible to assign methods to methods, for instance a method that estimates the running time of a method for a given problem specified as parameter. This is an easy way to represent knowledge about algorithms.

4.2. Automatic Classification of Specialized Models

In this subsection, I present concepts of M that may be used to find the most specific models for a given problem out of a hierarchy of models. In particular this means the recognition of special cases of problem instances. For these special cases, we may have more powerful methods.

Definition 1: We define an *optimization problem* $OP = (I,S,C,c,\theta)$ by:
(1) A set I of *problem instances*. This set represents the feasible input data.
(2) A set S of *solutions*.
(3) A *constraint function* $C: I \times S \to$ **Boolean**. If $C(i,s) =$ **true**, we say that s is a *feasible solution* for the problem instance i of OP. The set $S(i) := \{ s \in S \mid C(i,s) =$ **true**$\}$ is the set of all feasible solutions for the problem instance i.
(4) A *cost function* or *objective function* $c: I \times S \to$ **Real**
(5) θ in $\{ <, > \}$. If $\theta = <$, we say that the optimization problem OP is a *minimization problem*, otherwise it is a *maximization problem*.

Definiton 2: Let s_1 and s_2 be feasible solutions for a problem instance i of an optimization problem OP. We say that s_1 is a *better solution for the problem instance i* than s_2, written as $s_1 \theta(i) s_2$, if $c(i, s_1) \theta c(i, s_2)$. A feasible solution s that fulfills the condition:

$$\forall s' \in S : C(i, s') = \textbf{true} \Rightarrow \neg s' \theta(i) s$$

is an *optimal solution for the problem instance i* of OP.

Definition 3: Given are the optimization problems $OP = (I, S, C, c, \theta)$ and $OP' = (I',S',C',c',$ $\theta')$. We say OP' is a *special case* of OP if the following conditions are valid:

(1) There exists a set $I^* \subset I$ and a bijective function $h : I^* \to I'$. We call this function the *input mapping.*

(2) There exists a function $g : S' \to S$, and $g : S'(h(i)) \to S(i)$ is bijective for all i in I^*. We call g the *solution mapping.*

(3) The following condition holds:

$$s_1 \; \theta(i) \; s_2 \; \Rightarrow g^{-1}(s_1) \; \theta'(h(i)) \; g^{-1}(s_2)$$

The following Lemma obviously holds:

Lemma 1: Let OP' be a special case of OP and let h and g be the input resp. solution mapping. If s' is an optimal solution for a problem instance i' of OP', $g(s')$ is an optimal solution for the problem instance $h^{-1}(i')$ of OP.

Due to Lemma 1 it does not matter whether the problem is solved by the original or the special model. However, the special model may offer methods with a better performance, thus, it is rational to compute the most specific model that can be used for a given problem. M supports this by offering the *special case relationship* between models.

In M a special case relationship $SP = (M, P, \chi, h, g)$ is defined by:

(1) A model M that represents an optimization problem $OP_M = (I_M, S_M, C_M, c_M, \theta_M)$.

(2) The model P of the optimization problem $OP_P = (I_P, S_P, C_P, c_P, \theta_P)$. OP_P has to be a special case of OP_M.

(3) A *characteristic function* $\chi : I \to$ **Boolean** that characterizes the set I^* of Definition 3, i.e. $I^* = \{ i \in I_M \mid \chi(i) = \textbf{true} \}$.

(4) The *instance mapping* $h : I^* \to I_P$

(5) The *solution mapping* $g : S_P \to S_M$.

χ, g, and h have to be defined by lambda expressions. In this way, the classification operator of M can easily classify a given problem by using the characteristic functions and the instance mappings. For the retransformation of a problem solved via a specialized model, the solution mapping is used.

Example: I use the *subset-sum problem*, which is a special case of the knapsack problem. In the subset-sum problem, the profit value equals the weight value for all items. This results in a very hard problem because the profit per weight value is 1.0 for each item. Specialized solvers have been developed for this model.

We have:

χ:
```
$object.profit = $object.weight
```
h:
```
$special.capacity <- $object.capacity;
$special.item <- $object.weight
```
g:
```
$object.solution_val <- $special.solution_val;
$object.solution_set <- $special.solution_set
```

We simply check whether a knapsack problem is a subset-sum problem by comparing the profit and weight lists. To transform the knapsack instance in a subset-sum instance, we copy the capacity value and the weight values. `special` will be bound to the specialized problem instance and `object` to the general problem instance. The solution mapping is simply implemented by copying the solution set and the objective function value.

4.3. Method Plans

The strongest user support is achieved by *method plans*. These method plans are an adaption of skeleton plans, which are a common artificial intelligence technique for the solution of planning or configuration problems, see e.g., [17, 15]. Like skeleton plans, method plans can be viewed as and-or-trees. The sinks of a method plan represent the basic solution methods for the problem, e.g., optimization methods, integrity checks or transformation methods. Intermediate nodes of the method plan represent partial problems in the solution process. Such a node depends on other basic or intermediate nodes. We distinguish three types of nodes.

A *planning node* divides the associated problem into subproblems that have to be solved sequentially. For instance, to solve a knapsack problem, we have to do the following steps:
(1) Check whether the problem has been defined correctly.
(2) Sort the items according to decreasing values of the profit per unit weight. This is a precondition for all existing solution methods currently available.
(3) Solve the transformed problem with one of the existing optimization methods.
(4) Transform the solution back into terms of the original problem.

It seems to be adequate to represent this knowledge by a planning node.

The second type of nodes are *fork nodes*. These nodes represent alternative strategies in the solution process. For instance, step (3) in the solution of a knapsack problem can be achieved by applying a branch and bound algorithm, an algorithm based on dynamic programming, or a polynomial approximation scheme. What to do depends on the user's preferences and the input data, e.g., the number of items. For this reason, rules can be connected to a fork node. These rules control the expansion of the solution process by selecting at least one of the alternatives offered by the node. Selecting more than one node results in different strategies to achieve the desired goal. These strategies may be executed in parallel. Then a race between different methods (resp. strategies) can be started, and a solution emerges after the minimum of the running times.

The third type of nodes are *loop nodes*. They work like fork nodes with the exception that these nodes may start new methods if one of the methods earlier started has terminated.

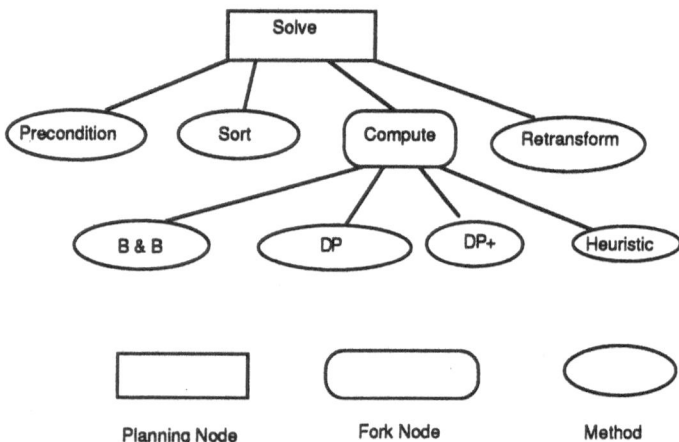

Figure 1. Method plan for knapsack problems

As an example, Figure 1 shows a method plan for knapsack problems. Its root is a planning node that represents the above mentioned solution steps. If this node is activated, the four methods resp. plans will be executed sequentially. The method plan *compute* represents a fork node that is responsible for the execution of the real solvers. If it becomes active, it will care for a proper selection of base methods, it will start these methods, and it will control the execution of these methods. How the method plan exactly will fulfill these tasks is defined by certain rules, which are typically represented by lambda expressions. These rules resp. lambda expressions have to be assigned to certain attributes offered by objects of the type method plan. An example is given below.

Analogous to methods, plans for an object may be called by using the dot operator. And similar to method calls, a *plan buffer* or *strategy call* will be created in the case of activation. By this plan buffer, the running plan and the running submethods resp. subplans can be controlled.

As an example, we take a closer look to fork nodes. A *fork plan* $FP = (I,S,F,E,R)$ is defined by:
(1) An *init rule I*. This rule will be called immediately after a plan has been started. It may be used to initialize the plan buffer properly.

(2) A *select rule S*. This rule does a preselection of the available methods. Usually in this step, the methods will be considered independently of other methods. For every method, we check, whether it may be useful to apply it. The surviving methods will be further considered by the filter rule, as explained below.

For knapsack problems the select rule is:

```
$object.list_methods
    *select '($item.second.kp_methodtype = "solver" and
              $item.second.utility > 0.0 )
```

utility is an *active value* for knapsack methods. Active values are attributes that compute the attribute value by some function. For each knapsack solver method, there is a lambda expression assigned to this attribute.

(3) A *filter rule F*. The filter rule chooses some of the methods proposed by the select rule. The filter rule typically represents interdependencies between the methods, for instance we never start more than one method per algorithmic paradigm (branch and bound, dynamic programming, heuristic). The methods resulting from the filter rule will be started and after it, we will have to wait for events that are handled by the event rule.

(4) An *event rule E*. This rule defines what happens in the case of an event. An event may either be a time out, a user defined event, or the termination of a method. For knapsack problems the event rule is:

```
if $event = STRAT_CALL_EVENT_TERM and
   $mcall.method.solution_quality = "optimal" and
   $mcall.exit_status = 0
then
   foreach mrun in $scall.active do
      $mrun.kill
   rof;
   $scall.terminate
fi
```

If the terminated method is a method to compute an optimal solution, all other active solvers will be stopped. Which methods are active is computable by sending the message active to the involved strategy call ($scall). By the means of the message terminate, the strategy call is informed about the fact that the strategy should be stopped.

84

(5) A *result rule R*. This rule computes a result of the strategy call. This result is stored in the strategy call buffer and may be used by the calling strategy.

The method plan concept has two advantages:
• Knowledge about the problem domain is structured in small pieces that are independent and reusable.
• Every intermediate node represents a powerful and sophisticated operator. Application of the source node results in an automatic solution.

5. Implementational Aspects

5.1. Overall Architecture

M is written in C and C++ and is based on the relational database system TRANSBASE as well as the software library LEDA [13]. It runs on a Sun Sparcstation under SunOS 4.1.3.

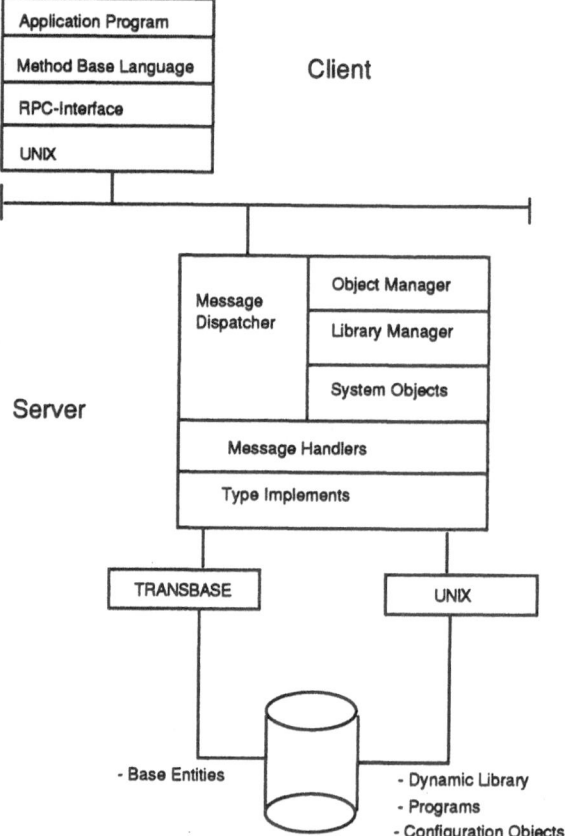

Figure 2. Architecture of M

The main features of the architecture are presented in Figure 2. M is based on a client-server concept: The server administers all objects of the method base, the client may be one of the generic user interfaces to M or any program that has connected to the method base by the means of a special library. This special library offers a C interface to a *MeBaL* compiler and interpreter. This approach has the advantage that *M* can easily be embedded in other systems. The interpretation of *MeBaL* statements leads to requests to the server of the method base system. For the transmission of these requests, the interpreter uses a *remote procedure call* based server interface.

Now imagine that an operation has to be performed on the method base, that means a data value or object identifier and an associated message arrives at the *message dispatcher*. The message dispatcher forwards this message to a *message handler*, which is the interface to the implementation of object types. There exist different implementations for the various object types that are used by *M*. The implementation performs the operation on the object.

The message dispatcher is supported in forwarding the messages by various system objects. The *object manager* is responsible for restoring and saving objects from resp. to disk. That means, that if an object not residing in main memory receives a message,then it will be restored automatically by the object manager. Moreover, the object manager is responsible for supporting a transaction concept, which is explained in more detail in the next subsection. The *library manager* is responsible for linking dynamic libraries on demand. Dynamic libraries may contain methods, user written message handlers, or other functions necessary for performing operations on objects, for instance, *before* or *after function* for methods, which may be used as interfaces to external programs.

The objects are stored as tupels in a database system or as special file structures. The latter is particularly useful for complex structured objects like graphs.

5.2. Integration of User Defined Data Types

To support complex mathematical structures like graphs or networks efficiently, the method base system offers a concept for the integration of user defined data types. A user written *message handler* for a new data type can be installed via a dynamic library. The library manager system object offers various messages for performing this task. In this way, it is easy to integrate new data types for mathematical structures by using software libraries, e.g., LEDA, see [13].

To fully support a transaction concept, the message handler has to implement several messages. These messages will be sent by the object manager in specific situations. In detail, these messages are:

CREATE	Create a new object
SAVE	Create an after image of an object
COMMIT_SAVE	Make an after image valid
DELETE_OBJECT	Delete an object
COMMIT_DELETE	Make a deletion valid
RESTORE	Restore an object from secondary storage
ROLLBACK	Cancel object updates
FREE	Delete an object from main memory

If the kernel receives the commit transaction request from an application, the object manager will send a SAVE message to all objects that have been updated by the transaction. Then the message handlers have to build after images of these objects. If no error has occured, the message COMMIT_SAVE is sent to the objects. The message handlers take care that the new object versions become valid. This proceeding corresponds to a two phase commit protocol.

By this architecture, it is easy to integrate new implementations of data types. For instance, the software library LEDA has been used as a base for the implementation of graphs in *M*. To achieve this I used the existing LEDA implementations and embedded them in a message handler. Most operations on an object of type graph are directly transformed in an adequate LEDA function call. Additionally, the message handler implements the above listed messages to fully support the transaction concept. To use objects of such a new type, we create a new class via *MeBaL* and set the implementation type of this class to the newly installed type.

Aside graphs, *M* offers a set of other common discrete structures, e.g., arrays, lists, matrices, and posets.

In the same way as integrating new data types, interfaces to other software systems can be built: one writes a message handler that delegates the requests to the system to be integrated and transforms any results delivered by that system, and creates a dedicated object that uses the newly created message handler. In this way, a general interface to the database system TRANSBASE has been established. The object `transbase` accepts data base queries in the following way:

```
transbase.query(database: <database name> , sqlquery: <sql query> )
```

If the object `transbase` receives a query, a connection to the desired data base will be established and the given SQL statement will be executed. An eventually returned result will be transformed into *M*'s data types. Further processing may follow. The next example shows, the retrieval of weight and profit values from a database to the knapsack problem kpp.

```
$tmp <- transbase.query ( database: "optbase@sunflower" ,
    sqlquery: "select profit, weight from kptable where id = 'mt2_2'")
kpp.profit <- $tmp %transform '($item.first)
kpp.weight <- $tmp %transform '($item.second)
```

The first command delivers the result relation of the data base query as a list of lists. This list is stored in the variable tmp. The other two commands transform this list in the desired format.

6. Summary

This article presented the method base system *M*. Its main features are:
- Facilities to define and solve models resp. problems in the area of discrete optimization in an object-oriented, persistent, and consistent way.
- Concepts for integrating implementations of complex mathematical stuctures and support for reuse of these structures in various models.
- User support by automatic selection of methods and specialized models.

Due to these aspects, *M* can be seen as one step towards a model managment system as proposed in [9].

Some aspects could not be considered in this article. For instance, there exists a graphical user interface for *M* called *Mint*, see [11]. This tool represents objects by graphical means, buttons are offered for applicable messages and methods, and the user is supported by explanations, e.g., for method parameters. At the moment, I am working on a WWW interface [2, 3] for *M*. Single objects should be presented by the means of Mosaic forms. Aim in the long run is to make a method base for discrete optimization available for the public via WWW.

7. References

1. H. Argenton, P. Becker, *Efficient Retrieval of Labeled Binary Trees*, to apear in: Proceedings of the International Symposium on Advanced Database Technologies and Their Integration, Japan, 1994
2. T. Berners-Lee and D. Connolly, *Hypertext Markup Language; A Representation of Textual Information and Meta Information for Retrieval and Interchange*; Internet Draft, CERN, 1993.
3. T. Berners-Lee, *Hypertext Transfer Protocol;* Internet Draft, CERN, 1993.
4. R. Cattell, *Object Databases: The ODMB-93 Standard*, Morgan Kaufman, San Mateo, CA, 1993.
5. Daniel R. Dolk, *A Generalized Model Management System for Mathematical Programming*, ACM Transactions on Mathematical Software, vol. 12, no. 2 pp.92-126, 1986.

6. Christoph Gauger, *Implementierung und Bewertung von Verfahren zur Lösung von Rucksackproblemen unter der Berücksichtigung der Integration in eine Methodenbank*, Studienarbeit, Universität Tübingen, 1993.
7. M. Grötschel, M. Jünger, and G. Reinelt, *Programmpaket zur Behandlung symmetrischer Hamilton-Wege-Probleme mit Ordnungsbeziehungen*, Internal Paper, 1991.
8. John G. Hughes, *Object-Oriented Databases*, Prentice-Hall, München, 1991.
9. M. Jarke and F.J. Radermacher, *The AI Potential of Model Management and Its Central Role in Decision Support*, Decision Support Systems, vol. 4 no. 4, pp. 287-404, 1988.
10. E. L. Lawler, J. K. Lenstra, A. H. G. Rinnooy Kan, and D. B. Shmoys, *The Traveling Salesman Problem*, Wiley, 1985.
11. Andreas Ludwig, *Erstellung einer graphischen Benutzerschnittstelle für das Methodenbanksystem M*, Studienarbeit, Universität Tübingen, 1992.
12. Silvano Martello and Paolo Toth, *Knapsack Problems*, Wiley, Chichester, 1990.
13. Kurth Mehlhorn and Stefan Näher, *LEDA - A Library of Efficient Data Types and Algorithms*, in Proceedings Graph-theoretic Concepts in Computer Science 1990, pp. 88-106, Springer, 1990.
14. F. H. Murphy and E. A. Stohr, *An Intelligent System for Formulating Linear Programs*, Decision Support Systems, vol. 2, pp. 29-47, 1986.
15. N. Nilsson, *Principles of Artificial Intelligence*, Springer, Berlin, 1982.
16. F.N. Paulisch and W. F. Tichy, *EDGE: An Extendible Graph Editor*, Software-Practice and Experience, vol. 20, no. S1, pp. 63-88, 1990.
17. Frank Puppe, *Problemlösungsmethoden in Expertensystemen*, Springer, Berlin, 1990.
18. Richard G. Ramirez, Chee Ching, and Robert D. St. Louis, *Model-Data and Model-Solver Mappings: A Basis for an Extended DSS Framework*, in ISDSS Conference Proceedings 1990, pp. 283-312.
19. Richard G. Ramirez, Chee Ching, and Robert D. St. Louis, *Independence and Mappings in Model-Based Decision Support Systems*, Decision Support Systems, vol. 10, pp. 341-358, 1993.

Modelling Events in Object-Oriented Analysis

L. Mathiassen*   A. Munk-Madsen[†]   P.A. Nielsen*   J. Stage*

Abstract: The concept of objects is widely applicable in software development. In this paper, we explore its capabilities in modelling various kinds of phenomena in object-oriented analysis and design. We argue that the dynamics of objects in the real world are different from the dynamics of objects within the computer system. There is much to be gained from explicitly modelling events in object-oriented analysis thereby concieving real-world objects differently from the classical way in which we understand and design objects as parts of a software system. The paper examines a well-known approach to object-oriented analysis, it provides specific advice on event modelling, and it outlines a way of representing events in object-oriented software design.

1   Introduction

The ability to use one powerful concept throughout analysis, design and implementation contributes significantly to the success of object-orientation. Objects are used to understand real-world phenomena in the context of a computer system as well as technical constructs in the computer system itself. We thereby avoid difficult conceptual transformations. A second factor contributing to this success is the coherent integration of both structural and dynamic aspects into the single notion of objects. We thereby negate the traditional separation of data and algorithms.

The many qualities of object-oriented approaches are, in other words, grounded in the generality of the concept of an object. We should, however, not neglect the important differences between the various kinds of phenomena involved in software development. Instead, we must acknowledge the important differences between real-world objects in the context of a computer system and objects that are parts of the software system itself. This line of reasoning has lead us to study how object dynamics can be modelled during object-oriented analysis.

In a well-known object-oriented method, OOA [2], Coad & Yourdon present object-oriented analysis as a 'natural' way of understanding and describing the problem domain of a computer system. They argue that the techniques and notation of OOA are based on the methods of organization that pervade all human thinking. OOA supports the selection and definition of classes which model objects in the

---

*L. Mathiassen, P. A. Nielsen, and J. Stage are with the Department of Mathematics and Computer Science, Aalborg University, Fredrik Bajers Vej 7, DK-9220 Aalborg East, Denmark.

[†]A. Munk-Madsen is with Metodica, Nyvej 19, DK-1851 Frederiksberg C, Denmark.

problem domain. It also guides selection and definition of structural relationships between classes.

Murphy [8] reports from a software development project in which the OOA method was used. He states that the OOA method provides an excellent set of general guidelines for approaching object-oriented analysis. However, portions of the approach still remain undefined. Murphy classifies OOA as a data-driven approach to analysis which originates from the field of information modelling. He argues that this is a questionable approach since it ignores the dynamics of objects.

Jackson's method, JSD [4], was developed a decade before the more recent object-oriented approaches. His method does, however, include a simple and elegant way of describing the dynamics of problem domain objects. An object is characterised by the structured set of actions in which it is involved throughout its lifetime. That which is described as an action in JSD is is denoted as an event in this paper. A major drawback of JSD is that structural relations between classes are ignored. The only relationship between objects occurs when data are transferred from one object to another.

This paper proposes and illustrates how OOA's guidelines for modelling problem domain objects and structure can be combined with JSD's notion of object dynamics. This proposal is based on the following experiences: (i) our teaching of first JSD and later OOA to both undergraduate students and practitioners for almost ten years, (ii) our own practising of JSD and OOA, (iii) our consultancy work, and (iv) our research efforts over the last three years to develop a new method for object-oriented analysis [6]. An earlier version of this paper has been published previously [7].

Section 2 introduces the concept of an event in object-oriented analysis. Section 3 discusses the modelling of problem domain dynamics and events, particularly in OOA and JSD. The basics of OOA and JSD are outlined and their major strengths and weaknesses concerning structural relations and object dynamics are emphasised. Section 4 presents our combined approach to problem domain modelling. Its use is illustrated by an example. Section 5 provides an outline of how to represent events from the problem domain in software design. Finally, Section 6 discusses directions for further improvement of methods for object-oriented analysis.

2 Events in Object-Oriented Analysis

Booch defines object-oriented analysis as an approach that "examines requirements from the perspective of the classes and objects found in the vocabulary of the problem domain," [1, p. 37], and he provides the following definition of the basic concept: "An object has state, behaviour, and identity" [1, p. 83]. This notion of an object is sufficiently general to support most modelling needs during software development; but how should we model the state, behaviour, and identity of objects to capture the variety of needs involved?

Inspired by the way objects are described in modern programming languages, we are invited to understand the behaviour of an object in terms of the methods or

90

services it makes available to other objects. We are also encouraged to describe the execution of such services by a sequence of simple statements. This notion is well-suited to understand and design objects which are integrated parts of programs, but do people, organizations, and machines in the real world outside the computer provide services that may be activated by other objects in the real-world? Is it necessary to describe the behaviour of a real world object by a detailed sequence of statements? Is this the most suitable way to understand and model the behaviour of objects not in the computer system, but in the context of a computer system?

Inspired by Jackson, we define an event as "an instantaneous action involving one or more objects," *cf.* [4]. From this point of view, objects do not provide services to each other. They perform or suffer actions, and these actions produce the events we can observe. In the following, we will explore this specialised notion of object behaviour as a basis for an analytic approach. Our argument is based on differences between objects from various domains involved in software development. Before proceeding, we therefore need to explicate the main domains involved, *cf.* Figure 1.

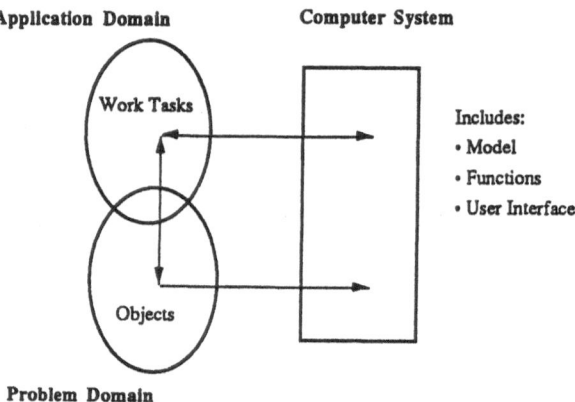

Figure 1: The computer system in context.

A computer system's *application domain* consists of its users and their way of applying the computer system in their work tasks. A computer system's *problem domain* denotes what the computer system is concerned with. It contains that part of reality to which the computer system is applied to administer, monitor, or control. With a car rental system, the application domain may be the work of desk clerks taking care of customers; they utilise the computer system to register customers, book cars, print contracts, etc. The corresponding problem domain may consist of cars, pricing rules, contracts, and what may happen to cars, pricing rules, and contracts; for example, cars are rented, cars are returned, cars are bought and sold, etc. The things in the problem domain are called objects and what happens to these objects are called events.

The idea of a *computer system* which we are promoting is that it must contain a model that keeps track of what happens in the problem domain [6, p. 7-8]. Simply, if the desk clerk wants to know whether a particular car is available, he only has to look at the state of the model and not at reality. This requires, of course, that the track-keeping is accurate and reliable. It also requires that the track-keeping is consistent with the desk clerk's perception of the real-world problem domain. Accordingly, we must choose our object and event abstractions of the real-world phenomena in a way that is relevant to the desk clerk.

The purpose of *analysis* is to understand and describe the users' requirements to the computer system. This involves building the model of the problem domain in object-oriented terms. In order to do this, objects and events must be described coherently. Analysis of the application domain is not particularly object-oriented as it must involve at least the description of the functionality provided by the system to support users in carrying out work tasks.

It should be noticed that what is termed an event in modern structured analysis, *cf.* [10], is not an event in the problem domain. It is merely denoting a request for information in the application domain.

3 Two Approaches to Event Modelling

Problem domain modelling is a key activity of object-oriented analysis. Event modelling, which we focus on in this paper, is a major part of this.

3.1 Event Modelling with OOA

Coad & Yourdon's object-oriented analysis method, OOA, comprises the following five activities, *cf.* [2]:

1. *Finding Classes and Objects:* The main criterion for selecting an object is either that the system is required to remember something about the object or that the object is required to provide some behaviour.

2. *Identifying Structures:* Structures include generalization-specialization structures, whole-part relations, and associations.

3. *Identifying Subjects:* Subjects are simply used to cluster classes in the problem domain model.

4. *Defining Attributes:* Attributes capture the data contents of objects.

5. *Defining Services:* A service is the data processing to be performed by an object upon receipt of a message.

OOA is a constructive contribution to the application of object-oriented concepts and ideas in problem domain modelling. The strength of OOA is the simple but powerful way in which it guides selection and definition of classes and their structural relations. A main weakness is its limited emphasis on problem domain dynamics.

Murphy [8] reports from a project in which an improved version of OOA was applied to analyse a network management application. OOA was initially selected through a review of ten object-oriented analysis methods, yet this review also indicated areas in which OOA had to be supplemented with other techniques. A major problem with OOA was its predominant focus on data as opposed to object behaviour.

In our experience, OOA is capable of handling events in two ways. If an event is worth remembering, it is considered as a major event and modelled as a special category of classes describing event-remembering objects. It is part of the first activity to identify events and classify these by finding a common denominator for a group of events which act like a whole. It is even part of a checklist to search. Study of a vast number of OOA models indicates that it is common practice to group significant events together into a single class.

Minor events may, instead, be treated as services. A service on an object can be used to register that something has happened to the object. For example, the services on an event-remembering class will typically be updating initiated by events, *e.g.* renting, or returning, a car can be modelled as a service on a contractual event. While this is in principle a possibility it is rarely used during analysis. Certainly, it is neither mentioned nor encouraged by OOA.

Neither of these two approaches is satisfactory. Events are intrinsically dynamic properties of the problem domain and it is truly misleading to model them as though they were objects. Objects and events are dual in nature and too much is lost if events are reduced to mere objects. To model events as services is to take the dynamic nature seriously, but a service is a computer construct which is not found outside the computer. The construct is useful in design where the computer system is described. In analysis, it reflects the mistake of thinking that the real-world outside the computer is acting exactly like a computer. The dynamics of the problem domain cannot usefully be thought of as processing carried out upon receipt of a message—no message is passed from a customer to a car and a car does not process anything, except petrol.

3.2 Event Modelling with JSD

JSD [4] was presented in 1983 as a reaction to the function-oriented approach of most contemporary analysis and design methods.

In many regards, Jackson's ideas correspond to the idea of a track-keeping system in a context of problem domain and application domain. Jackson argues that every computer system is concerned with the real-world, *i.e.* a part of reality outside itself, and the fundamental principle of JSD is that this reality should be modelled as an integrated part of the development of the computer system.

JSD is based on the notions of entities and actions in the problem domain. An *action* is a process that occurs in the real-world outside the computer system. An action must be regarded as being instantaneous and atomic in the sense that it is not relevant to decompose it into subactions. An *entity* is something that can be identified individually in the real-world. An entity must perform or suffer actions in a significant time-ordering. Ideally, each entity is thought of as a sequential process and a model as communicating, sequential processes.

The domain modelling of Jackson System Development comprises the following four activities, *cf.* [4]:

1. *Entity Action Step:* That which is relevant to the track-keeping model is listed as entities and actions.

2. *Entity Structure Step:* The lifetime of each entity is described by structured actions according to their ordering in time.

3. *Initial Model Step:* The problem domain is described as a process model consisting of connected entities.

4. *Function Step:* The functions that produce the desired output of the computer system are defined in terms of data processing and access to the entities of the model.

The JSD method was not originally presented as an object-oriented method. For that reason, some of the concepts used are different from conventional concepts of object-oriented thinking. On the other hand, most of the concepts resemble the object-oriented concepts. To avoid this potential for misunderstanding, we have chosen to exchange the designations of JSD for their object-oriented equivalents. We will use the more common notion of 'object' as a substitute for 'entity'. We have chosen to use the notion of 'event' to denote the mechanism by which a model object registers an action that involves the corresponding problem domain object.

Events and objects are equally important in JSD. They are both identified in the very first step of the method. Objects and events are closely related in Step 2 where object dynamics are expressed in terms of events. What we know about an object is the set of events with which it is involved and the order in which these events are happening. There is a notation and a whole range of hints, experience, and guidelines to support the description of the ordering of these events.

Regarded as a method for problem domain modelling the main drawback of JSD is that its notion of an object is too simple. JSD's notion of an object does not benefit from the advantages of abstract data types and the possibility to describe structural relations between objects and classes. In fact, JSD never introduces a class concept. It only deals with individual objects. In this respect, OOA offers a much more powerful approach.

3.3 Event Modelling with Other Methods

We have chosen to focus on OOA and JSD in our examination of event modelling because they have been the main inspiration in providing the combined method presented in Section 4. However, other methods also deal with events, one way or another.

Our discussion addresses the modelling of a problem domain during object-oriented analysis and in particular the intrinsic relation between the description of classes and their structural relations (static view) and the description of object dynamics (dynamic view).

Concerning the static view, we could have made another choice, *e.g.* the methods of Rumbaugh *et al.*, Martin *et al.*, or Booch [9, 5, 1]. There are differences in the support these methods provide to modelling the static aspects of the problem domain; but these differences are insignificant to our discussion.

Concerning the dynamic view, the ideas of JSD are still unique and not expressed or utilised in contemporary object-oriented analysis methods. All object-oriented analysis methods do, of course, address the dynamic aspects of objects as this is an inherent part of taking an object-oriented approach to modelling. JSD is, however, unique in its approach to modelling the dynamic aspects of the problem domain as we will illustrate by briefly reviewing two well-known methods which both emphasise the concept of event.

Rumbaugh *et al.* [9] distinguishes, amongst other things, between object modelling and dynamic modelling. The object model describes the possible patterns of objects, attributes, and links that can exist in a system. This corresponds to the static view represented by OOA in our discussion. The dynamic model consists of multiple state diagrams, one state diagram for each class, and shows the pattern of activity for an entire system via shared events. The view provided by this dynamic model corresponds closely to the view provided by JSD. However, the concern is quite different. Rumbaugh *et al.* propose to make a dynamic model of the computer system, whereas JSD propose to make a dynamic model of the problem domain to be used later as a basis for designing the computer system.

A similar difference can be found by reviewing Martin *et al.* [5]. Here, a distinction is made between object structure analysis and object behaviour analysis. Object structure analysis defines the classes we perceive and the ways in which we associate them. This corresponds to the object model of Rumbaugh *et al.* and the static view represented by OOA in our discussion. The object behaviour analysis takes an approach that is comparable to Rumbaugh *et al.*, i.e. the view taken is similar to JSD, but the concern is again quite different. Even though a distinction is made between events in general and external (to the system) sources of events, Martin *et al.* basically propose to model the dynamics of the computer system, not the problem domain as suggested by JSD.

4 The Combined Approach

We have conducted several analysis and design projects based on a method that combines the respective strengths of the two approaches described above. Below, we describe the domain modelling activities of this combined approach and illustrate its results by means of an example.

4.1 Problem Domain Modelling Activities

The combined approach to problem domain modelling comprises the following three activities:

1. *Classes and Events:* Selection and definition of the classes and events that are relevant to model the problem domain. All events that are considered relevant to a class are listed with it.

2. *Structure:* Description of structural relations between classes in terms of generalization structures and between objects in terms of aggregation and association structures.

3. *Dynamics:* Arrangement of the events in which an object is involved according to their potential occurrence in time. This also includes the definition of the attributes that are necessary to register certain states in the lifetime of an object.

These activities are carried out in a strongly iterative manner. Thus the sequence used here is mainly a matter of presentation.

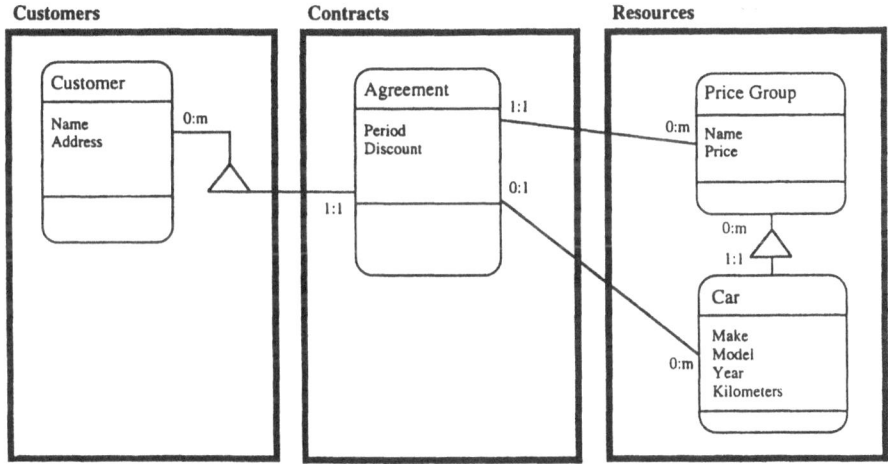

Figure 2: Structure diagram

4.2 A Problem Domain Model

To illustrate the results of this combined approach, we have chosen a small example: a car rental company. The classes and structures of this example are shown in the structure diagram, *cf.* Figure 2.

96

The structure diagram[1] illustrates the four classes that are used to describe the problem domain of the car rental company: Customer, Agreement, Price Group, and Car. The Customer and Car classes reflect the physical objects appearing in this problem domain. The Agreement class is chosen because it appears as a key document in the problem domain. The Price Group class is integrated in the model because the users insists it is the means for defining standard prices. Furthermore, reservations are made on price groups which pertain to specific categories of cars; the car itself is not allocated to a customer until he actually arrives to pick it up.

In the structure diagram, we have also outlined three clusters of classes. In [2] collections of classes are denoted as subjects. Instead, we prefer the word 'clusters,' which has, nevertheless, the same meaning. The clusters depicted here reflect the heart of the car rental case: resources are allocated dynamically to customers by means of contracts. For purposes of illustration, the model is deliberately kept as simple as possible. In a more elaborate version, each of these clusters will contain more classes. The dynamics of each class are described by a behaviour diagram. Figures 3, 4, 5, and 6 show the behaviour diagrams of the car rental case.

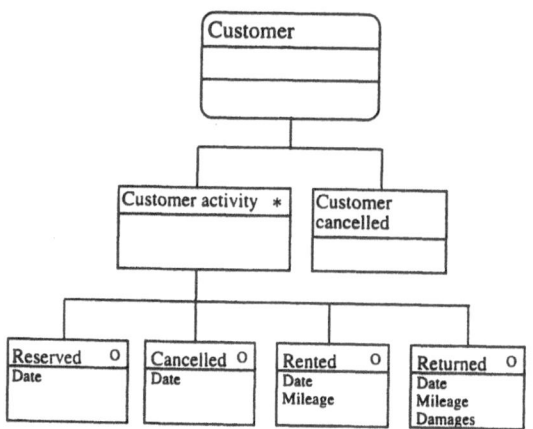

Figure 3: Behaviour diagram for the Customer class

Figure 3 shows a quite unrestricted way of describing object behaviour. This diagram shows that a customer object can be involved in any sequence of the four events described as options. Moreover, it describes how customer objects disappear beyond the problem domain boundary once the clerks decide to cancel them; in the case, this usually happens if a customer is inactive for more than a year.

Figure 4 is much more structured. It shows that an agreement object is created either when a reservation is made or when the empty event occurs. The latter situation indicates that a customer may rent a car without any prior reservation. The next event is either that the car is rented or the reservation cancelled. If the car

---

[1]The notation used in this diagram is borrowed from [2].

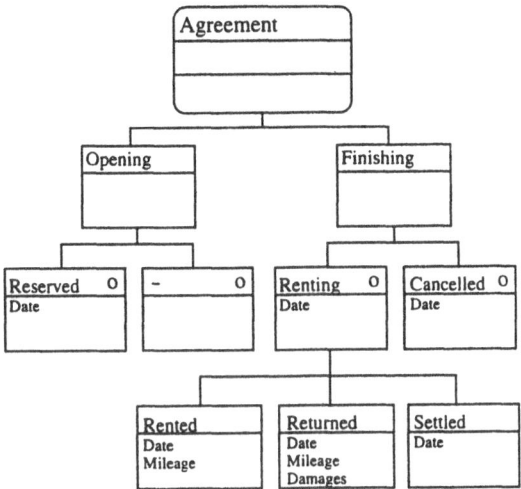

Figure 4: Behaviour diagram for the Agreement class

is rented, a simple sequence occurs, by which the car is returned and the customer's account is settled.

Figure 5 describes the ordering of events involving a price group object. Objects from this class are also characterised by a quite unrestricted behaviour. Price groups are explicitly created and deleted in the problem domain, implying that, in this case, actions of the car rental company are modelled as events. Otherwise, a price group can be involved in any sequence of reservation, cancellation, buying, and selling.

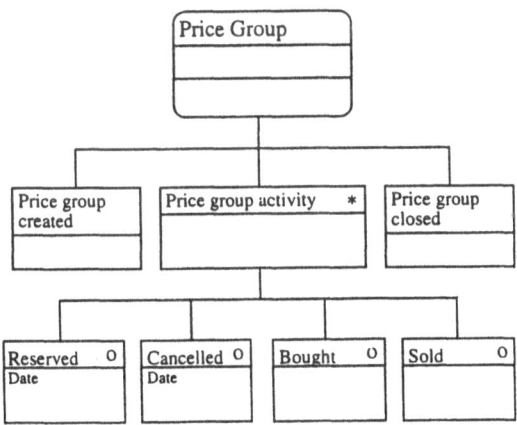

Figure 5: Behaviour diagram for the Price Group class

Finally, Figure 6 shows the behaviour of car objects. A car enters the problem domain once it is bought. Its main behaviour changes from renting to servicing, each being a small sequence of two events. When the car is inactive in the parking lot, it is waiting to be involved in either a 'rented' or 'delivered' event. The car disappears out of the problem domain when it is sold.

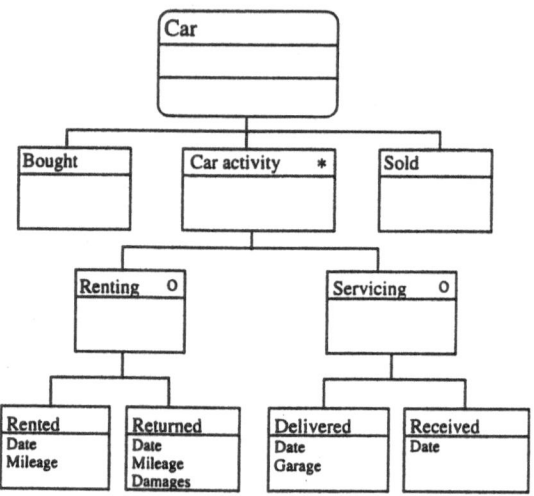

Figure 6: Behaviour diagram for the Car class

4.3 Private and Common Events

Figures 3, 4, and 5 illustrate how the behaviour diagrams of two or more classes may include events with the same names, e.g. 'reserved'. This indicates that the occurrence of such an event in the problem domain involves objects from each of these classes. In this sense, the event is common to objects from these classes. If the set of objects involved in a common event is important, a special diagram may be produced in order to describe the exact number of objects from each class that is involved in that particular event. The example used here is so simple that this description is unnecessary.

The use of common events implies that events have to be named globally, as opposed to local naming within each class. Events that only occur in the behaviour diagram of one class are private to objects of that class.

The purpose of introducing common events is to enable dynamic relationships between objects from different classes to be described. Usually, this dynamic relation is connected to a static relation between the objects involved.

4.4 Identifying Classes through Events

In the example above, we have illustrated a simple but sufficient way of describing the behavioural characteristics of problem domain objects. This is one important reason for focussing on events in object-oriented analysis. An equally important reason is that behaviour diagrams emphasise potential problems in our collection of classes.

Imagine, for a moment, that we had only identified the physical objects in the car rental case: customers and cars. With a conventional approach to object-oriented analysis we might convince ourselves that these were the relevant classes, yet the combined approach presented above provides systematic support in this respect by forcing us to make behaviour diagrams for each of the classes identified. Thus we have to make behaviour diagrams for the car and customer class.

The first problem occurs with the car class. We want to describe that the car is involved in a variety of reserved, rented, and returned events. However, we have difficulties describing how a car can be reserved at a future date once it is rented, since the event after renting should be the returning of the car. These problems should make us, again, ask the user whether reservations are made on the actual cars themselves. In this way, the price group class is identified.

The second problem is related to this. We want to describe in a simple way that a reservation is either fulfilled by a rented-returned sequence or cancelled. If we attempt to describe this on the price group, we have to ignore this dynamic relation between a particular reservation and its fulfillment or cancellation. If we describe it in the behaviour diagram of the customer class, we impose the unnecessary constraint that a customer cannot make a new reservation once he has started a reserved-rented-returned sequence. These problems should make us ask the user what actually connects a customer with a reservation and a subsequent allocation of the physical car. In this way, the agreement class is identified.

This imaginary analysis process illustrates the strength of any form of describing detailed dynamic object behaviour. The details enable us to see problems in an over-simplistic model. The additional strength of event modelling is its simplicity.

4.5 Requirements to Functionality and User Interface

So far, we have discussed and illustrated how the focus on structural relations of the OOA method can be combined with the focus on problem domain dynamics of the JSD method. In this sense, we have only dealt with the computer system's model of the problem domain.

In section 2 we emphasised functions and user interfaces as two equally important elements of a computer system. We have argued that the selection of objects and events defines our perspective on the problem domain. In a similar way, the functions of the computer system defines our perspective on the application domain. The application domain was defined as the collection of work tasks in the user organization in which the computer system is used as a tool to monitor, administrate, and control the problem domain. Hence the set of functions implemented by the computer system defines the set of work tasks that are supported and the way in which this support is achieved. This in turn defines the application domain.

The implication of this is that functional considerations have to be included in the analysis. The simple approach to this is to claim, as in OOA and JSD, that functional definitions should be made after the problem domain model is defined. This principle is theoretically sound, but it is impossible to practice, especially for a novice analyst, such as a student, still in the process of learning the method.

Without any concern for computer system functionality, we have no criterion for defining the model of the problem domain. The key point is that an object should be integrated in the problem domain model if, and only if, it is administered, monitored, or controlled by at least one function of the computer system. Otherwise, it is outside the boundary of the problem domain. In this sense, the functionality of the computer system provides the only criterion of relevance for the selection of objects.

With OOA and JSD this process of selection is based on a simple naming of the problem domain. Both methodologies suggest strongly that the problem domain is described before any systematic consideration of relevant functions. In this way, they imply that the simple naming of the problem domain introduces a logic which facilitates the selection of elements that are relevant to integrate into the model. Our experience is that the process of selection is more complicated.

The description of functions as part of object-oriented analysis serves two purposes. Firstly, it contributes to define the application domain more precisely, similar to the way classes are used to define the problem domain. Secondly, the description of functions facilitates a check of the completeness of the problem domain model. The model should contain only the information necessary to produce the required output of each function.

OOA and JSD both reflect a lack of emphasis towards the user interface. In JSD, the user interface is denoted as the input subsystem and it is implied that this can be added subsequently to the definition of model and functions. In OOA, it is postponed to the design activity, cf. [3]. Our experience is that software development with inexperienced users requires early emphasis on the user interface, for example through development and evaluation of early prototypes. The user interface is the only means to verify the contents and structure of the model when we are cooperating with users who are unable to cope with the abstract nature of object-oriented descriptions.

4.6 Principles of Analysis of Problem Domain Events

The combined approach is based on a number of principles fundamental to object oriented analysis. The principles state what the analysts should do, but not how it should be done. Five of these principles concern the analysis of events in the problem domain.

- *Investigate the problem domain.* It is imperative to study reality outside the computer. In this context it is important to focus on how the users of the future computer system will view the problem domain. It is their view on reality we try to express in the model.

- *Characterise objects by their events.* The set of classes and their structure forms the static properties of the model of the problem domain. The dynamic properties are modelled by means of events. It is not likely to have objects without events.

- *Describe objects' behaviour by patterns of events for classes.* The events are used to express the dynamics of the problem domain. As illustrated above an event is better described as a dynamic property than as a static property.

- *Consider events common to several objects.* Events common to two or more objects point to dynamic relationships in the model. Two objects with a common event must be related by either an aggregation or an association structure.

- *Derive the attributes of a class from its pattern of events.* The pattern of events of a class will point at central attributes necessary to keep historical data as well as state information.

These principles have been applied in the example above. In analysing problem domain dynamics there are many ways to apply the principles. Any approach aiming to deal properly with problem domain dynamics will need to adhere to these principles or similar principles covering the same contents.

5   Implications for Object-Oriented Design

Analysis based on the combined approach described above focusses on classes, events, structure, and dynamics. This approach differs from most other methods through the events and their use in describing object dynamics. This approach has consequences for design that can be explained by means of Figure 7.

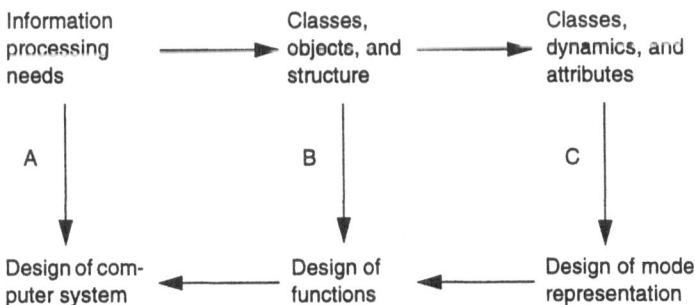

Figure 7: Different approaches to analysis and design

Approach (A) in the figure provides a simplified description of a traditional, function-oriented approach to analysis. We go straight from analysis of needs to computer system design.

Approach (B) is a typical object-oriented analysis. We analyse problem domain objects and their structural relations before we define the functions of the system. The strength of this is that we obtain an understanding of the essentials of the users' work and at the same time obtain a powerful language for expressing system requirements.

Approach (C) corresponds to the one introduced in this paper. Here, we go a step further as we *also* focus on problem domain dynamics. The advantages of this have been discussed above. However, this approach imposes further work during design as we have to decide how these dynamics should be represented. Thus the problem domain dynamics, described by the collection of behaviour diagrams, raise separate implementation considerations. Firstly, we must make sure that the information depicted in these diagrams is registered. Secondly, the computer system, once it is in operation, must support its users in controlling whether objects behave as prescribed by the behaviour diagrams.

The design may again be based on principles to transforming events to concepts known in object-oriented programming languages.

- *Events are represented as classes, structures and attributes.* Depending on the pattern to which the event belongs, it may be necessary to represent it as new attributes of the class (simple), new structures involving the class, or a new class (complex). See below.

- *Attributes of events are transferred to the appropriate classes.* These attributes are relevant to remember the events and are mostly transferred to the class into which the event is transformed. See below.

- *Updating services are defined based on patterns of events.* For each event there needs to be an updating service in every class it involves. An updating service must update the attributes of the object on which the event occurred and control whether the object is in a state where the event may occur according to the pattern.

Each of the three ways of assembling events into a pattern has a simple technique for transforming events into something else, *cf.* Figure 8. In addition to this come the updating services which in turn each follow the complexity and representation of the attributes, structures or classes representing the event.

Common events have to be treated with considerable care. This is not because they are common events in the model, but because they reflect a complication in the dynamic behaviour of the problem domain. Figure 9 explains the technique for treating common events.

Without going into detail of all the other aspects of object-oriented design let us mention that, as an integrated part of design, it is necessary to decide how the structural relationships are to be implemented. In particular, object relationships or links may impose serious problems on this activity. Furthermore, the design of functions which update or use the model, as well as the interface to users and other systems, are key issues in this context.

Sequence	A sequence is represented as a state attribute in the class above. The state attribute is assigned a new value each time an event in the sequence occurs. The attributes of the events are integrated into the class above.
Iteration	An iteration is represented as a new class. Each occurence creates a new object in the class. The attributes of the events are integrated into the new class. A subpattern below the iteration is treated as a pattern of the new class.
Selection	A selection is represented as a choice attribute in the class above. The value set of the choice attribute represents the choices in the selection. The attributes of the events are integrated in the class above.

Figure 8: Techniques for transforming private events

Common	If the event is part of unequally complex patterns, the primary rule is to represent the event in association with the class giving the least complex representation. If the event is part of equally complex patterns, trade-offs and choice of best solution has to be made by comparing alternative representations directly.

Figure 9: Techniques for transforming common events

6 Conclusion

We have argued in this paper that the dynamics of objects in the real world are significantly different from the dynamics of objects in the computer. In the computer services on objects seem to be sufficient while in modelling the real world outside the computer services are inappropriate. We have proposed to focus instead on events in the problem domain and on the patterns they form in reality. This we have taken as a starting point in the outline of an analytic approach.

Coad & Yourdon's OOA is, we have argued, a useful method for analysing the static properties of the problem domain but with insufficient focus on dynamic properties. Jackson's JSD is a useful method for analysing the dynamic properties of the problem domain but with insufficient means for modelling structural relationships.

We have proposed how static and dynamic properties of problem domain objects can be integrated in a combined approach leading to a coherent description.

Structure is modelled as in OOA and dynamics are modelled, as in JSD, by event patterns. We have illustrated that this combined approach has advantages beyond those of OOA and JSD.

Finally, we have finally how the behaviour may be represented in the computer system model during design. This involves transforming event patterns to new attributes, structures and classes as well as adding services to classes.

References

[1] G. Booch. *Object-Oriented Design with Applications*. Benjamin/Cummings, Redwood City, California, 2nd edition, 1994.

[2] P. Coad and E. Yourdon. *Object-Oriented Analysis*. Prentice-Hall, Englewood Cliffs, New Jersey, 2nd edition, 1991.

[3] P. Coad and E. Yourdon. *Object-Oriented Design*. Prentice-Hall, Englewood Cliffs, New Jersey, 1991.

[4] M. Jackson. *System Development*. Prentice-Hall, Englewood Cliffs, NJ, 1983.

[5] J. Martin and J. J. Odell. *Object-Oriented Analysis and Design*. Prentice-Hall, Englewood Cliffs, New Jersey, 1992.

[6] L. Mathiassen, A. Munk-Madsen, P. A. Nielsen, and J. Stage. *Objektorienteret analyse*. Marko, Aalborg, 1993.

[7] L. Mathiassen, A. Munk-Madsen, P. A. Nielsen, and J. Stage. Combining two approaches to object-oriented analysis. In *Proceedings from International Symposium on Object-Oriented Methodologies and Systems*, Palermo, September 21-22, 1994.

[8] G.C. Murphy. Experiences applying OOA. In *TOOLS USA '91*, 1991.

[9] J. Rumbaugh, M. Blaha, W. Premerlani, F. Eddy, and W. Lorensen. *Object-Oriented Modelling and Design*. Prentice-Hall, Englewood Cliffs, New Jersey, 1991.

[10] E. Yourdon. *Modern Structured Analysis*. Prentice-Hall, 1989.

An object-oriented design for modelling business rules in resource allocation jobs

S.Ramakrishnan

Department of Software Development
Monash University, PO Box 197, Caulfield East, Victoria 3145,
Australia.
email: sitar@pear.fcit.monash.edu.au fax: 61-3-903-2745

ABSTRACT. With the rapid economic restructuring and changes taking place in modern industrial organisations, it is essential that the software system used by a company is able to meet not only the present, but also the future demands of the company. This could be addressed by including strategic knowledge such as business policies and procedures explicitly in the software system development. This paper proposes a resource allocation model which considers the constraints to be satisfied by the resource allocation jobs (RAJ) at two levels. The constraints to be satisfied by the resource allocation jobs are expressed as the first level of constraints. The business policies and rules represent the second level of constraints and have been modelled as a wrapper layer of rules (RUG) around the resource allocation jobs objects. The paper shows how this resource allocation model allows an incremental evolution of the system by enabling the behaviour of resource allocation classes to be extended through reuse mechanisms, and how this facility of incremental evolution of systems can be extended to constraints by capturing the dynamic components of the system explicitly as a second level of constraints.

1. Introduction

An important aspect of software development is the software modelling, which is the process of creating a representation on a computer of the system under consideration. Software models based on rulebased expert systems have been developed to solve resource allocation problems [Solotorevsky et al. 1991, Onodera and Mori 1991]. Software models based on integer programming have also been developed, but in such models only single objectives are pursued [Berry 1992]. In this paper, a different approach has been followed and the system is modelled using an object-oriented (O-O) approach which enables real world problems to be modelled by identifying objects in the system and the interactions between those objects.

This paper introduces an object role model for capturing the business policy and rules explicitly in the system development. This need for business policies and rules to be considered explicitly in the system development process have also been recognised by other researchers [Tsalgatidou and Loucopoulos 1992].

A resource allocation model has been developed which extends the object-oriented approach of developing a system by including the business rules explicitly in a rulebased format. A static object model is presented for the *resource allocation job* (RAJ) objects to deal with the application domain objects. The RAJ objects are constrained by the business rules that may be specified.

2. Resource allocation model

In this paper, an aircrew scheduling example is used to discuss the proposed model. The planners involved in aircrew scheduling must satisfy the business rules or constraints prior to the allocation of crews to flights. Some of this domain knowledge can be captured and represented as rules to be considered in the allocation process. Other constraints such as a last minute change to the availability of an aircrew have to be handled by the planners online as part of the interactive scheduling system.

The model proposed here is shown in Figure 1 in which the component marked resource allocation jobs (RAJ) includes all the resources and job objects to describe all the entities related to the aircrew problem. A crew allocation task takes into consideration, resources such as flights, aircrafts, crew members and arrives at a duty for a crew member which is made up of a number of flights . The main feature of the model lies in its ability to treat business rules in a logical and systematic manner so that these rules can also be included as part of the reuse strategy in the incremental evolution of software. In this model, the constraints that may be satisfied by the resources and task objects involved in resource allocation job are considered at the following two levels: static type definition and context related information. The first level of constraints have been specified (where required) in the resource object's (static) type definition as part of its class definition. This constraint must be satisfied by an object when its behaviourial action(s) are invoked and is specified as assertions in Eiffel [Meyer 1988, Meyer 1992]. The business rules represent the second level of constraints that have to be satisfied by the RAJ objects and have been included as a wrapper layer of rules around those objects as shown in Figure 1. The RAJ object participates in the second level of constraint satisfaction by using the context information in the context header of the *rules using grammar* (RUG) object. The context header in the business rules represents the role played by the resource object. This second level of constraint is used to activate only those rules which match the active resource rule object and integrates the business rules and an application object in the resource object's constrain satisfaction. Some RAJ objects may not participate in any of these constraint satisfaction schemes, others may participate only at the first level and yet others may have constraints to be satisfied at both levels. The actions (methods, procedures or routines) of the objects have been qualified with these one or two levels of constraints, as dictated by the requirement of the objects in their interactions. One of the benefits of using the object-oriented approach is that the semantics of a system can evolve incrementally using the facilities provided by the paradigm for including new methods for various classes (types) over time [van Biema 1990]. The two levels of constraints used in this model, which allow an application object to have these varying levels of constraints, are a powerful additional mechanism through which software may evolve.

The language features that are used to describe the syntax and semantics of the RUG rules and the compilation of these rules which generate a parse tree are discussed in detail elsewhere [Ramakrishnan 1993]. The design framework integrates RAJ that has been represented using an object-oriented paradigm with the rulebased structure of the business rules (RUG) in a single language (Eiffel) formalism [Meyer 1989, Meyer 1990a, Meyer 1990b and Meyer 1990c].

The outcome of domain analysis of resource allocation problems is a domain model upon which the system architecture is based (refer to Figure 2). The high level architectural design (refer to Figure 3) shows the connection of the major components (clusters) at a given abstraction level. The knowledge elucidated from the study of scheduling theory, representation of business rules using O-O, artificial intelligence, compilation theory and attribute grammars has been encapsulated into component clusters to arrive at an initial version of domain taxonomy. The domain model is expanded to show the static structure of the objects and their relationships (refer to Figure 4) using Rumbaugh's object modelling techniques [Rumbaugh et al. 1991]. The diagram shows the relationships between the application classes, the reasoner class and the rulebase. The application classes such as Flight with its inheritance relationships with Uncrewed_flight and Crewed_flight; a Duty made up of a number of Crewed_flights and a Crew_allocation class associated with a number of Flights and Aircrafts. A Crew_allocation class interacts with the Reasoner and Rules to check for satisfaction of business rules. The business rules to be satisfied when assigning duties to a crew are included as Duty rules in the rulebase. A crew is allocated to a Flight and this Flight is included as part of his or her Duty application object only if the Duty rules are satisfied.

3. RUG wrapper for RAJ objects

Resource allocation job problems require the organisation's business rules to be included as part of the domain model. Business rules may be specified for a number of objects in the application cluster and an object may have to satisfy a number of rules. These rules may contain dependency information between attributes of an object. For example, a duty object may contain the following rule: "If duty is operating then total number of hours that this crew can work is 12 hours." The attributes in question are operating and total_number_of_hours. The total_number_of_hours attribute is a derived attribute (calculated) and the rule reflects the condition that must be met in allocating a crew member to a flight as part of his duty. These rules or constraints could be specified as assertions (preconditions, postconditions and invariants) in languages such as Eiffel. But, although assertions could be used to specify the constraints that an object and its descendants must satisfy, business rules expressed as a separate component makes them explicit and easy to read and extend. A rulebase component cluster should contain rules for resource application objects (refer to Figure 1). The wrapper represents an additional layer that must be satisfied by application objects apart from their usual constraint rules which can be specified as assertion rules. Encapsulating the rule semantics inside objects in the rulebase cluster and establishing interaction between the resource object and the rule object is how the RAJ objects are wrapped with RUG. The crew allocation process involves interaction between the resource objects. The application objects such as duty that have a wrapper layer interact with the rulebase component by instantiating a reasoner object. The reasoner object has access to stored rulebase application objects. In the prototype application, the resource object, aircraft, has been designed as an object without this semantic wrapper and hence there is no interaction between this object and the rulebase object. The aircraft object does have to satisfy a postcondition constraint included as part of its definition. But, more explicit business rules could be included as a wrapper in the rulebase cluster. Hence, the mechanism for including explicit rules about resource objects is to include the rules for these resource objects in the rulebase component and let the control be handled by the inference cluster. The business rules coded in the form of *context label: object, attribute, value* represent the left hand side of the condition in a rule in the rulebase. These rules have been represented as a structured document using a simple English language structure shown as follows:

```
setoperating: Given DUTY is operating
appo dtime maximum is 12.
setpaxing: Given DUTY equals paxing
appo dtime equals to 17.
mixoperatingandpax: Given DUTY equals mixoperpax
appo dtime maximum is 16
```

These rules have been described using Hedin's [Hedin 1989] object-oriented notation for attribute grammars and implemented in Eiffel by building a document processor for the rules [Ramakrishnan 1993]. These rules written as structured text are parsed and semantic actions are applied to the parsed document by collaborating with the Lexical and Parsing library classes of Eiffel.

The way in which the rulebase objects and application objects have been handled in this research is similar to the approach followed by Horn [1992] in his description of abstraction mechanisms called constraint patterns. Horn's constraint patterns combine the object-oriented concepts from the pattern abstraction of BETA [Kristensen et al. 1989] and Leler's [1989] Bertrand specification language to describe a constraint satisfaction system using augmented term rewriting rules. In this paper, constraint patterns for resource allocation problems combine the object-oriented features that have been developed for resource allocation objects using Eiffel with the rulebased paradigm of declarative rule specification using rewrite rules.

4. Integrating rules and application objects

The object-oriented paradigm provides good techniques for describing taxonomies of objects. But, in traditional object-oriented languages, the order of execution of methods is controlled through the statically defined class hierarchy. These languages do not provide mechanisms to code heuristics explicitly for the order of execution of methods. The methods can be specialised only according to their types through their inheritance relationships and not according to the state of the object. The notion of type is static whereas the notion of constraints being satisfied by an object at some point in the computation is dynamic.

Rules provide a natural way to describe heuristic problem-solving knowledge. Rule based production systems written using an object-oriented language such as Eiffel can access information in objects in the problem domain by using message passing. Rules can be stored using persistence facilities available in Eiffel as rulebase objects with active computational objects. *Triggers* are expressed in production systems as forward chaining production rules where a trigger [Eswaran et al. 1976] is a block consisting of a condition and body, and the body is executed if the condition is satisfied. In Boy's block representation [Boy 1993], contextual conditions or contexts are shown at a lower level than the triggering preconditions to express a different granularity of knowledge representation. Rules can, as shown in the business rules structure in the previous section, include context information in the condition part of the rule, to provide a more focussed triggering of the rules.

In this research, the constraints that may be satisfied by the resources and task objects involved in a resource allocation (refer to Figure 1) are achieved through the integration of a rulebased paradigm into the object-oriented language, Eiffel. Rules include a context header which precedes the if *condition* then *action*. This creates a context sensitive data driven rule based system which interacts with the application objects in the resource allocation process. The context header may match the messages sent to application objects. The resource allocation data activates only those rules which match the rule's context. This reduces the number of rules to be searched during the allocation process. This observation agrees with Chandrasekaran's observation [Chandrasekaran et al. 1992] that viewing knowledge at the appropriate level results in only a subset of the body of knowledge being relevant for consideration, thereby eliminating the need for conflict resolution.

Objects are been modelled in terms of their roles or responsibilities. The role is defined by the operations of the object [Wirfs-Brock et al. 1990; Jacobson et al. 1992]. A Duty application object has to satisfy the constraints specified by the Duty rule object, when the role of this application object (e.g. setoperating) matches the context header of the Duty rule object. The context header represents the role played by the rule object. A rule object specifies the action to be taken by the application object as the object's responsibility when the condition is met. A list of valid application objects for a resource allocation system and the responsibilities or roles of these objects are available to the system from obj_names class. Using this central information on valid objects and their roles, action is taken to invoke the appropriate message of the object.

5. Constraint satisfaction of business rules

Application cluster objects interact with the reasoner module to check for constraint satisfaction of rules. The reasoner class for the aircrew scheduling problem links the application object cluster to the rulebase objects. The reasoner object interacts with the stored application objects to access the duty object (refer to Figure 5). The stored application objects contain the various objects from the application cluster. The reasoner controls the interaction of the resource objects and the rulebase objects. The state diagram for the duty object (refer to Figure 6) shows the pattern of event that it receives and sends, and also the action performed by the duty object when the context value is matched. The application object involved in the crewing process is matched against that in the rule object and the state diagram (refer to Figure 6) shows the details of a crew allocation process in relation to the duty object. The rule object is retrieved from the object database of rules (rulebase). The reasoner controls the rules which are fired by matching the context of the application object against the context header of the rule object. Any extension to the behaviour or role or contextual information enacted by an application object affects the reasoner class as well. The new behaviours should be included in the relevant application objects and any new rules added to the rulebase to reflect this capability could be fired by adding the appropriate routines in the reasoner class.

6. Conclusion

The work presented in this paper emphasises the importance of including strategic knowledge such as business rules explicitly in the software system development. It presents an object-oriented (O-O) design framework for constraint based resource allocation problems. A systematic engineering approach has been followed to develop an object-oriented resource allocation model using the domain theory of scheduling, production rules approach and object-oriented technology. This model considers constraints that may be satisfied by the resource allocation process at two levels. The constraints to be satisfied by the resource allocation jobs (RAJ) are expressed as the first level of constraints and are specified as assertion rules in the static class description in an object-oriented language, Eiffel. The dynamic object role modelling of business rules represent the second level of constraints and have been included as a wrapper layer of rules around the resource allocation job objects. The rules are expressed in object-oriented attribute grammars as a separate component and represents the RUG layer over the RAJ objects. The wrapped application object interacts with a reasoner to satisfy constraints. The aim of the reasoner is to reduce the size of the search required when checking the business rules for constraint satisfaction. This reduction is achieved by introducing the concept of a context based search of the rulebase.

The object role modelling of business rules and the static modelling of application objects have been used to integrate a rulebased system into the object-oriented paradigm. The incrementally integrated prototype [Goldberg 1993] application of aircrew allocation may be extended by reusing the architecture and adding new behaviours by exploiting the facility of object-oriented languages for incremental evolution of the semantics of class types. This can be achieved by adding new methods for various class types. The constraint layer of RUG extends the evolution from types to constraints. This extension can be achieved by adding new roles or contextual information in the relevant application objects and updating the rulebase to include the business rules that govern these objects. This paper has shown that the benefits of using an object-oriented approach to evolve the semantics of a system incrementally by including new methods for various classes (types) can be extended to constraints by including dynamic constraints explicitly in the various stages of object-oriented system development including the programming phase.

References

[Berry 1992]   Berry P.A. (1992) A predictive model for satisfying conflicting objectives in scheduling problems. *AI magazine* 13(1)

[van Biema 1990]   van Biema M. (1990) *The constraint-based paradigm: The integration of object-oriented and the rule-based paradigms.* Columbia University 1990, UMI Dissertation services.

[Booch 1991]   Booch G. (1991) *Object-oriented design.* Reading (Mass): Addison-Wesley

[Boy 1993]   Boy G. (1993) Cognitive Science and Objects; the Agent perspective in *Technology of Object-oriented languages and systems* 10 (ed.)}. Magnusson B., Meyer B. and Perrot J. 297--318

[Chandrasekaran et al. 1992] Chandrasekaran B., Johnson T.R. and Smith J.W. (1992) Task-structure analysis for knowledge modelling, *Communications of the ACM* 35(9): 124--137

[Eswaran et al. 1976]   Eswaran K.P., Gray J.N., Loire R.A. and Traiger I.L. (1976) The notions of consistency and predicate locks in a database system *CACM* 19(11): 624--633

[Goldberg 1993]   Goldberg A (1993) Wishful thinking *Object magazine* 3(1) : 87--88

[Hedin 1989]   Hedin G. (1989) An Object-oriented Notation for Attribute Grammars in *ECOOP*, 1989 : 329--345

[Horn 1992]   Horn B. (1992) Constraint patterns as a basis for object-oriented programming in *ACM Sigplan Notices OOPSLA* 1992 27(10) : 218--234

[Jacobson et al. 1992]   Jacobson I., Christerson M., Jonsson P. and Overgaard G. (1992) *Object-oriented software engineering.* Readings (Mass.): Addison-Wesley

[Kristensen et al. 1989]   Kristensen B.B., Madsen O.L., Moller-Pedersen B. and Nygaard K. (1988) *Object-oriented programming in the BETA Programming language* Norwegian Computer Center, Oslo, and Computer Science Department, Aarhus University, Aarhus, Denmark, 1989.

[Leler 1988]   Leler Wm (1988) *Constraint programming languages - Their specification and generation.* Readings (Mass.) : Addison-Wesley

[Meyer 1988]   Meyer B. (1988) *Object-oriented Software Construction.* Prentice-Hall, Hemel Hemstead

[Meyer 1989]   *Interactive Software Engineering Inc., Eiffel: The Language* TR-EI-17/RM Version 2.2, Meyer B

[Meyer 1990a]   *Interactive Software Engineering Inc., Eiffel: The Libraries* TR-EI-7/LI Version 2.3, Meyer B. and Jean-Marc Nerson

[Meyer 1990b]   *Interactive Software Engineering Inc., Eiffel: The Environment* TR-EI-5/UM Version 2.3, Meyer B. and staff at ISE

[Meyer 1990c]   Meyer B. (1990) *Introduction to the theory of Programming Languages.* Prentice-Hall, Englewood Cliffs, New Jersey

[Meyer 1992]   Meyer B. (1992) Design by Contract in *Advances in software engineering* (ed.). Mandrioli D. and Meyer B., Object-oriented series, Prentice-Hall, Englewood Cliffs, New Jersey: 1--50

[Onodera and Mori 1991]   Onodera K. and Mori A. (1991) Cockpit scheduling and supporting system in *Operational expert system applications in the far east* (ed.). Lee J., Mizoguchi R., Narasimhalu D. and Yeung D. Pergamon press, New York, 133--161

[Ramakrishnan 1993]   Ramakrishnan S. (1993) *An object-oriented design for resource allocation problems.* Monash University, 1993. MComp. thesis

[Rumbaugh et al. 1991]   Rumbaugh J., Blaha M., Premerlani W., Eddy F. and Lorensen W. (1991) *Object-Oriented Modelling and Design.* Prentice-Hall, Englewood Cliffs, New Jersey

[Solotorevsky et al. 1991]   Solotorevsky G., Gudes E. and Meisels A. (1991) Specifying resource allocation and timetabling problems using a rule-based language *Proceeding 5th International conference on computer systems and software engineering*: 20--28

[Tsalgatidou and Loucopoulos 1991] Tsalgatidou A. and Loucopoulos P. (1991) Rule-based behaviour modelling: specification and validation of information systems dynamics *Information and software technology* 13(6): 425--432

[Wirfs-Brock et al. 1990] Wirfs-Brock R., Wilkerson B. and Wiener L. (1990) *Designing Object-Oriented Software*. Prentice-Hall, Englewood Cliffs, New Jersey

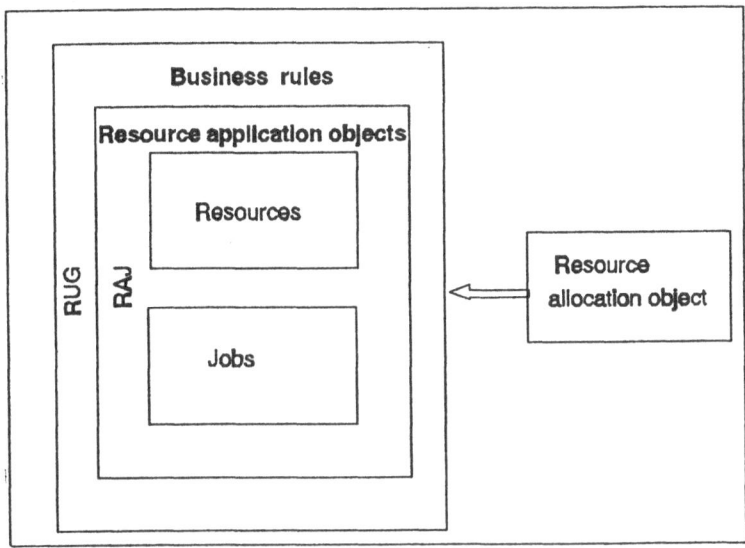

Figure 1: Resource application job objects wrapped with rules using grammar

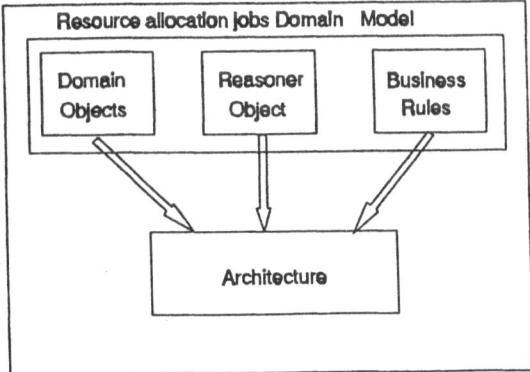

Figure 2: System architecture defined by the resource application jobs domain model

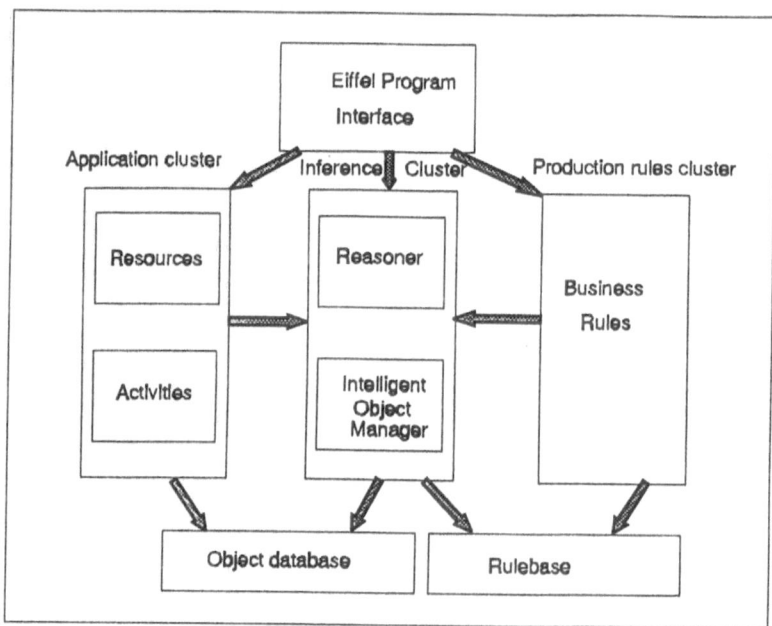

Figure 3: Resource allocation design framework

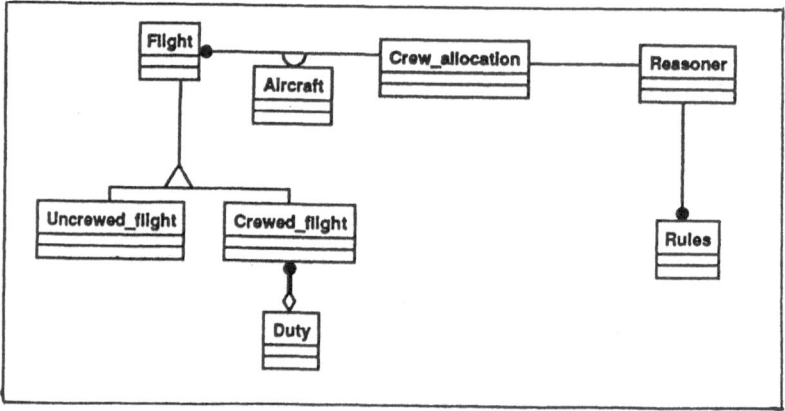

Figure 4: Aircrew scheduling object model diagram

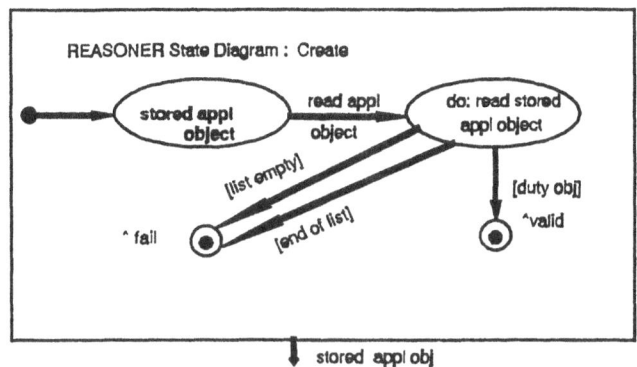

Figure 5: Reasoner collaborates with duty to set context values

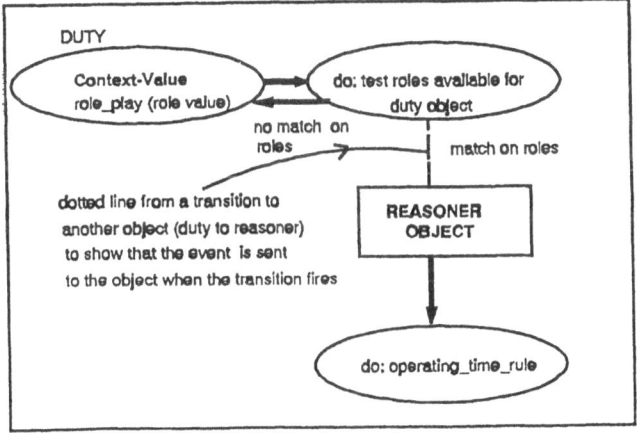

Figure 6: Matching roles of duty object against stored rules

Relational Implementation of Object Oriented Information System Design Using a Generic Model

Faïez Gargouri[1]   Faouzi Boufarès[2]   Charles François Ducateau[1]

[1] IUT de Paris, Université Paris 5, Département Informatique, Laboratoire LIASI
143, Ave de Versailles 75016. Paris. France.
[2] Laboratoire d'informatique Paris Nord, Avenue J.B. Clément. 93430, Villetaneuse. France.

ABSTRACT. *The emergence of the object philosophy in the new software development techniques gave birth to many object models. In this paper, Our aim, is to use a generic object-oriented model, to generate an optimized relational environment. This optimization concerns the best choice to implement, in the relational model, the structural links between classes using the set of treatments expressed on the information system studied. This approach presents the advantage, comparing to the classical structural methods, to choose a relational schema which will not be reconsidered later in the implementation stage.*

KEY WORDS: *Object oriented design; Generic model, Information System; Relational DBMS.*

1. Introduction

Most of the methods proposed for relational database design used to consider the users' needs as an independent part of the design process. This vision is supported by the dichotomy data/treatment, proper to the classical DBMS (codasyl or relational). Several methods were proposed to map from a given data model towards relational model [Bouzeghoub 86], [Lyngbeak 87], [Heurer 88] and [McCormack 93]. Unfortunately, those methods do not take into account the dynamic aspect of the information system. They just study the structural links (generalization and specialization relationships, association relationship, functional dependencies,...) between the information system components and thus, the relational database schema generated is, in most cases, not adequate to answer to the users' applications and needs in an optimum way. It is frequently modified, when mapping to the physical level, using the treatment in order to answer to the users' applications in an optimum way.

With the emergence of Object-Oriented approach in certain number of data processing domains, such as programming languages (Smalltalk, C++, Eiffel,...), software engineering, databases (Gemstone, O2, Ontos, ...),... many methods supporting conceptual modeling in an object-oriented way, have been proposed: OMT [Rumbaugh 91], OOA [Coad 91], OOD, GOOD [Booch 86], [Booch 87], HOOD [Heitz 89], OFM [Andonof 92], O* [Brunet 93] and MCO [Castellani 93] are some examples. The object-oriented approach enables the improvement of software quality, the reduction of future maintenance requirements, the reuse and the adaptation of specification and developments.

Our aim, in this paper, is to couple the object-oriented modelization power and the fact that the relational DBMS continuously increase their advantages in functionality and flexibility and catch up in performance [Rumbaugh 91] in order to generate a relational schema which will reflect exactly the conceptual representation and will be optimized according to the treatment expressed on the information system studied. The inheritance concept is not supported by the relational model. Thus, the relational implementation of this concept will need a formal study in order to choose, between the several possible relational implementations the more suitable one according to the set of treatments. The relational schema chosen will never be modified in the implementation level. This paper presents and justifies an algorithm which enables the choose of a relational implementation for an object-oriented representation according to the set of treatments expressed on it. Thus, we present an Object-to-Relational (OtoR) interface.

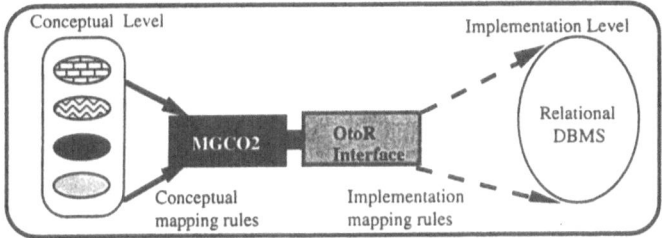

This article is organised as follows. Section 2 presents the MGCO2 generic concepts. Section 3 gives the 'Crude' transformation of an MGCO2 conceptual representation towards a relational schema. Section 4 and 5 give the mapping of inheritance and the choose criteria for the optimal relational implementation. The last section gives an ORACLE relational DBMS application.

2. Generic Concepts

Each method presents two kinds of models. The first one is the static model, the second is the dynamic one. The first model gives a static representation on the universe of discourse by describing its components and the relationships existing between them. The second model gives the interactions between the entities described by the static model and their interaction with the external environment. The following two sections introduce the concepts of the static and the dynamic models of MGCO2.

2.1. Static MGCO2 concepts:

Mainly three concepts represent the static MGCO2 model: class, object and properties. We will briefly introduce each of them hereafter.

A class describes a set of similar entities by defying their structural properties and their behaviour. Formally the class concept can be defined as follows:

$$\forall \kappa \in IS, \forall O_1, O_2 \in \kappa \Leftrightarrow \Omega(O_1) = \Omega(O_2) \text{ and } \Psi(O_1) = \Psi O_2)$$

Where: IS is the information system to built;

$\Omega(O_i) = \{a_{ij}\}_{j=1..n}$. the set of structural   properties of Oi,

$\Psi(O_i)$ the behaviour (dynamic) of Oi.

The general class specification is:

```
CLASS <class_name>:<class_type>
   [Inherits from: {<superclass_name>}+]
   Properties :{ <property_name>:<property_type>}+]
   [Relations: { <relation_name>}+]
   [Inheritance Constraint: {<inheritence_constraint}+]
   [Graphs: {<state_graph>+}]
   [Actions: {<action>+}]
   [Events: {<internal_event>}+]
END_CLASS -- <classe_name>
```

An object is a representation of a natural phenomenon belonging to the real world to model. Each Oi object belongs to a class and has a life cycle denoted $\vartheta(Oi)$. An object life cycle corresponds to the set of events arriving between the realisation of the $\xi_0(Oi)$ event creating the object and the realisation of the $\xi_m(Oi)$: event deleting the object. We admit that at a point of time only one event occurrence ξ_t can arrive. So, the life cycle of an object Oi can be formally describes as:

$$\vartheta(O_i) = \{\xi_{t0}(O_i), \xi_{t1}(O_i),..., \xi_{ti}(O_i),... \xi_{tm}(O_i)\}$$
$$\text{with } t_i < t_j \Leftrightarrow \xi_{ti} \text{ arrives before } \xi_{tj}$$

Example: The lifecycle of a room in a hotel can be: {reservation arrival, client arrival, client departure, deletion of the reservation} or {client arrival, client departure}.

The state of an object is given by a special attribute denoted *current_state*. The value of this attribute is:

. deduced from the value of one or more a_{ij};

. indicates the current state of the object.

During its life cycle an object can change from a state to an other. those changes correspond to the change of the current_state attribute value and are caused after the arrival of an event ξ_{tj} ($t_0 < t_j < t_m$). The state changes are expressed using a procedure *Change()* having as parameters: the initial state (before the event arrival), the event name and the new state of the object (after the event realisation). Example: for a room in a hotel:

States:
{free, occupied}
    Change(free, client arrival, occupied)
    Change(occupied, client departure, free)...

An object life cycle can be redefined as fellows:

$$\vartheta(O) = \{\xi_{ti}(O) / \textbf{Change}(state_1, \xi_{tj}, state_2)\}$$

Each object has a unique identity defines as follows:

$$\forall \kappa \in IS, \forall O_1, O_2 \in \kappa, \mathfrak{I}(O1) \neq \mathfrak{I}(O2) \Rightarrow O1 \neq O2$$

Where $\mathfrak{I}(O_i)$ is the O_i identity.

The structure of a class is given by its set of properties. Each property is defined by a signature giving its name and its domain. A property domain is either:

- predefined: Integer, Real, Character, Date or Boolean;
- user defined types expressed using:

. aggregation of other properties: aggregation_of (p_1: D_1, ..., p_n: D_n);

. using enumeration: {c_1, c_2,...};

- or the name of an information system class. This last case represents the inclusion and using links existing between the specified class and the other information system classes. The inclusion and using links will be defined later on. Some constructors can be used like: set_of(), liste_of(), ...

The definition of a class properties can be limited by some static constraints. They are expressed on the possible values of the properties.

The definition of existing links between an information system objects causes some problems to the designer for their definition and their use. Many researches were developed in order to define the different kinds of relationship between entities [Storey 92a], [Storey 92b]. Each method presents its own links used to represent the different relationships between the objects it represents. For MGCO2 model, the links between the object classes are defined using the relation between their life cycles. Three different types of links exist. The inclusion link, the using link and the relation link. Hereafter, we give the definition and some examples of those links.

An inclusion link, relating two classes κ_1 and κ_2 expresses a strong dependency between each object O1 of κ_1 and one or more objects O2 of κ_2. This dependency is unchangeable in time: the existence of O2 can not happen only if O1 exists and the deletion of a O1 causes the deletion of all its O2 objects. An inclusion link traduces an inclusion expressed on the O1 ad O2 life cycles and not on their classes like in [Peckhman 88] or [Hull 87] where the inclusion expresses an 'is-a' relationship.

As we admit that at a point of time only one event occurrence can arrive we assimilate the event name and its arrival time and so the inclusion link can be defined as follows:

$$\xi_0(O1) \leq \xi_0(O2) \ \& \ \xi_m(O2) \leq \xi_m(O1)$$

This formula can be generalised as follows:

$$\forall \ \xi_t(O2) \in \vartheta(O2) \Rightarrow t_{01} \leq t \leq t_{m1}$$

Each inclusion link relating two classes κ_1 and κ_2 can be mathematically defined using a function ∂:

$\partial : \kappa_1 \longrightarrow \kappa_2$
$O1 \longrightarrow \partial(O1) = \{ O2 \ / \ O2 \in \kappa_2 \}$
Using this function, each inclusion link must verify the following axioms:
a_0. the type of the inclusion link depends on the value of $Card(\partial(O1))$:

$$\text{If } Card(\partial(O1)) = 1 \Leftrightarrow \text{a simple inclusion link}$$
$$\text{If } Card(\partial(O1)) = n \Leftrightarrow \text{a multiple inclusion link}$$

a_1. the O2 objects of κ_2 related to the object O1 belonging to κ_1 can not be shared by different objects of κ_1 and this is true at any time in the application duration:

$$\forall \ t \ \forall \ O2 \in \kappa_2, \exists! \ O1 \in \kappa_1 \ / \ O2 \in \partial(O1).$$

a_2. if O1 is deleted than all the objects O2 belonging to $\partial(O1)$ will be automatically deleted too. Let's define a function called Delete(Object) which delete the object specified as a parameter than:

$$\text{If Delete(O1) Than Delete(O2)} \ / \ O2 \in \partial(O1).$$

Example: Graphical and textual representations of the inclusion link relating a hotel to its set of rooms are given hereafter:

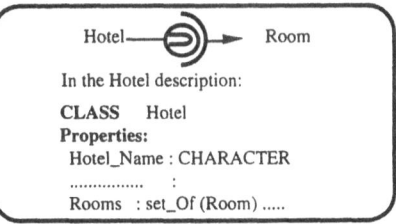

An using link relating two classes κ_1 and κ_2 (used by κ_1) expresses a dependency relation not durable between each object O1 belonging to κ_1 and one or more objects O2. the existence of O2 can happened if O1 is not yet created and the deletion of a O1 does not cause an automatic deletion of all the O2 objects to which it is coupled. An using link traduces an intersection expressed on the life cycles of the two objects O1 ad O2. Otherwise it can be defined as follows:

$$\exists\ \xi i \in \vartheta(O2) \Rightarrow \xi i \in \vartheta(O1)$$

Unlike the inclusion link, the definition of the using link does not expresses any condition on the creation events of the two objects neither on their deletion events.

Each using link relating two classes κ_1 and κ_2 can be mathematically defined using a function v as follows:

$v : \kappa_1 \longrightarrow \kappa_2$

$O1 \longrightarrow v(O1) = \{O2 \ / \ O2 \in k_2 \}$

Using this function, each using link must verify the following axioms:

a'$_0$. the type of the using link depends on the value of Card($v(O1)$):

$$\text{If Card}(v(O1)) = 1 \Leftrightarrow \text{a simple using link}$$
$$\text{If Card}(v(O1)) = n \Leftrightarrow \text{a multiple using link}$$

a'$_1$. the O2 objects belonging to $v(O1)$ can not be used by two different objects from κ_1 at the same time (t1). At an other time $t2 \neq t1$ it is possible that the using link between O1 and O2 let the place to an other using link relating O2 to O4 ($O4 \in \kappa_1$):

at t1 $\forall\ O2 \in \kappa_2$ if $\exists\ O1 \in \kappa_1/O2 \in v(O1) \Rightarrow \exists\ O4 \in \kappa_1\ /O2 \in v(O4)$
at t2 if $O2 \notin v(O1) \Rightarrow \exists\ O4 \in \kappa_1\ /\ O2 \in v(O4)$

A *relation link* between two classes κ_1 and κ_2 expresses a relationship between a κ_1 object: O1 and one or more κ_2 objects. This link is used to describe conceptual relations between objects having no intersection in their life cycles: their life cycles are independent. The relation that it describes does not affect the life cycles of the involved objects. Graphical conventions used to represent relation links are:

Link	Graphical convention
Relation link	(p,n) ◯ (p,n) role1 role 2

(p, n) are the cadinality ratio expressed on each relation link. The couple (p, n) determines the p minimum number (respectively the n maximum) of class κ_1 objects participating in the relation link. We use the same convention as in the entity relationship model. The notion of 'role' represents a temporal behaviour of the objects.

An *inheritance link* express an 'is-a' relationship between two classes G and S. The first class, named 'Generalization' and contains the structural properties, the behavioural properties and the constraints common two both classes. The second class in named 'Specialisation' and has its own set of structural properties,... We define four inheritance constraints restricting the possibilities of existence of the objects of several specialised classes, for each object of a generalised class. An inheritance constraint is specified within the generalised class. Four different constraints are used:
*. If the specialisation intersection is empty, the constraint is:

$$S_i \cap S_j = \emptyset \qquad \forall\ i \neq j$$

*. If the specialisation intersection is not empty the constraint is:

$$S_i \cap S_j \neq \varnothing \qquad \forall \; i \neq j$$

*. If the specialisation union is equal to the generalisation the constraint is:

$$\bigcup_{i=1}^{i=n} S_i = G \quad \text{n is the specialisation number}$$

*. If the specialisation union is not equal to the constraint is:

$$\bigcup_{i=1}^{i=n} S_i \neq G \quad \text{n is the specialisation number}$$

The four constraints can be combined.

2.2. Dynamic MGCO2 concepts

The static model gives a representation of the real model describing its different entities and relationships existing between them. Thus, the result of this model is a static point of view and can not give an idea about the interactions between the entities. In order to model the dynamic aspect of en information system we mainly use two concepts: events, actions and object state graphs.

An event describes a set of similar occurrences. An event occurrence is a projection of a real world fact and which has a result on the information system studied. At each point of time only one event occurrence can occur. An event occurrence triggers one or more actions on one or more objects. The result of the triggered actions is the change of the objet's state. Current_state can be modified as a consequence of an event arrival. An event can be external, temporal or internal. In the first case it is stimulated by the external environment of the information system represented. An internal event is caused by an object state change. Temporal events are the one for which the triggering is related to a precise time.
Example: "Client arrival" is an external event. One possible occurrence of this event is "Arrival of the client 'Alain Deloin". The arrival of Mr. Deloin changes the room #10 state, for example, from the 'free' state to the 'occupied' one (if we give him this room).

An Action is an operation triggered as an answer to an event arrival. It describes the object behaviour in front of events. It corresponds to a creation, modification or deletion of an object class. An other action type exists. It corresponds to actions using the classical instructions to express an algorithm.
Example: we associate to the event "Client arrival" the action: affect(Client, Room) which attributes a room to a client. So, this action changes the room #10 state from 'free' to 'occupied' after the arrival of Mr. 'Deloin'.
According to the object oriented encapsulation concept, a class can be affected only by its set of actions.
In order to restrict the possibilities of some action execution, we use the Dynamic constraints. Those constraints are expressed using object state graphs.
Let's note $£(O_i)$ the set of its different states. During its life cycle ($\vartheta(O_i)$), an object is submitted to some events $\xi_j(O_i)$, changing it from a state to an other. For each event, belonging to $\vartheta(O_i)$, we associate an action. This action will change, when the event is arriving, the value of one or more a_{ij} causing the state modification. Let's note $\delta(O_i)$ the set of action associated to O_i life cycle's events.

An object state graph can so defined as a graph having as nods the elements of $£(O_i)$ and as arcs those of $\delta(O_i)$. It describes the object evolution in time.

Example: for a room:

$£(\text{room}) = \{ \text{occupied, free, ..} \}$

$\vartheta(\text{room}) = \{ \text{Client arrival, Client departure, ...} \}$

$\delta(\text{room}) = \{ \text{affect, liberate, ...} \}$.

A room's possible states graph can be:

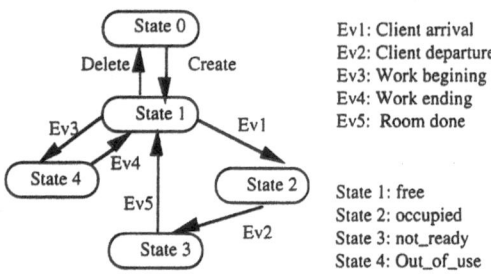

Ev1: Client arrival
Ev2: Client departure
Ev3: Work begining
Ev4: Work ending
Ev5: Room done

State 1: free
State 2: occupied
State 3: not_ready
State 4: Out_of_use

In the other hand, object state graphs enable the specification of some dynamic constraints. Thus, at an event arrival, the object's new state depends on its current state, and the nature of the arriving event. So, the state changing, can be represented by a function $\sum: £ \times \delta \longrightarrow £$. This function gives the list of events occurred on the object: its history and its future states.

The main idea of MGCO2 is to unify and to present a synthesis of all existing models. In order to map object oriented conceptual representations into MGCO2 model we define the following function:

$$T: M \times C \longrightarrow C_{mgco2}$$
$$(m, c) \longrightarrow c_{mgco2} / T(m, c) = \{ c_{mgco2} \}$$

Where $M = \{ \text{OOAD, OMT, MCO, O*,....} \}$ and C is the set of each model concepts.
This function transforms each source concept into its MGCO2 equivalent ones. The main transformations are presented in [Gargouri 95]. We distinguish four sets of rules:
. data structures transformation rules,
. static links transformation rules,
. inheritance transformation rules and
. dynamic aspects transformation

3. 'Crude' transformation of an MGCO2 conceptual representation towards a relational schema

Most of the methods proposed for relational database design used to consider the users' needs as an independent part of the design process. This vision is supported by the dichotomy data/treatment, proper to the classical DBMS (codasyl or relational).

3.1. Mapping of domains

In the relational model, each relation must have at least one attribute serving as a key to identify its set of tuples (a key-attribute). The distinction between tuples is done comparing the values of their keys. It is not the case in the object-oriented models where each object has an identifier -OID- apart of its properties and independently of its attribute values. So, when mapping the MGCO2 representations to the relational model, the problem of finding a key for each relation created will occur. The followed rule in this case is: if an object has, at least, one attribute which identifies it by its value, this attribute will form the key of the corresponding created relation. Otherwise, a key-attribute will be created for the generated relation. In order to simplify, we suppose in the following, that each object has a key-attribute.

When mapping the MGCO2 conceptual representations to the relational model, each class will be represented by a set of relations (depending on the inheritance links).

Each class is defined by a set of properties. Each property is implemented by an attribute in the generated relational schema. The attribute type is the same than the domain of the property it represents:

- **predefined domains**: INTEGER, STRING, DATE..., the translation will be done directly. Relational DBMS'- Oracle, Ingres, Sybase, DB2,...- support the MGCO2 predefined domains;
- **user-defined domains**: the type of the attribute will be either a semantic domain or a foreign key.

MGCO2	Relational DBMS
Predefined Domains	
INTEGER	INTEGER
REAL	REAL
CHAR	CHAR
DATE	DATE
User-defined domains	
Enumeration	Create Domain
Aggregation	Integrity Constraint
Interval	INTERVAL or CHECK
Class name	Integrity Constraint

Example:

Let's consider the following MGCO2 textual specification:

```
Class Person:C
properties
    Nss : CHAR[15]
    name : CHAR[30]
    age : [0 ...132]
    eyes_color : {black, blue, green}
    address : ADDRESS
Constraint
    Uniqueness: Nss
End_Class Person
```

The relational implementation of this class is given hereafter:

Relational Implementation	

Create table Person (
   Nss CHAR(15) **not null unique,**
   name CHAR(30),
   age INTEGER **check** (age in (0,132)),
   eyes_color COLOR,
   adr CHAR(6) **check**(adr in (select adr from Adress)));
	Create domaine COLOR is char (5) **check** (color in ('black', 'blue', 'green'))

Create table Address(adr CHAR(6) not null unique, street CHAR(40), city CHAR(35), country CHAR(26));	

The 'Person' class is translated by a standard SQL 'Create table'. The MGCO2 uniqueness constraint is expressed on the 'Nss' property. A semantic domain 'Color' is created with the enumerated values given within the MGCO2 textual description. A relation 'Address' is created with a referential constraint to verify that each address in the relation 'Person' corresponds to an other in the relation 'Address'. Nowadays, major relational DBMS support enumerated and interval domains. However, it is more complex to represent those domains whenever they are not supported. They may be expressed by two different ways. The first solution consists in using integrity constraints to express

122

the checking of the domain (the case of 'Age' attribute). The second solution is to generate some checking procedures within a programming language. Thus, explicit calls to those procedures must be specified when the corresponding properties are valued or changed.

3.2. Mapping of structural links

MGCO2 provides three kinds of structural links between objects: inclusion, using and relation links. One interest of these links is that they induce some behavioural dependencies. The rules used to translate the MGCO2 structural links are the same used to translate a classical E/R representations into the relational models. The cardinality ratio are used. In the case of the inclusion link the Extended SQL2 [ISO88] is used to translate the behavioural dependencies induced by this link (§2.1.). SQL2 offers the possibility to define which action have to be done when updating or deleting an attribute participating in a referential constraint. The SQL2 general syntax to define this action is given below:

```
FOREIGN KEY (<attribute>+)
REFERENCES <Relation_name> (<Attribute_name>)
ON UPDATE CASCADE/SET NULL/SET DEFAULT
ON DELETE CASCADE/SET NULL/SET DEFAULT
```

Example:
Let's consider the following MGCO2 representation:

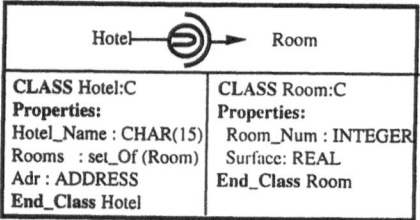

The SQL2 ensures that the deletion of an hotel implies the deletion of all its rooms:
The 'Hotel' and the 'Room' classes will be implemented as follows:

```
Create table Hotel (
Hotel_Name CHAR(15) not null unique,
Adr CHAR(6)
check( adr in (select Adr from Address))):
```

'Address' is a relation created to represent all the addresses.

```
Create table Room (
Room_Num Integer not null unique,
Surface REAL,
Nom_H CHAR(15)
References Hotel (Hotel_Name)
   ON DELETE CASCADE)
```

3.4. Mapping of operations and events

In MGCO2, three concepts are used to describe the dynamic aspect of the real world modelled: operations, events and object state graphs. In this paper we will not detail the relational implementation of those concepts. Three basic operations are provided by MGCO2. They correspond to the basic database operations: create, update, delete. They will be then translated towards the relational environment by using the similar SQL operations: INSERT INTO, UPDATE SET

WHERE, and DELETE FROM WHERE. Other kinds of operations can be represented in MGCO2, they are expressed by the classical instructions (DO WHILE, IF THEN ELSE....). The C/SQL language is used to translate them in the relational environment. The integration of the SQL standard language in the C is justified by the fact that alone, SQL is not adequate to translate all those operations.

An event represents a particular situation for which one or several actions must be triggered. An event is activated either by the outside of the system (external event), by a particular object state change (internal event), or by a clock (temporal event). The translation of events into the relational model is done according to their types. When the event is an external one, its translation is an interactive procedure. The inputs of this procedure are the parameters needed to activate the corresponding actions. The integrity constraint will be verified using the adequate SQL requests. Each internal event will be implemented using the trigger mechanism supported by relational DBMS. The trigger will verify the event predicates and activate the adequate actions. More details mechanism can be found in [Assar 92].

The previous sections propose the mapping from MGCO2 concepts towards relational model. Several papers have already presented simular results [Bouzeghoub 86], [Lyngbeak 87], [Heurer 88] and [McCormack 93]. Those methods did not take into account the dynamic aspect of the information system and they did not provide details for the relational implementation of the inheritance concept.

4. Mapping of inheritance

The MGCO2 inheritance mechanism is defined between two or more classes, named specialisation(s) and generalisation(s) class. The first inherits all the characteristics of the second, and has particular ones.

The relational model does not support the inheritance mechanism. The inheritance concept implementation can be done with creating a set of relations. Let's consider the following example:

	CLASS G:C	CLASS S1:C	CLASSE S2:C
G	Properties:	Inherits from: G	Inherits from:G
	p1	Properties:	Properties:
	p2	p11	p21
	....	p12	p22
S1 S2	pn	....	....
	End_CLASS G	p1m	p2p
		End_CLASS S1	End_CLASS S2

Different relational implementations (B1, B2, B3) are possible:

- **B1**: creating a single relation Rg having as attributes the properties of all classes G, S1 and S2. A flag attribute F is added. Its enables to distinguish between G. S1 and S2 instances:

$$Rg(\underline{p1}, p2,..pn, p11, p12,..., p1m, p21, p22, ..., p2p, F)$$

With: Domain(F) ={G, S1, S2}.

- **B2**: creating three relations Rg, Rs1 and Rs2. The S1 properties (respectively S2) are represented by the Rs1 (respectively Rs2) set of attributes. Rs1 (respectively Rs2) 'inherits' its key-attribute from Rg. G properties inherited by S1 (respectively S2) are represented by the Rg set of attributes. Each S1 (respectively S2) instance is then divided into two tuples: the first one is in Rg and the second is in Rs1 (respectively Rs2). An inclusion constraint is generated to have access to the S1 (respectively S2) properties represented in the Rg set of attributes.

$$Rg(\underline{p1}, p2,.....pn)$$
$$Rs1(\underline{p1}, p11, p12, ..., p1m)$$
$$Rs2(\underline{p1}, p21, p22, ..., p2p)$$

With: $\pi_{[p1]}(R_{s1}) \subset \pi_{[p1]}(Rg)$ and $\pi_{[p1]}(R_{s2}) \subset \pi_{[p1]}(Rg)$

- B3: creating three relations Rg, Rs1 and Rs2 representing the three classes G, S1 and S2. The S1 properties (respectively S2), and those inherited from G, are represented by the Rs1 (respectively Rs2) set of attributes. Thus the S1 (respectively S2) instances figure entirely in the Rs1 (respectively Rs2) set of tuples:

$$Rg(\underline{p1}, p2,....Pn)$$
$$Rs1(\underline{p1}, p2,....Pn, P11, P12, ..., P1m)$$
$$Rs2(\underline{p1}, p2,....pn, p21, p22, ..., p2p)$$

With: $\pi_{[p1]}(Rs1) \cap \pi_{[p1]}(Rg) = \emptyset$ and $\pi_{[p1]}(Rs2) \cap \pi_{[p1]}(Rg) = \emptyset$.

Example:
Let's consider the following MGCO2 conceptual representation:

CLASS Employee: C	**CLASS** Engineer: C	**CLASS** Department:C
Properties:	**Inherits from :**	**Properties:**
Number: INTEGER	Employee	Name: CHAR(15)
Name: CHAR(15)	**Properties:**	Strength: INTEGER
Salary: REAL	School: CHAR(5)	**Relations:**
Relations:	Experience: INTEGER	Work Employee (1,n)
Works_At Department (1,1)	Speciality: CHAR(5)	**END_CLASS** Department
END_CLASS Employee	**END_CLASS** Engineer	

The class 'Department' generates a relation, having the same name, and which attributes represent the class Department properties:

Department(NameD, Strength).

The relation link between an 'Employee' and the 'Department' where he works is translated with an attribute acting as a foreign key in the 'Employee' relation.(or the 'Engineer' relation) The three possibilities to translate the MGCO2 conceptual representation towards the relational model, are as follows:

B1:Employee(Number,Name,Salary,DepName,School, Experience,Speciality, F)
With: Domain(F) = {Engineer, others}

B2:Employee (Number, Name, Salary, DepName)
   Engineer(Number, School, Experience, Speciality)

B3:Employee (Number, Name, Salary, DepName)
   Engineer(Number, Name, Salary, DepName, School, Experience,Speciality)

5. Choose criteria for the optimal relational implementation

In MGCO2 the dynamic aspect of an information system is expressed with its set of actions. When mapping the MGCO2 conceptual representations into the relational model, each action will be translated using a sequence of algebraic operations. For each action, two kinds of operations will be generated. The first kind is generated to realise the action independently from the relational schema implemented and represent the action's semantic. The second kind, represents the algebraic operations generated according to the relational schema used because of the different distributions of data needed for the action execution. In order to choice an optimal relational schema, we distinguish three kinds of queries (actions) expressed on two classes: G the generalization class and S1 a specialization class. Those categories are given hereafter:

Q_1: queries using only the properties of G;
Q_2: queries using only the properties of S1;
Q_3: queries using both properties : of G and S1.

This classification is based on the properties requested and the classes used to answer to a given query, at the MGCO2 level. At the relational level, it gives the set of algebraic operations needed according to the database relational schema used. Thus, a given query q_{ij} belonging to Q_i may give birth to updating operations (insert, delete, update), selection operations (projection, restriction) or binary operations (Cartesian product, join, union...). So, the query cost varies from one solution to another.

Example:
Let's consider the following simple queries:

q_{11}: Give all the employee names;
q_{12}: Give for each employee, his name and his department name;
q_{21}: Increase the experience of each engineer;
q_{31}: Give the name, the salary and the speciality of each engineer;

The SQL requestes needed to implement these actions according to the relational schema used are:

B1 Relational schema:
q_{11}: SELECT Name FROM Employee;
q_{12}: SELECT Name,NameD
FROM Employee X, Department Y
WHERE X.DepName=Y.NameD;
q_{21}: UPDATE Employee
SET Experience=Experience+1
WHERE F='Engineer';
q_{31}: SELECT Name,Salary,Speciality
FROM Employee
WHERE F='Engineer';

B2 Relational schema:
q_{11}: SELECT Name FROM Employee;
q_{12}: SELECT Name,NameD
FROM Employee X, Department Y
WHERE X.DepName=Y.NameD;
q_{21}: UPDATE Engineer
SET Experience=Experience+1;

q_{31}: SELECT Name,Salary,Speciality
FROM Employee X, Engineer Y
WHERE X.Number=Y.Number;

B3 Relational schema:
q_{11}: SELECT Name FROM Employee
UNION
SELECT Name FROM Engineer;.
q_{12}: SELECT Name,NameD
FROM Employee X, Department Y
WHERE X.DepName=Y.NameD
UNION
SELECT Name,NameD
FROM Engineer X1, Department Y1
WHERE X1.DepName=Y1.NameD;
q_{21}: UPDATE Engineer
SET Experience=Experience+1;
q_{31}: SELECT Name,Salary,Speciality
FROM Engineer;

q_{11} and q_{12} gelong to the Q1 family. For their relational execution, the union algebraic operation is necessary on the B3 schema. On B1 and B2, no other operation is needed.
The properties needed by the q21 query belong to the specialisation ('Engineer'). When expresses on B2 and B3, this action needes no special operation as the relation 'Engineer' exists . On B1, this action needs a special algebraic operation: the restriction to consider only the 'Engineer' tuples.
q31 belongs to th third category. Thus, it uses the generalisation properties (Name and Salary) and the specialisation's ones (Speciality). It needes, when applied on B1, a restriction on the 'Engineer' tuples. On B2, this action needes a join algebraic operation because the properties it uses are dispersed between the two relations created.

The different action categories presented in the last section give birth to different algebraic operations according to the relational schema on which they are applied. The relational schema chosen, to implement an inheritance hierarchy, is the one which minimizes the execution complexity of all the queries expressed on this hierarchy. The execution complexity of a query is measured with:
- the number of tuples it uses and
- its activation frequency

In order to compare the different relational schemes we define an evaluation function as follows:

$$C(Bn) = \sum_{i=1}^{3} \sum_{j=1}^{N_i} f_{ij} * K_{q_{ij}n}$$

Where:
B_n: the relational schema B_n used;
q_{ij}: is the jth query belonging to the ith category;
N_i: the total number of the ith query category,
f_{ij}: the q_{ij} activation frequency;
$K_{q_{ij}n}$: the number of tuples 'used' by q_{ij} when activated on Bn.

This function evaluates a relational schema B_n according to the different queries expressed on it. Each query is evaluated with its activation frequency and the number of tuples used. This number depends on the relational schema on which the query is activated. Independently from the relational DBMS used we consider that the cost of the one-relation algebraic operations is N_a, and that the cost of the binary operations is $(N_a + N_b)$ where N_a (respevtivly N_b) is the number of the R_a (respevtivly N_b) tuples.
The solution Bi chosen is the one which verifies the condition below:

$$C(B_i) < C(B_j), i \neq j$$

Example:
For the set of queries (q11, q21, q31) presented above:

$C(B_1) = (N_e + N_i)*f_{11} + (N_e + N_i)*f_{21} + (N_e + N_i) * f_{31}$
$C(B_2) = (N_e + N_i)*f_{11} + N_i*f_{21} + (2*(N_e + N_i) + N_i) * f_{31}$
$C(B_3) = (N_e + N_i + (N_e + N_i)) * f_{11} + N_i * f_{21} + N_i * f_{31}$

With: N_e the employees number and N_i the engineers one.
The following table gives the execution complexity for each category of queries according to the relational scheme used:

B/Q	Q1	Q2	Q3
B1	Ne+Ni	Ne+Ni	Ne+Ni
B2	Ne+Ni	Ni	2(Ne+Ni)+Ni
B3	2(Ne+Ni)	Ni	Ni

Legend:

	The better B_n for this Q_i
	The B_k to avoid for this Q_i

Let Fi be the sum of frequencies of the Qi queries. So,

$$F_i = \sum_{q_{ij} \in Q_i} f_{ij}$$

Using this frequency and the table given before we established a set of rules specifying in which case it is better to avoid a given B_n relational schema:

Rule 1:	Avoid B_1 when $F_2 > F_1$ or $F_3 > F_1$
Rule 2:	Avoid B_2 when $F_3 > F_1$ or $F_3 > F_2$
Rule 3:	Avoid B_3 when $F_1 > F_2$ or $F_1 > F_3$

The choice algorithm enables an automatic choice of the best relational implementation for an inheritance hierarchy using the set of treatment expressed on the information system studied:

```
If Max(F1, F2, F3) = F1 Then
    If F2 > F3 Then Implement(B2)
    Else Implement(B1)
Else
    If Max(F1, F2, F3) = F2 Then
                    If F1 > F3 Then Implement(B2)
                    Else Implement(B3)
    Else Implement(B3)
```

6. Oracle BDMS implementation:

In order to proof this theorical study we implemented the database presented above using the Oracle DBMS (V6.2) under the Vax 6610 VMS system. The ruselts obteined confirm the algorithm choice and the set of rules presented in the previous section. The mesures have be done varing the table size (10^2, 10^3, 10^4 tuples) The two graphs given in the annexe section give the CPU time elapsed for the qij query execution. They, independently from the total tuple number, have almost the same orientations. We can easily notice that the CPU time needed to answer to a given query depends more from the query's category rather than the total tuple number. Those graphics confirm the rules established above to avoid some Bn according to the query category considered (Rule 1, Rule 2 and Rule 3). The q11 and q12 queries, belonging to the first category, disadvantage the B1 relational scheme. B2 and B3 request almost the same CPU time for the first category of queries. The q21 query belong to the second category of queries. It requests less CPU time when it is applied on the B3 relational scheme. This result is the same for both graphics. The q31 query requests lessees time when it is applied on the B3 relational schema. B2 is the relational scheme to avoid for this queries category. It gives the longest CPU time.

7. Conclusion:

In this paper we propose a Generic Model For Object-Oriented Information system Modelling: MGCO2. With the affluence of the object-oriented methods of information systems design and the terminology used by each one an intermediate step seems to be indispensable in the transition between the design and the different implementation environments. This step aims at the unification of the different concepts in a generic model representing all the concepts and independent of any method: MGCO2. We present an algorithm to map from an object-oriented conceptual representation towards a relational database envirnement including important constraints. MGCO2 fully integrates the object-oriented concepts. This work has many advantages for the development of applications. The use of the object-oriented approach at the conceptual level gives a powerfull set of concepts to modelize the real world. At the implementation level, relational DBMS, which are the focus of intense commercial activity, are utilized.
Our research, at present, are oriented to generate a set of application programs which represent the whole actions and events expressed on the information system.

Acknowledgements: we thank Gérard NOEL and Mehdi HANDOUS for their help during the implementation stage.

128

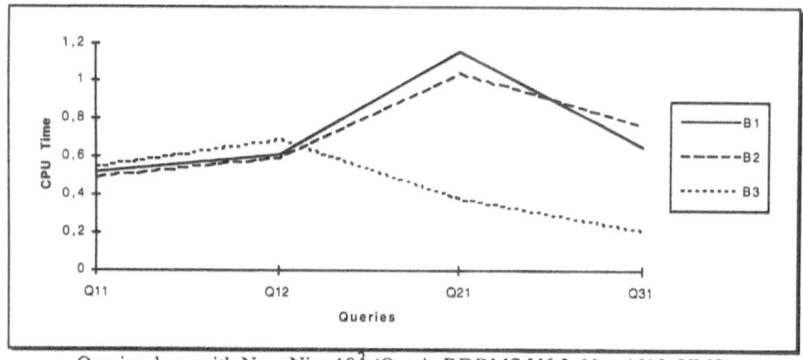

Queries done with Ne + Ni = 10^3 (Oracle RDBMS V6.2, Vax 6610, VMS)

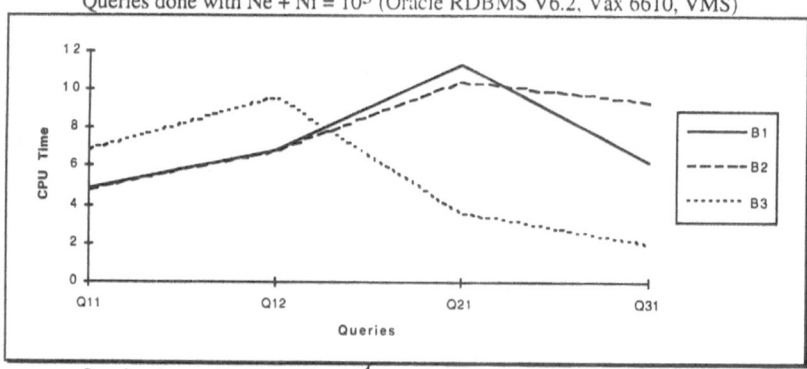

Queries done with Ne + Ni = 10^4(Oracle RDBMS V6.2, Vax 6610, VMS)

References

[Andonof 92] E. Andonof; "OFM : une méthode formelle pour la conception des bases de données orinetées objet", doctorat d'université Paul Sabatier, September 1992.

[Assar 92] S. Assar C. Rolland; "Traduction d'un schéma conceptuel Remora sur un SGBD relationnel", Congrès INFORSID. 1992.

[Bouzeghoub 86] M. Bouzeghoub, "SECSI un système expert en conception de systèmes d'informations", Thèse de doctorat de 3ème cycle Université de PARIS-SUD, 1986.

[Booch 86] G.Booch, "Object-Oriented Development", IEEE Trans. on S.E., Vol. SE-12, N°2, Feb. 1986.

[Booch 87] G.Booch, Software Engineering with Ada, 2nd Edition, Benjamin/Cummings Publishing Co., Menlo Park, 1987.

[Brunet 93] J. Brunet, "Analyse Conceptuelle orientée objet". Thèse de doctorat de l'université Paris 6. Paris 1993.

[Castellani 93] X. Castellani, "MCO Méthodologie Générale d'analyse et de Conception des Systèmes d'Objets, Tome 1 : l'Ingénierie des besoins" Edition Masson. Paris 1993.

[Coad 91] E. Yourdon, P. Coad "Object oriented analysis". second Edition, Yourdon press, 1991.

[Monarchi 92] D.E. Monarchi, G.I. Puhr. "A reaearch typology for object-oriented analysis and design. Communication of the ACM. Septembre 1992. Vol 35, N°9.

[Rumbaugh 91] J. Rumbaugh, M. Blaha, et al "Obiect oriented modeling and design". Printice Hall publishing compagny. Englewood Cliffs, 1991.

[Storey 92a] V.C. Storey "Understanding semantic relationships". VLDB Journal. October 1992.

[Storey 92b] V.C. Storey "Real Word Knowledge for Databases". Journal of Database Administration. 1992.

[Gargouri 95] F. Gargouri, C.F. Ducateau, F Boufarès "Towards a generic model for OO information system Modeling" International Conference on Industrial Engineering and Production Management. Marroco, April 4-7 1995.

[Peckhman 88] J. Peckhman, F. Maryansi "Semantic Data Models", ACM Computing surveys, Vol. 20, N°3, Sept. 1988.

[Hull 87] R. Hull, R. King "Semantic Database Modeling: Survey, Applications and Research Issues", ACM Computing surveys, Vol. 19, N°3, Sept. 1987.

[Heitz 89] M. Heitz, "HOOD, une méthode de conception hiérarchisée orientée objet pour le développement des gros logiciels techniques et temps réel", Déc. 1989, Journées Ada-France.

[Heurer 88] A. Heurer, "A data model for complex objects based on a semantic database model and nested relations", Lectures notes in computer science, Vol 361, Abiteboul S., Ficher P.C. and Scheck H.J.(Eds). 1988.

[ISO 88] ISO-ANSI Working draft, Database Language SQL2. December 1988.

[Lyngbeak 87] P. Lyngbeak, V. Vianu, "Mapping a Semantic Database Model to the relational Model", Sigmond record, Marsh 1987.

[McCormack 93] J.L. McCormack, T.A. Halpin, P.R. Ritson "Automated mapping of conceptual schemes to relational shemas", CAiSE 93. Paris. June 1993.

Object-Oriented Modelling and Simulation of an Expert System for Monitoring and Control of a Water Distribution System

Christine W. Chan, Nick Cercone, Aijun An   Paitoon Tontiwachwuthikul

Department of Computer Science   *Faculty of Engineering*
University of Regina
Regina, Sask., Canada S4S 0A2
E-mail: {chan, nick, aijun}@cs.uregina.ca   Fax: (306) 585-4745

ABSTRACT. *An object-oriented approach to modelling an expert system for monitoring and control of a water distribution system is presented in this paper. This approach generates the four models of object model, functional model, control model and user-interface model. Operational simulation of the water distribution system is combined within the functional model. The implementation of the expert system using G2 is discussed. The paper concludes with a short discussion of the advantages of the modelling approach.*

KEY WORDS: Object-oriented modelling, expert systems.

1. Introduction

An expert system that emulates the decisions and actions of a human expert for a well-defined domain functions as an aid for decision makers. The term "domain" refers to a group of processes about which the expert makes decisions. For real time domains in which the process changes rapidly over time, expert systems can operate in a monitoring or a controlling mode. In the monitoring mode they receive process information, present that information to the operator and recommend a course of actions to follow. In the controlling mode they initiate control actions within the system.

This paper describes an object-oriented approach to modelling an expert system for monitoring and control of a water distribution system. To emulate the domain knowledge and experience of application experts, it is essential to decompose the expertise into knowledge items. In our object-oriented modelling approach, the decomposition of knowledge items can be accomplished by defining objects and their class hierarchy, their functional relationships in formulas and the decision knowledge in rules. This delivers an object model, a functional model and a control model. Since user friendliness is critical to expert systems, a user-interface model is used to model the visual processing capability of the expert system. In order to test the problem solving expertise represented in the rules, we include an operational simulation of the water distribution system in our model. It simulates the changes of system states over a period of time and can test the decisions suggested by the system. Since the operational simulation reflects mathematical relationships among the values of object attributes, it is modeled within the functional model of the system. In the following, the water distribution system is described. We first present four models developed using the object-oriented approach and then describe the G2 implementation of these models. We conclude the paper by discussing some advantages of this approach to developing expert systems.

2. The Water Distribution System

The domain addressed is typical of a water distribution system of moderate-sized cities in North America. The sources of water are a lake and a number of underground wells. Water is pumped to reservoirs at a number of locations in the city and is pumped from the reservoirs to the distribution system, or to another reservoir when it is necessary to adjust water levels. Pressures and rates of flow throughout the system can be controlled by means of pumps and valves housed in pumping stations.

An ongoing control function is required to keep the system operating because conditions are never static. Parts of the control function are automated by means of Programmable Logic Controllers(PLCs) at the pumping stations, which send commands to perform actions like opening or closing a valve, starting or stopping a pump or a diesel generator, or adjusting chlorine levels. However, for the decisions that are based on economic, environmental and sociological factors, a human operator is needed. The operator employs heuristics to predict the customers' demand, to control the discharge pressures from pumping stations and to keep the water level of reservoirs within a reasonable range by sending commands to the PLCs to start or stop pumps. Documenting operators' heuristics and developing a consistent and optimal operating style are some of the chief benefits in developing the expert system.

3. Object-Oriented Modelling

An expert system has three main components: (1) the knowledge base -- a collection of information and knowledge from domain experts, (2) the inference engine -- a problem solving and reasoning mechanism, and (3) the user-interface -- an environment for the user to work in conjunction with the expert system. Since the inference engine is usually precoded and supplied in a shell, we focus on modelling the knowledge base and the user-interface in developing the system. Four models for modelling these two components are described as follows.

3.1 .Object Model

The object model represents the static data structure of the real-world system. Object modelling consists of identifying the objects of interest in the system, grouping the objects into classes, specifying attributes for the classes and organizing a class hierarchy from their common properties and inter-relationships.

Objects are used to represent physical and conceptual occurrences in the application environment. For example, reservoir-1, reservoir-2, ..., valve-1, valve-2, ..., pump-1, pump-2, ..., well-1, well-2, ..., etc., are occurrences of physical objects; today's weather, current demand, schedules of power rates, etc., are conceptual objects. Every object within the water distribution system belongs to a class, for example, all reservoirs belong to the class of *reservoir,* all inlet control valves belong to the class of *valve,* all water pumps belong to the class of *pump,* all demands at various times or from various customers belong to the class of *demand.* Each class has certain attributes that describe the common properties of that class of objects. For example, the class *reservoir* has the attributes of *current level, maximum level, area, depth, ground level, inflow, outflow, pressure-in, pressure-out, cut-in* (a level at which an operator makes a decision to open a valve or start a pump to fill up a reservoir) and *cut-out* (a level at which the operator makes a decision to close the valve or stop the pump to halt the inflow into a reservoir).

An efficient way of modelling is to arrange all classes of objects into a class hierarchy based on their common properties. For example, *process equipment* is created as a superior class of *pump, valve, reservoir, water source* and *water sink.* It contains the common attributes, such as *ground level, inflow* and *outflow,* of its subclasses. By declaring them once in the definition of the superior class of *process equipment,* common attributes are automatically passed into the subclasses. Similarly, *water source* is a superior class of *lake* and *well; pump* is a superior class of *large pump, medium pump* and *small pump;* and *valve* is a superior class of *on-off valve, throttling valve* and *manual valve.* They represent the common properties of their corresponding subclasses.

One of the advantages of using a class hierarchy is that many similar objects can be referenced by simply referring to a higher level class. For example, referring to a process equipment could mean a reservoir, a well, a pump, a valve or a water sink and a reference to a pump could mean a large, a medium or a small pump. Object reference is essential for writing generic rules and formulas which are described in more detail later in this paper.

3.2 .Functional Model

The functional model shows how values are computed without regard for sequencing, decision, or object structure. The functional model shows which values depend on which other values and the functions that relate them. Data flow diagrams are used for showing functional dependencies and functions are expressed by mathematical equations or formulas.

Values refer to the attribute values of objects in the object model. In this water distribution system, there are two kinds of values. The first kind represents the quantities such as ground levels, reservoir areas, reservoir depths, maximum levels, average demands, performance (H-Q) curves for pumps, etc. The second kind represents the time variant data, e.g., demands, reservoir current levels, inflows, outflows, weather, etc. The time variant data can be further subdivided into the data gathered from external sources, such as field instruments and weather office, and the data that are calculated according to the relationships with other data, for example, expected demand. Usually the functional model is used to describe the second kind of time variant data. However, the expert system presented in this paper is an off-line system in which the time variant data theoretically derivable from external sources in fact obtain their values through simulation. Therefore mathematical simulation formulas are included in the functional model along with the non-simulation formulas that calculate the second kind of time variant data.

Simulation formulas aim at providing the temporal change of the system states, similar to what would be obtained from the field instruments. For example, the simulation formula for the reservoir levels is

$$L_{new} = L + dt * (inflow—outflow)/area$$

where L is the current level of a reservoir and L_{new} is the new value of L after a time period dt. Since in the object model objects are grouped into classes, this formula needs to be written once only and applies to all the reservoirs in the system. This is an example of a generic formula.

Non-simulation formulas are used for providing new values for non-simulated time variant data that have functional dependencies with other simulated or non-simulated values.

3.3 .Control Model

The control model consists of rules that represent the heuristics that operators use to make decisions in monitoring and controlling their system.

The main operating decisions include setting up cut-in and cut-out levels in a reservoir, choosing a small, medium or large pump to start pumping water into a reservoir when the level of the reservoir reaches its cut-in level, and stopping pumping when the reservoir reaches its cut-out level. These decisions depend on many factors such as demand, reservoir storage capacity, required emergency storage, input capacity and also on the economics of supply such as the cost of pumping. Different operators may make different decisions in the same situation. In building the control model, different operating styles need to be recognized and rules belonging to the same operating style are grouped together to form a rule set. Within a single rule set, conflicts may appear when the conditions of two rules can be satisfied at the same time. Priorities are set to resolve this kind of conflicts among rules.

Since the object model is object-based, the rules can refer to a class of objects. This greatly reduces the total number of rules. For example, the following rule applies to any reservoir in the system.

If the level in a reservoir reaches its cut-in level and the time before next high demand is greater than 8 hours, then start the small pump connected to the reservoir.

3.4 . User-interface Model

The user-interface model describes an environment for the user to interact with the expert system. It consists of objects and classes that represent screens, buttons and explanation texts.

Screens provide system information to the operator and include the welcome screen, menu screen, system schematic screen, message screen, trend screen and data input screen. The schematic screens show the dynamic visual representations of the simulated operations on the system equipment. Message screens inform the operators on the actions that the expert system has initiated. Trend screens display values of variables over time. Menu screens have buttons which when triggered, the system provides more detailed information. Other user interface features such as buttons that enable users to input data or select subscreens, and texts that describe explanations, elicit user input or remind the user of their input values, are also used.

4. G2 Implementation of the Expert System

A prototype of the expert system has been implemented with the real time expert system shell G2[1]. G2 provides a graphic object-oriented development environment, an English-like language for creating rules, formulas, and procedures, and an inference engine that controls the execution of rules in the knowledge base. The implementation basically transforms the above models into a G2 knowledge base. Since G2 is object-oriented, the transformation is straightforward.

Classes in the object model and the user-interface model are created under the G2 predefined class hierarchy. Attributes are specified through creation of a definition item for each class that associates with a table where the common properties and characteristics can be described in standard formats. Using the G2 icon editor, an icon or a graphic image of an object class can also be drawn within its definition item. Thus by creating and cloning instances for different object classes and placing them on a workspace and connecting them according to their physical and logical relationships by a defined connection class, a system schematic is built. Simulation formulas in the functional model are implemented with generic and specific formulas in G2. A generic formula is a formula that applies to the whole class of objects while a specific formula is a formula that applies to a specific object or item in the system. The rules in the control model are translated into structured English-like rules with the help of the G2 editor for rule definitions.

The G2 real-time inference engine uses all the information in the knowledge base including rules, simulated values, and the values received from external sources to reason about the current state of the application and initiates other activity based upon what it has inferred. The essential techniques used in the G2 inference engine are backward chaining, forward chaining, scanning, focusing and invoking.

5. Conclusions

There are clear advantages to using an object-oriented approach in constructing expert systems. It provides a very structured and natural modelling environment and the inheritance feature among object classes means that there is less repetition in definitions. Rules and formulas can be written very generally and there need be far fewer rules and shorter formulas. For real time applications, user-defined variable types are defined that share a common scan interval, initial value or validity interval. This object-oriented approach to constructing a real-time expert system significantly streamlines an application.

References:

(Gensym, 1992): Gensym Co., *G2 Reference Manual, Version 3.0.* Gensym Corporation, Cambridge, MA, USA, July 1992.

---

[1] trademark of Gensym Corporation. U.S.A.

Reusing and Retrieving Software Components: An Object-Oriented Domain Analysis Approach

Muthu Ramachandran and Adil Al-Yasiri

Software Engineering Group
Philips Research Labs
Redhill RH1 5HA, UK
Email:ukrrama@prl.philips.co.uk

School of Computing and Mathematical Sciences
Liverpool John Moores University
Liverpool L3 3AF, UK
Email: cmsaalyasiri@vax.livjm.ac.uk

ABSTRACT: *Software reuse has promised to increase productivity by assembling systems from a large software library. Component retrieval mechanism is the key to library reuse. Existing approaches to this problem are inadequate. However, object class library can solve some of these problems. Components can be retrieved effectively based on an object-oriented domain analysis approach. Domain analysis has emerged to address the issue of identifying, classifying, analysing and reusing a classes of similar application systems. This paper also proposes a reuse-oriented domain analysis model that provides a framework for synthesising systems and developing reusable components.*

KEY WORDS: *Domain Analysis, Development for reuse, Library-based reuse, Software Components.*

1. Introduction

Composing application systems is one of the principle of library reuse (Biggerstaff and Perlis 1989). The idea is barrowed from other engineering disciplines that are proved to be successfull for many years. Software industry is still unable to practice a library based reuse systematically. This is partly due to difficulty in identifying, classifying and retrieving reusable components effectively. In the context of library based reuse, we need to address some of the issues specifically:

- What are the characteristics of a reusable component?
- How do we classify software components?
- Is there a method for retrieving components effectively?
- How do we provide a support for component understanding and documentation?

The component library is a necessary capital investment for reuse. To promote component reuse at all levels of the life-cycle, one of the main problems is automating the process of locating/ identifying and retrieving components. Current research hasn't addressed an effective way of classifying and retrieving components. The notaion of *software factories* are beginning to emerge. The Japanese have taken a different approach to programming; instead of software development, they view it as software production (Matsumoto 1987).

All these can be made possible if we can solve the problems of identifying reusable components and component cataloguing and retrieval mechanism. This article argues a mechanism based on an object-oriented domain analysis can be effective. This approach allows to:

- classify the application domain that is being modelled into a number of similar systems.
- identify commonality in those systems.
- identify frequently reusable systems, subsystems, classes and objects.

- retrieve components based on the application domain modelling can be more effective.
- use of the application domain knowledge for semantic description, scope for reuse, cost for modification and so on.

2. An object-oriented domain analysis

Let us firstly identify some of the key requirements of an analysis technique. We need an effective and detailed domain analysis technique which considers,
- the clients understanding of the required system,
- combining and integrating existing systems and methodologies (such as structured analysis techniques) with new systems and methods such as OOA
- support for reuse explicitly such as inheritance and object composition mechanisms,
- multiple viewpoints of the clients and the developers,
- an integrated tool support for the complete information systems life-cycle,
- risk analysis, business analysis, market analysis, and future maintenance information
- a family of similar systems in an application domain by analysing and identifying reusable resources,
- concurrency and distribution which are increasingly important for many applications such as multi-media, distributed, parallel, and real-time systems,
- guidelines and techniques.

Most of the existing methods (Structured and OOA methods) do not meet these criteria and we may never invent a method that can satisfy everything. Therefore, we need to select a method based on its suitability for specific application needs and the integrated tool support for the complete development life-cycle. Further investigation can be targeted for specific application needs and providing practical guidelines and techniques in using a selected methodology rather than inventing new notations.

Supporting the above criteria there are a number of application specific domain methods are emerging, known as domain analysis, an alternative technique proposed recently (Prieto-Diaz and Arango 1991; Booch 1989). The domain analysis techniques have emerged to support the identification and analysis of reusable objects or components or resources of a family of similar systems. This includes the notion of analysing multiple-views of the classes of systems.

The notion of domain analysis is introduced by Neighbors (1984) in the DRACO system. Neighbors (1984) points out that "the key to reusable software is best captured in domain analysis in that it stresses the reusability of analysis and design, not code". The Draco system has a domain language for describing programs in each different problem area. A domain analyst represents analysis information about a problem domain in terms of objects and operations in a domain language. A domain designer specifies different implementations for these objects and operations in terms of the other domains already known to Draco. However, the Draco system doesn't tell us clearly how to analyse and identify reusable abstractions.

At present, domain analysis is a slow, unstructured learning process. Knowledge of a domain is gained over time until sufficient experience and understnding lead to a threshold at which an abstraction can be synthesised and made available for reuse. Domain analysis is related to requirements analysis but it is performed in a much broader scope and generates different results. It encompasses a family of systems in a domain, produces a domain model with parameterisation to accomodate the differences, and defines a standard architecture based on which components can be developed and integrated.

A domain model and an associated dictionary represent the domain knowledge, and an architecture represents the framework for developing reusable components and for synthesising systems from the reusable components. An ideal domain model and architecture would be applicable throughout the life-cycle from requirements analysis through maintenance. This process should also provide a model for classifying, storing, and retrieving software components.

Our notion of reuse-oriented domain analysis is shown in Figure 1, this model supports the process of development for reuse & with reuse. There are number of stages to be followed which start from identifying an application domain, identify & classify reusable classes, identify reusable architectures, identify domain description language and specify the required system, formulate reuse guidelines and strategy, design components that are newly required, store & retrieve components, assessment for reuse, and synthesise systems.

This model proposes that we start identify the application domain, its boundary and scope precisely, and then produce a domain classification scheme which can be done by capturing from various domain experts if necessary. The next stage is to identify potentially reusable objects/abstractions/components. Formulate reuse guidelines which represent language knowledge and domain knowledge. Then make reuse assessment and improvement based on these guidelines against existing components and its reusability attributes. Design reusable components and describe systems. Finally deliver systems to the existing demands. In our earlier work (Ramachandran and Sommerville 1991) we have used this model successfully.

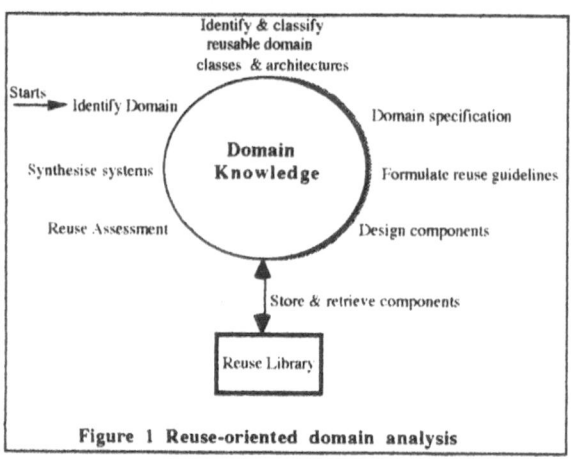

Figure 1 Reuse-oriented domain analysis

We believe the retrieval mechanism based on this description can be effective. We have also formulated specific guidelines for domain analysis and domain classification. Reusability is a complex component attribute and it is dependent on the effective use of the programming language used to implement the component and application domain knowledge. Application domain knowledge allows the abstractions in a domain to be identified and encoded as a set of reusable components. The objective of our work is to use language and domain knowledge to assess, with automatic assistance, the reusability of a component and to suggest to the software engineer how that component may be made more reusable. We have successfully used this model in our system.

The work described here addresses these problems and hence considers factors affecting reusability such as design, programming, language factors and domain factors. We believe objective and realizable guidelines will help to solve these problems. Our work has taken these existing studies as a starting point and has attempted to produce more detailed and practical guidelines on the way in which language and domain features affect reusability. Domain-oriented reuse knowledge should represent domain object identification, frequently reusable objects in that domain, and domain classification. For more detailed discussion on domain analysis, see Prieto-Diaz and Arango (1991).

Component templates play a major role in modelling reusable architecures and classes. Some of our domain guidelines (the application domain selected for study is abstract data structures) say:

- For all complex structures, provide two representations such as static and dynamic structures for each object class.
- Always select dynamic object representation for complex structures and hide detailed structural information.

We have successfully captured and represented reuse knowledge based on these guidelines. Therefore it is possible to reuse design knowledge and ideas when designing components for reuse. A rule-based approach has been taken when automating these guidelines. Component templates play a major role in creating and modifying reusable components by providing internal skeletons for various forms of reuse.

3. Conclusions

We believe our investigation on the domain analysis method described here can be effective in addressing reuse-oriented software development. Component retrieval mechanism is the key to library reuse. Existing approaches to this problem are inadequate. Domain analysis has emerged to address the issue of identifying, classifying, analysing and reusing a classes of similar application systems. This paper also proposed a reuse-oriented domain analysis model that provides a framework for synthesising systems and developing reusable components. Further investigation is underway on this technique.

4. References

Biggerstaff, T.J. and Perlis, A.J. (Editors) (1989): "Software Reusability: Concepts and Models", Vol.I & II, ACM Press, Addison-Wesley.
Booch, G. (1987): "Software Components with Ada", Benjamin/Cummings.
Matsumoto, Y. (1987): "A Software Factory: An Overall Approach to Software Production", In IEEE Tutorial in Software Reusability, Peter Freeman (Ed.), Computer Society Press, CA.
Neighbors, J M (1984): The Draco approach to constructing software from reusable components, IEEE Trans. on Software Eng, September, SE10(5).
Prieto-Diaz, R and Arango, G (1991): Domain Analysis and Software Systems Modeling, IEEE Computer Society Press Tutorial.
Ramachandran, M and Sommerville, I (1991): "Reuse Assessment", First International Workshop on Software Reuse, Dortmund, Germany, July.

Specification and Implementation of the Transmutation Concept

Xavier Castellani and Hong Jiang

CEDRIC-IIE (CNAM) research laboratory,
18 allée Jean Rostand, 91025 Evry Cedex, France
Email: {Castellani, jiang}@iie.cnam.fr   Fax: +33 1 69 36 73 05

ABSTRACT. *The concept of transmutation allows both representation of suppression of instances and creation of other instances by reusing possibly values of the suppressed instances. This paper presents the definition of this concept, the categories of the transmutations (mutations, disaggregations, merges, reflexive transmutations, opposite transmutations and cascade of transmutations), the end-user informal specification and the implementation of the transmutations with two solutions: a centralised solution and a distributed management solution.*

KEY WORDS: *Transmutation. Object design. Dynamic representation. Object state.*

1. Introduction

The change of state of an instance of a class may be made by modifying its characteristics and with keeping the instance in its class, or with generating its suppression and the creation of other instance(s) of other class(es). The first change of states of instances are represented with transition states' diagrams in numerous object-oriented methods. The second change are transformations that we call transmutations.
The transmutations are numerous in object-oriented information systems:
. in personnel management, an employee that has a promotion passes from a category of personnel to an other,
. in a hospital, a patient that has had all cares that a service can give it is transferred in an other service or leaves the hospital,
. in an assembly line, a mechanical and electronic component assemblage generates the creation of a car,
. during of a reorganisation of a company, its services and its departments are transformed into other units.

To our knowledge the concept of transmutation does not exist in object-oriented and non-object-oriented analysis and design methods. We studied the following object-oriented analysis and design methods: Booch method (Booch, 1991), BON (Nerson, 1992), CRC (Wirfs-Brock et al., 1990), HOOD (Heitz, 1987), Meyer method (Meyer, 1988), O* (Rolland and Cauvet, 1991), OBA (Gibson, 1990), ObjectOry (Jacobson, 1989), OMT (Rumbaugh et al., 1991), OOA (Coad and Yourdon, 1990), OOM (Rochfeld, 1991), OOSA (Shlaer and Mellor, 1988), OOSD (Wasserman and Pircher, 1991), and we studied object-oriented concepts presented in comparisons of methods: (Aksit and Bergams, 1992), (Ayache and Ou-Halima, 1992), (Bari and Rolland, 1990), (De Champeaux and Faure, 1992), (Henderson-Sellers and Edwards, 1990), (Hill, 1992), (Hutt, 1993), (Monarchi and Puhr, 1992), (Walker, 1992) and (Wirfs-Brock and Johnson, 1990).
Only Ptech method of Edwards presented in the method of Martin and Odell (Martin and Odell, 1992) allows the representation of change of instances between subclasses. It is the simplest form of transmutation, that we call mutation, only used in the Ptech method between subclasses. In the other methods, the mutations can only be represented with events between classes and

treatments.

The transmutation concept has been introduced in MCO publications (Castellani, 1991$_1$), (Castellani, 1991$_2$) and (Castellani, 1993). This paper presents the definition of the concept of transmutation, categories of transmutation, specification and implementation of this concept. The definition of this concept and the principal categories of transmutations (mutations, disaggregations, merges, reflexive transmutations, opposite transmutations and cascade of transmutations), are presented in Section 2. The specification and the implementation solutions of the transmutations are presented in Section 3.

2. The Concept of Transmutation

2.1. Definition

A transmutation is a transformation of one or several instances that are suppressed, in other instances of classes that are created.

The transmutation of one or several instances of classes CL-d1, CL-d2... CL-dT into instances of classes CL-a1, CL-a2... CL-aR (which may be CL-d1, CL-d2... CL-dT), is a change of states of these instances of the classes CL-d1, CL-d2... CL-dT, which generates:
. the suppression of instances of CL-d1, CL-d2... CL-dT,
. and the creation of instances of CL-a1, CL-a2... CL-aR by recuperating possibly values of the attributes of the instances of CL-d1, CL-d2... CL-dT.
The transmutation of instances is their death as instances of departure classes and their reincarnation, their metamorphose, as instances of arrival classes.

The comments of the graphical representation in Figure 1 specify how a transmutation is performed.

- Creations, suppressions and transmutations
Creations of instances which do not result of suppression of other instances are not transmutations.
Suppressions of instances which do not generate creation of other instances are not transmutations.
A suppression of a set of instances £-s following by a creation of a set of instances F-a is a transmutation if and only if this sequence of operations must not be interrupted. That is to say that if instances £-s are transmuted in instances F-a, the information system is stable if and only if it is in one of the two following states: the instances £-s exist and the instances F-a do not exist, the instances £-s do not exist and the instances F-a exist. The two following states are not stable: the instances £-s exist and the instances F-a exist, the instances £-s do not exist and the instances F-a do not exist.
Referential integrity constraints must be verified when suppressions of instances are executed during transmutations as simple suppressions. This verification is not recalled below.

- Departure conditions and creation conditions of a transmutation
The departure conditions and the creation conditions of transmutations are defined with formulations of "When" which take into account time and arrival events.
Examples:
- transmutation of a supervisor into an executive:
. departure conditions: at least four years of studies or at least fifteen years of seniority in rank,
. creation conditions: a position of executive is free in the firm and the candidate is the first of the candidate supervisor list;
- transmutation of a car into a wreck:
. departure condition: the car can not be repaired,
. creation condition: a wreck is created if a car can not run;
- transmutation of a potential customer into an active customer:
. departure condition: the first order of a potential customer is registered,

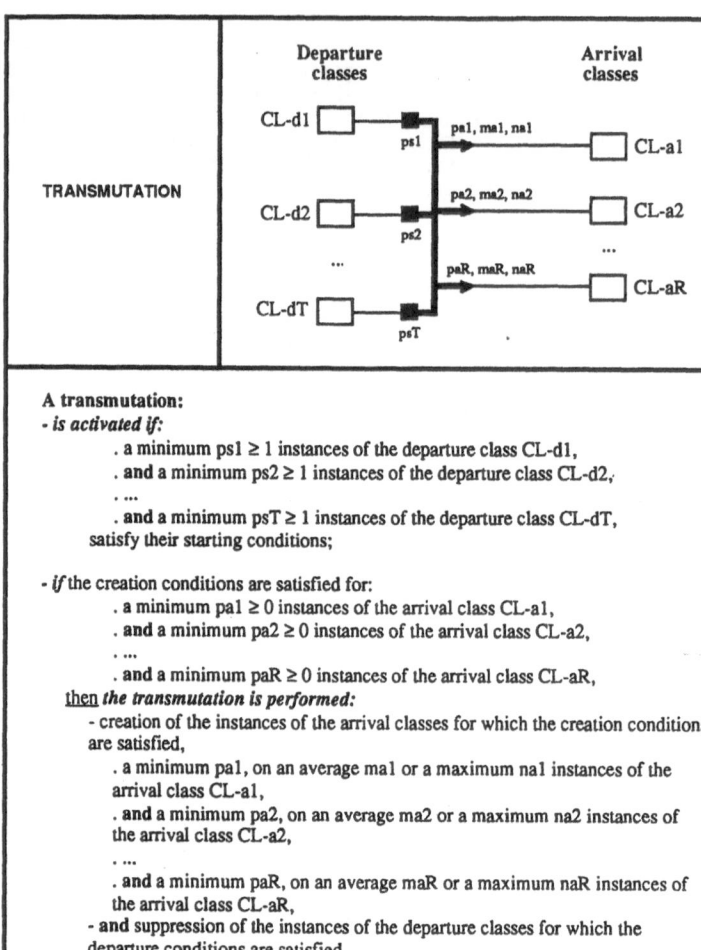

A transmutation:
- *is activated if:*
    . a minimum ps1 ≥ 1 instances of the departure class CL-d1,
    . **and** a minimum ps2 ≥ 1 instances of the departure class CL-d2,
    . ...
    . **and** a minimum psT ≥ 1 instances of the departure class CL-dT,
satisfy their starting conditions;

- *if* the creation conditions are satisfied for:
    . a minimum pa1 ≥ 0 instances of the arrival class CL-a1,
    . **and** a minimum pa2 ≥ 0 instances of the arrival class CL-a2,
    . ...
    . **and** a minimum paR ≥ 0 instances of the arrival class CL-aR,
<u>then</u> *the transmutation is performed:*
    - creation of the instances of the arrival classes for which the creation conditions are satisfied,
    . a minimum pa1, on an average ma1 or a maximum na1 instances of the arrival class CL-a1,
    . **and** a minimum pa2, on an average ma2 or a maximum na2 instances of the arrival class CL-a2,
    . ...
    . **and** a minimum paR, on an average maR or a maximum naR instances of the arrival class CL-aR,
    - **and** suppression of the instances of the departure classes for which the departure conditions are satisfied.

Figure 1: Graphical representation of a transmutation

. there is not creation condition: every potential customer who orders becomes an active customer.

- Cardinalities of a transmutation
Numbers (minimum, on an average and maximum) of instances of departure and arrival classes of a transmutation are called departure and arrival cardinalities of the transmutation.

A minimum departure cardinality of a transmutation must be superior or equal to one, because a departure class of a transmutation of which minimum cardinality is equal to zero is not used by this transmutation.

A minimum arrival cardinality of a transmutation is:
. *null* if the creation conditions of instances of the considered class are not always satisfied;

. *superior or equal to one* if the creation conditions of instances of this class are always satisfied; this case includes the case where creation conditions do not exist; if creation conditions exist and are always satisfied, they precise the numbers of instances to be created.

A transmutation is performed only if at least one instance of an arrival class is created, otherwise the operation is not a transmutation but a simple suppression of instances.

Example. Let us consider the following mutation in Figure 2.

Figure 2: Example of mutation

The minimum arrival cardinality of this transmutation is null because the creation conditions of an executive: a position of executive is free in the firm and the candidate is the first of the candidate supervisor list may not be satisfied, although the departure conditions of the transmutation of a supervisor are satisfied: General Certificate of Education plus at least four years of studies or at least fifteen years of seniority in rank.

The minimum, average and maximum cardinalities of a departure class or of an arrival class are noted respectively: p, m, n. The average is optional. If $p = m = n$, we note only one value.

By default, the minimum cardinalities of the departure classes, and the minimum, the average and the maximum cardinalities of the arrival classes of a transmutation are equal to 1.

- Recuperation of values of attributes of departure instances in the arrival instances of the transmutations

The creation of arrival instances of transmutation is done possibly with recuperation of some or all values of attributes of departure instances.

Examples

. a wreck is created by recuperating from a car the trade mark, the model, the registered date, the mileage;

. an engine is created by recuperating from a wreck the trade mark, the model, the registered date, the mileage;

. a wheel is created by recuperating from a wreck the trade mark, the model.

- When should we create several transmutations?

Several transmutations must be created if an exclusive OR exists between creations of instances of arrival classes.

Examples

. In personnel management (see Figure 3), an executive may be transmuted into a senior manager OR into a senior executive. Two transmutations must be created because it is an exclusive OR.

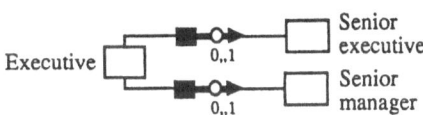

Figure 3: Example of several transmutations

. In a cassia (see Figure 4), a wreck of a car may be transmuted into its recovered components: engine OR wheels, etc. Only one transmutation must be created because it is not an exclusive OR.

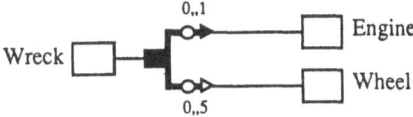

Figure 4: Example of unique transmutation

In Figure 4, Wreck is not linked with Engine and Wheel. After the suppression of a wreck, an engine and wheels are created, so that the transformation is a transmutation.

The suppression of an instance that referred other instances is not a transmutation. For example, if a wreck referred wheels and an engine the suppression of a wreck is not a transmutation into its components. So that it is a simple instance suppression because the instances referred with the suppressed instance pre-exist the suppression.

- Precision
Numerous transmutations are defined between subclasses of a class, in particular mutations, for example the mutation of potential customers into active customers. But the example of a wreck above-mentioned in Figure 4 shows that transmutations may be defined between classes which are not subclasses of a same class. Instances of departure classes may be transmuted into instances of classes which may be super classes of the departure classes, subclasses of the departure classes or classes which are neither super classes nor subclasses of the departure classes.

2.2. Principal Categories of Transmutations

On considering for one transmutation the numbers of its departure classes and their instances and the numbers of its arrival classes and their instances, we distinguish the following significant categories of transmutations: *mutations, disaggregations, merges and reflexive transmutations*. On the other hand, for several transmutations *the opposite transmutations and the cascade of transmutations* are significant.

- Mutations, disaggregations, merges
A mutation is a transmutation such that one instance of one class is transmuted into one instance of a class.

Figure 5: Mutation diagram

The mutations are generally performed between classes which are subclasses of a same class.

Examples: mutations in personnel management presented below in Figure 6.

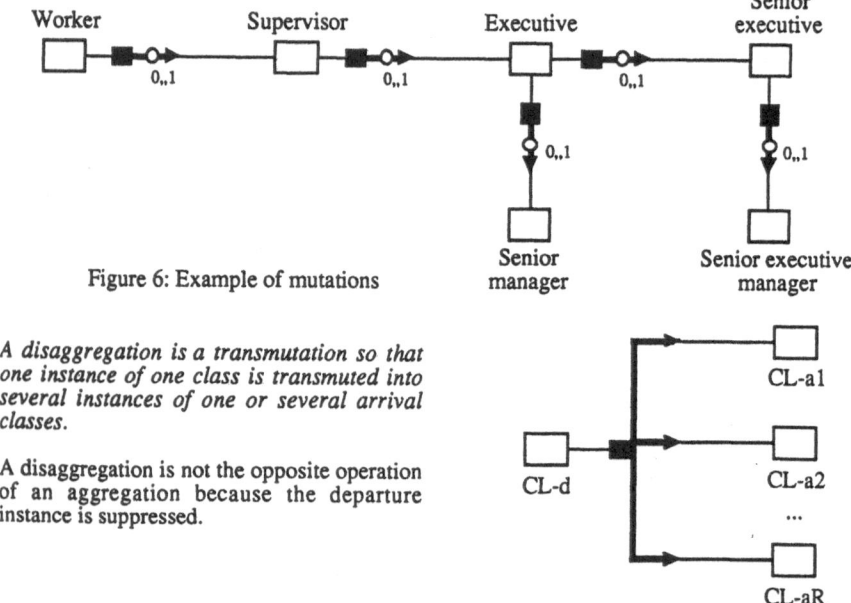

Figure 6: Example of mutations

A disaggregation is a transmutation so that one instance of one class is transmuted into several instances of one or several arrival classes.

A disaggregation is not the opposite operation of an aggregation because the departure instance is suppressed.

Figure 7: Disaggregation diagram

Example: in figure 8 a fresh fruit may be transmuted with three transmutations: a mutation into a crystallised fruit or a mutation into a failure or a disaggregation into its peel, its pips and its pulp.

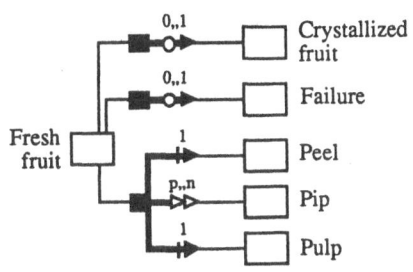

Figure 8: Mutations and disaggregation of fresh fruit

A merge is a transmutation such that instances of one or several departure classes are transmuted into one instance of an arrival class.

A merge is not an aggregation because the departure instances are suppressed.

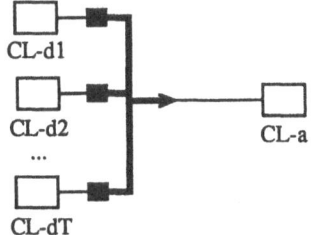

Figure 9: Merge diagram

Example: an atom of carbon and two atoms of oxygen are merged into a carbonic gas molecule in Figure 10.

Numerous chemical reactions are merges, others are disaggregations.

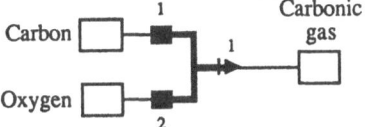

Figure 10: Example of merge

Some transmutations are not mutations, neither disaggregations nor merges.

Example: The chemical reaction of the chlorine on the soda is a transmutation that generates the creation of chloride of sodium, of water and of oxygen. The graphical representation of this transmutation is represented in Figure 11. This transmutation starts from instances of two classes and generates the creation of instances of three classes but it is not a mutation, neither a disaggregation nor a merge.

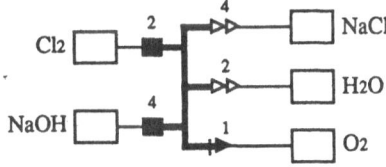

Figure 11: Chemical reaction

- Reflexive transmutations
A reflexive transmutation starts from one or several instances of a class and generates the creation of one or several instances of the same class.
Example: a reorganisation of a company is a reflexive transmutation which may be a merge or a disaggregation of its departments.

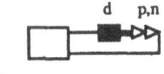

Department

Figure 12: Example of reflexive transmutation

A reflexive transmutation of an instance allows the creation of clones or copies of this instance with suppression of this instance.

A reflexive transmutation may be:
. a mutation if one departure instance generates the creation of only one instance of the same class; for example the mutation of a car model into an other car model;
. a disaggregation if every departure instance generates the creation of several instances of the same class; for example cellular division above-mentioned;
. a merge if several departure instances generate the creation of an instance of the same class; for example the merge of hay-cocks.

- Opposite transmutations

A transmutation T-i is the opposite of a transmutation T-j if the departure classes of T-j are the arrival classes of T-i and the arrival classes of T-j are the departure classes of T-i.

Figure 13: Example of opposite transmutations

Each transmutation does not necessarily have an opposite. Only the useful opposite transmutations must be defined.

- Cascade of transmutations

Two transmutations T-i and T-j are in cascade if at least one of the arrival classes of T-i is a departure class of T-j.
Cascades of transmutations represent in succession evolution of instances among classes of an object system.

Examples
. The transmutations of the personnel management above-mentioned in Figure 6 as examples of mutations are cascade of transmutations.
. The cascade of reactions of a nuclear explosion is a cascade of transmutations. Numerous chemical reactions are cascade of transmutations.
. In a cassia, a car is muted into a wreck and after a wreck is disaggregated into its recovered components: engine, wheels, etc. (see Figure 14).

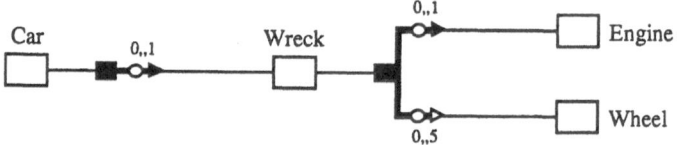

Figure 14: Example of cascade of transmutations

3. Specification and Implementation of Transmutations

The end-user specification of transmutations, the Petri-net representation of their execution and the two solutions of their implementation are presented in this Section.

3.1. End-user Specification of the Transmutations

The end-user specifications of the transmutations describe "What" and "When" they do. They are declarative because they describe "What" instead of "How". They define specifications relating to each departure class and each arrival class. They do not define the order of the treatments of these specifications. They do not precise anything on the suppressions of the departure instances because these suppressions are automatically performed if the departure and the creation conditions of a transmutation are satisfied. These specifications are conceptual because they are independent of the physical means used to implement them.

The end-user specification of a transmutation defines its departure conditions which must be satisfied by instances of departure classes and its creation conditions which must be satisfied for creation of instances of arrival classes.

The end-user specification of a transmutation specifies also:

. the attributes of the departure classes instances of which the values are sent to the instances of the arrival classes,

. and the attributes that define the arrival classes instances: the attributes of which values are received from departure classes instances and the complementary attributes of which the values are requested of external actors or of instances of other classes.

The schema of an end-user specification of a transmutation is presented in Figure 15.

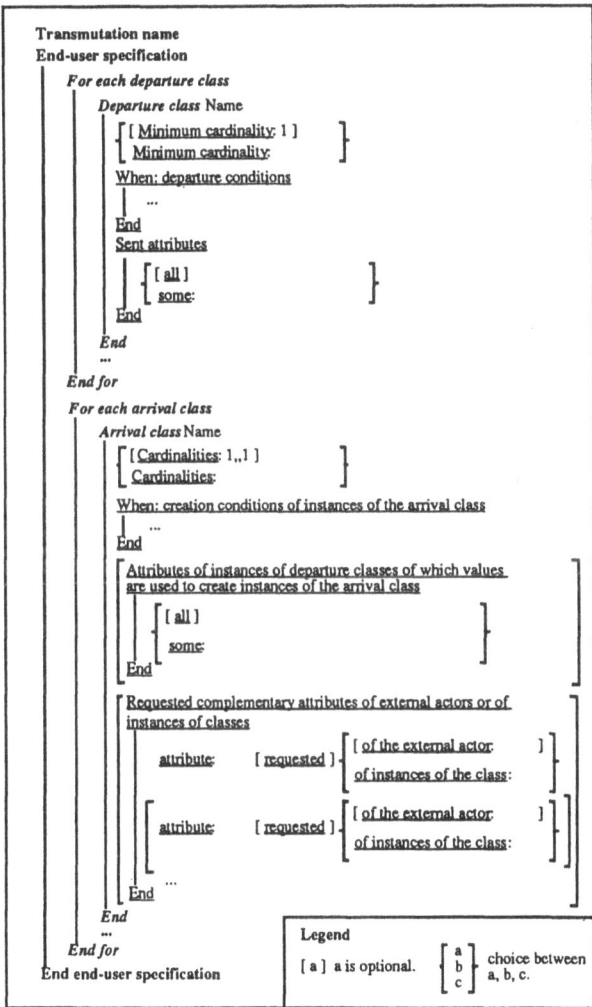

Figure 15: End-user specification of a transmutation

- For each departure class of a transmutation we define its cardinalities, its departure conditions and the attributes of the transmuted instances of which the values are sent to arrival instances.

- For each arrival class of a transmutation we define:
. its cardinalities,
. its creation conditions of instances,
. the attributes of instances of the departure classes of which values are used to create instances of the arrival class,
. and how the instances are created: with what attributes of the instances of departure classes of which the received values are used, and eventually with values of requested complementary attributes of external actors or of instances of other classes.

Example: the end-user specification of the transmutation of Wreck into Engine and Wheel is presented in Figure 16.

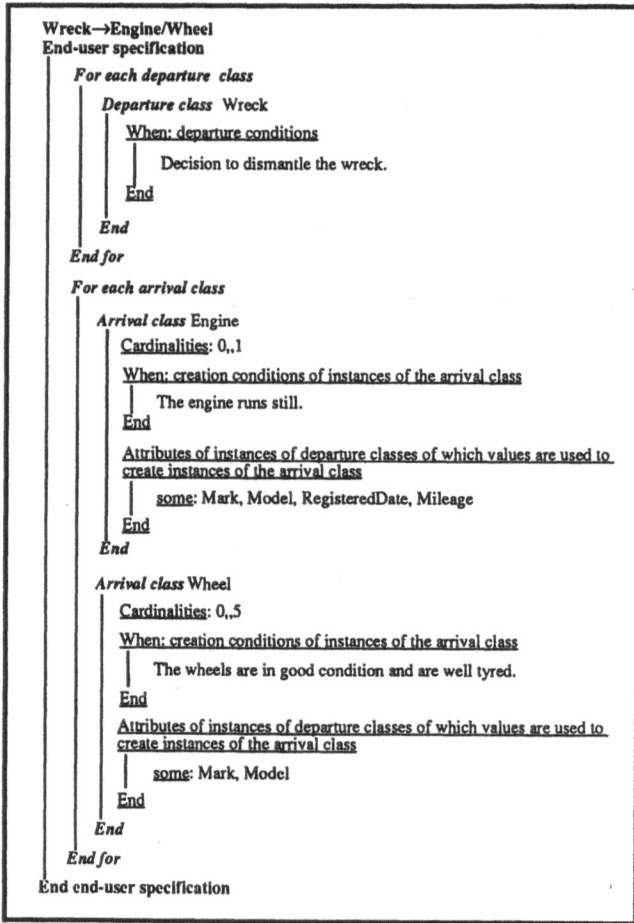

Figure 16: End-user specification of the transmutation Wreck→Engine/Wheel

3.2. Petri-net Representation of the Execution of a Transmutation

The execution of a transmutation is structured with three stages. The formal specification of this execution is represented with Petri-net (Petri, 1962).

First stage: *verification of the numbers of departure instances and of their departure conditions, and possible recuperation of values of attributes of these instances.*
A token starts the transition "Start verification and recuperation of values" which generates a token in every one of the T places such that each one allows us to start a transition to verify the number of instances of one of the T departure classes, to verify its departure conditions and to recover possibly values of attributes of these instances.

If all the transitions of the first stage have been performed, the second and the third stages are started *in parallel* by the transition "Start creations and suppressions". This transition generates a token in every one of R places associated to the R arrival classes and a token in every one of T places associated to the T departure classes.

Second stage: *verification of the creation conditions of instances of the arrival classes and creation of instances of these classes.*
Each of the tokens associated to R places associated to the R arrival classes starts a transition which verifies the creation conditions of instances of one of these R arrival classes following by a transition which creates instances of these classes.

Third stage: *suppression of instances of the departure classes.*
Each of the tokens of the T places associated to the T departure classes starts a transition which suppresses instances of one of the T departure classes.

The Petri-net representation of the execution of a transmutation is in Figure 17.

3.3. Implementation of the Transmutations

All the transmutations may be implemented by means of a centralised management solution presented in Section 3.3.1. The mutations may be implemented by means of a distributed management solution presented in Section 3.3.2. Comments about the implementation of the transmutations with object-oriented DBMS and languages are presented in Section 3.3.3.

3.3.1. Centralised Management of the Transmutations

The transmutations are ensured by servitude classes which are not semantic classes, that is to say they are not known by the end-users. A servitude class which has only one instance is created for each transmutation. Each servitude class co-operates with the departure classes and with the arrival classes of the transmutation and co-operates with the administrators of all these classes. The administrator of a class CL-a is a class which has only one instance which refers all the instances of the class CL-a.

A servitude class that manages a transmutation (see Figure 18):
- receives requests for transmutations from end-users or from instances (owing to events);
- co-operates with departure classes instances:
. to verify that the number of instances of each departure class candidate to be transmuted is equal or superior to its departure cardinality, and that their departure conditions are satisfied,
. possibly to recover values of attributes of these instances;
- manages the creation of arrival instances:
. verifies that their creation conditions are satisfied,
. requests administrators of the arrival classes to create instances,
. possibly sends values of attributes of the departure instances to the created instances,
- requests administrators of the departure classes to suppress the transmuted instances.

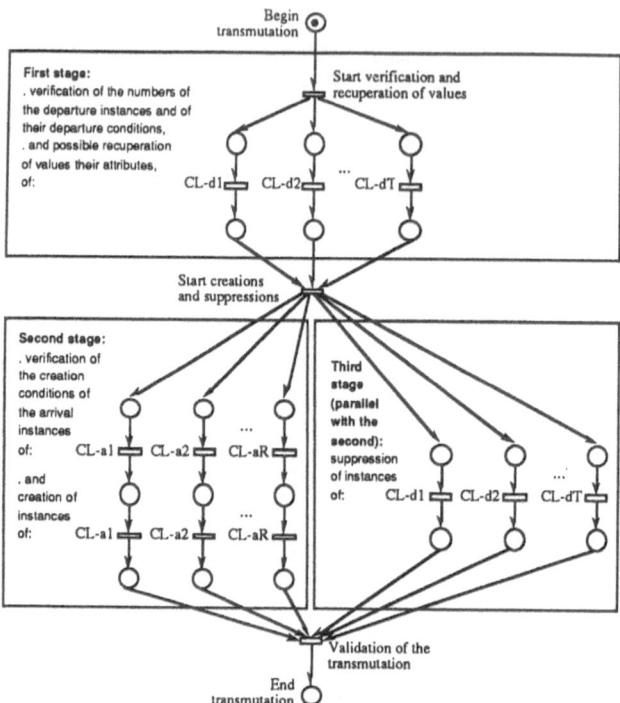

Figure 17: Petri-net representation of the execution of a transmutation

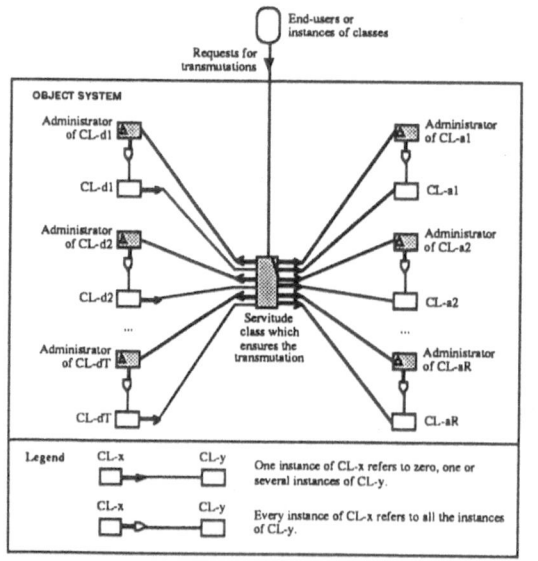

Figure 18: Centralised management of a transmutation CL-d1/CL-d2/.../CL-dT→CL-a1/CL-a2/.../CL-aR

3.3.2. Distributed Management of the Mutations

The mutations can be also implemented with a servitude class above presented. But a mutation is a particular transmutation defined only with a departure class and an arrival class. So a mutation may be ensured by services of the administrator of its departure class and by services of the administrator of its arrival class without a servitude class.

The administrator of the departure class of a mutation (see Figure 19):
- receives requests for mutations from end-users or from departure classes instances (owing to events);
- co-operates with a departure instance:
. to verify that its departure conditions are satisfied,
. and possibly to recover values of attributes of this instance;
- manages the creation of an arrival instance:
. verifies that its creation conditions are satisfied,
. requests the administrator of the arrival class to create an instance,
. possibly sends values of attributes of the departure instance to the created instance,
- suppresses the transmuted instance.

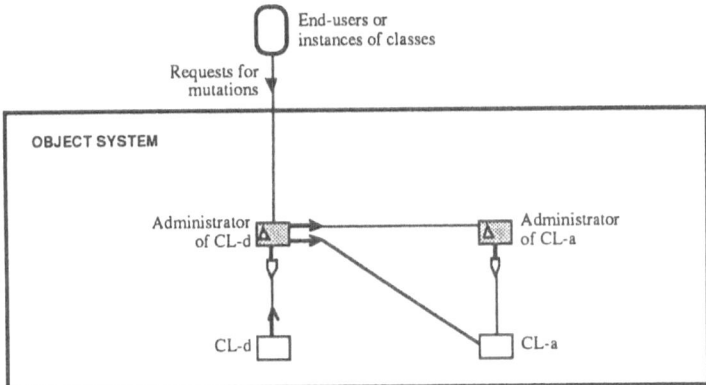

Figure 19: Distributed management of a mutation CL-d→CL-a

The distributed solution can be used with difficulty for the transmutations that use several departure classes or several arrival classes because the co-operation between the administrators of these classes imposes to create a servitude class to manage it. That results to the fact that it is difficult to choose an administrator to be the master manager of this co-operation.
A reflexive transmutation may be implemented with the administrator of the class of the transmuted instances.

3.3.3. Languages and DBMS about Transmutations

To our knowledge, the object-oriented and non-object-oriented programming languages give little possibility to implement the transmutations. In Smalltalk 80 and in Smalltalk/V the method *become:* defined in Object allows the change of the identifier (the OID) of an instance of a class into an other identifier of the same class and the modification of all references of all instances that referred to the old identifier with the new value. This method ensures functions of reflexive transmutations.
The other programming languages (object-oriented and non-object-oriented) propose neither concepts nor statements that allow the implementation of the transmutations. The transmutations must be programmed.

To our knowledge, DBMS propose neither concepts nor statements that allow the implementation of the transmutations, except GEMSTONE of Servio Logic Development Corporation. This object-oriented DBMS allows the mutations under precise conditions.

It is possible to change one instance of class with the help of the method *changeClassTo* defined in Object. This change is possible only if the arrival class is a subclass of the departure class, there is not new attributes, the departure class and the arrival class have the same storage format (pointers, unordered collections...), the same constraints are defined on the attributes of the departure class and of the arrival class.

Moreover, the transformed instance does not belong to an invariant class. The possibilities of representation of the mutations are limited with GEMSTONE.

4. Conclusion

The concept of transmutation represents suppressions of instances and creations of instances. These phenomena are rather frequent in management information systems and in industrial information systems. Without the concept of transmutation, these phenomena are represented with operations started by events. This solution is rather easy to represent mutations or reflexive transmutations as the implementation of the transmutations with a distributed management (cf. second solution presented in Section 3.3). On the other hand, for the other transmutations, this solution imposes to define classes which ensure them and it is difficult to represent their treatments without using the transmutation concept. This is equivalent to define classes which ensure transmutations as the servitude classes defined to implement transmutations with a centralised management (cf. first solution presented in Section 3.3).

Works on schema evolution allow evolution of classes and evolution of instances, for example the OTGen project ("Object Transformgen") (Lerner and Habermann, 1990). Actually, the transmutation concept allows evolution of instances. An outstanding research is being developed on the application of the transmutation concept to evolution of classes.

References:

(Aksit and Bergams, 1992): M. Aksit and L. Bergams. *Obstacles in Object-Oriented Software Development*. OOPSLA'92 Proceedings, 341-359 September 1992.

(Ayache and Ou-Halima, 1992): M. Ayache and M. Ou-Halima. *Représentation et identification des objets: modèle et méthode*. INFORSID '92 Conference, Clermont Ferrand, June 1992.

(Bari and Rolland, 1990): M. Bari and C. Rolland. *Une méthodologie pour la conception orientée objet*. Ada-France International French Conference Proceedings. Toulouse, December 5-6 1990.

(Booch, 1991): G. Booch. *Object Oriented Design*. Addison, 1991.

(Castellani, 1991₁): X. Castellani. *Le modèle de la méthode MCO d'analyse et de conception des systèmes d'objets*. INFORSID '91 Conference, Paris, June 1991.

(Castellani, 1991₂): X. Castellani. *L'implémentation de concepts fondamentaux de la méthode MCO d'analyse et de conception des systèmes d'objets*. Fourth International Conference Software Engineering and its Applications, December 9-13, 1991.

(Castellani, 1993): X. Castellani. *MCO: Méthodologie générale d'analyse et de conception des systèmes d'objets*. Tome 1: L'ingénierie des besoins, Preface of C. Rolland, Masson, 1993.

(De Champeaux and Faure, 1992): D. De Champeaux and P. Faure. *A comparative study of object-oriented analysis methods*. Journal of Object Oriented Programming, March/April 1992.

(Coad and Yourdon, 1990): P. Coad and E. Yourdon. *Object-oriented analysis*. Prentice Hall, second edition, 1990.

(Gibson, 1990): E. Gibson. *Objects Born and Bred. Object Behavior Analysis is a step-by-step, object-oriented approach to analysis*. Byte, October 1990.

(Heitz, 1987): M. Heitz. *HOOD, une méthode de conception hiérarchisée orientée objets pour le développement des gros logiciels techniques et temps réel*. Bigre n° 57, Journées Ada France: Le parallélisme en Ada, December 1987.

(Henderson-Sellers and Edwards, 1990): B. Henderson-Sellers and J. Edwards. *The object-oriented systems life cycle*. Communications of ACM, September 1990, Vol. 33, No 9.

(Hill, 1992): D.R.C. Hill. *Etude de quelques concepts pour une analyse et une conception par objets*. INFORSID'92 Conference, Clermont Ferrand, 1992.

(Hutt, 1993): A.T.F. Hutt. *Editor, Object Analysis and Design. Description of Methods. Object Analysis and Design Special Interest Group of the OMG (Object Management Group)*. A Wiley-QED Publication, John Wiley & Sons, Inc. 1994.

(Jacobson, 1989): I. Jacobson. *The industrial Development Of Software Using An Object-Oriented Technique*. Revue Objective Systems SF AB, 1989.

(Lerner and Habermann, 1990): B.S. Lerner and N.A. Habermann. *Beyond schema evolution to database reorganization*. ECOOP/OOPSLA '90 Proceedings, October 21-25 1990.

(Martin and Odell, 1992): J. Martin and J.J. Odell. *Object Oriented Analysis & Design*. Prentice Hall, 1992.

(Meyer, 1988): B. Meyer. *Object-oriented Software Construction*. Prentice Hall, 1988.

(Monarchi and Puhr, 1992): D.E. Monarchi and G.L. Puhr. *A research typology for object-oriented analysis and design*. Communication of the ACM, Vol. 35, No. 9, September 1992.

(Nerson, 1992): J.M. Nerson. *Applying Object-Oriented Analysis and Design*. Communications of the ACM, September 1992, Vol. 35, No 9.

(Petri, 1962): C. Petri. *Kommunication mit automater*. Phd Dissertation, Bonn, 1962.

(Rochfeld, 1991): A. Rochfeld. *Modèle externe de données et modèle externe objet*. Fourth International Conference Software Engineering and its Applications, December 9-13, 1991.

(Rolland and Cauvet, 1991): C. Rolland and C. Cauvet. *Modélisation conceptuelle orientée objet*. VIIèmes Journées Bases de données avancées, Lyon, September 25-27 1991.

(Rumbaugh et al., 1991): J. Rumbaugh, Blaham., W. Premerlani, F. Eddy and W. Lorensen. *Object-Oriented Modeling and Design*. Prentice Hall International, 1991.

(Shlaer and Mellor, 1988): S. Shlaer and S.J. Mellor. *Object-oriented systems analysis, Modeling the world in data*. Yourdon press computing series, 1988.

(Walker, 1992): I.J. Walker. *Requirements of an object-oriented design method*. Software Engineering Journal, March 1992.

(Wasserman and Pircher, 1991): A.I. Wasserman and P.A. Pircher. *Object-Oriented Structured Design*. Tutorial TOOLS' 91, Paris, 1991.

(Wirfs-Brock and Johnson, 1990): R.J. Wirfs-Brock and R.E. Johnson. *Surveying current research in object-oriented design*. Communications of ACM, September 1990, Vol. 33, No 9.

(Wirfs-Brock et al., 1990): R.J. Wirfs-Brock, B. Wilkerson and L. Wiener. *Designing Object-Oriented Software*. Prentice Hall, 1990.

OPUS: a Calculus for Modelling Object-Oriented Concepts

Tom Mens, Kim Mens, Patrick Steyaert

Department of Computer Science
Vrije Universiteit Brussel
Pleinlaan 2, B-1050 Brussels, BELGIUM
E-mail: { tommens@is1 | we34154@is1 | prsteyae@vnet3 }.vub.ac.be
Fax: +32 2 629 3495

ABSTRACT. *We propose a very concise calculus for modelling object-oriented concepts such as objects, message sending, encapsulation and incremental modification. We show how to deal with recursion and provide some object-oriented examples. State and encapsulated inheritance are modelled by means of an incremental modification operator.*

KEY WORDS: calculus, encapsulated objects, message sending, incremental modification, encapsulated inheritance.

1. Introduction

This paper proposes a foundation for modelling the essential concepts of object-orientedness (OO) by means of an elementary calculus called OPUS, which is an acronym for "Object-oriented Programming calculUS". Our calculus is based on the model of *substitutable objects*. This kind of object model was introduced in (Steyaert, 1994) to denote objects with explicit interfaces, a notion of encapsulation and polymorphism, and atomic message sending.

First of all, it is obvious that we need a notion of objects. Moreover, our object-oriented model is homogeneous since the only data structures are objects, while the only control structure is message sending. This makes our model very simple. For reasons of simplicity we have also chosen not to include state into our model. It is sufficient to provide only methods (behaviour), because state can be modelled by constant methods (i.e. methods that always return the same result). We will show that updating state can be modelled by an *incremental modification mechanism*. This mechanism is similar to the one described in (Wegner et al., 1988), and can also be used to model a form of *encapsulated inheritance*, as proposed by (Snyder, 1987) for reasons of reusability of software components.

To this extent we also need to provide an *encapsulation mechanism* that allows us to create objects with a public part and an encapsulated private part. This encapsulation operator will play an essential role in modelling recursive objects in our calculus *without needing explicit provisions for recursion*. Recursion can be dealt with by two alternative operators: a first one similar to the Y-operator of lambda-calculus, giving rise to infinite recursion; and a second one unfolding only one level of recursion, needed for updating state.

OPUS *explicitly uses names* in the method lookup mechanism. There is ample evidence that names simplify the modelling of object-oriented systems. In order to make the examples more concise and understandable, we will allow arguments to be passed with messages.

In the following section we will motivate from different perspectives why a formal model for OO can be useful. Section 3 describes the syntax and derivation mechanism of OPUS, gives an informal explanation, and shows how to deal with recursion and updating state using only this basic syntax. In the fourth section we present some object-oriented examples. More specifically we show how Booleans, numerals and class-based inheritance can be expressed. The subsequent section discusses some related work. In the last section we draw some conclusions, and discuss a few topics that might be worthwhile investigating in the future.

2. Motivation

In order to gain a consistent understanding of OO and its descriptions one first needs to find the key features for object-oriented programming languages (OOPLs). For obvious reasons we want these features to be as orthogonal as possible. Once the key concepts are found, a formalisation of OO can be developed in the form of a calculus with only a very restricted set of syntactic constructs. This calculus can then be used as a theoretical foundation of object-oriented languages, just as is the case for lambda-calculus in the functional programming paradigm. Such a formal framework is useful for many reasons.

First of all, many people lack a firm and rigorous ground when trying to prove general properties for OOPLs, partly because most concepts of OO have no generally accepted definition, and because there is still a lot of controversy about which features - classes, inheritance, delegation, encapsulation, message sending - are at the heart of OO, and how they relate to one another. By modelling these features in our calculus we will be able to get more insight in this matter.

An OO-calculus is also interesting from a more pragmatic standpoint. In analogy with the design of functional languages based on lambda-calculus, a concise OO-calculus might lead to development of new OOPLs with a more simple and orthogonal design but with the same expressivity as currently available OOPLs.

Most of the current research on formal models of OO consists of attempts to generalise lambda-calculus. A lot of these models suffer from difficulties in expressing the essential features of object-orientedness in a satisfying way. For this reason we feel that when developing a calculus one should stay closer to real OO languages, and only at a later stage one could investigate if the proposed model subsumes lambda-calculus. This is more or less the same methodology as followed by Laurent Dami, who first developed the HOP-calculus and later proved that this model can be regarded as an extension of de Bruijn lambda-calculus (de Bruijn, 1972) with names, combinations and alternations (Dami, 1994).

3. The calculus

3.1. Informal discussion of the syntax

In OPUS, an object consists of a *public part* and an encapsulated *private part* that is only accessible through the object's operations. Such an object is denoted as [*Public* | *Private*]. The public and private part of an object can contain a list of methods. The public part contains the methods visible for other objects, while the private part contains methods that are only used to implement public methods; hence they are not externally visible.

Methods will be invoked using the following message sending syntax: sending a message N with arguments A to an expression E is denoted by (E N:A). Apart from ordinary methods we need a special kind of methods to model state, namely constant methods. The difference with ordinary methods lies in the way they are executed. Furthermore, with constant methods the arguments in A will always be ignored.

An ordinary method will be represented by the symbol λ followed by a name, an equality sign and an expression (e.g. λgetx=x). Method execution is a combination of method selection and method application, and occurs as follows: if a message corresponding to a method is sent to an object, this method is looked up (method selection), unbound variables in the body of the method are bound to the arguments of the message (argument passing) or to values of corresponding attributes in the private part (static scoping), the method is evaluated (method invocation), and the result is returned. This result is typically again an object.

A constant method is represented by a name, followed by an equality sign, followed by an expression (e.g. x=xval). Constant methods have no arguments, and do not call attributes in the private part. If a message corresponding to a constant method is sent to an object, the body of this method is simply returned.

As a basic structure to create more complicated objects we use records, which is a common approach followed in literature (Cook, 1989), (Cardelli et al., 1989) and (Wegner et al., 1988). Objects in their most simple form have an empty private part and a public part which is a record of methods, for example [λgetx=x λgety=y |]. A more general form of objects are those containing a private part which is a record as well, e.g. [λgetx=x λgety=y | x=1 y=2]. In the most general case, the public and private parts of an object need not be records, but can be objects themselves. This is an important advantage of our calculus over lambda-calculus with records (Cardelli, 1988) and (Cardelli et al., 1989). It is essential on the one hand to model private methods, and on the other hand to have some form of binding of constant methods in different stages.

In many cases it is useful to have some kind of incremental modification mechanism. The incremental modification of an expression P (parent) with an expression M (modifier) is denoted by (P+M). This operator will prove useful when dealing with inheritance, because inheritance can be characterised as incremental modification with deferred binding of self-reference (Wegner et al., 1988). A further investigation of inheritance is delayed until section 4.3.

There is however a problem when defining an inheritance operator, because "inheritance may be considered a fundamental violation of encapsulation because of the change of self-reference" (Cook, 1989), or stated otherwise "the introduction of inheritance severely compromises encapsulation, by exposing implementation details to inheriting clients" (Snyder, 1987). An extensive discussion on the interaction between inheritance and encapsulation can be found in (Snyder, 1987). In our paper the incremental modification operator + is defined in such a way that it gives rise to a notion of *encapsulated inheritance* (each object can only refer to its own private methods and not to those of its parents, and vice versa). It is also possible to give an alternative definition of this operator so that it yields a form of *non-encapsulated inheritance*, but that is beyond the scope of this paper.

The operational semantics[1] of method lookup will be defined in a similar way as in object-oriented languages like Smalltalk. Sending a message to a modified object (E_1+E_2) is implemented by first sending the message to the rightmost object E_2, and if no corresponding attribute is found we continue searching in the object E_1 on the left. Hence the incremental modification operator is not commutative: if we compose two objects that both contain attributes corresponding to the same name, the attributes of the rightmost object will "overwrite" those of the leftmost object.

The following example illustrates the use of the incremental modification operator as well as the method lookup mechanism. Suppose we have a POINT-object with private constant methods x=1 and y=2, that defines the methods getx and gety as follows[2]:

POINT := [λgetx=x λgety=y | x=1 y=2]

We can modify this object to obtain a three-dimensional point object that inherits all methods of POINT and supplementary adds a public getz method, needed to access the private constant method z=3, by extending the POINT-object with the following modifier:

MODIFIER := [λgetz=z | z=3]
3DPOINT := (POINT + MODIFIER)

---

[1] A denotational semantics for the method lookup mechanism can be found in (Cook, 1989) or (Cook et al., 1989).
2 The operator := that binds expressions to variables, is not present in the syntax of the calculus. It is only used to make the examples more readable. Words written in uppercase refer to "predefined" objects that have to be replaced "in place".

Sending the parameterless message[3] gety to this 3DPOINT will result in first looking in the MODIFIER-object for an attribute corresponding to gety, but because no attribute will be found, we continue searching for this attribute in the POINT-object. The method gety found in POINT is then executed by evaluating its body in the context of the private part.

```
3DPOINT gety:[|]
=     ( POINT + MODIFIER ) gety:[|]
⇒     POINT gety:[|]
⇒     [ x=1 y=2 | ] y:[|]
⇒     2
```

Note that methods in the MODIFIER-object can never directly access the private attributes x and y of POINT, because the incremental modification operator + is defined in such a way that it gives rise to a notion of *encapsulated inheritance*. Similarly, the public methods of POINT can only access their own private attributes, and not those of MODIFIER.

3.2. Context free grammar

Formally, expressions in our calculus are defined by providing a context free grammar in EBNF-notation. The start symbol of this grammar is Expression, and all terminal symbols are written in bold between double quotes.

Expression	::=	Object | Message | Modification | Name
Object	::=	"[" ExtExpression "|" ExtExpression "]"
ExtExpression	::=	Expression | Record
Record	::=	{ Attribute }
Message	::=	"(" Expression Name ":" Expression ")"
Modification	::=	"(" Expression "+" Expression ")"
Attribute	::=	Constant | Method
Constant	::=	Name "=" Expression
Method	::=	"λ" Name "=" Expression
Name	::=	Character { Character }
Character	::=	"a" | "b" | "c" | ... | "z"

Notice that this syntax allows a Record to be empty. A Record can also contain different attributes corresponding to the same name, but only the last occurrence of this name will be significant, as will become clear in the reduction rules.

Message and **Modification** both require parentheses. To make the notation somewhat lighter, we will adopt the convention to omit parentheses whenever confusion is impossible. Furthermore, in case of ambiguity an expression will be parsed from left to right. E.g. A+B+C denotes (A+B)+C instead of A+(B+C), and similarly for message sending.

3.3. Reduction rules

For the rest of this paper, let N denote a meta-variable of type Name, E and E_i meta-variables of type Expression, F and F_i meta-variables of type ExtExpression, R and R_i meta-variables of type Record, and A a meta-variable of type Attribute.

Definition: An attribute A is called an **N-attribute** if A is of the form N=E or λN=E.

---

[3] We will see that the syntax of OPUS requires us always to send messages with arguments. Sending a message without arguments can be done by sending a message with the empty object [|] as argument.

Using this definition, the reduction rules can be expressed as follows:

<u>Rule 1</u>: Message sending to an object

a) [R | F] N:E   → ([|] + [R | F]) N:E   if R is not empty
                                          [|]   if R is empty

b) [(E_1 + E_2) | F] N:E   → ([E_1 | F] + [E_2 | F]) N:E

<u>Rule 2</u>: Message sending to an incrementally modified object

a) Constant method selection

    (E_1 + [R N=E_2 | F]) N:E → E_2

b) Method execution

    (E_1 + [R λN=E_2 | F]) N:E → { (F + E) }(E_2)   if F is no Record
                                        { ([F |] + E) }(E_2) if F is a Record

c) Attribute lookup

    (E_1 + [R A | F]) N:E   → (E_1 + [R | F]) N:E   if A is no N-attribute
    (E_1 + [| F]) N:E   → E_1 N:E

<u>Rule 3</u>: Currying

[[F_1 | F_2] | F_3]   → [F_1 | [F_2 | F_3]]   if F_2 is not empty
                             [F_1 | F_3]   if F_2 is empty

The notation → used in the reduction rules means "...reduces in one step to...", while ⇒ ("...reduces in zero or more steps to...") will be used in the subsequent examples to denote the transitive closure of →. An expression is in *normal form* if it cannot be reduced any further.

In rule 1, message sending to an object occurs by sending the message to the empty object [|] incrementally modified with the given object. If the message is not found in the object, the expression will automatically reduce to the empty object. For example:

[λgetx=x | x=1] sety:[y=1 |]
→   ([|] + [λgetx=x | x=1]) sety:[y=1 |]   (rule 1a)
→   ([|] + [| x=1]) sety:[y=1 |]   (rule 2c)
→   [|] sety:[y=1 |]   (rule 2c)
→   [|]   (rule 1a)

Rule 2b states that, to execute a method, we first bind all unbound variables in the body E_2 of the method N to the parameters E provided with the message, and next all remaining unbound variables are bound in the context of the private part F of the object of which the method was part of. This can be done by evaluating the body of the method in the context of the object (F+E). In other words, we implicitly use our incremental modification operator to model argument passing! To formalise the notion of evaluation in a context, a new notation { } will be introduced further. This notation does not belong to the syntax but can be seen as a kind of meta-level reduction scheme.

A problem still present in our approach is that the argument passing mechanism as proposed in this paper jeopardises encapsulation. The reason for this is that in rule 2b arguments have precedence over private methods. For example

[λgetx=x λgety=y | x=1 y=2] getx:[x=2 |]

yields 2 instead of the expected result 1. This problem can be solved by adding the restriction that argument names and private method names should be disjoint. Because we think that such issues will make the syntax needlessly difficult, we believe this problem should be solved by providing a higher level syntax.

Rule 2 formalises the method lookup mechanism that was explained earlier in the informal discussion of the syntax: to look up an attribute in a composed object, we search the record in the public part of the *rightmost* object *from right to left* for an attribute corresponding to the message name, and then execute the corresponding method. If no attribute is found in this object, we restart the whole process on the leftmost object. This process is illustrated in the following reduction:

$$([\ \lambda getx=x\ \lambda gety=y\ |\ x=1\ y=2\ ] + [\ \lambda getz=z\ |\ z=3\ ])\ getx:[|]$$

$\rightarrow$ $([\ \lambda getx=x\ \lambda gety=y\ |\ x=1\ y=2\ ] + [\ |\ z=3\ ])\ getx:[|]$	(rule 2c)
$\rightarrow$ $[\ \lambda getx=x\ \lambda gety=y\ |\ x=1\ y=2\ ]\ getx:[|]$	(rule 2c)
$\rightarrow$ $([|] + [\ \lambda getx=x\ \lambda gety=y\ |\ x=1\ y=2\ ])\ getx:[|]$	(rule 1a)
$\rightarrow$ $([|] + [\ \lambda getx=x\ |\ x=1\ y=2\ ])\ getx:[|]$	(rule 2c)
$\rightarrow$ $\{([\ x=1\ y=2\ |\ ] + [|])\}(\ x\ )$	(rule 2b)
$\Rightarrow$ 1	

The modification operator + is in fact an (implicit) delegation operator. The term *delegation* refers to the fact that an object can delegate responsibility of a message it cannot handle to objects that potentially could. Delegation is *implicit* because all messages that are not understood by the receiving object are automatically (= implicitly) delegated to its parent. Indeed, if a message N with arguments E is sent to an object E_2 with parent E_1 (i.e. (E_1+E_2) N:E) and E_2 does not contain any N-attribute, then rule 2c automatically delegates the message to the parent E_1 (i.e. E_1 N:E).

Rule 3 is needed because it is possible for a public part to be again an object, while the message sending mechanism only works with objects where the public part is a record.

3.4. Evaluation in a context

In rule 2b we used the meta-level reduction scheme $\{E\}(E_2)$ for the *evaluation of an expression E_2 in a context E*. The context E in which an expression is evaluated can be an arbitrary expression. The definition of evaluation in a context can be given inductively as follows[4]:

Inductive case:

$\{E\}(\ (E_1\ N{:}E_2)\ )$	equals	$(\ \{E\}(E_1)\ N{:}\{E\}(E_2)\ )$
$\{E\}(\ [\ F_1\ |\ F_2\ ]\ )$	equals	$[\ \{E\}(F_1)\ |\ \{E\}(F_2)\ ]$
$\{E\}(\ (E_1\ +\ E_2)\ )$	equals	$(\ \{E\}(E_1)\ +\ \{E\}(E_2)\ )$
$\{E\}(\ L\ \ A\ )$	equals	$\{E\}(L)\ \ \{E\}(A)$
$\{E\}(\ N{=}E_1\ )$	equals	$N{=}\{E\}(E_1)$

The inductive case captures the intuition that evaluation of an expression in a context corresponds to evaluation of the components of the expression in that context.

Base case:

$\{E\}(\ N\ )$	equals	$E\ N{:}[|]$
$\{E\}(\ \lambda N{=}E_1\ )$	equals	$\lambda N{=}E_1$
$\{E\}(\ \varepsilon\ )$	equals	ε

Intuitively the evaluation of an expression in a context corresponds to replacing all unbound names in that expression by their meaning in that context. Therefore evaluation of a name in a context simply corresponds to looking up that name, i.e. by sending the name as a message to the context. Evaluation of a method $\lambda N{=}E_1$ in a context leaves the method body unchanged. One might say that all free names in E_1 are bound by the λ.

3.5. Dealing with recursion

In most object-oriented languages it is very common that an object can call its own (public) methods using a recursive reference. Although we did not explicitly introduce recursion in our calculus we

---

[4] In this definition, ε is used to denote the empty expression.

will show how it can be implemented in a straightforward way. Our approach will be similar to the one followed by (Dami, 1994) for introducing recursion into λN-calculus.

Due to the special treatment of names in OPUS, we need a fixpoint operator μ_s for each name s, satisfying the property that taking the fixpoint over an expression yields a new expression that is exactly the same as the original one, except that every occurrence of s should be replaced by this new expression. In other words, the expression can refer to itself using the name s. Informally, the operator μ_s should behave as follows:

$$\mu_s \text{ fix:}[\text{ par=E } | \text{ }] \Rightarrow [\text{ E } | \text{ s } = [\text{ E } | \text{ s } = [\text{ E } | \text{ s } = \dots]]]$$

It is possible to define such an operator in the OPUS-syntax, using a rather difficult expression:

$$\mu_s := [\text{ } \lambda\text{fix=}[\text{ par } | \text{ s=}([\text{ } Z_s \text{ } | \text{ self=}Z_s \text{ e=par }] \text{ res:}[|]\text{ }) \text{ }] | \text{ }]$$
where $Z_s = [\text{ } \lambda\text{res=}[\text{ e } | \text{ s=}([\text{ self } | \text{ self=self e=e }] \text{ res:}[|]\text{ }) \text{ }] | \text{ }]$

The fixpoint operator μ_s can for example be used to calculate the factorial of an integer in a functional way. Due to space limitations we will only give an informal description of what this factorial should look like:

FACBODY := [λres=*if* n=0 *then* 1 *else* n*(fac res:[n=n-1 |]) |]
FAC := μ_{fac} fix:[par= FACBODY |]

In the approach followed above we observe that once the fixpoint μ_s fix:[par=E |] is defined for a given expression E, every reference to s will always return the same object [E | s=[E | s=[E | s=...]]]. This is not necessarily what we want in an OO approach. If the "internal state" of an object is changed, we want s to refer to this *updated* object, not to the original object. This problem can be solved by defining an operator that unfolds only one level of recursion. I.e. instead of using μ_s we will introduce an alternative operator σ_s with the property

$$\sigma_s \text{ unfold:}[\text{ par=E } | \text{ }] \Rightarrow [\text{ E } | \text{ s } = \text{ E }]$$

It is very easy to check that the expression below satisfies this property.

$$\sigma_s := [\text{ } \lambda\text{unfold=}[\text{ par } | \text{ s=par }] | \text{ }]$$

To simplify the examples in the rest of this paper we will abbreviate expressions of the form σ_s unfold:[par=E |] to σE.

The essential difference between μ_s and σ_s is that the former corresponds to an infinite recursive unfolding, whereas the latter expands only one level. The advantage of infinite recursion is that we only need to apply the fixpoint operator once, and that any future reference to s will yield the same object. However, this implies that the object cannot be updated. On the other hand, if we only unfold one level we have the disadvantage that the operator σ_s needs to be rewritten each time we want to unfold another level. But the advantage is that we can update the object at each level because every time we use the operator, s will refer to the latest version of the object instead of the original object.

3.6. Generator objects

When dealing with self-reference, things are quite similar to the generator functions of (Cook, 1989). A *generator* is an object that doesn't have a bound self-reference yet. To create objects that can refer to themselves, the self-reference needs to be bound. In our notation this is exactly done by the σ-notation.

For example, let G_1 be a generator object that makes use of self. Then $\sigma G_1 := [\ G_1\ |\ self = G_1\ ]$ corresponds to the same object where every self-reference is bound to the object G_1 itself.

$G_1 := [\ a=2\ \lambda double=(\sigma self\ a:[|])\ ^*\ 2\ |\ ]$
$\sigma G_1\ double:[|] \Rightarrow 4$

Generators may also be modified to define a new generator. This kind of use is unique to inheritance due to late binding of self-references: self calls of a parent should refer to the modified object instead of to the parent object. To insure that self-reference is handled properly, first the generator G_1 needs to be modified with a generator G_2 yielding (G_1+G_2), and only then the σ-operator should be applied. The example underneath clearly illustrates that this approach correctly handles late binding of self.

$G_2 := [\ a = 3\ |\ ]$
$\sigma(G_1+G_2)\ double:[|] \Rightarrow 6$

When the σ-operator is applied before the generators G_1 and G_2 are composed, we do not obtain late binding of self (because self-reference in G_1 refers to the unmodified version of G_1):

$(\sigma G_1+\sigma G_2)\ double:[|] \Rightarrow 4$

3.7. Updating state

Assume we want to define a POINT object with two private variables x and y that can only be accessed by means of the public methods getx and gety (that simply return the value of x and y respectively), and set (that stores a new value in x and y). The set method should be invoked by a message with two parameters x and y representing the new x- and y-values.

POINT := [λgetx=x λgety=y λset=σ(self+[λgetx=x λgety=y | x=x y=y])
         | x=0 y=0 λself=self]

Since state is modelled via incremental modification, we need the above described mechanism of generator combination: when we take a look at the set method, we see that to modify the POINT-object we have to modify self with the new values of x and y, and then apply the σ-operator. Also notice that because we work with encapsulated inheritance the modifier-object should contain in its public part all state-accessor methods, and in its private part the new values of the state.

The object σPOINT with bound self-references will satisfy our requirements, as we can see from the following reduction:

```
(σPOINT set:[x=1 y=2|]) gety:[|]
⇒ˉ   [ ( POINT + [ λgetx=x λgety=y | x=1 y=2 ] )
     | self = ( POINT + [ λgetx=x λgety=y | x=1 y=2 ] ) ] gety:[|]
→    ( [ POINT | self=(POINT+[ λgetx=x λgety=y | x=1 y=2 ]) ]
     + [   [λgetx=x λgety=y | x=1 y=2]
          | self=(POINT+[λgetx=x λgety=y | x=1 y=2]) ]
     ) gety:[|]                                              (rule 1b)
→    ( [ POINT | self=(POINT+[ λgetx=x λgety=y | x=1 y=2 ]) ]
     + [ λgetx=x λgety=y
          | [ x=1 y=2 | self=(POINT+[ λgetx=x λgety=y | x=1 y=2 ]) ] ]
     ) gety:[|]                                              (rule 3)
→    { ( [ x=1 y=2 | self=(POINT+[ λgetx=x λgety=y | x=1 y=2 ]) ]
     + [|] ) } (y)                                           (rule 2b)
⇒    2
```

4. Examples

We will illustrate how some basic object-oriented examples can be expressed in OPUS in a relatively straightforward fashion. More specifically we will define Boolean objects, numerals and classes.

4.1. Booleans

First we will show how to express the Booleans TRUE and FALSE. The standard way to do this is by defining Booleans as objects that understand the basic logical operators if, ifnot, and, or and not. As a first attempt, we simply define TRUE and FALSE as records understanding exactly those messages:

TRUE := [λif=then λifnot=else λand=second λor=TRUE λnot=FALSE |]
FALSE := [λif=else λifnot=then λand=FALSE λor=second λnot=TRUE |]

The problem is that those objects are mutually recursive, because TRUE is defined in terms of itself and FALSE, and vice versa. To solve this, we need two additional instance variables: a self instance variable referring to the object itself, and an instance variable other referring to the object with which the given object is mutually recursive. The revised versions of TRUE and FALSE are defined below:

TRUE   := [TRUE' | self=TRUE' other=FALSE']
FALSE   := [FALSE' | self=FALSE' other=TRUE']
TRUE'   := [λif=then λifnot=else λand=second λor=SELF λnot=OTHER |]
FALSE' := [λif=else λifnot=then λand=SELF λor=second λnot=OTHER |]
SELF   := [self | self=self other=other]
OTHER   := [other | self=other other=self]

Note that we cannot simply write TRUE := σTRUE' (or FALSE := σFALSE'), because we do not only need a recursive reference to TRUE itself, but also one to FALSE.
It is easy to see that these definitions yield the expected results, as can be verified by means of the following derivations:

TRUE if:[then=1 else=2 |] ⇒ 1
FALSE ifnot:[then=1 else=2 |] ⇒ 1
FALSE not:[|] ⇒ TRUE
TRUE and:[second=FALSE |] ⇒ FALSE
TRUE or:[second=FALSE |] ⇒ TRUE

4.2. Numerals

In a similar way, numerals can be defined as objects understanding the basic arithmetic operations. For the sake of simplicity, we will only deal with positive integer numbers (although negative numbers can be expressed in a similar way). Once the unary messages iszero, pred and succ are defined, all other operations plus, minus, times and fac can be expressed in terms of those:

a plus b =	b	if a is zero
	(a pred) plus (b succ)	otherwise
a minus b =	a	if a or b is zero
	(a pred) minus (b pred)	otherwise
a times b =	a	if a is zero
	((a pred) times b) plus b	otherwise
a fac =	a succ	if a is zero
	((a pred) fac) times a	otherwise

Note that in the previous definitions we defined zero minus b as zero, because we only work with positive numbers. In all these definitions we had to distinguish the special case where a is zero. For this reason we will need two kinds of objects: ZERO and POSITIVE, where the latter is a kind of template for all positive numbers:

```
ZERO := σ[   iszero=TRUE
             λpred=σself
             λsucc=σ( POSITIVE + [ pred=σself | ] )
             λplus=arg
             λminus=σself
             λtimes=σself
             λfac=σself succ:[|]
             | ]
```

```
POSITIVE := [   iszero=FALSE
                λsucc=σ( self + [ pred=σself | ] )
                λplus=σself pred:[|] plus:[ arg=arg succ:[|] | ]
                λminus=arg iszero:[|]
                              if:[    then=σself
                                      else=σself pred:[|] min:[arg=arg pred:[|] |]
                                      | ]
                λtimes=σself pred:[|] times:[ arg=arg | ] plus:[ arg=arg | ]
                λfac=σself pred:[|] fac:[|] times:[ arg=σself | ]
                | ]
```

Using these definitions the numerals can be defined as follows:

0 := *normal form of*   ZERO
1 := *normal form of*   **0** succ:[|]
2 := *normal form of*   **0** succ:[|] succ:[|]   = *normal form of*   **1** succ:[|]

One can check that these numerals are well defined (i.e. they express the arithmetic operators in a faithful way). A reduction of an expression with numerals is given below.

0 succ:[|] times:[arg=**2**|] minus:[arg=**1**|] ⇒ **1**

4.3. Class-based inheritance

In this section, we show by means of an example how to deal with class-based inheritance. Classes can be defined as templates from which objects are created. Different instances of a given class have the same behaviour, but can have a different internal state. For example we can define a point class where the private constant methods x and y differ between different instances of this class, while the getx, gety and set methods are the same for all instances. Moreover we add two new methods to illustrate late binding of self-reference. The move-method expects two arguments dx and dy, and updates the values x and y by invoking the set-method with x+dx and y+dy as arguments. The double-method doubles the coordinates x and y simply by invoking the move-method with the old values of x and y as arguments.

To simplify the subsequent examples, we will extend the meaning of σ_s:

σ_s := [λunfold=[par | s=par class=class super=super] |]

σ_{self} unfold:[par=E |] ⇒ [E | self=E class=class super=super]

As before we will abbreviate σ_{self} unfold:[par=E |] to σE.

Formally, a point instance without bound self- and class-references looks as follows:

```
POINT := [ λgetx=x
           λgety=y
           λset=σ( self + [ λgetx=x λgety=y | x=x y=y ] )
           λmove=σself set:[ x=σself getx:[|] plus:[arg=dx|]
                             y=σself gety:[|] plus:[arg=dy|] | ]
           λdouble=σself move:[ dx=σself getx:[|]
                                dy=σself gety:[|] | ]
           | x=0 y=0 λself=self λclass=class ]
```

Note that in the private part two methods occur. The self-method is used to be able to deal with recursive self-references, while the class-method is needed to refer to the point class itself. The bodies of both methods will be filled in via curried binding. Point instances can be created by invoking the new-method of the point class

```
POINTCLASS := [ λnew=[ inst | self=inst class=self ] | ]
```

where self and inst are bound to POINTCLASS and POINT respectively:

```
PC := [ POINTCLASS | self=POINTCLASS inst=POINT ]
PC new:[|] ⇒ [ POINT | self=POINT class=POINTCLASS ]
```

Subclasses of the point class can be created by incrementally modifying them for example with a MODIFIER implementing a move-method that only moves the x-coordinate while keeping the y-value unaltered:

```
MODIFIER := [ λmove=σself set:[ x=σself getx:[|] plus:[arg=dx|]
                                y=σself gety:[|] | ]
              | λself=self λclass=class ]
```

Instances of such a modified point class MODCLASS can be obtained by invoking its new-method. To illustrate the use of super, we will implement this new-method as a super call to the new-method of the point class.

```
MODCLASS := [ λnew=[ super | self=self inst=inst ] new:[|] | ]
```

Again self, inst and super need to be bound in order to become a meaningful object.

```
MC := [ MODCLASS | self=MODCLASS inst=(POINT+MODIFIER) super=POINTCLASS ]
```

In the above definition of inst we clearly see the incremental modification: POINT is incrementally modified with MODIFIER by using the + operator. Also note that the super variable in the above definition can only be used by class methods. In order to allow instance methods to perform super calls, another super variable needs to be introduced. We have chosen not to do this to keep the example simple.

Finally one can observe the correctness of all these definitions by looking at the reductions below. The first two create an instance of the point class, set the coordinates of the instantiated point, double these coordinates and return the x- and y-values respectively:

```
PC new:[|] set:[x=1 y=2|] double:[|] getx:[|]    ⇒    2
PC new:[|] set:[x=1 y=2|] double:[|] gety:[|]    ⇒    4
```

To illustrate the late binding of self, observe that invoking the double-method on an instance of the modified class exhibits a different behaviour than invoking the same method on an instance of the point class, since the double-method makes use of the move-method, which was overridden in the modifier instance!

```
MC new:[|] set:[x=1 y=2|] double:[|] getx:[|]    ⇒    2
MC new:[|] set:[x=1 y=2|] double:[|] gety:[|]    ⇒    2
```

There are still some difficulties with modelling classes in our object-based model. The dilemma is that normal message sending requires objects with an encapsulated self (e.g. PC and MC), while inheritance on objects requires objects with a non-encapsulated self (e.g. POINT+MODIFIER) in order to be able to ensure late binding of self.

5. Related research

In most formal approaches to OO, objects are modelled as records (Cardelli, 1988), (Cardelli et al., 1989), (Cook, 1989), (Dami, 1994), and (Wegner et al., 1988). In OPUS objects are more general since they are composed of a public and a private part, which are both records, or can even be objects themselves. This is an important advantage of our calculus over the more primitive approaches.

Most of the currently available object-oriented models (Castagna et al., 1992), (Dami, 1994), (Hofmann et al., 1993), (Pierce et al., 1994) are based on some extension or variant of lambda-calculus. OPUS on the other hand is not based on lambda-calculus, because we feel that it is necessary to stay closer to the object-oriented paradigm. Indeed, many of the proposed models such as (Hofmann et al., 1993), (Pierce et al., 1994), and (Dami, 1994) seem to have some problems because they are too functional. Apart from objects, functions are first class entities as well, and apart from message sending, function application is also a control structure. Therefore these models are not homogeneous.

According to (Steyaert, 1994), atomic message sending means that the syntax of message sending is always the same and that it is not composed out of more elementary building stones. Most models based on lambda-calculus with records do not have atomic message sending, since method selection and method application are considered distinct operations[5]. In OPUS on the contrary message sending is an atomic operation, since reduction rule 2 shows that method selection and method application are performed simultaneously.

For reasons advocated by (Canning et al., 1989) and (Steyaert, 1994), OPUS objects have explicit interfaces, i.e. an object's interface is determined totally by the object's definition: the object should always respond to the same messages, independent of the context in which it is used. Explicit interfaces are important in realising data abstraction, data encapsulation and separate compilation. They have many uses which bear on quality and productivity in object-oriented software development. These include compatibility checking, system design and documentation, and software reuse.

One of the calculi that is closest (in thought, if not in form) to ours is Dami's λN-calculus (Dami, 1994). Many examples expressible in λN are expressible in OPUS and vice versa. We even think that it is possible to define our calculus on top of λN. However, we do feel that λN-calculus is too low-level as a model for expressing and investigating object-oriented concepts.

Another calculus that seems close to ours is the one proposed by (Abadi et al., 1994). Just like OPUS, it is not based on lambda-calculus, although it subsumes lambda-calculus. But as opposed

---

[5] This also compromises object-based encapsulation, because it allows a method to be selected and temporarily stored somewhere, and later on this method can be retrieved and applied in a totally different context, gaining access to the object's encapsulated part without passing through its interface.

to OPUS, it contains a notion of recursion and self-reference in the basic syntax. There seem to be a lot of similarities between both calculi, although a more thorough comparison remains to be done.

6. Conclusions and future work

In this paper, we proposed an object-oriented programming calculus with a very simple syntax and only three reduction rules. Nevertheless we believe it can model all essential features of object-orientedness. We have shown that it is not necessary to include notions like recursion, numerals, inheritance and classes in the basic syntax, because they can be modelled straightforwardly using the basic syntactic constructs: objects, encapsulation, message sending and incremental modification. In a similar way state is not essential, because it can be modelled using constant methods and an incremental modification operator. Nevertheless it could be useful to find out how difficult it is to directly include state into our basic syntax and reduction rules, because this will strongly simplify the examples. However, it seems to be a non-trivial problem.

A problem still present in our calculus is that argument passing compromises object-based encapsulation to a certain extent. We believe however that these difficulties can be resolved in a reasonably straightforward way by providing a higher-level syntax. There are some problems with inheritance as well, due to the implicit interaction of encapsulation and inheritance. For example, in the approach presented in this paper, we were only able to model a form of encapsulated inheritance. Sometimes however non-encapsulated inheritance could also be useful. To solve this, one could uncouple the encapsulation mechanism from the inheritance mechanism by making the encapsulation operator explicit.

Another disadvantage of our calculus is that object-identity cannot be modeled with it because object identity is only meaningful when several distinct objects live together in the same space. This is clearly not the case in OPUS, since our calculus can only reduce one object (possibly containing different nested subobjects) at a time.

In the future we plan to show that OPUS subsumes lambda-calculus, thus proving its computational completeness. We have strong convictions that our calculus is computationally complete, because numerals can be modelled in it without any problems. It is also necessary to prove the consistency of OPUS, by means of a property similar to the Church-Rosser theorem for lambda-calculus. Showing the soundness and completeness of OPUS might be worthwhile too. OPUS might be extended to incorporate typing rules as well, in analogy with the extension of lambda-calculus to typed lambda-calculus.

7. Acknowledgements

We wish to express our gratitude to Niels Boyen and Wolfgang De Meuter for the heavy discussions, interesting suggestions and numerous remarks, and to the whole AGORA-group for their help and support. We would also like to thank our promoter Theo D'hondt and several anonymous referees for their comments.

8. References

(Abadi et al., 1994) M. Abadi and L. Cardelli. *A Theory of Primitive Objects: Untyped and First-order Systems*. Theoretical Aspects of Computing Software '94 Proceedings, Springer-Verlag, 1994

(Bracha et al., 1990) G. Bracha and W. Cook. *Mixin-based Inheritance*. Joint OOPSLA/ECOOP '90 Conference Proceedings, pp. 303-311, ACM Press, 1990

(Canning et al., 1989) P. Canning, W. Cook, W. Hill and W. Olthoff. *Interfaces for Strongly-Typed Object-Oriented Programming*. OOPSLA '89 Conference Proceedings, pp. 457-467, ACM Press, 1989

(Cardelli, 1988) L. Cardelli. *A semantics of multiple inheritance*. Information and Computation 76, pp. 138-164, Academic Press, 1988

(Cardelli et al., 1989) L. Cardelli and J. Mitchell. *Operations on Records*. Proceedings on Mathematical Foundations of Programming Semantics, LNCS 442, Springer-Verlag, 1989

(Castagna et al., 1992) G. Castagna, G. Ghelli and G. Longo. *A Calculus for Overloaded Functions with Subtyping*. LISP and Functional Programming '92 Conference Proceedings, pp. 182-192, ACM Press, 1992

(Cook, 1989) W. Cook. *A Denotational Semantics of Inheritance*. Ph.D.-Thesis, Brown University, 1989

(Cook et al., 1989) W. Cook and J. Palsberg. *A Denotational Semantics of Inheritance and its Correctness*. OOPSLA '89 Conference Proceedings, pp. 433-444, ACM Press, 1989.

(Dami, 1994) L. Dami. *Software Composition: Towards an Integration of Functional and Object-Oriented Approaches*. Ph.D.-Thesis, University of Geneva, 1994

(de Bruijn, 1972) N. de Bruijn. *Lambda-Calculus with Nameless Dummies, a Tool for Automatic Formula Manipulation*. Indag. Mat. 34, pp. 381-392, 1972

(Hofmann et al., 1993) M. Hofmann and B. Pierce. *A Unifying Type-Theoretic Framework for Objects*. Journal of Functional Programming 1, Cambridge University Press, 1993

(Milner, 1991) R. Milner. *The Poliadic π-calculus: A tutorial*. Technical Report ECS-LFCS-91-180, University of Edinburgh, 1991

(Nierstrasz, 1992) O. Nierstrasz. *Towards an Object Calculus*. ECOOP Workshop on Object-Based Concurrent Computing, LNCS 612, Springer-Verlag, 1992

(Pierce et al., 1994) B. Pierce and D. Turner. *Simple Type-Theoretic Foundations for Object-Oriented Programming*. Journal of Functional Programming, 1994

(Steyaert, 1994) P. Steyaert. *Open Design of Object-Oriented Languages, a Foundation for Specialisable Reflective Language Frameworks*. Ph.D.-Thesis, Vrije Universiteit Brussel, 1994

(Steyaert et al., 1993) P. Steyaert, W. Codenie, T. D'Hondt, K. De Hondt, C. Lucas and M. Van Limbergen. *Nested Mixin-Methods in Agora*. ECOOP '93 Conference Proceedings, pp. 197-219, Springer-Verlag, 1993

(Snyder, 1987) A. Snyder. *Inheritance and the Development of Encapsulated Software Components*. Research Directions in Object-Oriented Programming, MIT Press, 1987

(Wegner et al., 1988) P. Wegner and S. Zdonik. *Inheritance as an Incremental Modification Mechanism, or What Like is and Isn't Like*. ECOOP '88 Conference Proceedings, pp. 55-77, Springer-Verlag, 1988

MON: An Object Relationship Model Incorporating Roles, Classification, Publicity and Assertions

Glenn Maughan & Bohdan Durnota

Object Technology Group
Department of Software Development
Monash University, Caulfield Campus
PO Box 197, Caulfield East
Australia 3145

email: glennm@insect.sd.monash.edu.au
bdurnota@monash.edu.au
phone: 61-3-903 2660
fax: 61-3-903 2745

Abstract

This paper describes the current status of an object modelling notation that incorporates expressive, orthogonal assertions and different categories of relationships between objects.

The trichotomy of assertions (preconditions, postconditions and invariants) are now applicable to almost all system components. This paper describes examples of using assertions on relationships and classes.

The notation, called Monash Object Notation (MON), can be used to specify systems at differing levels of detail and provides the expressive power to specify temporal, creation, destruction and persistency constraints.

Keywords: object-orientation, visual notation, object notation

1 Introduction

Object-oriented programming is essentially programming by abstraction. An object-oriented programmer aims to build solutions to problems by building reusable abstract data types.

Current object-oriented modelling notations such as the Object Modelling Technique (OMT) (Rumbaugh, Blaha, Premerlani, and Lorensen 1991) and the Business Object Model (BON) (Nerson 1992), attempt to provide a notation for designing and specifying abstract data types. However, they fall short when trying to specify the semantics of data types.

The basic components of an abstract data type are: types, functions, preconditions and axioms (Meyer 1988). The components in an abstract data type express different properties:

types The types component lists the types of the abstract data type. For example, STACK[X] or SAVINGS_ACCOUNT

functions The functions are the services available on instances of the type. Possible functions for a STACK may be *push*, *pop* and *empty*. The signature of the function is given along with its name.

preconditions Preconditions express the requirements on the use of any of the functions. Preconditions express semantic properties of the abstract data type.

axioms The axioms express further semantic properties of the abstract date type.

A related issue is that of contract programming. To design and build correct and robust systems, the relationships between classes (and other system components) needs to be specified also. Meyer (1988) defines a contract to be a relationship between two classes; and the contract being the properties specified by the preconditions and postconditions of a routine. A class using a routine in another class is bound to abide by the preconditions of the routine. The class supplying the routine is also bound to satisfy the postconditions of the routine.

Specifying contracts such as these can help in building *correct* software. The BON notation (and extensions of the OMT notation) provide ways of specifying pre and postconditions on routines. Therefore these modelling notations allow contracts to be specified between classes.

To extend the expressiveness and power of object modelling, contracts can become orthogonal in nature. i.e., contracts can be specified not only between routines in classes, but between all components of a system, including the classes themselves and the relationships between classes.

This is exactly what the Monash Object Notation (MON) does. Preconditions and postconditions can be given to all components of a system. For example, a class itself (not just the routines in it) can have preconditions. One such use it the ability to specify how instances of a class are to be created. It may also have postconditions that specify how instances are to be destroyed. An association between classes may have pre and postconditions that specify special constraints on when the association comes into existence and when it may be removed. These uses of pre and postconditions gives a way to state the persistence of an association or class.

The MON notation also extends the language for specifying assertions. i.e., preconditions, postcondition and invariant boolean expressions. The language now incorporates some of the expressiveness of Object-Z (Duke, King, Rose, Smith 1991).

The body of this paper describes the new notation in detail. Section 4 details the notation with examples. This discussion outlines the different notations for all components in a system. A *non-trivial* example is then specified using the MON notation in section 5. Finally, we conclude with a discussion on the usefulness of the notation and further work.

2 Motivation

The development of the MON notation has come about because of its potential use in two projects at Monash University.

The first project is OZ-CASE. OZ-CASE is a project aimed at developing a visual CASE tool utilising formal specifications. The MON notation (and its underlying language) form the front-end language for OZ-CASE. Systems developed in OZ-CASE will be specified interactively using the MON notation.

The second project involves the re-engineering of object-oriented software through formal specifications. MON, in this project, forms the intermediate language for translation. The project is currently working on reverse-engineering Eiffel (Meyer 1992) to the MON language.

3 Related Work

The idea of combining formal specification languages with a graphical notation is not new. Similar work has been developed that combines the two types of notation effectively.

One such project involves the integration of visual notations with VDM (Dick and Loubersac 1991; Dick and Loubersac 1993). They developed a graphical notation that could be integrated with a formal specification language, such as the Vienna Development Method (VDM) (Jones 1990), thus easing the understanding for non-mathematitions.

The diagrams utilised are:

entity-structure diagrams Extended entity-relationship diagrams, that depict VDM specifications at two levels: decomposition into modules, and composite type definitions, also

operation-state diagrams Used to visualise the operations in VDM by stating pre- and post-conditions that constrain the possible effects of the operation.

It was concluded from this research that translating to and from VDM into entity-structure diagrams was a reasonably simple process. However, translation to and from VDM into operation-state diagrams was more complicated and required a specific style of VDM to be used.

Other related work includes the Clyder project developed under the ESPRIT project ICARUS (P2537) (Hagelstein, Roelants, and Wodon 1993). This project involved the development of a general-purpose formal requirements language that was an extension of the language Glider. One of the goals of this project was to incorporate a graphical notation to represent the structure of an application.

They found that there is no incompatibility between graphical notations and formal notations. Also the problem of mastering the complexity of large specifications was eased through the use of the graphical notation. It provided a means to display the hierarchies of software components and their interfaces.

Also the POLAR project (van den Bos, Feijs, and Van Ommering 1989) utilises a graphical notation on top of another formal specification language. This project aimed to find a solution to the problem of managing complexity. Their solution was the integration of a pictoral representation of the modular structure of possibly complex software system. POLAR is a graphical representation of the formal specification language COLD (Jonkers 1989).

4 The Graphical Notation

The MON graphical notation builds upon OMT and adds some features from the BON and Object-Z.

MON can be used in varying levels of detail, from a fully graphical notation to a fully linear notation. The different levels of detail provide the necessary power to create evolving analysis and design models using the same notation. Examples in this paper will show uses of the graphical form. All components in the graphical form have equivalent linear forms. The linear model is based loosely on Object-Z.

A case study is presented in section 5. This example specifies the loading and utilisation of transport vehicles.

4.1 The Assertion Language

In an object-oriented language classes are used to build abstract data type implementations. An abstract data type will generally have a number of operations that can be performed. Each of the operations performs some action. When specifying a system it is important to know what the formal properties of system components are. Assertions can be used as a mechanism for expressing these properties.

Assertions form a large part of specifying systems in formal specification languages such as Z (Diller 1991) and Object-Z (Duke et al. 1991). They are also appearing as part of the language definition in a number of programming languages such as Eiffel (Meyer 1992) and Sather (Omohundro 1993). However, they are generally restricted to class operations. The MON notation extends assertions so that they are orthogonal over all possible system components. Section 4.2 describes visibility and publicity of system components.

In current object modelling notations (and some object-oriented languages) assertions are boolean expressions that can appear in a number of forms:

1. as routine **preconditions** whereby they express the properties that must be satisfied before a routine will perform its specified action(s).

2. as routine **postconditions** whereby they express the properties that the routine will ensure upon completion and

3. as a **class invariant** that must be satisfied by every instance of the class at all times.

Assertions in the above forms can be used to specify both structural and behavioural constraints on an object. Structural constraints limit the way objects associate with each other while behavioural constraints limit the way object state changes may occur (Odell 1993).

The MON notation allows further assertion forms such as the following:

Class pre and postconditions, possibly specifying the constraints on the creation and destruction of objects.

Pre and postconditions on relationships A relationship in MON includes, inheritance, associations, aggregations, classification and roles., possibly specifying the dynamic nature of relationships between classes.

Invariants on relationships, possibly specifying the constraints on the relationship's existence.

Expressing assertions in MON is performed by writing Z-like expressions. A notation similar to the one used in BON has been adopted.

The basic Z formalisms include: logical symbols, terms, atomic statements and formulas. Some examples of assertions include:

$a < x$
$input = "Hello"$
$\forall x: N \bullet x \times x$

The logical symbols available in MON include: parenthesis, (typed) variables, connectives ($\neg$, $\wedge$, $\vee$, $\Rightarrow$ and $\Leftrightarrow$), quantifiers ($\forall$, $\exists$ and $\exists_1$) and the objects of an *environment*. The environment of an assertion is the set of all objects reachable either directly or indirectly.

The terms in an assertion can include all variables, objects in the closed environment and a sequence of object calls formed by passing in appropriately typed objects or variables within the closed environment. A further restriction on environments is visibility. A system component can restrict the *visibility* of its components to certain other components.

Atomic formulas can then be formed by grouping terms with logical symbols. For example, $t_1 = t_2$ is an atomic formula where t_1 and t_2 are terms. If P is a boolean-valued operation of an object o in the closed environment and with input signature $T_1 \times ... \times T_N$ and $t_1,...,t_N$ are terms with appropriate signatures respectively then $o.P(t_1,...,t_N)$ is an atomic formula.

Assertions can then be formed using atomic formulas. An assertion must have no free occurrences of variables. i.e., all variables must be bound to some object in the closed environment.

The side-effect of assertions is restricted. Preconditions and invariants can not be *mutable*. i.e., they can not change the values of any variables within their environment. Postconditions on the other hand may be mutable. Postconditions often specify how something has changed. This may take the form of changing the values of variables within the environment.

In Z there are two conventions concerning variable names:

1. Un-dashed names are used to denote the values of the state variables before an operation---the *start state*.

2. Dashed names are used to denote the values of state variables after an operation---the *ending state*.

Un-dashed names can be used in all assertions. Dashed names can only be used in postconditions. In a postcondition it is often necessary to refer to the values of both the before and after state of variables. This is generally because assertions are pure logic statements and assignment is not permitted. For example, the variable names *size* and *size'* refer to both the before and after states, respectively, of a variable called *size*. To assert a condition that the value of *size* will not change we could write:

$size' = size$

There is no exception handling built into the MON notation. Exceptions are quite often raised when assertions are not satisfied. When a system is correctly specified then exceptions, in the general sense, should not occur. MON does not include any specific exception handling notation as most exceptions can be specified as assertions.

4.1.1 Invariants

An invariant can be added to any system component. The invariants appear in a box with double edges on both sides. The following diagram specifies a possible invariant for class *Compartment* from the transport example.

$capacity > 0$

$volume \geq 0$

$volume \leq capacity$

This specifies that a particular *Compartment* has to satisfy the above restrictions at all times. The *capacity* has to remain above *0*, *volume* must be equal to or above *0* and the *volume* must be less than or equal to the *capacity*. If any of these invariants do not hold then the integrity of the class instances may have been compromised.

The above invariant uses a simple *infix* notation to specify assertions. This is permitted for the base class operations.

The invariants themselves are stated logically as in Object-Z. The variables mentioned in the invariants can only be those publicly defined in the current environment (see section 4.1).

4.2 Publicity

One often refers to the publicity of features within a class. This refers to the avalability of that feature to particular classes and the collective publicity of all features within a class is the class's public interface (Meyer 1988).

Therefore objects can only be manipulated through their interface.

In MON, all entities can have an associated publicity—not only objects, attributes and operations, but also associations.

A using object can either:

1. not see a particular feature

2. can both see and evaluate a feature

We use two icons to represent this information: an open eye
($\prec$) for visible and a closed eye ($\varnothing$) for not visible.

Both symbols can be used interchangeably and concurrently. A list of components that can see, or can not see, another component are listed within braces following the eye symbol. For example:

$$component\_name \prec \{component_1, \ldots, component_2\}$$

If a class is used in the visibility list it implies the specified class and all of its descendants.

Allowing visibility to apply to all system components add a small amount of overhead to specifying systems. *All* system components have to be given a unique name. The name may be appended by a short word or letter describing the type of component. For example, a relationship between classes may be named: *companiesA* if it is an association (*A*), or *companiesAgg* for an aggregation (*Agg*).

When specifying visibility, the notation with the smallest list of classes would normally be used. If an attribute is to be visible to almost all classes and not visible to a few, then the not visible symbol and list should be used.

There are also shorthand notations for specifying that a feature is visible to all classes or not visible to all classes. Using the open eye with no list implies visibility to all components and using the closed eye with no list implies visible to no components.

4.3 Classes

Classes are represented by boxes, with the class name appearing as an attached label at the top of the box. Apart from the class name, the class box is subdivided by a line into a number of sections. In the full linear model, there will be up to five sections for *name*, *inheritance*, *state*, *operations* and *class invariants*.

className
inheritance
state
operations
classInvariant

Each of these boxes will be described in detail in the following sections.

4.3.1 Class Parameters

Classes may be parameterized by a type. This includes constants, which are interpreted as singleton sets. Unless the parameter is completely generic, it must be typed. For example, Stack[X] is a stack over any elements of the generic type X. If we wished to define the class modular numbers with base 4 (0,1,2,3), we could specify Mod[$4:N_1$].

Constrained types allow the type of generic parameters to be restricted to a certain class hierarchy. For example, the following Eiffel class restricts the type of the generic parameter X to be of type HASHABLE or any of HASHABLE's descendants.

class HASH_TABLE[X->HASHABLE]
...
end; -- class HASH_TABLE

The restriction type may also be generic. The notation for constrained generics in MON is the same as in Eiffel. The class above would appear as:

HASH_TABLE [X $\rightarrow$ HASHABLE]

4.3.2 Classes and Types

We do not distinguish between types and classes. All classes are regarded as types, and all types are classes. Thus, what would be regarded as *basic types* such as the integers (Z) are also classes. This of course, means that these base types must follow the conventions for describing classes.

4.3.3 Base Classes

There are some basic constructors for creating

new types (classes) from existing ones. These include the different collection classes:

Power set   Set[X]
Bags   Bag[X]
Sequences   Seq[X[

where X is some type.

In MON all these constructors correspond to classes in their own right whilst in Z they would correspond to the type constructors P, bag and seq respectively.

4.3.4 Objects and Object Identity

Duke and Rose (1992) discuss the importance of object identity. The main points they identify include:

• The persistent identity of an object is of fundamental importance within object-oriented systems.

• The identity of an object uniquely identifies each object in a system.

• While the state of an object may change over time its identity will not change.

The current instance of a class can be identified by the reserved word *self*. The reference to the current instance can be used in all assertions. For example, the assertion that a parameter passed to an operation can not be equivalent to the current instance of the surrounding class would be written as:

$$self \neq parameter\_name$$

This would ensure that the value of is not equal to the value of .

The current instance can also appear as an actual parameter to operations.

The MON notation also allows the name of the system component to be used to designate all potential objects (instantiations) of the class. This is in the tradition of interpreting types in Z as set types. A calligraphic style is used to designate all current instances of a class. For example, all instances of class *A* would be written as A.

4.3.5 Object Creation and Destruction

In many object-oriented systems the method for creating and destroying objects can differ. Also there can be more than one way of creating a particular object.

In MON object creation is specified in class preconditions. A number of preconditions can be given to represent different initialisations. Object destruction may optionally be specified using class postconditions.

4.3.6 Attributes

Attributes encode the state of an object. They have a name and a type.

For each state variable in a class, an entry is made in the state box. The entry lists the name of the variable and its set type.

MON is not prescriptive as to what type of classes can be the types of attributes. One extreme modelling style is that:

• attributes have only base types such as N, Z, R and B, representing natural numbers, integers, real numbers, and booleans.

• more complicated objects are given as relationships between classes. (See section 4.4).

The class may have a number of state variables. The state box for a possible implementation may appear like figure 1.

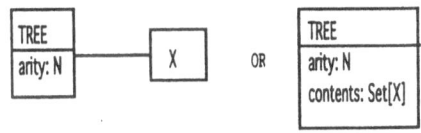

Figure 1. Attributes as associations and components

For the graphical notation the *basic* attribute *arity* is listed in the state box of the class. The second attribute has been modelled as an association constraint with the class X. The attribute *arity* could also have been modelled as an association. However, it is common to model basic class attributes within the state box. Section 4.4.2 discusses associations further.

At the other extreme, the base class attribute

arity is listed inside the class box and the attribute *contents* declared as a set of objects of type X.

However, these two styles do not have the same meaning. By modelling as an association we are allowing the possibility of class TREE being able to use the association. In the alternative style we have committed the association to be used only by TREE. Figure 2 expresses the same intent in the second style.

TREE	SET
arity: N	contents: X

Figure 2. Attributes as associations

MON allows mathematical/special symbols to appear in operation names. This can convey the traditional mathematical intent of the operation. For example, $\rightarrow$, and $\mapsto$.

4.3.7 Operations

Operations change the state of an object upon certain inputs, and produce certain outputs.

The signature of an operation names the input and output variables, together with their types in an Eiffel-like manner:

$$opName(in_1:Type_1,...,in_k:Type_k):$$

$$(out_1;Type_1,...,out_k:Type_k)$$

Operations differ from state in that they can have parameters and return values. Operations are listed with: the operation name, a parameter list within parenthesis, and the return value list within parenthesis. Operations *first_child*, *add_child* and from class may appear like the following operation box:

first_child: X
add_child (new_child: X)
append (tree: TREE): (new_tree: TREE, success: B)

Operation *first_child* takes no parameters and returns a value of type. In this case, if only one return result is listed, and has not been named, it can be referred to in assertions using the reserved word *Result* (as in Eiffel). Multiple return values can be listed. Operation *append* takes one parameter and returns two values: *new_tree* and *success*.

Similarly, operation *add_child* takes one parameter called *new_child* of some type X and

returns no values. However, it may change the state of the receiver object or itself.

Short hand forms of the operation notation also exist. An operation with no parameters can omit the parameter list (including the parenthesis). Also an operation with no return results can omit the result value list (including parenthesis). And finally, if an operation has only a return result it can be listed with just the operation name, a colon and the return type.

For example, the following operations are all valid in the MON notation:

$$add(obj_1,obj_2:X)$$

$$remove(obj_1:X)$$

$$item:X$$

$$items:(item_1,item_2:X)$$

The first example used an abbreviated form of parameter listing. If the parameters are of the same type, in this case X, then they can be listed in a comma separated list followed by the type. The order of the parameters does not effect the meaning. They are referred to by name only.

When multiple return values are listed, it is sometimes necessary to refer to one particular value in the list. Explicitly referencing particular return values can be performed using a similar notation to that used in mathematics. Referencing the return value *success* in operation *append* could be written as:

$$append \uparrow success$$

i.e., the *success* output variable of *append*. One could have used the common dot notation for this purpose, such as, *append.success*. However, this has the connotation of a function call in the evaluation of the expression and was replaced with the $\uparrow$ (filter) notation.

4.3.8 Meaning of Operations

The meaning of an operation is given by its preconditions and postconditions.

Preconditions for an operation are specified logically using Z-like syntax (see section 4.1). The variables mentioned in a precondition can be state variables or input variables.

Postconditions can reference state, input and output variables.

Preconditions are enclosed in a left hand sided box, with double edges. Postconditions are enclosed in a right hand sided box, with double edges.

In a graphic, the operation, precondition and postcondition are usually vertically aligned in that order. Postconditions are listed in a left sided box. The following diagram displays an operation called from a possible class . (It is assumed that *hour*, *minute* and *second* are declared as part of the state in class).

setTime(h,m,s: N)

```
h >= 0
h <= 23
m >= 0
m <= 59
s >= 0
s <= 59
```

```
hour = h
minute = m
second = s
```

For *setTime* to be valid all conditions in the precondition must be satisfied. At the end of processing all conditions in the postcondition must be satisfied.

Each of the assertions in pre and postconditions form a conjunction. i.e., the postcondition of setTime above, logically forms: $(hour = h \wedge minute = m \wedge second = s)$.

4.4   Relationships

A relationship models communication (either directly or indirectly) between two or more system components (Meyer 1988; Rumbaugh, etal 1991). They can also be seen as a named family of tuples from one particular class to another (de Champeaux, Lea and Faure 1993). Relationships in MON include inheritance, associations, aggregations, classifications and roles.

Each relationship is modelled by identifying the parties involved. Each *end* or *terminal* of the relationship will refer to a party. As classes have a unique identity, so do relationships. Each relationship is given a name.

Relationships can have preconditions, postconditions and invariants to denote creation, destruction and constraints on the component.

All relationships, except for inheritance, may be recursive in nature. i.e., the terminals in a relationship may refer to the same object.

At each end of the line a *multiplicity* can be given for how many instances of the respective object are in the relationship. If no multiplicity is explicitly given, it is taken to be one. The multiplicity annotation is given as a set of single values or a range in , or as a disjunction of these.

For example:

- > 4
- $2..6$
- $1 \vee 4 \vee 6..8$
- $\geq 10 \leq 15$

A relationship between system components can also be modelled mathematically. An association between classes A and B could be written as $A \Leftrightarrow B$. The domain and range of a relation can also be realised using the keywords dom and ran. This depends on the direction of traversal of the relation. From one side the range will be the set of objects on the opposite side.

4.4.1 Inheritance

Inheritance is a special relationship between *superclasses* (also called parent classes) and *subclasses* (also called child classes). *Single Inheritance* and *Multiple inheritance* is also supported by MON. A class can multiply inherit from a number of other classes. An issue that has to be handled is *shared inheritance*. when a class inherits from another class more than once. For example, figure 3 shows that class A is multiply inherited from both class B and class C.

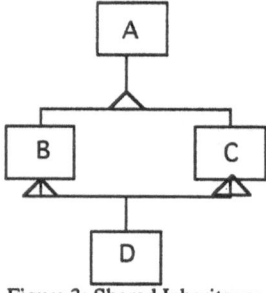

Figure 3: Shared Inheritance

The state and operations of superclasses are recursively inherited by a subclass. Therefore, a class's immediate environment contains itself and all of its superclasses recursively.

Superclass features can be overridden. given a new implementation. If a feature in a subclass has the same name as a feature in a superclass, then the subclass feature overrides the superclass feature.

A box drawn underneath the name of the class is the inheritance box. The inheritance box lists any direct parents of the class. In the graphical notation the inheritance subclass and superclass are linked by an inheritance line with a triangle directed towards the superclass. The linear notation includes the parents in a parent box (located under the class name box). Each parent class name can be decorated with a rename clause that identifies any renaming of state or operations from the parent. This feature is necessary in any language that provides multiple inheritance to resolve any name classes. It also provides for the customisation of a class to better suit its intended interface (Meyer 1988). The rename clause can appear on the inheritance link or after the parent name in the parent box.

For example, a programmer implementing a TREE class may inherit from another class LINKED_LIST to gain some existing functionality. However, the LINKED_LIST class may have features such as *first_element* , and *number_elements*, that do not convey the intended meaning when used in the context of a TREE. Renaming adds to the intended understanding of inherited state or operations.

In MON, the rename clause is similar to renaming in Z. It lists all features that will have new names in the current class. For the graphical notation each inheritance link can have an optional rename clause added. For the linear model, the rename clause is listed after

the name of the parent in the inheritance box.

The rename for TREE may look like figure 4.

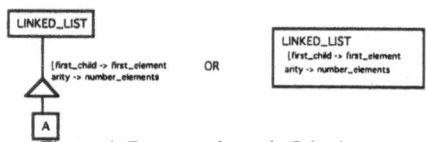

Figure 4: Rename clause in Inheritance

The forward left arrow is read as to. So for the first rename pair, *first_element* is renamed to *first_child*.

An inheritance invariant can be added to the relationship. The invariant may be used for dynamic class creation or other constraints on the inheritance relationship.

4.4.2 Associations

Associations designate relationships between classes, apart from those relationships pertaining to inheritance, aggregation or roles. They are represented as lines between classes.

Associations can also be seen as mappings (or relations) in the mathematical sense. For example, an association between class A and B could be written mathematically as: $A \leftrightarrow B$. If the association is named, as it generally would be, it may appear as: $relationName: A \leftrightarrow B$.

Figure 5 could represent the relationship between two classes, A and B.

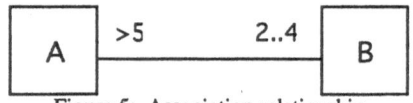

Figure 5: Association relationship

This diagram indicates that class A has an association with 2, 3 or 4 instances of class B. While class B is associated with at least 6 instances of class A. If an association constraint is omitted it is assumed to be 1.

This simple multiplicity annotation can be broadened to that of *association invariants*.

Odell (1993) describes an extended notation for association constraints. He discusses the use of similar techniques as above (with a different style) and also the use of constraints on mappings. For example, the use of describes mappings without duplicates, describes mappings where duplicate objects are allowed.

The MON notation also provides for this type of extended constraint, although in a more formal manner.

Generically defined associations can be defined to provide annotations for associations. For example, the constraint that an association must be *reflexive* can be defined as follows:

First the constraint is modelled as a generic relationship between two arbitrary classes as in 6.

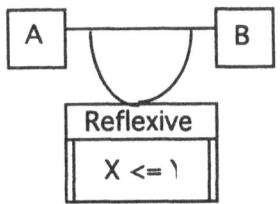

Figure 6: Generic association class definition

The constraint can then be used in any association invariants. An association invariant appears in a double sided box next to the association line. For example, the above association between class A and B could be written as in figure 7.

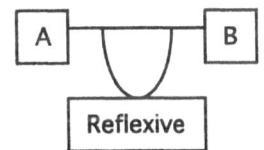

Figure 7: Utilising the generic Reflexive definition

Typical generic definitions can be found in the base class library in section 4.3.3. Examples include *Bag, Set, Sequence, TotalFunction* and *PartialFunction*.

Multiplicity and invariants can be specified separately. When multiplicity is specified within association invariants a notation for finding the number of instances of a particular class is useful. MON uses a bold (as in Greek) class name to refer to all instances of that class.

For example, **A** would refer to all instances of class A, and #**A** is the cardinality of instances of class A. So specifying that the number of instances (or multiplicity) of class A has to be greater than 4, can be written as: #**A** > 4.

Associations provide a mechanism for one class to view another class. To be able to talk about *viewed classes*, the *viewer class* needs a way to refer to these viewed classes. View names can be given at each end of the association. If no view name is given it is taken to be the name of the class itself. But views may be too public -- we may not wish all the information present in a viewed class to be available to a viewer class. The mechanism of publicity is provided here as described elsewhere.

Associations may have classes, called association classes, attached to the association. These classes are drawn with a hemisphere attached to the association. Their operations can refer to the publicly available portions of each end of the association. When association classes are present, multiplicities can be places in the class invariant box.

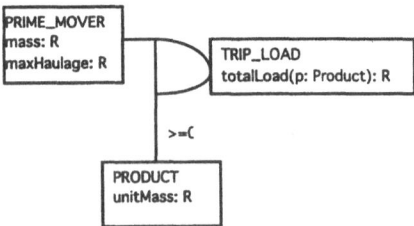

Figure 8: Association Link

Figure 8 specifies the association between and from the transport example in section 5. The association link is class TRIP_LOAD that keeps track of the current load for a certain product.

4.4.3 Aggregations

Aggregations are used to designate that certain objects are a *part* of another object. This relationship is represented as a line from the *whole class* to the *part class*, with a diamond drawn at the end of the line at the whole class.

Figure 9: Aggregation relationship

Figure 9 above shows the aggregation relationship between TANKER and COMPARTMENT. Each TANKER contains one or more COMPARTMENT.

Multiplicities are designated in the same fashion as described for associations, and are annotated at the part class end of the relationship. As for associations, we can also have *aggregation invariants*.

As with associations, aggregations can also have an *aggregation class* attached to them in the same way as association classes are attached to associations. When the aggregation class has its own class invariant the invariant becomes the aggregation invariant (or part thereof). Figure 10 shows a possible aggregation class.

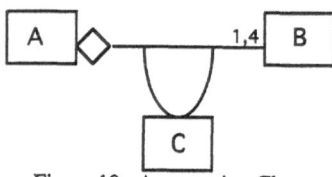

Figure 10: Aggregation Class

4.4.4 Classification

Objects (classes) may be classified in different ways. For example, a class Person may be classified as *Male* or *Female*. We call the classes Male and Female classifications. They are also classes, inheriting from Person. Person is called the *classified class*. An important property of a classification is that if it is active, then one and only one of the classifiers is chosen. More than one classification can be present for a class.

The classifiers in a classification are enclosed in a box, with a line drawn from the classified class to the box.

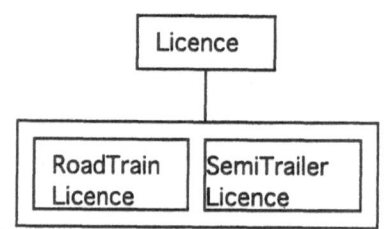

Figure 11: Classification relationship

Figure 11 shows the classification of a License. The Licence may be either a RoadTrainLicence or a SemiTrailorLicence. It must be one and only one of the choices at any one point in time.

A classification name, if needed, is annotated on the end of the line at the classified class. This is called a *classifier*, which is an operation of the classified class that determines the current classification, if any.

Classifications may or may not be *active* in certain circumstances. A classification may be committed to a single choice of the classifiers or it may be none of the choices. This is determined by the pre and post conditions attached to the classification relationship.

Consider the male/female example. If there was an attribute sex for Person, then the classifier would take the form:

$$sex = male \Rightarrow self \in Male$$
$$sex = female \Rightarrow self \in Female$$

However, if such an attribute does not exist and there is no classifier, the classification is taken to be implicit.

4.4.5 Roles

Objects can change their behavior at different stages of their life-cycles. If I consider myself as an object, then I am undertaking the role of an Author whilst I am typing this manuscript. Then, when I am finished, my role changes to a Driver when I am going home, and so forth. Sometimes roles can have many features in common. In other cases, the commonality is negligible. It is cumbersome to imbue a particular class with all possible operations and attributes which may be relevant to the many roles an object may need to take on. A better strategy is to encapsulate each *role* as a class, and then show the role relationship with the role-playing (owning) class.

If a class has a number of roles, they are represented as a line drawn from the role-playing class to a circle, and then lines emanating to the *role classes*.

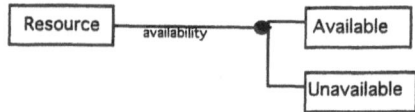

Figure 12: Role relationship

Figure 12 shows the role relationship of a Resource. A Resource may be just a Resource or either an Available-Resource or an Unavailable-Resource.

Just like classifications, roles also inherit from the role-playing class. Taking on a new role is a type of *dynamic functional inheritance*. Many object-oriented languages do not directly support roles. However, they are a useful modelling tool.

The roles in a role relationship are mutually exclusive. i.e., the Resource cannot have both the role of Available and Unavailable at the same time.

A *role determination* specifies the conditions under which roles change. The role relationship can also be annotated with pre and post conditions that further specify how roles are initiated and changed.

A class may also take on multiple, simultaneous roles. For example, a Person may have an *occupation* role of either Author or Driver. The Person may also have a particular *intoxication* of Drunk or Sober. A constraint that the Person cannot be a drunk driver can be specified in a role invariant. The following diagram shows this example:

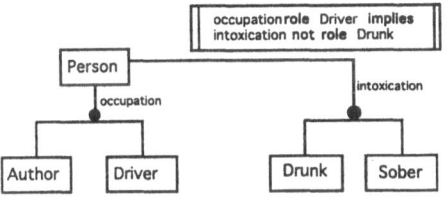

Figure 13: Multiple concurrent roles

5 Transport Loading System Specification

5.1 Introduction

Prime movers (or tractors) are motorized vehicles that haul tankers filled with products. Collectively, prime movers and tankers are called vehicles. There are two types of prime movers: Semi Trailers and Road Trains.

Products can only be loaded into tankers, which consist of a fixed number of compartments. Only one product can be filled into a given compartment.

Drivers can be licenced to drive either of the two prime mover types. A driver cannot drive a prime mover if he/she does not hold a valid licence for that type of vehicle.

Resources include both prime movers and drivers. A resource canbe available or unavailable. A prime mover can only be driven by a driver if both resources are available.

Our aim is to perform an object-oriented analysis and design for this system.

5.2 Object Model

MON has been used to model the system. Figure 14 on page stinkyfig shows the complete model. However, assertions have been omitted and are described after the diagram. The position of assertions can be ascertained by finding the bold numbers relating to the assertion on the model.

5.3 Model Constraints

A number of constraints are applicable to many of the system components in the transport model. These are modelled as invariants. Each of these invariants would normally appear on the model (in the position of the bold numbers). However, the lack of supporting tools for combining graphical models with mathematical assertions is a hindrance.

1. **Class PrimeMover** A prime mover has a current mass (load weight). This is the sum of the mass of all attached to the prime mover. A prime mover also has a maximum amount of haulage that can be carried. This must always be greater than zero. Also the current mass must be less that or equal to the maximum haulage.

$$mass = \sum (t.mass | t : Tankers)$$

$$maxHaulage > 0$$

$$mass \leq maxHaulage$$

2. **Class Tanker** A tanker holds a number of compartments. It has a mass that is the sum of the mass of each of its compartments.

$$mass = \sum (c.mass | t : Compartment)$$

3. **Class Compartment** A compartment can

hold a certain amount of product. This is determined by its capacity. The volume of a compartment is the current amount of product stored in that compartment.

$capacity > 0$

$volume \geq 0$

$volume \leq capacity$

4. **Class Product** A product has a certain unit mass. Obviously the mass is always greater than zero.

$unitMass > 0$

5. **Class Trip** A trip load determines the current total load for a prime mover. The total load for a particular product is the sum of the volume of all compartments in the prime mover.

$totalLoad(p) = \sum(\text{dom } (p.contents \triangleleft p)).volume$

$totalLoad \geq 0$

The totalLoad equation uses *bulk operators*. The operation volume is applied to all elements in the set of compartments. i.e., for the bulk operation $...,....,X$ apply operation to all elements of the set and return a set. The compartments are found by restricting the domain of the relation, given by p.contents, by the product p. The domain of that then gives a set of compartments of which we can apply the operation volume.

6. *Class SemiTrailer* A semi trailer has a different maximum haulage to a prime mover. This is specified in an assertion on the class.

$maxHaulage = 3$

7. **Class RoadTrain** A road train has a different maximum haulage to a prime mover. This is also specified in an assertion on the class.

$maxHaulage = 4$

8. **Aggregation** *Tanker $\leftrightarrow$ PrimeMover* This relationship models the ability of a PrimeMover to have zero or more Tankers. For this aggregation to be valid the tankers must be available.

$t.tankers \bullet t$ role   *Available*

This assertions specifies that for all tankers in the relation the tankers must be in the role of Available. The keyword can be used to check the current role of classes. This assertion also uses a short hand form of universal quantification. The assertion would appear in mathematics as:

$\forall t : Tankers | t \in tankers \bullet t$ role   *Available*

When referencing a relationship it is assumed that you are referring to the opposite side of the relation. For example, tankers is the name of the relation *PrimeMover $\leftrightarrow$ Tanker*. In the assertion above we are referencing the relation from the PrimeMover. This will return the Tankers in the relation.

9. **Association** *PrimeMover $\leftrightarrow$ Driver* This relation models the fact that a prime mover is driven by a particular driver. The invariant on this relationship specifies that the driver must have a valid licence for the vehicle that is being driven. Also both the prime mover and the driver must be available.

$drivenBy$ is $RoadTrain \Leftrightarrow drives.possesses$ is $RoadTrainLicence$
$drivenBy$ is $SemiTrailer \Leftrightarrow drives.possesses$ is $SemiTrailerLicence$
$PrimeMover$ role $Available$
$Driver$ role $Available$

The first assertion in this invariant uses the keyword **is** to identify the type (or class) of a variable. In this case the assertion checks whether the variable deivenBy is of type RoadTrain.

6. Conclusion and Further Work

This paper has discussed a new notation for *specifying* object-oriented systems. The main difference between this notation and existing graphical notations is the expressiveness and orthogonality of assertions.

One of the aims of the notation has been to increase the expressive nature of the diagrams. There are few implicit assumptions in the diagrams. For example, one such implicit assumption is when the multiplicity of a relationship is omitted it is implicitly one. The use of numbers to define multiplicity has also removed some of the symbols used in other notations. We believe that this creates an easier to understand notation without prior knowledge.

The power of orthogonal assertions provides the modelling of temporality and persistence.

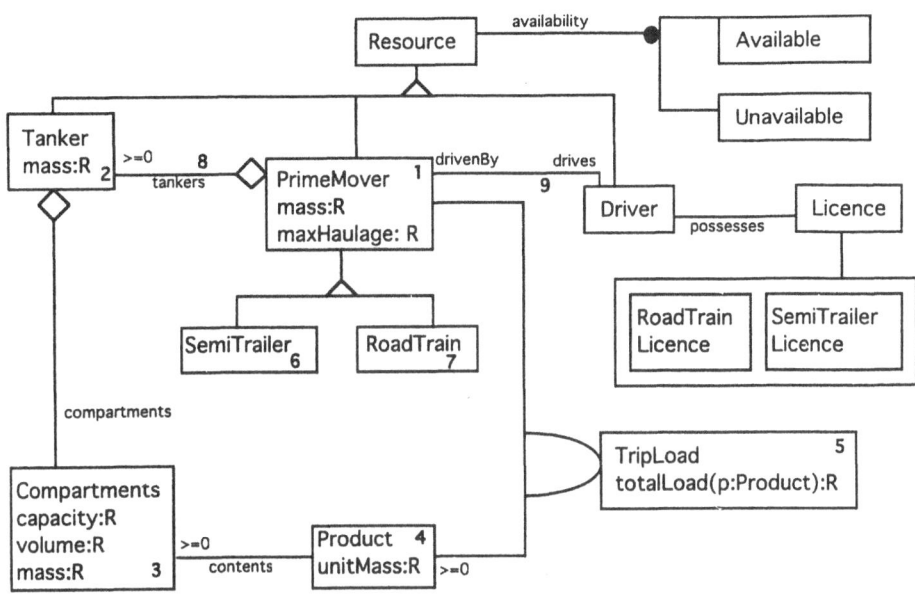

Figure 14: The Transport System Model

Pre and postconditions can specify the existence and lifetime of an object.

A number of additional features of the language have been omitted from this paper because of space limitations. They include:

• **Reflection** The ability to refer to ones self. Similar to the Smalltalk notion of Meta-class and the ability to distinguish between class and instance features.

• **Mutability Ascriptions** Notation for specifying whether an attribute is mutable or not. \ie is the attribute read only or writable? Preconditions and invariants can not perform mutable operations while postconditions can.

• **Usage Definitions** The redefinition of class features through inheritance can be specified.

• **Views and Morphisms** Interpreting (viewing) system components such as, classes, as other system components.

• **Temporality** Notation for specifying how things change in time using temporal logic.

Further development of the graphical notation and the expressiveness of assertions is being investigated in relation to the OZ-CASE project.

Also, an abstract syntax and axiomatic semantics for the notation is being developed. The axiomatic semantics are being specified using Object-Z.

The linear form of MON is also being developed concurrently with the graphical notation. It is based on Object-Z and used much of the notation found there. The linear notation will be the back-end language of OZ-CASE.

The MON notation can be used to *fully* specify a system. However, the amount of detail that can appear on a diagram can be cumbersome. This is where the notation lends itself well to automated tools that can provide interactive levels of detail for models. The introduction of both graphical and mathematical notation presents a problem for many of the current CASE tools. The OZ-CASE project is currently producing a tool that will provide this functionality.

References

de Champeaux, D., D. Lea and P. Faure (1993). Object-Oriented System Development. Addison-Wesley Publishing Company.

Dick, J. and J. Loubersac (1991). Integrating

visual notations with VDM. In Software Engineering Environments (SEE '91), Volume 3, pp. 219-231. Springer-Verlag.

Dick. J. and J. Loubersac (1993). Integrating structured and formal methods: A visual approach to VDM. In I. Sommerville and M. Paul (Eds.), Software Engineering - ESEC '93, pp. 37-59, Springer-Verlag.

Diller, A. (1991). Z: An Introduction to Formal Methods. John Willey & Sons.

Duke, R., P. King, G. Rose and G. Smith (1991, May). The Object-Z specification language. Technical Report 91-1, Software Verification Research Centre, Department of Computer Science, University of Queensland, Australia, Version 1.

Duke, R. and G. Rose (1992, December). Modelling object identity. Technical Report 92-11, University of Queensland, Software Verification Research Centre.

Hagelstein, J., D. Roelants, and P. Wodon (1993). Formal requirements made practical. In I. Somerville and M. Paul (Eds.), Software Engineering - ESEC '93, pp. 127-144. Springer-Verlag.

Jones, C. B. (1990). Systematic Software Development using VDM. Prentice-Hall Int. Second Edition.

Jonkers, H. (1989). An introduction to COLD-K. In M. Wirsing and J. Bergstra (Eds.), Algebraic Methods: Theory, Tools and Applications, pp. 139-205. Springer-Verlag. Lecture notes in Computer Science 394.

Meyer, B. (1988) Object-oriented Software Construction. Prentice-Hall International.

Meyer, B. (1992). Eiffel: The Language. Prentice-Hall Int.

Nerson, J-M. (1992). Extending Eiffel toward O-O analysis and design. In T. Korson, V. Vaishnavi, and B. Meyer (Eds.), Technology of Object-oriented languages and Systems (TOOLS 5), Santa Barbara, pp. 377-392, Prentice-Hall.

Odell, J. J. (1993, October). Analysis and design: Specifying structural constraints. Journal of Object-oriented programming 6(6), 12-16.

Omohundro, S. M. (1993, October). The Sather programming language. Dr. Dobb's Journal 18(11), 42-48.

Rumbaugh J., M. Blaha, W. Premerlani, and W. Lorensen (1991). Object-oriented Modeling and Design. Prentice-Hall Int.

van den Bos, R. L. Fiegs, and R, van Ommering (1989). POLAR: A picture-oriented language for abstract representations. In J. Bergstra and L. Fiegs (Eds.), Algebraic Methods II: Theory, Tools and Applications, pp. 233-247. Springer-Verlag. Lecture Notes in Computer Science 490.

KNOWLEDGEBASES

Objects with Views and Constraints :
from Databases to Knowledge bases

Ana Simonet and Michel Simonet

Laboratoire TIMC-IMAG, Faculté de Médecine de Grenoble
38706 LA TRONCHE CEDEX - FRANCE
e-mail : Michel.Simonet@imag.fr   Fax +33 76-51-86-67

ABSTRACT. *We present an object model which embodies views as a primitive notion. Assertions play a prominent role in defining classes and views in a declarative manner, and in implementation issues, through the partitioning of the object space which is derived from their analysis. Assertions may be interpreted as integrity constraints or production rules according to whether the class of the object is known (databases), or has to be inferred from the known attribute values (knowledge bases).*

KEY WORDS : *Database, Knowledge Base, Object modelling, Views, Integrity Constraints, Consistency, Expert Systems.*

1.   Introduction

The approach presented in this paper is the result of research undertaken in the early eighties into the possible relationship between algebraic data types and databases. In (Simonet, 1984) we proposed the concept of p-type, which proved later to be an object concept in its own right. The p-type concept embodies views as a primitive notion.

Views are organized in a class/subclass hierarchy. However, a hierarchy of views is conceptually distinct from a hierarchy of classes in object programming languages. Starting from a root view called the minimal view, views are built up by adding new attributes and/or specific assertions. The p-type itself is defined as the union of its views (see §2); this differs from the classical approach which would consider it simply as the root class.

An object may be attached to views in two manners : imperatively, by inserting it in a given view at creation time, or by letting the system determine the views it satisfies. In the former case the assertions of the view act as integrity constraints. In the latter, the object is created in the minimal view of the p-type (which is mandatory), and a classification process determines its other valid views, if any. This approach meets a preoccupation recently expressed in (Date et al, 1994) that *"the process of inserting a row can be regarded as a process of inserting that row into the database (rather than into some specific table)..."*.

The problem of determining the actual views of a given instance is very similar to that of classifying an object in a knowledge base. The aim of classification is to find the class of an object from the values of its known attributes (Clancey, 1985) (Napoli, 1992). According to whether the view of the object is determined by the user or by the system, the assertions are considered as integrity constraints to be checked, or production rules which direct the classification process.

Among the different kinds of assertions we consider in OSIRIS, domain assertions and inter-attribute dependencies play a special role in that they are used to build a partitioning of the object space into stability zones named Eq-classes. Eq-classes are equivalence classes for objects, according to the relation : "have the same validity according to the assertions". This means that all objects of a given Eq-class are either valid or invalid according to the assertions of the type or subtypes (views). As a consequence, dynamic checking of integrity constraints is replaced by determining the current Eq-class of the object. This is reduced to positioning every attribute concerned by the assertions in the right subdomain according to the partitioning which has been performed at compile time. The same process applies to the evaluation of production rules : reaching a "conclusion" is no longer performed through an inference engine : all valid (or conversely invalid) conclusions are known from the Eq-classes of the object, avoiding the need to perform dynamic inference. When dealing with incompletely known objects, the potential Eq-classes of the object implicitly encompass all possible instanciations, which avoids dealing explicitly with hypotheses (Simonet et al., 1989). For an object with n classifying[1] attributes, Eq-classes are hypercubes in the n-dimensional space of objects.

The dynamic process for assertion checking, i.e. determining the Eq-class of an object, is performed by a neural network, the input being the attribute values. This network needs no learning : it is fully determined from the partitioning into Eq-classes. Implementation by parallel processors is currently being studied and will improve still further the execution time of assertion checking.

At compile time, static analysis of assertions leads to the building of Eq-classes. They are the basis for the neural network design. Objects in external storage are indexed by their Eq-class. Queries using expressions based on domain predicates are therefore interpreted within the Eq-class structure. Procedural attachment, i.e. choosing the procedure best suited to a given object, is also governed by preconditions of the same kind. Thus assertions and the resulting Eq-classes are central to the whole system, both at compile time and at run time.

We first present the main aspects of the model, p-types and views, and their relationship with algebraic data types. We present two examples which illustrate the database and knowledge base capabilities of the model. We then present in detail the principle of static analysis of assertions and partitioning of the object space. Finally we discuss briefly some implementation aspects.

The model is currently implemented by the OSIRIS system, of which a UNIX version has been running on DEC Alpha since october 1994. A first prototype containing the basic functions associated with assertions and views was developed in 1993. It showed the feasibility of our approach and highlighted some problems, which we have since solved.

2. P-types and Views

Relational systems define a view as a virtual relation obtained by query or derivation operations : selection, projection, join ... (Stonebraker et al., 1990). In OSIRIS views are part and parcel of the conceptual schema, although they may be understood, to some extent, as virtual classes, as in (Abiteboul et al., 1987).

It is commonly recognized that object modelling eliminated the need for view definition, because of the higher expressive power of object concepts compared with relational ones. We do not agree with this opinion and the resulting choices. When using the sole notions of class and inheritance to create classes that are used to play the role of views, one has to build artificial classes which clutter up the data model. Just consider the example of a PERSON who may be and/or a STUDENT, a TEACHER, a SPORTSMAN, as well as being able to move from one to another, according to the class hierarchy below.

---

[1] Classifying attributes are those which appear in one assertion at least (domain assertion or Inter Attribute Dependency, precondition in methods), and whose domain is partitioned in at least two Stable Subdomains (see §4). Other attributes play no role in a classification process or constraint checking. For example, the *address* of a *person* will be in general a non-classifying attribute.

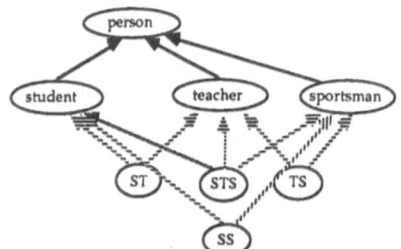

Because an object can be instanciated in only one class, four new classes must been created for the sole purpose of expressing that a person may at the same time be a STUDENT and a TEACHER (class ST), a TEACHER and a SPORTSMAN (class TS), a STUDENT and a SPORTSMAN (class SS) or the three of them (class STS).

Creating as ST class, which is necessary to express that an object may belong to the classes STUDENT and TEACHER, gives the user access to information of both superclasses. The user may thus access information which is non-pertinent to him when he is concerned by only one point of view : STUDENT or TEACHER. Moreover, when an ST object evolves and ceases to be a student, for example, it has to be moved explicitly to the TEACHER class. This, in many systems, including O2 (Deux et al., 1991), also implies changing its OID.

The proposed solution consists in considering the set of persons as a TYPE $\mathbb{P}$ERSON, and views as SUBTYPES in the algebraic sense (Liskov et al., 1974) (Guttag et al., 1978). A p-type is defined as an algebraic data type $<S, F, E>$ where S is a set of sorts $\{s_1, ..., s_n\}$, the carrier of the type, F a set of functions $s_{ix}s_{jx} ... {}_xs_k \rightarrow s_l$ and E a set of equations (Simonet, 1988).

The sorts of S are all the types necessary to define the functions of the type. One sort, $\mathbb{T}$, called the set of interest of the type, is central, in that the aim of the type definition is to establish the elements of the type and define their behaviour. In general, the type is given the name of its set of interest : $\mathbb{T}$. Among all possible **functions**, we call **attributes** those of the form $\mathbb{T} \rightarrow s$, $s \in S$. Other functions are called **methods**.

In relational systems, views are defined as restrictions of a set of relations, and they may themselves be used as relations in order to define other views. Contrary to this top-down approach, a p-type is defined from its views. One first gives its minimal view, then its other views by simple or multiple specialization, adding attributes and/or assertions. All the objects of a p-type are models of its minimal view. In OSIRIS, the p-type is given the name of its minimal view.

The algebraic type of the p-type is derived from the views declarations. The type $\mathbb{P}$ERSON contains all the attributes and methods which appear in its views. The domain of an attribute in type $\mathbb{P}$ERSON is the union of its domains in the views where it is declared.

Let $t_{min} : <S,F_{min},E_{min}>$, $t_1: <S,F_1,E_1>$, $t_2: < S,F_2,E_2>$, ... be the views of a P-type $\mathbb{T}$. $\mathbb{T}$ is defined as $<S, F, E>$ where :
- S is the support set of $\mathbb{T}$;
- $F = \cup_i F_i$;
- $E = E_{min}$

Views PERSON, STUDENT, TEACHER, TRAINEE-TEACHER, ... are subtypes of the p-type $\mathbb{P}$ERSON. The set of interest (domain) of the minimal view PERSON is identical to that of the p-type $\mathbb{P}$ERSON. The domain of another view is a subset of the domain of the view it specializes, or of the intersection of the domains of the views it specializes in case of multiple specialization.

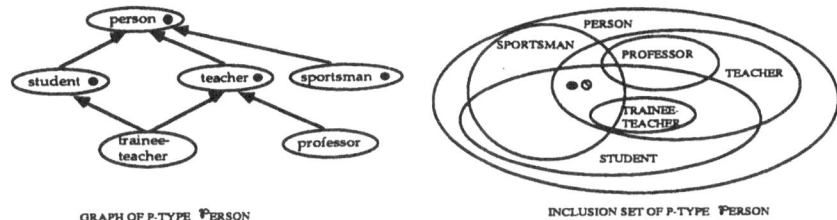

Access to the minimal view of an object only provides its attributes and methods. Access to the p-type provides the whole set of attributes and methods of the type; such access is necessary for the database administrator.

An object belongs to the p-type PERSON iff it satisfies the requirements of its minimal view. This means that the attributes of the external key[2] must be valued, and its assertions are valid. The criteria for an object to belong to a type (resp. subtype) is that the instance which represents it be a model of the equations of the type (resp. subtype).

Multiple inheritance is no longer necessary to express that an object may belong simultaneously to several views. It is used only to specify a strict subset of the views intersection, or to give an explicit name to such an intersection. The object ⊘ in the above diagram belongs to the views PERSON (all objects of the type satisfy the minimal view), STUDENT, TEACHER and SPORTSMAN, but not to the view TRAINEE-TEACHER, although it belongs to its two super-classes (super-views).

The class/subclass hierarchy is that deduced from constraint restriction and/or introduction of new attributes. This is different from (Bruce et al., 1986) (Cardelli et al., 1985) where subtypes are a binary relation between algebras. PERSON, STUDENT, TEACHER, TRAINEE, ... would be considered as distinct types, therefore different algebras (consequently disjoint OID domains), related by the subtyping relation. This is adequate for programming needs, where the main objective is to structure non-persistent and non-shared data, and to reduce the writing of methods.

Types are the logical unit for static checking and implementation issues. Within this perspective, an attribute, say IncomeTax, might be implemented in two different manners (by method overloading) in "types" STUDENT and TEACHER. This leads to the famous inheritance problem, where the system or the user has to decide which implementation of the attribute IncomeTax the TRAINEE-TEACHER class inherits. In OSIRIS, the implementation of methods is defined at the p-type level, independently from the class hierarchy. The different procedures which may implement a method are selected according to preconditions similar to the assertions.

Although the p-type concept is the most innovative aspect of the model, we must mention that we also distinguish **values**, in accordance with (MacLennan, 1982) and (Beeri, 1989). Values are modelled by v-types, which correspond to usual types in programming languages, where objects are neither shared nor persistent. They are used to define attributes whose values are not shared objects.

---

[2] In order to enable the system to determine whether the object under creation corresponds or not to some other existing object, one needs an external key which is a cartesian product of some attributes of the minimal view. Thanks to the existence of an OID (non-modifiable internal object identifier), the external key may be modified during the lifetime of the object.

3. A database example

This example is a very simple OSIRIS program which illustrates the notions of p-type and view. The universe modelled is that of PERSONS, which may be STUDENTS, TEACHERS and SPORTSMEN. A given *person* satisfies the minimal view and may belong to none, any or several other views. The view TRAINEE-TEACHER, which inherits STUDENT and TEACHER, is not necessary to express that a *person* can be a *student* and a *teacher* at the same time. It has been created to designate a subset of their intersection, characterized by some more assertions, which restrict its domain.

```
class PERSON                  -- Minimal view of p-type PERSON
  attr  Name : P_NAME;        -- P_NAME is declared elsewhere
        LivesAt : ADDRESS ;   -- ADDRESS is a v-type defined elsewhere
        Children : setof PERSON;
        Sex : CHAR In { "f", "m" };
        Age : INT ≤ 120 ;
        MilitaryService : STRING In { "yes", "no", "deferred", "exempt" };
        MaritalStatus : STRING In { "single", "married", "divorced", "separated" };
        IncomeTax : REAL calc;     -- procedural attachment
  key        Name               -- External key
  assertions
        Age < 17 ⇒ MilitaryService = "no";
        Age ≥ 18 ⇒ MilitaryService In { "yes", "deferred", "exempt" };
        Sex = 'f' ⇒ MilitaryService = "no";
end ;                         -- The minimal view automatically contains a private attribute  OID : t_oid.

view  STUDENT : PERSON                   -- STUDENT specializes PERSON
  attr  Studies : STRING In { "graduate", "postgraduate ", "doctorate"};
        Year : INT ;
end ;

view  TEACHER : PERSON                   -- TEACHER specializes PERSON
  attr  Diplomas : setof STRING In { "degree", "B.A.", "BSc" ,"M.A.","MSc","PhD"} ;
        Status : STRING In { "trainee", "lecturer", "professor", "instructor", "doctor" };
end ;

view PROFESSOR : TEACHER                 -- PROFESSOR specializes TEACHER
  assertions    Diplomas contain "PhD";
               Status = "professor";
end ;

view TRAINEE-TEACHER : STUDENT , TEACHER   -- specializes STUDENT and TEACHER
  assertions
        Status = "trainee";
        Studies = "graduate";
        Diplomas contain "degree";
end ;
...
```

The classes ADULT, MINOR, SENIOR and ADOLESCENT, defined as virtual classes in (Abiteboul et al., 1991), may be simply defined as views of the p-type PERSON, with the following definitions :

```
view ADULT : PERSON          assertions    Age ≥ 21    end ;
view MINOR : PERSON          assertions    Age < 21    end ;
view SENIOR : ADULT          assertions    Age ≥ 65    end ;
view ADOLESCENT : MINOR      assertions    Age ≥ 13    end ;
```

To some extent, these classes may be considered "virtual", in that no objects are instanciated in them specifically. Objects are instanciated as ℙERSONs. The attributes of the type ℙERSON are those of the minimal view, PERSON, plus those defined in views : Studies, Year, Status, Diplomas. Only the Database Administrator may access all the attributes of the type. Within a given view, the user may only use the attributes inherited from its super-views and the attributes proper to the view, if any. In the minimal view, the attributes Studies, Year, Status and Diplomas cannot be accessed. View definition may also be used as a basis to define confidentiality.

Encapsulation aims at data protection (public/private) and data independence, which is achieved by hiding the implementation aspects. In OSIRIS, the internal structure of the class is not known by the user. To **store** an attribute or not is an **implementation** decision, which may be changed without causing any modification to the user's programs (the implementation part has not been given in the example). This decision is independent of the way the value of the attribute is obtained.

Attributes may be calculated, or obtained from the user. When calculated, indicated by the **calc** qualifier, one or several procedures have to be provided in the implementation part. This way of triggering the calculation of attributes is called procedural attachment in knowledge representation systems (Winograd, 1975). Moreover, an attribute, whether calculated or not, may or may not be **stored**; this is an implementation choice. A non-stored attribute will be either calculated (if declared **calc**) or obtained from the user when its value is required. In either case, the encapsulation principle is respected in that the user knows the internal structure neither of an object nor of methods.

Most sytems (e.g. O2 (Deux et al., 1991)) make a distiction between attributes whose value is provided by the user and those which are calculated. The former are considered "real" attributes and are part of the tuple of the class, whereas the latter are methods. In this situation, a means to ensure a homogeneous way to access the values provided by the class, is to make attributes **private** and oblige the user to define methods to access their value. However, it is somewhat surprising to define methods simply for accessing attribute values, such as *readName* to access the *Name* value; moreover, this leads to encapsulation violation in queries, as quoted in (Adiba et al., 1993).

In OSIRIS, **Public** is the default choice. This seems natural to us in a Database context, where the main objective is to provide the user access to the values of the attributes. This is achieved most simply through the attribute name, which is also the choice in (Cattell et al., 1994).

4.   An expert system example

Most expert systems use production rules in the form of OSIRIS assertions. We give below some rules from an expert system for protein identification in molecular biology. A prototype of this system has been written in KEE (Fikes et al., 1985) and deals with five super-families of proteins (Langevin, 1993), whereas the final system should be able to identify 1000. The prototype contains 120 rules, which will lead to 25 000-30 000 rules for the final system.

KEE does not perform classification automatically : the programmer has to define a structure of classes which represent the taxonomy of proteins; he also has to write production rules and explicitly assign classes to some variables in order to keep track of the inference process. Rules are independent of class hierarchy, although, in practice, they are very similar. KEE does not perform any checking to ensure their compatibility. The programmer has absolute freedom and few protections; this opens the door to inconsistency problems, especially when the number of rules will be as many as 25 000-30 000.

In the example below, one-super family of proteins is considered : ABC. It is itself divided into subfamilies, according to the hierarchy shown on the right.

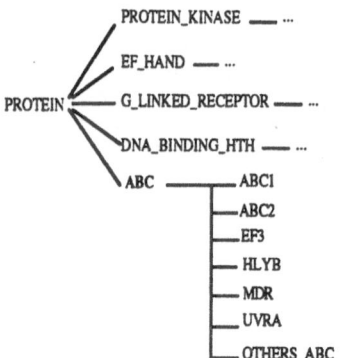

In OSIRIS, contrary to the KEE prototype, the rules are an integral part of the definition of the classes, since they are the assertions which **define** the class, all the attributes of the type being given in the root class, PROTEIN (although attributes might be defined at any level). OSIRIS will determine the class of a protein, given the values of its attributes : *Transmembrane*, *Prosites* and *q*. In the final version, about 100 attributes will be used.

We give the definition of the root class, PROTEIN, and two rules, along with the corresponding original KEE rules. In both programs, an intermediate class ABC12 has been defined in order to factorize assertions common to ABC1 and ABC2.

```
class PROTEIN                          -- root class of the taxonomy
  attr  Prosites setof ATOM;
        Transmembrane : INT;
        q : INT;
  end PROTEIN;

view ABC12 : ABC
  assertions   Transmembrane = 0;
               count atp_gtp_a in Prosites = 1;          -- "count v in X" returns the number
               count atp_bind_transport in Prosites  = 1;   -- of items v in the collection X
  end;
end ABC12;

view ABC1 : ABC12
  assertions   q>8;      end;
end ABC1;
```

KEE rules :

```
((abc12.rule
  (if   (lisp (zerop (get.value 's.protein 'transmembrane)))              /* transmembrane = 0 */
        (lisp (equal (sitecopynb prosites  'atp_gtp_a) 1)       /* occurrences of atp_gtp_a = 1*/
        (lisp (equal (sitecopynb prosites  'atp_bind_transport) 1))
     then
        (a family of s.protein is abc12))))          /* remembers that abc12 has been inferred */

((abc1.rule
  (if   (a family of s.protein is abc12)
        (lisp (> (sitecopynb (car (extract_data (cdr folder) 'composition)) 'q) 8))        /* q > 8 */
     then
        (a family of s.protein is abc1)               /* remembers that abc1 has been inferred */
  ...
```

Independently of the use of a LISP dialect, it is clear that the OSIRIS program is much closer to the expert specifications, in that it contains only declarative information. There is no need to "remember" the trace of the inferred classes as this is done by the attribute *family* of *s.protein*. In OSIRIS, classification is a built-in process and rules are part of the definition of the class in which they appear.

The assertions in this example are simply domain restrictions, since more general assertions were not necessary to express its production rules. Some predicates are not strictly in the form 'Attr **in** Domain'. An assertion '**count** atp_gtp_a **In** Prosites = 1' is a shortcut for the assertion 'X = 1' together with the definition of attribute 'X : INT **calc**', where the method which calculates its value returns '**count** atp_gtp_a **In** Prosites'. Assertions on collections (sets and lists) may use predicates **contain** and **in**, which represent the operators $\supseteq$ and $\in$ respectively.

5.   Partitioning of the Object Space

5.1. Eq-Classes

Memory management of a given type in external storage is based on the partitioning of the object space of the p-type into equivalence classes, according to the relation "have the same truth value according to the (entire set of) assertions of the type". These equivalence classes are called Eq-classes. By definition, all the objects belonging to the same Eq-class at a given moment are either valid or not valid for a given view; the validity may be different for different views, but all the objects of the Eq-class have the same behaviour. Moreover, the validity of an Eq-class for each view may be determined at compile time.

5.2. Domain partitioning

Several kinds of assertions may be expressed : domain assertions, Inter Attribute Dependencies, Inter Class Dependencies and global assertions (Inter Object Dependencies). We shall present in detail the first two because they govern the partitioning of the object space[3] . Any assertions may also be expressed by explicitly programmed functions.

Domain assertions are used to restrict the domain of an attribute. They can be written at the same time as the declaration of the attribute or in the assertion part of the language, as **Domain Predicates** (DPs), of the form $ATTR_i(X) \in D_j$, where $ATTR_i$ is some attribute of the type and D_j some subdomain of its definition domain.

Inter Attribute Dependencies (IADs) are Horn clauses (first-order formulas), the predicates of which are Domain Predicates.

The first step in assertion analysis consists in partitioning the domain of each attribute by all domain predicates into Stable Sub-Domains (SSDs). This is performed by the product of partitions obtained for each Domain Predicate of the attribute.

We shall present the method with attributes *Age, MilitaryService, Sex*, and assertions a1-a6 :

a1:   Age≤120

a2:   MilitaryService ∈ {"yes", "no", "deferred", "exempt"};

a3:   Sex ∈ { "f", "m" }

a4:   Age < 17 ⟹ MilitaryService = "no"

a5:   Age ≥ 18 ⟹ MilitaryService ∈ {"yes", "deferred", "exempt"}

a6:   Sex = "f" ⟹ MilitaryService = "no"   -- for the purpose of the example!

We show the partitioning of each attribute's domain into stable subdomains (SSDs) d_{ij}.

Age∈]INF,17[∪ [17,18[∪ [18 , 120]
                (a1, a4, a5,)

---

[3] Preconditions of methods are also used to determine this partition.

MilitaryService ∈ {"no"}∪{"yes", "deferred",
  "exempt"}   (a2, a4, a5, a6)

```
  ["no"]     { "yes", "deferred", "exempt" }
 |———————+———————————————————————————|
   d21                 d22
```

Sex ∈ {"m"}∪{"f"}   (a3, a6)

```
   {'m'}    { 'f }
 |————————+————————|
   d31      d32
```

The generic bounds INF/SUP are introduced whenever the lower and/or upper bounds of an ordered domain are unknown.

By definition, each subdomain d_{ij} has the following property : when an attribute value changes within a given subdomain d_{ij}, all domain predicates maintain their truth value and consequently the assertions do likewise. Divisions d_{ij} are therefore stability zones for the assertions, hence their name : Stable Subdomains (SSDs). Domain Predicates are transformed into more elementary ones of the form $ATTR_i \in d_{ij}$, where the d_{ij} are the SSDs of $ATTR_i$.

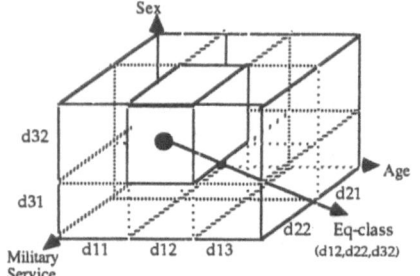

This partitioning of the domain of each attribute extends naturally to a partitioning of the space of the objects into stability hypercubes named Eq-classes. In our example, considering the three above attributes and assertions a1-a6 would lead to the partitioning in a 3-dimensional space.

There are $3_\times2_\times2 = 12$ Eq-classes.

The same partitioning mechanism is extended to multivalued attributes : sets and lists.

5.3. View determination

Within a given Eq-class, **all** the objects are either valid or invalid with respect to the set of assertions of a given view. Thus, one can speak of the validity of an Eq-class according to a view. The validity of each Eq-class for each view can be determined statically just by assessing the assertions of the view for any object of the Eq-class. Each view can then be associated with a map of Valid Eq-classes, as illustrated below in a two-dimensional case :

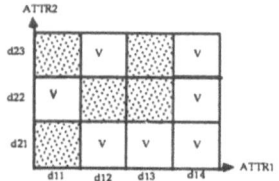
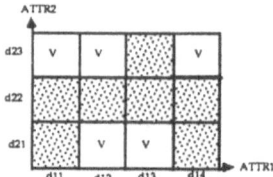

Valid Eq-classes of view V1   Valid Eq-classes of view V2

An object where all the attributes are known belongs to one Eq-class at a time; thus the knowledge of the Eq-class of an object determines which views are valid. For example, any object in Eq-class (d12, d21) is valid for both views V1 and V2, whereas an object in (d11, d22) is valid for V1 only, i.e. belongs to V1.

At a given moment, the information on an object may be incomplete (e.g. the object has been created by a user who is allowed a limited number of views). Reasoning with incomplete knowledge obeys the same rules. The known values will determine several Eq-classes instead of a single one. For example, if ATTR2 is unknown and ATTR1 is known to belong to d_{14} -even if its exact value is not determined-, view V1 is certain to be valid for that object, whereas view V2 remains potentially valid (depending on the final value of ATTR2). If ATTR1 is unknown and ATTR2 is known to belong to d_{22}, view V2 is certain to be invalid, whereas view V1 remains potentially valid.

Thus it may happen that incomplete information leads to an absolutely certain conclusion, without having to make hypotheses about unknown values of attributes. In some way, all possible hypotheses have been "compiled" through the Eq-classes.

Generalization to 3 dimensions is illustrated by the following diagram :

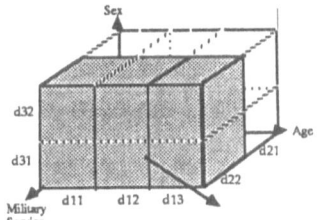

Given an object where attributes *Age* and *Sex* have unknown values, and *MilitaryService* is "yes", potentially valid Eq-classes are represented by 6 Eq-classes, denoted by (*, d_{22}, *). Such a set of Eq-classes is called a **semi-domain**.

Eq-classes can be checked as valid or invalid for each view. Semi-domains can be valid, invalid, or potential for a given view. It may occur that all the Eq-classes of a semi-domain are valid/invalid for a given view, in which case the semi-domain is valid/invalid for that view. When the Eq-classes of a semi-domain are of a mixed sort (valid and invalid ones), the semi-domain is **potential** for the considered view. According to further instanciation of the attribute, which will lead to the determination of one SSD for the attribute, and consequently one Eq-class for the object, the object will be known as certainly valid or invalid.

5.4. Consistency checking

The consistency of the base is ensured by the integrity constraints expressed by the assertions. However, assertions may themselves have consistency problems. They are checked for logical inconsistency, which is possible in spite of their first order general form, because the static process enables their transformation into an equivalent set of propositional formulas. Assertions a4-a5-a6 of the above examplemay be transformed into the following propositional system, where attributes are implicitly universally quantified, and where p_{ij} is the proposition expressing that attribute Attr$_i$ is in SSD d_{ij}, :

a4': $p11 \Rightarrow p21$

a5': $p13 \Rightarrow p22$

a6': $p32 \Rightarrow p21$

along with propositions of the form '$p_{ij} \Rightarrow$ **not** p_{ik} for all $k \neq j$', expressing the mutual exclusion of stable subdomains for the same attribute : $(\forall i)\ d_{ij} \cap d_{ik} = \emptyset$ for all $k \neq j$.

However, detecting logical inconsistencies is not sufficient when thousands of rules may have to be taken into account, possibly written by different users. Assertions are also checked for redundancy and for **domain-inconsistency**, which is weaker than logical inconsistency. An assertion is said to be domain-inconsistent when its antecedent is always invalidated by other assertions of the type. In the context of the above example, the assertion 'Sex = "f" **and** Age>30 ⇒ Some Conclusion' is always valid, whatever its conclusion, because its antecedent is always false, being contradictory to assertions a5-a6, which impose that there cannot be any female aged over 17 in the base[4] . One can assume that such Domain-inconsistent assertions are not written deliberately and their detection is essential to the user. Once they have been detected, it is up to the user to decide to maintain them or not.

Domain-inconsistencies as well as redundancies may be intended by the programmer; they may be harmless, but they may have unwanted hidden consequences. Detecting domain-inconsistencies is done by locating assertions whose antecedent contains a condition which is always invalidated by the other assertions.

6.   Implementation

6.1.   Memory organization

Eq-classes are the logical structure through which objects are accessed. However, Eq-classes are never represented explicitly in their totality, neither at compile-time nor at run-time. Only Eq-classes which represent actual objects are represented in the memory, thus avoiding combinatorial explosion. We use semi-domains, representing sets of Eq-classes where at least one attribute is undefined (Simonet et al., 1989), to index the actual objects. When all the attributes of an object are known, its semi-domain is an Eq-class.

The implementation unit is the p-type, and not the view. The record which is stored contains all the attributes of the p-type defined as "stored", not only those of its minimal view. Inner optimization may enable storing only attributes with a known value.

For each p-type, there is an indexing structure (ISD) which contains :

* an array of stable subdomains (SSD),
* view vectors (bit strings) representing valid, invalid and potential[5] views of the ISD,
* a pointer to the first object indexed by this semi-domain.

Objects belonging to the same ISD are chained together. As an object belongs to one (and only one) p-type, it is accessed through a unique ISD.

Updating an object entails the determination of its new ISD, if and only if at least one modified attribute changes its SSD. When the object does not change its semi-domain, it does not change its ISD either. The determination of the actual semi-domain of an object and its views is performed by a neural network (Simonet et al., 1994).

Physical object management is delegated to an existing object manager (Abecassis, 1994). A relational implemation is under way.

6.2.   Determination of the actual views of an object

Classification, i.e. determining the actual ISD and views of an object is performed by a three-layer neural network whose input is the attribute values. There is no intrinsic need to use a neural network, since algorithmic programming would achieve this task as well. Neural programming is used because it fits the problem and can later be optimised through parallel implementation. Contrary to neural networks usually used in classification, this network needs no learning in that it is completely determined from the analysis of the type structure and the assertions. As the

---

[4] This is due to assertion a5, which should have been written :

   Age $\geq$ 18 and Sex = 'm' $\Rightarrow$ MilitaryService $\in$ {"yes", "deferred", "exempt"}

This error was initially involuntary and we have maintained it to demonstrate Domain-Inconsistency.

[5] Potential views are those which are neither valid nor invalid for all the EQ-classes of the ISD, due to incomplete information.

understanding of this network is not necessary to the understanding of the OSIRIS system, we refer to (Bassolet, 1993) (Simonet et al., 1994a) (Simonet et al., 1994b).

The analysis of assertions and the construction of the neural network have been performed in a modular way such that when modifying, adding or suppressing assertions or views, consequences on the network and the indexing structure remain local. For example, on introducing the views ADULT, MINOR, SENIOR AND ADOLESCENT with their assertions, the partitioning of Age has to be modified. SSD d_{11} will be divided into $[0,13[$ and $[13,18[$, and SSD d_{13} into $[18,21[$, $[21,21]$ $]21,65[$ and $[65,120]$. Only the Eq-classes (and ISDs) containing the initial SSDs d_{11} and d_{13} are modified and divided into further Eq-classes. Among them only those which were valid before the modification are liable to become invalid Eq-classes; Eq-classes which were invalid will remain invalid and therefore do not have to be checked for validity.

7. Conclusion

The OSIRIS concepts possess many of the properties of the semantic model presented in (Abiteboul et al., 1987) and (Hull et al., 1987), while retaining unsullied object concepts. For example, Abiteboul and Hull's declaration *"Specialization can be used to define possible roles for members of a given type. Furthermore, an object may change such roles without changing its underlying or fundamental identity"* might stand for a description of a p-type and its views. An external key has been provided in order to allow several users to create objects according to their own views, while guaranteeing there cannot be any duplication of information concerning a physical object (Kim, 1993).

Many choices we had made in the design of the OSIRIS system are also those retained by the ODMG group (Cattell et al., 1994). An important difference is the notion of view, still absent from contemporary commercial object databases.

The existence of the theoretical framework of algebraic abstract data types enables the consideration of problems within another dimension. For example, the classical name conflict in multiple inheritance simply disappears when viewed in the p-types context. In a p-type, all attributes belong to the same type and a given name identifies only one attribute of the type.

Query answering is also optimized through the Eq-class indexing structure. Queries are transformed into a conjunction of elementary predicates. Thus answering a user's question consists in looking for those objects belonging to the Eq-classes of the query, thus reducing the search space; this is made possible by the indexation of objects by Eq-classes.

The last point we want to emphasize is the adaptation to user knowledge. A major criticism which is levied against expert systems is their need to ask many questions, necessary for their internal deductions but not at all applicable in the current user situation. In OSIRIS, any information given by the user is used to determine the possible Eq-classes of the current object. Further questions can then be asked, but only in the context of the restricted set of classes which are valid for these Eq-classes, thus reducing the risk of irrelevant questions.

OSIRIS is currently being evaluated on an expert system for protein identification in molecular biology. The existing prototype, written with classical expert system tools, has 120 rules and is going to expand by a factor of 300, which will lead to significant consistency and efficiency problems (Langevin, 1993). Through this application, we are able to examine whether or not our model is adequate for classical expert system writing. The whole system of rules is much simplified : a single structure replaces two structures which are very similar, that of the objects and that of the rules. Moreover, most "expert" rules are reduced to attribute domain restrictions, which corresponds more directly to their initial expression by the expert.

We consider that the approach presented here enables a unification of several important paradigms : databases, knowledge bases and constraint programming, within an object model where assertions play a central role, both at compile time and run-time. The programmer does not need to state explicitly whether he works in the database or the knowledge base context. Both paradigms, which are becoming more and more related (Brachman, 1993) (Ullman, 1992), are accessible through the OSIRIS capacities.

acknowledgements

We would like to thank Christabel Wellesley-Levasseur for her help in translating this paper.

8   References

(Abecassis, 1994): E. Abecassis, *YOODA user's guide,* APIC systèmes, Arcueil, France, 1994.

(Abiteboul et al., 1987): S. Abiteboul, R. Hull, *IFO; A Formal SemanticDatabase Model,* ACM Transaction on Database Systems, Vol 12, No. 4, Dec 1987, pages 525-565.

(Abiteboul et al., 1991): S. Abiteboul, A. Bonner, *Objects and Views,* ACM SIGMOD, Denver, Colorado 29-31 May 1991.

(Adiba et al., 1993): M. Adiba, C. Collet, *Objets et bases de données - le SGBD O2 ,* ed HERMES 1993.

(Bassolet, 1993): C.-G.Bassolet, *Couplage à un modèle objet d'une mémoire associative basée sur la partition de l'espace des objets par des règles.,* DEA informatique fondamentale, Univ. Claude Bernard - Ecole Normale Supérieure de Lyon, France, Juin 1993.

(Beeri, 1989):   C. Beeri, Formal models for object oriented databases. Procs of the first Int. Conf. on deductive and object-oriented databases (DOOD89). Kyoto, 4-6 Dec. 1989.

(Brachman, 1993): R.Brachman, *Viewing Data through a Knowledge Representation Lens,* KB & KS '93, Tokyo, 1993.

(Bruce et al., 1986): K. Bruce, P. Wegner, *An Algebraic Model of Subtypes in Objet-Oriented Languages,* SIGPLAN Notices V21 #10, Oct 1986.

(Cardelli et al., 1985): L. Cardelli, P.Wegner, *On understanding Types, Data Abstractions, and Polymorphism,* ACM Computing Surveys, vol17, 1985.

(Cattell et al., 1994): R. G. G. Cattell, T. Atwood, J. Duhl, G. Ferran, M. Loomis, D. Wade, *Object Database Standard : ODMG-93,* Morgan Kaufmann Publishers, 1994.

(Clancey, 1985): W. J.Clancey, *Heuristic Classification,* Artificial Intelligence 27 (1985), pages 289-350.

(Date et al., 1994): C. J. Date and David McGoveran. A New Database Design Principle. In DATABASE Programming and Design, July 1994.

(Deux et al., 1991): O. Deux et al., *The O2 System,* CACM, October 1991, Vol 34, No. 10, pages 34-48.

(Fikes et al., 1985): R. Fikes, T.,Keller *The role of Frame-based Representation in Reasoning,* CACM 85, 28(9) : pages 904-920, 1985.

(Guttag et al., 1978): J. Guttag, J. Horning, *The Algebraic Specification of Abstract Data Types,* Acta Informatica, 1978.

(Hull et al., 1987): R. Hull, R. King, *Semantics Database Modelling: Survey, Applications, and Research Issues,* ACM Computing Surveys, Vol 19, No. 3, Sept 1987, pages 201-260.

(Kim, 1993):   W. Kim, *Object-Oriented Database Systems : Promises, Reality, and Future*, Proceedings of the 19th VLDB Conference, Dublin, Ireland 1993.

(Langevin, 1993): E. Langevin, *Prototype de système expert à base de connaissances dédié à l'identification de fonctions cellulaires portées par la séquence proteique.* - DEA GBM, Univ. Cl. Bernard, Lyon, France 1993.

(MacLennan, 1982): B. J., MacLennan *Values and Objects in Programming Languages.* SIGPLAN notices, V17, #12, Dec. 1982.

(Liskov et al., 1974): B. Liskov, B. Zilles, *Programming with Abstract Data Types* - Proc. of a Symp. on Very High Level Language, Sigplan Notices 9, 4, April 74.

(Napoli, 1992):   A. Napoli, *Représentation à Objets et Raisonnement par Cassification en IA*, Thèse Docteur Es-Sciences, Université Nancy 1, France, 1992.

(Simonet, 1984): A. Sales-Simonet, *Types Abstraits et Bases de Données: formalisation du concept de partage et analyse statique de contraintes d'intégrité* - Thèse Docteur Ingénieur, Université Scientifique et Médicale de Grenoble, France, Avril 1984.

(Simonet, 1988): A. Simonet, *Les P-TYPES: un modèle pour la définition de bases de connaissances centrées-objets cohérentes* - R.R. 751-I laboratoire ARTEMIS - Grenoble, France, Novembre 1988.

(Simonet et al., 1989): A. Simonet, M. Simonet, *Les classes d'équivalence induites par des dépendances inter-attributs: fondements pour une représentation des objets partagés dans les bases de connaissances* - R.R. 769-I laboratoire ARTEMIS - Grenoble, France, Février 89.

(Simonet et al., 1994a): A. Simonet, M. Simonet, *OSIRIS : An Assertion-based Hybrid Object-Connexionist Knowledge Base System* - 14th International Conference on Artificial Intelligence, KBS, Expert-Systems and Natural Language, Avignon, France, may 30-june 3, 1994.

(Simonet et al., 1994b): A. Simonet, M. Simonet, C-G. Bassolet, J. Demongeot, *Une architecture connexionniste pour un système hybride de représentation de connaissances orienté-objet.*, Colloque sur le Neuromimétisme - Lyon, france, June 1994.

(Stonebraker et al., 1990): M. Stonebraker et al., *On rules, procedures caching and views*, ACM SIGMOD conference on management of data - Atlantic City - June 1990.

(Ullman, 1992): J. Ullman, *New Frontiers in Database System Research*, Proceedings on International Conference on the Occasion of the 25th Anniversary of INRIA Paris, France, Dec 1992.

(Winograd, 1975): T. Winograd, *Frame Representations and the Declarative/Procedural Controversy*, Representation and Understanding : Studies in Cognitive Science, pages 185-210, edited by D. G. Bobrow and A. M. Collins, New York: Academic Press, 1975.

An Integrated Expert Database System

Shi-Ming Huang*, Peter Smith and John Tait

*Tatung Institute of Technology, Department of Computer Science and Engineering,
Taipei, 10451, Taiwan, R.O.C.
E-mail:smhuang@cse.ttit.edu.tw   Fax: +886 2 5925252 2284
University of Sunderland, School of Computing and Information Systems,
Sunderland, SR2 7PR, U.K.
E-mail:cs0psm@isis.sunderland.ac.uk   Fax: +44 91 5152787

ABSTRACT. Information Technologists have moved from data processing into the information processing and are now moving then into the field of true knowledge processing. A new term "Expert Database System" (EDS) has emerged to refer to an important research area in this field. This paper presents an investigation into issues concerning the design of an Expert Database System Development Tool by using object oriented technology. The paper describes a system which has been developed by the authors and discusses the lessons learnt as a result of the work.

KEY WORDS: Expert Database System, Knowledge Base Management System, Database Management Systems and Expert System Shells.

1. Introduction

Current EDS research covers a very wide area of computing. Information Technologists view and apply it from different computing perspectives (such as DB technology, AI technology, Software Engineering, etc.). The conventional approach to EDS architecture is to enhance or couple existing database systems and expert system shells. A new research area is to try to find a unifying model which can satisfy the requirements of both a database and an expert system application to build a true Knowledge Base Management System (KBMS). There are several reasons for the existence of both of these approaches and it is difficult to distinguish either approach as being more useful than the other.

Through authors' survey in 1993 (Huang et al., 1993a), many people suggested that the feature EDS should include a new higher level synthesis model with re-engineering capability. For this reason, a project, called SEDSDT (Sunderland Expert Database System Development Tool), has been implemented by the authors which focuses on unifying these two issues to form a total integrated system.

In this paper, the authors will discuss the SEDSDT architecture, the FOODM (Frame Object Oriented data Model) higher level synthesis model, the SEDSDT prototype system, an application example (i.e. Human Resource Management System), and draw conclusions from the work.

2. The Architecture of SEDSDT

The main idea of SEDSDT is to use object oriented technology to build a hyper semantic data model (called FOODM; Huang et al., 1992) for a knowledge based management system and to use object-oriented semantic relationships to support a total integrated environment. Generally, the SEDSDT is an knowledge based management system with a peer-to-peer coupling of existing DBMSs (Database Management Systems) and ESSs (Expert System Shells) environment.

Figure 1 depicts the Architecture of SEDSDT (Smith et al., 1992). The architecture is divided into three general levels: internal, conceptual, and external. The outside user view of the system is a multi-user and multi-function system which includes many high level tools and an intelligent query and knowledge representational language. They can use different languages to represent knowledge in the external level. Through the mapping procedure, the knowledge will be represented as a FOODM at the conceptual level and the internal level control the knowledge physical storage.

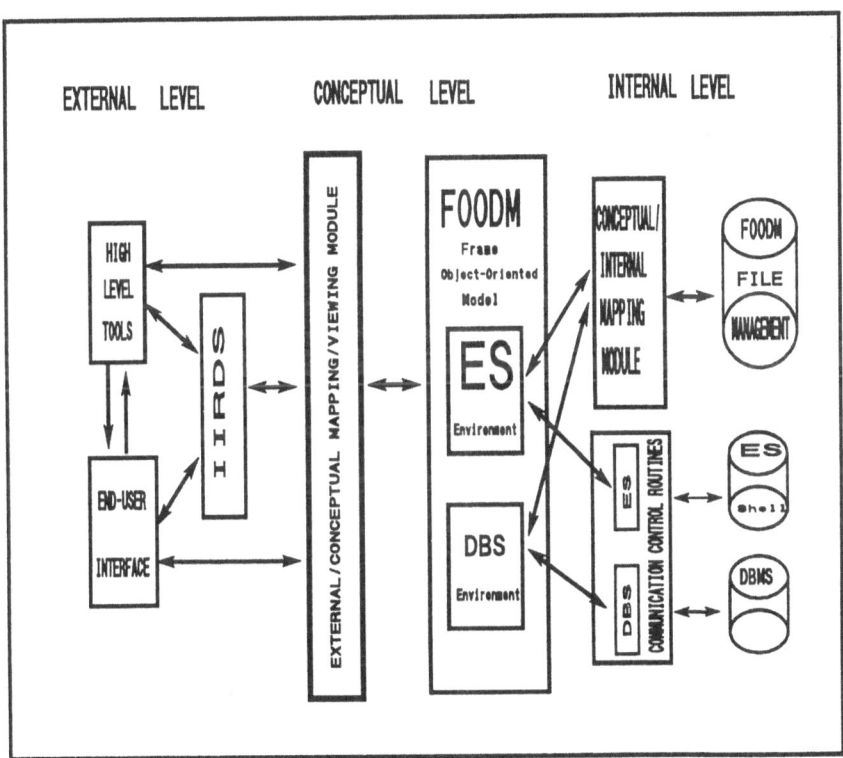

Figure 1 SEDSDT Architecture

2.1. External Level

The external level is the one closest to the users. It is concerned with the way that the system or knowledge is viewed by individual users. This is due to the fact that different classes of users will require different information from, or different ways of interacting with, the system. SEDSDT users include knowledge engineers, domain experts, EDS administrators, information engineers, and end-users. For example: Knowledge engineers want to build the knowledge base (i.e. a rule based system) and need to view the factual data structure in the existing database systems; EDS administrators want to view the expert database system structure, general and system information, ... etc.

The functionality of the external level contains a multi-view user interface to supply a different environment to different categories of users, high level tools to assist users in their use of SEDSDT to build EDSs, and on IIRDS (Intelligent Information Resource Dictionary System; Huang et al., 1993b) to assist the users when viewing the knowledge and integrating environment.

The external view is described by an external schema in the multi-view user interface. Users can change the schema through the external knowledge definition language to create their new view but can not change the entire knowledge base.

The high level tools module employs an open system architecture to allow users to link with other development tools. For example, it can include knowledge discovery tools, data integrity and quality-control tools, hypermedia management tools, data presentation and display tools, decision support and scenario analysis tools, data format management tools, intelligent-system design tools, or any other tools which are developed by the users.

The IIRDS is an integrated information resource dictionary system for a knowledge base management system and a peer to peer coupling expert database system. It is a communication control centre for all modules of SEDSDT. It supports the full-life cycle of EDS development. For this reason, IIRDS need to deal with database documents, expert system documents, knowledge base documents, expert database documents, and integrating documents.

2.2. Conceptual Level

The conceptual level is a "level of indirection" between the other two levels. This level will contain the algorithms which can individually create the different environments concerning the FOODM system, ES and DBMS. The kernel part of this level is the FOODM. It is the control centre of the SEDSDT and supports all the semantic relationships between the different modules of the system. Any system or high level tools which are developed in the system must use the FOODM structure. There are three main part modules in the FOODM, i.e. FOODM module, DBS module, and ES module. The FOODM module deals with the KBMS. The DBS module deals with the databases in the existing DBMS. The ES module deals with the existing ESs in the existing ESS. Each module can communicate by message passing or the object-oriented hierarchy generation or aggregation relationship.

The functionality of this level also includes an integrity maintenance module, privacy maintenance module, information retrieval module, inference engine module, deductive module, etc.

2.3. Internal Level

The internal level is the one closest to physical storage. That is, it is the level which is concerned with the way in which the knowledge types used by the system are actually stored. There are three kinds of physical storage structure. The FOODM file management system, existing database systems and existing expert systems. Each of these deal with the three main different knowledge modules at the conceptual level.

The FOODM file management system is the local storage management system for a true KBMS. It also will storage the really IIRDS. Another two systems, DBMSs and ES Shells, are to deal with the physical storage of coupling systems which are integrated into SEDSDT.

2.4. Mapping

Mapping technology has been widely used in DBMSs. It supports data independence. Many researchers have concluded that meta-rule or rule schema technology, combined with mapping technology, will achieve rule independence and multiple user environment (Pun and Kahn, 1989). SEDSDT uses mapping technology to build knowledge independence and a multi-user environment.

There are two mapping modules in this three level architecture. The conceptual/internal mapping defines the correspondence between the conceptual view and the physically stored knowledge; it specifies how conceptual views are represented at the internal level. If the structure of the internal view is changed (i.e. if a change is made to the storage structure definition), then the conceptual/internal mapping must also be changed accordingly, so that the conceptual schema may remain invariant. There are three environments in this module. One is the internal mapping module to deal with the FOODM module at the conceptual level and the FOODM file management system at the internal level. Another is the remote procedure calls for network management which deal with external systems (i.e. deal with the ES module and the DBS module at the conceptual level and existing DBMSs and ESSs at the internal level).

An external/conceptual mapping defines the correspondence between a particular external view and the conceptual view. For example, fields can have different knowledge types, field and record names can be changed, multiple conceptual fields can be combined into a single external field, and so on. Any number of external views can exist at the same time; any number of users can share a given external view and different external views can overlap.

The architecture of the SEDSDT is for the future EDS development tools which involve the re-engineering capability and a higher level synthesis model. It is based on modularity. Each separate subsystem (i.e. DBMS and ESS) is classified as a module. These separate subsystems are integrated by the IIRDS. The three level architecture (i.e. The architecture is divided into an internal level, a conceptual level, and an external level) has shown a great progress in achieving simultaneously data independence and a mulit-user environment over current DBMSs (Date, 1986) and KBSs (Pun and Kahn, 1989).

3. The Structure of FOODM

In this section, the authors propose a frame based object-oriented knowledge representation model, i.e. FOODM, within an extended entity-relationship (EER) framework which can be used to construct an effective knowledge base management system.

FOODM is the kernel of SEDSDT, i.e. the conceptual level. It is a higher-order synthesis which includes frame concepts, semantic data modelling concepts and object-oriented concepts to leave no real distinction between "data" and "knowledge" (in the form of rules). It can also support separate modules to allow existing systems to intercommunicate via it.

SEDSDT is an open architecture and can couple many different modules into the FOODM. For the purpose of this project these modules can be grouped into three generic classes; i.e. the knowledge representation module, the expert system coupling module, and the database coupling module (See Figure 2). The knowledge representation module presents the knowledge which is described by the language of SEDSDT, called the K-Language (Huang et al., 1994b). The expert system coupling module represents knowledge which is encapsulated in an existing external expert system shell, such as Crystal, GoldWorks, etc. The database coupling module represents the 'knowledge' which is encapsulated in an existing external database system, such as dBase, Oracle, etc.

FOODM structures an application domain into classes, where classes are organised via generalisation, aggregation, and user-defined relationships, and allows multiple inheritance within generalisation hierarchies. Knowledge-base or expert database system designers can describe each class as a specialisation (i.e. subclass) of other, more generic, classes. Thus attributes and methods of objects of one class are inherited by attributes and methods of another class lower in the ordering. Note that this ordering may not be hierarchical, since it is possible for a class to have more than one superclass. The model also allows associated information for attribute and method descriptions to be stored declaratively - this has the added advantage that the information is easily accessible, understandable, and modifiable.

The ability to attach procedures to objects enables behavioural models of objects and expertise in an application domain to be constructed. This allows an extremely effective and efficient form of object-oriented programming whereby objects represented by record like data structures can automatically respond to method calls. The attached procedure follows the IF-THEN structure which enables representation of production rules and normal procedures. The coupling procedure for an object is also an attached procedure within the object.

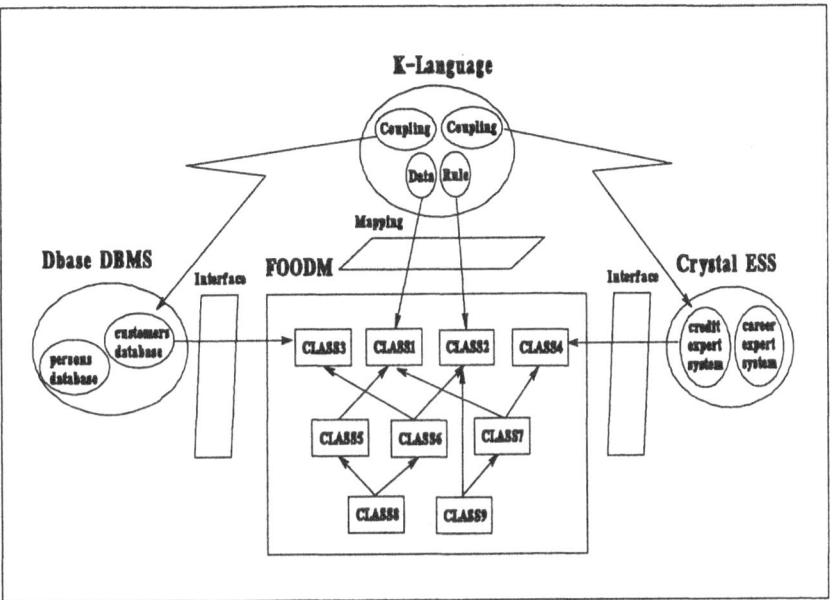

Figure 2 The Architecture of FOODM

Database researchers have recognised that integrating a production rule facility into a database system provides a uniform mechanism for a number of advanced database features including integrity constraint enforcement, derived data maintenance, triggers, protection, version control, and others (Hanson and Widom, 1993). These are referred to as active database systems and deductive database systems. FOODM unifies data and rules allowing these advanced features to be implemented. The knowledge processing mechanism, i.e. inference engine and data retrieval mechanism, has also been built into FOODM. It also supports very strong integrity constraint enforcement.

The representation of rules in the deductive and active database systems are fundamentally different, and both types of rules could theoretically by present in a single system (Hanson and Widom, 1993). Much research has shown that object-oriented techniques can be used to represent the deductive and active functionalities within the database. One of the important aims of the FOODM is to investigate this active and deductive single system by using object-oriented techniques. Another aim of FOODM is to represent rules and a peer to peer coupling architecture for the expert database system.

The architecture of FOODM also supports the semantics of data and knowledge communication by its generalisation and aggregation relationships. These semantic items link all modules of a system together to produce an integrated system.

Remember, FOODM is the conceptual level of SEDSDT. The authors' research focuses on the representation of the structure, i.e. the functionalities of the representation, but not the design of a user friendly language.

3.1 Knowledge Representation Schema

FOODM follows the object-oriented paradigm. All conceptual entities are modelled as an object. The same attribute and behaviour objects are classified into an object type, called a class. An object belongs to one, and only one, class. A fact is an object in FOODM and a rule is an object, too. There is much related research in this area, including that of Dayal et al., 1988; Cacace et al., 1990; Lee and Lee, 1990, etc.

FOODM is implemented with a knowledge representation schema (see Figure 3). A knowledge representation schema is a model of sets of objects which represent the inherent structure and properties of objects and relationships between sets of objects in a standardised form. In other words, a knowledge representation schema represents:

```
Description 5.1: Class
  Class {    Class_Name   /* a unique name in all system*/
             Primary_Key /*  an attribute name or default by class_name */
             Parents   /* a list of class names*/
             Description /* the description of the class */
             Attributes /*a list of attributes; see Description 5.2 */
             Methods /* a list of methods; see Description 5.3 */
             Constraints /* a list of constraint method for this class */
         }

Description 5.2: Attribute
Attribute   { Attribute_Name /* a unique name in this class*/
              Attribute_Type /* the data type for the attribute */
              Default_Value /* predefined value for the attribute */
              Cardinality /* define whether the attribute is a single or multi value */
              Description /* the description of the attribute */
              Constraints /*a list of  constraint method for this attribute */
          }

Description 5.3: Method
Method     {Method_Name /* a unique name in this class */
            Parameters   /* a list of arguments for the method */
            Type /* the final result data type */
            Description  /* the description of the method */
            Method_Body /* the processing function of the method */
                {If /* the rule conditions */
                    Then /* the rule actions or normal methods */}
            Constraints /* a list of constraints for this method */
          }

Description 5.4: Constraint
Constraints /* a list of constraint method for this class */
          {Method_Name /* constraint method name */
           Parameters     /* a list of arguments for the method */
           Ownership /*a class name to represent the ownership of the method */
           Event /* triggered event */
           Sequence /* method action time */
           Timing /* the method action timer */
          }
```

Figure 3 The Structure of FOODM

- object structure descriptions (i.e. classes),
- the user-defined relationship between each entity, and
- structure inheritance descriptions defined by taxonomies of structure which support data and behaviour inheritance (i.e. abstract relationships).

3.2 Objects

There are three different models of objects in the FOODM. One is a **static object** which is an instance of a static class and is used to represent factual data. Another is an **active object** which is an instance of an active class and is used to represent the rules. The final one is a **coupling object** which is an instance of a coupling class and is used to represent the coupling entity. Each object has an object identifier.

3.2.1 Static Objects

Static objects are similar to the usual sort of objects used in object-oriented technology. They are physically stored in the FOODM file management system. FOODM views a static class as a database, i.e. a set of factual data. The values of atomic attributes are stored in the object. The values of the virtual attributes are generated during the processing of the object. The value of the object attributes are object identifiers which point to further objects.

3.2.2 Active Objects

Active classes represent knowledge in the form of rules. There are instances called active objects which represent the event of the rule. The mapping module of SEDSDT will convert the rule into a FOODM active class. The attributes of the active class will include all factors in the condition part and action part of the rule. The type of these attributes will depend on the position of factors within the rule.

For example, consider the rule:
    Rule Name: Credit_Rating
        IF Customer-Status = "house-owner"
        THEN Credit-Rating = "good"

The system will present this rule as an active class. If there is an event to find the credit-rating of the customer Hector, the system will generate a new object for this event. If the customer-status of Hector is house-owner, the active object will be:

Object Identifier: Hector_Credit_Rating

```
Attributes:
      Customer= "Hector"
      Customer-Status= "House-Owner"
      Credit-Rating= Method(credit-rating)
Methods:
credit-rating (): Text;
      { IF Customer-Status = "House-Owner"
       Then Credit-Rating = "Good"}
```

'Method(credit-rating):' means the result value of the method 'credit-rating'.
'credit-rating (): Text;' means the 'credit-rating' method has a result value is a text.

Active objects are dynamic objects which are created as necessary on-line during processing. They exist only when the system needs them. They do not need to be stored in physical storage. This is the main difference between a static object and an active object. An active object is similar to a formula cell in a spreadsheet, but it is more powerful.

3.2.3 Coupling Objects

The coupling classes represent knowledge in the form used by external systems. An instance of a coupling class is called a coupling object. There are two types of coupling class in the FOODM. One is used to represent an external DB. The other is used to represent an external ES. Neither type of class tries to represent all of the knowledge present in the existing systems, but only represents those variables which are needed for communication with the FOODM. The conversion is implemented in the mapping module of the SEDSDT architecture. Both types of coupling classes require different formats for the conversion. The format for the DB coupling class is that of the external DB structure. All the attributes of the existing DB will be converted to the attributes of the coupling class in the FOODM. All the attributes are virtual attributes in the coupling class. The actual data type for an attribute will be the same as the type of the method for that attribute. The methods for each attribute describe the communication procedures to read the data from, and write the data to, the external system. For example: consider a DB 'Persons', in dBase III Plus format. The DB structure is shown in the following table:

Field name	Type	Field
Name	Character	15
Sex	Character	1
Father	Character	15
Mother	Character	15

The conversion procedure in the mapping module will convert this DB into the coupling class shown below:

Class Name: Persons

```
Attributes:
        Name: Method(name)
        Sex: Method(sex)
        Father: Method(father)
        Mother: Method(mother)
Methods:
        name (): Text; {............}
        sex (): Text;{............}
        father (): Text;{............}
        mother (): Text;{............}
```

The DB coupling class mirrors the DB structure (i.e. schema), but does not include all of the data in the DB. The reason is that it is difficult to hold a large amount of data in the integration system. DB conversion technology has been an area of research for more than 20 years. Schema conversion has been shown to offer a lot of advantages (Fong, 1992). The current FOODM can only convert a subschema of a DB (i.e. a table which is an entity or a relationship in the relational data model) as a coupling class in the system. It can not convert the full schema of a DB application which includes several tables and the relationships between these tables.

The ES coupling class represents the communication factors which need to perform data passing between the FOODM and an ES, but does not represent all the knowledge in the KB within the FOODM. The ES coupling class includes:
- Output Part Attributes: all the data which are required by the ES; and
- Input Part Attributes: all the results which are generated by the ES.

The conversion procedure will translate all input data variables which exist in the ES into the output part attributes of the class. The program developer will decide the variable name in which to save the resultant information from the ES. The simple view of the interface function between an ESS and the FOODM is to change the ES standard I/O interface to that of the FOODM. All the attributes of an ES coupling class are represented as virtual variables. The communication functions between the FOODM and the external system are built into the method of each attribute.

The ES coupling class only represents those variables which are required by the ES and the result variables which are required by the program developer, but not all of the rules which belong to the ES. The reason is that an ES may like a program and often include procedural rules. These are less structured and perform processing and user-interface activities, and are not of use to SEDSDT.

An instance of a coupling class is called a coupling object. The coupling object will be generated when information is required from the application system or users. They are dynamic objects, such as active objects, which are created as necessary during execution. They are not stored in the physical storage of FOODM, but in external systems which use different formats.

4. The SEDSDT Prototype System

SEDSDT has been built on a Sun SPARC Workstation, using Common LISP and C. The system environment includes two separate existing software systems, Oracle and GoldWorks, which run on two different Sun networked systems. A simple PC version system has also been implemented by using C language to integrate Crystal and Dbase III Plus.

The user interface of SEDSDT is a pull-down window system (See Figure 4). It supports the functions under the headings of System, Define, Find, Modify, Run, IIRDS, Browser, and Tools. Users can use this user-interface to easily couple the two existing systems or build a new EDS.

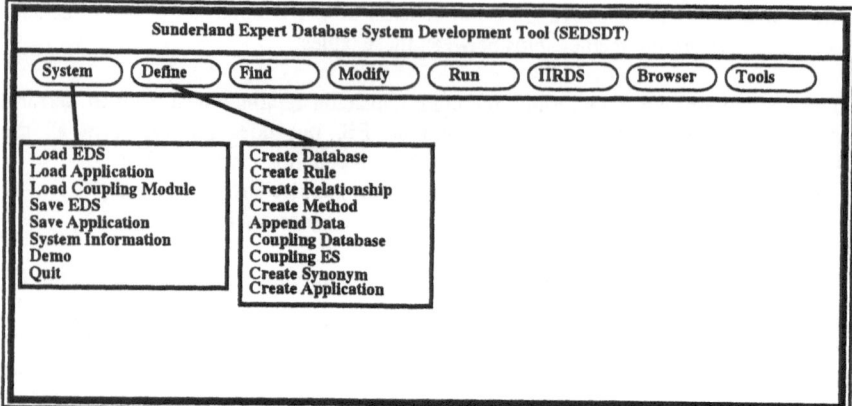

Figure 4 The Interface of SEDSDT

5. Implementation of a System in SEDSDT

Since SEDSDT is a development tool for the production of an EDS, it is, in effect, an EDS shell or knowledge management system. The inference mechanism and the data processing mechanism (i.e. the knowledge processing mechanism) has been built into the system. The principle steps for designing an EDS in SEDSDT are the following:

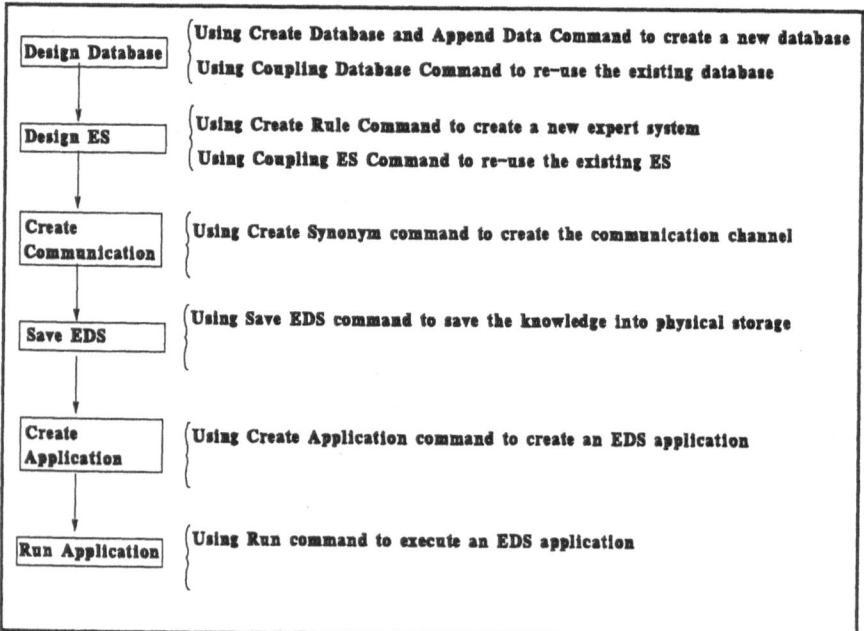

6. An Example: A Human Resource Management System

An example for job matching in a human resource management system has been applied in the SEDSDT. The main task of this application is to match staff with suitable placements with the ability to hold data relating to staff skills, location, availability, personal factors, and other human resource management knowledge. The new system was required to use the existing personal database and job vacancy database.

The overall prototype system is summarised in Figure 5. It is based on a simple PC version of SEDSDT. The personal, job vacancy, and skill/training databases are stored in the Dbase III plus. The HRM expert system was developed in the Crystal Epert System Shell (ESS). The SEDSDT forms a communication bridge between the two, as show in Figure 5.

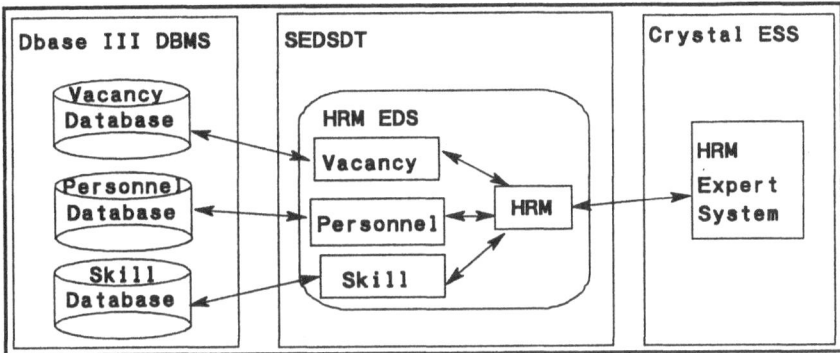

Figure 5 HRM Expert Database System

Figure 6 shows the top level data flow diagram of this system. The prototype system will advise the users (i.e. Resource Managers) of suitable people for a specific job. Users are asked to enter the vacancy job number and other special conditions, such as sex, location, personal factors, for a transaction (see Figure 7). The result will be a list of people who are suitable for a specific job. The result will also give reasons, suitability ratings, and advise on training courses that the candidate needs (see Figure 8).

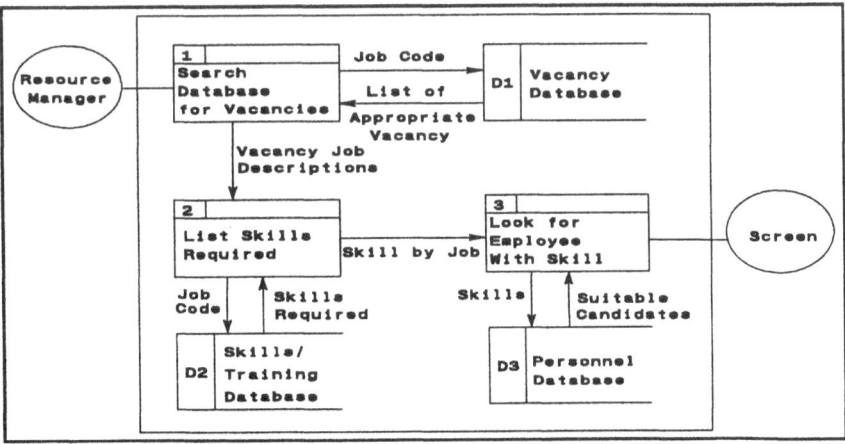

Figure 6 Top Level Data Flow Diagram For HRM EDS

```
+---------------------------------------------------------------+
|         Human Resource Management Expert Database System (HRM EDS) |
|                                                               |
| Please Enter Job Code: [0001   ]                              |
|                                                               |
| What Special Conditions Would You Like To Set Up In This Transaction? |
|         1. Skill                    2. Location               |
|         3. Family Situation         4. Hobby                 |
|         5. Sex                      6. Age                    |
|         7. Current Position         8. Others                |
|         0. No                                                 |
|         Please Select: [ 2 ]                                  |
+---------------------------------------------------------------+
```

Figure 7 Sample Interactive Session

```
+---------------------------------------------------------------+
| My Advice for the Job code  0001 (Chief Programmer in Project 2 of Directorate 1) is: |
| There are 3 persons who are suitable for this job.            |
+---------------------------------------------------------------+
| Name: Russell Parsons                          Person: 1/3    |
| Suitability Rating: 100%                                      |
| Current Position: Chief Programmer in Project 1 of Directorate 1 |
| Reasons: 1. 10 years experience in this type of job          |
|          2. Full skill requirement                           |
|          3. Review marking good                              |
|          4. Lives close to the work place.                   |
| Warning: He is also suitable for Job 0004 and Job 0007.      |
|                                                               |
|            Press Any Key to Display Next Person               |
+---------------------------------------------------------------+
```

Figure 8 Sample HRM EDS Conclusions

7. Conclusions

Re-engineering functionality and a higher synthesis model are not a tradeoff situation in EDS research. The SEDSDT project has demonstrated that they can be combined to form a very powerful and sophisticated EDS development tool by using object-oriented technology.

Object Oriented technology has achieved much in the AI, DB and AI-DB integration area during the last decade. The way in which one can use object oriented techniques to represent knowledge has given great hope for building a higher order synthesis model. Using object oriented technology to further improve EDS development tools has become a fashionable and worthy research topic.

It is certain that this field of research will continue to expand in the future, and that, as we gain a better understanding of the concept of knowledge and how to manage it, more sophisticated and yet practical systems will emerge.

References:

(Cacace et al., 1989):   "Integrating Object-Oriented Data Modelling With A Rule-Based Programming Paradigm", Internal Report, Politecnico Di Milano, Dipartimento Di Elettronica.

(Date, 1986):   Date, C.J., "An Introduction to Database Systems", Volume I, 4th Edition, Addison-Wesley Publishing Company, ISBN 0-201-14201-5.

(Dayal et al., 1988):   U. Dayal, et al., "The HiPAC project: Combining active databases and timing constraints", SIGMOD record 17(1), pp51-70.

(Fong, 1992):   Fong, J., 1992, "Methodology for Schema Translation from Hierarchical or Network into Relational", Information and Software Technology, Vol 34, No 3, pp 159-174.

(Hanson and Widom, 1993): Hanson, E.N. and Widom, J., 1993, "An Overview of Production Rules in Database Systems", The Knowledge Engineering Review, Vol 8:2, pp 121-143, Cambridge Press.

(Huang et al., 1992):   S.M. Huang, P. Smith, J.I. Tait, J. Clifford, and S. Pollitt, "FOODM: The Kernel of A New Expert Database System", EXPERSYS-92 conference, Paris, October 1992.

(Huang et al., 1993a):   S.M. Huang, P. Smith, J.I. Tait, and S. Pollitt, "A Survey of Approaches to Commercial Expert Database System Development Tools", Occasional Paper 93-4, University of Sunderland.

(Huang et al., 1993b):   S.M. Huang, P. Smith, J.I. Tait, and S. Pollitt, "An Information Resource Dictionary System for a Peer to Peer Expert Database system", Occasional Paper 93-7, University of Sunderland.

(Huang et al., 1994a):   S.M. Huang, P. Smith, J.I. Tait, and S. Pollitt, "Sunderland Expert Database System Development Tool (SEDSDT) User's Guide", Occasional Paper 94-15, University of Sunderland.

(Huang et al., 1994b):   S.M. Huang, P. Smith, and J.I. Tait, "Expert Database Systems: The Way Forward?", Database Management Horizons, 5th International Hong Kong Computer Society Database Workshop, Hong Kong, Feburary 1994.

(Lee and Lee, 1990):   K. Lee and S. Lee, "An Object-Oriented Approach To Data/Knowledge Modeling Based On Logic, IEEE Ch2840-7/0000/0289.

(Pun and Kahn, 1989):   P.K. Pun and H.J. Kahn, "Knowledge-based Applications = Knowledge Base + Mappings + Applications", Proceedings of the Data and Knowledge Base Integration Working Conference at the University of Keele, U.K., Editers S.M. Deen and G.P. Thomas, Pitman Pub.

(Smith et al., 1992):   P. Smith, S.M. Huang, J.I. Tait, J. Clifford, and S. Pollitt, "Knowledge Processing Tools: Proposal of a new architecture", The Third Annual IAKE Symposium 'New Generation Knowledge Engineering', Washington DC, November 1992.

Generic Methods in Deductive Object Databases

Elisa Bertino
Dipartimento di Scienze
dell'Informazione
Università di Milano
Via Comelico, 39 20133 Milano, Italy
bertino@hermes.mc.dsi.unimi.it

Giovanna Guerrini
Dipartimento di Informatica e
Scienze dell'Informazione
Università di Genova
Viale Benedetto XV, 3 16132 Genova, Italy
guerrini@disi.unige.it

Danilo Montesi *
Informatics Department
Rutherford Appleton Laboratory
Chilton, Didcot OX11 0QX, UK
danilo@inf.rl.ac.uk

Abstract

Deductive objects have been introduced in [3] to support declarative object specification in the database context taking advantage of the large body of results on Datalog-like language. However, the rigidity of logical languages does not reflect the flexible programming style of object-oriented systems. For instance the application of the same method to different objects. In this paper we propose an extension based on variable labels that allow to express generic methods through rules. The semantics of this approach is still based on fixpoint computation.

Keywords: Object-oriented paradigm, state evolution, knowledge bases.

1 Introduction

The object-oriented paradigm has being widely applied in several areas of computer science, such as programming languages, information systems, software engineering and user interfaces. In the specific case of a distributed information system the distribution of data/rules requires to consider the distribution of the database and thus the development of cooperative databases. Moreover, for some complex application domains (like Computer Integrated Manufacturing applications), the information system is inherently distributed. Many applications integrating and using data and services of local database systems [4] are designed and needed. In all cases, the specification of a cooperating information system presents strong analogies with the specification of composite (database) systems. Information systems can be seen as a collection of "objects" each of them incorporating some knowledge (like facts, rules, and constraints) and being a unit of design that can be composed with other objects. In this paper we consider the above problem in the context of deductive databases. The motivation for this choice is related to the formal model underlying deductive databases, which provides a formal behavior and also a computational model. Note that we will consider an extension called Obj-U-Datalog [3] considering deductive objects, that is objects expressed through a logic language and which can change the state. The relevant characteristic of U-Datalog is that updates are not executed as soon as they are evaluated, rather they are collected in a set and executed altogether at the end of the refutation process, if this process succeeds and the

*The work of D. Montesi has been partly supported by the ERCIM fellowship *Information and Knowledge Systems*.

set is ground and consistent (i.e. it does not contain complementary updates on the same fact). The feature of Obj-U-Datalog is instead to group data and rules to form deductive objects. Such objects interact through labeled atoms. The language we propose in this paper (called X-Obj-U-Datalog) is based on the notion of deductive object. Each deductive object is an U-Datalog database. Each object has a state (a set of facts) and a set of methods (rules) to manipulate the data. Methods may also contain update atoms to modify the object state. Moreover the computational model of our language is based on cooperation among objects through message passing. In Obj-U-Datalog such cooperation was fixed once for all at program development time. In this paper, instead we propose an approach to dynamic message passing where the label is a variable and can be instantiated at execution time. Our approach greatly improves the flexibility of deductive objects and is in the main stream of object calculus, according to [8]. In our approach, methods expressed through rules, cooperate with objects which are not fixed. They can change over time according to different instances for variable labels. We call them *generic methods*. Unfortunately, this dynamicity is paid with more computation. Indeed, in X-Obj-U-Datalog, the evaluation of a transaction must consider this new dynamic component which was not present in Obj-U-Datalog databases. The protptype has bee implementated translating the X-Obj-U-Datalog database into and U- Datalog database and by means of a bottom-up meta interpreter for U-Datalog [2]. The result of this paper is a rule language of cooperating objects expressed as deductive databases preserving the nice computational model of Datalog language. This allows the re-use of the already developed techniques for efficient query evaluation. Moreover, in databases an important issue is to ensure transactional behavior of a set of updates, that is all of them are executed or none of them is performed. Thus any collection of cooperating databases should ensure a transactional behavior. This is the second result of this paper, that is the semantics of cooperating databases has a transactional behavior. In the remainder of the paper we introduce the language and we show the flexibility through an example. We assume some previous knowledge of Datalog language [5].

2 X-Obj-U-Datalog

A deductive database $EDB_i \cup IDB$ expresses an object where the EDB part is the *object state* and the IDB part expresses *the methods* to manipulate the state. The deductive capability comes from the logical nature of the Datalog language. Rules are used to express simple methods which can query and/or update the object. Other languages use rules as methods. The approach proposed by Abiteboul et al. [1] does not consider state evolution. The approach proposed in [6] considers state evolution and has a formal semantics, but uses active rules (e.g., production rules extended with events) to express methods. An X-Obj-U-Datalog program consists of a set of object databases, each object in the program consists of the object state and the methods, that is $obj_j = \langle EDB_j, IDB_j \rangle$. obj_j is the object identifier which is defined over a fixed domain of constant object names OID. The *object state* is a set of facts, that is a set of ground atoms. The object state is a time-varying component, so in the following we may denote with EDB_j^i the possible states of object obj_j, i.e. EDB_j^i denotes the i-th state of object obj_j.

Definition 2.1 *A set of methods is a set of rules of the form*

$$H \leftarrow U_1, \ldots, U_i, B_{i+1}, \ldots, B_w, X_1 : B_{w+1}, \ldots, X_p : B_z.$$

where H is an intensional atom, $X_1 : B_{w+1}, \ldots, X_p : B_z$ are labeled conditions, that is they refer to specific objects. $B_{i+1}, \ldots, B_w$ (as in Datalog) are unlabeled conditions, that is they refer to the object itself where the rule is defined. $U_1, \ldots, U_i$ is the update part. To ensure encapsulation the updates refer to the object itself. The updates $(U_1, \ldots, U_i)$ and conditions $(B_{i+1}, \ldots, B_w, X_1 : B_{w+1}, \ldots, X_p : B_z)$ cannot be both empty. The variables $X_1, \ldots, X_p$ ranges over OID and must appear as arguments of an extensional predicate.

The intuitive meaning of a rule is: "if B_{w+1} is true in the object to which X_1 is instantiated , ..., B_z is true in the object to which X_p is instantiated, $B_{i+1}, ..., B_w$ are true in the object where the rule is defined and the updates $U_1, ..., U_i$ are consistent, then H is true". The notion of consistency is given informally. Intuitively, the updates $+p(X), -p(X)$, i.e. complementary updates, are not consistent. The updates $+p(Y), -p(X)$ could be consistent if the bindings for the variables were for example $X = tom, Y = bob$. By contrast with the bindings $X = tom, Y = tom$, they are not consistent. Cooperation among objects is supported using labeled atoms in rule bodies. If the object obj_i has a rule containing the labeled atom $obj_j : B_s$, this means that object obj_i cooperates with another object (the one to which variable X_J is instantiated), calling the method B_s. Note that a method call can involve updates only as side effect. This ensures the encapsulation. Thus a method call is a channel, where we have synchronous communication and parameter passing through unification. The use of labeled atoms in rules supports message passing among objects, thus we refer to labeled atoms also as message atoms.

Definition 2.2 *An Obj-U-Datalog program consists of a fixed set of cooperating objects*

$$O - DB = \{obj_1, obj_2, ..., obj_s\}$$

where each obj_j, $1 \leq j \leq s$, consists of an extensional component EDB_j, which is a set of ground facts, called object state, and an intensional component IDB_j, which is a set of methods, as in Definition 2.1.

A transaction has the form $B_1, ..., B_w, obj_1 : B_{w+1}, ..., obj_p : B_z$. and cannot contain update atoms. However its execution may indirectly generate updates, because of the invocation of rules with update atoms in their bodies. We do not allow update atoms in transactions to provide encapsulation, i.e., an object state can only be modified through its methods. Note that a transaction may contain two different kinds of atoms: labeled ones and unlabeled ones. Unlabeled atoms stand for the request for a refutation of the atom in any object constituting the database, while labeled atoms are directed to a specific object. The values to these objects can be given at transaction time. Note that the language does not support a strict encapsulation, in that it allows to directly access the attribute values (through queries on extensional predicates). We only disallow the modification of object attributes from outside the object. A *complex transaction* T is a sequence of transactions $T_1; ...; T_k$. It should be clear that a transaction provides different roles: the role of a query, in that it returns a set of bindings, an update role (even if indirectly, as seen) with a transactional behavior (all the updates are executed or, in case of inconsistencies, none of them is performed).

Example 2.1 *We assume a collection of cooperating rule based databases. Each of them can change its state through updates. Consider a cooperating databases containing four objects obj_1, obj_2, obj_3 and obj_4, where*

$obj_1 = $ name(computer_science), n_exams(18), good_score(S) $\leftarrow$ leq(S, 25)

$obj_2 = $ name(mathematics), n_exams(15), good_score(S) $\leftarrow$ leq(S, 27)

$obj_3 = $ dept(obj_1), year(3),
good(NEx, Avg) $\leftarrow$ dept(X), year(Year), X : n_exams(NE),
    X : good_score(Avg), obj_4 : ad(NEx, Year, NE),
chDept(NDept) $\leftarrow$ $-$dept(Dept), $+$dept(NDept), dept(Dept).

$obj_4 = $ contains a table of facts for the predicate ad.
This object does not have methods.

Since dept(obj_1) *is contained in* obj_3, *the rule for the good predicate contains two message calls to object* obj_1. *Suppose now to execute the transaction* obj_3 : chDept(obj_2), *then the rule for the good predicate contains now two message calls to object* obj_2. *In such a way, if the value for the attribute department of object* obj_3 *is changed, the good predicate refers automatically to the data of the new department.* ◇

From the above example we can note that there are different kinds of (synchronous) cooperation:

- $obj_3 \Rightarrow_{ad} obj_4$. This is a one way, one-to-one fixed cooperation on the channel *ad*.
- $obj_3 \Rightarrow_{good\_score, n\_exams} obj_1$. This is a one way, one-to-one dynamic cooperation on the channels *good_score, n_exams*. Indeed, after the execution of the transaction obj_3 : chDept(obj_2) this cooperation is substituted by $obj_3 \Rightarrow_{good\_score, n\_exams} obj_2$.

A labeled condition $(X_j : k(x))$ represents a channel (k) between the rule of the database where it is defined (obj_i) and the label (X_j) of the condition. The cooperation is provided through the condition and the parameters are transmitted through unification [7].

The semantics of an X-Obj-U-Datalog program is an extension of that introduced in [3]. Unfortunately, the dymanicity induced by variable labels do not allow to apply straightforward efficient query evaluation methods. However, the approach to transform an X-Obj-U-Datalog database into a U-Datalog one allow use to transform variable labels into special varible and the to apply efficient query evaluation strategies to the transformed database. On open interesting point is the application of extended efficient query evaluation strategies directly to X-Obj-U-Datalog.

References

[1] S. Abiteboul, G. Lausen, H. Uphoff, and E. Waller. Methods and rules. In P. Buneman and S. Jajodia, editors, *Proc. of the ACM SIGMOD Int'l Conf. on Management of Data*, pages 32–41, 1993.

[2] E. Bertino, B. Catania, G. Guerrini, M. Martelli and D. Montesi. A Bottom-up Interpreter for database languages with Updates and Transactions. To appear *Proc. Joint Conference on Declarative Programming Gulp-Prode*, Peniscola, 1994.

[3] E. Bertino, G. Guerrini, and D. Montesi. Deductive Object Databases. *Proc. Eighth European Conference on Objects-Oriented Programming*, Bologna, pages 213–235, Springer-Verlag, Bologna, 1994.

[4] M. L. Brodie. The Promise of Distributed Computing and the Challenges of Legacy Systems. In P. M. Gray and R. J. Lucas, editors, *Proc. BNCOD 10*, Lecture Notes in Computer Science, vol. 618, pages 1–28. Springer-Verlag, Berlin, 1992.

[5] S. Ceri, G. Gottlob, and L. Tanca. *Logic Programming and Databases*. Springer-Verlag, Berlin, 1990.

[6] D. Montesi and R. Torlone. A Rewriting technique for implementing Active Object Systems. To appear *Proc. International Symposium on Object-Oriented Methodologies and Systems (ISOOMS)*, Palermo, 1994.

[7] F.G. McCabe. *Logic and Objects*. PhD thesis, University of London, November 1988.

[8] O. Nierstrasz. Towards an object calculus. In *ECOOP '91 workshop on object-based concurrent computing*, Lecture Notes in Computer Science, vol. 612, pages 1–20. Springer- Verlag, Berlin, 1991.

SOFTWARE

DEVELOPMENT

Development of an Intelligent Object-Oriented CASE Tool

Daniela Mehandjiska-Stavreva, David Page and Paul Clark

Faculty of Information and Mathematical Sciences
Department of Computer Science
Massey University
Palmerston North, New Zealand
Email D.Mehandjiska@massey.ac.nz D.C.Page@massey.ac.nz P.K.Clark@massey.ac.nz

ABSTRACT. *A new intelligent methodology-independent CASE tool is proposed to support information systems development. Although a multitude of object-oriented analysis and design methodologies exist, neither these nor their corresponding CASE environments (i) support the building of integrated information systems, (ii) span the entire object-oriented life cycle, (iii) are customisable, (iv) utilise advanced data presentation techniques, and (v) exhibit intelligent behaviour. The aim of the paper is to address some of these unresolved problems through the development of a new CASE tool. The tool requirements and constraints are identified. A top level tool structure is outlined and different subsystems architecture is further explored and discussed. The intelligent environment and some aspects of the user interface are also addressed.*

KEY WORDS: *Object-Oriented, CASE, Expert Systems.*

1. Introduction

The object-oriented (OO) movement at present is split into many factions. As a result no standards have been defined. There are a multiplicity of object-oriented analysis (OOA) and object-oriented design (OOD) methodologies (Champeaux et al., 1992). The descriptions of these methodologies do not distinguish clearly between what is considered analysis and what is considered design (Mehand et al., 1993). Some of the reasons for this are:
- it is not clear when OOA ends and OOD starts, since they are related by refinement, and the distinction between them is blurred. As Coad and Yourdon (Coad et al., 1991) state, moving from OOA to OOD is a progressive expansion of the model;
- many OOD methodologies specify how initially objects, classes, attributes and operations are identified. This is analysis. Examples are described in (Coad et al. 1991, Booch 1994, Wirfs-Brook et al. 1990);
- many OOA methodologies allow sufficiently expressive models to be developed such that they could be described as designs.

A direct consequence of this lack of consensus is that there are no mature CASE tools available. Current object-oriented CASE tools (ooCASE) are methodology dependent. They are not driven by the need to enable the successful construction of OO software but rather to sell a particular methodology (at this time there are over 27 different OO methodologies). The existing methodologies and their corresponding CASE tools support single phases of the development process, are not customisable, do not exhibit intelligent behaviour and do not exploit state-of-the-art data presentation and interaction techniques.

Many of these issues are also relevant and affect the construction of Object-Oriented Information Systems (OOIS). The most important are:
- the large number of existing object-oriented methodologies and dialects of these methodologies (for example Wirfs-Brook's responsibility driven design and its dialect adopted by Budd (1991));
- most object-oriented methodologies (OOMs) are still undergoing modifications, for example

Booch (1994). In addition as Brough (1992) stated methodologies must evolve;
* current commercial ooCASE tools are methodology dependent and support single phases of the development process.

To successfully build OOIS powerful CASE tools are required. The effectiveness of current CASE tools is limited as they:
* lack flexibility (dictate which methodology an organisation should use as the tools are vendor specific);
* lack integration between specification tools and construction tools (typically focus on a narrow portion of the system development process (Sumner, 1992));
* lack support for specifying methodology knowledge;
* are targeted to specific methodologies (Nilsson, 1990, Papahristos, 1991) (for example ObjecTool, Rational Rose/C++, OMTool, etc.);
* are not customisable;
* do not provide information interchange between analysis and design results expressed in different methodologies;
* do not provide means to successfully navigate complex structures of classes;
* do not utilise state-of-the-art data presentation and interaction techniques;
* do not support the emerging concept of frameworks.

The aim of the paper is to address some of these unresolved problems through the development of a new CASE tool. As the number of commercially available ooCASE tools is growing very quickly, only their common features and characteristics have been identified and addressed in this paper. The rapid emergence of new tools makes specific tool comparison a difficult, even meaningless task.

2. Methodology Independent CASE, Meta-CASE and CASE Shells

In the past few years the research into CASE technology has been concentrated in two main areas. The first one addressed the development of software environments with an open architecture aiming at the integration of independently developed CASE tools. Attempts have been made to create an open environment in which different methodologies and their supporting CASE tools coexist. This approach provides reusability of information. For example, communication among diverse methodologies is addressed in the Federated CASE Environment (FCE) by a common data dictionary (Papahristos et al., 1991).

A lot of research has also been done to address the problems of CASE tools methodology dependence. A metamodelling approach has been utilised to allow the generation of customised software specification environments. The goal of a meta system is to (semi) automatically generate the software necessary for a specific environment. Research prototypes adopting this approach include Metaview, MetaEdit, MetaPlex RAMATIC, etc. (Smolander et al. 1991 Sorenson et al. 1988). The environment for a given methodology is specified in two parts: conceptual definition and graphical definition. The conceptual definition is based on different data models. For example, MetaEdit is based on the Object-Property-Role-Relationship (OPRR) model. Metaview is based on Entity-Aggregate-Relationship-Attribute (EARA) model. RAMATIC is based on the set-oriented data model. The developed prototypes support mechanisms to express the mapping between the metamodelling concepts and corresponding graphical representations.

In general, none of these systems are aimed at OO software construction. The utilised underlying models (e.g. EARA, OPRR, etc.) do not directly support the object-oriented concepts of Inheritance and Message Passing. The developed research prototypes do not also address the important Human Computer Interaction (HCI) issues.

An alternative metamodelling approach is being undertaken in a prototype ooCASE tool, MOOT (Massey Object Oriented Tool). Instead of extending the existing conventional models to permit advanced semantic based data modelling (e.g. aggregation, generalisation and classification) the MOOT approach is to use the object model which naturally and directly supports all these concepts. MOOT is based on the object-oriented concepts of Objects, Classes, Inheritance and

Message Passing. To express the mapping between metamodelling concepts and graphical representations MOOT uses a methodology specification language. A notation definition language is used to support the definition of a graphical representation of the underlying object model (Page et al., 1994). MOOT has a common persistent store and a common methodology knowledge base which models the core (generic) OO concepts. Non generic features of OO methodologies require specialised knowledge bases to achieve the migration of analysis and design results.

The goal of the development of MOOT is to build a useable, intelligent, modifiable ooCASE tool which supports arbitrary OO methodologies and utilises state-of-the-art HCI data presentation techniques. MOOT is an intelligent environment which supports the specification of new methodologies' knowledge. MOOT will be used as a vehicle for research into other aspects of the OO approach as well as in teaching the principles of the object-oriented paradigm.

MOOT incorporates some of the characteristics referred to as features of an ideal CASE tool (Gibson 1988, Papahristos 1991). It supports a range of methodologies, has an open architecture and is configurable. Methodology-independence avoids conflicts resulting from:
- having to choose one and only one methodology;
- becoming CASE vendor dependent;
- being unable to extend the methodology to meet the special requirements of information systems, such as having additional annotation for hardware and people related activities;
- information interchange between analysis and design results expressed in different methodologies.

There are several advantages to this approach:
- The tools is open so it may be altered and extended to verify ideas about different methodologies and techniques;
- The activities of a company will not be restricted by the architecture and notation of third party CASE tools;
- A flexible and expressive tool can be used to develop systems to explore other applications of the object-oriented paradigm, e.g. concurrent object-oriented expert systems;
- The built in user model allows the tool to be used to teach the principles of the object-oriented paradigm.

The greatest advantage of a methodology-independent ooCASE is the flexibility to model different information systems of an enterprise with different methodologies and still retain a joint repository. Real-time production control systems deal with timing constraints and thus require a different OOM than cost accounting systems. Nevertheless both types of systems have to be merged to design effective Computer Integrated Manufacturing (CIM) systems. Company-wide repositories are therefore required to model information systems successfully across departmental boundaries and provide input for strategic information planning.

A justification for designing an ooCASE is the need for an open tool, i.e. a CASE tool which allows "other software development support systems" to be integrated into the ooCASE. Although this openness seems to be primarily a research requirement there is a distinct advantage for larger corporations to extend the tool to meet the companies' competitive-edge information requirements. As the development approach for the tool itself is object-oriented the design will give valuable insight into how to build object-oriented information systems.

To accelerate work on the tool our research group is monitoring but not implementing the OMG Common Object Request Broker Architecture (QED, 1992) and PCTE (PCTE, 1988) standards.

3. Tool Requirements

Based on identified limitations and drawbacks of the existing tools the generic ooCASE tool requirements have been identified.

The tool must be flexible to:
- support any of the current OO methodologies;

- allow customisation based on individual company requirements;
- support the specification of new methodology knowledge;
- be extendible when required;
- support the specification of new graphical notation;
- redefine the notation when required;
- change the conventions incorporated in the methodologies installed in the tool.

The tool must have a persistent storage facility to store and retrieve information:
- about the systems to be modelled;
- about any user-input such as drawing settings and supplementary textual input. This information is additional to the information kept about the user's current work.

The tool has to support the principles of the object-oriented paradigm:
- presentation of class/object hierarchies (is-a and part-of);
- presentation of object relationships (connected to, instantiation);
- presentation of message flows;
- clustering of classes/objects into subject areas or class categories with the ability to implode all class/objects belonging to the same subject area/ category into a single symbol;
- effective support for object behaviour analysis, such as events, triggers and state transitions.

The tool also should:
- exhibit intelligent behaviour through the application of acquired high level expertise;
- be able to hide and unhide information for the sake of better viewing clarity;
- use colour to highlight dynamic aspects of instantiation and message passing;
- utilise new distortion-oriented data presentation techniques.

Modern CASE tool development, apart from requiring well formulated methodologies to form the basis for the tool itself, is critically related to issues of human-computer interaction (HCI). One of the common problems associated with any computer representation of complex data, is the relatively small window through which an information space can be viewed. CASE tools, which generally provide multiple orthogonal representations of the model being developed, share this problem. The small window effect gives rise to difficulties in locating a given item of information (navigation), in interpreting an item once it has been located, and in relating a given item to others, if that item cannot be seen in its full context. These items, in a CASE environment, may be classes, objects, or subjects.

A range of techniques have evolved to overcome some of these difficulties, and these have been broadly classified as either distortion-oriented or non-distortion oriented. Whilst the non-distortion techniques may be adequate for limited text-based applications, they generally do not provide sufficient context to the user to support navigation of larger graphical data spaces. The developed CASE tool will utilise new distortion-oriented presentation techniques (Leung and Apperley, 1993). The common feature of these techniques is to allow a user to examine a local area in detail on a section of the display screen (eg a number of classes with their attributes and methods), and at the same time to present a global view of the entire object-oriented architecture diagram to provide an overall context and to facilitate navigation.

3.1 Core object-oriented requirements

The ooCASE tool meets the following requirements supported by each methodology (core OO principles and concepts):

- Class and Object diagrams, showing:
  - generalisation-specialisation (is-a);
  - part-of;
  - associations;
  - message passing.
- Subject / category diagrams, grouping of classes;
- Attributes belonging to each class and object;

• Services (operations) offered by each class and object.

The core OO principles and concepts are supported by each object-oriented methodology and are therefore "hard coded" into the tool. A generic knowledge base is constructed to support these common features of the methodologies. Additional information requirements resulting from the special information needs of each installed methodology are "soft coded" into the tool by a knowledge engineer.

4. Subsystem decomposition

Three different approaches can be utilised to build a CASE tool which is modifiable:

1   Build a Super Methodology which encompasses everything required to model systems.

2   Maintain the projects in a common persistent store. All projects are stored in the same way. Each methodology provides different views of information in the persistent store. Information interchange is simple as the information is stored in a common way for all projects.

3   Each methodology requires a distinct persistent store. Information is exchanged between projects by filters which translate between methodologies.

Approach one is infeasible since the modelling techniques which will be required in the future cannot be predicted. Maintaining projects in a common persistent store is difficult as the different methodologies often incorporate unique modelling techniques. Approach three describes the current state of CASE technology.

The approach taken in the methodology independent ooCASE tool is a combination of approaches two and three. The core principles and concepts of the object-oriented paradigm have been modelled and stored in the same way for each methodology. The unique conceptual structures and models each methodology supports are stored separately. Hence filters are only required to translate those aspects of a methodology which are unique. All parts of a project which is consistent with core OO concepts and principles can automatically migrate to different methodologies.

In addition to its open architecture the tool under development supports the specification of new methodologies. The conceptual and graphical definitions of a new methodology's environment are specified with notation and methodology editors. The notation editor is a graphical metamodelling editor. It allows the conceptual structures of the user methodology to be modelled with a user defined graphical notation. The methodology editor allows the definition of the conceptual structures supported by the methodology. The notation and methodology editors allow the tool to be tailored in the areas of the user interface and the conceptual structures and rules used in the methodologies.

The overall tool structure is shown in Figure 1.

4.1. Graphical User Interface

A CASE tool which can support different methodologies and whose Graphical User Interface (GUI) has a consistent look and feel reduces the amount of effort required to fully utilise these methodologies. Each methodology may use distinct notation but the interaction mechanisms and interaction items are the same.

As each methodology has its own notation the ooCASE tool has a notation editor to define new notations. A language which facilitates abstract definitions of graphical notations and the human-computer interaction with them has been developed. The notation editor generates a template description of the symbols, connections and the Human Computer Interaction (HCI) with the notation.

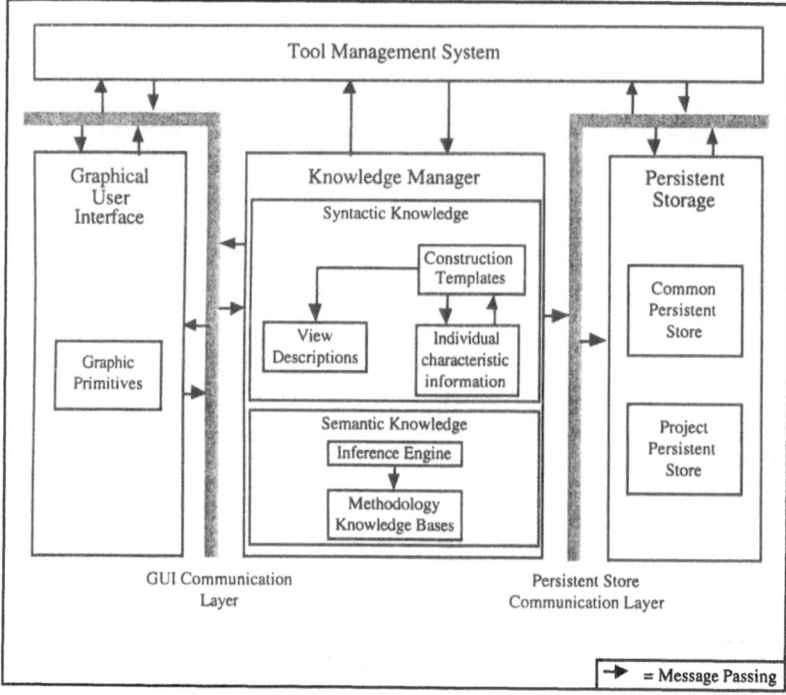

Figure 1 Tool top level decomposition

A template is a blueprint for creating graphical representations (views) of symbols and connections and describes the allowable interaction with these views (Page 1994, Egbert et al. 1992). Whenever the user wants to enter a new piece of information, such as a new class, the corresponding template is invoked and the template creates a view of the class. Figure 2 illustrates the relationship between the classes Template, View and Viewable_Thing.

The class Window_Manger is responsible for maintaining multiple windows on the display screen. Each instance of class Window manages its component instances of class View. The implementation of classes Context and CASE_Context are specific to the interface development tool kit used. Primitive low level operations needed for the interface development environment are provided by the class Context. The class CASE_Context provides the standard GUI communication layer. In the development of MOOT Tcl/Tk is used to build the interface. A more detailed description of the template mechanism explored and implemented is given in (Page et al., 1994).

A template generator has been developed which generates methodology notation descriptions in the utilised notation definition language. The basis of the template language are the rules describing how a view may be created. Views change dynamically in response to changes of the height and width of the enclosed textboxes. The primary basis of the template generator tool is the automatic generation of the template code which describes how each drawing object responds to variable sized textboxes. It is necessary to model this response so that the tool can generate the template code with minimal user intervention. The tool uses a visual programming approach to allow graphical notations to be described.

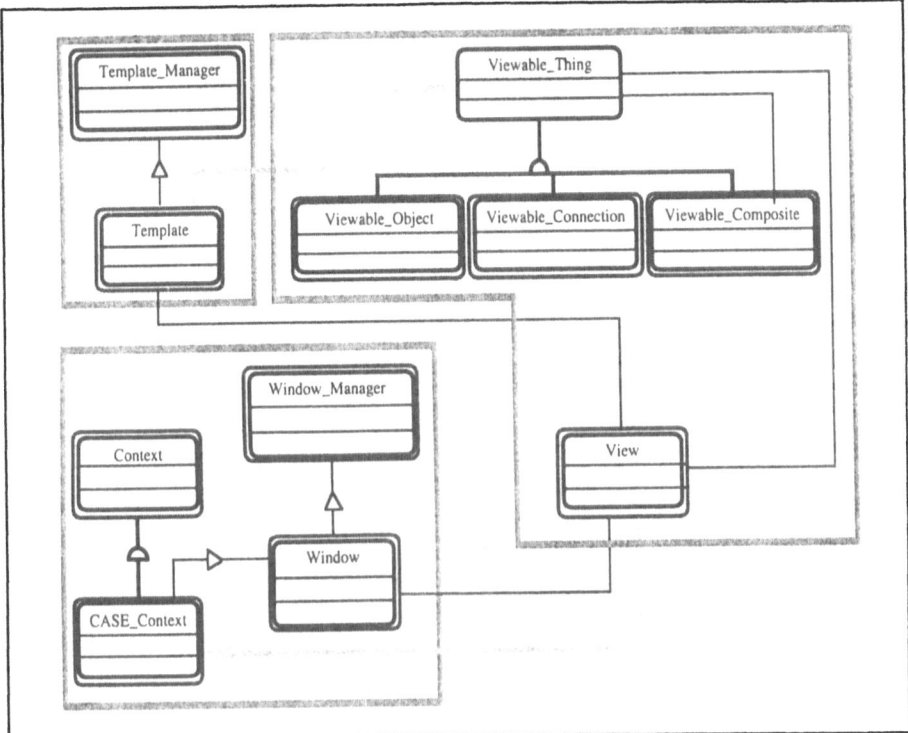

Figure 2 Template mechanism explored

4.2. Knowledge Manager

The developed CASE tool adopts the expert system approach and exhibits intelligent behaviour. The user model will be built to help monitoring and control of the user's progress. A knowledge base will be constructed containing past experience.

A generic knowledge base incorporating the object-oriented principles and concepts valid per all methodologies will be built into the tool. A methodology editor will be designed to allow the specification of the conceptual structures of different methodologies. It will also handle the incorporation of specific methodology dependent guidelines and rules.

The knowledge manager is responsible for maintaining knowledge of two different categories, semantic and syntactic knowledge. Semantic knowledge specifies how particular data is handled within the methodology. An example is whether two classes in a diagram can have the same name.

Syntactic knowledge describes the construction of the different components of a methodology notation. A construction template is used to generate a view description. This is a combination of individual characteristic information and the internal specification of the construction template.

The knowledge manager has a set of knowledge bases, one for each installed methodology plus the hard-coded knowledge base (the generic knowledge base) for the core OO principles. Installed methodologies inherit the core OO principles from the generic knowledge base as well as define their own specific features and characteristics. The knowledge manager semantic subsystem object diagram using Coad and Yourdon's notation is shown in Figure 3.

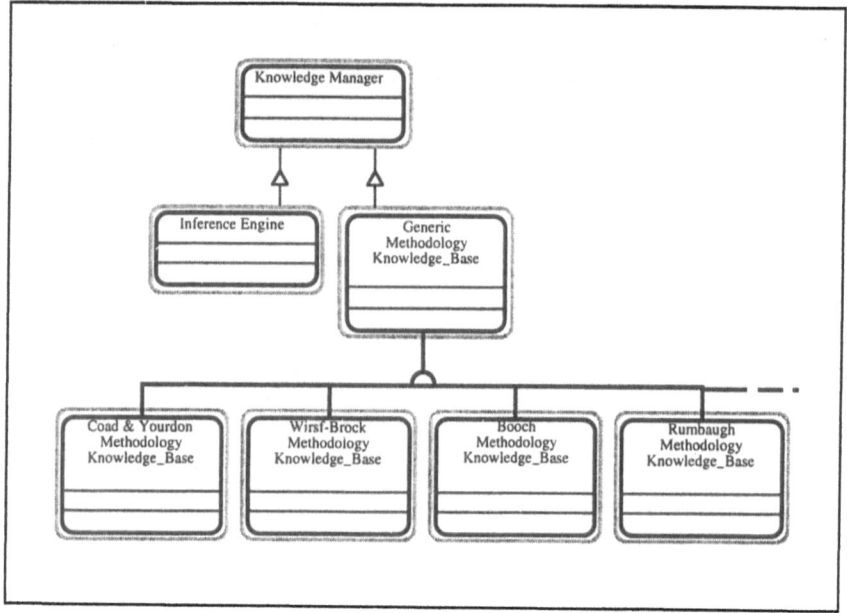

Figure 3 Knowledge Manager

By providing the tool with a generic knowledge base:
- the installation effort for new methodologies is reduced;
- all methodologies installed have a non-empty intersection of object-oriented features thus allowing transformation from one methodology to another.

The hard-coded generic knowledge base does not allow the knowledge engineer to build other methodologies than object-oriented ones.

4.3. Persistent Storage

The persistent storage consists of a common persistent store and a project persistent store. The common store holds the results of completed analysis and designs. The project store holds work-in-progress.

Ode 3.0 (Biliris et al., 1994) has been chosen for the implementation of the persistent store. Ode is a database system and environment based on the object-oriented paradigm. Ode, similar to other object-oriented databases (Cattell 1991, August-Wilhelm, 1992) allows any class to be automatically added to the persistent store by declaring it "persistent". By having such tight coupling between the C++ code and the object-oriented database the systems developer is freed from writing a database schema.

O++, a language which is an extension of C++, is used to define, query and manipulate databases. It provides facilities for creating persistent objects, defining sets and queries.

There are many OO databases which would satisfy the requirements of the project. Ode is chosen primarily because of the constraints imposed by the development platform (Sun SPARCstation running Solaris 2.3) and the lack of funding for purchasing a commercial OO database.

4.4. Tool Management System

The Tool Management System controls the access to the tool, its components and contains utilities to uphold the integrity of any data in the system. The functionality includes:
• Importing new information into the common persistent store;
• Printing information;
• Generating syntactic or semantic information;
• Translating information from one notation to another.

5. Tool Development

The tool is currently under construction using iterative, incremental development consisting of three stages. The construction has started with the implementation of the GUI, as the flexibility required to represent varying notations has been considered the most time consuming part of the tool development. A prototype of the GUI has been completed. Two snapshots of the graphical user interface of the system configured to support Rumbaugh's methodology is shown in Figure 4.

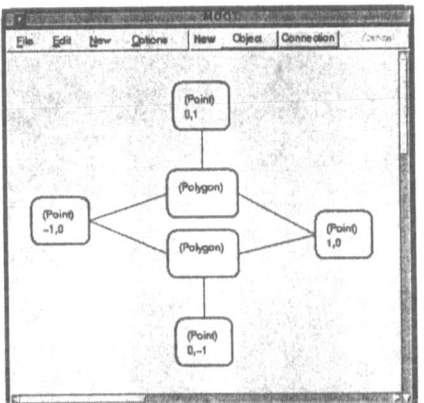
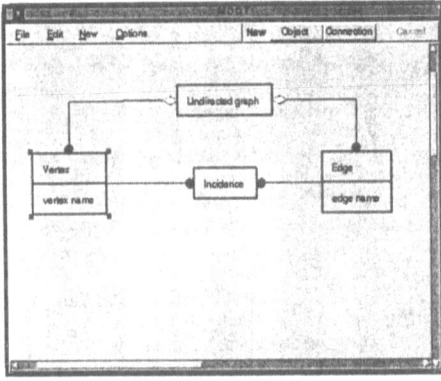

Figure 4 a) Instance diagram b) Object diagram

TCL 7.3, TK 3.6 and XF 2.3 is used to implement the GUI. The tool itself is written in SparcWorks C++ 2.0. Ode 3.0 is used for the object oriented database. The system runs on a SPARCstation LX under Solaris 2.3 and X/Windows.

Work on the knowledge manager and persistent store has already commenced. An object oriented knowledge representation mechanism is adopted. The inference mechanism explored to build the inference engine is based on inheritance and message passing.

The next two stages are addressing the following tasks:
• Installing different methodologies as well as addressing conflicts and non generic commonalties between methodologies;
• Creating multiple views, importing into and exporting from the persistent store and providing report writer capabilities.

The knowledge manager and persistent store are currently in their design phase. Two approaches are being investigated:

In the first approach the instances, which are stored and used in the inference process, are those of the subclasses of Viewable_Thing. That is Viewable_Object, Viewable_Connection and Viewable_Composite (Page et al., 1994). Each of these classes have a type as an attribute. A Booch class would have type Class, a Coad and Yourdon Class&Object would have type Class&Object and a Rumbaugh Process would have type process.

The advantage of this mechanism is that only four types exist at compile time, each representing the methods of structuring employed in a model: symbols, relationships and groups. New models are easily added without any recompilation of the CASE tool. A high level OO knowledge representation language will be constructed to facilitate building of the knowledge base. The disadvantage of this high level of abstraction is that there are only four types to store in the OODB which makes writing an efficient schema difficult. This problem can be alleviated if objects can be structured in the OODB by using each object's type attribute.

The second approach uses C++ to build the knowledge base for each new methodology and an object-oriented database as the persistent store. The knowledge engineer constructs new methodology knowledge bases by writing C++ code reusing existing classes where possible. Classes for reuse already exist in the generic knowledge base and in the knowledge bases of existing methodologies. Using inheritance the knowledge engineer can modify the behaviour of existing classes to match the requirements of the new methodology.

For methodologies which make use of new types not covered by the core OO principles the knowledge engineer has to construct classes from the very beginning. The generic knowledge base also contains classes which support the creation of new methodologies. In addition there exist classes which support the translation of new types into "Viewable_Things". The extra C++ code is compiled without having to recompile the tool itself (Segal and Frieder, 1993).

A tailored user interface will be built to allow the installation of new methodologies by entering their semantics without programming in C++.

Future enhancements are:
- Multi-user access and version control;
- Automatic code generation;
- Reverse engineering facilities;
- Class/ framework browser;
- Integration with project management tools.

6. Conclusions

The advantages of the object-oriented paradigm are that:
- it applies to the whole software development life cycle;
- any additional models necessary to meet the extra requirements of new OO methodologies do not violate the core OO principles, in other words: all OO methodologies share a common core.

These two advantages make the design of a methodology-independent ooCASE tool feasible as no transformation of models along the software development life cycle is necessary.

The main benefit of a methodology-independent CASE tool is building company-wide object-oriented information systems. It also provides a powerful environment to investigate object-oriented methodologies and concepts.

With software reuse being the main issue of object-oriented information systems (Griss, 1993), a methodology-independent ooCASE helps to "glue" systems together which have been built using different methodologies.

The CASE tool of tomorrow must be customisable, open and multi-methodology to give designers methodologies which suit their needs. To have an all-embracing methodology which suits all types of information systems is not foreseeable in the near future. As it is the case with operating systems, programming languages and expert systems we will most likely have to live with a diversity in object-oriented methodologies. The key question is whether this diversity is mastered by having a number of different object-oriented CASE tools side by side which exchange their information via interfaces or whether that diversity will be mastered by having a methodology-independent ooCASE tool.

The future of a methodology-independent ooCASE tool will largely depend on how diverse the different methodologies will be and how much "knowledge" the knowledge engineer has to enter to install a new methodology.

The generic features of the tool, its flexibility, adaptability, advanced user interface and intelligence will allow the tool to benefit all sectors and companies dealing with software construction.

References

(August-Wilhelm, 1992):   August-Wilhelm Scheer, *Architecture of Integrated Information Systems: Foundations of Enterprise Modelling*, Springer-Verlag, New York, 1992.

(August-Wilhelm, 1990):   August-Wilhelm Scheer, Wirtsschaftsinformatik:*Informationssysteme im Industriebetrieb*, Springer-Verlag, Berlin, 3rd edition, 1990.

(Booch, 1994):   Grady Booch, *Object-Oriented Analysis and Design with Applications*, The Benjamin/Cummings Publishing Company, Inc., Redwood City, CA, 2nd edition, 1994.

(Berard, 1993):   Edward V. Berard, *Essays on Object-oriented Software Engineering, Vol. 1*, Prentice-Hall, Inc, Englewood Cliffs, NJ, 1993.

(Biliris et al, 1994):   A. Biliris, J. Gava, N. Gehani, D. Lieuwen, E. Panagos and T. Roycroft. *Ode 3.0 User Manual*, AT & T Bell Laboratories, Murry Hill, New Jersey 07974.

(Budd, 1991):   T. Budd, An Introduction to Object-Oriented Programming, Addison Wesley Publishing Company, Reading, MA, 1991.

(Brough, 1992):   Mike Brough, *Methods for CASE: a Generic Framework*, Advanced Information Systems Engineering: 4th International Conference CAiSE'92, Springer-Verlag, Berlin, 1992.

(Cattell, 1991):   R.G.G. Cattell, *Object Data Management*, Addison-Wesley Publishing Company, Reading, MA, 1991.

(Coad et al., 1991):   Peter Coad and Edward Yourdon, *Object-Oriented Analysis*, Yourdon Press, Englewood Cliffs, NJ, 2nd edition, 1991.

(Champeaux et al., 1992):   Dennis de Champeaux and Penelope Faure, *A comparative study of object-oriented analysis methods*, Journal of Object-Oriented Programming, Vol 5, No 1, March / April 1992.

(Egbert et al., 1992):   Parris K Egbert and William J. Kubitz, *Application Graphics Modelling Support Through Object Orientation*, IEEE Computer, Vol 25, No 10, October, 1992.

(Embley et al., 1992):   David W. Embley et al., *Object-Oriented Systems Analysis, A Model-Driven Approach*, Yourdon Press, Englewood Cliffs, NJ, 1992.

(Gibson, 1988):   M. Gibson. *A Guide to Selecting CASE Tools*. Datamation, July 1, 1988, pp 65-66.

(Griss, 1993):   M.L.Griss, *Software reuse: From library to factory*, IBM Systems Journal, Vol 32, No 4, 1993.

(Harrison et al., 1993):   William Harrison and Harold Ossher, *Subject-Oriented Programming (A Critique of Pure Objects)*, IBM T.J. Watson Research Center, in OOPSLA'93 (published as: ACM SIGPLAN Notices, Vol 28, No 10, October, 1993).

(Lang et al., 1993): Neil Lang, Shlaer-Mellor, *Object-Oriented Analysis Rules*, ACM Sigsoft Software Engineering Notes, Vol 18, No 1, January, 1993.

(Leung et al,, 1993): Y. Leung and M. D. Apperley, *A Taxonomy of Distortion-Oriented Display Techniques for Graphical Data Presentation*, Proceedings of HCI International'93, Orlando, Florida, 1993.

(Martin, 1993): James Martin, *Principles of Object-Oriented Analysis and Design*, Prentice-Hall, Inc, Englewood Cliffs, NJ, 1993.

(Mehand. et al., 1993): D. Mehandjiska-Stavreva and D. Page, *Object-Oriented Development of Expert Systems*, in ANNES'93 (published as: IEEE Computer Society Press November, 1993).

(Nilson, 1990): E. G. Nilsson. *CASE Tools and Software Factories* in Advanced Information Systems Engineering, CAiSE '90 edited by G. Goos and J. Hartmanis, Springer-Verlag, Berlin, 1990.

(Page, 1994): David Page et al., *An abstract Definition of Graphical Notations for Object-Orientated Information Systems*, OOIS'94.

(Papahristos et al., 1991): S. Papahristos, W. A. Gray. *Federated CASE Environment* in Advanced Information Systems Engineering, CAiSE '91 edited by G. Goos and J. Hartmanis, Springer-Verlag, Berlin, 1991.

(PCTE, 1988): European Computer Manufacturer Association (ECMA), *PCTE*, Geneva, 1988.

(Poet Software, 1993): Poet Software GmbH, *POET Programmer's & Reference Guide*, Release 2.0, Poet Software GmbH, 22359 Hamburg, Germany, 1993.

(QED, 1992): Object Management Group, *The Common Object Request Broker: Architecture and Specification*, distributed by QED Publishing Group, Wesley, MA, 1992.

(Rumbaugh et al., 1991): James Rumbaugh et al., *Object-oriented modelling and design*, Prentice-Hall, Inc, Englewood Cliffs, NJ, 1991.

(Segal et al., 1993): Mark E. Segal and Ophir Frieder, *On-The-Fly Program Modification: Systems for Dynamic Updating*, IEEE Software, Vol 10, No 2, March, 1993.

(Shlaer et al., 1988): Shlaer, S. and Mellor S., *Object-Oriented Systems Analysis: Modelling the World in Data*, Yourdon Press, Englewood Cliffs, 1988.

(Smolander et al., 1991): K. Smolander et al. MetaEdit: *A flexible Graphical Environment for Methodology Modelling* in Advanced Information Systems Engineering, CAiSE '91 edited by G. Goos and J. Hartmanis, Springer-Verlag, Berlin, 1991.

(Sorenson et al., 1988): P. G. Sorenson et al. *On-The Metaview System for Many Specification Environments* IEEE Software, Vol 5, No 2, March, 1988.

(Sumner, 1992): M. Sumner. *The Impact of Computer-Assisted Software Engineering on Systems Development*. IFIP Transactions - The Impact of Computer Supported Technologies on Information Systems Development edited by Kendall K.E, Lyytinen K, DeGross J I, Elsevier Science Publishers, Amsterdam, 1992.

(Wirfs-Brook et al., 1990): Wirfs-Brook, R et al., *Designing Object-Oriented Software*, Prentice-Hall, Inc, Englewood Cliffs, NJ, 1990.

Identifying Internal and External Characteristics of Classes likely to be useful as Structural Complexity Metrics

Brian Henderson-Sellers

Centre for Object Technology Applications and Research
School of Computing Sciences
University of Technology, Sydney
P.O. Box 123
Broadway, NSW 2007, Australia
E-mail: brian@socs.uts.edu.au   Fax: +61 2 330 1807

ABSTRACT. *Metrics appropriate to object-oriented information systems development are urgently required. As part of an ongoing evaluation of existing OO metrics and the development and validation of new ones, here we systematically consider the various perspectives of an object-oriented system: inside a class, external at the class level, system level, system level relationships and inheritance coupling.*

KEY WORDS: Metrics, object-oriented systems

1. Introduction

Metrics appropriate to object-oriented information systems development are urgently required. As part of an ongoing evaluation of existing OO metrics (particularly the six of Chidamber and Kemerer, 1991) and the development and validation of new ones (e.g. Cant *et al.*, 1994; Pant *et al.*, 1994), here we systematically consider the various perspectives of an object-oriented system: inside a class, external at the class level (i.e. the specification or interface), system level (but ignoring relationships), system level relationships (excluding inheritance), inheritance coupling. By focussing on the code and design level characteristics, we are considering only "structural complexity" metrics — Figure 1 sets these in perspective. These proposals, which provide a "pool" of potential measures for adoption within a specific application of Basili and Rombach's (1988) GQM framework, remain to be evaluated and their practicality assessed within specific contexts and "questions".

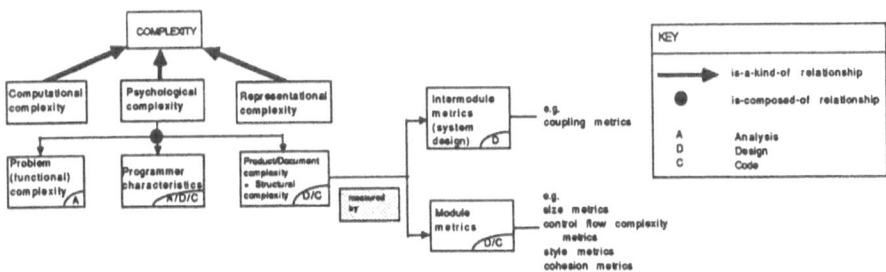

Figure 1 Classification of complexity metrics

2. Inside a class

A class can be considered to contain n public methods (those that appear as services in the interface) and, in some languages, m public attributes. There are also r private methods and s private attributes. Each method is a piece of procedural code which may or may not send messages to other objects. For each of these $n + r$ methods, we can calculate a control flow complexity. This can be accomplished by local application of the cyclomatic complexity, $V(G)$ (McCabe, 1976) or $V_{LI}(G)$ (Henderson-Sellers and Tegarden, 1994). Since there is a $V(G)$ for each method, there must be $n + r$ such values.

For each class, we can therefore count or calculate a distribution of $V(G)$ ($n+r$ values) — from this we calculate measures of central tendency and dispersion[1] and a class total $V(G)$ — this last tallies with WMC of Chidamber and Kemerer (1991).

As well as cyclomatic complexity, we could characterize each method by its size (assuming that a consistent definition for size is used). This gives $n + r$ values in the class for method size.

For each class, we can therefore count or calculate a distribution of method size ($n+r$ values) — and consequently median, mean, standard deviation (as appropriate) and a class total method size — this is labelled TMS.

For each class, we can also do a straightforward count of the total number of methods = NOM of Li and Henry (1993) and the total number of attributes = NOA.

These values give one way of representing overall *class size*, S_C, as (i) a weighted calculation of method and attribute sizes = NOA + TMS or (ii) an unweighted calculation of method and attribute sizes = NOA + NOM = SIZE2 of Li and Henry (1993).

The final structural "complexity" measure internal to a class is the LCOM (lack of cohesion of methods) metric of Chidamber and Kemerer (1991). Again this is a value that can be calculated *for each class*.

3. External at the class level

External to the class, we see only the interface or the specification. We can characterize this as a total number of services, some of which are queries and some of which are commands. We see, from outside, no indication of (internal) size or complexity. We can thus count (a) the number of commands for the ith class, c_i and (b) the number of queries for the ith class, q_i. We might alternatively prefer to weight these with the number of arguments by adding one for each argument to the unweighted count i.e. the number of weighted commands, $c_i' = \left(c + \sum_{j=1}^{c} C_{arglist_j} \right)_i$ and the number of weighted queries, $q_i' = \left(q + \sum_{k=1}^{q} C_{arglist_k} \right)_i$ where $C_{arglist_j}$ is the cardinality of the argument list for the jth service.

4. System level but ignoring relationships

At this level, we simply gross up some of the measures we have already identified. A first, simple measure is the total number of classes in the system, C_S. This is an extremely rough measure but one can say that a system with 1000 classes in it is likely to be bigger (in all senses of the word) than one with only 20 classes.

---

[1] For measures on an ordinal scale we must use the median; whereas for measures on an interval or ratio scale we can also use means and standard deviations.

We can then look at system-wide averages, assuming we have the appropriate interval or ratio scale, derived from the lower-level measures: mean and standard deviation for c_i, c'_i, q_i, q'_i, S_{C_i} and NOM_i.

5. System level relationships but excluding inheritance

Coupling is epitomized at a design level where only a single client–server relationship between any pair of classes is considered. This is the CBO metric of Chidamber and Kemerer (1991) and the more detailed message passing metrics, discussed above, of Li and Henry (1993). Collaborators which require such connections are related to the declarations of ADTs within the class body and are thus also equivalent to Li and Henry's DAC metric. The CBO measure or "design fanout", is easily calculable from a design diagram. Since multiple objects from the same class will probably not add significantly (a hypothesis that we have yet to test) to the psychological complexity of the class being measured, this design level metric can be done at the class level. Another way of thinking about this metric is simply as the "number of other classes referenced".

A useful insight into the "object-orientedness" of the design can be gained from the systemwide distribution of the class fan-out values. For a system in which a single class has a very high fan-out and all the other classes have low or zero fan-outs, we really have a structured, not an OO, system (Kreindler and Mickel, 1993, p.c.). This also agrees with the guidelines of Wirfs-Brock et al. (1990) about ensuring that the total behaviour is distributed fairly evenly across the system.

At the detailed design level, however, CBO is inadequate. The establishment of a connection between two classes permits several services of the server class to be used. The sum of the services used across all the server classes (i.e. the colloborators) gives a value for the metric NRM (number of remote methods). Of course, NRM $\geq$ CBO. This leads to two further metrics: RFC and MPC. RFC is the sum of the number of local methods (NLM $\equiv$ NOM) and the number of remote methods (NRM) i.e. RFC = NLM + NRM (and is one of Chidamber and Kemerer's, 1991 six metrics).

However, RFC simply addresses the notion of "how many methods do I have access to from within the class in question?" It does not make any statement regarding the frequency of use, from different parts of the class, of those methods. This can be addressed, for the external methods by MPC (the message-passing coupling of Li and Henry, 1993) and for the internal methods, to some degree, by $V(G)$.

6. Inheritance coupling

Inheritance can be addressed initially by those metrics already proposed; although it should be noted that no-one has yet seriously addressed, theoretically, the "complexity" introduced by the use of polymorphism. Thus we have (i) DIT = depth of each class in the hierarchy; (ii) maximum depth of inheritance tree; (iii) mean depth of inheritance tree; and (iv) NOC_i = number of children for each class (also distribution and "averages" (means or medians) across the whole inheritance tree).

Kolewe (1993) also suggests that the number of distinct inheritance hierarchies might reflect the number of broad domain foci within the system; although there seems little reason to start averaging the NOC values listed above (per hierarchy) across the whole system.

Finally, the reuse metrics U and S are available (Yap and Henderson-Sellers, 1993). These are (i) the reuse ratio, U, which gives an indication of developers inheriting from existing classes, and is always less than 1. A value nearer 0 indicates a shallow, broad hierarchy; and (ii) the specialization ratio, S, which also gives an indication of width (large values of S) and, additionally, gives an indication of the extent to which MI is used since (a) for a leafy (broad, shallow) structure, $S \gg 1$ and (b) for extensive use of multiple inheritance, $S \ll 1$.

7. Summary

In the first stage of this research project we have clarified OO metrics which can be collected at various levels of resolution (class, system etc.). Empirical evaluation is under way using industrially supplied data sets.

8. Acknowledgements

This is Contribution number 94/10 of the Centre for Object Technology Applications and Research of the University of Technology, Sydney

9. References

(Basili and Rombach, 1988): V.R. Basili and H.D. Rombach, The TAME project: towards improvement-orientated software environments, *IEEE Trans. Soft. Eng.*, **14(6)**, pages 758–773, 1988

(Cant et al., 1994): S.N. Cant, B. Henderson-Sellers and D.R. Jeffery, Application of cognitive complexity metrics to object-oriented programs, *J. Obj.-Oriented Programming*, **7(4)**, pages 52–63, 1994

(Chidamber and Kemerer, 1991): S. Chidamber and C. Kemerer, Towards a metric suite for object-oriented design, in *Proc. OOPSLA'91, Sigplan Notices*, **26(11)**, pages 197–211, 1991

(Henderson-Sellers and Tegarden, 1994): B. Henderson-Sellers and D. Tegarden, Clarification concerning modularization and McCabe's cyclomatic complexity, *Comm. ACM*, **37(4)**, pages 92–94, 1994

(Kolewe, 1993): R. Kolewe, Metrics in object-oriented design and programming, *Software Development*, pages 53–62, October 1993

(Li and Henry, 1993): W. Li and S. Henry, Object-oriented metrics that predict maintainability, *J. Systems Software*, **23(2)**, pages 111–122, 1993

(McCabe, 1976): T.J. McCabe, A complexity measure, *IEEE Trans. Soft. Eng.*, **2(4)**, pages 308–320, 1976

(Pant et al., 1994): Y.R. Pant, J.M. Verner and B. Henderson-Sellers, S/C: a software size/complexity measure, *Procs First IFIP/SQI International Conference on Software Quality and Productivity (ICSQP 94)*, Hong Kong, 5–7 December 1994 (in press)

(Wirfs-Brock et al., 1990): R.J. Wirfs-Brock, B. Wilkerson and L. Wiener, *Designing Object-Oriented Software*, Prentice Hall, 368pp, 1990

(Yap and Henderson-Sellers, 1993): L.-M. Yap and B. Henderson-Sellers, Consistency considerations of object-oriented class libraries, Centre for Information Technology Research Report No. 93/3, University of New South Wales, Sydney, Australia, 110pp, 1993

An Application Sensitive Repository Search Technique.

Donald McFall   George Wilkie.

Department of Information Systems, University of Ulster,
Newtownabbey, Co Antrim, N. Ireland, BT37 OQB

Abstract. *Object modelling provides a rich mechanism for representing analysis concepts. Reuse is a critical activity for commercial organisations anxious to reduce development costs. A significant problem for CASE is the absence of application sensitive mechanics for searching tool repositories. By enhancing the semantics of an Object Model with the descriptive qualities of Repertory Grid this paper proposes an Application Sensitive and semantically rich method for locating re-usable object model components within a CASE Repository.*

Keywords. *Reuse, Repository, Repertory Grid, CASE.*

1. Introduction.

Two problems which are obvious in practical modelling scenarios are:

- the informal means of semantic clarification often used for associations and object types in Object Modelling

- the difficulty of finding reusable Object Models stored in a repository.

The former problem is not immediately evident in well understood application domains. If an association 'Uses' exists between an object type 'Person' and an object type 'Vehicle' the semantics of the association is often left unexplained; it is taken as evident from the application context. A Vehicle may be used by a Person for spare parts, a meaning not immediately obvious but taken by the analyst to be obvious during modelling. Narrative is the means employed by a traditional CASE approach for capturing and storing the domain meaning of the relationship. In a CASE environment, the analyst may or may not enter a written description of the association into a dialogue box (Misra 90) (Biggerstaff et al 89).

When a description is entered into the repository it offers a degree of semantic clarity. In order to retrieve the model at some point in the future the only practical strategy is browsing (Gorla 91) (Oman 90). This activity is time consuming and tedious and would be greatly reduced if an automated tool could search for and provide a selection of models from the repository which are semantically close to the type of model needed in the current application. Unfortunately narrative does not make the most efficient search argument.

One solution is to provide a more structured explanation of each class and association when prompted by a CASE tool. Repertory Grid Technique (Kelly 55) offers a useful way to specify the semantics of an object type or association through the construction of a Repertory Grid and has the benefit of compatibility with metrics for analysing the 'closeness of fit' with other Repertory Grids.

2. Application Analysis Tool Architecture.

The architecture of our proposed solution is detailed in fig 1. The Application Analysis Tool (AAT) has two roles. Firstly it assists an analyst during Object Modelling with the construction of a Repertory Grid for each object type and each association within the model. The Repertory Grids are then stored, as an addition to the model, in the repository. The second role of the AAT is to search the repository for reusable model candidates, AAT will elicit from the analyst a Repertory Grid description of the model required and utilise metrics to search the repository for models which most closely match the application domain meaning of the input requirement.

3. Repertory Grid Technique.

Psychologists have always been interested in how a person classifies their experiences and categorises the world. The concept of a modifiable structure which a person utilises to categorise experiences is common in theories of human cognition (Bartlett 32) (Brunner et al 65) (Skemp 62). Kelly argues that each individual builds a lattice of constructs which is used in any attempt to classify the world.

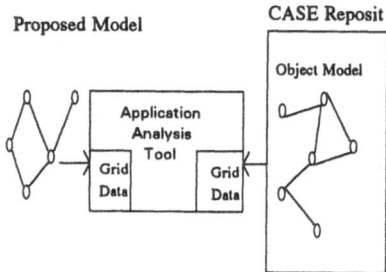

Proposed Model   CASE Reposit

Fig 1. AAT Architecture

In a Repertory Grid test Kelly asked people to list, compare and rate elements within a particular domain of interest. Care was taken to choose meaningful elements. For example in an analysis of automobile technology the elements might be cars or maybe different parts of an engine. The elements are rated against a set of constructs. A construct is a bipolar dimension which is a basic dimension of appraisal.

Many clearly defined methods for eliciting the constructs exist (Fransells et al). One such method involves consideration of elements in triads. Here elements are presented in groups of three and the client is asked in what way two of the elements are alike and thereby different from a third. The clients answer is noted and is referred to as the emergent pole. The opposite of the emergent pole is referred to as the implicit pole and is often unspecified. Kelly implies that the existence of the implicit pole is guaranteed.

For example, when considering three elements such as

VEHICLE

PERSON

LIBRARY

an emergent pole such as HUMAN may arise with its implicit pole NOT HUMAN. When a construct is elicited all elements are rated against it. The process continues with another triad of elements until a complete or at least satisfactory number of constructs have been elicited.

Two commonly used techniques for assigning elements to constructs are ranking and rating. In the ranking method elements are rank ordered from the emergent pole. An element (person in this example) may be ranked differently in each of the following constructs:

HUMAN -- NOT HUMAN

HUMAN -- ANIMAL

even though the emergent pole is identical in both constructs. In rating, an element is rated along a five point scale from 1 at the left pole to 5 at the right pole. Rating involves the participation of both poles and is therefore favoured in the majority of Repertory Grid tests. Both the scale and the meaning associated with points on the scale can be varied to suit a domain.

The well defined triadic mechanism for manually eliciting constructs for a Repertory Grid lends itself to automation. Further: statistical methods exist for determining relationships between elements in a Grid and this is used as a control mechanism for focusing on the elicitation of relevant constructs. When elements are shown to be highly matched they are distinguished by eliciting a new construct on which all the elements are matched. This will have the effect of reducing the correlation between the matched elements to below a predetermined level.

4. Classifying object types using repertory grids.

Each object type within an application will form an element in a Repertory Grid. AAT assists in the creation of the constructs which act to differentiate between the object types. Each object type will also have a Repertory Grid for its associations; the associations forming the elements and the constructs here differentiating between the associations. See Fig 2.

The form of the constructs is application dependent but the same constructs should be used for all classification within a given domain. Some constructs will imply specific relationships while others will be more application oriented. For example consider fig 3.; given two classes PERSON and CUSTOMER and a relationship where PERSON is a generalisation of CUSTOMER. This may be reflected in a construct

generalisation of PERSON -- not generalisation of PERSON.

All object types will be categorised on this construct; 1 implying the relationship holds and 5 implying that the relationship does not hold. Aggregation relationships can be dealt with in a similar way.

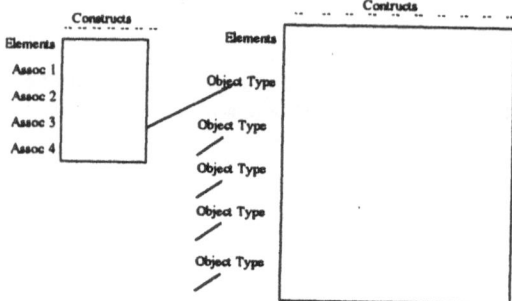

Fig 2. Object Model repertory Grid Template

Other more application oriented constructs might include;

CENTRAL TO APPLICATION -- not CENTRAL TO APPLICATION
CONCEPTUAL -- not CONCEPTUAL
TRANSACTION -- not TRANSACTION
EXPENSIVE -- NOT EXPENSIVE
PHYSICAL -- not PHYSICAL

The object type Person is linked to another repertory grid which contains only two elements, 'uses' and the implicit generalisation. A set of constructs for differentiating in this context might include;

SEMANTICS OBVIOUS -- not SEMANTICS OBVIOUS
OBTAINS A SERVICE -- not OBTAINS A SERVICE
MANDATORY -- not MANDATORY
GENERALISATION -- not GENERALISATION
AGGREGATION -- not AGGREGATION

All associations would be categorised on each construct with aggregations and generalisations returning a value 3.

This description forms the basis of the application context of the object types and associations. The metric used to differentiate between object types and between associations is also used to locate Grids within the repository which most closely match the required application. The exact mechanics for achieving this are under review but will include the possibility of searching on individual object types alone.

The methods for the analysis of Grid data can be divided into the simpler correlation methods and the much more complex multivariate methods. The correlational methods examine the interrelations between the constructs or elements and the multivariate techniques examine the underlying structure of interrelations between constructs or elements.

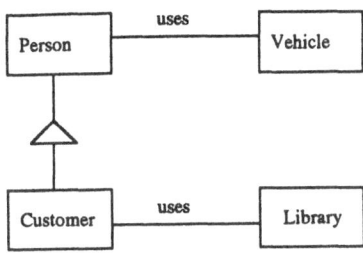

Fig 3 Simple Object Model.
(Triangle Notation implies   generalisation).

5. Conclusion.

The approach outlined in this paper is currently being researched and several issues are being examined. The nature of the constructs required to differentiate between object types and between associations is not well understood. These constructs are the implicit criteria used by the analyst when forming a class in the first place and must be made explicit. The precise mechanism for performing the repository search is under investigation. The form of representation of the model in a Repertory Grid and the possibility of processing the Grids with a neural network are being considered.

References.

Bartlett F.C.   'Remembering'. 1932 Cambridge University Press London 1932

Biggerstaff T, Perlis A, 1989 'Software Reusability', Addison Wesley 1989

Bruner J.S et al 1965   'A study of thinking' Wiley, New York 1965

Fransella F. & Bannister D. 'A Manual for Repertory Grid Technique'. Academic Press, London, New York, S.F.

Gorla N, 1991   'Techniques of application software maintenance', Inorfmation and Software Technology, Jan/Feb 1991

Kelly G.A. 1955   'The psychology of personal constructs' vols 1 & 2 (1955) Norton.

Misra S. 1990   'Analysing CASE system characteristics:an evaluative framework', Inorfmation and Software Technology, July/August 1990

Oman P, 1990   'Maintenance Tools', IEEE Software, May 1990

Skemp R.R 1962   'The need for a schematic learning theory' in The British Journal of Educ. Psychology. 1962

Don McFall is a lecturer in Information Systems at the University of Ulster, where he is investigating software maintenance problems. He is the author of several papers on the topic.

George Wilkie is a lecturer in Information Systems at the University of Ulster and is the author of a book 'Object Oriented Software: the Professional Developers Guide'.

INTERFACE DESIGN

GOMI: A Graphical User Interface
for Object-Oriented Databases

Yong S. Jun and Suk I. Yoo

Department of Computer Science
Seoul National University
Shilim-dong, Kwanak-ku, Seoul, Korea
E-mail: yooailab@krsnucc1.bitnet   Fax: +082-2-887-8991

ABSTRACT. *This paper presents a graphical user interface for object-oriented databases, called GOMI(Graphical Object Manipulation Interface). It allows inexperienced users to easily perform complex operations such as selection, projection, navigation, naming, persistence, display, creation, deletion, and update against objects. Since these operations can be easily and uniformly posed on graphs, the objects and the reference relationships between them can be intuitively displayed and manipulated.*

KEY WORDS: Graphical User Interface, Object-Oriented Database, Query

1. Introduction

In order to help users express their data manipulation requirements, database management systems(DBMSs) provide one or more nonprocedural data manipulation languages(DMLs) such as SQL to users. The users find it difficult to learn the formal syntax and semantics of these languages and tend not to be familiar with the logical structure of the database. These problems become worse if the database has a large and complex schema. Consequently, recent research on the database area has concentrated on making DBMSs easier to use.

During recent years workstations with bit-mapped displays, pointing devices, icons, multiple windows, and pop-up menus allow users to point directly to objects on the screen and manipulate them in a two-dimensional graphical manner. The availability of advanced graphics facilities has stimulated research on graphical interfaces for various computer applications.

These research trends have resulted in a number of graphical user interfaces(GUIs) for DBMSs(Kim, 1986)(Ozsoyoglu et al., 1993). They resemble each other in terms of manipulating data by means of a two-dimensional, graphically aided examples and in their user friendliness. However, the focus has been on GUIs for databases organized with traditional data models such as the entity-relationship model and the relational model. In these traditional data models, there is typically a small fixed set of operations that the user can perform on the data, and the data itself consists of values of predefined types.

With the increasing popularity of object-oriented DBMSs(OODBMSs), there is a need for GUIs to databases organized according to the object-oriented data model. In OODBMSs, the classes defined in the database schema can be arbitrarily complex and the objects can refer to other objects. Thus, the objects of all types and the reference relationships between them should be displayed by the interface in a uniform and intuitive way. Several GUIs for OODBMSs have been already introduced and some of them are surveyed and compared in Section 6. However, these GUIs are insufficient to display and manipulate the objects and the references between them in a uniform and intuitive way.

This paper presents the graphical object manipulation interface for OODBMSs, called GOMI(Graphical Object Manipulation Interface). It provides facilities for browsing the database, performing queries on the database, and examining the database schema. In particular, it allows users to perform complex operations against objects in a uniform and easy way. These include selection, projection, reference, naming, persistence, display, creation, deletion, and update of objects. Since these operations can be easily and uniformly posed on graphs, the objects and the reference relationships between them can be intuitively displayed and manipulated. We have completed the implementation of GOMI. It is being used as a GUI of the Obase OODBMS developed at Seoul National University in Korea(Yoo et al., 1994).

The organization of the rest of the paper is as follows. We briefly introduce the object definition facility in Section 2. In Section 3-5, the object browsing, the object manipulation, and the query facility are described, respectively. In Section 6, we discuss related work. Our conclusions are presented in Section 7.

2. Object Definition

GOMI is based on one integrated data model for both database and general purpose manipulations. This model borrows and extends the object model of C++(Ellis et al., 1990). The object definition facility is called the class, which supports data encapsulation and multiple inheritance. If a class inherits from the root class OBJECT, it is called a database class; otherwise, we call it a volatile class(ordinary C++ class). According to multiple inheritance, users can define new database classes as subclasses of existing database classes and manipulate all database classes uniformly. Database class declarations in Obase(Jun et al., 1994)(Yoo et al., 1994) are similar to those in C++, except for the following:

(1) A database class has only virtual superclasses in order to ensure that only one copy of the virtual superclass appears in an instance of the subclass.
(2) Only atomic types(such as char, int, float, and string), pointers to atomic types, pointers to database classes, and pointers to volatile classes are allowed. Pointers to system-defined database classes such as Collection and Set should be specified together with a domain type.
(3) The attributes whose types are pointers to atomic types or pointers to volatile classes are used mainly by application programmers, and the values of these attributes are volatile. Thus, these values cannot be manipulated by GOMI.
(4) The inverse keyword is used to define the inverse relationships between attributes whose types are pointers to database classes. The unique keyword is used to define the uniqueness integrity constraints about attributes whose types are atomic or pointers to database classes. The required keyword is used to define the non-null integrity constraints about attributes whose types are string or pointers to database classes. The constraints keyword is used to specify the code section for user-defined integrity constraints.

A database object is defined as an instance of a database class, and a volatile object(ordinary C++ object) as an instance of a volatile class. If a database object has its physical space in disk and it can be accessed in other transactions, it is called a persistent object; otherwise, we call it a temporary object. A temporary object can become semipersistent explicitly by using makePersistent method in OBJECT, or implicitly by being transitively referenced by any persistent or semipersistent objects. A semipersistent object is dealt with just like a persistent one within the transaction, and is actually made persistent only if the transaction commits. Also, if at least one of attributes of a database object is modified within the transaction, the database object is called updated. A dirty object is an updated object whose constraints are not evaluated yet after the last change. A clean object is an updated object whose constraints are satisfied.

Every database object is associated with a system-wide unique object identifier(OID). An OID consists of a database identifier, a class identifier, and an instance identifier. Thus OIDs are unique over a number of databases and then database objects can be referenced through their own OID elsewhere.

In Obase, a database consists of a schema and an extension. The schema, a persistent type catalog to store information about types of database classes, provides the type information about objects in run-time. The extension, a collection of objects, divides into class extensions. A class extension of a database class groups the objects belonging to it. A hierarchical extension is logically treated as a union of class extensions of a database class and its subclasses.

Unless ambiguous, we use the unqualified term "object" and "class" to refer to a database object and a database class, respectively.

240

We end this section by introducing an example database, called BANK. This database will be used throughout the paper to illustrate functionalities of GOMI. The schema of the BANK database is shown in Figure 1. The attribute relationship between two classes indicates that the domain of an attribute of one class is the other class. The set-attribute relationship between two classes indicates that the domain of an attribute of one class is Set and the domain of its elements is the other class. The IS-A relationship between two classes indicates that one class is a superclass of the other class.

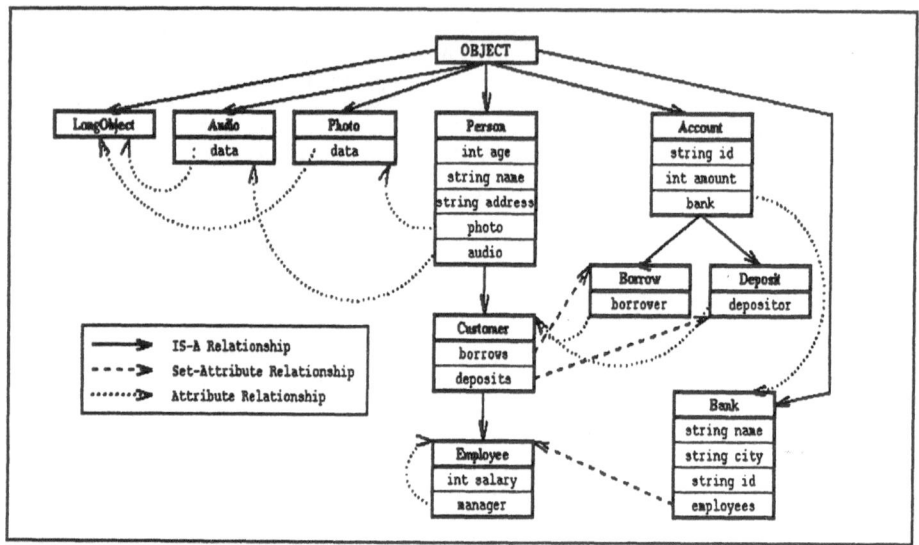

Figure 1. Schema of the BANK database

In addition, this schema includes some integrity constraints. First, the referential integrity constraints are defined in all of attributes whose types are pointers to database classes. Secondly, the borrows of Customer and the borrower of Borrow are declared to be a many-to-one inverse relationship of one another. Similarly, there is a many-to-one inverse relationship between the deposits of Customer and the depositor of Deposit. For example, as soon as a customer A has a new deposit account B, B's depositor is automatically set to A. Conversely, as soon as B's depositor is set to A, B is automatically inserted to A's deposits. Thirdly, the uniqueness integrity constraints are defined in the id of Account and the id of Bank. Fourthly, the non-null integrity constraints are defined in the id of Account, the id of Bank, and the name of Person. Lastly, Employee has a user-defined integrity constraint that an employee must have accounts only in the bank which he works for.

3. Object Presentation

An execution of GOMI corresponds to a transaction. When the user starts GOMI, he should be specify a database and an integrity modes within the transaction. GOMI supports three integrity modes(Jun et al., 1994)(Yoo et al., 1994):

(1) *Immediate mode.* At the point where an object is updated, its integrity constraints are evaluated.
(2) *Deferred mode.* Constraint evaluations for all of updated objects are deferred until just before the end of the transaction.

(3) *User mode.* Whenever the user selects the Fire menu, constraints of dirty objects are evaluated.

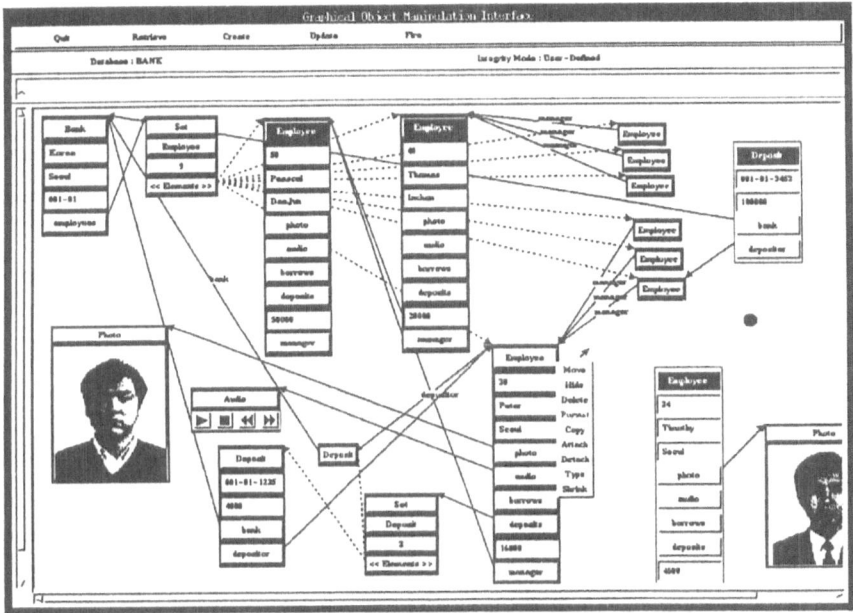

Figure 2. Object presentation in GOMI

Figure 2 presents a state of the GOMI screen that consists of three subwindows: a base menu subwindow, a message subwindow, and a graphic subwindow. The message subwindow indicates the current status such as the database name, the integrity mode, and the guidance to the user. The base menu subwindow provides a set of commands. Quit menu has two submenus: Commit which commits the transaction, and Abort which aborts it. Other menus are described in Section 4. The graphic subwindow displays several database graphs, each of which is a set of vertices connected by directed edges. The objects and the connections among them are depicted by the vertices and edges, respectively.

A vertex represents an object in two modes. In the shrinking mode a vertex appears as only a title button whose label is the class name of the corresponding object. In the expanding mode it basically consists of a title button and a set of attribute windows, each of which corresponds to an attribute of the object. If the type of an attribute is a pointer to a database class, its attribute window is a button whose label is the attribute name; if the type of an attribute is atomic, its window is an editable text which presents its value; otherwise, its window is a button whose label is "Invisible". The boundary color of the vertex of a (semi)persistent object is black, while that of a temporary object is white. The title button of an updated object are reversed. For example, *Peter* is a persistent object, and *Timothy* is a temporary, updated object.

A directed edge represents a connection between two objects in two modes. The solid line indicates that one object refers to the other object, while the dashed line does that one Set object contains the other object. An edge incident from the shrinking vertex indicates the attribute's name in the middle of it. In Figure 2, we intuitively know the manager of the employee *Peter* working for Seoul branch of the Korea bank is *Paascal*.

The layout of vertices is explicitly determined by the user. This is because the automatic location of vertices requires very complicated computation and wastes the space of the graphic subwindow. The anchor, where a vertex will be created, copied, or moved, appears as a filled circle in the position where the user presses the mouse button within the graphic subwindow. For example, when the photo button of *Paascal* is clicked in Figure 2, a vertex of a Photo object are created in the current position of the anchor, and an edge from the photo to the new vertex is drawn.

In some cases an object may have embedded semantics. For example, in the case of a Photo object, displaying the pictorial representation of its data will be more intuitive than displaying its data itself. We decided that it is the responsibility of the class designer to implement several virtual functions for displaying objects of the class in the expanding mode, since he knows best how an object is to be displayed. Thus, as shown in Figure 2, the vertex of a Photo object consists of a title button and a drawn button displaying the pictorial representation of its data. Also, in order to hide the internal structure of Set class, the vertex of a Set object consists of a title button, a button indicating the number of its elements, a button indicating the domain type name of its elements, and the button with the label "<<Elements>>". When the last button of a Set object is clicked, its elements are displayed. If its domain type is atomic, a dialog window listing its elements is created; otherwise, the dashed edges between the last button of a Set object and each of vertices of its elements are drawn.

4. Object Manipulation

GOMI provides facilities for manipulating objects. When the title button of a vertex is clicked, a title menu with some operations against the corresponding object pops up, as shown in Figure 2. In addition, the base menu subwindow provides facilities for retrieval, creation, modification, and integrity.

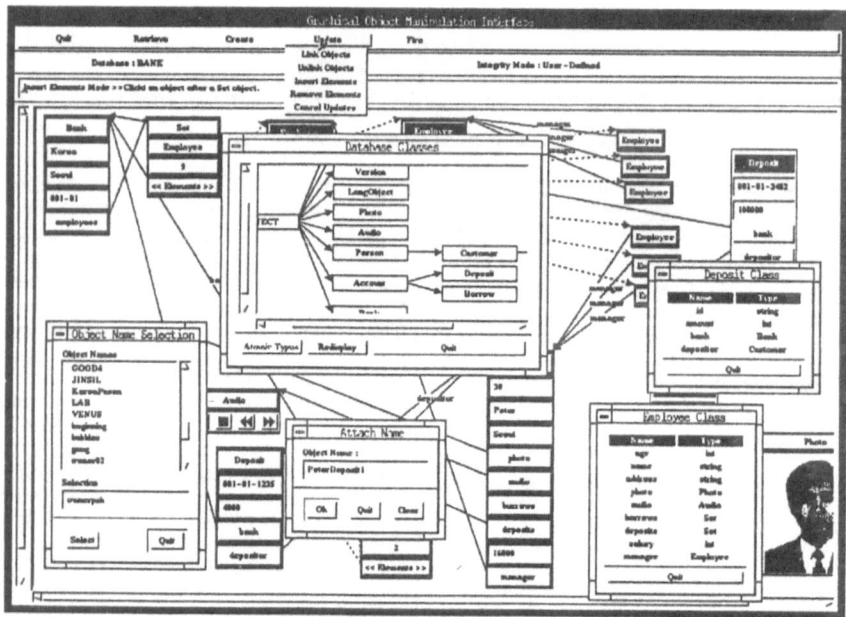

Figure 3. Object manipulation in GOMI

4.1 Object Creation

When `Create` in the base menu subwindow is clicked, a class selection window which displays the class inheritance hierarchy pops up. This window is shown in Figure 3. If the user selects a class, a temporary object of the class is created using the default constructor of the class and its vertex is displayed in the current anchor position. The user selecting `Set` must specify the domain type of the new `Set` object.

4.2 Object Copy

When `Copy` in the title menu of a vertex is clicked, a temporary object is shallow-copied and its vertex is displayed in the current anchor position.

4.3 Object Deletion

When `Delete` in the title menu of a vertex is clicked, the corresponding object is deleted from the database. Then the vertex and the edges incident with it disappear from the graphic subwindow.

4.4 Object Modification

Since the attribute whose type is atomic appears as an editable text window, the user can change its value directly from keyboard. In order to change the value of the attribute whose type is a pointer to a database class, GOMI provides four submenus in `Update` base menu:

(1) *Link.* If the user clicking this submenu presses a title button after the attribute button which he wants to modify, an edge from the attribute button to the title button is drawn. This edge indicates the object with the attribute button refers the object with the title button through the attribute corresponding to the attribute button. Of course, the previous edge incident from the attribute button disappears. If the type of the attributes incompatible with that of the object with the title button, the error message appears in the message subwindow and this update is canceled.

(2) *Unlink.* If the user clicking this submenu presses an attribute button which he wants to nullify, the edge incident from it disappears.

(3) *Insert.* When the user clicking this submenu presses the last button of a `Set` vertex whose domain type is atomic, an input window is created. If the user types a new element and then press `Ok` button in the input window, the new element is inserted into the `Set` object. When the user clicking this submenu presses the title button of a vertex after the last button of a `Set` vertex whose elements is objects, the object with the title button is inserted into the `Set` object and a dashed edge between two objects is drawn. If the type of the inserted object is incompatible with the domain type of the `Set` object, an error message appears in the message subwindow and this update is canceled.

(4) *Remove.* When the user clicking this submenu presses the last button of a `Set` vertex whose domain type is atomic, an input window is created. If the user types an element and then presses `Ok` button in the input window, the element is removed from the `Set` object. When the user clicking this submenu presses the title button of a vertex after the last button of a `Set` vertex whose elements is objects, the object with the title button is removed from the `Set` object and an edge between two objects disappears.

4.5 Object Persistence

If `Persist` in the title menu of a vertex corresponding to a temporary object is clicked or a vertex of a temporary object is reachable from (semi)persistent objects, this temporary object and all of temporary objects reachable from it become semipersistent.

4.6 Object Naming

When Attach in the title menu of a vertex is clicked, an input window is created. If the user types a new name and then press Ok button in the input window, the new name is attached to the corresponding object. In the case of clicking Detach, the input window is also created. If the user types one of the names attached to the object and then press Ok, the name is detached from the object. Results of the naming operations are immediately reflected into the name selection window, which is created by clicking the By Name submenu of Retrieve base menu. As soon as one of names listed in the name selection window shown in Figure 3 is selected by the user, the vertex of the corresponding object is displayed in the current anchor position if it is not displayed yet.

4.7 Object Display

When Move in the title menu of a vertex is clicked, the vertex is moved to the current anchor position. When Hide is clicked, the vertex and the edges incident with it disappear. Shrink shrinks the vertex, while Expand expands it. Type shows the class definition table for the class of the object as shown in Figure 3.

4.8 Integrity Processing

Integrity constraints are used to maintain a database consistency beyond what is typically expressible using the type system. Constraints, which consist of a condition and an action, are associated with class definitions(Jun et al., 1994)(Yoo et al., 1994). This action is executed when the condition is violated. All objects of a class must satisfy all constraints associated with the class. A subclass inherits the constraints of its superclasses and new constraints can be added. Depending on the integrity mode within the transaction, constraint checking can be performed immediately after modifying the object or at some later point in time. Thus, the user must specify the integrity mode within when he starts GOMI. As described above, GOMI supports three integrity modes.

In the case of the immediate mode, as soon as the user modifies an object, all of its constraints are evaluated. The modification is detected by using callbacks of the Motif widget set(Young, 1986). If a constraint is evaluated, the action corresponding to it is executed. If, during the execution of the action, other objects are modified, their constraints are recursively evaluated. Then, the result of the constraint evaluation is immediately reflected in the graphic subwindow. Thus, this mode ensures that objects are internally consistent at all times. For example, if a customer opens a deposit(i.e. the deposit's depositor is linked to the customer), the deposit, after the constraint evaluation, is automatically inserted into the customer's deposits(i.e. a dashed line from the customer's deposits to the deposit is drawn). If an employee opens an account whose bank is not equal to the bank for which he works, the transaction aborts and then GOMI ends.

In the case of the deferred mode, constraint checking is delayed until just before the transaction commits. All constraints associated with objects that have been modified are then checked. Thus, this mode ensures that objects are consistent after the end of the transaction.

The user mode is similar to the deferred mode. But, in this mode, whenever the user clicks Fire base menu or just before the transaction commit, all constraints associated with dirty objects are checked. In the case of clicking Fire base menu, the result of the constraint evaluation is reflected in the graphic subwindow.

5. Query Facility

Recently many graphical query interfaces have been introduced(Kim, 1986)(Ozsoyoglu et al., 1993). The approaches taken so far for them can be broadly classified in to the table-based approach and the graph-based one. In the first approach. the user specifies an example output or a selection predicate by directly making entries into table skeletons. On the other hand, in the second approach the user formulates a query using graphs. This approach helps users to formulate queries more easily than the first one does. Eliminating join expressions and tuple variables in queries, the second approach allows users to pose complex queries without knowing the details of first-order predicate calculus or algebra. Nested queries can be also easily formulated in the second approach. More importantly, sharing nodes and arcs in the query specification eases the task of users. Most of graphical query interfaces have taken the table-based approach while, to the best of our knowledge, only PICASSO(Kim, 1986)(Kim et al., 1988), GVF(Noik, 1992), and GOMI the graph-based approach. However, PICASSO is a GUI for a universal relational database system and GVF is a hypothetical GUI for relational databases.

A query session of GOMI goes roughly as follows. In order to give the starting point from which navigations or manipulations begin, GOMI provides Retrieve base menu with two submenus: By Name and By Query. The former manages the name selection window described in Section 4.6, while the latter does the query specification window upon which the user formulates queries using mouse and menus. After the user formulates a graphical query, he asks GOMI to translate the query into the OQL++ query language(Yoo et al., 1994) by selecting the Generate command. Then he sends it to Obase through the Run command. After executing the query, Obase sends the result of the query to GOMI. In OQL++, query results are temporary Set objects, and hence they appears as vertices of temporary Set objects in the graphic subwindow. Therefore these vertices are uniformly manipulated just like other vertices and are used for formulating queries in future queries.

In GOMI, the user specifies a query using a query graph, which consists of nodes connected by directed arcs. Nodes are divided into four types as follows:

(1) *Collection Node* represents a collection of objects. It consists of a title button and a set of attribute buttons. Each attribute button corresponds to an attribute of the collection's domain class. The reversed buttons in this node indicate the projection. The reversed title button indicates that elements of the collection will be projected themselves. The reversed attribute button indicates that the corresponding attribute of the elements will be projected. Collection nodes are again divided into two types:

    * *Extension Node* represents a class(hierarchical) extension of a class. In the case of the class extension, the title button has the label with the class name. In the other case, the button has the label with the class name preceding '@'.

    * *Set Node* represents a Set object of objects. The title button has the label with the name which is used to retrieve this Set object.

(2) *Operator Node* consists of a button representing a symbol of an operator.

(3) *Value Node* consists of a title button and a value text. The user can enter a value into the value text. The title button indicates the value's type.

(4) *Name Node* consists of a button with the name corresponding to an object.

Arcs between nodes are divided into two types. The reference arc between two collection nodes is used to represent the path expression. For example, in Figure 4, the path from Deposit node to Bank node indicates a path expression "p2->bank" if p2 is a tuple variable for Deposit's extension in the equivalent OQL++ query. The reference arc with the '@' symbol in the middle of the arc indicates the transitive closure. On the other hand, the operand arc between an operator node and a node is used to represent a term of a predicate concerned with an attribute or a path expression. A predicate consists of one or more terms. For example, in Figure 4, a path from the name attribute of Bank to the value node with its value "Seoul" indicates the predicate (p2->bank->name LIKE "Seoul").

When the user builds an arc, GOMI checks the validity of the arc. For instance, if the LIKE node adjacent from the name attribute of Bank node is connected to the Integer value node, this arc is rejected and an error message is shown to the user. This validity checking is performed using the finite parsing automata. Also, this automata is used to transform the graphical query into the OQL++ query.

Hereafter, we show the expressibility of GOMI query through various examples which demonstrate the power of graphics to provide a simple method of stating what would be a complex query if traditional query interfaces are used. Because of space limitation, we avoid the details of the finite parsing automata, pop-up menus, mouse interactions, and step-by-step query formulation in GOMI. Those details are in (Yoo et al., 1994).

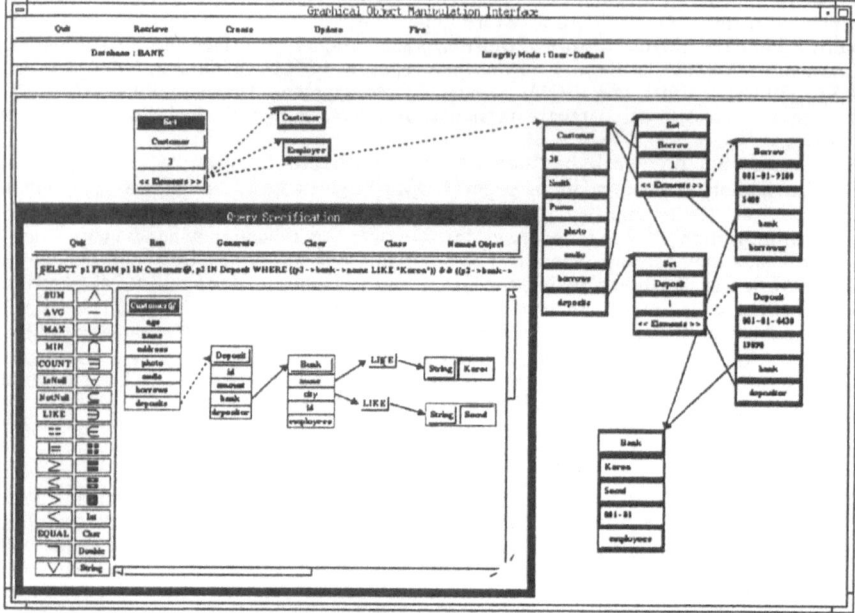

Figure 4. A graphical query for Example 1

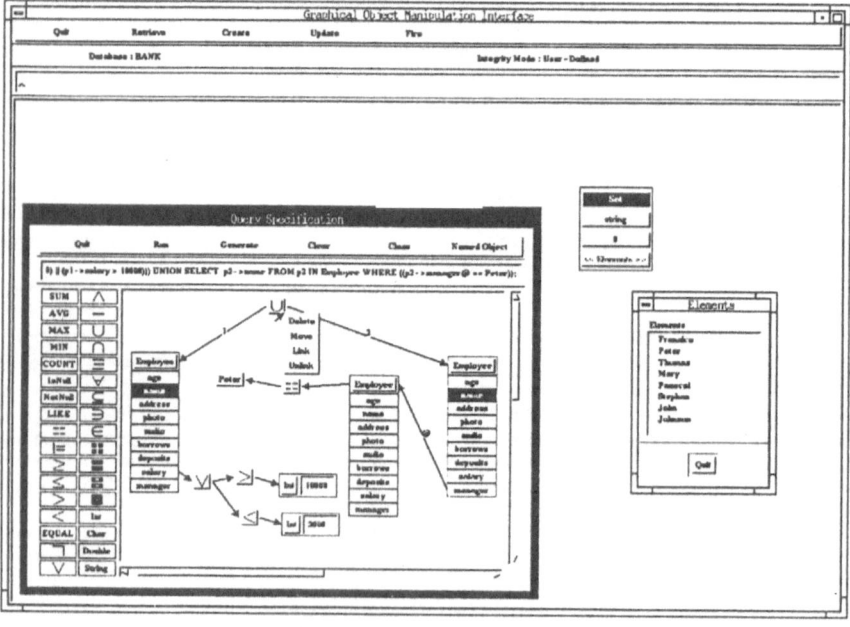

Figure 5. A graphical query for Example 2

Example 1. Consider the query "Find customers(or employees) who have at least one deposit at Seoul branch of Korea bank, and then display themselves". Figure 4 shows one of the equivalent graphical queries and its result. The equivalent OQL++ query is generated as follows:

```
SELECT p1
FROM p1 In Customer@, p2 IN Deposit
WHERE (p2->bank->name LIKE "Korea")
             && (p2->bank->city LIKE "Seoul")
                          && (p2 IN p1->deposits);
```

Example 2. Consider the query "Find employees whose salaries are greater than 10000 or less than 3000 or who are directly or indirectly managed by Peter, and then display their names". Figure 5 shows one of the equivalent graphical queries and its result. The equivalent OQL++ query is generated as follows:

```
SELECT p1->name
FROM p1 IN Employee
WHERE ((p1->salary < 3000) || (p1->salary> 10000))
UNION
SELECT p2->name
FROM p2 IN Employee
WHERE (p2->manager@ == Peter);
```

Example 3. Assume that the user attaches the name "QueryResult" to the result of Example 1. Consider the query "Find customers who have a deposit at Seoul branch of Korea bank and who have one or more loans, and then display the name and the number of deposits for each of these customers". Figure 6 shows one of the equivalent graphical queries and its result. The equivalent OQL++ query is generated as follows:

```
SELECT TUPLE<cnt:COUNT(p1->deposits), name:p1->name>
FROM p1 IN QueryResult
WHERE (EXISTS p1->borrows);
```

Example 4. Consider the query "Find customers who live in the same city of the bank at which they have at least one deposit, and then display their names, their address, and banks at which they have deposits". Figure 7 shows one of the equivalent graphical queries and its result. The equivalent OQL++ query is generated as follows:

```
SELECT TUPLE<_Bank:p2->bank, addr:p1->address, name:p1->name>
FROM p1 IN Customer@, p2 IN deposit
WHERE ((p2->bank->city == p1->address)
                          && (p2 IN p1->deposits));
```

6. Related Work

Numerous GUIs for databases have emerged in recent years. In this section, we introduce some of those GUIs and compare each of them with GOMI.

Most of GUIs for databases organized with the entity-relationship data model or the relational model are example-based graphical query languages. Some of them have been surveyed and compared in (Kim, 1986)(Ozsoyoglu et al., 1993). They resemble each other in terms of formulating a query by means of a two-dimensional, graphically aided example and in their user friendliness. These languages expand or revise Query-By-Example(Zloof, 1977) significantly to

248

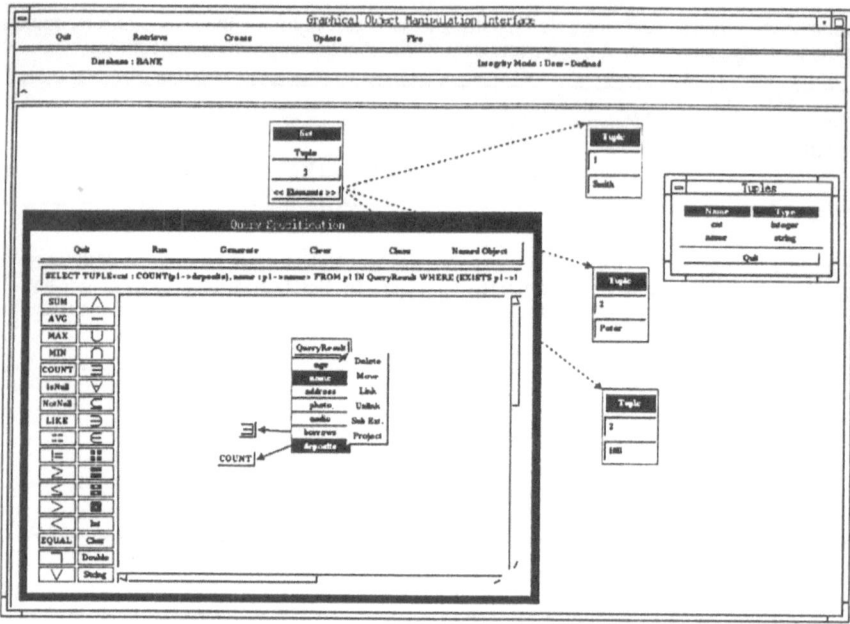

Figure 6. A graphical query for Example 3

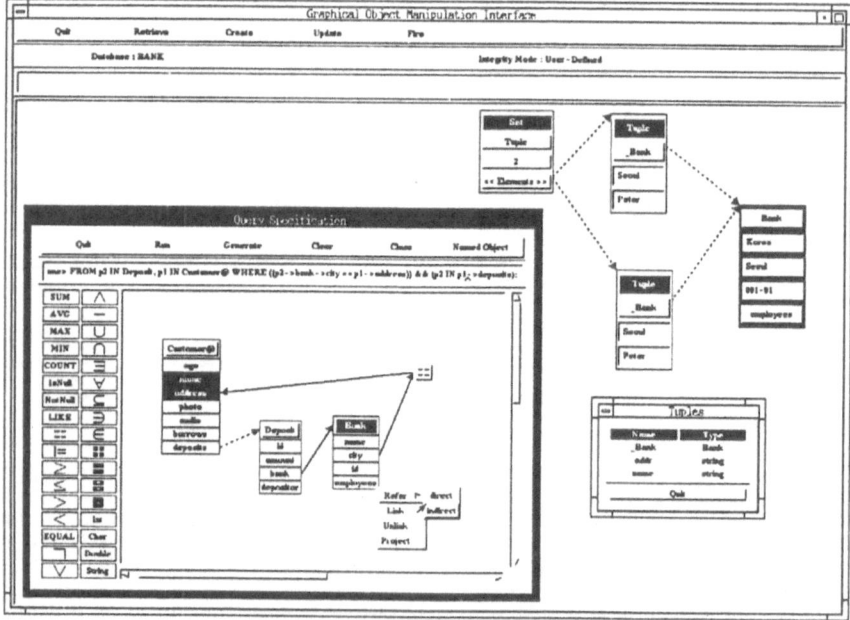

Figure 7. A graphical query for Example 4

serve different applications. However, these languages are inadequate for advanced applications such as CAD/CAM design, hypermedia systems, and knowledge bases.

Related to the query formulation model of GOMI is that of PICASSO(Kim, 1986)(Kim et al., 1988), which is a graphics-based database query language designed for use with a universal relational database systems. The hypergraph semantics of the universal relation are used as the foundation for PICASSO. The hypergraph is formed whose nodes are the attribute of the universal relation and whose hyperedges, called maximal objects, represents maximal sets of the related attributes in which queries make sense. Query formulation is done directly on hypergraphs using the mouse. However, PICASSO does not support any update operations.

Pasta-3 graphical query language(Kuntz et al., 1989) is an interface to KB2, which is a knowledge base system embedded in Prolog. KB2 uses the entity-relationship data model, extended with inheritance and deductive rules. Pasta-3's query capability has been designed to support all queries that are expressible in KB2's linear language. However, Pasta-3 does not appear to use any type information to assist the user in specifying queries, and its logical operators are treated specially.

SIG(Maier et al., 1986) generates interactive displays for complex objects. The display for an object is created by interpreting the associated class type. In SIG, the display for the object referenced by an object must be embedded into the display for the referencing object. This display mechanism is not suitable in case that an object is referenced by more than one object as well as in case that an object references itself directly or indirectly.

The navigation model of GOMI is inspired of KIVIEW(Motro et al., 1988). KIVIEW is an object-oriented browsing interface to databases whose internal model is characterized as a semantic network. KIVIEW browsing sessions interleaves two activities: navigation and manipulation. To speed up repetitive searches, KIVIEW supports the synchronized browsing. However, it allows the user to display only the immediate attributes which is newly defined in the class of the given object. Moreover, KIVIEW supports no update operations for objects and no graphical query facilities.

The O_2 user interface generator, O2Look(Deux et al., 1991), supports the display and manipulation of large, complex, and multimedia objects on the screen. In O2Look, ready-made presentations are automatically built while customized presentations can be created by means of masks and resources. O2Look can be extended to fit new application requirements. However, relationships between objects are not shown, and a query facility is not provided.

SMARTIE(Zoeller et al., 1992) is a forms-based GUI for the ITASCA OODBMS. It is composed of several abstract class methods that automatically configure visual presentations based on domain information for each attribute in the class. These display methods are capable of handling the dynamic modification of any part of the database schema, and require no programming by the system designer. However, SMARTIE provides only a simple textual query capability rather than a graphical query interface.

Closely related to GOMI is OdeView(Agrawal et al., 1990)(Dar et al., 1992) in the Ode OODBMS. It examines the database schema, browses the database, and performs arbitrary queries on the database. OdeView also supports facilities for the set iteration, the synchronized browsing, and the method invocation. GOMI has not supported these facilities yet, but we are investigating the application of them to GOMI. GOMI represents an object as a vertex within a graphic subwindow and a relationship between objects as an edge. However, in OdeView, an object appears as a window and a relationship between objects appears in the title bar of the window indicating the path from the root of the display tree to this window. It is easily recognized that OdeView represents relationships between objects less intuitively than GOMI. Moreover, if an object is referenced by more than one objects, several copies of its window are displayed at the same time. This problem becomes worse if an object references itself directly or indirectly(i.e. a cyclic reference occurs). OdeView allows the user to perform a query on only one window for a set of objects while in GOMI the user can specify a query on a number of sets or extensions. Thus, explicit join expressions are hard to formulate in OdeView. The query specification of OdeView is table-based while that of GOMI is graph-based. This graph-based query specification reduces the burden of the user by sharing selection predicates. For example, consider the query in the Example 1. In GOMI the path from a customer to a bank is specified only once while in OdeView it is specified twice.

7. Conclusion

We defined and implemented GOMI that is a graphical object manipulation interface for OODBMSs. We benefited from previous studies on GUIs·particularly from the ones implemented for OODBMSs. The major contribution of GOMI is that all of facilities such as object manipulation and query formulation are based on graphs. Therefore the user can manipulate objects and relationships between them in a uniform way, recognize relationships between objects intuitively, and formulate complex queries easily.

We have completed the implementation of GOMI. It has been implemented in C++(Ellis et al., 1990) on top of the X window system using the OSF's Motif widget set(Young, 1986). At the moment, GOMI is integrated into the Obase OODBMS(Yoo et al., 1994) developed at Seoul National University in Korea. It is possible to port GOMI onto any OODBMSs with minor effort and to extend it to fit new requirements. We are investigating the application of some facilities such as set iteration, synchronized browsing, and method invocation.

Acknowledgements

The work presented in this paper has been supported by Hyundai Electronics Industries Co. in Korea. We especially deeply appreciate Mr. M. H. Chung, the chairman of Hyundai Electronics Industries Co., for his financial support and encouragement. We are also grateful to members of our laboratory, including E. Hong, Y. Lee, J. Lee, and H. Park.

References:

(Agrawal et al. 1990):   R. Agrawal, H. Gehani, and J. Srinivasan. *OdeView: The Graphical Interface to Ode*. In the Proceedings of the 1990 ACM SIGMOD International Conference on Management of Data, pp. 34-43, 1990.

(Dar et al. 1992):   S. Dar, N. Gehani, H. Jagadish, and J. Srinivasan. *Queries in an Object-Oriented Graphical Interface*. In the Technical Report ATT-DB-92-12, AT&T Bell Labs., 1992.

(Deux et al. 1991):   O. Deux et al. *The O₂ System*. In the Communication of the ACM, Vol. 34, No. 10, pp. 34-48, 1991.

(Ellis et al. 1990):   M. Ellis and B. Stroustrup. *The Annotated C++ Reference Manual*. Addison-Wesley, 1990.

(Jun et al. 1994):   Y. S. Jun and S. I. Yoo. *The spareC++ Object-Oriented Database Programming Language*. In the Proceedings of the 4th International Conference on Data and Knowledge Systems for Manufacturing and Engineering, pp. 89-94, 1994.

(Kim, 1990):   H. J. Kim. *Graphical Interfaces for Database Systems: A Survey*. In the Proceedings of the 1986 Mountain Regional ACM Conference. 1986.

(Kim et al. 1988):   H. J. Kim, H. F. Korth, and A. Silberschatz. *PICASSO: A Graphical Query Language*. In the Software-Practice and Engineering, Vol. 18, No. 3, pp. 169-203, 1988.

(Kuntz et al. 1989):   M. Kuntz and R. Melchert. *Pasta-3's Graphical Query Language: Direct Manipulation, Cooperative Queries, Full Expressive Power*. In the Proceedings of the 15th International Conference on Very Large Data Bases, pp. 97-105, 1989.

(Maier et al. 1986):   D. Maier, P. Nordquist, and M. Grossman. *Displaying Database Objects*. In the Proceedings of the 1st International Conference on Expert Database Systems, pp. 59-74, 1986.

(Motro et al. 1988):   A. Motro, A. D'Atri, and L. Tarantino. *The Design of KIVIEW: An Object-Oriented Browser*. In the Proceedings of the 2nd International Conference on Expert Database Systems, pp. 17-31, 1988.

(Noik, 1992):   E. Noik. *Challenges in Graph-Based Relational Data Visualization*. In the Technical Report, Department of Computer Science, University of Toronto, 1992.

(Ozsoyoglu et al. 1993):   G. Ozsoyoglu and H. Wang. *Example-Based Graphical Database Query Languages*. In the IEEE Computer, Vol. 26, No. 5, pp. 25-38, 1993.

(Yoo et al. 1994):   S. I. Yoo et al. *Obase: An Object-Oriented Database Management Systems*. In the Journal of the Korea Information Science Society, 1994. *(to appear)*

(Young, 1986):   D. Young. *The X Window System Programming and Applications with Xt*. Prentice Hall, 1986.

(Zloof, 1977):   M. Zloof. *Query-By-Example: A Data Base Language*. In the IBM System Journal, Vol. 16, No. 4, pp. 324-343, 1977.

(Zoeller et al. 1992):   R. Zoeller and D. Barry. *Dynamic Self-Configuring Methods for Graphical Presentation of ODBMS Objects*. In the Proceedings of the 8th International Conference on Data Engineering, pp. 136-143, 1992.

A Layered Approach to Dedicated Application Builders Based on Application Frameworks

Patrick Steyaert- Koen De Hondt - Serge Demeyer

Marleen De Molder

Programming Technology Lab
Brussels Free University
Pleinlaan 2, 1050 Brussel, Belgium
E-mail: {prsteyae, kdehondt, sademeye}@vnet3.vub.ac.be
WWW: http://progwww.vub.ac.be/

OO Partners bvba
Romeinse steenweg 464
1853 Strombeek-Bever, Belgium
Fax: +32 2 2677151

ABSTRACT. *In this paper we investigate what is needed to make user interface builders incrementally refinable. The need for dedicated user interface builders is motivated by drawing a parallel with programming language design and object-oriented application frameworks. We show that reflection techniques borrowed from the programming language community can be successfully applied to make user interface builders incrementally refinable.*

KEY WORDS: *User Interfaces, User Interface Builder, Object-oriented Framework, Reflection.*

1. Introduction

Graphical user interfaces for workstation applications are inherently difficult to build. To help programmers create such interfaces, tools are being developed. Those tools range from tool kits (libraries providing primitive building blocks for managing simple widgets, sometimes machine dependent) to user interface management systems (application frameworks and user interface builders supporting higher level user interface concepts). The major goal of those tools is to reduce the effort to build a good user interface and, more importantly, to promote the reuse of application code. Application code is not specific for the problem domain but deals with the interaction of a program with its environment independently from its problem domain. The problem domain is handled by domain code.

In analogy with programming paradigms (e.g. functional and imperative programming), it can be observed that different user interface paradigms (Tesler, 1986) exist. Although the notion of user interface paradigms has not been developed to the same degree as programming paradigms, different user interface paradigms can be tentatively identified. Most popular is the direct manipulation paradigm in which an interface models the real or an imagined world without using intermediate structures such as command languages or menus (Shneiderman, 1983). The exact opposite is the menu driven user interface paradigm. Another popular paradigm, the navigational paradigm, can be found in the area of hypertext systems. Here the idea is to allow users to explore different ideas by supporting the navigation through complex information structures.

As with programming paradigms, user interface paradigms also can be divided into sub-paradigms. For example in (Akscyn, 1991) a distinction is made between domain specific and domain general hypertext systems, whereby domain specific hypertext systems are possibly expressed in particular refinements of the navigational paradigm.

Generally one can say that a particular set of user interface tools is specialised to generate the user interface for applications expressed in a particular paradigm or sub-paradigm. Moreover, it can be observed that some applications can be more easily expressed in one paradigm than others. For example, the navigational paradigm is more suited to express hypertext applications. Similar to programming languages there is a trade-off between generality and the ability to compactly express applications in it. The more general the tool is, the less concise applications can be expressed in it. In principle, dedicated tools minimise, and in some cases eliminate, the need for additional programming. This is because features are absorbed in the system supporting the dedicated paradigm. The absorption makes the dedicated tools less general of course.

The trade-off has lead to a proliferation of user interface tools that cannot co-operate. Instead of defining a user interface tool for each paradigm, we want to be able to define a family of cooperating user interface tools that support different paradigms. One way to achieve this is to define one customisable user interface builder.

But – and here we come to the central theme of this paper – user interface builders are in most of the cases "closed systems": they generally lack the ability to be adapted or specialised to support new or refined user interface paradigms. A symptom for this illness is the fact that most user interface builders are expressed as 'black box' abstractions (Kiczales, 1992).

This paper discusses techniques for creating open user interface builders. We will investigate the different aspects involved in specialising a general purpose user interface builder based on an application framework to a dedicated user interface builder based on a specialised application framework. Therefore, after covering some basic vocabulary, we will propose a fairly general application framework serving as a basis for our user interface builder. Afterwards, we will show how reflection can be used for specialising user interface builders. Finally our approach will be demonstrated by a well documented experiment.

2. Terminology and Examples

Application frameworks aid in building applications and their user interface by providing a skeleton or abstract implementation that can be reused (Wirfs-Brock, 1990)(Johnson et al., 1988)(Deutsch, 1987). In the object-oriented community, researchers observed that inheritance and late-binding polymorphism are powerful abstraction mechanisms, and that programs expressed in an object-oriented programming language can be reused by incrementally adapting them to different needs. As such, object-oriented techniques are especially useful when building application frameworks. An object-oriented application framework consists of abstract and concrete classes that together form a theory on how to build applications and their user interface. Among the earliest examples of object-oriented application frameworks was the Smalltalk Model/View/Controller framework (Krasner et al., 1988) (Goldberg et al., 1989)(Lalonde et al., 1991). Other examples are MacApp (Schmucker, 1986) and InterViews (Linton et al., 1989).

Since application frameworks are expressed as object-oriented skeleton programs, standard object-oriented techniques such as refinement by inheritance can be applied to it. A skeleton can be incrementally modified into a new, more specialised skeleton. An example can be found in (Meyrowitz, 1986) where MacApp, a fairly general application framework, is refined to Intermedia, an application framework for hypermedia applications.

User interface management systems (UIMS) promote visual user interface design and development to minimise the need for conventional programming. A *user interface builder* (UIB) is a particular kind of UIMS. Conventionally UIBs are interactive meta-programs that allow visual painting of user interfaces and generation of application code. The generated programs are skeleton implementations to which the programmer must further add the user interface logic and domain logic. In the ideal case where the target language is object-oriented, the generated code can fit in some application framework that can be reused incrementally to build an application. In other cases the application code and domain code must be added, e.g. by text editing the generated skeleton. In all cases the need for conventional programming is minimised, since the bulk of the interface management is absorbed in the underlying user interface model.

To illustrate these ideas, we will discuss two examples of user interface builders: HyperCard and VisualWorks. The former is a dedicated purpose user interface builder, promoting an iterative development process where no programming is necessary to build running applications. The latter is general purpose in nature, supports an iterative development process, and requires programming to build an application. Both of the examples will be used later on in this paper.

HyperCard (Goodman, 1987) is a kind of hypertext. Conceptually, a HyperCard application is a stack of cards. Each card contains some information and links to other cards in the same or other stacks. The information on the cards is shown using text and graphics. The links to other cards are presented as buttons, typically complete with an icon representing the destination card. A user of HyperCard browses the cards of a stack using the link buttons. Only one card of a stack is displayed at a time. Clicking a link button results in the display of the destination card.

HyperCard not only lets a user browse prefabricated stacks (browsing and typing level), it also allows the creation of new stacks (authoring level). On the authoring level, the stack developer designs cards using the small set of HyperCard-dedicated interface components. Text fields and pictures are used to display information. Link buttons are used to link cards. After painting an interface component, its contents is to be specified in order to complete its appearance. In case of a link button, its destination card must be specified by selecting it.

At any time the stack developer can switch from painting to browsing and back to try out the new cards and to fine-tune his design. This iterative development ensures a very smooth transition from development to a running stack. For simple information-oriented stacks, the developer does not need to write a single line of code. Only the destination cards of the link buttons need to be specified. However, when a stack not only has an informational nature, but also has to exhibit a more active behaviour, the stack designer has to develop cards on the scripting level, on which programming in the dedicated language HyperTalk is supported. For example, a button can be assigned another behaviour than simple card linking.

VisualWorks[1] (VisualWorks, 1992) is a development tool used in conjunction with the ObjectWorks\Smalltalk environment. We refer to section 3.3 for a discussion on the concepts used in VisualWorks; here we will illustrate the development process with the construction of an example application.

Imagine a dialog window to manipulate an integer: a possible interface might consist of a text field and two buttons. In the text field the user is allowed to edit the value using the keyboard; the buttons are used for incrementing or decrementing the value. Figure 1 shows how such an interface may look like.

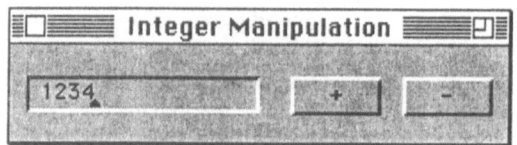

Figure 1: a running application to manipulate an integer

To create this interface, the interface designer opens a new canvas (an editor representation for the interface being developed) and shapes it using the painter. He drags visual components (here two buttons and one text field) from a palette onto the canvas and positions them appropriately. Afterwards he uses the properties editor to define properties of these components.

After stepping through this procedure, he has created the user interface for the application without writing a single line of code. But to incorporate the user interface logic, programming is required. First, a class must be created as a repository for the code. Second, the interface designer uses VisualWorks tools to generate code for every visual component on the canvas. Regular interface development forces designers to extend the application framework with user interface logic afterwards.

In this example, the VisualWorks tools are able to create an instance variable holding the text entered in the text field; the appropriate initialisation and accessor methods are generated as well. For every button an empty action method is generated, which must be completed by the interface designer. Here is where the user interface logic is defined (i.e. the fact that when pressing a button, the value in the text field is incremented or decremented).

As with normal Smalltalk development, it is possible to build and test applications incrementally. In this example, one can build a window with one text field, test it, and install the buttons afterwards. The incremental development idea is not completely supported though, since the VisualWorks system is unaware of modifications to generated code.

3. Related Work

As explained before, user interface management systems are software tools that enable designers to create a complete and working user interface and minimise the coding effort.

The main concerns of UIMSs are listed by Alan Dix (Dix et al., 1993 - p. 353):"

---

[1] VisualWorks. ObjectWorks and ObjectWorks\Smalltalk are trademarks of ParcPlace Systems Inc.

- a conceptual architecture for the structure of interactive systems which concentrates on a separation between application semantics and presentation,
- techniques for implementing a separated application and presentation while preserving the intended connection between them,
- support techniques for managing, implementing and evaluating a run-time interactive environment."

Main reasons for using UIMSs are portability and reusability, arguments we recognise as advocating for application frameworks too.

In the following paragraphs we will discuss some important UIMSs and match them to the above criteria. Afterwards we will tentatively define a purified application framework and associated UIB.

3.1 The Model-View-Controller Framework

The Model-View-Controller (MVC) framework (Krasner et al., 1988)(Goldberg et al., 1989)(Lalonde et al., 1991) can not be omitted from this overview, as it is generally regarded as being one of the first object-oriented frameworks (Johnson et al., 1988)(Johnson et al., 1991). Its main contribution was the distinction between three important roles (namely data, output and input) that should be reflected in the design of a user interface framework. Those roles were reflected in three abstract superclasses — Model, View, Controller — composing the heart of the framework. It also provided a dependency mechanism between objects: a construction for change propagation (Weinand et al., 1988) which is necessary when developing highly interactive software. As such it was used in building the graphical user interface for the Smalltalk programming environment.

In (Tesler, 1986) it is argued that the MVC framework is very broad, and can be used to explore different user interface paradigms. Nevertheless, it needs more refinement to allow for actual code reuse. In the ObjectWorks\Smalltalk 4.1 (ObjectWorks, 1992) class library this is accomplished with a group of 'pluggable views'. In practice we feel that this is not enough to call it a real UIMS: there is still too much burden left on the programmer (e.g. the positioning of the visual elements). Moreover, it is hard to scale up MVC applications since all of the synchronisation between the visual elements is encoded in the model: a better separation of responsibilities is needed. These are well known problems and they were addressed with the introduction of VisualWorks (section 3.3).

3.2 The MoDE Framework

One of the first extensions of the MVC framework was the MoDE framework (Shan, 1990). The motivation for the experiment was the observation that the MVC concepts provide convenient divisions at the abstract level, but maintaining this division on the implementation level is much harder. This hinders the reuse of software components and produces awkward inheritance structures.

MoDE (Mode Development Environment) is what we call a UIB. It consists of a direct manipulation interface editor (the Mode Composer) on top of (and created with) an object-oriented framework. The basic building block of the framework is a mode, which is responsible for managing a certain area on the screen. A mode is defined by its appearance, its semantics and its interaction: three orthogonal axes in the user interface component space, each of them corresponding with different classes in the framework. The interaction between the different modes is coded in the *computing component*. MoDE has been used to develop several user interfaces supporting different user interface paradigms (direct manipulation, navigational, ...). The framework is easy to extend for experienced programmers. The composer promotes the reuse of modes: newly created modes may be pasted in a library for later application.

Our main objection against MoDE is the vague definition of the "computing component". This encourages the intertwining of user interface logic with domain logic (constraints independent of the user interface) and obstructs the reuse of software components.

3.3 VisualWorks

The problems of the class library provided with ObjectWorks\Smalltalk (see section 3.1) were tackled with the introduction of VisualWorks (VisualWorks, 1992). The major improvement came with the direct manipulation interface editor. Similar to the NeXT interface builder (Webster, 1989)(Shneiderman, 1992) it provides the interface designer with a palette of widgets that may be pasted on a canvas (an editor representation for the actual window). Each of these widgets (visual components) communicates with the underlying model through an *aspect*, which is responsible for the user interface behaviour of a certain piece of information[2]. To control the interrelationships between those aspects, the notions of *application model* and *domain model* were introduced: the former being responsible for the user interface, the latter for the data consistency.

There exist other commercial products providing graphical interface editors for Smalltalk, but none of these possesses fundamental improvements compared to VisualWorks. In fact they all lack an important property we feel as being essential for the success of user interface builders: extensibility. Indeed it is possible to expand the set of available widgets, but this is not enough. First of all because the process is too difficult (it is poorly documented and requires some tricky hacks). Secondly because incorporating new interface paradigms takes a lot more than the ability to include new widgets. For example, when we want to simulate HyperCard, we would like to include a "home button" into the palette of available widgets. To do this we need a way to provide semantic information for the widget. We refer the reader to the last section of the paper for a detailed discussion on the subject.

What is needed is a well defined architecture and an open and extensible implementation. And here we touch upon another severe drawback of the VisualWorks system: the lack of a well-defined application framework. A symptom for this is the fact that there are no classes for important concepts like "DomainModel" and "Aspect".

3.4 Conclusion

Over the years many developers used object-oriented frameworks as the kernel of a UIMS. We mention HotDraw (Johnson, 1992) and Tigre (Tigre, 1991) as additional UIMSs for Smalltalk. Other languages served as implementation vehicle as well: MacApp (Schmucker, 1986) for C; ET++ (Weinand et al., 88), Vamp (Ferrel et al., 1989) in C++; Picasso (Konstan et al., 1991) for CLOS.

It is our opinion that all of today's UIMSs fail in making a clear separation between user interface logic and domain logic. This is necessary for an orthogonal design enabling code reuse. Moreover, when providing the means for extending the UIMS, they are biased towards user interface details. Adding new kinds of widgets is feasible, but incorporating semantic information needed to assimilate interface paradigms is nearly impossible.

In the next section we will see how we can improve on these shortcomings by introducing a new architecture for user interface management systems.

4. Building Application Builders

As explained before, user interface management systems promote visual user interface design and the reuse of visual components in user interfaces. Some of these systems even permit experienced users to extend the library of widgets. In spite of all these powerful properties, we feel that too much attention is directed towards the visual characteristics and not enough to the underlying user interface model.

We claim that a higher level of reuse and extension is needed to incorporate user interface paradigms into a user interface management system. We will call a system that enables such high level manipulation an *application builder*.

In what follows we will try to explain how such a system might be conceived. Afterwards we will guide the reader through an experiment demonstrating the philosophy of an application builder.

---

[2]   The notion of an aspect resembles in many ways the notion of a mode in MoDE (see section 3.2).

4.1 An Application Framework Sustaining Application Builders

In order to successfully incorporate user interface paradigms into a user interface management system, we propose a scheme of incremental extensions on an underlying framework. We will start with the definition of the concepts serving as the foundation for our UIMS.
It is not a claim of this paper to propose the ultimate UIMS framework. As a matter of fact, we don't think such a framework exists. Rather, we want to argue that the use of a framework allows the construction of an "open" user interface builder. Moreover, reflection makes it possible to migrate seamlessly from the user interface design level to the paradigm design level.
For easy refinement of a framework, a set of orthogonal concepts is essential (Johnson et al., 1988). We adopt the terminology of VisualWorks (see 3.3), mainly because we like its clear distinction between the application model and domain model. We purify these concepts to fit them into the framework.
In figure 2 the foundation of the framework is depicted. The core of the model consists of three basic concepts: user interface component, application model and domain model. An auxiliary concept, aspect, is needed to separate the domain model from the user interface component. The relations between the four concepts are display, notify and control.

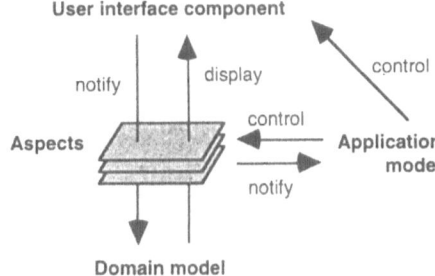

Figure 2: the framework architecture

A *domain model* models the overall functionality of the problem domain and maintains user interface independent constraints. From the viewpoint of the user interface components, its main goal is to serve as a storage for the information to be displayed. Features like printing, persistence (database storage) and network communication are included in the domain model as well. There can exist several application models for one domain model.
An *aspect* is a container for a reference to a piece of information (supplied by the domain model) that is to be represented on the screen and can be modified by the user. Such information may be simple (e.g. strings, numbers, dates) or complex (e.g. lists, matrices). The main function for an aspect is to interpret operations from user interface components and translate them into operations on the domain model. As such, aspects can be layered on top of each other to encapsulate user interface specific operations from the domain model.
A *user interface component* controls the display and the user interaction of a particular piece of information. The information is supplied by the domain model, but a series of aspects will be used to hide implementation details, e.g. the message that is needed to retrieve the information from the domain model, or the last choice from a pop-up menu. Among the responsibilities of a user interface component are properties like colour, font and position (display), and functions like mouse tracking and keyboard control (user interaction). Note that every interface component has exactly one aspect, but that one aspect can be shared between several components. Normally an interface component will not stand on itself: it is grouped with other interface components to act as a whole.
An *application model* manages the global behaviour of such a group of interface components. It is responsible for the user interface logic and controls user interface behaviour like: When should what information be displayed ? What operations affect the information and how should the display be updated ? As such, an application model is an aggregation of aspects that are to be

considered as a whole and interact with each other. Actually, almost all of the programming effort that goes into an application model is specifying the interaction between the different aspects. Readers should be aware that the same application model can be reused on different domain models.

It is recognised that user interface tools require a mechanism to synchronise the different interface components (Krasner et al., 1988)(Weinand et al., 1988). That is precisely the motivation for the relations between the basic concepts.

After setting up a complete data structure, the system starts with an initial display. This is accomplished by activating the user interface components for all aspects contained in the application model. The user interface component requests the aspect for the information to display, the aspect translates this request in the appropriate operations on the domain model (or on the next aspect). This explains the *control* relation from the application model to the user interface component and the *display* relation from the domain model to the interface component.

When the user activates a user interface component (by clicking a button, selecting an item in a list or a pop-up menu, typing some characters in a text field, etc.) it applies a *notification* operation on the domain model (through the aspect) which takes the appropriate actions. Most of the aspects also *notify*[3] the application model. The application model might decide to alter interface components (e.g. disabling a text field) or to modify the domain model through other aspects. This explains the two *notify* relations (from the interface component to the domain model and from the aspect to the application model) and both of the *control* relations (from the application model to the interface component and to the aspect).

4.2 An Example

In this section we will illustrate the architecture of our framework with the integer manipulating application from section 2.

The domain model for such an application is a simple object with one instance variable being an integer. Let us call this variable 'number' (with accessor methods number and number:) and the class representing the domain model 'UserObject'. We define three user interface components for this application: a text field and two buttons. The text field should allow numeric characters only, the label of the increment button is a plus sign and the label of the decrement button is a minus sign.

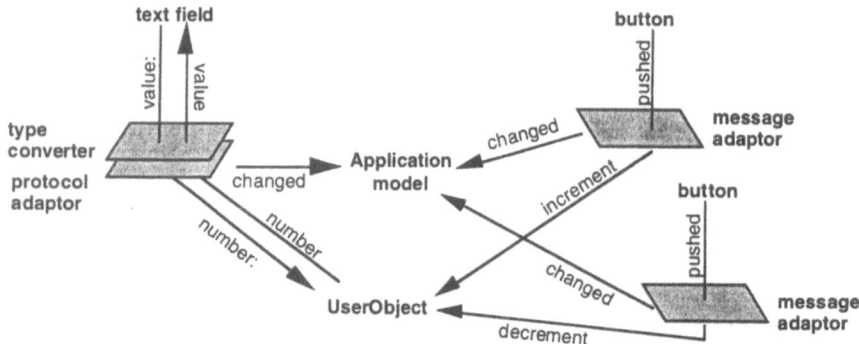

Figure 3 : the structure behind the number application

Some aspects are needed to glue these user interface components together with the application and domain model (see figure 3) :

---

[3]   The mechanism is similar to the dependency mechanism of Smalltalk (see section 3.1).

- A protocol adaptor to translate the protocol of the text field (i.e. `value` / `value:`) into the protocol of the domain model (i.e. `number` / `number:`) and to notify the application model using the `changed` message.
- A type converter to convert the type of the text field (a string) into the type of the domain model (an integer).
- A message adaptor to translate the protocol of the buttons (i.e. `pushed`) into the protocol of the domain model (i.e. `increment` / `decrement`) and to notify the application model using the `changed` message.

4.3 User Interface Builder with an Open Implementation + Reflection = Application Builder

In our view a user interface builder consists of a range of tools. The *painter* is the tool to create a user interface layout. It consists of a canvas and a palette of visual components. Aspects are chosen from the aspect palette and associated with visual components on the canvas. Visual properties and aspects are modified with the *visual properties editor* and the *aspect editor* respectively. User interface logic is generated by the *definer*, and modified using the *code browser* or other conventional coding tools.

A particular configuration of tools determines how well the UIB fits into a certain user interface paradigm. Adapting the UIB to a new interface paradigm amounts to the reconfiguration of this set of tools. As already argued in the introduction, today's UIBs do not support this reconfiguration, because they are expressed as 'black box' abstractions (Kiczales, 1992).

'Open implementations' (Rao, 1991) do support this reconfiguration of tools by providing a meta-level interface (Rao, 1991)(Kiczales, 1992)(Steyaert, 1994) besides the traditional base-level interface. The latter is the interface to the basic system's functionality. The former is the interface to the system's implementation and reveals aspects of how the base-level interface is implemented.

A UIB with an open implementation is a UIB with a meta-level interface to adapt the configuration of the tools it consists of. For example, to adapt the painter tool the meta-level interface supplies the methods `installComponentPalette:`, `installAspectPalette:` and `installDefaultCanvas:` for the installation of custom palettes and custom default canvasses.

Only providing a meta-level interface has the severe drawback that the UIB modifications have to be hand-coded. This means that an interface designer who finds the UIB not suited for his target applications must use a completely different set of tools to adapt the UIB to his needs. To reconfigure the UIB, he must leave the UIB environment, hand-code the modifications, install them into the UIB-framework and return to the UIB environment. As a consequence only skilled users would be able to customise the UIB. Moreover, switching levels gives rise to certain 'paradigm mismatches', e.g. inconsistencies between hand-coded specifications and specifications generated by the UIB.

New tools need not be hand-coded as is typically the case for their built-in counterparts. Since they have a user interface, they can be created by a UIB. A UIB with an open implementation capable of reconfiguring itself is called reflective. It uses its meta-level interface for its own specialisation. A reflective UIB can be used for both the construction of traditional applications and the specialisation of itself. Reflective UIBs enable incorporation of user interface paradigms without leaving the UIB environment. This is precisely the higher level reuse and extension aimed at in the introduction of section 4. Thus, a UIB with an open implementation and reflection is an application builder.

The reflective nature of an application builder introduces layers of abstraction in the user interface building process. At any level, the application builder is used to refine the framework introduced in section 4.1. At the bottom layer the basic application builder is used; at any level above all refinements of the previous levels can be reused. This is illustrated in the next section.

5. Experiment : a HyperCard-like Application Using Specialised UI Components

To substantiate the idea of a reflective application builder, experiments were carried out in VisualWorks. Natively VisualWorks does not support customisation. Therefore it was extended with reflective facilities. Moreover VisualWorks uses a slightly different application framework than the one proposed in this text. We will point out the differences when needed.

The experiment described here uses specialised user interface components in order to build HyperCard-like applications. Figure 4 shows a card of the target application. In the remainder we will call the HyperCard-like application 'Card'. We aimed to create user interface components and one application model that are so dedicated to the Card application that the Card application programmer need not write a single line of user interface logic. The dedication lies in the fact that all of the features needed for the definition of the user interface logic can be absorbed in the user interface components.

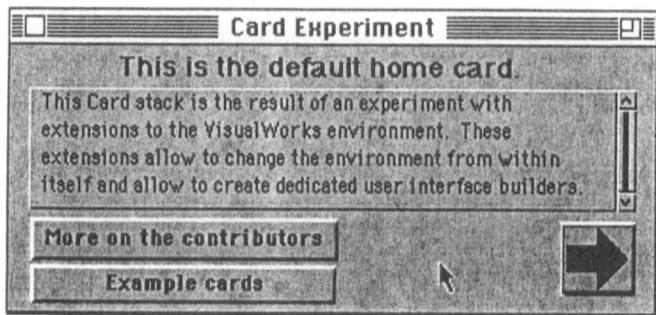

Figure 4 : an example card

First a description will be given of how the Card application can be designed with standard VisualWorks. VisualWorks' shortcomings will be discussed as well. Then some light will be shed on how VisualWorks was extended to turn it into a reflective variant. Finally, the development of the Card application using the reflective variant of VisualWorks will be discussed.

5.1 Description of the User Interface Components and the Application Model

The description of HyperCard was given in section 2. For simplicity, we will restrict the information to be textual. Conceptually, five link button types can be distinguished: the general link button and four special link buttons: the home button, the previous button, the next button and the return button. The general link button links with an arbitrary card in the stack. The home button connects with the first card in the stack. The previous and the next button are used to follow a sequential path through the stack and the return button jumps to the last visited card. These five button types will be made explicit in the Card application.

Labels, text fields and buttons are placed on a card. Cards are represented as complete interfaces. In order not to get a proliferation of non-reusable application models representing cards, all cards share the same application model, being the Card application. There is no explicit domain model (i.e. a stack); the order of the cards is determined by explicit linking through the previous button and the next button.

5.2 Designing a HyperCard-like Application with Standard VisualWorks

When using standard VisualWorks components, the different Card buttons can be implemented using the standard action button. The properties of an action button are specified using the properties dialog shown in figure 5. The contents of the 'Action:' field is the name of the message that will be sent to the application model when the action button is clicked.

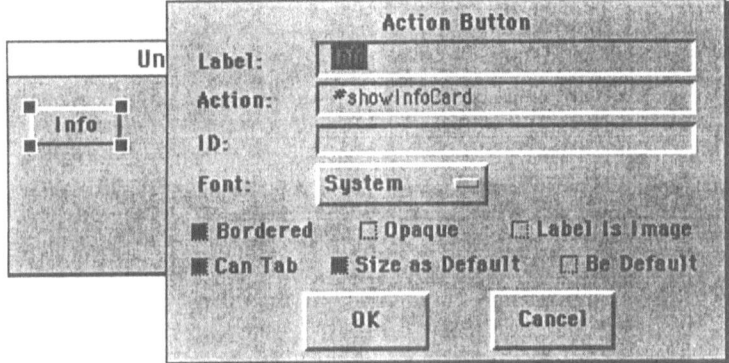

Figure 5 : standard action button properties dialog

In order to make action buttons behave as link buttons, the application model using the action buttons has to provide one action method per action button, each different in the destination card name used (see figure 6). Since our intention was to have only one application model, the Card application model has as many implemented action methods as there are action buttons on all the cards of the stack. Note that the designer of a stack has to implement all the action methods by hand to give each button its specific behaviour.[4]

Figure 6 : an implementation of Card buttons directly based on action buttons

5.3 Arguments for Customisation of the UIB

It is clear that an extra abstraction level is needed to eliminate the multiple action methods. The kernel of a Card application is an application model for navigating through a stack of cards. Therefore it should have a very simple protocol. It should only respond to gotoCard: messages to display another card. In contrast with general purpose action buttons, where the different action methods are unary messages, this message takes a parameter: the card to go to when the button is clicked. The destination card of a link button is encapsulated as a variable in the link button aspect. In figure 7 the link button is represented in terms of our conceptual model of section 4.1.

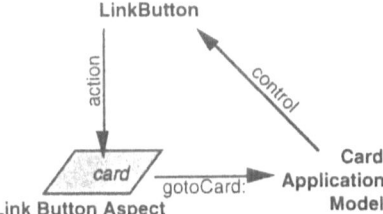

Figure 7 : conceptual representation of a dedicated link button in an abstract application model

---

4 Having several application models, i.e. one application model per card, would not inhibit the hand-coding of the action methods.

The extra abstraction level can be realised by means of a dedicated UIB and a dedicated Card application model. Instead of using standard action buttons, dedicated link buttons are painted on a canvas. They have dedicated properties dialogs, as shown in figure 8. Link buttons now have a *card* property which specifies the name of the destination card. The name supplied in the 'Card:' field is the actual argument for the gotoCard: method of the Card application model. Since all link button aspects use the same method and the method is part of the Card application model's protocol, the designer of a stack does not have to write a single line of code.

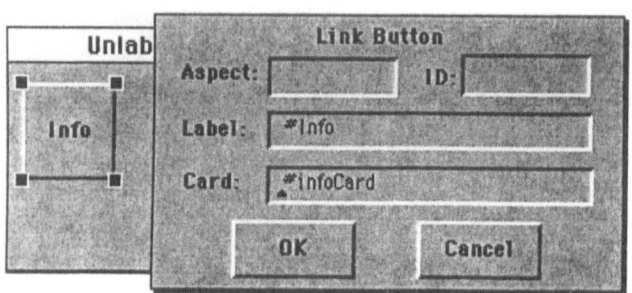

Figure 8 : the dedicated link button properties dialog

Note that the properties editor shown in figure 8 mixes visual properties (e.g. the label of the button) and aspect properties (e.g. the card name). This follows from the fact that VisualWorks does not make an as clean separation between aspects and application models as our framework does. In an ideal UIB there would exist a visual properties editor and an aspect editor to reflect this separation of concepts.

5.4 Customisation of the UIB

To customise the UIB three steps must be taken:
1. creation of dedicated application models
2. creation of properties dialogs for the dedicated application models
3. creation of a palette containing the dedicated application models

The standard VisualWorks UIB does not support steps 2 and 3. Therefore the standard UIB was turned into a reflective variant.
A palette containing user interface components for painting palettes (i.e. palette buttons) was created using the VisualWorks UIB. The palette application model, not present in VisualWorks, and the palette button application models were hand-coded. Then the standard UIB was parameterised with the palette to be used. When opened with the palette for painting palettes, the UIB can now be used to paint dedicated palettes which, in turn, can be used in conjunction with the UIB to paint dedicated user interfaces. The UIB was extended to be able to install a canvas as custom properties dialog, and modified to open the appropriate custom dialog on a dedicated application model.
The UIB is now reflective and will be used to design the HyperCard-like application.

5.4.1 Step 1 : Creation of Dedicated Application Models

The dedicated application models corresponding to the five button types (i.e. general link button, home button, previous button, next button and return button) and the text field are defined using conventional programming, i.e. with a browser. Their user interfaces are specified using the UIB with the standard palette.
The definition of a customised link button aspect is straightforward and depicted below. It is important to mention that this definition is not VisualWorks source code, but rather a definition that fits into the conceptual framework.

```
class LinkButtonAspect extends AbstractAspect
instance variables
    card
methods
    card
        return card
    card: aCard
        card := aCard
    action
        self changed: #gotoCard: with: self card
endclass
```

The link button aspect contains its destination card name. When triggered by an action method, it notifies its application model via the dependency mechanism to go to the destination card. Notice that in the philosophy of section 4.3 the `card` and `card:` methods belong to the meta-level interface and the action method is part of the base-level interface of the link button. The explanation for this is straightforward: the `card` messages are sent by the aspect editor for the definition of the aspect, the `action` message is sent when the button is triggered by user interaction.

5.4.2 Step 2 : Creation of Properties Dialogs

Using the reflective UIB, the properties dialogs of the custom components are specified. The properties dialog for link buttons was depicted in figure 8. The VisualWorks properties dialogs allow editing of aspects as well as visual properties. In our conceptual framework only the aspect editor part is of concern. The responsibility of the aspect editor is to fill in the destination card of the link button aspect. As shown in figure 9, the link button aspect editor is an application which must have the above defined link button aspect as domain model. This is what makes the dedicated UIB special: it allows the installation of aspects, e.g. link buttons, as domain model for aspect editors, e.g. link button aspect editors.

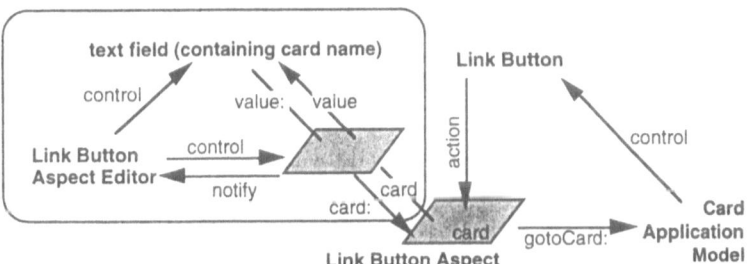

Figure 9 : conceptual representation of the link button aspect editor

5.4.3 Step 3 : Creation of the Dedicated Palette

With the reflective UIB the dedicated palette for Card applications is defined. For all palette buttons the appropriate icons and the target user interface components are specified with the properties editor. In figure 10 on the left the finished custom palette is shown.

5.5 Building an Example Application

Now we are ready to paint canvasses using the new specialised components. For each card a canvas is painted and installed under a different name. The cards are linked through the 'Card' property of the buttons. Figure 10 shows how the dedicated palette is used to paint dedicated Card components on a canvas. Note that the home button aspect editor, as shown, has no card field because the destination card for home buttons is implicit.

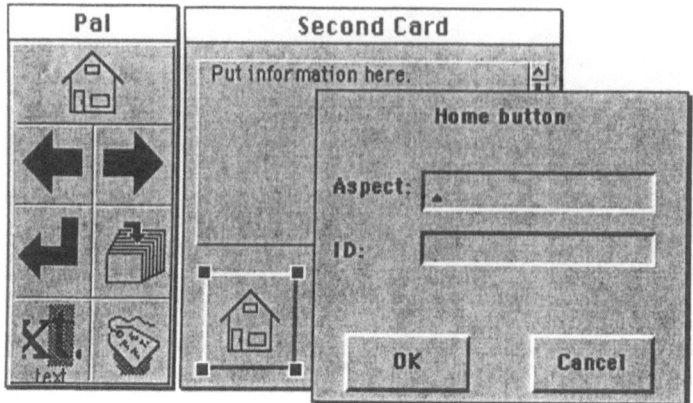

Figure 10 : the Card application builder in action

For a screen dump of a complete card built with the dedicated Card application builder we refer the reader to figure 4.

6. Conclusions

Over the last years we have seen a proliferation of interface tools. Such tools range from simple machine dependent tool kits to full-blown direct manipulation environments. On the other hand, in the object-oriented research community, application frameworks have been successfully applied on diverse problem domains. We feel that for the next generation of user interface builders much can be learned from the experiences gained in application framework research. Especially the concept of incremental refinement seems appropriate.

In this paper we have shown that application frameworks and reflection are essential for the construction of full-blown specialisable user interface builders, because they support such an incremental refinement through a layered approach. Experiments sustain this viewpoint. The experiment described in the paper is a good example of the absorption of the HyperCard user interface paradigm into an application builder. It shows clearly that reflection makes it possible to migrate seamlessly from the user interface design level to the paradigm design level.

Emphasis has been put on the use of reflection, rather than on the technical aspects of making a user interface builder reflective. Although the latter is a very interesting topic, it is out of the scope of this paper.

References

(Akscyn, 1991)   R. M. Akscyn. *Design Tradeoffs for Advanced Hypertext Technology.* Tutorial Notes, Third ACM Conference on Hypertext, December 91.

(Cox, 1986)   B. Cox. *Panel: User Interface Frameworks.* In Proceedings of OOPSLA'86 conference, pp. 497-501, printed as SIGPLAN Notices, 21(11), 1986.

(Deutsch, 1987)   L. P. Deutsch. *Levels of Reuse in the Smalltalk-80 Programming System.* In Peter Freeman (Ed.) Tutorial: Software Reusability, IEEE Computer Society Press, 1987.

(Dix et al., 1993)   A. Dix, J. Finlay, R. Beale. *Human-Computer Interaction.* Addison Wesley, 1993.

(Ferrel et al., 1989)   P. J. Ferrel, R. F. Meyer: Vamp. *The Aldus Application Framework.* Proceedings of OOPSLA'89 conference, p. 185-189, ACM Press, October 1989

(Goldberg et al., 1989) A. Goldberg, and D. Robson. *Smalltalk-80, The Language.* Addison-Wesley Publishing Company, Reading Massachusetts, 1989.

(Goodman, 1987) D. Goodman. *The Complete HyperCard Handbook*. Bantam Computer Books, September 1987.

(Johnson et al., 1988) R. E. Johnson, B. Foote. *Designing Reusable Classes*. Journal of Object-Oriented Programming, 1(2), pp. 22-35, 1988.

(Johnson et al., 1991) R. E. Johnson, Vincent F. Russo. Reusing *Object-Oriented Design*. University of Illinois tech report UIUCDCS 91-1696,1991.

(Johnson, 1992) R. E. Johnson. *Documenting Frameworks using Patterns*. Proceedings of OOPSLA'92 conference, p. 63-76, SIGPLAN Notices, ACM Press, October 1992

(Kiczales, 1992) G. Kiczales. *Towards a New Model of Abstraction in the Engineering of Software*. In Proceedings of IMSA'92, International Workshop on Reflection and Meta-Level Architectures, pp. 1-11, November 1992.

(Konstan et al., 1991) J. A. Konstan, L. A. Rowe. *Developing a GUIDE Using Object-Oriented Programming*. Proceedings of OOPSLA'91 conference, p. 75-88, SIGPLAN Notices, ACM Press, November 1991

(Krasner et al., 1988) G. E. Krasner, S. T. Pope. *A Cookbook for Using the Model-View-Controller User Interface Paradigm in Smalltalk-80*. Journal of Object Oriented Programming, August 1988, p. 26-49.

(Lalonde et al., 1991) W. R. Lalonde, J. R. Pugh. *Inside Smalltalk - Volume II*. Prentice Hall 1991.

(Linton et al., 1989) M. A. Linton, J. M. Vlissides, P. R. Calder. *Composing User Interfaces with InterViews*. IEEE Computer, p. 8-22, February 1989

(Meyrowitz, 1986) N. Meyrowitz. Intermedia: *The Architecture and Construction of an Object-Oriented Hypermedia System and Applications Framework*. In Proceedings of OOPSLA'86 conference, pp. 186-201, printed as SIGPLAN Notices, 21(11), 1986.

(ObjectWorks, 1992) ParcPlace Systems. *Objectworks\Smalltalk Release 4.1 User's Guide*. ParcPlace Systems 1992.

(Rao, 1991) R. Rao. *Implementational Reflection in Silica*. In ECOOP'91 Proceedings, Lecture Notes in Computer Science, P. America (Ed.), pp. 251-267, Springer-Verlag, 1991.

(Schmucker, 1986) K. J. Schmucker. *Object-Oriented Programming for the Macintosch*. Hayden Book Company, 1986.

(Shan, 1990) Y. P. Shan. *MoDE: An Object-Oriented User Interface Development Environment Based on the Concept of Mode*. PhD Thesis, University of North Carolina at Chapel Hill - Department of Computer Science, 1990.

(Shneiderman, 1983) B. Shneiderman. *Direct Manipulation: A Step Beyond Programming Languages* IEEE Computer, August 1983.

(Shneiderman, 1992) B. Shneiderman. *Designing the User Interface: Strategies for Effective Human-Computer Interaction*. Addison Wesley 1992.

(Steyaert, 1994) P. Steyaert. *Open Design of Object-Oriented Languages, A Foundation for Specialisable Reflective Language Frameworks*. PhD Thesis, Vrije Universiteit Brussel, 1994.

(Tesler, 1986) L. Tesler, position statement in (Cox, 1986).

(Tigre, 1991) Tigre Object Systems. *The Tigre Programming Environment, User's Guide, Version 1.6*. Tigre Object Systems, 1991

(VisualWorks, 1992) ParcPlace Systems. *VisualWorks release 1.0 User's Guide*. ParcPlace Systems 1992.

(Webster, 1989) B. F. Webster. *The NeXT Book*. Addison-Wesley 1989.

(Weinand et al., 1988) A. Weinand, E. Gamma, and R. Marty. *ET++: an object-oriented application framework in C++*. In Proceedings of OOPSLA'88, pp. 46-57, November 1988, printed as SIGPLAN Notices, 23(11).

(Wirfs-Brock, 1990) Allen Wirfs-Brock. *Panel: Designing Reusable Designs: Experiences Designing Object-Oriented Frameworks*. SIGPLAN Notices Special Issue OOPSLA-ECOOP'90 Addendum to the Proceedings (Jerry L. Archibald and K.C. Burgess Yakemovic eds.), pp. 19-24, 1990.

An Abstract Definition of Graphical Notations for Object Orientated Information Systems

David Page, Paul Clark and Daniela Mehandjiska-Stavreva

Faculty of Informational and Mathematical Sciences
Department of Computer Science
Massey University
Palmerston North, New Zealand
E-mail: D.C.Page@massey.ac.nz, P.K.Clark@massey.ac.nz, D.Mehandjiska@massey.ac.nz

ABSTRACT. *A language which facilitates abstract definitions of graphical notations and the human-computer interaction with them has been developed. It supports a methodology independent Computer Aided Software Engineering (CASE) tool for the construction of Object Orientated (OO) software but can be applied to information systems which employ graphical notations. Arbitrary notations and dialogues for OO models can be described and modified using this language without reconstruction of the CASE environment. Its utilisation allows an experimental approach to CASE tool development and OO methodology evaluation.*

KEY WORDS: *Object-Orientated, Human Computer Interaction, CASE.*

1. Introduction

HCI research has identified that consistency in the look and feel of an interface is important for user productivity due to the facilitation effect and chunking of information (Johnson 1992). Most companies have a large investment in training staff to use existing and new software (Powers et al. 1984). Often this software is not utilised to its full potential as users lack any means to understand it in terms of software or procedures they already use. People learn how to use new systems faster if they are consistent with existing software as there is a smaller cognitive load placed on the user. The HCI consistency issue is especially inherent in Computer Aided Software Engineering (CASE) tools as an organisation may require a range of different tools to support their business.

A methodology provides a means of solving a problem by forming abstract descriptions (models) of the problem in a systematic way. Each model a methodology employs has a notation which consists of a set of symbols and a set of rules (Olle et al., 1991). Typically different methodologies and hence different CASE tools are required to support a company's activities. The reason for this is that existing CASE tools focus on a narrow slice of the software life cycle (Sumner 1992) or are targeted to specific methodologies (Nilsson 1990, Papahristos 1990) (for example ObjecTool, Rational Rose/C++ and OMTool). In addition if a company is using different CASE tools then information interchange between them is difficult to achieve. The choice of which methodologies a company uses should be made by the company not enforced by CASE tool vendors (Nilsson 1990). Ideally a CASE tool should support a range of methodologies, have an open architecture and be configurable (Gibson 1988, Papahristos 1991). An additional drawback of using different CASE tools is that users find it difficult to extract the maximum benefit from their use as the interaction with each tool is unique.

A CASE tool which can support many different methodologies and has a consistent look and feel would reduce the amount of effort required to fully utilise these methodologies. If in addition the tool is modifiable and new methodologies could be added then the tool's lifetime increases as the tool can be tailored to satisfy the company's needs. Each methodology may use distinct notations but since the interaction mechanisms and interaction items are the same the users productivity will increase. These reasons motivated the formulation of an abstract definition of graphical notations for Information Systems.

The paper outlines work on a notation definition language which facilitates an abstract description of a models notation and the possible human computer dialogue with it. The results of this work is being used in the development of an intelligent methodology independent CASE tool which is described in (Mehand et al., 1994). The proposed language is applicable to any information system which utilises graphical notations. Possible applications are Computer Aided Operation and Simulation software.

2. Graphical Notations and the Notation Definition Language

Experience has shown that users tend to deal more effectively with concepts when they can visualise them in graphical form. A model is expressed diagrammatically using a notation. A notation consists of symbols which contain semantic information, connections which represent semantic relationships between symbols and text which may be free or associated with the connections. A notation may consist of a variety of symbols, some of which may represent compositions of other symbols and relationships.

The term view is used to describe the visual rendering of symbols and connections on a computer display. Views are graphical representations of semantic information. The semantic information for which a corresponding view is constructed is referred to as a viewable thing. Examples of viewable things are Classes, Objects, Entities, Processes, Relationships and Subject Areas. We define Two types of view, connection and symbol, have been defined which represent the two types of viewable thing rendered graphically. The user of the tool constructs and modifies the semantic model by interacting with the views. The notation definition language must allow the description of how views are constructed, how connections are made and all of the possible interactions with these views.

The notation definition language is a pseudo English definition of the semantic characteristics of a notation. The basis of the notation definition language are the rules which describe how views are created and manipulated. For example: Figure 1 (a) shows a Coad and Yourdon (Coad et al., 1991) abstract superclass; Figure 1 (b) shows the corresponding changes required when two new methods are added. The size of a view depends dynamically on textbox height and width changes. Figure 1 (c) illustrates one possible realisation of such dynamic changes using simple scaling.

A simple scaling of the Coad and Yourdon abstract class symbol to accommodate the text (class name, attributes and operations) is insufficient in general. Some parts of the symbol will change size and position according to one or more textboxes whilst some may only change position or even be invariant in size and position. For example the curves in the Coad and Yourdon abstract class must always maintain the same curvature but some may vary in position. A template mechanism is utilised to build descriptions of a notation and forms the basis of the notation definition language.

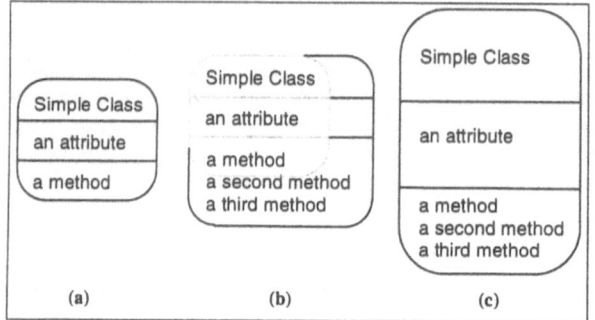

Figure 1 - (a) an abstract class (b) dynamic changes (c) simple scaling

3. Templates

A template is a description of how a view is to be constructed for a particular viewable thing. The size of the view and its orientation depends on the information stored in the viewable thing. In the system, view is modelled as a class View, viewable things are organised in a hierarchy with class Viewable_Thing at the root and templates are realised as a class Template.

To provide a configurable tool the graphical representation of the model must be constructed without a reliance on the viewable things it represents. The 'view creation' process should not have a dependency on the viewable things for which the views are constructed and this dependency should not be hard coded in the system (Brough 1992). A template mechanism is utilised to avoid such dependencies.

An instance of class Template, when provided with an instance of class Viewable_Thing, creates a corresponding instance of class View. Each time a user action at the interface results in a semantic change (for example renaming) the corresponding instance of class Template will be used to update the appropriate instance of class View. An object diagram of the relationship between the classes Template, View and Viewable_Thing adopting Coad and Yourdon's notation is shown in Figure 2.

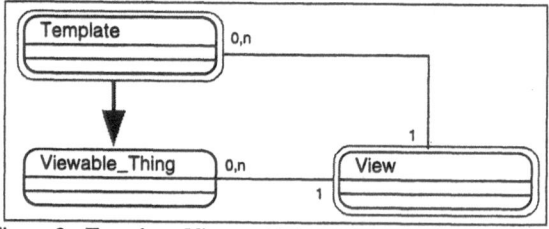

Figure 2 - Template, View and Viewable_Thing relationships.

The template also describes the permissible actions and the steps the user follows to invoke them. A view may have zero or more active areas which the user may select to invoke an action. The template must define these active areas and the actions which are bound to them. Figure 3 shows two classes before and after the user has selected an active area.

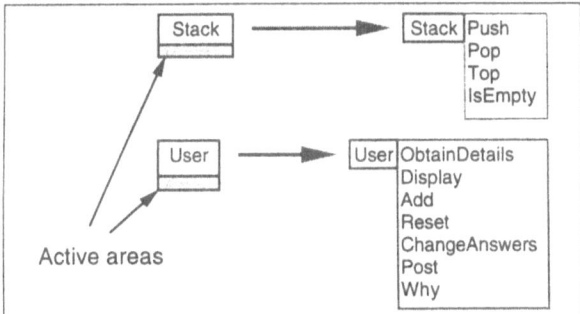

Figure 3 - Two classes before and after selection of an active area

Selecting the grey active area results in displaying the operations for that class. The same template will be used to construct each view and to define the result of selection of active areas. The size of each symbol (including their active areas) is different as the amount of text in each symbol is different.

In an initial analysis phase there was a specialised template for each viewable thing. The template knew about the state and behaviour of its corresponding viewable thing. The dependency existed as the template must send specific messages to the viewable thing to extract the required information (eg class name, list of attributes or process name). Each specialised template had a compile-time dependency on the class for which it was creating views. The template knew the <u>name</u> of the operation which it needed to access the private state of the viewable thing.

If the template knows the names of any of the operations of the viewable thing it then contains semantic information about the viewable thing. It is essential that the template does not posses this knowledge. The template is simply responsible for constructing views and as such is not required to understand the viewable thing it is constructing views for. An analogy may be drawn with the relationship between view and viewable thing where view possesses no understanding of the information the viewable thing represents and is simply a means to facilitate user interaction. The mechanism used to specify the required information of the viewable thing must identify that information by a means other than name.

In the present phase an id number scheme is utilised to specify the required information. Each property of the viewable thing is given a unique id number. All viewable things are described by an inheritance hierarchy with an abstract superclass Viewable_Thing at the root. Viewable_Thing has three subclasses, Viewable_Connection, Viewable_Object and Viewable_Composite. Viewable_Thing defines an operation Get. The class Template does not need to know the name of specific messages it can send to an instance of Viewable_Thing. It is the responsibility of the receiving object to determine if it may respond to the message Get. This mechanism is similar to dynamic binding in pure OO languages such as Smalltalk.

An instance of Template builds an instance of View when sent a message GetView with an instance viewable thing as a parameter. The template is essentially an interpreter with a 'template program' as part of its state. This 'template program' is defined in a template file which is read when the system is started. The view may be altered by changing the 'template program'. Figure 4 shows the relationship between the classes Template, View and Viewable_Thing in more detail.

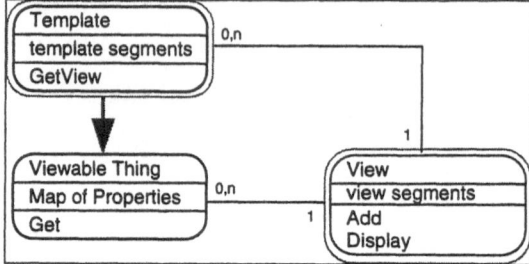

Figure 4 - Attributes and Operations of Template, View and Viewable_Thing

4. Template Design

A template must provide the necessary rules to generate a particular view from the stored information. As such a template must provide:

- lines, arcs, text, fill and pattern styles, fonts and font size from which views are composed.
- a means of specifying relationships between subparts of a view. For example the length of one part of the view may depend on the length of one or more lines of text;
- connection docking areas and annotations. We may require connections to be made to specific parts of the view;
- a facility to bind actions to parts of the generated view.

Figure 5 shows the notation for an abstract class in Coad and Yourdon's Object-Orientated Analysis (OOA) with a topographical description. The equations describe the lines and arcs which compose the view of an arbitrary abstract class. The equations depend on three text fields, the size of which will only be known at run-time. This description forms the basis of the language developed to describe templates.

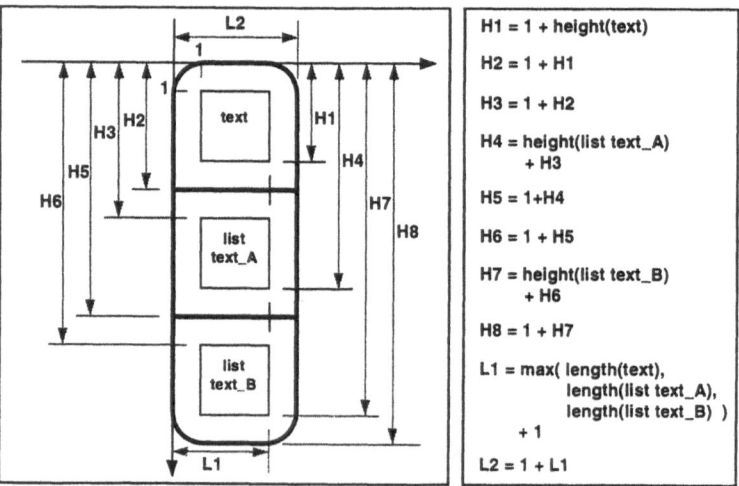

Figure 5 - A topographical description of a template

The abstract class icon in Figure 5 is described by a series of equations and expressions. These expressions are classified as arithmetic expressions, functions, expression references and numerical constants. This is reflected in the expression class hierarchy shown in Figure 6. The four subclasses of class Expression are E_Value (a numerical value), E_Complex (an expression using +, -, * or / between two other expressions), E_TextFunc (a function which calculates the height or length of a text item) and E_Function (a function such as minimum or maximum).

Text functions calculate either the height or width of a particular line or a group of lines of text. A text function names the operation to be performed and the id number of the text on which it is to be performed. The width and height of a text item depends on the context it is viewed in. This includes the particular font, the font size and maximum and minimum constraints for the block of text.

Two manipulation functions have been identified, minimum and maximum. Both of these functions take an arbitrary number of arguments. These functions are used when the size of one part of a view depends on several other parts.

An expression reference names a predefined equation. Expression references remove the duplication of common sub-expressions.

Both floating point and integer numerical constants are supported. All numerical values throughout the evaluation of an expression are type converted to floating point numbers.

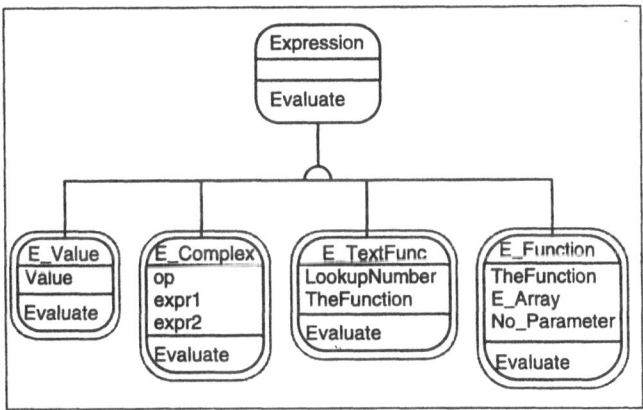

Figure 6 - The Expression class hierarchy

A Template is composed of five different sub-template types. Collectively these sub-templates are used to describe a notation and the allowable human computer interaction with it. The sub-templates are object, group, connection, composite and region templates.

4.1 Group Template

A group template describes a common shape which would be needed more than once within a definition for either an object or a connection template. An example of this is shown is Figure 7.

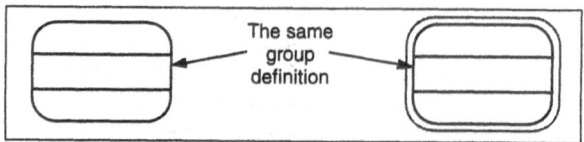

Figure 7 - Reduced redundancy through grouping

A group template is described by the class Group_Template and is composed of six different types of template segment as shown in Figure 8.

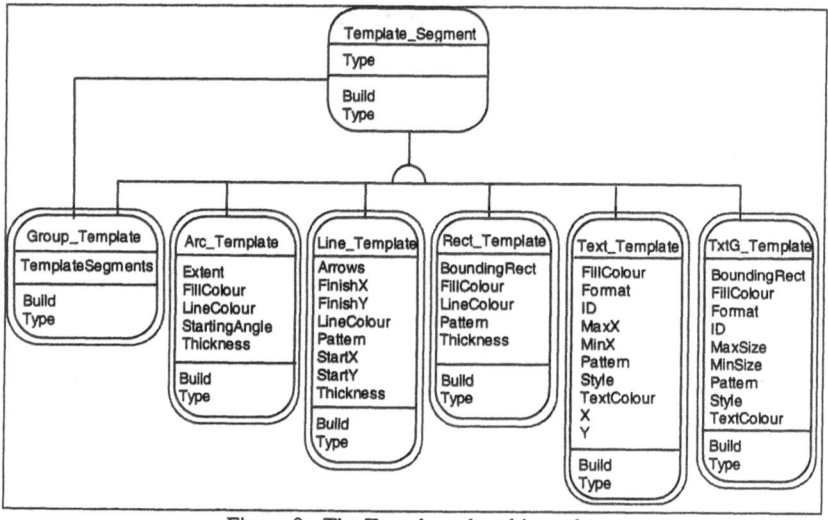

Figure 8 - The Template class hierarchy

The class Template_Segment defines an operation Build which subclasses of Template_Segment override. Instances of Arc_Template, Line_Template and Rect_Template construct arcs, lines and rectangles respectively when sent the message Build with a Viewable_Thing as an argument. A Text_Template defines a single line of text with a particular format, style and up to a maximum length. The class TxtG_Template builds a list of text items in a bounding box up to a maximum width and height. Both Text_Template and TxtG_Template have an id number as an attribute so they can request the actual text from the Viewable_Thing. If the amount of text to be displayed is outside of the specified maximum allowable then Text_Template and TxtG_Template also construct scroll bars so all the text may still be viewed. Instances of class Group_Template contain previously defined instances of class Template_Segment. The relationship between Group_Template and Template_Segment is expressed by the instance connection between Template_Segment and Group_Template.

4.2 Object Template

Symbols such as process bubbles in a data flow diagram, as used by Rumbaugh (Rumbaugh et al. 1991), or abstract classes used in Coad and Yourdon are described by object templates. An object template is a collection of template segments and group templates.

4.3 Connection Template

Connection templates build views of relationships. They describe which Viewable_Object or Viewable_Composite the connections can be joined to, how the connections are made and how they will be drawn. Figure 9 shows some possible connections.

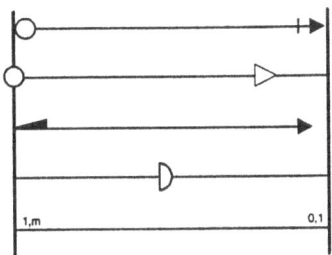

Figure 9 - Connection Types

Each symbol has several docking areas, each of which is described by a template segment. Each area specifies a type of connection that is accepted and a minimum distance between connections. Figure 10 shows two possible docking areas for a symbol. A connecting line may be: a single straight line, a poly line or a poly line composed of horizontal and vertical line segments. Curved lines are not yet supported.

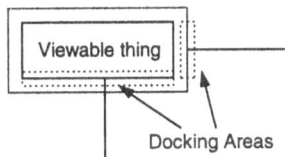

Figure 10 - Symbol Docking Areas

A connection and its annotations are described by template segments. Additional proximity information indicates which end of the connection an annotation is associated with, the position on the connection line and the offset from the connection. This information allows the annotation to be placed at any position along, or beside, the connection line.

4.4 Composite Template

A composite template describes how a view is constructed for a viewable thing which is a grouping of other viewable things. This view will depend on the view of each component viewable thing. An example is the subject area in Coad and Yourdon's OOA. The view of a subject area is either a single symbol (when collapsed) or drawn as a border around the views of the component viewable things (when exploded).

4.4.1 Region Template

A region template describes an active area which may be selected with a logical pointing device (such as a mouse). The 'active areas' for each view may differ in size depending on the viewable thing it is created for. Region templates describe rectangular areas that cause a specific action to be invoked when they are selected. This is the mechanism employed to specify dialogue control.

4.4.2 Relating Actions to Templates

Drawing a notation on the screen through templates is only one aspect of describing a notation. The user interaction with the notation (the set of allowable actions) must also be described. Some actions specify a semantic change (such as deletion or editing) and some actions only affect the syntax (such as formatting or querying). Actions such as dragging and resizing are considered primitive actions and cannot be redefined. Each object template specifies the actions that are available for use with the constructed view. The specification may also include additional information necessary for the action. The same action may be associated with more than one template.

5. Implementation

The system has been implemented on a Sun SPARCstation LX running Solaris 2.3 using SparcWorks C++ 2.0 (SunPro 1992), Tcl 7.3, Tk 3.6 (Ousterhoust 1993) and XF 2.3 (Delmas 1993). Tcl is a general purpose interpretive programming language. Tk is an extension of Tcl that supports graphical windowing applications. XF is an interface development tool that allows the construction of applications based on Tcl and Tk. Together these tools allow the rapid construction of graphical interfaces.

Figure 11 (a) and (b) show snapshots of the systems graphical user interface. Each example is using a different template. The first supports Coad and Yourdons' OOA notation and the second supports structure charts.

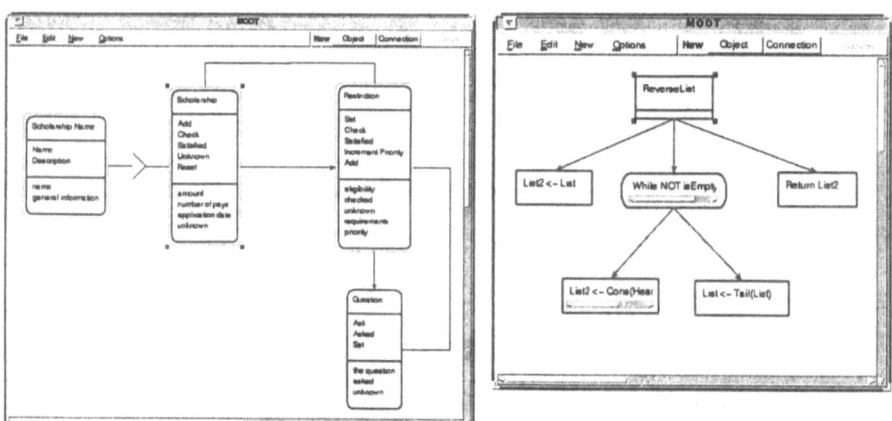

Figure 11 - (a) Coad and Yourdon OOA model (b) Structure Chart.

Figure 12 is an excerpt from a template program which is used to describe Coad and Yourdon's notation in Figure 11 (a). This portion defines how an abstract class is constructed.

```
Template Object "Abstract Class" // An abstract class from Coad and Yourdons notation
        Equations
                    = 10 + Property(1,Height)
                    = 10 + EQ(1)
                    = 10 + EQ(2)
                    = EQ(2) + Property(3,Height)
                    = 20 + EQ(4)
                    = 10 + EQ(5)
                    = EQ(6) + Property(2,Height)
                    = 10 + EQ(7)
                    = 10 + MAX( Property(1,Length), Property(2,Length), Property(3,Length) )
                    = 10 + EQ(9)
        End
        Segments
            Line 10,0 to EQ(9),0 Thickness 2 Colour "black" Pattern "" Arrows none
            Line EQ(10),10 to EQ(10),EQ(7) Thickness 2 Colour "black" Pattern "" Arrows none
            Line 10,EQ(8) to EQ(9),EQ(8) Thickness 2 Colour "black" Pattern "" Arrows none
            Line 0,10 to 0,EQ(7) Thickness 2 Colour "black" Pattern "" Arrows none
            Line 0,EQ(2) to EQ(10),EQ(2) Thickness 2 Colour "black" Pattern "" Arrows none
            Line 0,EQ(5) to EQ(10),EQ(5) Thickness 2 Colour "black" Pattern "" Arrows none
            Arc in box 0,0,20,20 start 90 extent 90 Thickness 2 Colour Line "black" Fill "" pattern ""
            Arc in box EQ(9)-10,0,EQ(10),20 start 0 extent 90 Thickness 2 Colour line "black" Fill "" pattern ""
            Arc in box EQ(9)-10,EQ(7)-10,EQ(10),EQ(8) start 270 extent 90 thickness 2 colour line "black" fill "" pattern ""
            Arc in box 0,EQ(7)-10,20,EQ(8) start 180 extent 90 Thickness 2 Colour line "black" Fill "" pattern ""
            Text at 10,10 Width EQ(9)-10 MaxX 300 MinX 10 Style "BU" Format 'R' ID 1
            Group at 5,EQ(2)+5 to EQ(9)+5,EQ(5)-5 MaxX 300 MinX 10 MaxY 300 MinY 10 Style "BU" Format 'C' ID 3
            Group at 5,EQ(5)+5 to EQ(9)+5,EQ(8)-5 MaxX 300 MinX 10 MaxY 300 MinY 10 Style "BU" Format 'C' ID 2
        End
        // + regions and action binding.
End // Object template Abstract Class
```

Figure 12 - Object template for Coad and Yourdons notation

6. Conclusion

Many of today's Information Systems require the representation of information in a graphical form, with symbols, connections and groups. The notation definition language described facilitates an abstract definition of a graphical notation and the allowable human-computer interaction with it. The addition of such a language to user interface toolkits and User Interface Management Systems will provide greater flexibility in interface development. Therefore even though notations may be different the interaction mechanisms and interaction items can be the same. The advantages of the notation definition language have been incorporated in a prototype of a methodology independent object orientated CASE tool. A notation generation tool is under construction which utilises a 'program by example approach' to automate the generation of template programs in this language. Symbols are drawn and the topographical definition is inferred.

7. Further Work

The types of viewable things that have been considered are static in their appearance. The mechanism described here will not be sufficient to describe views which change dynamically. For example a bubble, the symbol for a class in Booch's (Booch, 1994) methodology, which changed the number of ripples according to the length of the class or object name cannot yet be described. The text in views is of a default font, size and colour. Specification of a specific font and font size will be added.

276

References:

(Booch, 1994):   G. Booch. *Object-Oriented Analysis and Design with Applications.* The Benjamin/Cummings Publishing Company Inc., Redwood City, CA, 2nd edition, 1994.

(Brough, 1992):   M. Brough. *Methods for CASE: A generic framework.* Advanced Information Systems Engineering: 4th International Conference CAiSE '92, Springer-Verlag, Berlin, 1992.

(Coad et al., 1991):   P. Coad, E. Yourdon. *Object-Oriented Analysis.* Yourdon Press, Englewood Cliffs, NJ, 2nd edition, 1991.

(Delmas, 1993):   S. Delmas, *XF - Design and Implementation of a Programming Environment for Interactive Construction of Graphical User Interfaces*, Technische Universitat Berlin, Institut fur Angewandle Informatik, Fachbereich 20 (Informatik), Lehngebiet Softwaretechnik, 1993.

(Gibson, 1988):   M. Gibson. *A Guide to Selecting CASE Tools.* Datamation, July 1, 1988, pp 65-66.

(Johnson, 1992):   Johnson P. *Human Computer Interaction.* McGraw-Hill Book Company, London, 1992.

(Mehand, 1994):   D. Mehandjiska-Stavreva, D. Page, P. Clark. *Development of an Intelligent Object-Oriented CASE Tool*, OOIS'94, 1994.

(Nilsson, 1990):   E. G. Nilsson. *CASE Tools and Software Factories* in Advanced Information Systems Engineering, CAiSE '90 edited by G. Goos and J. Hartmanis, Springer-Verlag, Berlin, 1990.

(Olle et al., 1991):   T. W. Olle, J. Hagelstein, I. G. Macdonald, C. Rolland, H. G. Sol, F. J. M. Assche, A. A. Verrijn-Stuart. *Information Systems Methodologies: A Framework for Understanding.* Addison-Wesley, Amsterdam, 1991.

(Ousterhout, 1993):   J. K. Ousterhoust, *An Introduction to Tcl and Tk*, Addison-Wesley, Amsterdam, 1992.

(Papahristos et al., 1991):   S. Papahristos, W. A. Gray. *Federated CASE Environment* in Advanced Information Systems Engineering, CAiSE '90 edited by G. Goos and J. Hartmanis, Springer-Verlag, Berlin, 1991.

(Powers et al., 1984):   M. J. Powers, D. R. Adams, H. D. Mills. *Computer Information Systems Development: Analysis and Design.* South-Western Publishing Co, Cincinnatti, Ohio, 1984.

(Rumbaugh et al., 1991):   Rumbaugh J et al. *Object-oriented Modeling and Design.* Prentice-Hall, Inc, Englewood Cliffs, NJ, 1991.

(Sumner, 1992):   M. Sumner. *The Impact of Computer-Assisted Software Engineering on Systems Development.* IFIP Transactions - The Impact of Computer Supported Technologies on Information Systems Development edited by Kendall K.E, Lyytinen K, DeGross J I, Elsevier Science Publishers, Amsterdam, 1992.

(SunPro, 1992):   SunPro, *SPARCworks Reference Manuals*, Sun Microsystems Inc, 2550 Garcia Avenue, Mountain View, California 94043-1100, USA, 1992.

OBJECT DATABASES

The OODB Ownership Relationship

Oscar (0u) Yang[†], Michael Halper[‡], James Geller[†], and Yehoshua Perl[†]

[†]*CIS Department and CMS*
New Jersey Institute of Technology
Newark, NJ 07102 USA
e-mail: oscar@earth.njit.edu, {geller, perl}@vienna.njit.edu
fax: (201) 596-5777

[‡]*Dept. of Math & Computer Science*
Kean College of New Jersey
Union, NJ 07083 USA
e-mail: viking@ earth.njit.edu

Abstract. *The notion of "ownership" is prevalent in many social, economic, and political activities. In this paper, we show that an "ownership" semantic relationship can be a powerful addition to the repertoire of object-oriented database (OODB) modeling primitives. The motivation for such a relationship is provided by example OODB schemata. Using these schemata and some (informal) legal definitions, the varied semantics of ownership are identified. A formal ownership relationship is presented as an extension to an OODB data model.*

KEY WORDS: *Semantic Relationships, Ownership Relationship, Semantic Modeling, Commercial Applications, Integrity Constraints*

1. Introduction

Object-Oriented Database Systems have become powerful tools in many advanced application domains due to their data modeling capabilities (Kim et al., 1989; MacKellar et al., 1992; Woelk et al., 1986). While sharing with semantic data models some common notions such as classes and inheritance among classes (Hammer et al., 1978), OODBs possess additional properties like encapsulation and late binding. Their utility is derived in no small part from the semantic relationships — e.g., IS-A (SUBCLASS) (Brachman, 1983; Snyder, 1986) and PART-OF (Halper et al., 1992; Halper, 1993; Kim et al., 1989b; Nguyen et al., 1991) — used in the construction of their schemata. By "semantic relationship" we mean a connection between classes whose interpretation does not lie solely "in its name" (Woods, 1975) but in its constraint-satisfaction, inheritance, and operational mechanisms. Our data model not only captures important static constraints, as most semantic data models do, but also includes as part of the schema many dynamic constraints, i.e., constraints on the state transition of the database (Gray et al., 1992). In other words, such a relationship is a built-in modeling primitive with rich semantics. In this paper, we demonstrate the usefulness of including an "ownership" semantic relationship in an OODB data model. The motivation for this revolves around the following issues:

1. The richness and complexity of "ownership" in real-world applications. There are many different kinds of ownership encompassing a variety of semantics with respect to owner, possession, and their connection.
2. The frequent use of ownership in everyday life and the corporate world.
3. The hierarchical nature of ownership in the corporate world, where, for example, a company can own other companies. This may be represented by one reflexive ownership relationship at the schema level.

For our motivation of an ownership semantic relationship, we shall employ two example schemata. The first is abstracted from the following scenario. Joe owns a manufacturing business that produces an item for which he holds a patent. The business resides in a building which Joe owns and for which a bank, First National Trust, holds a lien. Joe and his wife Jackie rent their house from Tom. Jackie is a professional writer and owns the copyrights for two books. She owns a car, and Joe uses another which is legally owned by his business. Together, they own another car, used by their son John, and a joint bank account. Their individual investment portfolios consist of corporate stocks and government bonds. In addition, each possesses a life insurance policy. Both jointly own the appliances in their home.

The second schema is abstracted from the following. General Motors (GM) owns Chevrolet which in turn owns subsidiaries, manufacturing plants, industrial equipment, etc. GM and Toyota jointly own the Geo Corporation. GM also is a public company and issues stock which is owned by shareholders who are persons or other corporations.

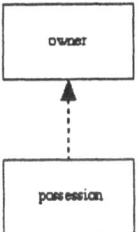

Figure 1. The generic ownership relationship.

We graphically represent "ownership" in an OODB schema (Halper et al., 1993b) by a bold, dotted arrow (Fig. 1). The two above scenarios and their corresponding schemata are shown in Fig. 2 and 3, respectively. As we will discuss, the various ownership relationships which appear in these schemata exhibit a wide range of distinctions. In the next section, we will categorize these different sorts of ownership.

The remainder of this paper is organized as follows. In Section 2, we discuss the legal definition of and terminology relating to ownership. In Section 3, we formally define the ownership relationship as a quintuple comprising a number of "characteristic" dimensions. Section 4 contains concluding remarks.

280

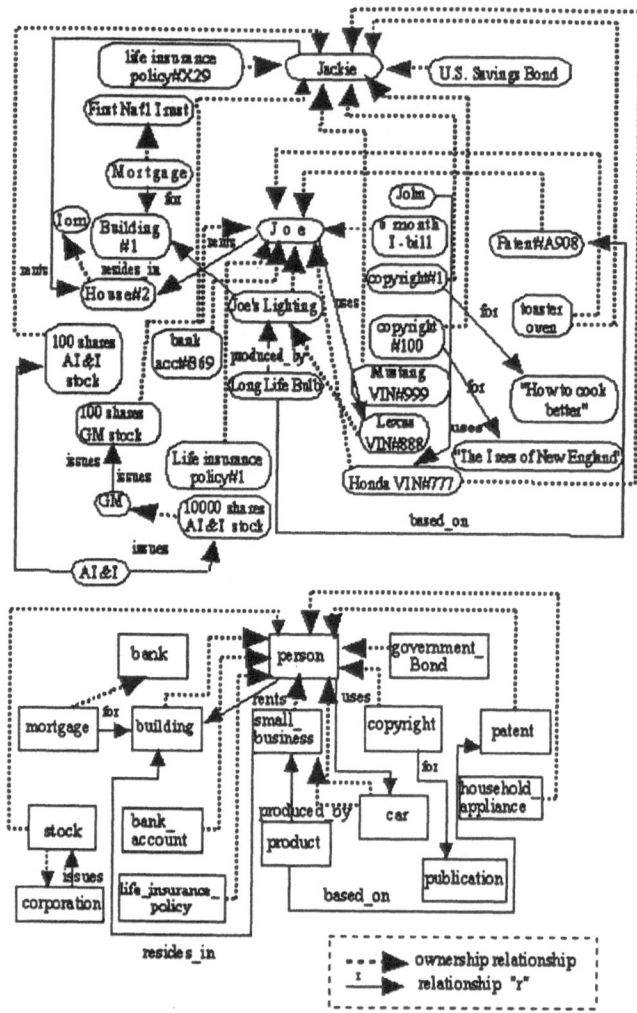

Figure 2. Instance and schema diagrams for first scenario.

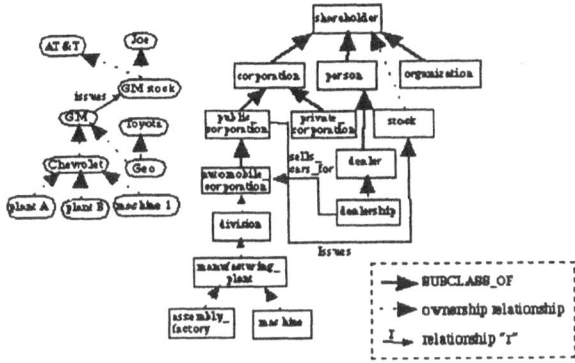

Figure 3: Instance and schema diagrams for second scenario.

2. The Definition of Ownership

When we describe a state of "ownership", we must in general include the following three features: (1) The owner, (2) the possession that is owned, and (3) the characteristics of the relationship between the two (Fig. 1). We are interested in identifying what types of objects can fi2.ll the roles of (1) and (2), and what the characteristics that distinguish the various kinds of ownership are.

According to *Webster's Dictionary*, ownership is defined as follows:
1. The state or fact of being an owner.
2. Proprietorship; Legal right of possession; Legal or just claim or title (to something); in law, the right to use for one's own advantage some possession.[1]

The owner referred to above can, by law, be a natural person, a corporation, or an organization. The latter two are, in general, referred to as *legal entities*. Under the law, legal entities are vested with certain powers, some of which are also held by natural persons. Others, like the power to exist in perpetuity, are unique to legal entities. In our databases, we see that Joe as a natural person owns his business. The GM Corporation as a legal entity owns Chevrolet. In Fig. 2, the following classes can be characterized as legal entities in ownership relationships: *bank*, *small_business*, and *corporation*. All "owner" classes in Fig. 3 represent legal entities.

Ownership of an item is often distributed among persons and legal entities. For example, Joe and Jackie together own a toaster oven, a bank account, and their son's car. Also, the Geo Corporation is a joint venture of GM and Toyota. We describe such a situation as *joint ownership*. It is perfectly legitimate to have a person and a company jointly own the same thing. In Fig. 2, Jackie and GM hold stock in AT&T and are thus among the group of its joint owners. The ownership need not be divided into equal portions, either. Stock holdings partition the ownership of a public company into various percentages. Joe, for example, owns one thousand shares of GM, making him a small percentage owner.

---

[1] The technical legal term for possession is *property*, however, due to the widespread use of that term in the database field, we will avoid it here.

In law, *possession* means the rights which one has in anything subject to ownership, whether it be mobile or immobile, tangible or intangible, visible or invisible. Ownership is used synonymously with rights in possession. Thus, a person is said to be the owner of a possession if he has certain rights in it. The term ownership is often used to indicate that one has the "highest rights" (Anderson et al., 1971) in a possession, but it may be used even when one does not have a the rights; thus, we say that a person is an owner of a house even though he has rented it to a tenant who has exclusive rights to the use of the house during the term of the lease (Anderson et al., 1971).

A possession can be classified as *real, intellectual,* or *personal.* A real *possession* refers to the rights that one has in land or things closely related to it. An *intellectual possession* is the rights held on an idea (e.g., the design of an invention) or a creative work (such as a musical composition or a novel). For such possessions, the rights apply to a potentiality-no claim is made on any tangible item. Copyrights and patents are the ordinary forms of intellectual possessions. *Personal possessions* encompass everything that is not a real or intellectual possession.

As examples, Joe's business resides in a building which is his real possession. The patent (number A908) for the Long_Life Bulb is his intellectual property. Bank account 369 and a toaster oven are among his and Jackie's personal possessions. In Fig. 2, the class building denotes a real possession. *Copyright* and *patent* are intellectual possessions. The remainder of the "possession" classes represent personal possessions. In Fig. 3, the only real possession is *manufacturing_plant.* The rest are personal possessions.

The major distinguishing characteristic of the ownership relationship itself centers around the existence of a legal document that verifies the owner's rights to a possession. A copyright owner, e.g., is granted a legal certificate giving him exclusive rights to possess, make, publish, and sell copies of his intellectual production, or to authorize others to do so. In contrast, the owner of a household item does not have a legal document to support his ownership, but he has the right to use it as he pleases.[2] We call ownership of the former kind *de jure* and ownership of the latter kind de facto. So, Jackie's copyrights are owned *de jure,* while her toaster oven is owned *de facto.*

In Fig. 2, the following ownership (written as: owner class - possession class) are among those that can be classified as *de jure: bank - mortgage, person - building, person - small_business, person - bank_account, small_business - car.* The relationship between the classes *person* and *household_appliance* is *de facto.* All ownerships in Fig. 3 are *de jure.*

3. Ownership as an OODB Semantic Relationship

To incorporate ownership into an OODB data model, we need to provide a formal description for it. As discussed earlier, there are different kinds of ownership. Our investigation has revealed characteristics which describe the required functionality to support the different kinds of ownership. Such characteristics are called dimensions, and we will give formal definitions for each dimension of the ownership relationship. We first introduce the definition of a generic ownership relationship, from which all others will be derived. Let $E(C)$ denote the extension of

---

[2]Yes, he may have kept the sales receipt, but technically that documents the purchase transaction, not the ownership.

a class C, i.e., the set of all instances of C. The generic ownership relationship between a possession class B and an owner class A (Figure 1) is a relation Ω_B^A, from $E(B)$ to $E(A)$. The pair $(b, a) \in \Omega_B^A$ indicates that the instance b of class B is the possession of (i.e., is owned by) the instance a of class A. We will ordinarily express this fact as $b\Omega_B^A a$.

3.1 The Formal Definition of the Ownership Relationship

To describe the characteristic dimensions of ownership, we employ the following quintuple.

$$O_{B,A} = <\Omega_B^A, \lambda, \chi, \delta, v> \tag{1}$$

Ω_B^A is defined as above. The remainder of the quintuple represents the values of four characteristic dimensions. For each dimension we list its name and domain as follows:

$$
\begin{aligned}
&\textit{Exclusiveness: } \chi \in X = \{exclusive, free\text{-}joint, percentage\text{-}joint\}, \\
&\textit{Dependency: } \delta \in D = \{owner\text{-}to\text{-}possession, nil\}, \qquad\qquad (2)\\
&\textit{Legality: } \lambda \in L = \{de\ jure,\ de\ facto\}, \\
&\textit{Value Propagation: } v \in V = \{up, down, upTrans, downTrans, up\&down, nil\}.
\end{aligned}
$$

Formal descriptions of each dimension will be given in subsequent sections. For this, we need the following definitions. Assume that there exists an ownership relationship $O_{B,A}$.

Definition 1: $\forall a \in E(A)$, let $Po_s^A(a) = \{b \mid b \in E(B) \wedge b\Omega_B^A a\}$. $Po_s^A(a)$ is called the *possession* set of a with respect to $O_{B,A}$, i.e., the set of instances of B which are possessions of a.

Definition 2: $\forall b \in E(B)$, let $No_s^A(b) = \{a \mid a \in E(A) \wedge b\Omega_B^A a\}$. $No_s^A(b)$ is called *the owner* set of b with respect to the ownership $O_{B,A}$, i.e., the set of instances of A of which b is a possession.

3.2 The Exclusiveness Dimension

Ownership relationships, in general, can be divided along the lines of exclusive and joint. In other words, a possession may be owned by only one owner or jointly owned by several owners. As a basic characteristic of ownership in the real world (Anderson et al., 1971; Moore, 1968), exclusiveness represents an intuitive constraint which may be imposed on objects in an ownership relationship. The formal definition for the exclusive ownership relationship follows:

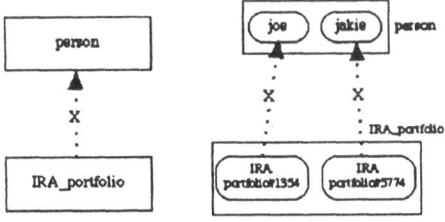

Figure 4: An example of exclusive ownership.

284

Definition 3: The ownership relationship $O_{B,A}$ is exclusive (i.e., $\chi = exclusive$) if $\forall b \in E(B), |N_{\alpha_A}(b)| \leq 1$. That is, an exclusive possession cannot have more than one owner.

We add in our graphical notation an **X** on the dotted arrow to indicate eXclusive (Fig. 4). Those ownership relationships which are not exclusive are referred to as *joint*, in which case a possession may be either jointly owned freely (e.g., a joint bank account is freely shared by a couple — we call this *free joint*), or jointly owned such that each owner takes a certain percentage of the ownership (e.g., the husband and the wife each owns 50% of their house — we call this percentage joint). We call the case where all owners have the same percentage *equal joint*. Although the exclusiveness dimension has been included in some OODB models (e.g., SHOOD (Nguyen et al., 1991) and OODINI (Halper et al., 1992)), percentage joint is unique to ownership. Percentage joint plays an important role in economic activities. A shareholder has the right to receive his proportion (i.e., percentage) of dividends; or to call a special meeting of the shareholders, if he owns the shares in a stated percentage.

In our graphical notation, a plain dotted arrow indicates free joint (Fig. 5). Percentage joint and equal joint are denoted by labels of **P** and =, respectively (Figs. 6, 7).

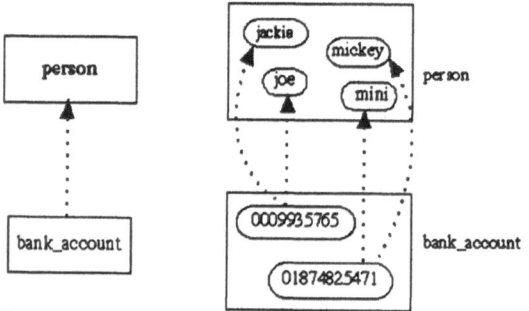

Figure 5. Jointly owned bank accounts.

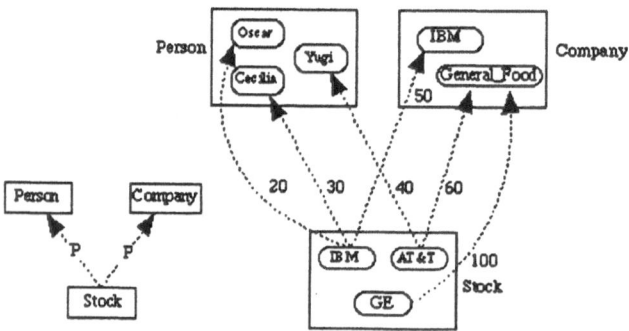

Figure 6. Stocks are owned (percentage) jointly by person and company.

Definition 4: The ownership relationship $O_{B,A}$ is *free joint* (i.e., χ = *free-joint*) if $\forall\, b \in E(B), |N\alpha_B^A(b)| \geq 0$, i.e., there is no constraint on the owner set of b.

Definition 5a: The ownership relationship $O_{B,A}$ is *percentage joint* if there exists a total function (called the individual share function) $f : E(B) \times E(A) \rightarrow [0, 100]$ such that $\forall\, b,\; \sum\limits_{a \in N\alpha_B^A(b)} f(b,a) = 100$.

Definition 5a defines the *percentage joint* ownership relationship when the possession class has only one owner class. At times, the ownership may be distributed among owners from different classes. This "multiple ownership" case is defined as follows.

Definition 5b: The ownership relationships $O_{B,A_1}, O_{B,A_2}, ..., O_{B,A_n}$ (n is an integer) are percentage joint if there exists a total function $f : E(B) \times \bigcup\limits_{i=1}^{n} E(A_i) \longrightarrow [0, 100]$ such that

$\forall b,\; \sum\limits_{a \in M} f(b,a) = 100$, where $M = \bigcup\limits_{i=1}^{n} N\alpha_B^{A_i}(b)$.

To better understand Definition 5b, refer to Figure 6 , where $O_{Stock, Person}$ and $O_{Stock, Company}$ are two percentage joint relationships. For any instance of class Stock, the ownership is distributed among its owners such that each of them takes a certain percentage and that the sum of the percentages is 100 (percent). In Figure 6, the stock IBM's owners are Oscar and Cecilia of class *Person*, and IBM of class *Company*, with 20, 30, and 50 percent of the ownership, respectively.

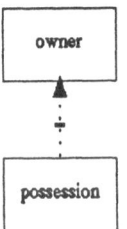

Figure 7: The equal ownership relationship.

3.3 The Dependency Dimension

The dependency dimension of ownership relationship $O_{B,A}$ regulates the semantics of deletion of owner class A or possession class B. It defines when deletion of one should cause deletion of the other. Intuitively, there seems to be no need of a dependency dimension for ownership; neither the owner nor the possession ceases to exist if the other is deleted from the database.

Nevertheless, after looking at some examples, we find that we need such a dimension. Consider the relationship between a person and his car. Neither is dependent on the other. However, suppose that in the application domain, say, of an insurance company, we need to distinguish people who own cars from people who do not. Car owners have some specific properties which are modeled by creating a specialization class *car owner* of the class *person*. The class car owner inherits properties from person and have extra properties. The ownership relationship for the car refers to the car owner class rather than to the person. This way of modeling in OODBs

286

is described in (Kifer et al., 1992) as shifting information from the data to the schema. In this way, if we model the class car owner as a subclass of *person*, then the car owner is dependent on the car. For example, if a car owner *Lisa* owns only one car, and if it is "deleted" (e.g., destroyed in an accident), *Lisa* should be deleted from the class car owner — since she is no longer a car owner — but not from the class person. Now, if the query "list car owners" is executed, *Lisa* will not be returned (Fig. 8). In general, we may have such a dependency for specialization classes which are actually categorized according to the possession.

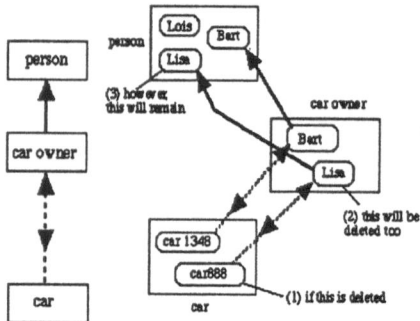

Figure 8: Car owner depends on car.

On the other hand, the possession-to-owner dependency is not justified by our analysis, though there are some examples that seem to require. Consider a corporation that owns several subsidiaries. Usually, if the corporation goes bankrupt, all its subsidiaries will also go out of business. This looks like a case of possession-to-owner dependency, but a closer look reveals that besides the ownership relationship, there is also PART-OF relationship between subsidiary and corporation, i.e., the subsidiaries are not only possessions, but also parts of the corporation. Furthermore, the ownership relationship itself does not cause any possession-to-owner dependency; it is the PART-OF relationship (Halper et al., 1993), that causes this dependency. Therefore, the possession-to-owner dependency does not appear in the dependency dimension of the ownership relationship. This dimension is, therefore, specified by the following set of values:

$$\delta \in D = \{owner\text{-}to\text{-}possession,\ nil\}$$

The second value indicates that the ownership relationship lacks any dependency semantics. This is desirable in most cases (e.g., a person is not deleted if he sells his car).

In the following, we use the notation *del(x)* to denote the application of a method to delete the instance *x*, and use "x => y" to indicate that action *x* implies action *y*.

Definition 6: The ownership relationship $O_{B,A}$ is *owner-to-possession dependent* (i.e., δ = *owner-to-possession*) if $\forall b \in E(B), del(b) \Rightarrow \forall a \in E(A)$ such that $b\Omega_B^A a \wedge P_{\Omega_s^A}(a) = \{b\}, del(a)$.

We draw an extra arrow head pointing to the possession on the dotted line to indicate this dependency (Fig. 8).

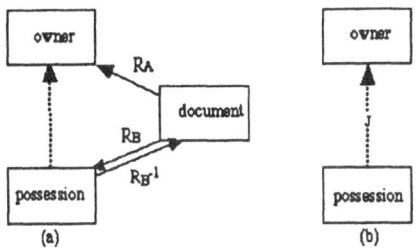

(a)   (b)

Figure 9: Ownership *de jure*: (a) document relates to both owner and possession (b) the graphical notation

3.4 The Legality Dimension

De jure ownership always has a supporting legal document, while *de facto* ownership does not. To represent *de jure* ownership, we need an extra class document which relates to both owner and possession. We label the relationship between *document* and *owner* as R_A, between *document* and *possession* as R_B. We assume a one-to-one correspondence between the instances document and possession, and define the inverse relationship R_B^{-1} for R_B (Fig. 9(a)).[3] The inverse relationship is necessary to maintain information integrity endowed with ownership *de jure*. For example, if we are given $b\Omega_B^A a$, and wish to find the document that supports it, we need to go from class *possession* to class *document*. Without R_B^{-1}, we would not be able to do so.

To be consistent with the notations for other dimensions and to simplify the graphical representation of the schema, we will denote ownership *de jure* with a **J** on the dotted arrow (Fig. 9(b)). That is, we omit the class *document* and its relationships from the graphical schema, assuming their existence.

In the following, A and B are the owner class and possession class respectively, C is the documentclass, and R_A, R_B and R_B^{-1} are defined as above. In addition, $del(x)$ is defined as the application of a method to delete the instance x, $break(x, y)$ $(con(x, y))$ to break (establish) the connection between the instances x and y, and $add(x, Y)$ to add the instance x to the class Y.

Definition 7: The ownership relationship $O_{B,A} = <\Omega_B^A, de\ jure, \chi, \delta, \nu>$, where Ω_B^A, χ, δ and ν are defined as in (1) and (2) above, is called an ownership *de jure*, if $\forall a, b$ such that $a \in E(A), b \in E(B)$, and $b\Omega_B^A a$ holds, there exists $c \in E(C)$ such that $(c, a) \in R_A, (c, b) \in R_B$ (i.e., there exists a legal document verifying the ownership $b\Omega_B^A a$), and if it satisfies the following modification conditions:

(1) **delete owner:** $\forall a \in E(A), del(a) \Rightarrow \forall b \in P_{\Omega_a^A}(a), break(b, a) \land \forall c \in E(C)$ such that $(b, c) \in R_B^{-1}, break(b, c), del(c)$.

---

[3]Note that R_A is not one-to-one as an owner may possess several instances of the same kind of possession. Thus it is not so simple to access the document through the owner class.

(2) **delete possession:** $\forall b \in E(B)$, $del(b) \Rightarrow \forall c \in E(C)$ such that
$(b, c) \in R_B^{-1}$, $break(b, c)$, $del(c)$.

(3) **delete ownership relationship:** $break(b, a)$ such that $b\Omega_B^A a \Rightarrow \forall c$ such that
$(b, c) \in R_B^{-1}$, $break(b, c)$, $del(c)$.

(4) **establish ownership relationship:** $con(b, a)$ such that
$b\Omega_B^A a \Rightarrow add(c, C)$, $con(c, a)$, $con(c, b)$, $con(b, c)$.

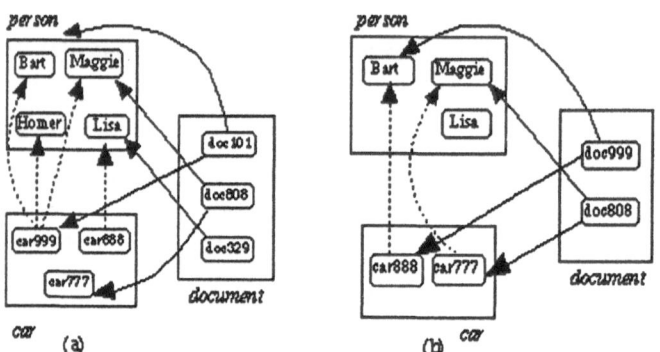

Figure 10: The ownership *de jure*. (a) before operations performed, (b) after operations performed.

The methods in Definition 7 are basic operations. Complex operations can be implemented by combining those methods. An example of such operations is ownership transfer, which is a common transaction in the commercial world. This can be characterized by "the ownership of b is transferred from a_1 to a_2". The method *transfer* (a_1, a_2, b) can be implemented by "$break(b, a_1)$" and "$con(b, a_2)$". In Figure 10, *Bart* lost his car *car999* in an accident and bought a second-hand car *car888* from *Lisa*. In the meantime, *Homer* died of old age, and left his car *car777* which was formally jointly owned with his wife *Maggie*. The changes in the database can be described by the following sequence of operations: $del(car999)$, $transfer(Lisa, Bart, car888)$, and $del(Homer)$. By forcing the database schema to adhere to those constraints, the integrity of the data model is guaranteed.

Definition 8: The ownership relationship $O_{B,A}$ is *de facto* if it is not *de jure*.

3.5 The Value Propagation Dimension

There are times when a certain feature of a possession is naturally assimilated as a feature of its owner, or vice versa. For example, the address of a person may be modeled as the address of his house rather than as an intrinsic attribute of the person. Likewise, the name that appears on the passport can be taken to be the name of its owner. In the former case, the value of *address*, rather than being duplicated, should be stored solely with the house and propagated upward on demand (Figure 11). *Address*, in this sense, is a *derived attribute* of person. In our data model, the value propagation dimension may take on six different values:

$V = \{up,\ down,\ upTrans,\ downTrans,\ up\&down,\ nil\}$

Due to space limitations, we will present only the definition for transformational upward propagation, which is expressed by $\delta = upTrans$. For the other cases, refer to (Halper, 1993; Halper et al., 1993), where we use similar definitions for part modeling.

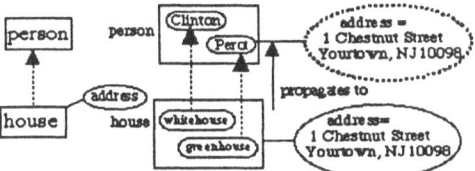

Figure 11: Address propagated from home to person

Definition 9: Let $\pi_B : E(B) \to \tau$ be a possession of B. The *transformational upward propagating ownership relationship which propagates* π_B is defined as $O_{B,A} = \left\langle \Omega_B^A, \lambda, \chi, \delta, \left(upTrans, D_{\pi_B}, \{T^{(n)}\}\right), \nu \right\rangle$. Here, τ is any data type, $\{T^{(n)}\}$ is a family of symmetric operators $T^{(n)}: \tau^n \to \tau$ with $n > 0$, and the function $D_{\pi_B}: E(A) \to \tau$, called a derived attribute, is defined in terms of $\{T^{(n)}\}$ as follows. (Note that the possession set of an instance a of A is taken to be $P\Omega_a^A(a) = \{b_1, b_2, ..., b_m\}, m \geq 0.$)

$$D_{\pi_B}(a) = \begin{cases} T^{(m)}[\pi_B(b_1), \pi_B(b_2), ..., \pi_B(b_m)], & m \neq 0 \wedge \pi_B(b_i) \text{ is defined}, \\ C, & \text{otherwise.} \end{cases}$$

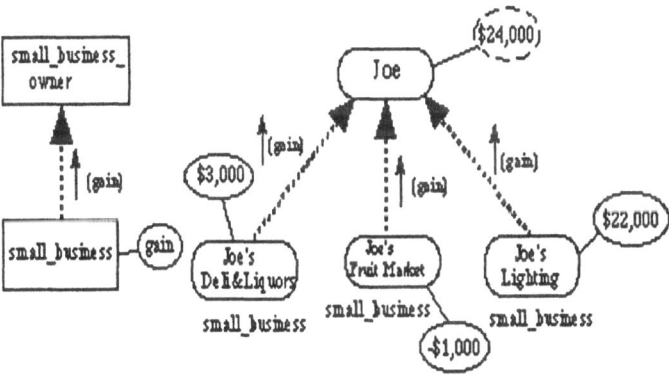

Figure 12: An example of the value propagation.

Here C is a pre-set default value. For example (Fig. 12), Mr. *Joe* owns three businesses, *Joe's Deli & Liquors, Joe's Fruit Market*, and *Joe's Lighting*. At the end of a year, he wants to know how much money he has made from his businesses. This can be done by having a transformational upward propagation. That is, the derived attribute D_{gain} of the class *small business owner* can be written in terms of the attribute *gain*: $E(small\ business) \to REAL$ of the class *small Business*, as follows:

$$D_{gain}(a) = \begin{cases} sum[gain(b_1),\ gain(b_2),\ ...,\ gain(b_n)], & n \neq 0 \wedge gain(b_i)\ \text{is defined for}\ 1 \leq i \leq n, \\ 0, & \text{otherwise.} \end{cases}$$

4. Conclusion

We have addressed the issue of representing ownership relationships in OODBS, with a model that captures a variety of semantics. In particular, we have distinguished a number of aspects for the roles of the owner and possession in such relationships. These aspects define notions like exclusive and joint owners. Ownership relationships themselves were shown to be either *de jure* or *de facto*, the former being distinguished by the presence of a legal document. Formal definitions for the various ownership relationships were presented. To complement these, we have presented graphical symbols for each of the ownership relationships which expand the graphical schema representation language for OODBs developed in (Halper et al., 1993b). In future work, we will investigate the interaction between ownership transactions and the above ownership dimensions. We plan to integrate the ownership relationship as an integral part of a commercial OODB system supporting the necessary dimensions. Such an addition to OODB systems will increase their appeal for commercial applications.

References

(Anderson et al., 1971): R. Anderson, W. Kumpf, and R. Kendrick. Business Law - *Principles and cases*. South-Western Publishing Co., Cincinnati, OH, 1971.

(Brachman, 1983): Ronald J. Brachman. What IS-A is and isn't: An analysis of taxonomic links in semantic networks. *Computer*, 16(10):30-36, October 1983.

(Gray et al., 1992): P. Gray, K. Kalkarni and N. Paton. *Object-Oriented Databases: A Semantic Data Model Approach*. Prentice Hall, 1992.

(Halper, 1993): M. Halper. *A Comprehensive Part Model and Graphical Schema Representation for Object-Oriented Databases*. PhD thesis, CIS Department, New Jersey Institute of Technology, 1993.

(Halper et al., 1992): M. Halper, J. Geller, and Y. Perl. An OODB "part" relationship model. In *Proceedings of the First International Conference on Information and Knowledge Management*, 602-611, Baltimore, MD, 1992.

(Halper et al., 1993): M. Halper, J. Geller, and Y. Perl. Value propagation in object-oriented database part hierarchies. In *Proceedings of the 2nd Int'l. Conference on Information and Knowledge Management*, 606-614. Washington, DC, 1993.

(Halper et al., 1993b): M. Halper, J. Geller, Y. Perl, and E. J. Neuhold. A graphical schema representation forobject-oriented databases. In R. Cooper, editor, *Interfaces to Database Systems*, 282-307. Springer-Verlag, London, 1993.

(Hammer et al., 1978):   M. Hammer and D. McLeod. The Semantic Data Model: a Modeling Mechanism for Database Applications. In Proc. of *ACM SIGMOD*, 1978.

(Kim et al., 1989):   W. Kim, N. Ballou, H.-T. Chou, and J. F. Garza. Features of the orion object-orienteddatabase system. In W. Kim and F. H. Lochovsky, editors, *Object-Oriented Concepts, Databases, and Applications*. Addison Wesley, Reading, MA, 1989.

(Kim et al., 1989b):   W. Kim, E. Bertino, and J. Garza. Composite objects revisited. In Proc. of the 1989 ACM SIGMOD International Conference on the Management of Data Portland, Oregon, appeared as SIGMOD RECORD, pages 337-347,1989.

(Kifer et al., 1992):   M. Kifer, W. Kim, and Y. Sagiv. Querying object-oriented databases. In *Proceedings of the 1992 ACM SIGMOD Int'l Conf. on Management of Data*, 393-402, San Diego, California, June 1992.

(Moore, 1968):   Clarence C. Moore. *Business Law*. The Bruce Publishing Company, USA, 1968.

(MacKellar et al., 1992): B. MacKellar and J. Peckham. Representing design objects in sorac: A data model with semantic objects, relationships and constraints. In *Second International Conference on Artificial Intelligence in Design*, Pittsburgh, PA, June 1992.

(Nguyen et al., 1991):   G. T. Nguyen and D. Rieu. Representing design objects. In *AI in Design '91*. Butterworth-Heinemann Ltd., 1991.

(Snyder, 1986):   Alan Snyder. Encapsulation and inheritance in object-oriented programming languages. In *Proc. OOPSLA-86*, 38-45, 1986.

(Woelk et al., 1986):   D. Woelk, W. Kim, and W. Luther. An object-oriented approach to multimedia databases. In *Proc. ACM SIGMOD Int'l Conf. on Management of Data*, 311-325, Washington, D.C., May 1986.

(Woods, 1975):   W. A. Woods. What's in a link: Foundations for semantic networks. In D. G. Bobrow and A. M. Collins, editors, *Representation and Understanding*, 35-82. Academic Press, New York, NY, 1975.

Function Materialization in Object-Oriented Databases

T W Carnduff[1] and W A Gray[2]

[1] Cardiff Institute of Higher Education and University of Wales College of Cardiff
e-mail tom.carnduff@cm.cf.ac.uk

[2] Department of Computing Mathematics,University of Wales College of Cardiff, PO Box 916, Cardiff CF2 4YN, UK.

Abstract: This paper considers aspects of object-oriented database support for engineering design. In particular we consider function materialization, that is the use of stored, precalculated function results to optimize the return of a function result. We review the materialization of functions in the relational data model and an object-oriented data model implementation. We present a new approach to function materialization in object-oriented databases, as implemented in our class library TOMS. This approach is fundamentally different to a previous approach, due to the context in which we see function materialization being used; an environment where complex engineering design objects evolve through a series of versions. The objects storing the precalculated function results - MFOs, will themselves exist in several versions. We describe the means of managing these complex version evolution configurations, and detail the expression of relationships which exist between MFOs and dependent objects. We go on to describe the way in which rematerialization of functions after changes to objects within a database, can be supported by object versioning in a time efficient manner. The designer must carefully consider the trade-off between improved function result response times and the storage costs of maintaining complex version hierarchies. Finally we show that MFOs may be extracted from their associated version evolution trees and checked in to a public database in a hierarchically partitioned engineering design database environment.

KEY WORDS: OODB, Function Materialization, Versioning, Engineering Design.

---

1. Introduction

The object-oriented data model can be extremely effective for modelling the complex structure and semantics of engineering design artefacts [Carnduff et al, 1991; Carnduff et al, 1991]. We have been investigating the way in which object-oriented databases can be extended to provide facilities to support the engineering design process, particularly through design object versioning and function materialization [Carnduff et al, 1993]. Function materialization is the process by which the value of a function is determined by the system evaluating it. In a database management system, functions can have a direct or an indirect data materialization [Date, 1981]. If a function has an indirect materialization then it is evaluated in the normal way by calling a procedure to compute the function value, given the current parameter values. If it has a direct data materialization, the values of the function for given parameters have been precomputed and stored in the database. It is these stored values that are returned in this situation, giving in the case of complicated functions a faster response time. If a direct data materialization is being used for function materialization and the stored values for the current parameters are unavailable, then the function value can either be materialized indirectly (full function materialization) or by an interpolative materialization, where the stored values are used to evaluate the unavailable value by interpolation. In an object-oriented database supporting object versions, where the object attributes may be defined by complex functions which will have to be materialized every time the object version is accessed, considerable time savings can be achieved by using a non-full function materialization, which is a mixture of direct data materialization and interpolative materialization. In this paper when we refer to function materialization without a prefix, we will be referring to non-full function materialization.

The intention behind function materialization in an object-oriented database system, is to reduce the time between calling a function and returning a result. The technique is particularly useful where function evaluation involves the complex, CPU intensive, time consuming processes typical of engineering design, particularly where the result for a particular set of parameter values may be required more than once. This situation prevails with engineering analysis and design within a cycle of tentative and iterative design artefact evolution and development.

During the early stages of a design, the design engineer will be "feeling his/her way", exploring alternatives and establishing the general suitablity of design fragments by means of coarse boundary condition parameter evaluation. When the calculated boundary conditions for a design fragment are found to be within acceptable limits, the next iteration of the "design spiral" (figure 1) may take place. As the designer moves closer to design completion, he/she is less likely to accept time penalties associated with complex functional evaluation by indirect materialization, particularily if these calculations have previously been performed and have not been invalidated by changes in the design. The approach presented in this paper as a means of overcoming, or at least alleviating the processing bottleneck that can result from such re-evaluation, is function materialization in conjunction with object versioning, in an object-oriented design environment, i.e. a design environment supported by an object-oriented database system.

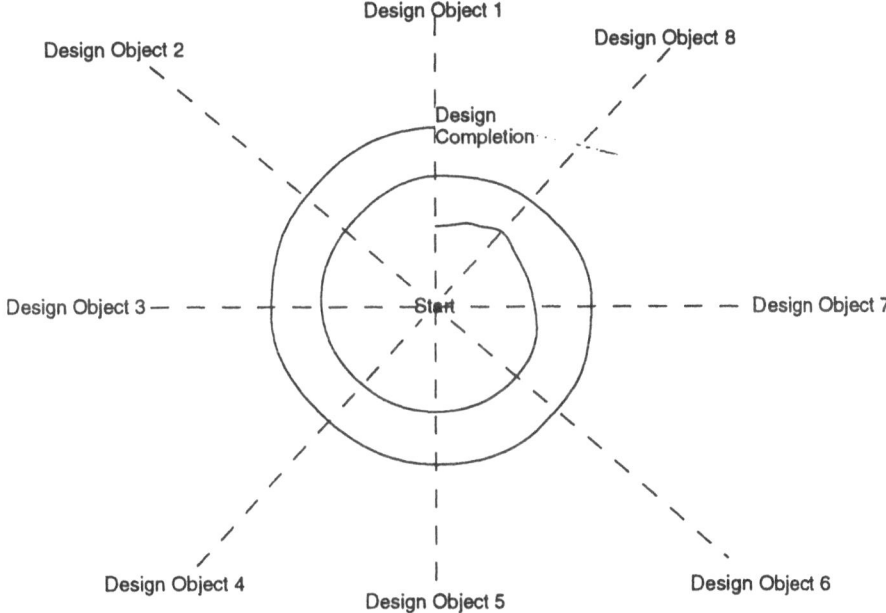

Figure 1: Design Spiral

2. Various Approaches to Non-Full Function Materialization

Access to precomputed function results may be achieved in several different ways. Before the widespread use of database systems, precomputed function results were stored in data files.

The difficulty with this approach is a lack of data independence, which is overcome in a relational database approach, where the database management system provides the necessary degree of data independence.

2.1 Function Materialization in the Relational Data Model

There are several difficulties in replacing data files of precomputed results with relational tables and using the query language of a relational database management system to access them. This access to table values can only be made via the retrieval features of its query language, and a query predicate will be required to specify the search conditions for returning a precomputed function result. This predicate must express the function parameter values which together with the result make up the attributes of the relation.

For example, consider the function:

$z(a, b, c) = a * b - c$

then if a, b and c are parameters of the function $z(a, b, c)$, we require a relation

$R1(\underline{a}, \underline{b}, \underline{c}, z)$

where the attributes a, b and c, comprise the primary key of R1, and z, the only non-key attribute, is the function result. This approach, while adequate for attributes belonging to the basic types supplied with most relational database system implementations, cannot cope in a simple way, with complex attribute types [Dayal et al, 1987; Lorie et al, 1983; Maier, 1991], other than by spreading the constituent parts of a complex object as tuples in several relations, and on retrieval, recomposing the object by means of explicit multiple join operations as illustrated in figure 2.

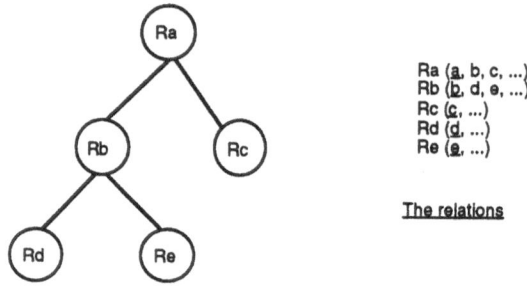

Ra (<u>a</u>, b, c, ...)
Rb (<u>b</u>, d, e, ...)
Rc (<u>c</u>, ...)
Rd (<u>d</u>, ...)
Re (<u>e</u>, ...)

The relations

Composition Hierarchy

```
SELECT Ra.a, Ra.b, Ra.c, Rb.d, Rb.e, ...
FROM Ra, Rb, Rc, Rd, Re
WHERE Ra='A1'
AND Ra.b=Rb.b
AND Ra.c=Rc.c
AND Rb.d=Rd.d
AND Rb.e=Re.e
```

Recomposing Complex Object 'A1'

Figure 2: Complex Object in Relational Database

Another difficulty with this approach is that the function, whose precomputed results may be stored in a relational table, is probably expressed in some 3rd generation language program, where access to the materialized result is made through an embedded declarative query of the form:

SELECT z FROM R1
WHERE a = 1 AND b = 5 AND c = 2

This query must be mapped from the equivalent function call, $z(1, 5, 2)$, and this process may take longer than the time saved through using the full function materialization. Another difficulty concerns floating point function parameters. In this case since we cannot store every possible parameter value, we need to use an interpolative materialization and tuples must be held for reasonable increments of floating point parameter values, to allow interpolation values to be calculated. This raises the problem of forming queries to return the attribute results required for the interpolation. If such a query has a predicate which includes a floating point value which does not exist as an attribute value in the target table, no result will be returned. Thus this interpolative approach would be difficult to implement in a relational system, even with the approach used to materialize relational views [Blakely et al, 1986; Blakely et al, 1989; Hanson, 1987]. The motive for view materialization is similar to that for function materialization, however, views are entirely defined by a query language and cannot meet the expressive and semantic complexity requirements of functions expressed in computationally complete programming languages. For this reason, view materialization is not discussed further in this paper.

2.2 Function Materialization in an Object-Oriented Data Model

The experimental object-oriented database system GOM [Kemper et al, 1990; Kemper et al, 1991] supports complex objects, single inheritance, encapsulation of attributes and routines, and includes function materialization facilities as a feature of the kernel object base system. A generalized materialization relation (GMR) data structure is used to store object function results against arguments and a validity flag. A function result is invalidated when any of the objects visited in calculating the result has been changed. Recalculation of an invalidated function results in an update to the GMR, that is a rematerialization, carried out lazily, where the old result is replaced by the new result and the validity flag is updated to *true*. A reverse reference relation (RRR) is maintained to store the object identifier of objects against their named materialized functions and the object identifiers of the objects visited during materialization. Thus if an object in the database is changed, the RRR is checked to see if the object identifier of the changed object exists as an argument of a function materialization. If it does exist, then the appropriate GMR validity attributes are set to false, and rematerialization of the invalidated functions is carried out.

3. Object-Oriented Function Materialization with Design Object Versioning

The approach to function materialization in object-oriented databases which we present in this paper, is broadly similar to that taken in GOM, however, there are fundamental differences, principally due to the context in which we see this technique being used, namely computer-aided engineering design. Engineering design objects evolve through a series of versions, all of which remain accessible to the designer. Every object version, barring the first, is derived from some predecessor version, and may in its turn, give rise to a series of successive or alternative versions. This situation has a profound effect on the materialization of object functions. When an object is changed, and a new version of that object is derived from it, then the original version of that object still exists with its own set of precalculated function results. We call the objects containing the precalculated results, MFOs (materialized function objects). If the change to the object invalidates an MFO, then the new object version will require a rematerialization of the affected function. This rematerialization does not replace the original MFO, but results in a new MFO version. This approach to function materialization has been realized in our object versioning, configuration management and function materialization class library **TOMS**

(Temporal Object Management Server).

3.1 Design Object Versioning

In the TOMS version model, a set of versions of an object is managed by a generic version. This generic version maintains a version evolution history and provides a means of access to each of the object versions in the version set, through a dynamic reference. Versioned objects may also be referenced statically without reference to the generic version. A structurally complex object consists of a set of arbitrarily complex objects. The objects making up the composition hierarchy of a complex object may be versionable. This leads to the need for a configuration management facility, where a configuration groups a root object version in a composition hierarchy with a set of identified, versioned subobjects at lower levels in the hierarchy. Thus, if we consider a versionable complex object A , which consists of an aggregation of versionable complex objects B, C and D, where B consists of an aggregation of versionable objects E, F and G, and so on, then configuration 1 of object A, might be made up as shown in figure 3.

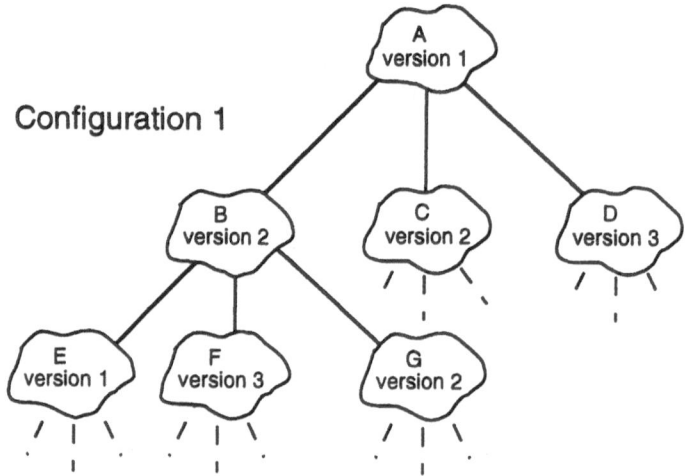

Figure 3: Composition Hierarchy for Configuration 1 of Complex Object A

Complex objects of this type are constructed at each level in the composition hierarchy using sets of subobject generic versions, that is to say that references to subobjects are dynamic, or indirect. The process of constructing a configuration involves converting the dynamic references at each level in the composition hierarchy, to static references. We refer to the resulting dereferenced, complex, configuration objects as **monolithic versions**.

3.2 Function Materialization

Function materialization is achieved in TOMS, by reimplementing full function materialization routines so that they retrieve the function result from an MFO, according to the parameter values. An MFO is created as a result of an explicit materialization creation call. MFOs contain function results for every combination of parameter values specified at MFO creation. The types of function parameters and results may be atomic or complex, although the extent of the MFO will vary, dependent upon these types. In the case of a function with at least one atomic floating point parameter, it is clearly impossible to precalculate the function result for every possible value of this parameter. Instead, a range of values and an increment size must be specified, and the access method to the MFO must incorporate some means of interpolation. Every materialized function has its own MFO. The equivalent to our MFO structure is, in the GOM database system, the GMR. A single GMR stores the precalculated results of several functions for several objects of the same type, whereas an MFO stores the set of results for a single object function. The reason for this is, as will be described presently, that a particular MFO may exist in several versions.

3.2.1 Change Management

Having initially materialized an object function, its results may be invalidated by some change to a feature of the object itself, or some other object. An MFO is dependent on other objects or **components** as we call them. Such dependencies are specified explicitly in our model, as it is our belief that complete dependency semantics can only be fully understood and captured by the software developer who is a computerate application domain expert. We introduce an example to aid the discussion.

Consider a class *RIGHT_PRISM*, whose instances are described as cubes. We use a simplistic representation of a cube which is described by the attributes *length, breadth* and *height*. *RIGHT_PRISM* has a materialized function *volume*, whose MFO is dependent on each of the components *length, breadth* and *height*. If we change the value of any of these components for a cube object, then its MFO for *volume* will be invalidated. The dependency described above is termed a dependent-component relationship. Transitive dependencies may also be declared, for example if we had another materialized function, *weight(substance)*, where

*weight = volume * substance.density*

then *weight* is dependent on *volume* and hence transitively dependent on the dependents of *volume* . This transitive dependency is resolved by TOMS into direct dependent-component relationships between the *weight* and *length, breadth* and *height* . Clearly, a *weight* MFO would contain a set of results, one for each value of *substance* .

The generic version for an object containing a materialized function maintains a set of materialization triples. Each triple consists of references to an MFO, a component in the MFO dependent-component relationship and the version number of the version object to which the relationship occurence belongs. In fact, the set of triples in a generic version results from the union of sets of version-specific materialization triples, held in each of the object versions presided over by a generic version.

When a versioned object with a materialized function is updated, there are three consequent activities. The update results in the automatic creation of a new version of the object, and the generic version is inspected to determine whether this update involves a change of value in one or more components. Lastly, if there is a change to a component, the dependent MFO is added to a set of references to MFOs requiring rematerialization, stored in the generic version. Rematerialization is carried out lazily as a background task, and when a rematerialization is completed, reference to its MFO is removed from the rematerialization set.

3.2.2 Rematerialization

As described earlier, rematerialization of a function in GOM results in the replacement of precalculated results in a GMR. Our approach, however, demands that when an MFO is invalidated by some component change, the rematerialization caused by this change instigates the creation of a new MFO, which does not replace or overwrite the previous MFO, but results in a new version of it which will be the current version of the MFO.

To clarify the mechanisms of rematerialization, evolution of object versions and version

298

configuration management we introduce a further example. To the class *RIGHT_PRISM* whose instances are cubes, we add classes describing spherical and cylindrical objects. The geometrical objects which are instances of these classes have the functions *volume_to_depth(depth)* and *weight_to_depth(depth, substance)*. The volume_to_depth function returns the volume of a geometrical object up to some vertical distance above its base *(depth)* . Similarly, weight_to_depth returns the weight of an object made of, or filled with *substance* up to the specified depth . Cuboid, spherical and cylindrical objects can be grouped together into *assemblies* , where the volume_to_depth of an assembly object is the sum of the volumes of its constituent geometric units up to the specified depth. The value of depth is translated into the local coordinate systems of each of the geometric units.

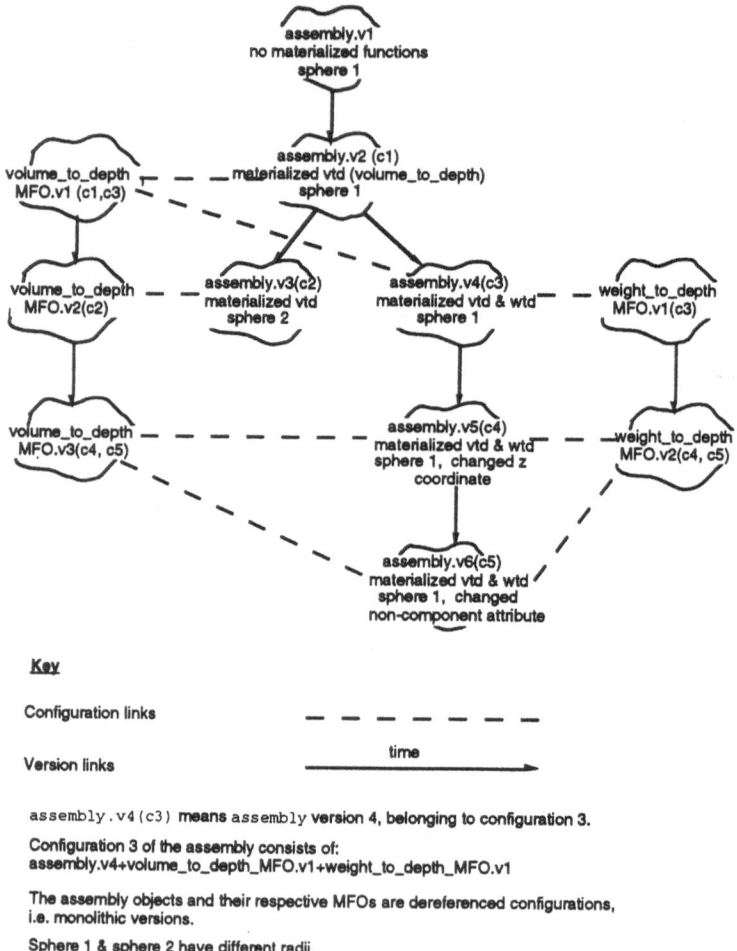

Key

Configuration links   — — — — —

Version links   ⟶ time

assembly.v4(c3) **means** assembly **version 4, belonging to configuration 3.**

Configuration 3 of the assembly consists of:
assembly.v4+volume_to_depth_MFO.v1+weight_to_depth_MFO.v1

The assembly objects and their respective MFOs are dereferenced configurations, i.e. monolithic versions.

Sphere 1 & sphere 2 have different radii.

Figure 4: Evolution of complex object with materialized functions

Figure 4 documents the evolution of an assembly object as its functions are progressively materialized and geometrical units are changed or repositioned within the assembly (an artefact version evolution tree). For clarity, the figure refers to only one of the constituent geometrical units in the assembly, namely a sphere, which at various stages of assembly evolution has two different radii denoted as sphere 1 and sphere 2 - actually two versions of the same sphere. The evolution of the assembly from version 1 to version 2 is caused, not by any change of attribute value or unit composition, but rather by the decision to materialize the volume_to_depth function. This is an important feature of TOMS, that initial function materialization and any subsequent rematerialization automatically causes the creation of a new object version.

The public interface of each of the object versions making up a particular version set remains invariant. Only the attribute values or function implementations may change. Versions 2 to 6 of the assembly object with their respective MFOs, consist of dereferenced configurations, that is monolithic versions. The configuration mechanism expresses the binding that exists between a versioned assembly object, its composition hierarchy of specific versioned geometric units and the versioned MFOs that express the materialization of assembly functions. For example, configuration 3 of the assembly is composed of a set of identified versions of geometric units including sphere 1, and the two MFOs, volume_to_depth version 1 and weight_to_depth version 1, bound together in a monolithic version.

Version 2 of the assembly has only one materialized function, namely volume_to_depth, as weight_to_depth is implemented in its full function materialization form. It is interesting to note that weight_to_depth benefits from the materialization of volume_to_depth and may thus be termed partially materialized. The decision as to whether or not a function requires materialization depends on a number of factors, including whether it is already partially materialized. Partial function materialization may provide a sufficiently improved performance, in a particular application of the function.

All of the evolutions of the assembly from version 1 to version 5 have been as a result of either initial function materialization or subsequent rematerialization. Version 6 of the assembly, on the other hand, has been created as a result of a change of value to one of the attributes of the assembly, and not as a result of some function materialization-related change. This is the conventional reason for version evolution. Version 6 of the assembly object differs in only one respect to its predecessor, that is in the value of the changed non-component attribute. It shares the MFO references and version-specific composition hierarchy of its predecessor, version 5.

3.2.3 Version Evolution

Figure 5 illustrates an enhanced design spiral showing the development of an artefact consisting of components A, B, ..., H. The figure shows that each component may evolve through multiple versions, but that some components may require more versions than others. For each iteration of the spiral some, but not all of the components may evolve into new versions. If we analyse the evolution of a particular component, say for example component A, version 1 might result from empirical estimates (preliminary design), and version 2 from detailed design calculations (functions). Having selected the second version of this component as being appropriate to the final design, it would be inappropriate to re-evaluate the design calculations when using the complete, integrated artefact if the function evaluations take a substantial amount of time. Instead, these design functions should be materialized in a new, final version (version 3) of component A. As we go out along a radial line for a design component, we see where new versions of it were created by changes effected by the designers.

3.3 Evaluation of TOMS Function Materialization

Function materialization, while providing significant time savings in the return of complex function results, is not without cost. Returning to figure 4, it will be appreciated that versioning results in a proliferation of stored objects. For example, the materialization of functions in the

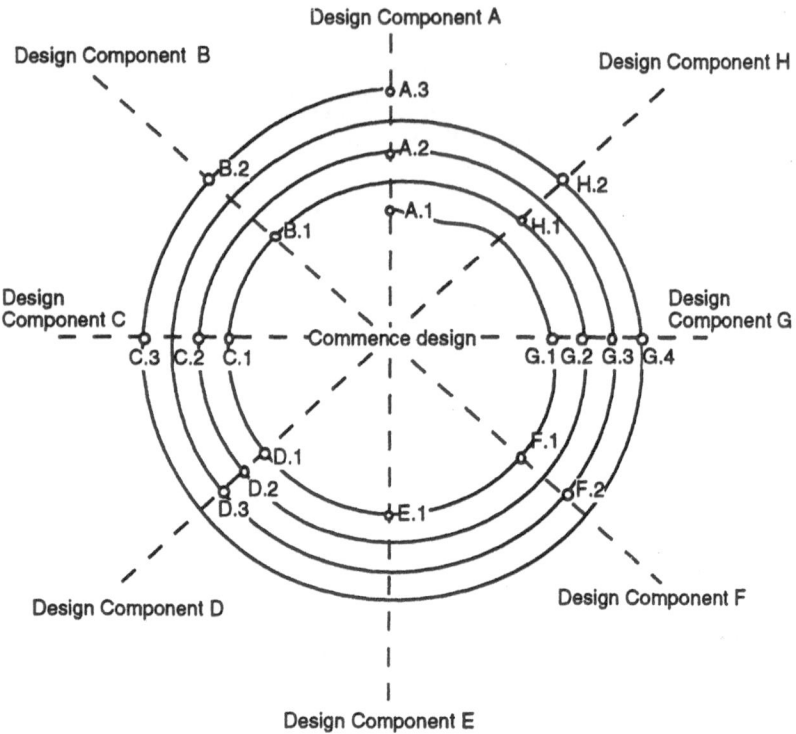

Final design = (A.3 + B.2 + C.3 + D.3 + E.1 + F.2 + G.4 + H.2)

<u>Notation</u> A.1 indicates version 1 of component A

Figure 5: Design Spiral Showing Version Evolution

original assembly object, has resulted in another 10 MFO and assembly objects. This does not include a potentially large number of unspecified geometrical unit, versioned subobjects, which may themselves have materialized functions with resulting MFOs. In addition, each family of versioned objects within a version set, has its own generic version.

In this section we present the results of tests carried out to investigate the effectiveness of the TOMS approach to function materialization with object versioning. The engineering design artefact in these tests is conceptually similar to the simple geometrical assembly artefact introduced in section 3.2.2, however, the constituent subobjects making up the assembly are both structurally and semantically complex (ship hulls). These subobjects have complex

geometrical forms described by means of polynomials. There are four functions of interest in our artefact, and the non-full materialization implementation of three of these functions, $f1$, $f2$ and $f3$, involves the double integration of the polynomials for the subobjects. This is a substantial processing task which can take a long time.

The test system is designed to evaluate the fourth function $f4$, for a range of values of a single parameter p, where $f4$ is a function of $f1$, $f2$ and $f3$, that is

$$f4(p) = F(f1(p), f2(p), f3(p))$$

where F expresses a simple arithmetic relationship between $f4$ and $f1$, $f2$ and $f3$.

3.3.1 Temporal Metric

The test program concerned with the temporal metric generates a sequence of four versions of the assembly artefact. The specification for each of these versions is as follows:

- in version 1 of the artefact, none of the three functions $f1$, $f2$ and $f3$, is materialized,
- version 2 of the artefact is identical to version 1, except that $f1$ has been materialized,
- version 3 of the artefact differs from version 2 only in terms of the materialized implementation of function $f2$, and
- in version 4 of the artefact all three of the functions $f1$, $f2$ and $f3$ are materialized.

The results for the test program are summarised in figure 6, which shows the time taken in seconds, to evaluate $f4$ for each of the versions 1 to 4, over a range of values for parameter p. The test programs were run on a DECStation 5000/120 graphical workstation.

Timings in Seconds for Evaluation of f4						
Parameter p	2.0	2.4	5.0	5.4	9.0	9.4
Version 1	23.233	26.183	30.300	33.150	42.533	46.067
Version 2	18.933	20.967	22.833	25.150	30.450	36.417
Version 3	10.017	11.700	16.417	18.017	25.000	27.067
Version 4	0.000	0.017	0.000	0.017	0.000	0.017

Figure 6: Timing Test

These results show that:

- for each of the versions 1 to 3, the time taken to return a result for function $f4$ increases with the value of parameter p,
- for a given value of parameter p, the time taken to return a result for function $f4$ decreases with an increasing version number, i.e. as each of the constituent functions $f1$, $f2$ and $f3$ is materialized in turn, in artefact versions 2, 3 and 4 respectively, there is a significant reduction in the time taken to return a result for $f4$.

The precision of the system clock used to measure the user time for function evaluation is $^1/_{60}$ (0.017) second. It can be seen in figure 6, that the time benefits of function materialization are considerable where, for example, a function evaluation time of around 46 seconds for unmaterialized functions is reduced to less than 20 micro seconds for materialized functions $f1$, $f2$ and $f3$. However, this improvement in performance is not without cost, as the next section will show.

302

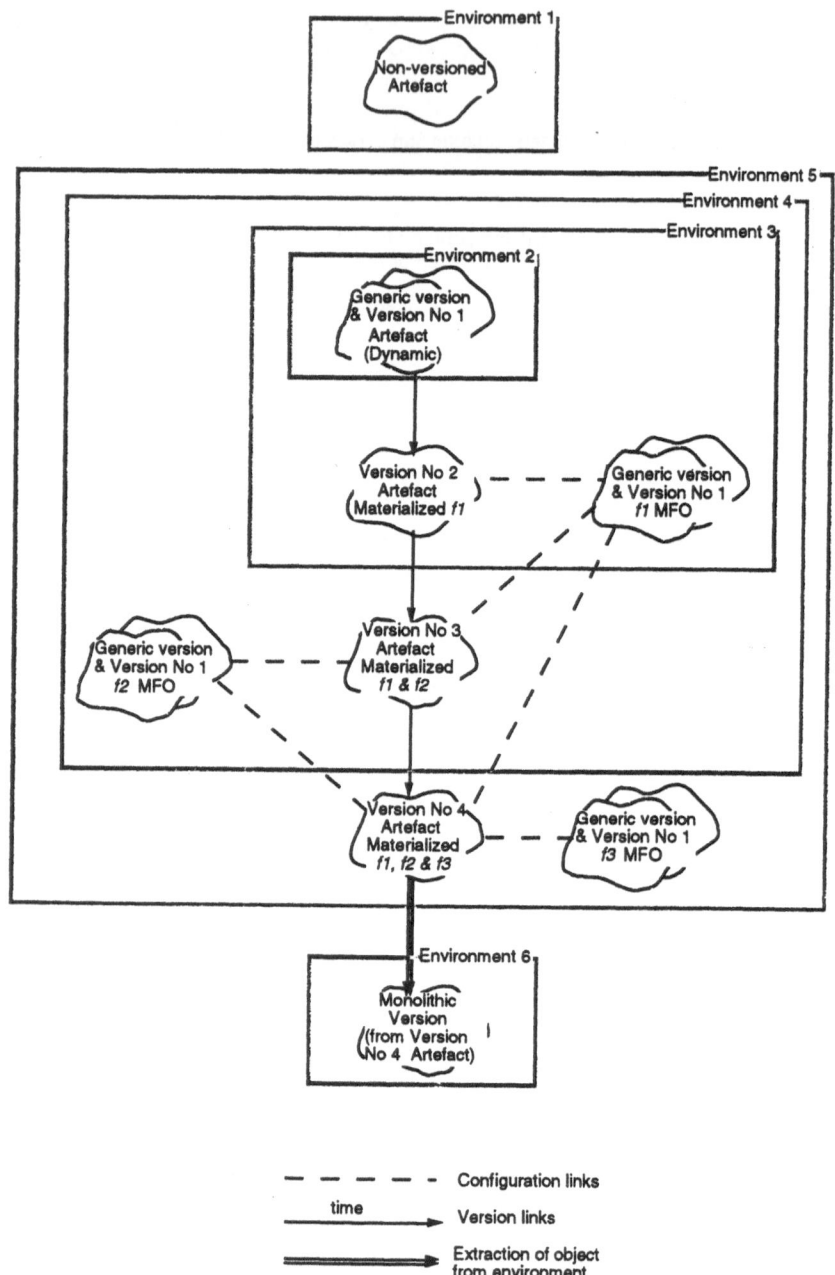

Figure 7: Storage of Environments

3.3.2 Storage Metric

Our test program determines the storage requirement for the polynomial assembly artefact just described. Figure 7 indicates graphically (on the previous page), the object environments numbered 1 to 6, for which we have determined the storage requirement. These environments can be summarised as:

- the artefact in a non-versioned form - environment 1,
- the generic artefact object immediately following the creation of each of the artefact versions 1, 2, 3 and 4 - environments 2 to 5, respectively, and
- a monolithic version, extracted from version 4 of the artefact - environment 6.

The object environment file sizes are summarised in figure 8.

Environment	Description	Stored Size
1	Non-versioned artefact:	22,223 Bytes
2	Up to Version 1 of artefact:	24,143 Bytes
3	Up to Version 2 of artefact:	50,324 Bytes
4	Up to Version 3 of artefact:	79,204 Bytes
5	Up to Version 4 of artefact:	111,304 Bytes
6	Monolithic version from Ver.4:	27,511 Bytes

Figure 8: Storage Test

From these results, assuming a certain, fixed file structure storage overhead, for each of the stored object environments, the following conclusions can be made:

- there is little extra storage overhead (approximately 2 kBytes) in progressing from a structurally complex (large) non-versioned artefact, to the equivalent versioned artefact,
- the extra storage required for a new function materialization with the new artefact version object and the associated MFO, is around 30 kBytes, for each of the three functions represented,
- a stand-alone monolithic version with all three functions materialized, requires only 28 kBytes, which is not much bigger than the non-versioned artefact at 22 kBytes.

3.3.3 Appraisal of Timing and Storage Tests

We conclude that although function materialization with object versioning is costly in terms of storage, there are real benefits in terms of the greatly reduced time for complex object function evaluation. The designer must weigh the storage costs against the timing benefits and possibly consider partial function materialization as a compromise strategy to provide more modest time response improvement with limited storage cost.

4. Use of Monolithic Versions in a Partitioned Design Database

When a design engineer settles on a complex object configuration that suits his/her needs, he/she may extract a monolithic version with fully materialized functions from the artefact version evolution tree, to gain the maximum temporal benefit from function materialization, with very little extra storage cost. In a hierarchically partitioned engineering design database as described in [CHO86, CHO88, LOR83], we believe that the monolithic version is a useful unit for check out and check in. Monolithic versions may be checked in to the public database as mature released versions, as illustrated in figure 9.

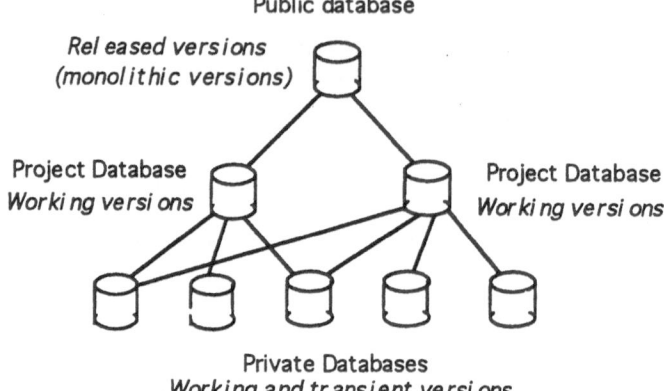

Figure 9: Database Partitions

5. Conclusions

Although function materialization is possible in a restricted sense in a relational database, as described in section 2.1, a major shortcoming of this approach is that the functions for which precalculated results are required are external to the database schema. Function materialization in GOM, as described in section 2.2, is both comprehensive and rigorous. However, GOM is unable to support the evolutionary design process where objects with materialized functions are not replaced when updated, but evolve into new object versions within a design artefact version evolution environment.

The TOMS versioning, configuration management and function materialization system described in this paper, has been implemented as an Eiffel class library. We believe that as these data management facilities are only required by specialist applications, they are better implemented outside the kernel object management system. Our approach permits modifications and extensions to be made to the library, through inheritance, so that users may customize function materialization to their own requirements. We are currently investigating the semantics of interpolative materialization to deal with the case of a direct function materialization, where the MFO does not contain a particular parameter value, and the user wishes to avoid a complete rematerialization.

Although we recommend that initial function materialization and subsequent rematerialization are undertaken as background processes, the database system may be heavily loaded by such operations. The functions requiring materialization are by definition process intensive, and each function requires precomputation for every parameter value combination. The choice of whether or not to materialize a function should be taken very carefully, therefore, as although considerable time savings can be made in returning function results, the materialization facility has to be paid for in terms of both storage and time taken in precalculating function results.

References

[Blakely et al, 1986]
Blakely, J A; Larson P et al; Efficiently Updating Materialized Views, Ed Zaniolo, *Proc ACM SIGMOD'86 Conf.*, ACM, 1986, pp 61-71.

[Blakely et al, 1989]
Blakely, J A; Coburn, N   et al; Updating Derived Relations: Detecting Irrelevant and Autonomously Computable Updates, *ACM Transactions on Database Systems* , 4, 3, 1989, pp 369-400.

[Carnduff et al, 1991]
Carnduff, T W; Gray, W A; Object-Oriented Computing Techniques in Ship Design, *Proc. ICCAS 91*, North Holland, Elsevier, Amsterdam, 1991.

[Carnduff et al, 1992]
Carnduff, T W; Gray, W A; An Eiffel Class Library for Ship Design, Eds Heeg, Magnusson & Meyer, *Proc. Tools 7*, Prentice-Hall, Dortmund, 1992, pp 233-245.

[Carnduff et al, 1993]
Carnduff, T W; Gray, W A; Function Materialization Through Object Versioning in Object-Oriented Databases, *Proc British National Conference on Databases (BNCOD11)* , Springer Verlag, 1993, pp 111-128.

[Chou et al, 1986]
Chou, H T; Kim, W; A Unifying Framework for Versions in a CAD Environment, Eds Chu, Gardarin & Ohsuga, *Proc VLDB 86*, 1986, pp 336-344.

[Chou et al, 1988]
Chou, Hong-Tai; Kim, Won; Versions and Change Notification in an Object-Oriented Database System, *Proc 25th ACM/IEEE Design Automation Conference*, ACM/IEEE , 1988, pp 275-281.

[Date, 1981]
Date, C J; An Introduction to Database Systems, 3rd edition, Addison-Wesley, 1981.

[Dayal et al, 1987]
Dayal, U; Manola, F et al; Simplifying Complex Objects: The Probe Approach to Modelling, *Proceedings German Database Conference* , Burg Technik Und Wissenschafts, Darmstadt, 1987, pp 390-399.

[Hanson, 1987]
Hanson, Eric N; A Performance Analysis of View Materialization Strategies, Eds Dayal & Traiger, *Proc ACM SIGMOD '87 Conf,* ACM, 1987, pp 440-453.

[Kemper et al, 1990]
Kemper, Alfons; Kilger, Cristoph et al , Function Materialization in Object Bases, Universitat Karlsruhe, Fakultat Fur Informatik, Karlsruhe, Germany, 1990.

[Kemper et al, 1991]
Kemper, Alfons; Kilger, Christof et al; Function Materialization in Object Bases, Eds Clifford & King, *Proc ACM SIGMOD '91 Conf* , ACM, Denver, 1991, pp 258-267.

[Lorie et al, 1983]
Lorie, R; Plouffe, W; Complex Objects and their Use in Design Transactions, *Proc Engineering Design Applications* , IEEE, 1983, pp 115-121.

[Maier, 1991]
Maier, David; Making Database Systems Fast Enough for CAD Applications, Eds Kim & Lochovsky, *Object-Oriented Concepts, Databases and Applications* , Addison Wesley, Reading, Mass, 1989, pp 573-581.

Safe Derivations in Object Hierarchies

Stefan Conrad[1], Martin Gogolla[2], and Rudolf Herzig[2]

[1] Universität Magdeburg, Fakultät für Informatik,
Postfach 4120, D–39016 Magdeburg, Germany
[2] Universität Bremen, FB3 Mathematik und Informatik,
Postfach 33 04 40, D–28334 Bremen, Germany
E-mail: conrad@iti.cs.tu-magdeburg.de   Fax: +49 391 5592 2020

ABSTRACT. *We present a language for specifying structure and behavior of objects in information systems. This language is restricted to a set of core concepts for conceptual modeling. But it includes powerful concepts for specifying constraints and derived data. We present an algorithm for deciding on safe computation of derived information and demonstrate how this algorithm works with an example.*

KEY WORDS: *object oriented databases, object specification, TROLL light, object hierarchies, derived attributes, safe derivation / safe queries.*

1. Introduction

In the last years two important directions for developing databases for non-standard applications have evolved: object-oriented databases and deductive databases.

Object-oriented databases [Ban88, ABD90] aim to support conceptual modeling features known from semantic data models, like SDM [HM81], IRIS [LK86], IFO [AH87], EER [EGH92], and data models for complex objects (e.g., [SS86, PA86, Heu89]). Moreover they come along with object-oriented programming languages, thereby overcoming the well-known impedance mismatch in relational database systems (an example of a popular object-oriented databases systems is O_2 [Deu90]).

In principle, deductive databases are based on the relational data model. Relations are treated as predicates in order to apply the machinery of logic programming. The basic declarative language DATALOG [CGT89, CGT90] has been extended for capturing sets and functions in many different ways. Well-known examples are LDL [NT89, BNST91], LPS [Kup90], and COL [AG91].

The integration of object-orientation and deduction promises to unify the advantages of both areas [Abi90, Bee90]. First efforts resulted, e.g., in F-Logic [KL89, KLW90] and LOCO [STV91, STVV91], two deductive languages incorporating object-oriented features like object identity and inheritance. Although principle problems in integrating object-oriented and deductive databases were stated in [Ull91], there seem to be several meaningful ways for their combination. For instance, object-oriented features can be embedded into declarative languages (e.g., as in IQL [AK89] and OIL [Zan90]). More references on object-orientation, deduction, and their integration can be found in [CG92].

In this paper we present a core language for specifying objects in information systems [CGH92, GCH93, HCG94]. This language called TROLL *light* is a dialect, but not a subset of TROLL [JSH91]. Because our aim in the KorSo project is to study aspects of validating and verifying object specifications we have restricted TROLL *light* to a small number of concepts for modeling structure and behavior of object communities. Nevertheless our language includes a powerful sublanguage for specifying derived data and static integrity constraints in a declarative way. This sublanguage is an offspring of a calculus for an Extended Entity-Relationship model [GH91] and marks one of the mayor differences between TROLL and TROLL *light*.

With our language we specify derived data, not derived objects. This is in contrast to approaches where derivation rules may create new objects (F-Logic [KL89], HiLog [CKW89] or Living in a Lattice [HS91]). Usually, derived objects represent a special form of views. The problem occurring in those approaches is how to classify the derived objects with regard to an existing class structure [HS91]. In our comprehension the result of a query is a complex value [AFS89] which, of course, may contain object identifiers. We consider values like 42 or { flight(HAJ,JFK), flight(JFK,DAL), flight(HAJ,FUE) } as time-independent things. In contrast, objects are persistent items showing (apart from their identity) time-dependent features which can be observed by values [EGS90].

But we can specify derived attributes for objects. The question arising here is whether we can ensure that the values of these attributes can always be computed. For this problem we present an algorithm which gives a sufficient criterion for the safety of a large class of derivations. This algorithm is based on the principle of stratification (cf. [ABW88, CGT89, etc.]) which however had to be modified due to the fact that we use a language conceptually richer than Horn-clause languages and due to the fact that our specification language requires to organize objects into object hierarchies. This is why we will talk about hierarchical stratification.

In the sequel we briefly introduce TROLL *light* and the sublanguage which we will call query calculus for convenience (Sect. 2). In Sect. 3, we first present our algorithm for deciding on safe computation of derived information, then we demonstrate this algorithm with an example, and finally we give a short example for safe computation which our algorithm cannot detect. We conclude with some remarks on the presented algorithm and on future work.

2. Concepts of TROLL *light*

In the sequel we present the concepts of TROLL *light*, a dialect of TROLL [JSH91]. In our project, we need a simple but powerful language for investigating aspects of validating and verifying specifications. Therefore, TROLL *light* offers only a small number of core concepts for specifying objects and object communities in information systems. However, with regard to certain aspects, TROLL *light* is richer than TROLL. For example, we integrated a well-founded query calculus. This offers the possibility to formulate (static) integrity constraints and to query objects. Furthermore, this calculus is used to describe derived information, i.e., derived attributes. We will consider this query calculus in more detail after having given a brief overview of TROLL *light*.

2.1 Concepts for modeling object structure and behavior

In TROLL *light* objects are described by templates which have the following structure.

```
TEMPLATE name of current template
   DATA TYPES     data types used in current template
   TEMPLATES ·    other templates used in current template
   SUBOBJECTS     slots for subobjects
   ATTRIBUTES     slots for attributes
   EVENTS         event generators
   CONSTRAINTS    restricting conditions on object states
   VALUATION      effect of event occurrences on attributes
   DERIVATION     rules for derived attributes
   INTERACTION    synchronization of events in different objects
   BEHAVIOR       description of object behavior by CSP-like processes
END TEMPLATE;
```

In the following we will explain each section which may appear in a template. First, the DATA TYPES and TEMPLATES sections are explained because they provide the context for object descriptions. Then, the ATTRIBUTES, CONSTRAINTS, EVENTS, VALUATION, and BEHAVIOR sections are considered. With these concepts we are able to describe single objects. Afterwards, we deal with the SUBOBJECTS and INTERACTION section which we need for forming object communities. The DERIVATION section will be treated in more detail in Sect. 2.2.

In the DATA TYPES section we have to list which data types are used in the current template, i.e., sorts, operations, and predicates specified for these data types are made known. Please note that TROLL *light* is not intended for specifying data types. Instead we assume data type specifications to be already given. For this, we may use other specification languages, like SPECTRUM [BFG93] (used in the KorSo project), ACT ONE [EFH83], PLUSS [Gau84], or OBJ3 [GW88].

Analogously, other templates used in the current template must be declared in the TEMPLATES section. We employ a certain convention concerning data types, templates, and associated sorts. Names starting with an upper case letter denote data types and templates, i.e., complete modules, whereas the corresponding sort names start with a lower case letter. For example, Nat refers to the complete specification of the natural numbers including the sort nat and constants and operations like 0 : -> nat or + : nat nat -> nat . The sorts corresponding to templates are called object sorts.

Observable properties of objects are attributes which are specified in the ATTRIBUTES section. The general form of an attribute declaration is $a\,[\,([p_1:]s_1,\ldots,[p_n:]s_n)\,]:d$, where a is an attribute name generator, d is a sort expression determining the range of an attribute, and $s_1, \ldots, s_n$ $(n \geq 0)$ denote optional parameter sorts (data or object sorts). To describe the intuitive meaning of parameters, optional parameter names p_i might be added. The sort expression d may be built over both data and object sorts by applying the predefined type constructors TUPLE, LIST, BAG, SET, and UNION. This allows to specify arbitrary complex attributes which can be data-valued, object-valued, multi-valued, composite, and alternative. We allow attribute names to be provided with parameters, e.g., the attribute SoldBooks(Year:nat):nat in a template Author. Thereby, an infinite number of attribute names, like SoldBooks(1993), can be introduced. However, only a finite number of attributes of an object can have a defined value.

Static integrity constraints restricting the allowed object states, in particular restricting the values which attributes may take, are specified in the CONSTRAINTS section. Here, we omit details on constraints because in Sect. 2.2 the construction of terms and formulas for specifying derivation rules of derived attributes is described. In principle, the same kind of terms and formulas may be used for constraints.

Events are specified in the EVENTS section of a template by $e[([p_1:]s_1,\ldots,[p_n:]s_n)]$, where e denotes an event generator and $s_1,\ldots,s_n$ represent optional parameter sort expressions. In order to give an intuitive meaning to parameters, optional parameter names p_i may be added. Events are used for modeling incidents which may happen in an object's life. Special events are birth and death events (marked by BIRTH and DEATH, resp.). Several birth or death events may be specified for the same object. In any case there must be at least one birth event description in a template.

The effect of events on attribute values is described in the VALUATION section by valuation rules having the following form:

$$[\{precondition\}]\ [event\_descr]\ attr\_term = term$$

Such a valuation rule describes that after the occurrence of an event matching *event_descr* the attribute denoted by *attr_term* has the value given by *term* provided the optional *precondition* is fulfilled. Both terms as well as the precondition are evaluated in the state before the event occurs. There is a frame rule saying that attributes which are not caught by a suitable valuation rule remain unchanged. Before the birth event, all attributes of an object are assumed to be undefined. Thus if the event in question is a birth event, some attributes may remain undefined. Of course, derived attributes cannot directly be manipulated by valuation rules.

In the BEHAVIOR section admissible life cycles may be specified for objects. Life cycles are described by so-called process patterns. Each object has a finite number of possible o-machine states (o for object). For these o-machine states, state transitions caused by event occurrences are specified in the process patterns. Event sequences as well as event dependent branchings may be described here. Additional preconditions for state transitions allow to forbid event occurrences, i.e., if in an o-machine state the precondition for an event is not fulfilled the event is not permitted to occur. Thereby, the admissible life cycles can be restricted further. Life cycles must start with a birth event and possibly end with a death event. Omitting the BEHAVIOR section in a template allows arbitrary event occurrences after a birth event and before a possible death event.

For relating objects in an object community we can specify subobject relationships in the SUBOBJECTS section. A subobject declaration $u [([p_1:]s_1, \ldots, [p_n:]s_n)] : o$ resembles an attribute declaration. Here, however, the sort expression o is restricted to object sorts. Such a subobject declaration provides possible subobject names. Subobject relationships organize the objects of an object community into a hierarchy.

Communication between objects is specified in the INTERACTION section by event calling schemes of the following form:

$$[\{precondition\}] \ [source\_object.] source\_event >> [destination\_object.] destination\_event$$

Such an event calling scheme expresses the following dependency: Provided the precondition is fulfilled the occurrence of an event matching *source_event* in an object matching *source_object* causes the simultaneous occurrence of the event described by *destination_event* in the object described by *destination_object*. If *source_object* or *destination_object* are missing, we assume that the corresponding event refers to the object for which this interaction is specified.

2.2 Employing the query calculus for derivation of attributes

Now, we will put the focus on derived attributes. TROLL *light* offers this concept because it enables the specification of information which can be computed from other information already present. Thereby, redundant storage of data can be avoided. Furthermore, it is possible to query objects. Here, we concentrate on derived attributes, but the presented calculus can also be used for general query purposes.

Derived attributes are marked by the keyword DERIVED in the ATTRIBUTES section of a template. The evaluation of a derived attribute is specified in the DERIVATION section by an equation with the derived attribute as left hand side and a defining term as right hand side.

Example:

```
TEMPLATE Node
   DATA TYPES   Nat;
   SUBOBJECTS   Child(nat) : node;
   ATTRIBUTES   Content : nat;
                DERIVED  Total : nat;
   ...
   DERIVATION   Total = SUM ( SELECT Total(PRJ(X,2)) FROM X IN Child )
                        + Content;
   ...
END TEMPLATE;
```

The above template describes objects which can appear as nodes in a tree. Each node has a finite number of private subobjects. For instance binary trees could be described as objects with at most two subobjects, say Child(0) and Child(1) giving the left and right subtree, respectively. Objects described by this template have a non-derived attribute Content and a derived attribute Total. In each object state the value of the derived attribute is given by the defining term

```
SUM( SELECT Total(PRJ(X,2)) FROM X IN Child )
+ Content;
```

which is a term of our query calculus. In the SELECT expression, Child is used as a term of sort SET(TUPLE(nat,node)). This will be explained below. The term describes that we have to sum up the values of the attributes Total of all existing subobjects of the considered object and to add the value of the attribute Content. In the sequel, we discuss this query calculus in more detail in order to give an impression of its expressiveness. First, we have to distinguish terms and formulas.

Terms may be built with variables and operation symbols as usual. As already mentioned in the previous section we assume a data specification including a data signature to be given. So, data sorts and operation symbols are known. Additional sorts are object sorts which correspond to templates.

Attribute and subobject symbols are special operation symbols. Recall that attributes are specified by a declaration $a:d$ for non-parameterized attributes and by $a'(s_1,\ldots,s_n):d$ for parameterized attributes. Now, we have to distinguish where we want to use attribute symbols for constructing terms. If they shall refer to the object itself, then we may use a respectively $a'(t_1,\ldots,t_n)$ as terms of sort d (with $t_1,\ldots,t_n$ being terms of suitable sorts), e.g., we use Content for referring to the object's own attribute. If we want to refer to another object we have to add a parameter denoting this object, e.g., $a(o)$ respectively $a'(o,t_1,\ldots,t_n)$. For example Total(PRJ(X,2)) denotes the attribute Total of an object referred to by PRJ(X,2). Additionally, there is a further use of parameterized attributes. a' (resp. $a'(o)$) is a term of sort SET(TUPLE($s_1,\ldots,s_n,d$)) denoting the set of all tuples which can be constructed from parameter values for which the attribute has a value different from undefined. Subobject symbols can be used in the same way. For a parameterized subobject declaration $u(s_1,\ldots,s_n):s_o$ the term u (resp. $u(o)$) is of sort SET(TUPLE($s_1,\ldots,s_n,s_o$)) and includes all tuples for which the corresponding subobject (of object sort s_o) is currently existing. For instance, we have used the term Child in the defining term of the derived attribute Total.

Two additional constructs are offered: The conditional (IF...THEN...ELSE...) and the query construct (SELECT...FROM...[WHERE...]). A term (IF φ THEN t_1 ELSE t_2) is admissible if φ is a formula and t_1, t_2 are terms of the same sort. This sort also determines the sort of the complete term. The query construct requires some more explanation. The general form of a query term is as follows:

$$(\text{SELECT } t_1,\ldots,t_n \quad \text{FROM } decl_1,\ldots,decl_k \text{ [WHERE } \varphi \text{] })$$

In the FROM-part there is a list of variable declarations. Each declaration has the form var IN $range\_term$ where var is a variable and $range\_term$ is a multi-valued term giving a finite range to var. In $range\_term$ there may occur other variables which must be declared before. Thereby, dependent ranges can be specified. In the SELECT-part a list of terms $t_1,\ldots,t_n$ is given in which the variables introduced in the FROM-part may occur. The sort of such a query term is given by BAG(TUPLE($sort(t_1),\ldots,sort(t_n)$)) where $sort(t_i)$ denotes the sort of term t_i. The value of a query term is the least multi-set computed as follows. For each instantiation of the variables (according to their declarations) the tuple consisting of the values obtained by evaluating the terms $t_1,\ldots,t_n$ is an element of the result provided the optional selection condition φ is fulfilled. If the WHERE-part is missing the selection condition is assumed to equal TRUE.

To round off the construction of terms some additional operations are used. For converting multi-sets or lists into sets the operations BTS or LTS, respectively, can be used (Bag To Set or List To Set). The operation PRJ is necessary for projecting components from a tuple. Moreover, there are several aggregate functions like CNT (for counting elements) and SUM which can be applied to sets, lists, or multi-sets.

Next, we briefly sketch the possibilities to build formulas. Because we assume a data signature containing predicate symbols to be given, these predicate symbols applied to terms yield atomic formulas (e.g., $p(t_1,\ldots,t_n)$ for some predicate symbol p; of course, infix notation for binary predicates could be used for convenience). Furthermore, there are pre-defined predicate symbols: IN for testing whether a value is an element of a set (list, multi-set), and DEF for testing whether a term yields a value different from the undefined value.

Formulas may be connected by the connectives AND, OR, and IMPLIES. Furthermore, formulas can be built by applying NOT. For quantifying variables we have a universal quantifier FORALL and an existential one EXISTS. A variable declaration as explained for query terms must follow each of these quantifiers. Thereby, quantifiers bind variables to finite ranges only. The above assumptions guarantee that formulas can be evaluated in each state of an object community.

Now, we close this section by explaining the example for a derived attribute given above. In the query term the variable X is given the finite range Child. Child is a term of sort SET(TUPLE(nat,node)) yielding a set of pairs consisting of a natural number and an object of sort node. As explained above only those pairs are elements of Child where the second component is a living subobject of the considered object, and the first component is the number n contributing to the subobject's name Child(n). In consequence, X ranges over these pairs. This is why we have to project the second component of such pairs by PRJ(X,2) in order to get the subobject itself. The application of Total(...) yields the value of the attribute Total of the respective subobject. The aggregation function SUM adds up all these attribute values which are in the result of the query term. Finally, the value of the object's own attribute Content is added. For objects having no subobjects the SELECT term evaluates to the empty set and the aggregation function SUM yields 0 as result.

The usage of other attributes for defining the value of derived attributes imposes the problem that cyclic dependencies can be specified such that it might be impossible to safely compute the values of derived attributes. In the next section we deal with this problem by presenting an algorithm for checking TROLL *light* specifications whether their derived attributes can be safely computed.

3. Ensuring safe computation of derived attributes

In the sequel we develop an algorithm for checking a TROLL *light* specification for safe derivation. For this we have to analyze the defining terms of derived attributes and to construct a dependency graph for derived attributes. If this dependency graph fulfills certain conditions the computation of derived attributes is guaranteed to be safe. However it should be noted that there may be specifications which guarantee safe computation of derived attributes where the dependency graph does not fulfill these conditions.

Next we present our algorithm for ensuring safe derivations. Afterwards we will apply our algorithm to a small example, and, finally, we will give an example which shows that our algorithm cannot cover any case in which the computation of derived attributes is safe. Therefore, we have a sufficient but not necessary criterion.

3.1 The algorithm

The algorithm for ensuring safe computation of derived attributes is based on a syntactical analysis of the defining terms of derived attributes. The result we want to obtain is a graph which reflects the computation of derived attributes. If this graph fulfills a certain condition which we call *stratification condition* then the computation of derived attributes is guaranteed to be safe.

The main idea of the following algorithm is that the computation of a derived attribute is unsafe if its computation may become cyclic. Then, there is a directly or indirectly self-recursive definition of that derived attribute. In consequence, we have to check whether such self-recursive derivations have been specified. Therefore, the algorithm constructs a graph from the defining terms of derived attributes. Nodes are attribute and subobject symbols specified in the object descriptions. Edges reflect computational order, i.e., a path starting at a symbol of a derived attribute goes to symbols of attributes and subobjects which are used for computations of that derived attribute. Going to a subobject symbol means that the following symbols (on the path) refer to attributes or subobjects of a subobject. This is the positive case because we are moving downwards in the object hierarchy. The negative case is going to a symbol of a non-derived, object-valued attribute. Here, we cannot make a general statement to which object consequent symbols on a path are referring. Because this might result in self-recursive computations we cannot guarantee safe computation.

The graph construction algorithm:

Input: a collection of TROLL *light* templates as a specification of
an object community

Output: a directed graph with attribute and subobject symbols as
nodes and edges denoting access dependencies provided by
the specification of derived attributes

Execute the following steps for each derived attribute:

1. *Build the syntax tree of its defining term.*

2. *Eliminate variables from the syntax tree.*

   Two cases may occur:

   - The considered variable is free in the defining term. This may only occur for parameterized derived attributes because for such an attribute the defining term may have free variables referring to parameters of the attribute. In consequence, when evaluating such an attribute these variables are substituted by the actual parameters. Therefore, these variables cannot introduce dependencies on other attributes, and we may ignore these variables.

   - The considered variable is bound by a variable declaration in which a multi-valued term describing the range for the variable is given. This term may involve attributes and subobjects. Therefore, we must substitute each occurrence of the variable by the syntax tree of that term. The occurrence of the variable in its own declaration may be totally ignored, because, here, the substitution does not affect the further steps.

3. *Eliminate all operation symbols from the modified syntax tree which are neither attribute symbols nor subobject symbols.*

   Thereby, we remove operation symbols from the tree which do not affect the safe computation of derived attributes. Among these symbols there are symbols given by data types (e.g., symbols like 2 and +), symbols standing for predefined operations (e.g., PRJ) or for special constructs of TROLL *light* (e.g., IF, SELECT). The edges of the resulting graph have to be constructed as follows: There is an edge between two remaining symbols if and only if there was a path from the root to a leaf in the former tree and both symbols lie on that path.

4. *Interpret the edges in the sense of computational order and construct the dependency graph.*

   Each edge in the graph obtained in the previous step can be interpreted as a computational dependency. This is quite easy to see because syntax trees can be used for determining computational orders. The dependencies given by a syntax tree are that each term represented by a node n in the syntax tree can only be evaluated if all its subterms (represented by nodes which are successors of n in the syntax tree) have been evaluated before. Therefore we orientate the edges in a way that they are going upwards, i.e., from subterms to root terms.

   Now, we know that the derived attribute we are considering depends on those attributes and subobjects for which there is a node with the corresponding symbol in the obtained graph. But, if there is a chain $n_1 \rightarrow \ldots \rightarrow n_k$ in that graph then the dependency on $n_2, \ldots,$ and n_k is not a "direct" one. We have first to evaluate n_1, then $n_2, \ldots,$ and finally n_k. Thereby, the edges reflect the navigation through templates necessary for evaluating a derived attribute. And this navigation starts at the considered derived attribute itself. In consequence, we build the final dependency graph by adding a node with the symbol of the considered derived attribute and by drawing edges from this new node to each starting node of a chain. Please note that isolated nodes are considered to be trivial chains and, thereby, they are also starting nodes of chains. Now, nodes labeled by the same symbol are collapsed – as well as multiple edges from one node to another.

After having constructed a dependency graph for each derived attribute, we can bring together these graphs by collapsing nodes labeled with the same symbol and by eliminating multiple edges. Next, we have to find all (minimal) cycles in the resulting graph. For this, standard graph algorithms can be applied. Then the following condition must be checked for fulfillment:

Stratification condition:
>The computation of derived attributes is safe if in the dependency graph each cycle, which contains a symbol of a derived attributes, also contains at least one subobject symbol and does not contain any symbol of a non-derived attribute.

This property ensures that the computation can be hierarchically stratified. This is because a cycle containing a subobject symbol represents the fact that the computation of a derived attribute is based recursively on the computation of the same derived attribute but the computation is done for subobjects which are strictly lower in the object hierarchy. This recursion makes no problems because the objects in an object community form an object hierarchy in each instant of time. Moreover, in each state this hierarchy is finite. In consequence, such a recursive computation is safe.

However, if the cycle contains a symbol of an object-valued attribute (or a complex-valued attribute where an object value occurs as part of the complex value) we have a problem. Because object-valued attributes of an object may have for instance the object's own superobject as values such a cycle could be an indication for a non-terminating computation.

3.2 Applying the algorithm

In this section we will give a concrete example for the application of the algorithm presented before. For this we will use the following TROLL *light* specification of persons which may have other persons identified by a name as direct offsprings (modeled as subobjects):

```
TEMPLATE Person
  DATA TYPES String, Nat, Real;
  SUBOBJECTS DirOffspring(string):person;
  ATTRIBUTES Age:nat;
             DERIVED Offsprings:SET(person);
             DERIVED OffspringNames:BAG(string);
             DERIVED OffspringCount:nat;
             DERIVED SumAge:nat;
             DERIVED AvgAge:real;
  ...
  DERIVATION
    Offsprings =
      BTS(SELECT PRJ(X,2) FROM X IN DirOffspring)
      +
      BTS(SELECT Y FROM X IN DirOffspring, Y IN Offsprings(PRJ(X,2)));
    OffspringNames =
      SELECT PRJ(X,1) FROM X IN DirOffspring
      +
      SELECT Y FROM X IN DirOffspring, Y IN OffspringNames(PRJ(X,2));
    OffspringCount =
      CNT(Offsprings);
    SumAge =
```

```
        SUM(SELECT SumAge(PRJ(X,2)) FROM X IN DirOffspring) + Age;
    AvgAge =
        SumAge / (OffspringCount+1);
    ...
END TEMPLATE
```

There are several derived attributes for persons.

Offsprings: The set of direct and indirect offsprings of a person.

OffspringNames: The bag of all names of direct and indirect offsprings of a person.

OffspringCount: The number of direct and indirect offsprings of a person.

SumAge: The sum of ages of all direct and indirect offsprings of a person plus the age of the person itself.

AvgAge: The average age of all direct and indirect offsprings of a person including the person itself.

The four steps for constructing the dependency graph for a derived attribute will be demonstrated by the derivation rule for Offsprings:

```
BTS(SELECT PRJ(X,2) FROM X IN DirOffspring)
+
BTS(SELECT Y FROM X IN DirOffspring, Y IN Offsprings(PRJ(X,2)));
```

Step 1:

The syntax tree of the considered term is depicted in Fig. 1.

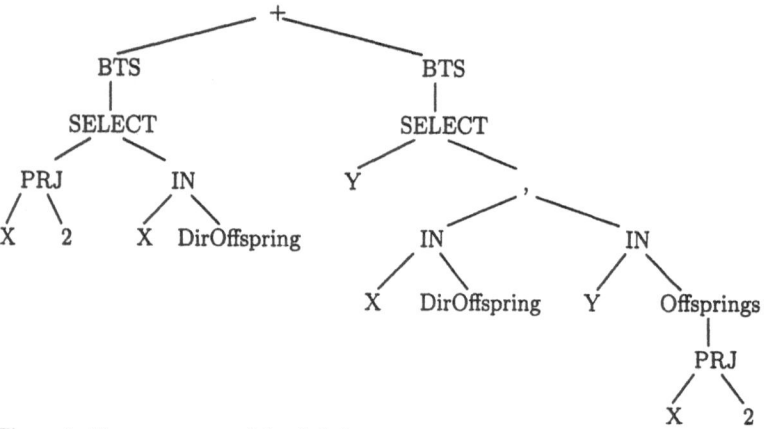

Figure 1: The syntax tree of the defining term.

Step 2:

The elimination of variables from the syntax tree results in a modified tree given in Fig. 2.

Step 3:

By eliminating all symbols from the modified syntax tree which are neither attribute nor subobject symbols we obtain the following graph:

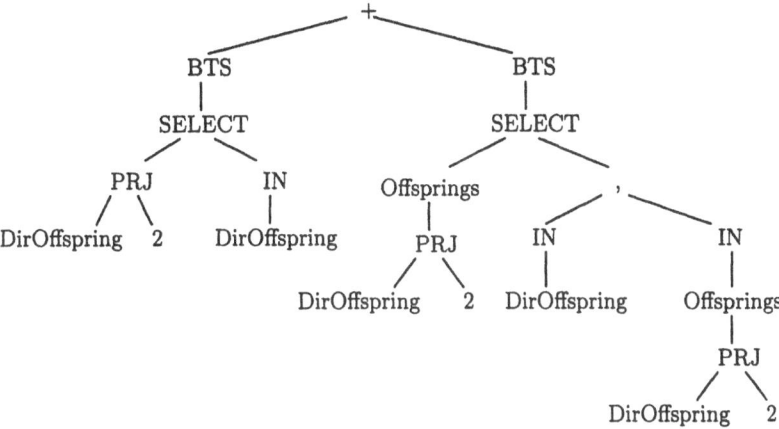

Figure 2: The modified syntax tree.

Step 4:

Giving an orientation to the edges as explained, adding the symbol of the considered derived attribute as a node, and connecting this node by directed egdes to the starting nodes of chains yields the following graph:

Collapsing nodes labeled by the same symbol and eliminating multiple edges lead to the dependency graph for the considered derived attribute Offsprings:

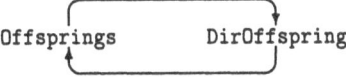

Now these four steps must be repeated for the other derived attributes. We skip this here and give the final dependency graph in which all dependency graphs of derived attributes are embedded:

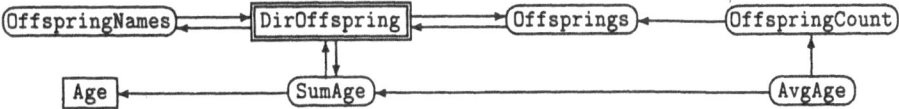

In the graph we have marked the different kinds of symbols by different kinds of frames: double frames for subobject symbol, frames with rounded corners for symbols of derived attributes, and square frames for symbols of non-derived attributes. It can easily be checked that each cycle in that graph goes through a subobject symbol, i.e., goes through DirOffspring. Furthermore, there is no symbol of a non-derived (and object-valued) attribute in any cycle. In consequence, the graph fulfills the stratification condition and the computation of derived attributes is guaranteed to be safe.

3.3 Safe computations not detected by the algorithm

The algorithm described in the last section provides only a sufficient criterion, not a necessary one. Take for example the following template.

```
TEMPLATE Strange
  ATTRIBUTES  DERIVED A: nat;
              DERIVED B: nat;
              C: nat;
  . . .
  DERIVATION  A = (IF C > 100 THEN B ELSE C );
              B = (IF C < 100 THEN A ELSE C );
  . . .
END TEMPLATE
```

Here, the dependency graph has a cycle which violates the stratification condition. Nevertheless, we can safely evaluate the values of the attributes A and B in each possible state. For this we have to consider the value of attribute C:

C = 100: A as well as B have the same value as C.

C > 100: A must have the same value as B, and B gets the value of C. In consequence, A gets the value of C, too.

C < 100: B must have the same value as A, and A gets the value of C. In consequence, B gets the value of C, too.

In any case A and B have the same value as C. Thus investigating the semantics of if-terms one may verify the derivation to be safe.

On the other hand it is possible to construct derivation rules where safety totally depends on the current state of an object community. For example replace the subobject relationships of person by object-valued attributes. Then it is no longer guaranteed that offspring relationships establish a tree structure, and hence the derivation process may lead into cycles.

4. Conclusions

We have presented TROLL *light*, a core language for specifying structure and behavior of objects in information systems. This language includes a powerful query calculus which can be used to define derived attributes. We have given an algorithm which guarantees safe computation for a class of syntactical decidable derivation rules. The algorithm is based on the idea of hierarchical stratification as a modification of standard stratification.

However, as we have shown there are cases in which safe evaluation could be guaranteed, but which cannot be found by our algorithm. This is due to the fact that in those cases we need semantical knowledge for deciding the safety of computation.

Our algorithm is designed for hierarchies of objects as they are specified in TROLL *light*. It would be interesting whether this algorithm could be transferred to more comfortable specification languages which offer more or other structuring concepts for object communities, for instance, hierarchies of classes together with inheritance. In our specification language we do not offer inheritance because it is often used in a way which contradicts usual declarative approaches. For instance, verifying object properties becomes nearly impossible in the presence of inheritance because, in general, inheritance causes non-monotonicity. As far as we know, the approaches of [BL91, BL92] and [LSV90, LV90, LV91] are the only ones which try to overcome this problem.

However, these and several further questions are lying outside the current scope of our project. Instead we focus our work on a development environment for reliable information systems [VHG93]. For this environment we implement an animation system which can be used for validating object specifications. Furthermore, for verifying TROLL *light* specifications we have developed a verification calculus [Con94] which is realized with the help of the generic proof system Isabelle [Pau90]. The algorithm presented in this paper is thought to be the basis for automatically checking consistency of specifications. Thereby, we hope to support the development of reliable information systems.

Acknowledgement

Work reported here has been partially supported by the German Ministry for Research and Technology (BMFT) under Grant No. 01 IS 203 D (KorSo = Korrekte Software) and by the CEC under Grant No. 6112 (COMPASS). This work originates in Braunschweig where the authors had worked together.

References:

[ABD90] M. Atkinson, F. Bancilhon, D. DeWitt, K. Dittrich, D. Maier, and S. Zdonik. The Object-Oriented Database System Manifesto. In W. Kim, J.-M. Nicolas, and S. Nishio, eds., *Deductive and Object-Oriented Databases*, pages 223–240. Elsevier (North-Holland), 1990.

[Abi90] S. Abiteboul. Towards a deductive object-oriented database language. *Data & Knowledge Engineering*, 5(2):263–287, 1990.

[ABW88] K.R. Apt, H.A. Blair, and A. Walker. Towards a Theory of Declarative Knowlewdge. In J. Minker, ed., *Foundations of Deductive Databases and Logic Programming*, pages 89–148. Kaufmann, 1988.

[AFS89] S. Abiteboul, P.C. Fischer, and H.J. Schek, eds. *Nested Relations and Complex Objects in Databases*, Springer, LNCS 361, 1989.

[AG91] S. Abiteboul and S. Grumbach. A Rule–Based Language with Functions and Sets. *ACM Trans. on Database Systems*, 16(1):1–30, 1991.

[AH87] S. Abiteboul and R. Hull. IFO — A Formal Semantic Database Model. *ACM Trans. on Database Systems*, 12(4):525–565, 1987.

[AK89] S. Abiteboul and P.C. Kanellakis. Object Identity as a Query Language Primitive. In *ACM SIGMOD Conf. on Management of Data*, pages 159–173, 1989.

[Ban88] F. Bancilhon. Object-Oriented Database Systems. In *Proc. 7th ACM Symp. Principles of Database Systems*, pages 152–162, 1988.

[Bee90] C. Beeri. A Formal Approach to Object-Oriented Databases. *Data & Knowledge Engineering*, 5(4):353–382, 1990.

[BFG93] M. Broy, C. Facchi, R. Grosu, R. Hettler, H. Hussmann, D. Nazareth, F. Regensburger, and K. Stølen. The Requirement and Design Specification Language SPECTRUM — An Informal Introduction (2 parts). Technical Report TUM–I9311/9312, TU München, 1993.

[BL91] S. Brass and U.W. Lipeck. Semantics of Inheritance in Logical Object Specifications. In C. Delobel, M. Kifer, and Y. Masunaga, eds., *Deductive and Object-Oriented*

Databases (DOOD'91), pages 411–430. Springer, LNCS 566, 1991.

[BL92]   S. Brass and U.W. Lipeck. Generalized Bottom-Up Query Evaluation. In A. Pirotte, C. Delobel, and G. Gottlob, eds., *Advances in Database Technology – EDBT'92*, pages 88–103. Springer, LNCS 580, 1992.

[BNST91] C. Beeri, S. Naqvi, O. Shmuelli, and S. Tsur. Set Constructors in a Logic Database Language. *Journal of Logic Programming*, 10(3):181–232, 1991.

[CG92]   S. Conrad and M. Gogolla. An Annotated Bibliography on Object-Orientation and Deduction. *ACM SIGMOD RECORD*, 21(1):123–132, 1992.

[CGH92]   S. Conrad, M. Gogolla, and R. Herzig. TROLL *light*: A Core Language for Specifying Objects. Informatik-Bericht 92–02, TU Braunschweig, 1992.

[CGT89]   S. Ceri, G. Gottlob, and L. Tanca. What You always wanted to Know About Datalog (And Never Dared to Ask). *IEEE Transaction on Knowledge and Data Engineering*, 1(1):146–166, 1989.

[CGT90]   S. Ceri, G. Gottlob, and L. Tanca. *Logic Programming and Databases*. Springer New York, 1990.

[CKW89]   W. Chen, M. Kifer, and D.S. Warren. HiLog as a Platform for Database Languages (or why predicate calculus is not enough). In D. Stemple R. Hull, R. Morrison, ed., *Proc. Int. Workshop on DB Programming Languages*, pages 315–329. Kaufmann, 1989.

[Con94]   S. Conrad. On Certification of Specifications for TROLL *light* Objects. In F. Orejas, ed., *Proc. 9th Workshop on Abstract Data Types – 4th Compass Workshop (WADT/Compass'92*. Springer, LNCS, 1994.

[Deu90]   O. Deux. The Story of O_2. *IEEE Transaction on Knowledge and Data Engineering*, 2(1):91–108, 1990.

[EFH83]   H. Ehrig, W. Fey, and H. Hansen. ACT ONE: An Algebraic Specification Language with Two Levels of Semantics. Technical Report 83-03, Technische Universität Berlin, 1983.

[EGH92]   G. Engels, M. Gogolla, U. Hohenstein, K. Hülsmann, P. Löhr-Richter, G. Saake, and H.-D. Ehrich. Conceptual modelling of database applications using an extended ER model. *Data & Knowledge Engineering, North-Holland*, 9(2):157–204, 1992.

[EGS90]   H.-D. Ehrich, J. A. Goguen, and A. Sernadas. A Categorial Theory of Objects as Observed Processes. In J.W. deBakker, W.P. deRoever, and G. Rozenberg, eds., *Proc. REX/FOOL Workshop*, pages 203–228, Noordwijkerhood (NL), 1990. LNCS 489, Springer, Berlin.

[Gau84]   M.-C. Gaudel. A First Introduction to PLUSS. Technical Report, Université de Paris-Sud, Orsay, 1984.

[GCH93]   M. Gogolla, S. Conrad, and R. Herzig. Sketching Concepts and Computational Model of TROLL *light*. In A. Miola, ed., *Proc. 3rd Int. Conf. Design and Implementation of Symbolic Computation Systems (DISCO'93)*, pages 17–32. Springer, Berlin, LNCS 722, 1993.

[GH91]   M. Gogolla and U. Hohenstein. Towards a Semantic View of an Extended Entity-Relationship Model. *ACM Trans. on Database Systems*, 16(3):369–416, 1991.

[GW88]   J.A. Goguen and T. Winkler. Introducing OBJ3. Research Report SRI-CSL-88-9, SRI International, 1988.

[HCG94]   R. Herzig, S. Conrad, and M. Gogolla. Compositional Description of Object Communities with TROLL *light*. In C. Chrisment, ed., *Proc. Basque Int. Workshop on Information Technology (BIWIT'94): Information Systems Design and Hypermedia*, pages 183–194. Cépaduès-Éditions, Toulouse, 1994.

[Heu89]   A. Heuer. A Data Model for Complex Objects Based on a Semantic Database Model and Nested Relations. In S. Abiteboul, P.C. Fischer, and H.-J. Schek, eds., *Proc. Nested Relations and Complex Objects in Databases*, pages 297–312. Springer, LNCS 361, 1989.

[HM81]   M. Hammer and D. McLeod. Database Description with SDM: A Semantic Database

Model. *ACM Trans. on Database Systems*, 6(3):351–386, 1981.

[HS91]   A. Heuer and P. Sander. Classifying Object–Oriented Query Results in a Class/Type Lattice. In B. Thalheim, J. Demetrovics, and H.-D. Gerhardt, eds., *Math. Fundamentals of Database Systems MFDBS*, pages 14–28. Springer, LNCS 495, 1991.

[JSH91] R. Jungclaus, G. Saake, T. Hartmann, and C. Sernadas. Object-Oriented Specification of Information Systems: The TROLL Language. Informatik-Bericht 91-04, TU Braunschweig, 1991.

[KL89]   M. Kifer and G. Lausen. F-Logic: A Higher-Order Language for Reasoning About Objects, Inheritance, and Scheme. In *ACM SIGMOD Conf. on Management of Data*, pages 134–146, 1989.

[KLW90] M. Kifer, G. Lausen, and J. Wu. Logical Foundations of Object–Oriented and Frame–Based Languages. Informatik-Manuskript 3/1990, University of Mannheim, 1990.

[Kup90] G. Kuper. Logic Programming with Sets. *Journal of Computer and System Sciences*, 41(1):44–64, 1990.

[LK86]   P. Lyngbaek and W. Kent. A Data Modeling Methodology for the Design and Implementation of Information Systems. In K.R. Dittrich and U. Dayal, eds., *Proc. of the Int. Workshop on Object-Oriented Database Systems (California)*, pages 6–17, 1986.

[LSV90] E. Laenens, D. Sacca, and D. Vermeir. Extending Logic Programming. In *ACM SIG-MOD Conf. on Management of Data*, pages 184–193, 1990.

[LV90]   E. Laenens and D. Vermeir. A Fixpoint Semantics for Ordered Logic. *Journal of Logic and Computation*, 1(2):159–185, 1990.

[LV91]   E. Laenens and D. Vermeir. On the Relationship between Well–Founded and Stable Partial Models. In B. Thalheim, J. Demetrovics, and H.-D. Gerhardt, eds., *Math. Fundamentals of Database Systems MFDBS*, pages 59–73. Springer, LNCS 495, 1991.

[NT89]   S.A. Naqvi and S. Tsur. *A Logical Language for Data and Knowledge Bases*. Computer Science Press, 1989.

[PA86]   P. Pistor and F. Andersen. Designing a Generalized NF2 Model with an SQL-Type Language Interface. In W. Chen, G. Gardarin, and S. Ohsuga, eds., *Int. Conf. on Very Large Data Bases VLDB*, pages 278–285. Kaufmann, 1986.

[Pau90] L.C. Paulson. Isabelle: The Next 700 Theorem Provers. In P. Odifreddi, ed., *Logic and Computer Science*, pages 361–385. Academic Press, 1990.

[SS86]   H.-J. Schek and M.H. Scholl. The Relational Model with Relation-Valued Attributes. *Information Systems*, 11(2):137–147, 1986.

[STV91] F. Staes, L. Tarantino, and B. Verdonk. A Logic Approach for Supporting Queries in Object Oriented Databases. In F. Van Assche, B. Moulins, and C. Rolland, eds., *Proc. IFIP Working Conf. on the Object–Oriented Approach in Information Systems*, pages 193–208. North–Holland, 1991.

[STVV91] F. Staes, L. Tarantino, B. Verdonk, and D. Vermeir. Supporting User Interaction with OODB's: A Declarative Approach. In D. Karagiannis, ed., *Proc. Int. Conf. on Database and Expert System Applications (DEXA'91)*, pages 210–215. Springer, 1991.

[Ull91] J.D. Ullman. A Comparison of Deductive and Object-Oriented Database Systems. In C. Delobel, M. Kifer, and Y. Masunaga, eds., *Deductive and Object-Oriented Databases (DOOD'91)*, pages 263–277. Springer, LNCS 566, 1991.

[VHG93] N. Vlachantonis, R. Herzig, M. Gogolla, G. Denker, S. Conrad, and H.-D. Ehrich. Towards Reliable Information Systems: The KORSO Approach. In C. Rolland, F. Bodart, and C. Cauvet, eds., *Proc. 5th Int. Conf. on Advanced Information Systems Engineering (CAiSE'93)*, pages 463–482. Springer, Berlin, LNCS 685, 1993.

[Zan90] C. Zaniolo. Object Identity and Inheritance in Deductive Databases — an Evolutionary Approach. In W. Kim, J.-M. Nicolas, and S. Nishio, eds., *Proc. Int. Conf. on Deductive and Object-Oriented Databases (DOOD'89)*, pages 7–24. North–Holland, 1990.

DISTRIBUTED
DATABASE SYSTEMS

Jupiter/MDD : The Jupiter Interoperator Multidatabase Dictionary

John Murphy,
Dublin City University,
Dublin 9, Ireland.
E-mail: jmurphy@ca.dcu.ie

Jane Grimson,
Trinity College Dublin,
Dublin 2, Ireland.
grimson@cs.tcd.ie

Abstract

This paper describes the formal model of the dictionary component of the Jupiter Interoperator using the Z notation. The Jupiter Interoperator is a system which supports interoperability between a federation of autonomous heterogeneous database systems. A feature of Jupiter is that it has been constructed with reference to a formal framework which allows us to model applications, system components and data models in the formalism. We develop the basic state model for Jupiter/MDD and we describe a subset of the operations available.

KEY WORDS: MULTIDATABASE, DICTIONARY, FORMAL MODEL, FEDERATED

1 Introduction and Motivation

Formal techniques in software development have been controversial; advocates assert that they revolutionise software development and detractors claim they are impossibly difficult to use [10]. It has been claimed that a major benefit of formal methods is that they make a designer think very hard about the system which is to be specified [12]. An important application of Formal Methods will be the modelling of legacy applications [3]. Legacy applications are often impossible to rewrite for cost reasons and integrating these systems with other systems is a difficult and expensive task. While legacy systems may be impossible to bring into a *Laboratory* type environment for studying, we propose that a formal model of such a system can simplify the integration process and facilitate a precise understanding of the legacy application. Whether the integration solution is a *gateway*, a *data warehouse* or a *federation* a formal model will clarify many aspects of the integration process.

Our motivation comes from Legacy Applications in Health-care Computing environments which typically consist of a heterogeneous collection of autonomous information systems. These range from centralised hospital-wide systems such as patient administration systems to departmental systems such as pharmacy stock-control, laboratory information systems, accident and emergency systems and so on. Many of these applications have been operational for many years and are difficult to integrate and virtually impossible to rewrite.

The major contribution of the Jupiter project is that we are attempting to model the Legacy Systems Environment along three related dimensions in a *uniform* formal framework. These dimensions are : the Legacy Application dimension, i.e. the formal models of the enterprises legacy systems; the Model/Language dimension, i.e. the formal model of the database model and database language; and the Subsystem dimension, i.e. the formal descriptions of the subcomponents which support interoperability between legacy applications. A great deal of useful work can be done using formal models to understand properties of legacy systems along these dimensions before constructing systems to facilitate interoperability between them.

The work in the field on multidatabase, federated and heterogeneous systems is characterised by the diversity of techniques and approaches taken [1, 2, 4, 5, 6, 8, 9, 11, 13, 14, 15, 16, 17, 18, 21, 25, 26]. In this paper we illustrate the approach by constructing a formal model of the Jupiter dictionary Jupiter/MDD, i.e. we specify a subcomponent on the Subsystem dimension. Thus we have a model of the language, its underlying semantics and algebra, and in the same formalism a model of an important system component.

The dictionary specification is developed, as would be expected without reference to any particular implementation considerations. The dictionary could be implemented from the specification in a number of environments and is thus *implementation independent.* In [19, 20] we discuss the primary advantages that accrue from the use of Formal Methods.

2 Jupiter Given Sets

The development of the specification proceeds from the definition of some *given* sets, i.e. sets which are of interest but where we are not concerned with the internal structure of the sets. The given sets we will use are:

[*USER*, *HOST*]

The given set *USER* is the set of all possible users from which the users and database administrators will take their identifiers. As the set is a given set we are not worried about whether the elements of the set are *names* which are strings or *identifiers* which may be numbers. The only property which is relevant is that each element of the set USER will represent a federation user.

We will assume that the set named RELATION contains all of the valid relations in all databases in the federation. This assumption is made on the grounds of simplification: we do not want to have to over-specify the Z schemas in the dictionary specification. A function *RELID* is defined in the first Z schema and is used to uniquely identify each relation in the federation, the argument to the function is an *IDENT* and we will not clutter the specification by concerning ourselves with the possible internal structure of elements of IDENT, i.e. a structure which designates a pathway to a relation (MDB.DB.R). Thus, we are allowed to

```
┌─ JILschema ──────────────────────────────────────────────
│  Expschema : IDENT ⇸ 𝔽 IDENT
│  Fedschema : IDENT ⇸ 𝔽 IDENT
│  Federation : 𝔽 HOST
│  Location : IDENT ⇸ HOST
│  Relid : IDENT ⇸ RELATION
├──────────────────────────────────────────────────────────
│  ran Location ⊆ Federation
│  dom Location = dom Relid ∪ dom Expschema ∪ dom Fedschema
│  ∪(ran Fedschema) ⊆ dom Expschema
│  ∪(ran Expschema) ⊆ dom Relid
└──────────────────────────────────────────────────────────
```

Figure 1: The *JILSCHEMA* Z schema

use *RELATION* in our specification of the data dictionary component; additionally we allow access to any of the properties defined for a relation r (r : RELATION), i.e. *schema(r)*, *ext(r)* denoting the schema and extension of a relation respectively.

The resources of the federation, i.e. relations and export and federation schemas, are accessible to federation users who have certain privileges over the resources. The privileges are defined by *PRIV* :

$$PRIV \ == \ export\_rel \ | \ list\_rel \ | \ upd\_exp \ | \ list\_exp \ | \ rem\_exp \ | \ export\_exp$$
$$| \ del\_exp \ | \ rem\_fed \ | \ list\_fed \ | \ del\_fed \ | \ none \ | \ query\_fed \ | \ upd\_fed$$

These privileges are discussed in detail in section ??.

As is usual in this type of formal specification we present first of all the *state space of the system*. The state space will be represented in terms of two Z schemas: *JILschema* and *JILuser*. *JILschema* will specify and constrain information relating to *HOSTs*, *Export Schemas*, *RELATIONs* and *Federation Schemas*.

3 Jupiter Dictionary State Spaces

Now that we have outlined and motivated the formal approach and defined the relevant given sets. We are in a position to describe the state space of the system. The first state space is called *JILschema* and it defines the relationship between hosts, schemas and relations. We will define a second state space which will describe the relationships between different classes of users and the access they have to dictionary resources , i.e. export schemas, federation schemas and relations, this schema is known as *JILuser*. Eventually we will combine the the Z schemas *JILschema* and *JILuser* in our final state space *JUPMDD*. The state space *JILschema* contains a number of *declarations* above the middle line of the schema and below the line is a list of predicates which constrain and interrelate the declarations. For example, *Expschema* is declared as a partial function from identifiers which represent the name of an export schema to a *set* of identifiers representing the relations which are elements of a particular export schema. *Fedschema* is a partial function from identifiers which name export schemas in the federation, to a set of identifiers denoting the export schemas which constitute a particular federation schema. *Relid* maps relation identifiers to relations. In database terminology, *Fedschema*, *Expschema* and *Relid* represent the mapping from federation schemas to export schemas and subsequently to relations.

The declaration *Federation* is a finite set of HOSTs and the elements of this set are the current participant hosts in the federation. Every object of interest in the federation, i.e. *Relations*, *Export schemas* and *Federation schemas* is assumed to have a unique identifier which can be used as an argument to the partial function *Location* to determine the location of the object, i.e. its host. The constraint part of the schema is the list of predicates below the middle line. The first constraint states that:

The location (the host) of every federation object is a member of the set of federation participants, **Federation**

The second constraint specifies that the domain of the partial function *Location* is equal to the union of the domains of the partial functions *Relid*, *Expschema* and *Fedschema*. This is what we would expect as location information is required for all federation objects.

The third constraint states that the distributed union of the range of *Fedschema* is a subset of the domain of Expschema. That is, the only valid components of a federation schema are those export schemas which can be mapped using *Expschema*. We use the distributed union operator, $\cup$, as the range of *Fedschema* is a set of sets.

The last constraint in the *JILschema* Z schema states that the only valid components of an export schema are relations which can be mapped to from *Relid*. Again the distributed union operator is used as the range of *Expschema* is a set of sets.

The second state space that is defined in the Federation Dictionary specification is *JILuser*. This Z schema describes information relating to classes of users. The primary classes of users are database administrators and ordinary users. These sets of users are disjoint, that is, it is not possible for a federation user to be a DBA and an ordinary user at the same time.

In the declaration part of the Z schema *JILuser*, the set of all users in the federation *User*, is defined. This set contains elements from the given set *USER*. The set of federation users *User* is partitioned into the two sets *DBA* and *nonDBA* representing database administrators and ordinary users respectively. The first four constraints in the schema assert that DBAs and non-DBAs are federation users and that the union of these sets equals the set of all known federation users *User*. Also, the intersection of *DBA* and *nonDBA* is the null set indicating that they are disjoint.

The partial function *Group* designates groups of users, it will be useful in the formal specification to be able to manipulate a group of users simultaneously. The partial function *Owner* maps the identifier of a federation object to a single user, that is, the user having

```
┌─ JILuser ─────────────────────────────────────────────────────────
│ User : 𝔽 USER
│ DBA : 𝔽 USER
│ nonDBA : 𝔽 USER
│ Group : USER ⇸ 𝔽 USER
│ Owner : IDENT ⇸ USER
│ Access : USER ⇸ 𝔽 IDENT
│ Userpriv : USER → (PRIV ⇸ 𝔽 IDENT)
├───────────────────────────────────────────────────────────────────
│ DBA ⊆ User
│ nonDBA ⊆ User
│ nonDBA ∪ DBA = User
│ nonDBA ∩ DBA = ∅
│ ran Owner ⊆ User
│ dom Group ⊆ nonDBA
│  ∪(ran Group) ⊆ nonDBA
│ dom Userpriv = nonDBA
└───────────────────────────────────────────────────────────────────
```

Figure 2: The *JILUSER* Z schema

ownership rights over the federation object. The range of *Owner* is constrained to be a subset of the set of known federation users. The set of users which has privileges over federation resources is exactly equal to the the set of nonDBA users. Every resource is *owned*, i.e. the domain of *Owner* is equal to the union of the domains of *Relid*, *Expschema* and *Fedschema*. also, the resources which users have privileges over is exactly equal to the set of resources which are owned.

There is a relationship between the declarations in the state spaces *JILschema* and *JILuser*. The state space *JUPMDD* is defined using *JILschema* and *JILuser* and specifies relationships between the declarations in each schema. *JUPMDD* contains in its declaration part the names of the schemas *JILschema* and *JILuser*, that is, it incorporates these schemas and states additional constraints and declarations. An additional declaration *Hostuser* appears and this is a partial function which maps users to the host which they are associated

```
┌─ JUPMDD ──────────────────────────────────────────────────────────
│ JILschema
│ JILuser
│ Hostuser : USER ⇸ HOST
├───────────────────────────────────────────────────────────────────
│ dom Owner = dom Relid ∪ dom Fedschema ∪ dom Expschema
│  ∪(ran ran Userpriv) = dom Owner
│ ran Hostuser ⊆ Federation
│ dom hostuser = User
└───────────────────────────────────────────────────────────────────
```

Figure 3: The *JUPMDD* Z schema

```
┌─ Create_Host ─────────────────────────────────────────────
│ Δ JILschema
│ Ξ JILuser
│ h? : HOST
│ u? : USER
├───────────────────────────────────────────────────────────
│ Precond
│ h? ∉ Federation
│ u? ∈ DBA
│ Transform
│ Federation' = Federation ∪ {h?}
│ No state change
│ Expschema' = Expschema
│ Fedschema' = Fedschema
│ Location' = Location
│ Relid' = Relid
└───────────────────────────────────────────────────────────
```

Figure 4: The Create Host Z schema

with in the federation. The constraint part of the *JUPMDD* schema specifies that all of the objects in the federation have an owner and that the only objects which can be accessed by a federation user are objects which have been defined in the federation. The set of hosts to which the users in the federation are mapped is a subset of *Federation*, the set of participant hosts. All users are mapped to a single participant host, this assumes that a user cannot be a user at two or more hosts in the federation.

4   Jupiter/MDD Z Operation Schemas

4.1   Host Operation schemas

Now that the state space of the Z specification has been defined the specification of the operations which manipulate the state space can begin, i.e. we have formally defined the static aspects of the Jupiter Dictionary state space and we can begin the process of formally defining the dictionary operations. We will not specify all of the operations available in Jupiter/MDD for space reasons.

Our first operation schema specifies the action of adding a new host to the federation. The first two lines below the centre line of the Z schema *Create_Host* are *pre-conditions* and the first pre-condition asserts that the proposed new host $h?$ is not an existing participant of the federation. The input is decorated by a ? and the output (if any) is decorated by a ! as is the usual Z convention. We would like to have some control over the creation of new federation hosts and the second pre-condition states that the user $u?$ must be a database administrator, i.e. a member of the set *DBA*. The transformational part of the

```
┌─ Delete_Host ──────────────────────────────────────────────
│ ΔJUPMDD
│ h? : HOST
│ u? : USER
├────────────────────────────────────────────────────────────
│ Precond
│ h? ∈ Federation
│ u? ∈ DBA
│ Hostuser(u?) = h?
│ Transform
│ Federation' = Federation \ {h?}
│ Location' = Location ▷ {h?}
│ Hostuser' = Hostuser ▷ {h?}
│ Fedschema' = Location⁻¹(| {h?} |) ◁ Fedschema
│ Expschema' = Location⁻¹(| {h?} |) ◁ Expschema
│ User' = User \ {u : USER | Hostuser(u) = h?}
│ Relid' = dom(Location ▷ {h?}) ◁ Relid
│ Userpriv' = dom(Hostuser ▷ {h?}) ◁ Userpriv
│ Group' = dom(Hostuser ▷ {h?}) ◁ Group
│ Owner' = dom(Hostuser ▷ {h?}) ◁ Access
└────────────────────────────────────────────────────────────
```

Figure 5: The *Delete Host* Z schema

schema starts below the word *transform* in the predicate part of the schema. The only action or transformation assertion is the addition of the new host to the federation. The assertion states that the after-state *Federation'* is equal to the union of the before-state *Federation* and $\{h?\}$, the singleton set containing precisely the host we want to add to the federation. The *No state change* part of the schema asserts that there is no change to the mappings *Expschema*, *Fedschema*, *Location* and *Relid*. The fact that there is no change in these mappings is asserted by stating that the after-state of each mapping is the same as the before-state.

In the declaration part of the schema (above the middle line) we define the state space operated on by *Create_Host*. The definition of each operation has to include declarations of both before and after-states. To avoid having to write these declarations in full for each operation schema we prefix the schema state space name with Δ, e.g. ΔJILschema, this denotes a schema which contains both before and after state components. The Ξ*schemaname* notation declares a schema state space's before and after-states but with the constraint that the after-states are equal to before-states, i.e. there are no updates. When we use the 'Δ' notation in a declaration we assert that there will be a state transformation and when we use 'Ξ' we assert that there will be no state changes.

The operation for removing a host from a federation is somewhat more complicated and as this operation is more pervasive the declaration part of the schema declares ΔJUPMDD. Removing a host requires two input parameters: the name of the host $h?$ and the user who is removing the host $u?$. The pre-condition states the host is required to be an existing member of the federation and that the user removing the host is a DBA *and* a registered user of the host which is to be removed. This constraint means that only *local* DBAs can remove a host from the federation. The transformation part of the schema is more complicated than that of *Create_Host*. The first predicate in the transformation part states that the after-state *Federation'* is equal to the before-state with the host $h?$ removed. The second transformation predicate uses the range subtraction operation (see appendix for definition of range subtraction, $\triangleright$ and the relational image operation, $(\!|\!|)$) to assert that the after-state *Location'* is equal to the before-state restricted to those mappings which do not include $h?$ as their second component, i.e. the after-state of *Location* has no knowledge of resources which were made available to the federation by the removed host. *Hostuser* is a partial function which maps each user in the federation to their corresponding host. When a particular host is removed we will want to remove all knowledge of the users associated with that host. The after-state of *Hostuser* is equal to its before-state with the removed host subtracted from its range. *Relid* is the function which maps identifiers to relations in the federation and once a host has been removed we require that all knowledge of its relations be removed from the mapping *Relid*. The after-state *Relid'* is equal to the before-state minus the mappings concerning relations located at the host being deleted, i.e. $h?$. User groups which have been defined at a deleted host are also removed. The after-state Group' is equal to the before-state with user groups from the deleted host removed from its domain. *Hostuser* $\triangleright \{h?\}$ restricts *Hostuser* to those mappings which have $h?$ as a second component, i.e. representing all of the users and user groups at $h?$. When a host is removed from the federation we no longer require knowledge of ownership of the resources it has contributed to the federation and consequently we remove this information from its domain. The after-state *Owner'* is equal to the before-state with the resources from $h?$ removed from its domain.

We make no mention of what happens to the sets *DBA* and *nonDBA* in the operation *Delete_Host*. A consequence of the invariants in *JILuser* and *JILschema* is that we can deduce the fact:

*If all of the users (**User**) are removed which are associated with a deleted host then this implies the removal of **DBA** and **nonDBA** users which are associated with the deleted host.*

1. The after state *User'* in the operation schema is :

$$User \setminus \{u : USER \mid Hostuser(u) = h?\}$$

   i.e. all users are removed as:

$$\mathrm{dom}\, Hostuser = User \qquad\qquad Invariant\ JUPMDD$$

2. All DBAS associated with the deleted host are removed as $DBA \subseteq User$ is an invariant of *JILuser* and all nonDBAs are likewise removed as $nonDBA \subseteq User$ is also and invariant of *JILuser*.

From this example it can be seen that it is possible to infer properties of the dictionary system from the specification.

```
┌─ Create_Export ──────────────────────────────────────────
│ ΔJUPMDD
│ h? : HOST
│ u? : USER
│ i? : IDENT
│ exp_rels? : 𝔽 IDENT
├──────────────────────────────────────────────────────────
│ Precond
│ (u? ∈ DBA
│ ∨ (exp_rels? ⊆ Owner(u?) ∧ exp_rels ⊆ Userpriv u? export_rel)
│ h? ∈ Federation
│ i? ∉ dom Expschema
│ Hostuser(u?) = h?
│ Transform
│ Expschema' = Expschema ⊕ {i? ↦ exp_rels?}
│ Owner' = Owner ∪ {(i?, u?)}
│ Location' = Location ∪ {(i?, h?)}
│ Userpriv' = Userpriv ⊕ {(u, p, fi) : USER × PRIV × 𝔽 IDENT |
│             u ∉ DBA ∧ u = u? ∧ (p = export_exp ∨ p = list_exp)
│             • (u, p, fi ∪ {i?})}
│ No state change
│ Fedschema' = Fedschema
│ Federation' = Federation
│ Relid' = Relid
│ Hostuser' = Hostuser
│ User' = User
│ Access' = Access
│ Group' = Group
└──────────────────────────────────────────────────────────
```

Figure 6: The *Create Export* Z schema

4.2 Export Schema Operations

In order for federation participants to be able to make visible the information they would like to share we define the operation for creating an export schema. In this section we specify a number of dictionary operations for the maintenance of export schemas.

The information which a federation user is willing to share is described by an *export schema*. Export schemas are a mechanism for making sharable data visible in the federation. Export schemas are constructed from the relations a federation user is willing to share and *federation schemas* are constructed from export schemas and provide the mappings which support interoperability across multiple export schemas. Users and DBAs can create export schemas at a given host by providing a name for the export schema and a set of identifiers denoting the component relations in the export schema. The security restrictions for this operation are that the user is either the local DBA or has owner and export authority over the component relations (pre-condition 1). *Userpriv* is a curried function and *Userpriv u p* returns the set

---
$\_$ Delete_Export $\_$
$\Delta JUPMDD$
$h? : HOST$
$u? : USER$
$i? : IDENT$

$Precond$
$h? \in Host$
$i? \in \text{dom } Expschema$
$((Owner(i?) = u? \wedge i? \in Userpriv \ u? \ del\_exp) \vee u? \in DBA)$
$Hostuser(u?) = h?$
$Transform$
$Expschema' = \{i?\} \triangleleft Expschema$
$Fedschema' = Fedschema \oplus \{(i, e) : IDENT \times \mathbb{F} IDENT \ |$
$\qquad\qquad Fedschema(i) = e \wedge i? \in e \bullet (i, e \setminus \{i?\})\}$
$Location' = \{i?\} \triangleleft Location$
$Owner' = \{i?\} \triangleleft Owner$
$Userpriv' = Userpriv \oplus \{(u, p, fi) : USER \times PRIV \times \mathbb{F} IDENT \ |$
$\qquad\qquad i? \in fi \bullet (u, p, fi \setminus \{i?\})\}$
$No \ state \ change$
$User' = User$
$Federation' = Federation$
$Hostuser' = Hostuser$
$Relid' = Relid$

Figure 7: The *Delete Export* Z schema

of federation objects over which user u has privilege p. The host, $h?$, at which the export schema is being created must be a registered host, i.e. a member of the federation. The name of the new export schema must be unique, that is there is no other export schema in the federation which has the same name ($i?$). The constituent relations of the new export schema must all be *known* relations which are defined in the federation, this constraint is implied by pre-condition 1 as dom *Relid* $\subseteq$ dom *Owner*.

The transformation part of the schema describes the state changes which occur if the pre-conditions are satisfied, namely the addition of knowledge to the dictionary regarding the contents, ownership and location of the export schema. The user who creates the export schema is granted initial privileges for including the export schema in a federation schema (export_exp) and for viewing the export schema (list_exp).

Deletion of an export schema can only be invoked by a DBA or by the user who owns the export schema if they have delete privilege on the export schema. Using the domain subtraction operation, $\triangleleft$, the export schema identified by $i?$ is removed from the *Expschema* mapping. The deleted export schema may itself be a component of a number of federation schemas in which case it is removed from these federation schemas (line 2 transformation part of the schema). The function override operation, $\oplus$, is used to set the after-state *Fedschema'* to the before-state *Fedschema*, except where a federation schema in the before-

---
__ *Create_Federation* _____

$\Delta JUPMDD$
$h? : HOST$
$u? : USER$
$i? : IDENT$
$Fed\_exps? : \mathbb{F}\ IDENT$

Precond
$h? \in Federation$
$i? \notin$ dom *Fedschema*
$Fed\_exps? \subseteq$ dom *Expschema*
$(u? \in DBA \vee (Fed\_exps? \subseteq Userpriv\ u?\ export\_exp)$
$Hostuser(u?) = h?$
Transform
$Fedschema' = Fedschema \oplus \{i? \mapsto Fed\_exps?\}$
$Owner' = Owner \oplus \{i? \mapsto u?\}$
$Location' = Location \oplus \{i? \mapsto h?\}$
$Userpriv' = Userpriv \oplus \{(u, p, fi) : USER \times PRIV \times \mathbb{F}\ IDENT\ |$
$\qquad\qquad u? \notin DBA \wedge u = u? \wedge Userpriv\ u\ p = fi\ \wedge$
$\qquad\qquad (p = list\_fed \vee p = query\_fed) \bullet (u, p, fi \cup \{i?\})\}$
No state change
$Expschema' = Expschema$
$Federation' = Federation$
$Relid' = Relid$
$Hostuser' = Hostuser$
$User' = User$

Figure 8: The *Create Federation* Z schema

state contains the deleted export schema in which case the federated schema maps to a set of export identifiers *excluding* the deleted export schema identifier. The domain subtraction operation is again used to remove the location and ownership knowledge about the deleted export schema from the dictionary. The privileges other users had over the deleted export schema are removed by the mapping transformation in the predicate part of the Z schema :

$$Userpriv' = Userpriv \oplus \{(u, p, fi) : USER \times PRIV \times \mathbb{F}\ IDENT\ |$$
$$i? \in fi \bullet (u, p, fi \setminus \{i?\})\}$$

4.3 Federation Schema Operations

The operation of creating a federation schema is invoked by a user who has access to the component export schemas and has permission to include these export schemas in a federation schema (*export_exp*). The federation schema is created at the host at which the user is registered. A DBA can create a federation schema with any available export schemas whereas ordinary users can only create a federation schema from export schemas they have

$$
\begin{array}{l}
\rule{0pt}{0pt} \\
\underline{\quad Create\_User} \\
\Delta JUPMDD \\
u_1? : USER \\
u_2? : USER \\
h? : HOST \\
\hline
Precond \\
u_1? \in DBA \\
u_2? \notin User \\
Hostuser(u_1?) = h? \\
Hostuser(u_2?) = h? \\
Transform \\
Hostuser' = Hostuser \oplus \{u_2? \mapsto h?\} \\
nonDBA' = nonDBA \cup \{u_2?\} \\
Userpriv' = Userpriv \oplus \{(u_2?, none, \varnothing)\} \\
No\ state\ change \\
Expschema' = Expschema \\
Fedschema' = Fedschema \\
Federation' = Federation \\
Location' = Location \\
Relid' = Relid \\
DBA' = DBA \\
Group' = Group \\
Owner' = Owner
\end{array}
$$

Figure 9: The *Create User* Z schema

been granted access to. The export schema identifiers in the input set *Fed_Exps* must all be registered export schemas, i.e. members of the domain of the mapping *Expschema*. If the pre-conditions are met the operation specifies that the *Fedschema* mapping is overridden ($\oplus$) by the maplet from the federation schema identifier $i?$ to the set of its component export schema identifiers *Fed_Exps*. Also, the knowledge that the user invoking the operation is the owner of the new federation schema is recorded by the transformation $Owner' = Owner \oplus \{i? \mapsto u?\}$. The location of the new federation schema is also recorded and the user is granted an initial set of privileges over the new federation schema.

4.4 User Schema Operations

In this section we describe the operations available in the dictionary for the management of *users*, individuals who are registered to the dictionary and who are allowed to invoke the operations provided by Jupiter/MDD depending on the privileges they have. We describe two simple operations for the addition of new users (*Create_User*) and the deletion of users (*Delete_User*).

```
┌─ Delete_User ──────────────────────────────────────────
│ ΔJUPMDD
│ u₁? : USER
│ u₂? : USER
│ h? : HOST
├────────────────────────────────────────────────────────
│ Precond
│ u₁? ∈ DBA
│ u₂? ∈ nonDBA
│ Hostuser(u₁?) = h?
│ Hostuser(u₂?) = h?
│ Transform
│ Hostuser' = {u₂?} ◁ Hostuser
│ nonDBA' = nonDBA \ {u₂?}
│ Owner' = Owner ▷ {u₂?}
│ Userpriv' = {u₂?} ◁ Userpriv
│ Group' = Group ⊕ {(u, fu) : USER × 𝔽 IDENT |
│                  Group(u) = fu ∧ u₂? ∈ fu • (u, fu \ {u₂?})}
│ Userpriv' = {u₂?} ◁ Userpriv
│ No state change
│ Expschema' = Expschema
│ Fedschema' = Fedschema
│ Federation' = Federation
│ Location' = Location
│ Relid' = Relid
│ DBA' = DBA
└────────────────────────────────────────────────────────
```

Figure 10: The *Delete User* Z schema

Create_User is a dictionary operation which allows the DBA at a particular host create a new user identified by u_2? at that host. The identifier u_2? must not be the identifier of an existing federation user. The host h? must be a member of the federation and this is implicit in the precondition $Hostuser(u_1?) = h$?, as ran $Hostuser \subseteq Federation$ is an invariant of the Z state space schema *JUPMDD*. This is another example of reasoning from already known properties of the specification to implicit properties. The transformation part of the schema shows the modification of the mapping *Hostuser* to record the knowledge of the location of the new user; and the knowledge that the new user is an ordinary user, that is, a *nonDBA*.

5 Conclusions

This paper presented the formal specification of a subcomponent of the Jupiter Interoperator, i.e. Jupiter/MDD the multidatabase dictionary component for legacy applications in the Health-care computing environment. We have shown only a subset of the operations from the specification, in particular we have not shown the operations for access control, security, federation DBAs, bindings and other auxiliary operations. We are currently developing a framework for formal systems development in a legacy systems environment and we reiterate our view here that legacy systems can be characterised along three dimensions: the legacy applications themselves; the models and languages which are used to express these applications; and the system subcomponents which support interoperability. We have developed a formal semantics of the Jupiter Interoperator Language, JIL. Embedded in this semantics is a novel multirelational algebra which is the subject of a forthcoming paper. Our future and continuing work relates to the completion of our formal model; the extension of this model to heterogeneous database languages; and the implementation of the Interoperator itself using a CORBA based architecture, i.e. Iona Technologies' ORBIX system.

References

[1] E. Bertino. Integration of heterogeneous data repositories by using object-oriented views. In *Proc. 1st workshop on interoperability in Multidatabase systems*, pages 22–29, Kyoto, Japan, April 1991.

[2] Y. Brietbart and L. Tieman. *ADDS: Heterogeneous and distributed database system.* North-Holland Publishing Co. The Netherlands, 1985.

[3] M. Brodie. The promise of distributed computing and the challenges of legacy information systems. In *Proceedings of IFIP DS5 Semantics of Interoperable Database Systems*, pages 1–25, Lorne, Victoria, Australia, November 1992.

[4] C. Chung. Dataplex: A heterogeneous distributed database management system. Technical Report GMR-5973, General Motors Research Laboratories, 1987.

[5] C. Chung. Datapiex: An access to heterogeneous distributed databases. *Communications of The ACM*, 33(1):70–80, 1990.

[6] Shen Collet, Nuhns. Resource integration using a large knowledge base in carnot. *IEEE Computer*, January 1991.

[7] A. Diller. *Z : An Introduction to Formal Methods.* John Wiley, 1990.

[8] G. Thomas et al. Heterogeneous distributed database systems for production use. *ACM Computing Surveys*, 22(3):237–266, 1990.

[9] M. Castellanos F. Saltor and M. Garcia-Solaco. Suitability of dat models as canonical models for federated databases. In Amit P. Sheth, editor, *SIGMOD Record*, number 4, pages 44–48. ACM Press, 1991.

[10] A. Hall. Seven myths of formal methods. *IEEE Software*, pages 11–19, September 1990.

[11] N. Roussopulos J. Grant, W. Litwin and T. Sellis. Query languages for relational multidatabases. *VLDB Journal*, 2:153–171, 1993.

[12] R. Kemmerer. Integrating formal methods into the development process. *IEEE Trans. Soft.*, pages 37–50, September 1986.

[13] William Kent. The breakdown of the information model in multi-database systems. In Amit P. Sheth, editor, *SIGMOD Record*, number 4, pages 10–15. ACM Press, 1991.

[14] W. Kim and J. Seo. Classifying schematic and data heterogeneity in multidatabase systems. *IEEE Computer*, December 1991.

[15] W. Litwin. The future of heterogeneous databases. In *Proceedings of the Fall Joint Computer Conference*, Dallas, Texas, October 1987.

[16] W. Litwin. An overview of the multi-database manipulation language mdsl. In *Proceedings of the IEEE*, pages 621–632, May 1987.

[17] W. Litwin and A. Abdellatif. Multidatabase interoperability. *IEEE Computer*, December 1986.

[18] D. Chen A. Dao S. Lund E. MacGregor M. Templeton, D. Brill and R. Ward. Mermaid: A front-end to distributed heterogeneous databases. *Proc. IEEE Special Issue on Distributed Database Systems*, 75(5):695–708, 1987.

[19] John Murphy and Jane Grimson. An Object Model in Z. *Database Technology*, 4(4):297–304, 1992.

[20] John Murphy and Jane Grimson. Formal Specification of a Persistent Object Manager. *Information and Software Technology*, 35(7), 1993.

[21] A. Sheth and J. Larson. Federated database sytems for managing distributed, heterogeneous, and autonomous database systems. *ACM Computing Surveys*, 22(3):183–236, 1990.

[22] J. Spivey. An Introduction to Z and Formal Specifications. *Software Engineering Journal*, 4:40–50, 1987.

[23] J. Spivey. *Understanding Z : A Specification language and its formal semantics*. Cambridge Tracts in Theoretical Computer Science 3, 1992.

[24] J. Spivey. *The Z Notation : A Reference Manual, Second Edition*. Prentice Hall International, 1992.

[25] R. Rosenberg T. Landers. *An overview of Multibase*. North-Holland, 1982.

[26] Susan Urban and Jian Wu. Resolving semantic heterogeneity through the explicit representation of data model semantics. In Amit P. Sheth, editor, *SIGMOD Record*, number 4, pages 55–58. ACM Press, 1991.

[27] J.B. Wordsworth. *Software Development with Z : A Practical Approach to Formal Methods in Software Engineering*. Addison–Wesley, 1992.

Building component schemata of an heterogeneous federated database with the IFO$_2$ model.

Christian SOUTOU

U.R.A.CO.M. - 9, Avenue de l'Europe - 31527 Ramonville St-Agne. FRANCE
E-mail : uracom@cict.fr   Fax : (33)-61-75-50-25.

ABSTRACT. *The bottom-up development process of an heterogeneous federated database schemata is divided into four steps. The first one consists in translating a local schema into a common data model. This paper offers a method to transform a relational schema into an equivalent object-oriented (OO) one. The purpose of our work is to improve the communication between different databases administrators when analysing and comparing schemata, two stages which precede schemata integration. The common data model we are using is the IFO$_2$ model (Poncelet et al.,1993a). We translate a relational schema into three stages : deduction of the basic types, deduction of edges and functions, deduction of fragments.*

KEY WORDS : *relational and Object-Oriented schema, federated database, IFO$_2$ model.*

1. Introduction

The interoperability is the concept which releases the user from the technological constraints inherent to computer systems. The main idea consists in offering the user universal and transparent access to these information. A lot of constructors and programmers have already designed some tools in order to promote the interoperability, notably between their own softwares and some of the greater standards on the market. One of the aims of distributed databases and specifically federated ones is, partly, to answer to this interoperability. A federated database is a compromise between non-integration (for which the user has to connect to a unique database at a time) and a whole integration (for which the autonomy of each component does not exist and the user manages data access through a global schema). A federated database allows existing databases to cooperate through five levels of schemata (Sheth et al., 1990). Upstream these implementation problems, the information must be described in these different levels. The bottom-up process used to design federated database schemata includes the four steps we described below.

-1- Translation of local database schemata into a common data model.
-2- Division of available information to the users of the federated database.
-3- Integration of the schemata to export.
-4- Definition of the views assigned to the users.

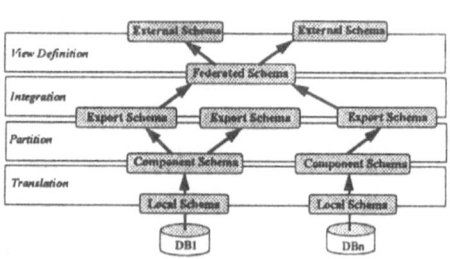

Our study is based on the first of these four phases and then consists in deducing from local schemata the component schemata in the common data model environment. The process we propose is related to "*Reverse Database Engineering*" (Whang et al.,1992). We have chosen an heterogeneous context made up of relational and object-oriented database managing system (DBMS). Though the OO DBMS have not got the extent and maturity of their predecessors yet because of incompatibility (Kim,1993), most relational DBMS constructors propose object extensions of their SQL today. We present a methodology to transform a relational schema into an equivalent OO one. The purpose of our work is double :

- ensure timelessness of relational databases which are susceptible of being transformed into OO databases;
- improve the communication between the different administrators of heterogeneous local databases by facilitating the analysis and comparison of schemata in an identical field in order to integrate them.

The common data model of an heterogeneous federated database must offer local database administrators a real help owing to its textual and graphic formalization. We have chosen the IFO_2 model (Teisseire et al.,1992), (Poncelet, 1993a & b). The object approach offers some advantages to database designers. The schema of an object database is easy to understand : the inheritance concept permits to factorize the properties in classes. The object identity notion makes the sharing of objects easier. The associations between objects are clearly represented with references between them. Complex objects are directly designed, without any decomposition.

This paper is composed of four parts. Chapter 2 refers to some works on schema transformations. Chapter 3 reminds the main characteristics of the data model IFO_2. Chapter 4 describes the process we propose to transform a relational schema into an equivalent IFO_2 schema. This method includes three steps : deduction of the IFO_2 basic types from the main relations, deduction of the edges and IFO_2 functions from the secondary relations, deduction of the IFO_2 fragments. Chapter 6 presents an example.

2. Related work

Most of the works relating scema transformations deal with database design, and precisely with the mapping of a conceptual model into a logical one. The design of a federated DBMS implements the reverse operation because the databases to integrate already exist. We refer to studies concerning the transformation of Entity-Relationship (ER) schemata and relational ones into an OO schema.

2.1 From an ER schema to an OO schema
The independence between static and dynamic aspects represents one of the limits of methods based up on the ER model. The natural objects model of Concis corporation allows to formalize dynamic object behaviour built with the enriched ER model (Robineau,1993). Moreover, the group O_2 Technology develops some tools to generate an OO schema from an ER schema automatically (Ferran,1993). However, the works using extensions of ER models are not easily exploitable because these models cannot be directly applied to logical object data models. Moreover, the ER schema must be in conformity with the physical schema of a database, which is is rarely verified.

2.2 From a relational schema to an OO schema
The schema migration could be very simple : each relation will become a class. However, we will do not use any references between classes. The BLOOD system (Descamps et al.,1990) makes the coupling between the SPOKE language and a relational DBMS. In this study and in (Fresnais,1993), each N-M association is represented with a class. Another surveys (Sull et al.,1992), (Gardarin,1994) describes the transformation of a relational schema into an oriented graph representing an OO schema more formally. The modelization is not implemented by constructors but by attributes. A semantic enrichment process of a relational schema towards BLOOM classes is proposed in (Castellanos,1993). This model takes into account rich abstractions (four kinds of specialization and three kinds of aggregation). This survey deals with an exhaustive way with the inclusion dependencies according to the nature of the attributes concerned. There is neither graphical formalism, nor mapping to a target model. (Atzeni et al.,1993) deals with many data models but do not take into account inheritance. The most

detailled survey (Chiang et al.,1994) deals with only one of kind of aggregate (we will see below that three kinds of aggregate exist).

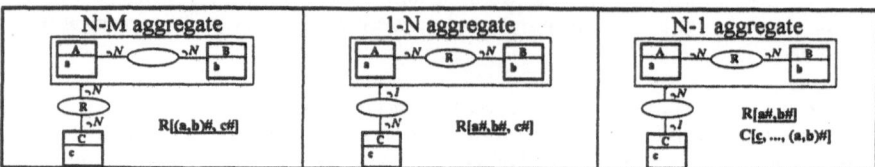

N-M aggregate	1-N aggregate	N-1 aggregate

If we take only static features (properties) into account, we can retrieve some notions formalized by the object approach such as inheritance (see 4.1.2.2) and composition in a relational schema (Soutou et al.,1993). Moreover, we can deduce an alternative structure from a relational schema (see 4.2.5). Each n-ary relation represents C_n^2 associations N-M (one association with each pair of principal relation). We stabilize the schema as follows : we regroup the main pair of principal relation by an 2-ary relation, then we connect another one to this grouping by an 2-ary relation... We obtain (n-1) 2-ary relations instead of an n-ary relation. This process enhances the integrity control and facilitates the mapping to IFO$_2$ model in translation of N-M associations.

We describe an example of unstable schema. The 3-ary relation REGISTRATION represents three N-M associations (PERSON-DIPLOMA, DIPLOMA-UNIT, PERSON-UNIT). We cannot control the integrity of this schema if a person is registered in a diploma with incorrect units. The foreign keys are noted #.

```
R =     { PERSON [CodeP, Name ...], DIPLOMA [CodeD, Designation], UNIT [CodeU, Department#]
        REGISTRATION [CodeP#, CodeD#, CodeU#]  /* 3-ary relation */
I = { REGISTRATION[CodeP] ⊆ PERSON[CodeP], REGISTRATION[CodeD] ⊆ DIPLOMA[CodeD],
        REGISTRATION[CodeU] ⊆ UNIT[CodeU] }
```

The stabilized schema has only 2-ary relations :

```
R =     { PERSON [CodeP, Name, ...], DIPLOMA [CodeD, Designation], UNIT [CodeU, Department#],
        COMPOSITION [CodeD#, CodeU#],              /* 2-ary relation */
        REGISTRATION [CodeP#, (CodeD + CodeU)#]  /* 2-ary relation */}
I=      { REGISTRATION[CodeP] ⊆ PERSON[CodeP],
        REGISTRATION[CodeD,CodeU] ⊆ COMPOSITION[CodeD,CodeU],
        COMPOSITION[CodeD] ⊆ DIPLOMA[CodeU], COMPOSITION[CodeU] ⊆ UNIT[CodeU] }
```

3. The IFO$_2$ model, reminders

The IFO$_2$ model (Teisseire et al.,1992), (Poncelet, 1993a & b) is an extension of the IFO model. This model is called intermediate because it is placed upstream physical implementation problematics and, downstream conceptual problematics. It will be carried out, in its downstream stage, automatically into a target model (O$_2$, ORION, ...). The objects are the instances of the different types presented as follow. The particularity of abstract types is that their value domain is empty : they represent an entity without any internal structure but nevertheless identifiable.

3.1 Basic types

Three basic types are proposed in that model :
- The **abstract type** (TOA);
- the **printable type** (TOP) represents the Input/Output application (attributes);
- The **represented type** (TOR) allows to handle another type through the inheritance link *IS-A*.

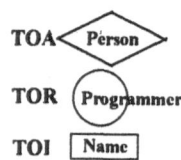

3.2 Constructors types

Five type constructors (TC) are proposed in that model which makes a distinction between an exclusive and a non-exclusive building. These constructors are orthogonal : they can be recursively applied for building more complex types. These constructors are :

- **Aggregation** which consists in regrouping different types into a new one of an upper level. From a formal point of view, an aggregate type is defined by the cartesian product of aggregated types.
- **Composition** is enriched, in relation to aggregation, with an exclusivity constraint. This one allows to verify that each object participates in the building of a unique aggregate type object.
- **Collection** represents the same type object set constructor : the collected type.
- **Grouping** is enriched, in relation to collection, with an exclusivity constraint. This one allows to verify that each object participates in the building of a unique collected type object.
- **Alternative** (union type) allows to manipulate types that are structurally different. From a formal point of view, alternative describes type unions.

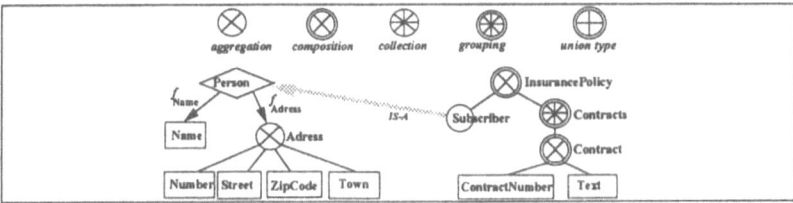

3.3 IFO$_2$ Fragments

The aim of an IFO$_2$ fragment is to describe properties of the principal type called : the heart. A schema includes many fragments linked between them with specialization links (*IS-A*). It is possible, with the represented type concept, to have an interest to only one part of the schema and to use already defined and validated components : that provides reusability and modularity in softwares.

3.4 Synthesis of IFO$_2$ model

The types could be linked by functions f (simple or complex i.e. multi-valued) if the origin is an abstract (TOA) or represented type (TOR) ; by edges if the origin is a constructor type (TC). Only the represented type can be an origin of *IS-A* links. Leaves of IFO$_2$ schemata are the printable types (TOP) linked by either function or edge. The union type represents the exclusion and totality functionnal integrity constraint (FIC) (every object of a root type participate either in an associated type, or another one, but not both (when the root type is linked to several associated types)). The *IS-A* link represents the inclusion FIC. However the IFO$_2$ model does not clearly represent the totality FIC (every object of a root type participate in one or more associated types (when the root type is linked to several associated types)). Moreover, the simultaneity CIF (every object which participate in an associated type will participate in another one) is not clearly proposed.

4. Mapping a relational schema to an IFO$_2$ schema

The mapping we propose is a three-step process (Soutou,1994) :

- The first step consists in analysing the principal relations (primary key composed of one attribute) and the n-ary relations (primary key composed of n attributes) having non-keys attributes. So, we can deduce the printable types IFO$_2$ (TOP) and the basic types IFO$_2$ (TOA, TOR, TC). In this step, we connect the TOP associated to the basic type.

- The second step consists in studying the foreign keys and the n-ary relations. We can deduce the links between IFO$_2$ basic types (mapped from principal relations). We connect these types either by IFO$_2$ edges, or IFO$_2$ functions.

- The third step consists in extracting fragments from the set of IFO$_2$ types deduced previously.

We can deduce an inheritance association and a union association from a set of relations. Our study is based on an analysis of the domain of primary keys and the inclusion dependencies between a pair of principal relations. A definition and an example are given as follows :

▪ Two principal relations $R_1[\underline{K_1},...]$ and $R_2[\underline{K_2},...]$ are inheritance associated such that :
   - K_1 and K_2 have the same domain of values;
- $R_1[K_1] \subseteq R_2[K_2]$ or $R_2[K_2] \subseteq R_1[K_1]$.

▪ Two principal relations $R_1[\underline{K_1},...]$ and $R_2[\underline{K_2},...]$ are union associated such that :
   - K_1 and K_2 have the same domain of values;
   - $R_1[K_1] \not\subseteq R_2[K_2]$ and $R_2[K_2] \not\subseteq R_1[K_1]$;
   - $R_1[K_1] \cap R_2[K_2]=\varnothing$.

Each 2-ary relation represents either an 1-1 association 1-1, or an 1-N association, or an N-M association (usually), or an inheritance association relating two principal relations.

4.1 Step 1 : Deduction of IFO$_2$ types

4.1.1 Printable types (TOP)
We deduce the IFO$_2$ printable types from non-foreign keys and artificial attributes. We regroup some attributes either in an IFO$_2$ aggregation type or an IFO$_2$ composition type. "Aerodrome" contains "RunwayLenght",

Aerodrome [OACIcode, AerodromeName, Adress, RunwayLenght, Orientation, Altitude]

OACIcode   Location   Substructure
AerodromeName   Adress   RunwayLenght   Orientation   Altitude

"Orientation" and "Altitude" which we regroup into the IFO$_2$ aggregation type "Substructure". If we consider that an object cannot occur in several constructions, we use the IFO$_2$ type composition (here "Location").

4.1.2 non-printable types
Each non-printable IFO$_2$ types deduced from a relation may be connected to an IFO$_2$ basic type (TOA, TOR, TC). The printable types become the object type component of this IFO$_2$ basic type.

4.1.2.1 Creation of abstract types (TOA)
We infer an abstract type from a principal relation when it is neither in N-1 association, in inheritance association, nor in union association with another principal relation. We map a relation to an IFO$_2$ abstract type (TOA) in three steps :

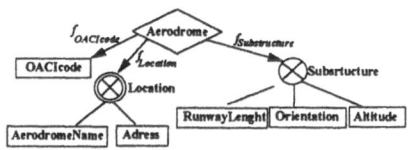

- assignment of the relation name to the abstract type name;
- creation of printable types and associated aggregates;
- creation of functions connecting the abstract type to the printable types.

4.1.2.2 Creation of represented types (TOR)
We infer a represented type from a principal relation when it is in inheritance association with another principal relation. We map a relation to an IFO$_2$

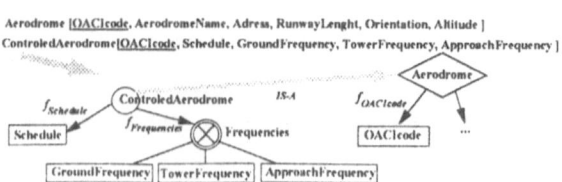

represented type (TOR) in four steps :

- assignment of the relation name to the represented type name;
- creation of printable types and associated aggregates;
- creation of functions connecting the abstract type to the printable types;
- creation of *IS-A* link(s).

The inclusion dependency following ControledAerodrome[OACIcode] ⊆ Aerodrome[OACIcode] allow us to deduce an inheritance association relating these principal relations.

4.1.2.3 Creation of constructors types (TC)

We infer a constructor type from a principal relation when it is either in N-1 association, or in union association and it is not in inheritance association with another principal relation. We deduce the kind of this constructor in the

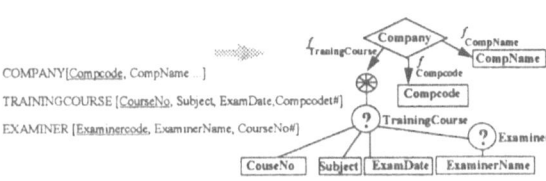

COMPANY[Compcode, CompName ...]

TRAININGCOURSE [CourseNo, Subject, ExamDate,Compcodet#]

EXAMINER [Examinercode, ExaminerName, CourseNo#]

second step (see 4.2).We map a relation to an IFO₂ constructor type in three steps :

- assignment of the relation name to the constructor type name;
- creation of printable types and associated aggregates;
- creation of edges connecting the constructor type to the printable types.

In this exemple, we deduce two IFO₂ constructor types from the principal relations EXAMINER and TRAININGCOURSE which are respectively in N-1 association with TRAININGCOURSE and COMPANY.

4.2 Step 2 : Deduction of edges and functions

In this chapter, we map all the associations in the relational schema to the IFO₂ model. We deduce the IFO₂ edges and functions from the associations (1-1, 1-N, N-M, inheritance and union). We examine each pair of relations (noted R_1 and R_2).

4.2.1 1-1 Associations

The figure describes the feasible 1-1 associations with the IFO₂ model. We propose our solutions for the impossible cases in converting one (or two) IFO₂ basic type(s).

4.2.1.1 Transformed cases : 1-1 (TOA,TOA) associations

We transform an 1-1 (TOA,TOA) association either to an 1-1 (TOA,TC) association or 1-1 (TOA,TOR) association. In the first case, we convert the TOA deduced from R_1 into a TC. We connect the abstract type deduced from R_2 to this TC by a function. In the second case, we convert the TOA deduced from R_1 into a TOR. We connect the abstract type deduced from R_2 to this TOR by a function. We apply an *IS-A* link from R_1 to a new generic type. Another solution consists in merging the TOAs. This is possible if the objects of the included type are not referenced in other types. We convert the included type into a constructor type. The result is an 1-1 (TOA,TC) association.

The figure illustrates two principal relations (STUDENT, TRANINGCOURSE) 1-1 associated. In order to avoid an 1-1 (TOA,TOA) association 1-1, we transform the abstract type "Student" into a represented type.

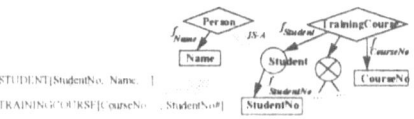

STUDENT[StudentNo, Name, ...]

TRAININGCOURSE[CourseNo ... StudentNo#]

We create a generic type "Person" with an *IS-A* link. The result is an 1-1 (TOA,TOR) association. The function $f_{Student}$ connects the abstract type to the new represented type.

4.2.1.2 1-1 (TOA,TOR) associations
The relation R_1 is inheritance associated. We deduce a function connecting the abstract type to the represented type. See the previous example describing an 1-1 (TOA, TOR) association with "TrainingCourse" and "Student".

4.2.1.3 1-1 (TOA,TC) associations
This case is the more frequent in an IFO_2 schema. We deduce a function connecting the abstract type to the constructor type. The example describes an 1-1 (TOA,TC) association with "Student" as TOA and "TrainingCourse" as TC. The created function is $f_{TrainingCourse}$.

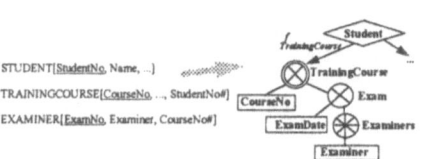

STUDENT[StudentNo, Name, ...]
TRAININGCOURSE[CourseNo, ..., StudentNo#]
EXAMINER[ExamNo, Examiner, CourseNo#]

4.2.1.4 Transformed cases : 1-1 (TOR,TOA) associations
A TOR is linked with a TOA in a particular case (see reciprocal link in the definition of IFO_2 fragments (Poncelet et al,1993a)). We adopt the 1-1 (TOA,TOR) association by creating a function which connects the abstract type to the represented one. The figure illustrates an 1-1 (TOA,TOR) with "Student" as TOA and "TrainingCourse" as TOR. The function we define is $f_{TrainingCourse}$.

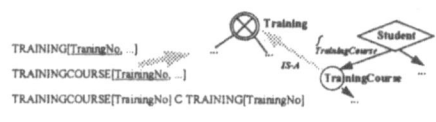

TRAINING[TraningNo, ...]
TRAININGCOURSE[TrainingNo, ...]
TRAININGCOURSE[TrainingNo] C TRAINING[TrainingNo]

4.2.1.5 Transformed cases : 1-1 (TOR,TOR) associations
An IFO_2 schema is composed of several fragments related by *IS-A* links. If we connect two TOR (belonging by definition to separate fragments), we have to merge the two types into a unique fragment. The solution consists in converting one of the two TOR into a constructor type (aggregation or composition). The consequence is the lost of the initial *IS-A* link. Then, we define in the new TC, a component (represented type) in order to maintain the pre-existing *IS-A* link (see figure 4.2.1.8).

4.2.1.6 1-1 (TOR,TC) associations
We deduce a function connecting the represented type to the constructor type. The figure illustrates an example of 1-1 (TOR,TC) with "Student" as TOR and "TrainingCourse" as TC. The function we define is $f_{TrainingCourse}$.

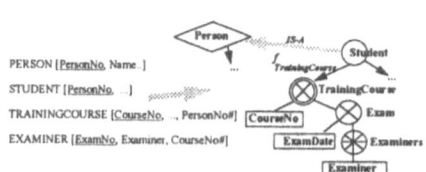

PERSON [PersonNo, Name]
STUDENT [PersonNo, ...]
TRAININGCOURSE [CourseNo, ..., PersonNo#]
EXAMINER [ExamNo, Examiner, CourseNo#]

4.2.1.7 Transformed cases : 1-1 (TC,TOA) associations
We transform these associations in 1-1 (TOA,TC) associations. The reason is that TC types are either target of functions or source of edges to another TC or TOR. We define a function from the TOA to the TC (see figure 4.2.1.3).

4.2.1.8 1-1 (TC,TOR) associations
We define these associations by defining an edge from the constructor type to the represented one. The figure illustrates an 1-1 (TC,TOR) association with "Student" as TC (the STUDENT relation is N-1 associated with

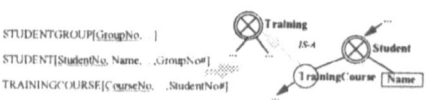

STUDENTGROUP[GroupNo,]
STUDENT[StudentNo, Name, ,GroupNo#]
TRAININGCOURSE[CourseNo, ,StudentNo#]

STUDENTGROUP) and "TrainingCourse" as TOR. The edge created goes from the constructor type to the represented one.

4.2.1.9 1-1 (TC,TC) associations

We create an edge connecting the two constructor types deduced from the principal relations (R_1 and R_2). Suppose a Training course is defined as §4.2.1.3, we will connect the constructor type "Student" to the constructor type "TrainingCourse" by an edge.

4.2.2 1-N Associations

The figure describes the feasible 1-N associations with the IFO$_2$ model. We propose our solutions for the impossible cases in converting one (or two) IFO$_2$ basic type(s).

Particular cases : reflexives associations (see appendix 6.1.2.).

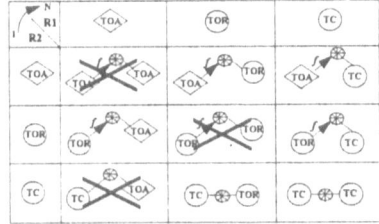

4.2.2.1 Transformed cases : 1-N (TOA,TOA) associations

We transform an 1-N (TOA,TOA) association either to an 1-N (TOA,TC) association or an 1-N (TOA,TOR) association. In the first case, we convert the TOA deduced from R_1 (for example) into a TC and we connect to it the abstract type deduced from R_2 (see 4.2.2.3). In the second case, we define a new TOR which compound one of the two TOA. We connect the abstract type upgraded to this TOR by a complex function. The 1-N association between the two TOA is acheived by this complex function via a *IS-A* link.

The following figure illustrates two principal relations (DRIVER and CAR) 1-N associated. In order to avoid an 1-N (TOA,TOA) association, the TOR we define

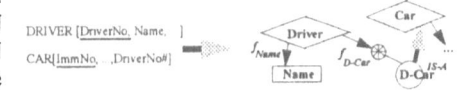

is "D-Car". "Driver" and "Car" are 1-N associated by the complex function $f_{D\text{-}Car}$ via the *IS-A* link.

4.2.2.2 1-N (TOA,TOR) associations

The relation R_1 is inheritance associated. We deduce a complex function connecting the abstract type to the represented type. See the previous example describing an 1-N (TOA,TOR) association with "Driver" and "D-Car".

4.2.2.3 1-N (TOA,TC) associations

This case is the more frequent in a IFO$_2$ schema. We deduce first the kind of the constructor type. The TC is a collection or a grouping IFO$_2$ type. Then, we create a function connecting the abstract type to the constructor one.

The example describes two 1-N (TOA,TC) associations with "Driver" as TOA and "Cars" as grouping constructor type. For the associated printable types (TOP) we define a complex function from the TOA ($f_{FirstName}$).

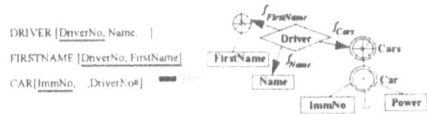

4.2.2.4 1-N (TOR,TOA) associations

This case is impossible because we do not map a principal N-1 associated relation into a TOA (see 4.1.2.1).

4.2.2.5 Transformed cases : 1-N (TOR,TOR) associations

The reason of this transformation is explained 4.2.1.5. We connect the non-converted TOR to the new TC by a complex function. The result is a 1-N (TOR,TC) or (TC,TOR) association.

4.2.2.6 1-N (TOR,TC) associations

We deduce first the kind of the constructor type (aggregation or composition). Then ,we create a complex function which connects the abstract type to the constructor one.

4.2.2.7 1-N (TC,TOA) associations

This case is impossible because we do not map a principal N-1 associated relation into a TOA.

4.2.2.8 1-N (TC,TOR) associations

We deduce first the kind of the constructor type (aggregation or composition). Then, we create an edge connecting the constructor type to the represented one via a collection or a grouping type.

4.2.2.9 1-N (TC,TC) associations

We deduce first the kind of the constructor types (one of them must be either a collection or a grouping type, the other must be either an aggregation or a composition type). Then, we create an edge connecting the two constructor types.

4.2.3 N-M Associations

The following figure describes the feasible N-M associations with the IFO_2 model. We propose our solutions for the impossible cases in converting one (or two) IFO_2 basic type(s).

Particular cases : N-M associations with properties (see appendix 6.2.2.2).

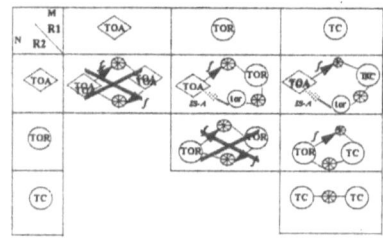

4.2.3.1 Transformed cases : N-M (TOA,TOA) associations

We transform an N-M (TOA,TOA) association either to an N-M (TOA,TC) association, or via a TOR. In the first case, we convert the TOA deduced from R_1 (for example) into a TC. Then, we

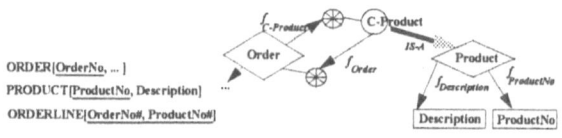

ORDER[OrderNo, ...]
PRODUCT[ProductNo, Description]
ORDERLINE[OrderNo#, ProductNo#]

connect the abstract type deduced from R_2 to this TC (see 4.2.3.3). In the second case, we define a new TOR which compound one of the two TOA. We connect the abstract type upgraded to this TOR by a complex function. The N-M association between the two TOA is acheived by two complex function via a IS-A link. The following figure illustrates two principal relations (DRIVER and CAR) 1-N associated. In order to avoid an 1-N (TOA,TOA) association, the TOR we define is "D-Car". "Driver" and "Car" are 1-N associated by the complex function $f_{D\text{-}Car}$ via the IS-A link.

4.2.3.2 N-M (TOA,TOR) and (TOR,TOA) associations

We deduce two complex functions connecting the represented type to the abstract type and vice-versa.

4.2.3.3 N-M (TOA,TC) and (TC,TOA) associations

We deduce first the kind of the constructor type (aggregation or composition type) and we define a complex function connecting the the abstract type to the constructor type. Then, we implement a new TOR (which compound the constructor type). This TOR gives a way to link the constructor type to the abstract type via a collection (if the TC is an aggregation) or a grouping type (if the TC is a composition).

4.2.3.4 Transformed cases : N-M (TOR,TOR) associations

The reason of this transformation is explained 4.2.1.5. The TOR component gives a way to link the new TC to the non converted TOR via a collection (if the TC is an aggregation) or a grouping type (if the TC is a composition). The result is a N-M (TOR,TC) or (TC,TOR) association.

4.2.3.5 N-M (TOR,TC) and (TC,TOR) associations

We deduce first the kind of the constructor type (aggregation or composition type). Then, we implement a complex function which connects the TOR to the TC and a constructor (collection if the TC is an aggregation, or grouping type if the TC is a composition) which connects the TC to the TOR via a *IS-A* link.

4.2.3.6 N-M (TC,TC) associations

We deduce first the kind of the two constructor types (aggregation or composition). Then, we implement a constructor for both of them (collection if the TC is an aggregation, or grouping type if the TC is a composition) which connects the two TC via a *IS-A* link. See 6.3 an example of N-M (TC,TC) association between "Order" and "Product".

4.2.3.7 Particular N-M associations (n-ary relations, n>2)

See chapter 2 the three kinds of aggregate, we propose to represent these particular N-M associations with multple inheritance. The entities of the agggregate are A, B, C. The link between the aggregate and the third entity is defined by an association (1-N, N-1, N-M) between the basic type representing this entity and the basic type representing the aggregate.

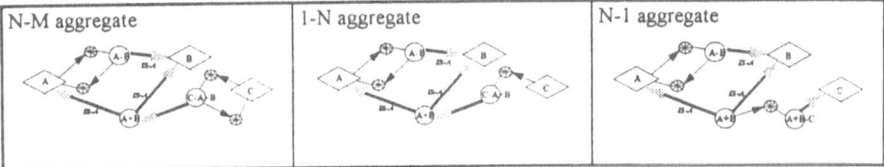

| N-M aggregate | 1-N aggregate | N-1 aggregate |

4.2.4 Inheritance associations

The figure describes the feasible inheritance associations with the IFO$_2$ model.

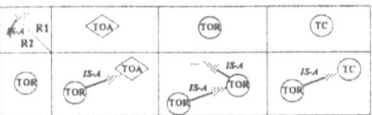

4.2.4.1 (TOR,TOA) Inheritance

This case is the more frequent in an IFO$_2$ schema. We define the inheritance from a represented type to an abstract type by creating an *IS-A* link. This link goes from the IFO$_2$ TOR deduced from R$_2$ to the IFO$_2$ TOA deduced from R$_1$. See the example 4.1.2.2.

4.2.4.2 (TOR,TOR) Inheritance

We define the inheritance related to two represented type by creating an *IS-A* link. This case corresponds to several levels of specialization (see appendix 6.3).

4.2.4.3 (TOR,TC) Inheritance

We define the inheritance from a represented type to a constructor type by creating an *IS-A* link. We deduce here the kind of the constructor type (aggregation, composition, union type).

346

4.2.5 Union associations

Several relations may be in union associations. In this case, we study each pair according to their IFO_2 basic types deduced. The figure describes the feasible union associations with the IFO_2 model. We propose our solutions for the impossible cases in converting one (or two) IFO_2 basic type(s).

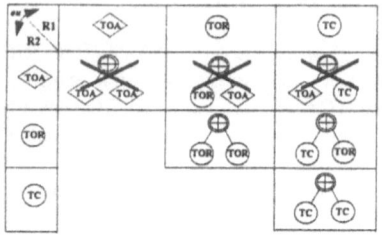

In order to conform to the IFO_2 model, we convert TOA either in TOR or TC by using principles described before.

4.3 Step 3 : Deduction of IFO_2 fragments

This step consists in extracting fragments from the set of IFO_2 types deduced previously. The aim of the fragment is to describe properties of the principal type called heart (see 3.4). An IFO_2 fragment is a graph H=(X,A) with X the set of types and A the set of fragments links, the root of H is the heart of the fragment.

4.3.1 Process

The aim of the process we propose is to verify the following properties :
- An IFO_2 schema is a set of fragments related with *IS-A* links.
- For each link connecting the heart to a represented type (TOR), there is a reciprocal function.

First, we regroup in sets the IFO_2 types deduced previously without taking into account the *IS-A* links. In order to verify the second property, in particular cases we create an IFO_2 function connecting a TOR to an abstract type.

4.3.1.1 Creation of a fragment with a reciprocal function

Each TOA becomes a root of a fragment and we regroup the types which are connecting directly or indirectly to it by edges or functions (but not by *IS-A* link). For each function connecting the TOA to a represented type, we add the reciprocal function to the IFO_2 schema.

The example illustrates two IFO_2 heart types ("Vehicle" and "Driver"). We give the name of the hearts to the fragments. The reciprocal function we create is f_{Driver}.

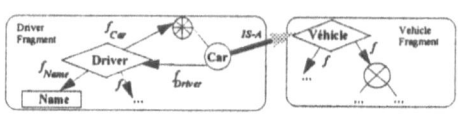

4.3.1.2 Creation of a fragment without a reciprocal function

Each constructor type target of one (or more) of *IS-A* link(s) becomes root of a fragment. Each constructor root of a direct tree having a source type of one (or more) *IS-A* links becomes root of a fragment. In both cases we assign the name of the constructor to the name of the fragment.

The types which are connecting directly or indirectly to its constructor by edges or functions (but not by *IS-A* link) become types of the fragment. We do not add any reciprocal function. The example describes three IFO_2 heart types ("Vehicle", "Car" and "Engine").

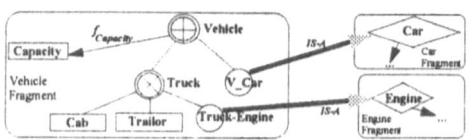

5. Conclusion and prospects

This study describes the first step of the bottom-up process to develop an heterogeneous federated database. The methodology proposed is related to a "*Reverse Database Engineering*" technology. It allows to change a relational logical (or physical) schema into an equivalent oriented-object conceptual one. The aim is to ensure Information Systems durability regarding to their evolutions or their foreseeable merging.

This paper summarizes the results of more complete and detailed researches (Soutou,1994) in which we described procedures to determine the various associations in a relational schema more formally. Based from these associations, the links between IFO_2 types have been defined. In the same way, this study presents the algorithms to implement in order to deduce IFO_2 basic types from the principal relations. The evolutions of this study will follow the bottom-up process to conceive federated database schemata, namely :
- Definition of exportation schemata (subparts of IFO_2 component schemata). The intent is to describe the information which are potentially available to a federation users. The evolution rules of an IFO_2 schema will permit to formalize allowed updates to preserve the integrity of exportation schemata.
- Integration of exportation schemata into one or more federated schemata. The aim is to propose one or more global IFO_2 schemata, without any redundancy. In order to achieve this stage, we will adjust existent methodologies which can be applied to extended ER schemata.

Acknoledgements
I would like to acknowledge Pascal Poncelet for his helpful comments on the IFO_2 model.

References :
(Atzeni et al., 1993) P.ATZENI, R.TORLONE, "A Metamodel approach for the management of multiple models and the schemes", *Journal of Information Systems*, Vol 18, N°6, 1993.

(Castellanos,1993) M.CASTELLANOS, "A Methodology for Semantically Enriching Interoperable Databases", *Proceedings of the 11th British National Conference on Databases*, Keele, 1993.

(Chiang et al.,1994) R.CHIANG, T.BARRON, V.STOREY, Reverse engineering of relational databases : Extraction of a from a relational database", *Journal of Data and Knowledge Engineering*, Vol 12, N°2. 1994.

(Descamps et al.,1990) V.DESCAMPS, C.DAMIER, G.BENSOUSSAN, L.HENNINGER, "BLOOD: extension d'un langage à objet.", *VI Journées BD Avancées*, Montpellier. 1990.

(Ferran,1993) G.FERRAN, "En attendant les vrai SGBDOO, faisons dialoguer l'objet avec le relationnel.", *Le Monde Informatique*, Mars 1993.

(Fresnais,1993) P.FRESNAIS, "Comparaison des SGBD relationnels et orientés-objets à travers une étude de cas.". *Congrès Biennal AFCET*, Versailles, 1993.

(Gardarin,1994)] G.GARDARIN, "Convergence des modèles relationnels et à objets", *Ingénierie des systèmes d'infor* N°3, Hermès, 1994.

(Kim,1993) W.KIM, "Object-Oriented Database Systems : Promises, Reality, and Future", *Proceedings of the 19th International Conference on Very Large Databases*, Dublin, 1993.

(Poncelet et al.,1993a) P.PONCELET, M.TEISSEIRE, R.CICCHETTI. L.LAKHAL, "Towards a Formal Approach for Object Database Design". *Proceedings of the 19th International Conference on Very Large Databases*, Dublin, 1993.

(Poncelet.1993b) P.PONCELET "Conception d'applications avancées : modèles, mécanismes d'évolution et dérivation", *INFORSID*, Lille, 1993.

(Robineau,1993) O.ROBINEAU. "L'objet associé au modèle entité-association", *Le Monde Informatique*, Avril 1993.

(Sheth et al.,1990) A.P.SHETH. J.A.LARSON. "Federated Database Systems for managing distributed heterogeneous and autonomous databases.", *ACM. Computing Surveys*, Vol 22, No 3, 1990. ,

(Soutou et al,1993) C.SOUTOU, M.COBOS. "SGBD Coopérants. Les étapes du développement d'une fédération". *INFORSID*, Lille. 1993.

(Soutou.1994) C.SOUTOU. "Contribution à la conception d'une base de données fédérée hétérogène. Dérivation. Evolution et Intégration de schémas.", *PH.D Thesis*, Université Paul Sabatier Toulouse. *to appear* 1994.

(Sull et al.,1992)   W.SULL, R.KASHYAP, "A Self-Organizing Knowledge Representation Scheme for Extensible Heterogeneous Information Environment", *Transactions on Software Engineering*, Vol 4, No 2, 1992.

(Teisseire et al.,1992) M.TEISSEIRE, P.PONCELET, L.LAKHAL, "IFO2, Modèle et Principe pour la Conception de Base de Données Avancées.", *VIII journées Bases de Données Avancées*, Trégastel, 1992.

(Whang et al.,1992) JW.K.WHANG, S.CHAKRAVARTHY, S.B.NAVATHE, "Heterogeneous Databases : Inferring Relationships for Merging Component Schemas, and a Query Langage.", *Research Report UF-CIS-TR-92-048*, University of Florida, 1992.

6 Appendix : Mapping a relational schema

6.1 Analysis

We deduce from the relational schema inspired from (Fresnais,1993) an equivalent component IFO$_2$ schema.

CATEGORY	(cat-No, designation, turn-over-min)
PERSON	(pers-No, name, street, no, zip-code)
PAYEE	(pers-No, payment-type)
EMPLOYEE	(pers-No, post, salary, commission, chief-No#)
CUSTOMER	(pers-No, turn-over, comment, cat-No#)
ORDER	(order-No, order-date, total, delivery-date, payee-No#, cust-No#, emp-No#)
ORDER-LINE	(order-No, product-No, quantity, sale-price, state)
FAMILY	(fam-No, designation, vat-rate)
PRODUCT	(product-No, designation, unit-price, inventory, fam-No#)

6.1.1 Inclusion dependencies

CUSTOMER(cat-No) ⊆ CATEGORY(cat-No)	ORDER(cust-No)	⊆ CUSTOMER(pers-No)
PAYEE(pers-No) ⊆ PERSON(pers-No)	ORDER(emp-No)	⊆ EMPLOYEE(pers-No)
CUSTOMER(pers-No) ⊆ PERSON(pers-No)	ORDER-LINE(order-No) ⊆ ORDER(order-No)	
EMPLOYEE(pers-No) ⊆ PERSON(pers-No)	ORDER-LINE(product-No) ⊆ PRODUCT(product-No)	
EMPLOYEE(chief-No)⊆ EMPLOYEE(pers-No)	PRODUCT(fam-No)	⊆ FAMILY(fam-No)
ORDER(payee-No) ⊆ PAYEE(pers-No)		

6.1.2 Deduction of associations

1-N associations :	N-M associations :	Inheritance associations :
(CATEGORY,CUSTOMER)	(ORDER,PRODUCT)	(PAYEE,PERSON)
(PAYEE,ORDER)		(CUSTOMER,PERSON)
(CUSTOMER,ORDER)		(EMPLOYEE,PERSON)
(EMPLOYEE,ORDER)		(EMPLOYEE,EMPLOYEE)
(FAMILY,PRODUCT)		
(EMPLOYEE,EMPLOYEE)		

6.2 Mapping to an IFO$_2$ schema

6.2.1 Step 1 : deduction of basic types

Each attribute becomes a printable type (TOP) except "chief-No" in EMPLOYEE, "cat-No" in CUSTOMER, "payee-No", "cust-No", "emp-No" in ORDER, "fam-No" in PRODUCT.
We regroup some attributes in IFO$_2$ (aggregation or composition) as follow :

IFO$_2$ composition types :	IFO$_2$ aggregation type :
- **CatType** regrouping "designation","turn-over-min" in CATEGORY;	- **Adress** regrouping "street", "no", "zip-code" in PERSON.
- **Function** : "post", "salary" and "commission" in EMPLOYEE;	
- **CustType** : "turn-over" and "comment" de CUSTOMER;	
- **Content** : "order-date", "total" and "delivery-date" in ORDER;	
- **FamType** : "designation" and "vat-rate" in FAMILY;	
- **ProdTyp** : "designation" and "unit-price" in PRODUCT.	

The following principals relations CATEGORY, PERSON et FAMILY are neither inheritance associated nor N-1 associated with an another principal relation. We deduce three IFO$_2$ abstract type **"Category"**, **"Person"** and **"Family"**. The following principal relations CUSTOMER, EMPLOYEE and PAYEE are inheritance associated with PERSON (see 4.0). We deduce three

IFO$_2$ represented types "**Customer**", "**Employee**" and "**Payee**". The relations ORDER and PRODUCT are N-1 associated with other principal relations. We deduce two IFO$_2$ constructor types "**Order**" and "**Product**". We determine the kind of these constructors during the second step (aggregation or composition type).

6.2.2 Step 2 : Deduction of edges and functions

6.2.2.1 1-N associations

We follow the process described 4.2 in order to deduce the IFO$_2$ edges and functions connecting the basic types deduced previously. We verify in this step the compatibility of the IFO$_2$ basic types linked. There is a particular 1-N association : the reflexive association in EMPLOYEE. We define a new represented type "**Boss**".

6.2.2.2 N-M associations

There is a particular N-M (TC,TC) association between "Order" and "Product" with properties (quantity, sale-price, state). See the process 4.2.3.6, the grouping type "**OrderedProducts**" and "**Pr-Orders**" give a way to connect the two TC via the TOR "**OrdredProduct**" and "**Pr-Order**".

6.2.3 Step 3 : Deduction of fragments

We create the reciprocal function $f_{Category}$ connecting "Customer" to the heart "Category". The other fragments are "Person", "Boss", "Employee", "Payee", Order and "Family".

6.3 IFO$_2$ schema

Integrating Distribution and Mobility into an Object-Oriented Database[*]

Dietmar A. Kottmann, Ludwig Keller
University of Karlsruhe, Institute of Telematics, 76128 Karlsruhe, Germany
email: [kottmann/keller]@telematik.informatik.uni-karlsruhe.de

Abstract

Most distributed database systems of today are build around a client-server paradigm. Nowadays development of distributed systems technology has gone beyond client-server systems. Especially for distributed object-oriented systems, many promising concepts have been proposed and evaluated. One of them are mobile objects. This idea has proved to be of great importance for applications that need fine grained tuning at run time. Mechanical engineering applications in the area of simultaneous/concurrent engineering call for support of this kind, as the structure and distribution of application needs often is not known when setting up the underlying database system. As on the other hand, object-oriented databases are tailored to handle the complex entities of engineering applications, integrating mobile objects into such databases is one step on the way to qualify them as a company-wide information backbone. In this paper an approach to integrate mobility in an existing object-oriented client-server system is presented. We concentrate on object management and on architectural aspects besides presenting the seamless integration of the necessary extensions to the object model in a strongly typed language.

Keywords: Distributed Systems, Object Model, Object-Oriented Databases, Distributed Databases, Mobile Objects

1.   Introduction

Distributed Database Systems employ a great number of potential advantages, cf. (Öszu et al., 1991). Numerous research projects investigated mechanisms like distributed query processing, managing distributed transactions, distributed scheduling, composing multi-databases or improving fault-tolerance through replication or reconfiguration. On the other hand, most systems are build using some kind of client-server approach.

Considering the state of the art in distributed systems technology, development has gone beyond the client-server model (Bever et al., 1993). This shift is not incorporated in todays distributed databases, as much of the novel aspects base on object-oriented technology, cf. (Chin et al.,1991). One of the most prominent features is object mobility. In a nutshell, the advantages of mobile objects include the ability to dynamically share load between processors, reducing communication cost and increasing availability through reconfiguration[1]. Furthermore this technique is a convenient way to move application data to the point where it is needed.

Mobile objects become even more important if there is only little a priori knowledge about the way and the place objects will be used by applications. Concurrent/simultaneous engineering is one example where preplanning usage patterns is doomed to fail (Kemper et al.,1990) (Hayashi, 1993). This correlates to the fact that mechanical engineering is one of the most important application domains for object-oriented database system. This observation is further strengthened by the fact

---

[*] This work was partially supported by the German Research Council (Deutsche Forschungsgemeinschaft DFG) under grant SFB 346 project A6.

[1] The advantages of mobile objects have often been discussed. For further information the reader is referred to (Black et al., 1987) (Levy et al. 1988).

that mobile persistent objects have already proved to be a useful paradigm for building applications in related fields (Black et al.,1989) (Schill, 1992).

This paper follows the sketched guideline in presenting an approach to mobilize the objects of an object-oriented database. Our goal is to build a system that qualifies for a company-wide information backbone. We know that our current work only represents the first few steps, but nevertheless the long term target plays its role in several design decisions. For example, we cannot rely on global structures, as this would defy scalability.

The presentation is organized as follows: After giving a brief introduction to our object-oriented data model in section 2, the main section 3 describes our approach to managing mobile objects inside the database and central aspects of our system architecture. In section 4 our current UNIX implementation is presented. Finally section 5 discusses related approaches and section 6 concludes with a summary and a brief outlook.

2. An Object-Oriented Model

This section first briefly introduces the basic concepts of our object-oriented data model, preparing the ground for an extension that will become important when focusing on distribution. As the discussion in this paper mainly concentrates on object management and system architecture, the presentation is restricted to those aspects having consequences for the necessary run time support. Readers interested in more details are referred to (Kemper et al.,1994).

2.1 The Basic Object Model

In essence, our object model *GOM* (Generic Object Model) provides all the compulsory features identified in (Atkinson et al.,1989) in one orthogonal syntactical framework. Objects incorporate a *structural* and a *behavioral* description. Objects with similar structure and behaviour are classified into *types*. A new object type is introduced using an *object type definition frame* (cf. the example in figure 1).

```
type tool
   supertype ANY is
      body  [ident: string;
             .... ]
      operations
            declare tool: string -> void;
            declare assign: job -> bool;
            ...
      implementation  ...
   end type tool;
```

Figure1 : An Example for an Object Type Definition.

The structural representation of a type is defined in the **body** clause. Besides tuple-structured objects, collection types (sets and lists) are part of the language. The behaviour of objects is specified by type-associated operations. The signatures of these operations, consisting of an operation name, a list of input parameter types and a result type, is contained in the **operations** clause. The operations are finally coded in the **implementation** clause, using a C-like syntax. The state of an object may only be accessed by invoking the type-associated operations. Types could be refined in a super-/sub-type taxonomy using the **supertype** clause.

Objects are created using a system-defined or type-specific constructor. An unique immutable object-identifier *OID* is assigned to each object on instantiation. The OID is independent of the object's physical address or state. Hence, objects could be understood as triples *(OID, type, state)*, where state represents the internal state, i.e., the current attribute values in case of a tuple-structured object.

GOM is designed as a strongly typed language. Hence, type conformance of operation invocations is guaranteed at compile time. As subtyping of collection types in a strongly typed language is impossible (Kemper et al.,1994), the language provides bounded polymorphic operations besides the inclusion polymorphism within the super-/sub-type taxonomy. This feature will be used in section 3.4 to minimize the compiler modifications necessary to integrate object mobility and distribution.

2.2 Active Objects

Objects are collected into an object base because of a presumed need for cooperation among them. Classically, the cooperation is initiated by synchronous calls to operations. Such a strategy requires a clear a priori understanding of how cooperation among objects contributes to the problem solution. But many modern applications such as industrial automation with their high volume of concurrent, interleaved, and iterative actions defy preplanning and call for the support of dynamic relations between objects.

Our approach to such a dynamic strategy are active objects. From the system point of view, active objects differ from their passive counterparts in having an own thread of control, comprise abilities for asynchronous communication besides synchronous invocations, and a rule system that realizes the dynamic cooperation strategy (cf. (Lockemann et al.,1993) for details). Active objects are instances of active types which may be subtypes of normal types – the reverse is forbidden. Figure 2 gives a glimpse of the most simple way (the **send** primitive) to access an active object asynchronously.

```
!! Type Declarations
type tool is ... endtype tool;
type hammer supertype tool is ... endtype hammer;
active type drilling_machine supertype tool is ... endtype drilling_machine;
...
!! Variables
persistent var mytool: tool;
persistent var myhammer: hammer;
persistent var mydrill: drilling_machine;
...
mytool := myhammer;
send mytool.assign(...); !! operation performed synchronously.
mytool := mydrill;
send mytool.assign(...); !! operation performed asynchronously.
...
```

Figure 2: Using active types.

3. Integrating Distribution and Mobility

This section first presents our basic system architecture that is designed along the guiding principle of renouncing from global structures. Afterwards we present the run time object management, necessary to mobilize active and passive objects. Finally it is shown how bounded polymorphic operations are used to realize the extensions to the object model.

3.1 System Architecture

The cornerstone of our project is to build an object-oriented database that qualifies as a company-wide information backbone for CAx-technology. As the system has to have the ability to support hundreds or thousands of nodes, the usual one-level client-server approach is unacceptable. Stretching this kind of architecture to a multi-level hierarchy still does not match many user requirements, as activities are often highly interconnected with no intrinsic hierarchical structure in their need for information and cooperation, cf. (Hayashi, 1993). This mismatch has often been identified in distributed systems projects. A promising remedy is to use loosely coupled systems, providing access transparency but no ubiquitous view of all the available information.

We follow this paradigm in composing our system from loosely coupled clusters. Each cluster is self contained, as it contains all the necessary run time support. If activities cannot be completed within a cluster, transparent access to information located outside is possible. The guiding principle of the design to renounce from using global structures is realized in fetching needed information on demand. This reflects the information needs of activities like concurrent engineering that incorporate only few preunderstanding about what information will sometimes be accessed.

3.1.1 Architecture

The resulting system architecture consists of a set of *logical nodes* and *server nodes*, as depicted in figure 3. Each logical node comprises user programs, active objects and an *endpoint mapper*, that keeps track of the active objects within the logical node. Several logical nodes are grouped into a cluster, together with a server node (hereafter called *local sever*) that provides stable storage to all entities within the cluster. Thus intra-cluster communication is far more common than inter-cluster communication. A server node can reside in the same physical address space as logical nodes of the same cluster. Clusters could be set up reflecting the physical topology of a network – e.g., a cluster for each LAN -- or administrative requirements – e.g., a data intensive application that is started in a logical node colocated to its local server in the same physical address space.

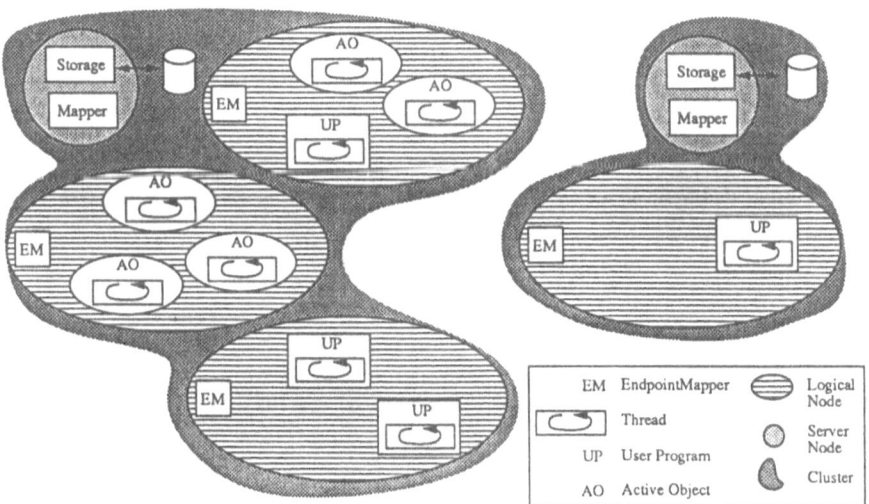

Figure 3: The basic system architecture

3.1.2 Operation invocation

Passive objects are not explicitly represented in the architecture. Their state resides on the stable storage of a server node and is mapped into the buffer of user programs on demand. The computation of a user program can span passive objects on multiple servers. This is synchronized using distributed transactions and a 2-Phase-Commit protocol. Thus, there could be copies of the state of one passive object in multiple buffers, if only read operations are performed. Each active object manages its state in a passive object with the same structural description. In order to allow active objects to rearrange operation invocations and reactions according to their dynamic cooperation strategy, they are never allocated in a buffer. Moreover, invocations are directed to a run time incarnation, using normal operation invocations or asynchronous calls on the level of the database programming language.

3.1.3 Logical vs. physical identity

On creation, the state of an object is stored in the stable storage of the local server and an unique OID is generated. The OID codes the creating cluster. Furthermore a tupel containing the OID and the physical address of the object's state on stable storage is inserted into the object table of the local server. This tuple is not forwarded to other servers. Thus the object tables of the servers normally comprise different mappings. Moreover, there is no global structure that contains the mapping from all OIDs to their physical addresses. How nevertheless transparent access is provided and object tables are lazily enlarged -- compliant to usage patterns -- will be discussed in section 3.3.

3.1.4 Transient vs. persistent internal structures

As logical nodes have no direct access to stable-storage, all persistent system- and user-information is kept on their local server. Buffers of user programs and endpoint mappers only keep transient copies of persistent information. Additionally endpoint mappers keep information about the internal structure of their logical node. This is possible as the lifetime of an endpoint mapper is limited by the lifetime of its logical node. As logical nodes normally reside on workstations, they are not persistent themselves. Rather multiple incarnations are allowed, but never more than one at each instance of time. On creating a new incarnation, the endpoint mapper starts from scratch. It fetches needed information from the local server on demand (section 3.2). This approach has the advantage that logical nodes are loosely coupled themselves, defying the need for expensive coordination protocols among them.

3.2 Mobile Active Objects

Run time incarnations of active objects are located on logical nodes. They can freely move among nodes, using a **migrate** operation (cf. section 3.4) -- e.g. to colocate active objects that will closely cooperate in the near future. We have to manage the incarnations – e.g., to route invocations to it – besides managing the persistent states. In the following we present how incarnations are managed, while the treatment of persistent information is defered to section 3.3.

3.2.1 Localization

The most vital problem in realizing mobile entities in distributed systems is their localization. Among the numerous proposed solutions, forward addressing has proved to be adequate for a broad range of usage patterns (cf. (Fowler, 1986) (Schill et al.,1993)). In this scheme, a reference to an object is directed to a location, where the object once resided. When an object migrates, a new reference is installed at its former location. If references were directed to active objects, a migration could invalidate many references. Thus references are directed to endpoint mappers that encapsulate the location within logical nodes. Generally, forwarding chains result, that may – at least theoretically – become very long. In practice, however, the expected length is below 2 (Fowler, 1986). The impact of migration on reference chains is depicted in part a and b of figure 4.

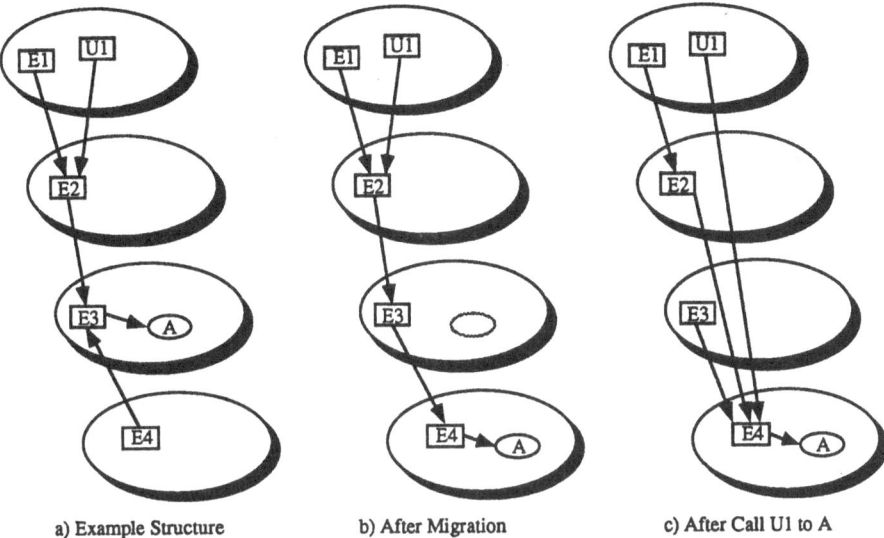

| a) Example Structure | b) After Migration | c) After Call U1 to A |

Figure 4: Using Forward References as a Method for Localizing Objects.

Now the question arises what measures should be taken to shrink the length of reference chains. Our approach is to shrink chains as a side effect of synchronous or asynchronous operation invocations. Each invocation has to be directed to the callee. As soon as the invocation is recorded at the callee, a return message is produced that follows the reverse way of the invocation and updates the intermediate forward addresses. In case of an asynchronous call we are done. In the synchronous case, the active object produces a result message, which it directly sends to the caller. Here we have 2 return messages. One that performs housekeeping on the chain and a second containing the result of the invocation which directly reaches the caller. It is possible that the caller gets the result before housekeeping has been completed. Part c of figure 4 shows the reference structure after a housekeeping operation.

As a result of this approach, references on nodes that rarely use an active object may become far out of date, whilst references on nodes with remarkable communication to the object are generally very short. This behaviour automatically adapts to the pattern, an object is used. To improve performance, references are not only stored in endpoint mappers, but are also cached in user programs or active objects (cf. the reference of user program U1 to active object A in figure 4).

3.2.2 Backup mechanism for localization

Looking back to our guiding principle of not to use persistent information solely for purposes of endpoint mappers, the problem of broken chains arises. This originates from crashes or simply from the fact, that logical nodes may be temporaly unavailable, before they reappear in a new incarnation. Thus we need a secondary mechanism for locating active objects. Here we employ the fact, that logical OIDs code the generating cluster. On migrating an active object, its new address is not only stored in the endpoint mapper, but also sent to the mapper on the local server of the cluster, the object once was created in (hereafter called birth-cluster). The mapper keeps a table of the current locations of all active objects, ever created inside its cluster. Now if an endpoint mapper couldn't reach the next one in the chain, it contacts the mapper of the object's birth-cluster to inquire its current location. Then it forwards the request to the new location and updates its reference as usual. Note that this design is not always sufficient to keep completely transparent. It may happen, that an object is physically reachable, but no operation on it could be invoked as the chain is broken and the birth-cluster is unreachable. We tolerate this behaviour, as alternative locating mechanisms that guarantee a higher degree of transparency (e.g. broadcasting) are too expensive.

The same mechanism is used to bootstrap endpoint mappers. If a user program or active objects wants to send an invocation to another active object, it first consults its local cache. If a reference is obtained, the usual forwarding procedure begins. Otherwise the local endpoint mapper is contacted. If it has a reference, we proceed as usual. Otherwise the endpoint mapper consults the mapper on the local server of the object's birth-cluster. In this way, an endpoint mapper becomes aware of new references. This strategy is not only necessary for bootstrapping endpoint mappers, but also for handling OIDs of unknown objects.

We can restate this procedure in other words to make the principles more transparent. The current address of active objects is always recorded in the mapper of the birth-cluster of an active object. To improve performance, a two-level caching strategy -- endpoint mappers and local caches -- is overlayed. The caching strategy is further improved in linking the caches of endpoint mappers through forward references, to reduce the number of remote messages[2].

3.2.3 Terminating incarnation

Due to the possible number of active objects it is impossible to have steadily run time incarnations for all of them. Each active object can decide to leave its incarnation at any time. This is possible, as the state of active objects is managed in corresponding passive objects. Nevertheless, leaving incarnations requires some housekeeping.

Terminating incarnations has to be synchronized with invocations, especially those that are on their way to the object. If an active object wants to leave its incarnation, it contacts its local endpoint mapper. If the endpoint mapper still has some outstanding calls to the object, it gives a negative acknowledge, as those calls would create a new incarnation (see below) immediately. Otherwise the endpoint mapper grants a lock for the object and records all further arriving invocations. It forwards the leave-request to the mapper of the object's birth-cluster, which notes that the object has currently no incarnation and returns an acknowledge. On receiving this acknowledge, the endpoint mapper gives the object the permission to exit its incarnation, deletes its reference for the object and finally releases the lock. Recorded invocations are treated as if they appeared after lifting the lock, which normally results in creating a new incarnation. Note that after deletion, the last endpoint mapper in the reference chains has no reference for the object any more.

Deleting an active object from the database generally proceeds along the same lines. In addition, the passive object corresponding to the active one is deleted from the database and its entry in the mapper of the object's birth-cluster is removed.

3.2.4 Creating incarnations

As noted above it is inevitable to allow active objects to sleep on stable-storage, without having a run time incarnation. As invocations to active objects only could be processed through incarnations, they have to be created somehow. The need to create an invocation occurs, when an invocation proceeds along a forward chain, reaching an endpoint mapper that has no reference for the object. The endpoint mapper is not able to tell the situation when itself has to be bootstrapped from the situation when a new incarnation has to be created. This could only be percepted through the mapper of the object's birth-cluster. Consequently – to reduce complexity –, creating incarantions should be handeled transparently to the endpoint mapper.

---

[2] Remember, that forward chains are in general shorter than 2, whilst a mapper-lookup always comprises an inquire- and a result-message.

The following procedure for creating incarnations is slightly simplified for the sake of presentation. The special case of removed objects and some issues necessary for fault-tolerance are ignored. The procedure is also depicted in figure 5.

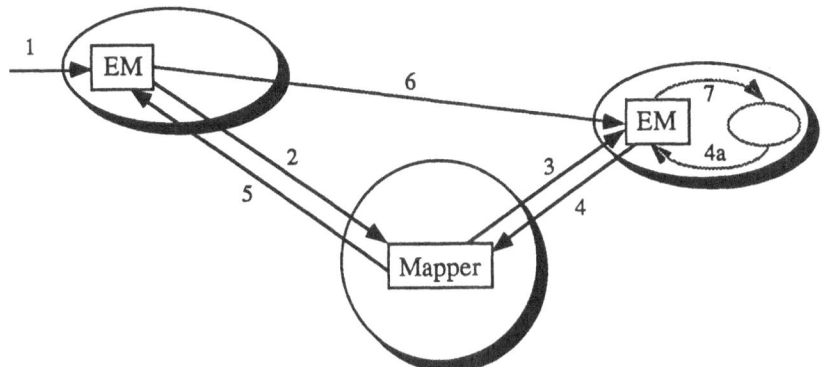

Figure 5: Creating Run Time Incarnations.

Step 1 & 2: An invocation arrives at an endpoint mapper that has no reference for the object. Thus the invocation is forwarded to the mapper of the object's birth-cluster.

Step 3: The mapper percepts that the object has no current incarnation. Thus it forwards the request to the endpoint mapper of the logical node, the object logically resides on and records that a run time incarnation exists[3]. The endpoint mapper grants a lock for the object and creates a new incarnation which is initialized.

Step 4 & 4b: Before initialization has completed, the mapper is informed that a new incarnation exists (message 4). After initialization has completed, the active object informs the endpoint mapper, so that the lock could be released (message 4a).

Step 5: The mapper returns the address of the object to the calling endpoint mapper.

Step 6: The endpoint mapper receives the new address, updates its reference and forwards the recorded invocation from step 1.

Step 7: If the lock from step 3 has already been lifted (message 4a), the invocation is immediately directed to the object. Otherwise it is queued until message 4a arrives.

Note that the endpoint mapper that stores the invocation (message 1) can't tell the mapper's answer from the case when the mapper must not create a new incarnation, but only has to reply an existing address.

The initial creation of an active object follows the same procedure. The difference occurs in step 3, when a request reaches the mapper and the mapper has no information about the active object. In this case the mapper creates an incarnation of the active object on the node, the calling sequence originated. Hence active objects are always created locally and only relocated using the migrate primitive.

---

[3] Note that objects don't move by accident. They always keep the address they were migrated to, even if they temporarily cease to have an incarnation.

3.3 Migrating Passive Objects

As most objects in the database are passive, mobilizing them is of equal importance as mobilizing active ones. Even though we generally assume that networks are transparent, their performance will become obvious at the database layer. Under the assumption, that intra-cluster communication is cheaper, passive objects should be able to move to the cluster where they will be used in the near future without loosing the ability to access them transparently from their former location. Hence the **migrate** operation is also valid for passive objects. In contrast to active objects, migration is meaningless within a cluster, as we only have one server that provides stable storage. Thus a migrate primitive specifying a logical node as its target is reinterpreted as if the server node of the target cluster would have been specified. This is transparent to the program that invokes the migration. In addition, migrating an active object implicitly migrates the passive object holding the state on behalf of the active one.

Again we use forward addressing to locate passive objects. As passive objects normally are accessed through consulting the object table on the local server, the mapping from OIDs to physical addresses has to be extended. Besides coding an address of the server´s stable-storage, a forwarding reference is regarded as a valid physical address. This reference points to a cluster, as passive objects could only be stored at server nodes. Hence the entity to be contacted is clear from the cluster address.

Again we incorporate the birth-cluster concept as a backup mechanism. This is necessary, as once again foreign OIDs could become visible through accessing objects from foreign clusters. Now we have either the possibility to install mappings for the transient closure of referenced objects in the local object table or to provide a mechanism for accessing objects that are unknown in the local table. As the former may incorporate extensive updates that might never be of use, we follow the latter concept. Once again we employ the fact, that OIDs code the birth-cluster of an object. Hence if a lookup at the local object table neither returns an address on stable storage, nor a forwarding address, we consult the object table of the creating-cluster. Migrating an object now comprises the installation of a forward pointer in the local object table and updating the object table of the object's birth-cluster.

Note that this approach once again follows the principle of lazily propagating information and renouncing from the use of global structures. In contrast to the endpoint mappers we also have the necessity to remove entries for deleted objects from the object table. For this purpose we keep deletion-logs for removed objects in the server of the birth-node cluster and use anti-entropy maintenance sessions (Golding, 1992) among servers to shrink the tables and finally remove the deletion-logs.

3.4 Implications to the Object Model

The described approach relies on **migrate** operations that must be valid for all objects. We integrated the operation as a bounded polymorphic operation inside the strongly typed framework of our language. The declaration in figure 6 is contained in a default header file which is included automatically by the compiler. Its implementation is part of the default link library. This way, we are able to enrich our language without compiler modifications.

```
polymorph declare migrate(\Typ<=ANY):\Typ // ANY -> void
    code_migrate;
```

Figure 6: Polymorphic Declaration of the **migrate** Operation.

The method is also used to answer another question: how can active objects decide on terminating their current incarnation. Here we introduced two operations along the line of the migrate operation:

sleep and **nosleep**. Normally the run time incarnation of an active object is terminated as soon, as there is no outstanding invocation or response. Using the **nosleep** operation an active object could prevent its incarnation from being terminated. This is useful, when the active object knows that it is still participating in a cooperation even if at the moment no messages are on their way. The operation increments a counter inside the run time system of the active object, that is initialized with 0 when the incarnation is created. The **sleep** operation decrements the counter. Termination only occurs if the counter is reset to 0.

4   Implementation

Implementing the presented concepts started at our existing one-level client-server prototype, which is currently used in about 20 mechanical engineering projects. Our main goal is to investigate whether our extensions are sensible and useful for engineering applications. Thus, we decided minimize changes to the existing prototype to bring the extensions to the field as soon as possible.

The one-level client-server prototype is build on top of the EXODUS storage-manager (Carey et al, 1991). This manager currently only provides one transaction per client process. Hence using lightweight processes within an address space to realize incarnations of active objects would interfere with transaction management. Furthermore, the development system we rely on -- for reasons of portability -- currently isn't able to produce thread-safe code from C++ sources -- the language employed for implementing the current run time system. Due to this limitations we decided to realize endpoint mappers, user programs and active objects as UNIX processes. To be more precise, an endpoint mapper is realized as a daemon process. Thus, a logical node currently corresponds to a workstation[4]. This rather heavyweight approach can only be justified as we are only interested in functionality and not in performance at the moment.

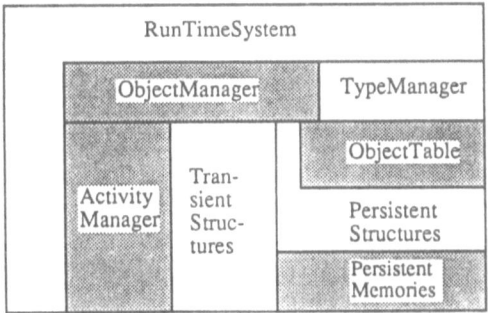

Figure 7: The modified run time system.

Figure 7 depicts the simplified structure of our run time system. In order to realize the extensions we had to modify the gray shaded modules. First, it was necessary to include a new module: the activity manager. This module realizes communication to active objects or mappers and runs the client parts of the protocols explained in section 3. Furthermore, the object manager had to be modified in order to redirect invocations of active objects to the activity manager. The persistent memory module incorporates all access operations to the storage manager and provides a buffer to map passive objects into the address space of user programs. Integrating multiple servers needs on demand buffering for each of them. Hence we modified the persistent memory module to enable communication with multiple servers, relying on the EXODUS feature to work with multiple

---

[4] It is still possible to colocate logical and server nodes.

servers. Finally, support for indirections which is necessary for realizing mobility of passive objects is included in the client side of the object table.

Besides these modifications and the realization of the daemons, slight compiler modifications were made in order to supply additional information for active objects to the run time system and to include asynchronous invocations.

5. Related Work

A number of existing approaches have been concerned with distributed object-based systems (Chin et al.,1991). We concentrate the related work to those systems that mobilize objects, as the novel aspects of our system lies in the integration of object mobility into a database system. The basic principles of distributed databases are covered in (Öszu et al, 1991). Readers interested in an overview of other problems that are currently investigated in the area of distributed database systems are referred to (Öszu et al.,1994).

Object mobility has first been treated for transient objects. The best known approach is the *Emerald* system (Black et al.,1987) (Levy et al.,1988), that supports fine-grained mobile objects in a distributed environment. It offers operations to locate and move objects explicitly and makes object invocations location transparent. A specific feature is the ability to move objects even if they are currently computing on an invocation. Moreover, mobile objects could contain internal objects that are tied and cannot be moved independently. Thus, the grain of mobility could be tailored in declaring objects as mobile or internal objects. A follow-on project of Emerald is the *Amber* system (Chase et al., 1989), that implements a distributed version of C++. Most important the architecture of Amber is tailored to use the facilities of a combination of tightly and loosely coupled multiprocessors. Using C++ as the object model rises a great number of complications that are solved in restricting the use of memory pointers within mobile objects. Other approaches that employ object mobility are *Electra* (Maffeis, 1992), *Peace* (Schröder-Preikschat, 1992), Trellis/DOWL (Achauer, 1993) and *DC++* (Schill et al.,1993). Even more systems enabling either object or process mobility in distributed systems are described in (Borghoff, 1992). A common feature of those systems is that they assume an existing incarnation able to process invocations somewhere in the system. Thus our main problem that generally only a small subset of the objects has current incarnations are unknown to those approaches.

Systems supporting mobile persistent objects are not that numerous. One of them is *Hermes* (Black et al.,1989). It employs a subset of nodes as storesites. Objects can move freely between nodes with volatile memory and can checkpoint their state and log state changes to a storesite. An object can dynamically be assigned to a different storesite. Contrary to our approach, persistency is not transparent at the object model level. The *Comandos* system (Krakowiak et al.,1990) also supports persistent objects and mobility. Application programs in Comandos are implemented in the integrated language *Guide*. Comandos includes a dynamic cluster management facility that enables to configure units of execution on runtime. Another system supporting persistent mobile objects is presented in (Schill, 1992). Besides the basic features it provides special support for accessing system objects, like printers or terminals where total transparency would become contraproductive. Neither of those systems is fully integrated inside an object-oriented database, though, some employ databases for managing their persistent components. There is no distinction between passive and active object at the type level that allows for transparent support of mobility and persistence. Consequently, the incarnation problem often appear, as persistent objects could simply be mapped into the address space of the clients. Normally, passive objects only comprise trivial operations, whereas active objects model the complex entities of the real world, which is reflected in the different run time support for both in our system. In addition, our approach of propagating information lazily is novel and leads to automatic adaption to usage patterns at run time.

6. Conclusion

The paper described the design and implementation of a system that integrates object mobility in an object-oriented database. We presented the protocols necessary for object management and the architectural concepts to enable scalability. We also showed how the extensions are seamlessly integrated into the strongly typed object model.

Future work will especially concentrate on mechanisms to propagate knowledge about the object population between clusters. Nowadays propagation relies on references and global persistent variables. Global type extensions are not supported but could be integrated by the designer of a new type in inserting each newly created instance in a set object through using type-specific constructors.

Disseminating information in big distributed systems nowaday bases on name servers or traders (ANSA, 1991). We plan to inquire how the features of traders could be exploited and integrated to solve the disseminating problem in the database system. Compared to using type extensions or global sets, this approach has the advantage, that the underlying run time protocols could be tailored especially for the propagation purpose. This was the reason why we decided not to support global type extensions. In addition the extended prototype is up to be shipped to the mechanical engineering projects in order to evaluate the usefulness of our extensions.

Acknowledgements
We thank Alfons Kemper, Christoph Kilger, Guido Moerkotte, Hans-Dirk Walter, and Andreas Zachmann for their work on the original one-level client-server prototype and the design of the GOM database language. Andreas Zachmann also modified the original compiler. Finally we are indebted to our students Thomas Arens, Arnd Grosse, Sascha Helfrich, Thomas Hübsch, Nils Lorenscheidt, Anke Otto, and Keyvan Seiraffi for their help in implementing the current system.

References

(Achauer, 1993) B. Achauer: *The DOWL Distributed Object-Oriented Language*, Communications of the ACM, Vol. 36, No. 6, Sept. 1993, pp. 48-55

(Atkinson et al.,1989): M. Atkinson, F. Bancilhon, D.J. DeWitt, K.R., D. Maier, and S. Zdonik: *The object-oriented database system manifesto*. Proc. Int. Conference on Deductive and Object-Oriented Databases, Kyoto, Japan, Dec. 1989, pp. 40-57

(ANSA, 1991): ANSA: *ANSAware 3.0 Implementation Manual*, document RM.097.01, Feb. 1991

(Bever et al., 1993): M. Bever, K. Geihs, L. Heuser, M. Mülhhäuser, and A. Schill: *Distributed Systems, OSF DCE, and Beyond*. In: A. Schill (Eds.): *DCE - The OSF Distributed Computing Environment: Client/Server Model and Beyond*, Springer, Lecture Notes in Computer Science, No. 731, Berlin, 1993, pp. 1-20

(Black et al.,1987): A. Black, N. Hutchinson, E. Jul, H. Levy, and L. Carter: *Distribution and Abstract Types in Emerald*. IEEE Transactions on Software Engineering, Vol. SE-13, No. 1, Jan. 1987, pp. 65-75

(Black et al.,1989): A. Black, and Y. Artsy: *Implementing Location Independant Invocation*. Proc. 9th Int. Conference on Distributed Computing Systems, Newport Beach, 1989, pp. 550-559

(Borghoff, 1992): U. M. Borghoff: *Catalogue of Distributed File/Operating Systems*. Springer, Berlin, 1992

(Chase et al., 1989): J.S. Chase, F.G. Amador, E.D. Lazowska, H.M. Levy, and R.J. Littlefield: *The Amber System: Parallel Programming on a Notebook of Multiprocessors*. Internal Report, Univ. of Washington, Seattle, 1989

(Chin et al.,1991): R.S. Chin, and S.T. Chanson: *Distributed Object-Based Programming Systems*. ACM Computing Surveys, Vol. 23, No. 1, Mar. 1991, pp. 91-124

(Fowler, 1986): R.J. Fowler: *The complexity of using forwarding addresses for decentralized object finding*. Proc. 5th Int. ACM Synmposium on Principles of Distributed Computation, Calgary, Canada, Aug. 1986

(Golding, 1992): R.A. Golding: *Weak-Consistency Group Communication and Membership*. Ph.D. Dissertation, University of California at Santa Cruz, Tech. Report UCSC-CRL-92-52, Dec. 1992

(Hayashi, 1993): H. Hayashi: *Manufacturing: A Preview of the 21st Century*. IEEE Spectrum, Sept. 1993, pp. 82-85

(Levy et al.,1988): E. Jul, H. Levy, N. Hutchinson, and A. Black: *Fine-Grained Mobility in the Emerald System*. ACM Tranactions on Computer Systems, Vol. 6, No. 1, Feb. 1988, pp. 109-133

(Carey et al, 1991): M.J. Carey, D.J. DeWitt, D. Frank, G. Graefe, J.E. Richardson, E.J. Shekita, and M. Muralikrishna: *The Architecture of the EXODUS Extensible DBMS*. In: K. R. Dittrich, U. Dayal, A. P. Buchmann (Eds.): *On Object-Oriented Database Systems*, Springer, Berlin, 1991

(Kemper et al.,1994): A. Kemper, G. Moerkotte: *Object-Oriented Database Management: Applications in Engineering and Computer Science*. Prentice-Hall Inc., Englewood Cliffs, New Jersey, 1994

(Kemper et al.,1990): A. Kemper, P.C. Lockemann, G. Moerkotte, H.-D. Walter, and S.M. Lang: *Autonomy over Ubiquity: Coping with the Complexity of a Distributed World*. Proc. 9th Int. Conference on the Entity Relationship Approach, Lausanne, Oct. 1990

(Krakowiak et al.,1990): S. Krakowiak, M. Meysembourg, and H. Van Nguyen: *Design and Implementation of an Object-Oriented Strongly Typed Language for Distributed Applications*. Journal of Object-Oriented Programming, Vol. 3, No. 3, Pept./Oct. 1990, pp. 11-22

(Lockemann et al.,1993): P.C. Lockemann, and H.-D. Walter: *Activities in Object Bases*. Proc. 1st Int. Workshop on Rules in Database Systems, Edinburgh, 1993

(Maffeis, 1992): S. Maffeis: *The Electra Approach to Object Oriented Programming*. Tech. Report IFI TR 92.23, Institute for Informatics, University of Zürich, 1992

(Öszu et al, 1991): T.M. Öszu, and P. Valduriez: *Principles of Distributed Database Systems*. Prentice Hall, Englewood Cliffs, 1991

(Öszu et al.,1994): T.M. Öszu, and P.Valduriez: *Distributed Data Management: Unsolved Problems and New Issues*. In: T. L. Casavant, M. Singhal: *Readings in Distributed Computing Systems*, IEEE Computer Society Press, Los Alamitos, 1994

(Schröder-Preikschat, 1992): W. Schröder-Preikschat: *PEACE -- The Evolution of a Parallel Operating System*. Reports of GMD No. 646, 1992

(Schill, 1992): A.B. Schill: *Distributed Object Management within a Loosely-Coupled Repository Environment*. Proc. OpenForum'92, Utrecht, pp. 289-304

(Schill et al.,1993): A.B. Schill, M.U. Mock: *DC++: Distributed Object-Oriented System Support on Top of OSF DCE*. Distributed Systems Engineering Journal, Vol. 1, No. 2, 1993

SCHEMA EVOLUTION
AND
ACTIVE DATA

From Conceptual Specification to Object Oriented Design

Moncef BARI

Université Paris XII - Val de Marne and
Labo MASI - IBP - CNRS UA 818
Université Pierre et Marie Curie
4 place Jussieu, F75252 Paris Cedex 05
Email : Moncef.Bari@masi.ibp.fr - Fax : + 33 1 44 27 62 86

ABSTRACT. *We present a mapping of a conceptual specification into an object oriented design product in order to build Information Systems.*
This represents part of a methodology based, for each step of the software life cycle, on (1) a model and (2) a step by step process. Thus, analysis is based on the information systems design methodology REMORA (Rolland et al., 82 & 88), design is based on a particular object model (Bari, 92) and implementation is based on Ada language.
The main benefit of this approach is to bring into operation traceability and to favor weak coupling between software components.

KEY WORDS: *Information Systems, Object Oriented Design, REMORA, Traceability, Mapping Rules.*

1. Introduction

By the time the object paradigm had reached the design phase, a major question aroused : how to integrate an object oriented design in the whole software life cycle?

One of the most representative object oriented design methods is probably Booch's (Booch, 86), even though it does not deal with inheritance. This method, let us call it OOD, aims at building software so that each composite module (1) closely matches a real-world entity and (2) is weakly coupled with the other components. In this way, long term maintainability is improved.

Nowadays, many new methods claim to be influenced by its approach, eg. GOOD (Seidewitz et al., 87) and HOOD (Delatte et al., 93). But very few existing methodologies, if any, cover the whole software life cycle according to OOD principles, although Ladden has made out the requisites for such methodologies (Ladden, 89). Moreover, it has been shown that many analysis methods could successfully integrate OOD, eg. JSD (Poo, 91) and Data Flow Diagrams (Solsi, 91). A controversy has aroused about the compatibility between structured methods and OOD. Indeed, (Shumate, 91) and (Ward, 89) have, respectively, shown that SA and SA/SD are compatible with OOD, whereas (Firesmith, 91) and (Brookman, 91) have shown the opposite.
In addition, we have showed (Bari et al., 90) that the information systems design methodology REMORA (Rolland et al., 82 & 88) can successfully be used front-end to OOD.

Nevertheless, OOD suffers from a number of limitations some of which have been made out at least by (Ladden, 89). To deal with these limitations (parallelism, semantics of dependencies between modules, identification of objects, ...) we have developed (1) an object model (Bari, 92) and (2) a step by step process that enables the translation of a conceptual schema into a design product.
Covering a single field limited just to Information Systems is one of the characteristics of the proposed object model.

The main benefit of our approach lies in its capacity to bring traceability into operation and to favor weak coupling between software components. These two points are a major answer of the object oriented approach to the software crisis (Booch, 86), (Meyer, 88).

Traceability is achieved according to the two following ways :
- the correspondence between each real-world phenomenon or class of phenomena and a software component;
- the translation from the product of each step to a product of another one (conceptual schema, design product and software system) is achieved according to precise rules enabling an automatic mapping.

Weak coupling is achieved by means of the object model used for the design. This model is based on a taxonomy wherein objects of each type are given a specific role. Therefore, they have a particular structure, behavior and visibility inherent to their type. The object visibility expresses its dependencies in relation to other objects by stating which ones "see" it and which ones it "sees".

In this way, we can define generic components to make an advantage out of the strong "functional redundancy" going along with Information Systems (Fussichen, 91).

Each step of the methodology we propose is based on a specific model and a step by step process (figure 1).

	Model	Step by Step Process	Product
Analysis	Remora Model	Remora Process	Conceptual Schema
Design	Object Model	Mapping rules *atd*	Design Product
Implementation	Generic Components	Mapping rules *dti*	Software System

Figure 1 *The three steps*

The analysis step is entirely based on REMORA and the design step is based on the object model presented in section 3; the related process consists in (1) a translation of the elements of a conceptual schema to the elements of a design product according to mapping rules *atd* (analysis to design) and (2) a re-organization of the initial design product in order to decrease its complexity.

The implementation step is based on Ada generic units; the related process is based on (1) a translation of the elements of a design product into software components according to mapping rules *dti* (design to implementation) and (2) a possible re-organization of these components in order to consider some implementation constraints (distribution, optimization, ...).

The paper is outlined as follows : next section presents the analysis model ; the third section presents the design model ; the fourth section presents the *atd* mapping rules ; a stock-control case study illustrates our presentation.

2. The Analysis Model

The basic idea of REMORA is that reality is made of *objects* handled by *operations*, themselves being triggered by *events* corresponding to specific state changes of *objects* (figure 2).

A REMORA specification is set through a conceptual schema describing both the static and the dynamic aspects of the real world, in accordance with (ISO, 82).

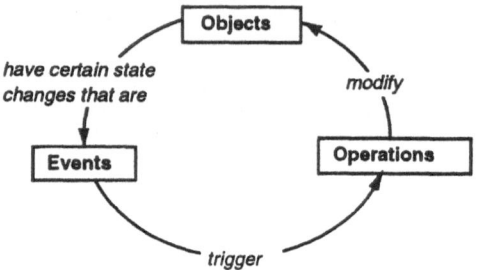

Figure 2 *The Remora Functional Schema*

2.1. The static model

The static dimension of reality is captured, first, using the E/R model (Chen, 76). Then, the introduction of the *permanent functional dependency* (pfd) provides a more accurate definition of interdependencies between entities.
A *pfd* between two entity types A and B states that to each instance of A corresponds a single instance of B, and that associated instances are always the same. To build the static conceptual schema, REMORA basic concept is the **c-object** that represents a temporal aspect of a real-world entity or relationship type, (ie. the largest set of properties of an entity or a relationship type having the same temporal behavior).

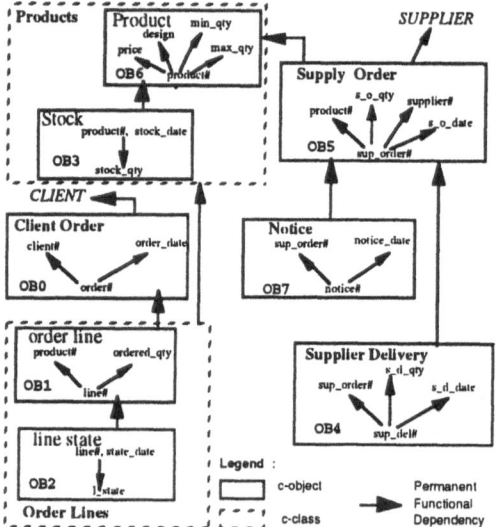

Figure 3 *Example of static conceptual schema*

There are two kinds of c-objects, each one describing a particular aspect of an entity or a relationship type : permanent and variable c-objects. The former describes real world aspects that do not evolve through time, whereas the latter describes real world aspects subject to changes. A permanent c-object and its related variable c-objects form a "c-class".

Figure 3 gives an example of a static conceptual schema related to a stock-control case.

For instance, c-class *Products* comprises (1) the permanent c-object *Product*, ob6, whose attributes are *product#, design, price, min_qty* and *max_qty*; and (2) the variable c-object *Stock*, ob3, whose attributes are *product#, stock_date* and *stock_qty*. Similarly, ob1 and ob2 describe the entity type *order_lines*. The remaining c-objects are permanent.

2.2. The dynamic model

Once the c-objects are known, their dynamic properties, ie. their behavior, are established and the dynamic conceptual schema is developed using two main concepts :
- the **c-operation** that represents an elementary transformation of only one c-object,
- the **c-event** that represents the state change of only one c-object, at which time some operations are triggered, eventually under some condition and/or iteratively.
In addition to these three basic concepts, two notions are used to model the dynamic of an information system : the *condition* and the *factor*.
A condition refers to the state of some c-objects. A factor selects the c-object instances to serve as parameters for the execution of an iterative c-operation.
Triggering conditions or factors may be simple or complex. They deal with a unique c-objet in the first case, with several c-objects in the second.

Figure 4 gives an example of a dynamic conceptual schema that describes the relationships between c-objects, c-operations and c-events related to the stock-control case.

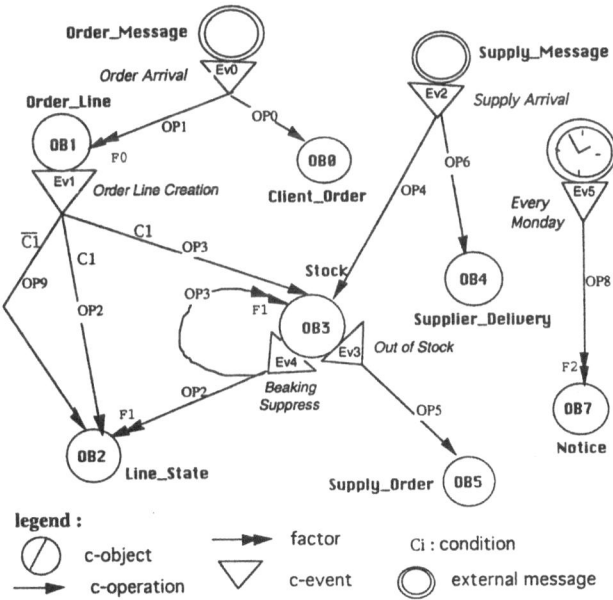

Figure 4 *Example of dynamic conceptual schema*

Two external events, namely "*order arrival*", (Ev0) and "*supply arrival*", (Ev2), correspond to the interactions between the environment and the system. This interaction is described through out the arrival of messages : the *Order_Message* and the *Supply_Message*.

The system reacts to external events by executing c-operations on c-objects. For instance, Ev0 triggers two c-operations : OP0 to create the *order* and OP1 to create the *order_lines*; OP1 is triggered as many times as there are order lines related to the order (this is expressed by the factor F0).

In addition, internal c-events (Ev1, Ev3 and Ev4) show the way c-objects react to the changing of their state. For example, Ev1 is due to the creation of a new instance of *order_line*. Depending on the condition C1 (the stock quantity of the ordered product is higher than the ordered quantity), this creation will trigger :

- OP3 on OB3 (to decrease the stock quantity) and
- OP2 on OB2 (to set the line_state to "*satisfied*");

or

- OP9 on OB2 (to set the line_state to "*to be satisfied*").

Temporal c-events are the last kind of events REMORA deals with. For instance Ev5 "every Monday, a notification will be sent to the suppliers who did not answer a supply order sent a month earlier."

All the information related to an IS are not supplied by the graphical specification of the conceptual schema. In fact, the complete specification is established on the basis of textual formalism, which is not described in the present article.

The main benefit of REMORA is to cover the whole analysis step and to allow the building of validated specifications to serve as a rigorous basis for following steps.

REMORA is nowadays supported by CASE tools among which the expert design tool known as OICSI (Cauvet et al., 88) and the prototyping tool RUBIS (Rolland et al., 88).

3. The Design Model

One of the object oriented approach goals is to allow the building of weakly coupled and highly coherent modules in order to improve software maintainability.

The properties of weak coupling together with high cohesion come basically from the way software components and their relationships are built up. This is the aim of the design step, based, in our methodology, upon an object model and a step by step process.

The design model we suggest is based on :

1- A taxonomy of objects including passive and active ones. The former manage data whereas the latter take charge of the system dynamics and may be of message-awaiting, time-watching, internal agent or sender agent type. The fact that the dependencies of each object among the others are limited by its type favors the mastering of the coupling between software components.
2- A set of communication protocols to define with concision the cooperation mode between objects according to their type.
3- A set of relationships expressed by typical visibilities between software components. We make out *composition*, *inheritance*, *genericity* and *use* relationships. The *use* one may be structural or operational. In the first case, it expresses that client objects make use of some data types defined within the interface of the server objects, whereas, in the second case, it expresses the use of operations.

In the present article we only present the taxonomy of objects. Each type of object is characterized by the operations it offers, those it requires and, for active objects, the specific elements that constitute formal generic parameters.

3.1. Passive objects

Passive objects are the basic objects of an IS. All other types of objects are organized around them.
A passive object is related to a real world abstraction and takes charge of its data management. Such an object acts as an administrator of a real world abstraction.
On one hand, a passive object allows all the operations that manage access, transformation, memorization and restitution of the data related to that abstraction. On the other hand, it does not require any operation from any other visible object of the system.
A passive object may have as components passive and active objects of internal agent type that take in charge its interactions with other objects.

Figure 5 shows graphical symbol of passive objects and an example of visibility among objects.

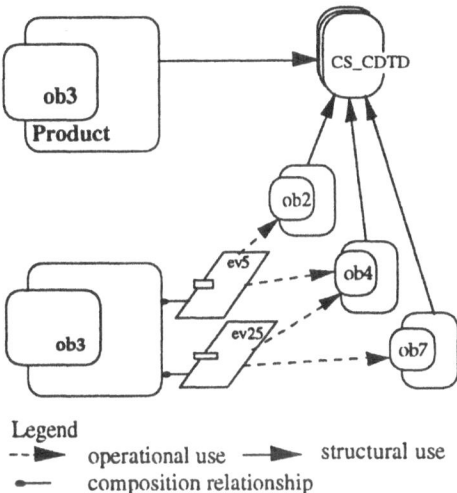

Legend
- - ▶ operational use   ───▶ structural use
─● composition relationship

Figure 5 *Graphical symbol of passive objects and an example of visibilities. The passive object ob3 structurally uses CS_CDTD; its components are agents ev5 et ev25. They operationally use ob2, ob4 and ob7.*

3.2. Active objects

While passive objects manage data, active objects ensure the dynamics of IS. Active objects are specialized into *time-watching*, *message-awaiting*, *internal agent* and *sender agent*. They are presented in turn.

3.2.1. Time-watching objects

Time-watching objects supervise the out flow of time in order to detect the temporal situations from which actions are to be triggered.

Temporal situations may be repeated during the whole system life cycle, an interval of time or occur only once.
According to the temporal situation supervised, a time-watching object is called periodic unbounded, periodic bounded or simple.

Figure 6 shows graphical symbols and behaviors (expressed in an Ada-like formalism) of time-watching objects. The specific elements of this type are : the function *NextOccurrence*, the operation *Action* and, depending on its kind, the functions *Calculate* and *LastTime* .

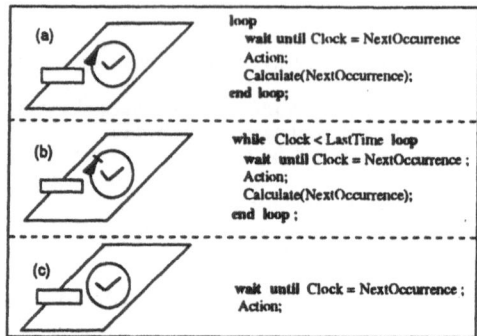

Figure 6 *Graphical symbols and behaviors of time-watching objects*
((a) periodic unbounded, (b) periodic bounded, (c) simple)

3.2.2. Message-awaiting objects

Each message-awaiting object watches out the arrival of external messages belonging to a given type. Their role is to check and filter all the external world information brought in. No information is allowed in if not validated. The validation concerns :
- domain constraints,
- referential constraints,
- qualitative checks.

Figure 7 shows graphical symbol and behavior of message-awaiting objects. The specific elements of this type are : the function *Validate*, the operation *Action*, the exception *InvalidMessage*, and the data type *Message* .

On one hand, each message-awaiting object offers one operation to the external world in order to receive messages. On the other hand, it requires one operation, called here *Action*, from the system's passive objects in order to pass on the information resulting from the received messages.

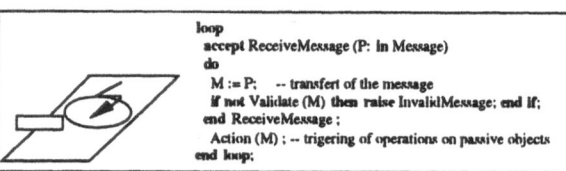

Figure 7 *Graphical symbol and behavior of message-awaiting objects.*

3.2.3. Agent objects

Agent objects are active objects acted on by other objects. Internal agents manage interactions between passive objects, whereas sender agents take in charge the production and sending of messages to the system environment.

Internal agent

Internal agent objects are components of passive objects. The former rule the interactions occurring among the latter. Each internal agent is specialized in a particular service. For example, when an out-of-stock happens, the passive agent in charge of *Product* entities sends a message to its agent that takes charge of supplying. While the passive object may respond to other

solicitations, the agent triggers all the necessary operations to operate the corresponding supply service (determination of the quantity to order, choice of the supplier, etc...).
Agent objects are part of the elements that favor weak coupling by discoupling the main objects in an Information System : the passive ones.

On one hand, each agent object offers one operation to its passive object in order to get its service invoked. On the other hand, it requires all the necessary operations to get into action from passive and sender objects .

Figure 8 shows graphical symbol and behavior of internal agent objects. The specific elements to each object of this type are the data type *Parameters* and the operation *Action*.

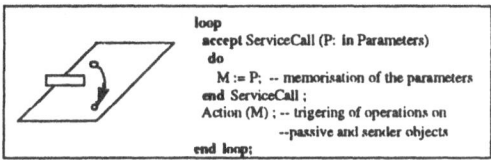

Figure 8 *Graphical symbol and behavior of internal agent objects*

Sender agent

An organization communicates with its environment by means of input and output messages.
The part played by sender objects is contrary to the one played by message-awaiting objects. A sender object is associated to every kind of message dedicated to the system environment (client-invoice, supply-order, ...).
Every sender object :
   - contains the description of the associated message type,
   - requires the necessary operations for their production (these operations are offered by passive objects) and
   - requires an operation from the system environment to send the messages.

Each sender object offers a unique operation to receive the message parameters. The clients of this operation are internal agents (when the messages are produced and sent as soon as events occur) or time-watching objects (when the messages are sent at given dates).

Figure 9 shows graphical symbol and behavior of agent sender objects. The specific elements to each object of this type are the data type *MessageParameters* and the operations *MessageProduce* and *MessageSending*.

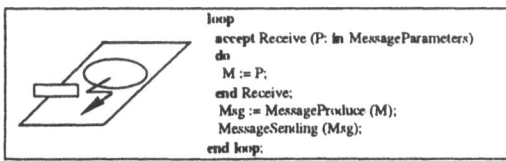

Figure 9 *Sender agent objects graphical symbol and behavior*

3.3. Common Data Types Dictionary Objects (CDTD)

Object structural visibility establishes the set of the components of the system that contain declarations required for the definition of the data types of that object.
The structural visibility consists of two parts :
   - the first one deals with structural links reflecting referential dependencies. These dependencies express the use of data types related to identifiers;

- the second one deals with non-identifier data types that are common to several objects (eg. *Price, PhoneNumber, Quantity, ...*).

One of the software engineering principles is to set a data type once for all, even when used by several components. That is why one has (1) to select from the very beginning the modules in which every common data type is to be defined and (2) to establish the structural visibility associated to every component.

Nevertheless, this may increase the amount of the system dependencies and induce choices quite hard to justify.

A possible solution for such a difficulty is the use of "Common Data Types Dictionary" (CDTD) objects. This way, every system is granted with a single module CDTD, wherein all the common data types are defined, so that the structural visibility of each component is reduced to its CDTD that comprises only an interface grouping the data types describing the domains related to the universe of discourse.

Such a solution favors weak coupling between components as it reduces their dependencies. In this way, the system complexity also decreases (Bari et al., 91).

This solution works only with small and medium systems. For larger systems we suggest :
1- to define a CDTD component for each subsystem composed of components related to an application domain;
2- to define every two or more subsystems a common CDTD "interface".

This way, we can create a hierarchy of CDTDs in which the higher an object is, the greater the number of subsystems that use its data types is.

As an example, figure 10 shows a portion of the CDTD related to the stock-control case.

```
With Calendar ;
Package CS_CDTD is
.........
  type PRICE is -- UoD depending
  type PRODUCT_NUM is -- UoD depending
  type QTY is -- UoD depending
  type LABEL is -- UoD depending

  type PRODUCT is record
       PRODUCT# : PRODUCT_NUM ;
       THE_PRICE : PRICE;
       MIN_QTY : QTY;
       MAX_QTY : QTY;
       DESIGNATION : LABEL;
  end record;

  type STOCK is record
       PRODUCT# : PRODUCT_NUM ;
       STOCK_DATE : CALENDAR.DATE;
       STOCK_QTY : QTY;
  end record;
............
end CS_CDTD;
```

Figure 10 *Example of CDTD*

4. Mapping rules from the analysis model to the design model

Let us now have a look at the mapping rules according to the first four steps of Booch's method (Booch, 86). Even though his more recent work (Booch, 91) has brought in new items (introduction of the notions of class and inheritance), the *process* remains basically the same.

4.1. Identify the objects and their attributes

Passive objects

Rule 1.1 - Each *c-object* is mapped into a *passive object*. From figure 3, we can identify eight passive objects (ob0 to ob7) and their attributes (eg. the attributes of ob3 are *product#, stock_date and stock_qty*).

Rule 1.2 - *Passive objects* related to a permanent c-object and its variable c-objects are grouped into one passive object (ie. a *c-class* is mapped into a *composed passive object*). It is the case for *Products* that will contain ob3 and ob6, and *Order_Lines* that will contain ob1 and ob2.

Active objects

Rule 1.3 - Each *external c-event* is mapped into a message-awaiting object. Its attributes describe the message type it handles. From figure 4, we can identify two such objects: ev0 and ev2.

Rule 1.4 - Each *temporal c-event* is mapped into a *time-watching object*, which is the case for ev5.

Rule 1.5 - Each *internal c-event* is mapped into an *internal agent*. This is the case for ev1, ev3 and ev4. Each one of them is embedded within the passive object it is related to.

CDTD objects

Rule 1.6 - Data types related to attributes identified within the static conceptual schema are defined within a CDTD object; let's call ours *CS_CDTD*.

4.2. Identify the operations

Remora dynamic schema identifies all the relevant operations for the set of objects defined in the static schema. These operations correspond to the real-world rules that are the requirements for the system behavior. Due to the definition of c-event and c-operation concepts, it grants a complete and not redundant set of operations.
The operations we deal with may be :
- *constructors* if they alter the state of objects,
- *selectors* if they return the state of objects,
- *iterators* if they allow access to parts of objects.

Rule 2.1 - All the c-*operations* acting on a c-object are part of the definition of the corresponding passive object as *offered constructors*. This can be done by simply looking at the graphical representation (eg. ob3 definition is completed by adding op3 and op4 as offered constructors).

Rule 2.2 - All the c-*operations* triggered by a c-event are added to the related active object definition as *required constructors*. For example, op2 and op5 are required by ob3 whereas op4 and op6 are required by ev2.

Rule 2.3 - Each *elementary triggering condition* is mapped into a *selector*. This one is *offered* by the passive object related to the c-object whose state is evaluated by that condition. This is the case for condition *c1* that is transformed into a selector offered by ob3 and required by ev1.

Rule 2.4 - Each *complex triggering condition* (CTC) is mapped into a *selector* requiring elementary conditions necessary to evaluate the state of the related objects. Whenever a CTC is required by several active objects, it is turned into a free (ie. non-embedded) component. Otherwise it is embedded within the object that requires it.

Rule 2.5 - Each *elementary triggering factor* is mapped into an *iterator*. This iterator is *offered* by the passive object related to the c-object from which the factor returns the parameters. This is the case for factor f1 offered by the composite object *OrederLines* and required by ev4.

Rule 2.6 - Each *complex triggering factor* (CTF) is mapped into an operation requiring elementary factors to return the necessary parameters. Whenever a CTF is required by several active objects, it is turned into a free component. Otherwise it is embedded within the unique object requiring it. This is the case for factor f2 that requires elementary iterators from ob4 and ob5 and is required by ev5.

4.3. Establish the visibility

The structural visibility of the overall objects is the same. They see the CDTD related to the application domain. The operational visibility is deduced from the dynamic conceptual schema and the rules of the previous step.
From our example of stock-control, the visibility of the component *Products* is established as follows :
- its interface sees *CS_CDTD* (ie. the CDTD of the domain),
- its body sees *OrderLines* and *SupplyDelivery*,
- it is seen by *OrderLines* and *ev2*.

The visibility is used to build the software architecture related to a problem domain. As an example, let us show in figure 11 the software architecture related to the stock-control case from the point of view of the operational dependencies that express operational *use* relationships.

In this architecture, the components are organized according to layers : at the top (layer a), there are the actor (Booch, 91) or director (Walters, 91) objects; at the bottom (layer c) there are the server objects and between these two layers we find the relay objects.

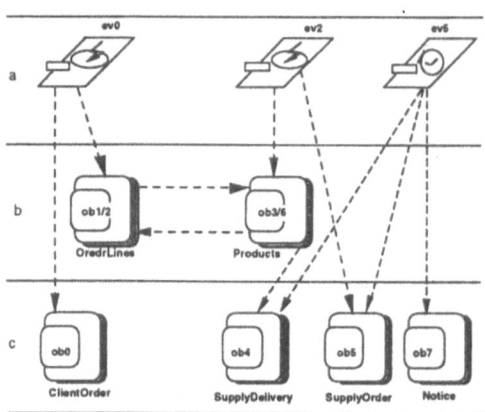

Figure 11 *Operational software architecture related to the stock -control problem*

This kind of architecture is called senior-junior hierarchy (Seidewitz et al., 87), (Delatte et al., 93) : objects of each layer may depend on each other or on objects of lower layers (each layer represents a virtual machine). This way, weak coupling between objects is improved. In this case we can build two hierarchies (structural and operational) exhibiting the complete range of dependencies among the objects.

4.4. Establish the interface

The interface of each object contains all the elements used by other objects, essentially offered operations and exceptions attached to that object. In order to complete the interface, a rule related to integrity constraints is added.

Rule 4.1 - Each *integrity constraint* is transformed into an *exception* (the control related to the exception is hidden within the object body). For instance, all the referential integrity constraints are mapped into an exception (eg. the NON_EXISTENT_PRODUCT exception related to the object *Products* in figure 12; a hidden function checks the raising of that exception).

Using an Ada-like formalism, the *Products* interface contains the following elements (figure 12) :

```
with CS_CDTD, CALENDAR; -- CALENDAR is the package managing the data type DATE
package PRODUCTS is

  procedure OP3(ORDERED_QTY : in CS_CDTD.QTY; PRODUCT# : in CS_CDTD.PRODUCT_NUM);
  procedure OP4(S_D_QTY : in CS_CDTD.QTY; PRODUCT# : in CS_CDTD.PRODUCT_NUM);
  function C1(ORDERED_QTY:in CS_CDTD.QTY; PRODUCT#: in CS_CDTD.PRODUCT_NUM) return
    Boolean;
  function IMAGE(NUM : in CS_CDTD.PRODUCT_NUM) return CS_CDTD.T_STOCK;
  OVERFLOW, NON_EXISTENT_PRODUCT : exception;

end PRODUCTS;
```

Figure 12 *Component Products interface*

As a conclusion to this section, figure 13 shows the correspondences between REMORA elements and our object model elements.

REMORA	Object Model
c-object	passive object
internal event	internal agent
external event	message-awaiting object
temporal event	time-watching object
c-operation	constructor
condition	selector
factor	iterator
integrity constraint	exception

Figure 13 *Correspondences between REMORA and our object model elements*

5. Conclusion

We have presented a mapping of a conceptual specification into an object oriented design product in order to build Information Systems. This is part of a methodology that combines an information systems design methodology, an object oriented design and the Ada language. This methodology favors mainly traceability and weak coupling between software components.

The first property is due to the compatibility between the models used throughout the software life cycle. Precise mapping rules enable an automatic translation of the product of a given step into the product of the next step.

Weak coupling between software components is improved by the object model. This one is based on a taxonomy of objects comprising passive and active objects. Passive objects manage data whereas active objects take charge of the system dynamics. Active objects may be message-awaiting, time-watching, internal or sender agents. According to their type, each object has an inherent and limited visibility.

Tools supporting the methodology are under development : the first is based on HyperCard®, the second is based on a full-Ada solution and the third uses a CASE tool developed in our laboratory.

Future works will concern extensions of REMORA to take into account :
  - modeling of messages sent to the external world,
  - management of complex objects, operations and events.

6. References

(Bari et al., 90): Bari, M and Rolland, C "A Methodology for the Object-Oriented Design", in: N. Prakash (eds), Data Management, Current Trends, Tata-McGraw-Hill, New-Delhi, Proc. of the Intern. Conf. on Management of Data, COMAD'90, (Dec. 1990) pp 244-259

(Bari et al., 91): Bari, M and Rolland, C "Optimizing Object-Oriented Software Systems Architecture", SERF'91 (Software Engineering Forum Research), Tampa, USA, 7-8 (Nov. 1991) pp 133-142

(Bari, 92): Bari, M "Le modèle objet de la méthode rAdar", intern. conf. Ada-France (Afcet), Paris, (26-27 oct. 1992), pp 89-100

(Booch, 86): Booch, G "Object-Oriented Development", IEEE Trans. on S.E., Vol. SE-12, N°2, (Feb 1986) pp 211-221

(Booch, 91): Booch, G *Object-Oriented Design with Applications*, Benjamin/Cummings Publishing Co., Menlo Park (1991)

(Brookman, 91): Brookman, D "SA/SD vs OOD", SIGAda Ada letters, vol. 11, n° 9, (1991) pp 96-99

(Cauvet et al., 88): Cauvet, C and Rolland, C , Proix "Information Systems Design : an Expert System Approach", in Proc. of the Intern. Conf. on Extended Database Technology, Venice, (March 1988)

(Chen, 76): Chen, P.P.S "The entity-relationship model : towards a unified view of data", ACM Trans. on Data Base Systems, Vol.1, N°1 (1976) pp 9-36

(Delatte et al., 93): Delatte, B., Heitz, M and Muller, J.-P. *Hood Reference Manual, 3.1,* Masson/Prentice-Hall, Paris 1993

(Firesmith, 91): Firesmith, D "Structured Analysis and Object-Oriented Design are not Compatible", SIGAda Ada letters, Vol. 11, No 9, (1991) pp 56-66

(Fussichen, 91): Fussichen, K "Ada in Information Systems", SIGAda Ada Letters, Vol. XI, N° 6, (1991) pp 77-79

(ISO, 82): ISO "Concepts and Terminology for the Conceptual Schema and the Information Base", Report N° 695, ISO/TC/9/SC5/WG3 (1982)

(Ladden, 89): Ladden, R.M "A Survey of Issues to be Considered in the Development of an Object-Oriented Development Methodology for Ada", SIGAda Ada Letters, Vol. IX, No 2 (March/April 1989) pp 78-88

(Meyer, 88): Meyer, B *Object-Oriented Software Construction*, Prentice Hall, Hemel Hempstead (1988)

(Poo, 91): Poo, C_C D "Adapting and using JSD modelling technique as front-end to Object-Oriented systems Development", Information and Software Technology, vol 33, n° 7 (Sept. 1991), pp 466-476

(Rolland et al., 82): Rolland, C and Richard, C "The Remora Methodology for Information Systems Design and Management", in Olle, T.W., Sol, H.G., Verryn-Stuart, A.A. (eds) Information Systems Design Methodologies : A Comparative Review, North Holland (1982) pp 369-426

(Rolland et al., 88): Rolland, C , Foucaut, O and Benci, G *Conception de Systèmes d'Information, la méthode Remora* , Ed. Eyrolles, Paris (1988)

(Rolland et al., 88): Rolland, C et al. "The RUBIS system", CRIS88, Computerized Assistance during the Information System Life Cycle, London (1988) pp 193-239

(Seidewitz et al., 87): Seidewitz, E and Stark, M "Towards a General Object-Oriented Software Development Methodology", SIGAda Ada letters, Vol. 7, No 4, (July-August 1987) pp 54-67

(Shumate, 91): Shumate, N "Structured Analysis and Object-Oriented Design are Compatible", SIGAda Ada letters, Vol. 11, No 4, (1991) pp 78-90

(Solsi, 91): Solsi, S.C "Simple Yet Complete Heuristics for Transforming Data Flow Diagrams into Booch Style Diagrams", SIGAda Ada letters, Vol. 11, No 2, (1991) pp 115-127

(Walters, 91): Walters, N. L "An Ada Object-Based Analysis and Design Approach", ACM Sigada, Ada Letters, Vol.11, N° 5, (1991) pp 62-78

(Ward, 89): Ward, P.T "How to integrate Object Orientation with structured analysis and design", IEEE Trans. on S.E., Vol. SE-15, N°3 (1989) pp 74-82

Identifying the requirement for history of time-varying objects during an object-oriented analysis

L.C.Valet and S.A.Roberts

*Division of Operational Research and Information Systems,
School of Conputer Studies, University of Leeds,
Leeds LS2 9JT - UK*

E-mail : {laurent,sar}@scs.leeds.ac.uk   Fax : +44 532 33 54 68

ABSTRACT *A number of temporal object-oriented data models deal with the problem of preserving the history of changes. In practice, an application may not want to preserve the changes of all time-varying objects. As this question needs to be answered at the analysis stage, this paper presents a model to identify the history requirements during an object-oriented analysis.*

KEYWORDS : *Object-oriented analysis, Temporal modelling, Temporal Databases*

1. Introduction

During the past few years, a number of temporal object-oriented data models have appeared in the literature (Sciore, 1991), (Su et al., 1991) and (Rose et al., 1993). These models deal with the problem of preserving the history of changes of objects by using historical objects. In practice, an application may not want to preserve the changes of all time-varying objects. The question then arises as to which time-varying object-classes should allow historical objects as their instances. This question needs to be addressed at the analysis stage because the purpose of this stage is to identify the requirements of the application. To this end, we introduce a model for temporal modelling and history requirement modelling.

This paper is organised as follows. Section 2 describes briefly the application that motivated this work. Section 3 presents existing temporal data models and object-oriented analysis techniques. Our extension, and how it can be used are described in section 4. Finally, we draw some conclusions in section 5.

2. Motivation

This work was motivated by the study of a real application in the context of the RODOS Project which is partly funded by the Commission of the European Communities (Ehrardt et al, 1993).The RODOS Project aims at developing a Decision Support System for accidental releases of radio-activity (such as the Chernobyl accident). One of the components of this system is a forecasting system that predicts the dispersal of a plume of radioactive material in the atmosphere according to the parameters of the release and the wind (Chien-Seng, 1993).

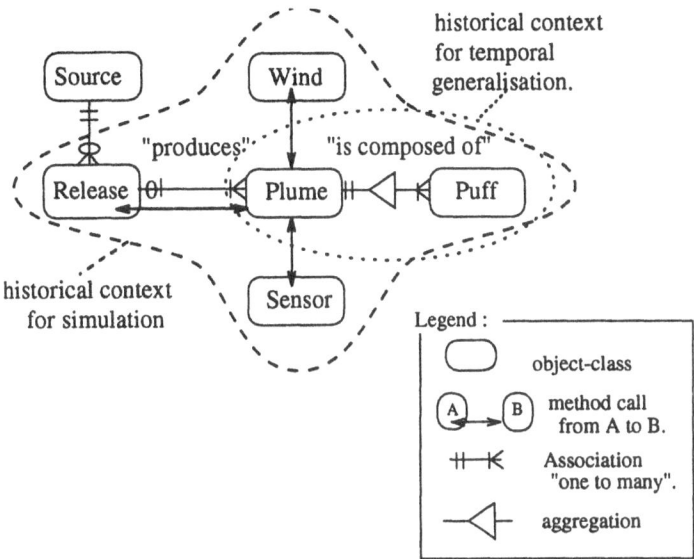

Figure 1: Object Interaction Model of the forecasting system

Figure 1 shows a simplified version of the object-oriented analysis of this dispersal with the notation of (Coad et al., 1991). A plume of radioactive material is being released by a source and is dispersed by the wind. The readings of radioactivity level are provided by the sensors to update the estimations of radioactivity material within the plume (French et al., 1993).

This application was chosen because many of the objects are varying over time and their histories are needed. However, which classes are varying over time and which classes would be required to be historical was not clear from the outset.

3. Related Work

3.1. *Temporal Models*

There are a number of temporal conceptual models and temporal data models reported in the literature. The conceptual models provide a framework for representing the real-world whereas data models specify how the data are organised and manipulated in a database (Kim, 1991).
The temporal conceptual models incorporate the time dimension either by extending the Entity-Relationship model (Klopproge, 1981), (Dubois et al., 1986), (Loucopoulos, 1991) or the object-oriented model (Wuu et al., 1991), (Edelweiss et al., 1993). Temporal conceptual models differ from other conceptual models in that the notion of passage of time forms a fundamental part of the model. They usually provide a model of time and the concepts of activity or event, of object and relationship. Objects are described by properties (or attributes) and static properties are distinguished from time-varying ones.

The temporal data models studied are those based on the object-oriented model. They have in common the concept of temporal object (Sciore, 1991), (Su et al., 1991), (Rose et al., 1993). A temporal object is an object that contains many states that are valid at different times. At its simplest, it contains its past and/or future states (historical object) but it can also contain the sequence of corrections of its states (revised object) (Sciore, 1991), (Rose et al., 1993) or alternative versions of states (versioned object) (Sciore, 1991).

We found in the literature few works describing the mapping between a temporal conceptual model and a temporal data model. Most make the implicit assumption that there is a history requirement for every time-varying object-class. Every time-varying object-class is therefore implemented as a class of historical objects. Where the mapping is described (for example, for the ERT conceptual model and the object-oriented language AMORE (Oelmann, 19991)) the same assumption is made, only this time explicitly.

3.2. *Object-oriented analysis methods*

Object-oriented analysis methods guide the analysis of an application in the context of the object-oriented approach. The reader is referred to well-known methods such as the Object-Oriented Analysis method (Coad et al., 1991), the Object Modelling Technique (Rumbaugh et al., 1991) and the Object-Oriented Analysis and Design method (Booch, 1994). Evaluations of object-oriented analysis techniques may be found in (McGinnes, 1992) and (Aksit et al., 1992).

Most object-oriented analysis models are composed of three models : the object model, the object interaction model and the object behaviour model. Object-oriented analysis techniques provide these models under one form or another although the nomenclature varies between them. In essence, the object interaction model describes what happens, the object behaviour model describes when it happens and the object model what it happens to (Rumbaugh et al., 1991).

The object model describes the properties of the objects and their relationships (aggregation, generalisation, specialisation and user-defined associations). The object interaction model describes the interactions between objects by means of message passing. An object may be seen as providing services by means of its methods to other objects (Coad et al., 1991). The object behaviour model describes the behaviour of the objects in response to service requests using state transition diagrams and specification templates for the services. A state transition diagram specifies which message modifies the state of an object from one particular state to another.

Object-oriented analysis models therefore support a description of the evolution of the real-world. Although they support description of the dynamics of the real-world entities, they do not support explicitly the modelling of history requirements.

We borrow from these techniques some important concepts: the concept of object state, mutator and observer methods. The state of an object encompasses all the current values of the object properties and relationships (Booch, 1994). A **mutator** is a method that changes the state of the object. Conversely, a method that simply reads the state of the object without changing it, is named an **observer**. An initialiser is the method that sets the state of an object (like the `init' method in Smalltalk) at its creation. We now define the concept of **mutation server** ; it will be used during the modelling of history requirement to define the context of change of an object. Informally, a mutation server of a class 'A' is either a class of objects which mutate the objects of class 'A' or a class of objects that are observed by the mutators of class 'A'. A mutation server of a class 'A' may be formally defined as either the class of objects that invoke a mutator of 'A' or the class of objects that are invoked by the objects of the class A' within a mutator, where the method being called is an observer.

4. Analysing the history requirement

4.1. *Temporal modelling*

At the analysis stage, a set of properties, a set of methods and a set of relationships with other object classes are defined for each object-class. In general, object instances of each class have a life cycle involving creation, initialisation, mutation and destruction (Coad et al., 1991). For some object classes, there will be no instances which can change state, during the time-scale of interest (i.e. the time-scale of the Universe of Discourse).These will have no mutators and are therefore easily recognised. We shall call these object-classes **static** object-classes. We note that instances of static object-classes may be created, initialised or destroyed during the time-scale of interest.

Other object classes which do have instances that undergo state changes during the time-scale of interest are termed **time-varying** object classes. These will have mutators which either change the value of one of their properties or else establish, or break a relationship with another object.

Temporal modelling is the activity which assigns each object-class to either the static class or the time-varying class. For example, in the RODOS application all classes are found to be time-varying. The 'Puff' class is time-varying because the wind calls a mutator that changes its shape and position. The 'Source' class is time-varying because its state changes when an accidental release occurs. The 'Release' is also a time-varying class because its mutators are called regularly to represent the continuous release of radioactive material.

4.2. *Modelling of history requirements*

Once the temporal analysis is complete, the analyst must consider the requirements for histories to be kept in order to support the applications of interest. The history of a static object is composed of the times at which it was created and destroyed (i.e. the lifespan of the object (Rose et al., 1993), (Wuu et al., 1991)). The history of a time-varying object includes all the states of the object during its lifespan together with the times at which the state transitions occurred.

In order to distinguish between object-classes which have a history requirement and those which do not, we introduce four new concepts. A **historical** object-class is a time-varying object class for which there is a history requirement. A **snapshot** object-class is a time-varying object-class for which there is no history requirement. Furthermore, we classify object-classes as being either **preserved** or **ephemeral** depending on whether a trace of their existence is required after they have been destroyed.

The purpose of the requirements modelling phase is to further classify time-varying object classes into either snapshot, historical preserved or historical ephemeral classes, and to classify static object-classes into either preserved or ephemeral static object-classes. The new concepts and their classification hierarchy is shown in figure 2. Notice that we do not allow snapshot classes to be preserved since, by definition, we have no use for their history.

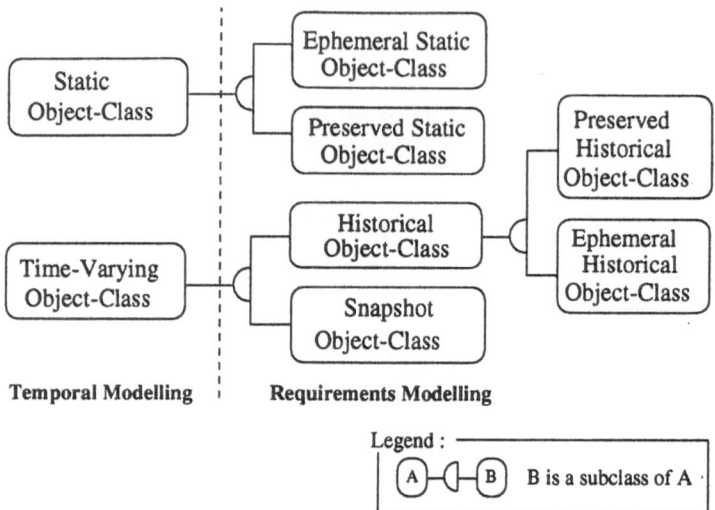

Figure 2: The class model for the modelling of history requirement

4.3. *Achieving a comprehensive modelling of the history requirements*

In our experience, modelling the history requirements is not a trivial task for an unfamiliar application domain. For some classes, it will be immediately obvious whether there is a need to maintain the history, for others it is less clear. For example, in the RODOS application, it was clear that the history of the plume must be kept, since this was required for the analysis of how much radioactive material had been deposited on the ground over a certain time. This in turn led us to classify 'Puff' as a historical class because a 'Plume' is an aggregation of 'Puffs'. What was not so clear, for example, was whether the history of the wind and the sensors which were responsible for changing the plume needed to be preserved, since they have had their effect on the history of the plume.

The difficulty of modelling history requirements comes from the number of objects of the application that might be connected to a given object, at the same time, either by method calls or associations. If preserving the histories of all these objects is to be avoided, a way must be found to delimit which set of objects will be historical or static preserved. To this end, we propose to study the operational requirements for time-varying classes. They represent the reasons why the histories are required and correspond to operations usually performed on historical data. Like atemporal operational requirements, they are represented by the methods of the object-classes of the application. A **historical context** is defined for each operational requirement on a time-varying class. The historical context is the set of classes that might be preserved among those connected to this class in order to satisfy the operational requirement. We note that static classes might be among these classes since a static class can be connected to a time-varying one.

Defining a historical context simplifies the task of the analyst: any time-varying class (or static class) that is outside the historical context of all history requirements can not be a historical class (or static preserved class). Conversely, any time-varying class (or static class) that is within a historical context is a candidate to be classified as a historical object-class (or static preserved class).

Although we would not claim that this is necessarily a complete set, four different types of operational requirement have been identified. These are:

1. **re-construction:** to reconstruct a past snapshot or series of snapshots;
2. **temporal generalisation:** to analyse a time series;
3. **simulation or prediction:** to perform a 'what if' or extrapolation exercise;
4. **influence analysis:** to analyse the consequences of the actions of an object.

We describe below how these can be used. For each of them, the historical context is defined. The time-varying object-class on which the operational requirement applies is denoted as the target class.

4.3.1. Re-construction

If there is a requirement to reconstruct past snapshots, then the object-classes involved in the reconstruction should be preserved. A snapshot is composed of the states of objects connected at a given time to the target object by structural associations like aggregation, generalisation and user-defined relationship.
Hence, the historical context is the transitive closure of all object-classes related to that target class by generalisation, aggregation or user-defined association as well as its superclasses. This historical context might extend to many object-classes; however, it excludes any class that is connected to the class of interest only by virtue of method calls. The analyst will pick the classes that are of interest for the re-construction among this historical context.

For example, there might be a requirement to re-construct the snapshots of a particular release of radioactive material. The historical context then contains the class 'Source', the class 'Release' by virtue of its association with the 'Source' and the classes 'Plume' and 'Puff' because a release produces a plume (see figure 1).

Any subclass of the target-class is excluded from the historical context for this operational requirement because it obviously does not influence the structure of the target class. The operational requirement of reconstruction should be applied to the class that is at the lowest level in the class hierarchy unless it defines properties that are of no interest for this application or that are not time-varying.

4.3.2. Temporal generalisation

The requirement for temporal generalisation refers to the analysis of the time series held within the objects of the target class. Typically, the properties of the objects will contain the time-series and access to these time series is provided by the observers of this class. The time-varying attributes may either be inherited from a superclass (the target class and this class are linked by a generalisation association) or be aggregated from a component class (aggregation association). The historical context therefore comprises the superclasses and the components classes of the target class.

For example, the classes `Puff` and `Plume` must be historical when the time-series of doses of radioactive material is to be analysed since a `Plume` is an aggregation of `Puffs` (see figure 1).

4.3.3. Simulation

Simulation of what will or would have happened to a target class is the third operational requirement and implies that some kind of predictive model is being employed by the application. This predictive model is embedded in the mutation servers of the target class whose behaviour is being forecast. In order to simulate what would have happened with a different premise, the context of change created by the mutation servers must be preserved. It therefore follows that, if some of these mutation servers are themselves time-varying, their histories should be maintained. If some of them are static, they should be classified as preserved static classes.

The historical context is thus the set of mutation servers. Note that according to the substitution semantics associated with the specialisation association (Coad et al., 1991), the subclasses of a mutation server of the target class are also mutation servers because they inherit the methods that participate in the mutation of the objects of the target class. Unless these methods are overridden, subclasses are mutation servers by transitivity through the specialisation association.

In the case of the RODOS project, it is interesting to note that the 'Plume' and 'Puff' are the only object-classes candidates to be historical if there is a requirement of time-series analysis upon the class 'Plume'. However, if there is a requirement of simulation of what will happen to the 'Plume' from some point in time, then the mutator servers ('Wind', 'Release' and 'Sensor'), which form its context of change, are candidate historical classes as well (see figure 1).

Some real-world entities do not vary because of the influence of other entities but as a result of the passage of time. This kind of entity is often modelled as an object that is "self-mutating" in that its state transition diagram shows that state changes are triggered by the 'tick' of a clock object (Rumbaugh et al., 1991). In this particular case, the set of mutation servers of this object-class contains no other class than this one. There is no such object-class in the RODOS application. However, an example of "self-mutating" object may be found in air traffic control applications, for instance, where the position of a plane in the air is changed by the passage of time.

4.3.4. Influence analysis

Finally, we consider the operational requirement for tracing the influence of a particular object on others. The target class is the class of this particular object. This operational requirement aims at analysing the influence that this object may have in mutating other objects. This requirement is similar to the idea of a log book where the identities of persons responsible for some actions are preserved. Hence, all objects that receive a mutation request from a particular object are within its "sphere of influence". The historical context is then the set of object-classes called from the target class, where the method called is a mutator.

As the RODOS system is a decision support system, it needs to learn from past situations. It might be useful, in particular, to trace the influence that the judgement of human experts has in the process of decision making. The estimations of experts regarding the strength of release of contaminated material are stored in the RODOS system by the objects of the class 'Expert' that invoke the mutator methods of the class 'Release'. For the requirement of influence analysis of the object-class 'Expert', the time-varying class 'Release' is candidate to be historical as it belongs to the historical context (or "sphere of influence") of this class for this operational requirement.

For each operational requirement, table 1 summarises the composition of the historical context of a target class. It indicates whether a class connected to the target-class belongs to the historical context of the operational requirement depending on the type of its relationship with the target-class.

Operational Requirement upon class 'A' Type of relationship 'B' is connected to 'A' by ...	Reconstruction	Time-series analysis	Simulation	Influence Analysis
user-defined association	yes	no	no	no
specialisation ('B' is a subclass of 'A')	no	no	no	no
generalisation ('B' is a superclass of 'A')	yes	yes	no	no
aggregation ('A' is composed of 'B')	yes	yes	no	no
a method call such that 'B' is a mutation server of 'A'	no	no	yes	no
a method call such that 'A' calls a mutator of 'B'	no	no	no	yes

Table 1: Does class 'B' belong to the historical context of the target class 'A' ?

5. Conclusion

We presented a model to identify the history requirement of classes during an object-oriented analysis. The phases of temporal modelling and history requirement modelling were distinguished. This allowed us to express a history requirement about some time-varying classes only, those for which the application needs historical objects.
We found that operational requirements must be used to delimit the sets of object-classes that are candidates to be historical classes or static preserved classes. Indeed, this selection can not be done on the basis of the type of connection between classes only, because too many classes would be retained.

Some operational requirements (re-construction and temporal generalisation) select candidate objects that are linked by structural connections while the requirements of simulation and influence analysis select candidate objects that are dynamically linked (method calls).

Future work will focus on the development of an object-oriented data model that enforces the semantics of the concepts of our analysis model. This data model will have to manage the interactions (message passing) within a mixed collection of objects that may include objects belonging to the five classes previously defined. It will then be possible to implement applications that mix historical objects, snapshot objects and static preserved objects.

Acknowledgements

This work has been funded by a fellowship grant from the Commission of the European Communities under the Human Capital and Mobility programme. We gratefully acknowledge this sponsorship.
We would like to thank Torben Mikkelsen and Soren Thykier-Nielsen from Riso, Denmark for providing the source code for the plume dispersal. We would also like to thank Professor Simon French and Dave Ranyard from the School of Computer Studies of the University of Leeds.

References

(Aksit et al., 1992) : M.Aksit and L.Bergmanns, *Obstacles in Object-Oriented Software Development*, OOPSLA'92 : 7th International Conference on Object-Oriented Programming Systems, Languages, and Applications, pp. 341-358, A.Paepcke (editor), Vancouver, Canada, ACM Sigplan notices, v.27, no.10, October 1992.

(Booch et al., 1994) : G.Booch, *Object-oriented analysis and design with applications*, The Benjamin/Cummings Series in Object-Oriented Software Engineering, The Benjamin/Cummings Publishing Company, Inc., Second edition, 1994.

(Chien-Sieng, 1993) : L.Chien-Seng, *Development of the Object-Oriented RIMPUFF System* , MSc.Thesis, University of Leeds, School of Computer Studies, England, 1993.

(Coad et al. , 1991) : P. Coad and E.Yourdon, *Object-oriented Analysis*, Yourdon Press Computing Series, Prentice Hall, 1991.

(Dubois et al. 1986) : E.Dubois, J.Hagelstein, E.Lahou, F.Ponsaert, A.Rifaut and F.Williams,*The ERAE model : A Case Study* , IFIP WG 8.1: Working Conference on Comparative Review of Information Systems Design Methodologies : Improving the Practice, Noordwijkerhout, The Netherlands, 5-7 May 1986, T.W Olle, H.G. Sol and A.A.Verrijn-Stuart (editors), North Holland.

(Edelweiss et al.,1993): N.Edelweiss, J.P.M.de Oliveira and B.Pernici, *An Object-Oriented Temporal Model* , CAiSE'93, 5th International Conference on Advanced Information Systems Engineering, Paris, France, pp. 397-415, June 1993.

(Ehrardt et al., 1993) : J.Ehrardt, J.Pasler-Sauer, O.Schule, G.Benx, M.Rafat and J.Richter, *Development of RODOS, a comprehensive decision support system for nuclear emergencies in Europe - an overview*, Radiation Protection Dosimetry, 1993.

(French et al., 1993) : S.French and J.Q.Smith, *Using Monitoring Data to Update Atmospheric Dispersion Models with an application to the RIMPUFF model* , The Statistician, Vol 42 (1993) pp. 501-511.

(Kim, 1991) : W.Kim, *Introduction to Object-Oriented Databases*, Computer Systems Series, MIT Press, 1991.

(Klopproge, 1981) : M.R.Klopproge, *TERM : An Approach to include the Time Dimension in the Entity-Relationship Model*, 2nd International Conference on the Entity-Relationship Approach, P.P.S. Chen (editor), ER Institute, pp. 477-512, 1981.

(Loucopoulos et al., 1991) : P.Loucopoulos, P.McBrien, F.Schumacker, B.Theodoulidis, V.Kopanas and B.Wangler, *Integrating database technology, rule-based systems and temporal reasoning for effective information systems : the TEMPORA paradigm*, Journal of Informations Systems, No. 1, pp. 129-152, 1991.

(McGinnes, 1992) : S.McGinnes, *How Objective is Object-Oriented Analysis ?*, CAiSE'92 : 4th International Conference on Advanced Informations Systems Engineering, pp. 1-16, P.Loucopoulos (editor), Manchester, UK, May 1992.

(Oelmann, 1991) : A.Oelmann, *Representing a System Specification with a Temporal Dimension in an Object-Oriented Language* , pp.540-560, CAiSE'91, 3rd International Conference on Advanced Information Systems Engineering, Trondheim, Norway, May 1991.

(Rose et al., 1993) : E.Rose and A.Segev, *TOOA : A Temporal Object-Oriented Algebra*, ECOOP'93, 7th European Conference on Object-Oriented Programming, pp.297-325, Kaiserlautern, Germany, July 1993.

(Rumbaugh et al., 1991) : J.Rumbaugh et al.,*Object-oriented modeling and design*, Prentice Hall, 1991.

(Sciore, 1991) : E.Sciore, *Using Annotations to Support Multiple Kinds of Versioning in an Object-Oriented Database System* , ACM Transactions on Database Systems, pp. 417-438,Vol. 16, No. 3, September 1991.

(Su et al., 1991) : S.Y.W.Su and H.M.Chen, *A Temporal Knowledge Representation Model OSAM*/T and its Query Language OQL/T* , pp. 431-442, VLDB'91, 17th International Conference on Very Large Data Bases, Barcelona, Spain, September 1991.

(Wuu et al., 1991) : G.T.J.Wuu and U.Dayal, *A Uniform Model for Temporal Object-Oriented Databases*, 8th International Conference on Data Engineering, pp. 584-593, February 1991.

INTEGRITY CONSTRAINTS

IN AN OBJECT ORIENTED INFORMATION SYSTEM

Nachouki J
Département Informatique
IUT de Nantes
3 rue du Maréchal Joffre
44 000 Nantes
FRANCE

Chastang MP, Briand H
IRESTE
La Chantrerie
44300 Nantes
FRANCE

ABSTRACT

The main feature of this paper is the definition of generic modules in order to check the integrity constraints defined upon an object oriented database without needing to define those ones in each class of the application. This proposal is applied to the O2 database system developed by O2 TECHNOLOGY.

KEY-WORDS

integrity constraints, object database design, generic modules, O2 database system.

1- Introduction

Object oriented databases result from the merging of database and object oriented programming technologies. Nowadays, a number of object oriented databases have been implemented : GEMSTONE (Servio-Logic, USA), ORION (MCC-Arthemis, Austin USA), ONTOS (Burlington, Massachussetts USA), IRIS (Palo Alto, USA), O2 (O2 TECHNOLOGY, France) (Adiba & al., 1993), (Bancilhon & al., 1992). But methodologies for conceptual modeling which take advantage of the object paradigm are still being investigated (Pernici 1990).

In this paper, we propose a method which permits to obtain an object oriented database schema starting from the study of the Entity-Relationship (ER) model (Chen 1976). The resulting object schema, is based on the use of generic modules.
Similar work is proposed in (Bouzeghoub & al., 1991). This paper shows how to integrate the concept of generic module in order to check the integrity contraints on any object defined in users applications.

2- Improvement of an object schema with the use of generic modules

Genericity is the ability to define parameterized modules (Meyer 1988). Such a module, called a generic module, is not directly usable. The parameters (called formal generic parameters) stand for types. Actual modules, called instances of the generic module, are obtained by providing actual types (actual generic parameters) for each of the formal generic parameters.
The main feature of generic modules is their reutilizability in users applications. This concept of reutilizability permits to avoid the rewriting of the same methods in several different classes of one or more applications.
The generic modules that we have defined in this proposal , deal with integrity constraints that any object in any user application must verify.

In this section, we describe first the architecture of the object schema which permits to define the generic modules.

2-1 Generic schema design

The design of the object Generic schema is based on the definition of a class whose type is "any" or "empty". The Generic schema (figure 1) is made of one main class called Constraints and some others sub_classes as class Integer, String, ... Those sub-classes inherit the properties and the behavior of the super_classes (Constraints).

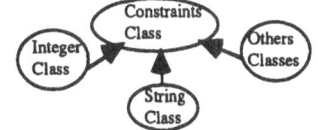

Figure 1 :Design of the Generic schema

The **Constraints** class defined in the Generic schema (like in each of its sub-classes) can be imported into any working schema (figure 2) in order to check the integrity constraints on the objects in the users applications. The Constraints class must be declared in the working schema as a superclass.

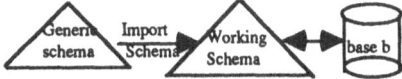

Figure 2 : Importing the Integrity_Constraints schema into a working schema

2-1-1 Definition of the class Constraints

The Constraints class doesn't need a particular data structure. This class can be assigned to any type of class defined in users applications (Personn, Car, ...) with the concept of inheritance between the super-class Constraint and its sub-classes (figure 3).

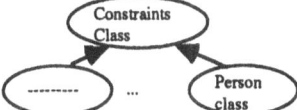

Figure 3 : Inheritance relationship between the Constraint class and the Person class

The Constraint class contains a set of modules or generic methods that permit to check the integrity constraints defined upon the object database.
The relationship between the class Personn and the class Constraints is an inheritance relationship. In Figure 6, every Person type object is also a Constraints type object. The person class inherits generic methods of its super-class. The integrity constraints on an object person arechecked by calls to the generic modules instances.
The Constraints class definition in the O2 model (O2 Technology 1994) is the following :

Class Constraints
        type tuple (any)
method public Check_Unicity (object: Constraints, persistant_object_set: set(Constraints))) : boolean in class Constraints
method public Check_Totality_role (role1 :set(Constraints), role2 : set(Constraints)) boolean in class Constraints
method public Check_Equality_role (role1 : set(Constraints), role2 : set(Constraints)) : boolean in class Constraints,
method public Check_Inclusion_Relationship(ta1: set(Constraints), ta2 : set(Constraints)) : boolean in class Constraints
        ...

end

"Any" can be any type in the O2 model, Check_unicity, Check_totality, Check_Equality_role, Check_Inclusion_Relationship are four examples of generic modules which can be defined in the Contraints class. This class can also own other modules.

Every method contains two parameters. Each of one is Constraints type (or set (Constraints). They express two sets of objects of the same type.

* The Check_unicity method checks the unicity of a candidate key defined upon a class. The values of two parameters (object and persistant_object_set) of this method are often one of the two object types (integer or string) studied latter. Those two types are chosen because the definition domains used by candidate keys in Entity types are often simple types like integer or string.

The Check_unicity method uses the concepts of methods redefinitition and dynamic links : depending on the type of its actual parameters (integer or string), this method executes a method called Check which is defined in the Constraints class and redefined in each class Integer and String. The Check method verifies if an object belonging to the class Integer or String also belongs to the persistant object set of the same type.

* The Check_Totality_role method checks the totality constraint between two roles. The values which can be assigned to the two parameters role1 and role2 of this method are any object types of users applications.
This method checks the following constraint : role1 $\cup$ role2 $\neq$ {nil}.

* The Check_Equality_role method checks the equality constraint between two roles. The values which can be assigned to the two parameters role1 and role2 of this method are any object types of users applications.
This method checks the following constraint : role1 $\neq$ {nil} and role2 $\neq$ {nil}.
* The Check_Inclusion_Relationship method checks the equality constraint between two relationships. The values which can be assigned to the two parameters ta1 and ta2 of this method are any object types of users applications.
This method checks the following constraint : ta1 $\subseteq$ ta2 (or ta2 $\subseteq$ ta1).

2-1-2 Definition of the Integer class

The integer class is defined as a sub-class of the Constraint class. .An object of the type integer is also an object of the type "anThe integer class is defined as a sub-class of the Constraint y". The structure of this class in the O2 model is the following:

```
Class Integer inherits Constraints
        type tuple ( ...,
                val : integer)method...
        check ( x : Integer, y: set(Integer)) : boolean
end
```

The Check method is a method which exists in the Constraints class and which is redefined in the Integer class . This method checks the existence of the object x in the set of objects y.The Check method returns the value "True" if x is included in y and "false" otherwise. The body of this method is the following :

```
method body check (x : Integer, y : set(Integer)) : boolean in class Integer
                {       for (o in y)
                        if  (x->val == o->val)
                        return (true);   ...
                }
```

2-1-3 Definition of the String class

The definition of the String class is similar to the definition of the Integer class but here the type is string. The Check method is also redefined in the String class and it returns the value "True" if x is included in y and "false" otherwise.

3- Conclusion

In [Nachouki et al., 1991] starting from the study of the use of data, we have provided some rules in order to define an object oriented database.

In this paper, we have used the concept of generic modules in order to check the integrity contraints on any object defined in users applications. A prototype has been developped under the O2 system.

Some other types of constraints must also be considered such as constraints between a composite and it is components. Those constraints are required in knowledge based systems (for example: the CAD/CAM applications (Djeraba & al., 1993)) . In knowledge based systems the semantic dependencies between a composite object and its component objects doesn't exist. For example, the sharing of a component object between several composite objects cannot be described in those systems. So it seems to be important to study the implementation of this new type of constraints , and, in particular, how to express :

- the existential dependencies between a composite object and its components ;
- the sharing dependencies between a composite and its components ;
- the exclusively dependencies between a composite and its components.

References:

(Adiba & al., 1993):   M Adiba and al. Objets et bases de données le SGBD O2. Edition Hermes, Paris, 1993

(Bancilhon and al., 1992):   F Bancilhon and al. Building an Object Oriented Database System - The story of O2. The Morgan Kaufmann series in data management systems - 1992

(Bouzeghoub & al., 1991):   M Bouzeghoub and al. Semantic modeling of object oriented databases.Proceeding of the 17th International Conference on Very Large Data Bases, Barcelona 1991

(Chen 1976):   P.P Chen.The Entity-Relationship model : Toward a unified view of data. ACM Transactions on database systems mars 1976

(Djeraba 1993):   C. Djeraba, and al. Objets composites et liens de dépendance dans un système à base de connaissance. Inforsid 93- Lille

(Meyer 1988):   B Meyer. Object-oriented software construction.Prenticd Hall International edition Edition 1988

(Nachouki & al. 1991):   Nachouki and al.From entity relationship diagram to an object oriented database. Proc. of the 10th Int. Conf. on the Entity-Relationship Approach . San Mateo - USA 1991

(Pernici 1990):   B. Pernici. Requirement specification for object oriented systems Nouvelles perspectives des Systèmes d'Information. Inforsid 1990- Biarritz Eyrolles 1990

(O2 Technology 1994) :   O2 Technology : The O2 user Manual, version 4.0, 1994

HYPERMEDIA

HyperMART
Hypermedia and Multimedia Authoring
and Rendering Tool

Canice Lambe, Ray McGuigan, Jane Grimson

Knowledge and Data Engineering Group,
Dept. of Computer Science,
Trinity College
Dublin 2.
email: Canice.Lambe/Ray.McGuigan/Jane.Grimson@cs.tcd.ie

ABSTRACT. *This paper describes HyperMART, an object oriented Hypermedia and Multimedia Authoring and Rendering Tool for multimedia presentations. It allows authoring, using point-and-click mechanisms, of multimedia presentations, without compromising the original data . Multimedia assets are presented in a seamless, transparent environment with a unified set of interaction methods, offering services to a range of users from naive to experienced.*

KEY WORDS: *multimedia, hypermedia*

1. Introduction

In this paper we hope to illustrate deficiencies in current approaches to multimedia and hypermedia technology and detail a solution for the PC platform that uses object oriented techniques. [1]

1.1 Current multimedia technology

The developing use of multimedia computing, including the introduction of multimedia information presentations to the PC platform, has highlighted a number of gaps in the software applications available for authoring and presenting such material.

Currently multimedia presentations can be authored using specifically designed proprietary applications or written in a conventional programming language typically object oriented (OO) such as C++.

The applications (which require a smaller investment in training time) such as Macromedia Director and Authorware tend to be proprietary tools which *hard code* a specific multimedia presentation where the data is linked, using embedded coding in a

---

[1] This work has been partially funded by Multimedia Information Presentation System (MIPS) ESPRIT III Project 6542

closed system. This does not allow for its easy interchange with other systems in contrast with the programmed route using directly coded OO programming languages which offer greater flexibility and power but require a much greater investment in training and programming time.

Another problem to be addressed in multimedia computing is the presentation of the multimedia assets (the text, graphics, audio and video material) on a standard size screen while minimising complexity and clutter. If standard display tools are used (for example MS Word for text and graphics, Video for Windows for video etc.) the result is a mixture of Window frames with different tool bars, menu options and interactions with resulting confusion for the user.

Clearly the user is less interested in *how* the information is presented than *what* is there when it is presented. A desirable solution is a transparent, seamless presentation mechanism where the assets are presented democratically in what appears to be a single window with unified interaction methods.

The multimedia author wants a package which combines the simplicity of the *point and click* mechanism with the power of object orientation perhaps through a scripting language but without the complexity of learning a specific programming language. The application developer wants tools which will interface to a programming language such as C++.

1.2 Hypermedia

The concept of hypermedia has developed from that of hypertext expounded by Nelson in the 1960s and based on the seminal ideas of Vannevar Bush published in 1945 [Bush 1945]. Bush pointed out that, even then, there was a growing mountain of data and looked for new ways of linking together information. He described the idea of *associative links* in an attempt to model the way the human mind absorbs information and proposed a machine (analogue at that time) which would enable *associative trails* to be marked though disparate but associated data.

Bush's proposals, and his detailed plans for a machine *Memex* to implement them, did not progress beyond the academic paper expounding them but advances in technology, and computing in particular, enabled Ted Nelson to take them one step further when he envisaged a *docuverse* with the overall aim that [Nelson 67]:

> *Everything should be available to everyone. Any user should be able to follow origins and links of material across boundaries of documents, servers, networks and individual implementations. There should be a unified environment available to everyone providing access to the whole docuverse.*

The development of affordable computing, and in particular of the personal computing, led to a number of commercially available hypertext products. Recent advances incorporating time-based multimedia material such as audio, video and animation have led to hypermedia products. These enable data to be authored and accessed with embedded links which allow a user follow the associative trails envisaged by Bush.

However as Andries Van Dam pointed out in 1987 [Van Dam 1987] the proprietary nature of these products and their incompatibility, plus the fact that they compromise the data by *hard-coding* link pointers into the data meant that individual hypertexts were ending up as a series of *unconnected islands of information* rather than Nelson's docuverse.

Hugh Davis, Wendy Hall and others have pointed out that [Davis 1992]:

> *In order to make use of a document in a hypermedia system it must generally first be imported to the system. As soon as links are added to the system the data to represent the link will be stored in the file as some form of mark-up. The data is now in a closed system; it is no longer possible to process the data with the package that created it as it is now stored in a format private to the hypermedia system.*

They have followed Kathryn Malcolm and others [Malcolm 1991] and Frank Halasz [Halasz 1991] in suggesting that what is needed is a third generation of hypermedia systems which incorporate the presentational power of multimedia with the information richness of associative linking, or hyperlinking, in an open system where the data remains available and is not compromised in an data dead-end.

To address these needs researchers at Trinity College Dublin (TCD) are working on a vertically integrated suite of tools which will utilise OO techniques to enable authoring and presentation of a multimedia package within a seamless environment where the integrity of the data is not compromised by the application but remains available to other users in its original form.

This suite of tools comprises

- a screen builder - a package to allow *point-and-click* screen design
- an application builder - to parse the screen design to a scripting language and allow the introduction of flow-control
- an hypermedia object manager - to manage multimedia / hypermedia data exchange and linking
- a presentation tool - to enable seamless integration of multimedia assets in (apparently) a single window.

A detailed description of HyperMART's architecture and these modules follows in later sections.

2. Industrial requirements of hypermedia authoring systems

There follows three scenarios that illustrate the range of demands industry might make on a hypermedia tool suite.

2.1 A publishing solution

One possible use of the tool suite would be to integrate legacy databases in the publishing area into multimedia/hypermedia information systems.

Major publishers, whether they publish in text, electronic, or broadcast form, preserve their information in computer databases. In most cases this repository of data is used in a limited number of ways.

Firstly it is used in the primary publication of the data. In many cases this is the only use made of the data. Given the cost of assembling and storing the information this is not very cost effective. Secondly it is sometimes used as an archive source within the organisation - for example as an on-line research resource. In a very few cases the data is made available on a *pay-as-you-use* on-line database.

In most cases this data is capable of wider use and a hyperlinked environment would greatly add to its value. For example a newspaper may be publishing business and financial information, news and analysis every day. Much of this information is intricately inter-related e.g. the cross ownership of companies, their competing and complementary interests, trends in related industries, trends in comparable time periods and developments in world markets. The use of associative links or hyperlinks can add greatly to the reference value of the data.

Hyperlinking can make the most of the cross-related information but the data may be stored in formats not readily compatible with other data which would further enrich the information (graphics, pictures, video clips, radio interviews, TV programmes). HyperMART would enable a hypermedia database to be constructed using a publisher's existing data and overlaying the data with hyperlinks within that data and to other existing data sources, including multimedia data. The result would be a hypermedia document with a data value that is, in many ways, greater than the sum of all its parts. This data could be issued as a CD title or made available for remote log-in on a fee paying basis. The information would be available in read-only form to the end user.

2.2 Multimedia software project uses C++

Quite often a multimedia application requires complexity and/or performance that are not available from existing off the shelf authoring environments. Programmers have indicated dissatisfaction with performance where proprietary products were used to encode multimedia presentations. For example developers building a kiosk information system for the London Underground have stated [Rogers 1994]:

> *Authorware and Toolbook were analysed and subsequently rejected because they couldn't offer the required user response time of <3 seconds.*

Their data structure handling is typically quite simple and their interpreted environments lead to poor performance when compared to compiled languages.

Writing the application in a compiled language provides its own difficulties. Ideally the programmer would like to visually build the screens to be used and then place hooks for the code behind them. It would improve things if the assets used could be authored separately from the code (i.e. no details of hotspots, etc. hard-coded in the application.) An effective solution would seem to be a persistent store of multimedia asset objects with appropriate support for their rendition. The client code could then access these using a suitable protocol.

By the same token, support for a visual description, separate from the code (like a resource compiler for dialog boxes), saves unnecessary information from being hard coded into the application.

2.3 Naive user and simple presentation.

Many multimedia applications are no more than slideshow presentations with perhaps some logic offering branching or choice to the users. The authors of such systems do not need much experience in computing technology - often it is more important that they have good presentation skills. Such users will require tools to markup assets, build screens and introduce simple control flow logic. Systems such as Hypercard, Toolbook, etc. use this approach, however, all marking up and linking of assets exists within the application.

3. Architecture of HyperMART

This section describe the various modules that comprise HyperMART and how, combined, they attempt to solve some of the problems mentioned above. The architecture appears in Figure 1.

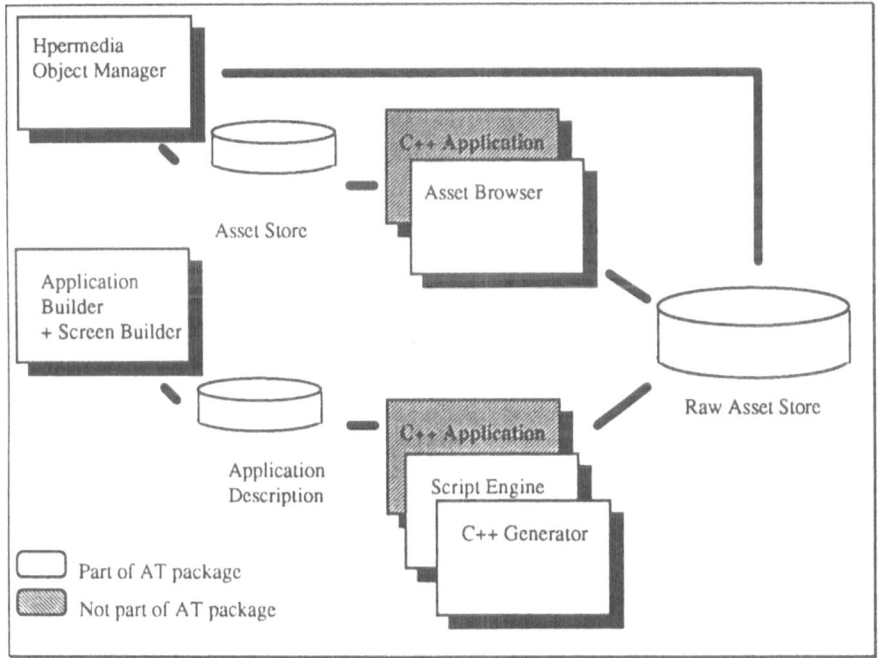

Figure 1 Architecture of HyperMART

3.1 Hypermedia Object Manager

The *Hypermedia Object Manager (HOM)* is responsible for the managing of the multimedia objects within the hyperdocument. It can be divided into two modules - the *Asset Manager* and the *Link Manager*

The Asset Manager (AM) will store information about the assets, their formats and link ends defined for them while the Link Manager (LM) will enable the semantics of the link to be communicated to the user and information about the use of the link mechanism to be displayed. The *Raw Asset Store* is the repository for the unmarked up or raw assets - this may be a read only network drive, a legacy database etc. The *Asset Store* is HyperMART's asset storage system. This contains all required asset information including references where necessary (filenames, SQL statements, etc.) to the Raw Asset Store.

Since most hypermedia links are explicitly made by authors the use of a single environment means that the author can, in establishing links, provide the information needed by the object manager to enable linking in an open hypermedia context. This is particularly useful with legacy databases where the data may not be available for export to another system or where it is required to be available to existing users. The HOM additionally ensures that the data is not compromised as a result of incorporation into a hypermedia document as it remains free of specific mark-up or tagging.

3.2 Asset Browser

An *Asset Browser* (AB) will provide a GUI front end for retrieving assets stored using the AM and LM. This will have rendering capability for each type of asset stored, will follow links between the assets, and will have some navigational aids when using links.

3.3 Application Builder and Screen Builder

Developers can use an *Application Builder (AB)* and *Screen Builder (SB)* to develop their applications. The SB allows the user to visually construct the set of *interaction mechanisms* (window controls that render assets and accept user interaction) required and bind them to existing assets if desired. The AB further accepts script language input that can be associated with events generated by user interaction.. The output is a file that contains the visual description of the screen and the control logic.

3.4 Script Engine

The *Script Engine* (SE) reads the files produced by the AB and uses an instance of the dispatch object to render the specified application. The application file is effectively interpreted.

3.5 C++ Generator

Having built the multimedia application using the AB:

- The user may be happy that the application is complete and wants a stand alone version that is not interpreted and is not reliant on the Engine
- The user may have achieved a certain subset of the desired functionality and wishes to use a more powerful language to achieve the rest.

In either case, translation of the application from script to C++ solves the problem. In the former case, once compiled, a faster stand alone version is produced.

In the latter case, the application is now represented in C++ code, the necessary hooks can be inserted to complete functionality. A strongly object oriented representation to isolate the HyperMART modules from the application specific modules is highly desirable.

3.6 Interfacing with C++

A client programmer can interface C++ to the system at a number of points.

- The client may simply access assets from the Asset Store. A C++ interface is provided that will instantiate the asset requested in a C++ object. The multimedia control objects for rendering are also available at this level.
- The client may use the visual aspects of the screen builder (much like a dialog resource) but. not use the Application Builder's script language.
- As mentioned above, the client might use the C++ translation facility.

4. Implementation of HyperMART

Before construction of the HypcrMART system could begin a representation for the information that facilitated both storage and rendering had to be identified.

4.1 The Hypermedia Common Object Model

The issues relating to open hypermedia have been outlined already. The Hypermedia Object Manager is central to an architecture which enables the authoring and accessing of a hyperdocument using existing data (possibly in legacy data systems)

- with uniform access - through a common user interface
- with heterogeneous data sources - incorporating different assets and formats
- in a distributed system - across a network

The Hypermedia Object Model defines data to enable its access and display while a Link Model defines the data to be accessed from the perspectives of the link operations, the mechanisms used (in authoring and browsing), and the semantics of the link.

400

4.1.1 Hypermedia Object Model

The Hypermedia Object Model enables access to the hyperdocument through

- a common user interface - transparent and seamless
- a common data access - not dependent on asset type or format
- common communication methods
- common link definition and typing
- common object structure - allowing for aggregated or decomposed assets objects

The model encompasses the properties of the assets which constitute the hyperdocument. Many of these properties are common across the range of assets (though with varying, and sometimes dynamic, values) such as:

```
id
extent
access mode
anchor
```

where *id* is a unique system wide identifier for the asset, *extent* is the size of this asset, *access mode* indicates the access level for this asset as between author, mark-up or render mode and anchor would indicate the point within the asset (typically, but not necessarily, the start) which the link actually links to.

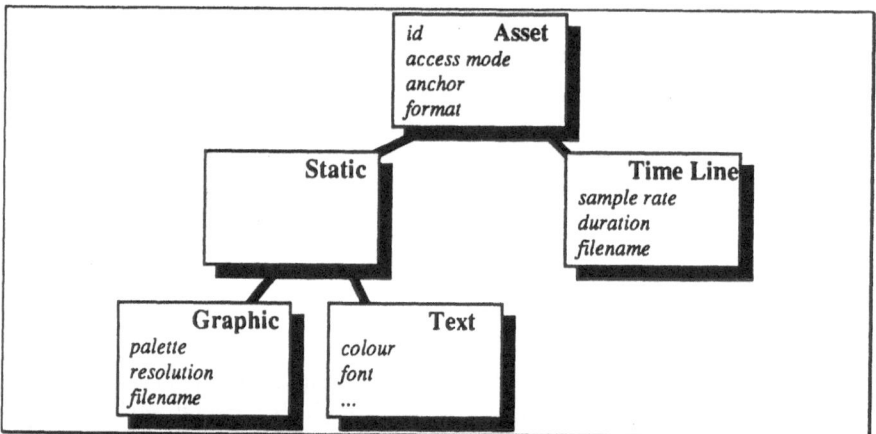

Figure 2 - Simplified hierarchy of asset types

One fundamental division is that which divides all assets into either time-line assets or static assets with associated properties and values in each (see Figure 2).

Thus a class hierarchy can be established which concentrates the commonality of data objects within the hyperdocument while allowing for their classification according to properties and values.

4.1.2 The Link Object Model

The *Link Object Model's* role is common to the authoring and rendering modes of HyperMART. Since all links have to be established manually by an author it is logical that the author should classify the links according to basic information about the assets being linked, the possible associative trail being authored and the semantics of the link.

The overhead of the authoring process can be reduced by much of the link object properties being pre-filled upon selection of the asset.

The link model defines

- link object properties
- link mechanisms
- link semantics

4.1.2.1 Link object properties

This is a hierarchy of objects concentrating on the commonality of the linking process with object properties such as:

```
chosen/ not chosen
internal/ external
uni-directional/ bi-directional/ n-directional
to_static/ to_time-line
```

4.1.2.2 Link mechanisms

These are the operations which the link object is able to perform and which would differ depending whether the user was in *render mode* or *author mode* (see section 4.3).

```
create_link_to
create_link_from
delete_link (to and from)
traverse_link
reverse_link
ignore_link
composite_link_with
```

4.1.2.3 Link descriptors

A recognised problem of hypermedia and hyperlinking is that described as *informational myopia* by Jeff Conklin [Conklin 87] or *the rhetoric of arrival* by George Landow [Landow 87] which describes the fact that the user may not know what they are linking to until it actually arrives on their screen. They may then find that the information is actually of no interest to them, or is too detailed, or is on parallel lines. This problem may be aggravated if the data is a large graphic or video file which takes some time to be loaded.

Thus link semantics would give the user a sense of the semantics of the link by classifying all links under a small number of headings. These might include

detail	further detail on this specific topic
explanatory	definition of the terms used, e.g. reference to a glossary
supplementary	additional data such as a picture or animation
parallel	additional data on similar topics

4.2 The HyperMART Presentation Tool

The rationale for the *HyperMART Presentation Tool (PT)* uses the metaphor of a *whiteboard* where the user's screen is a *blank page* waiting to be worked on. All the assets to be presented are shown within a uniform context where the environment is seamless and the commands transparent.

The uniform context is provided through the architecture of the PT which, using OO techniques, encapsulates existing presentation mechanisms to produce a common method of programming and interaction for the presentation tool.

The seamless environment follows from the uniform context which enables the various assets to be displayed within one window as far as the user is concerned. In fact the assets are in separate, seamless, child windows.

The commands are transparent in that the same look and feel can be used between different assets and within assets, for example, buttons, menus and hot-spotted pictures (all offer choice to the user). In a different environment separate tools might be used creating a multiplicity of interaction methods and interfaces.

The net effect of these three features is that the PT provides a user-and programmer friendly interface by providing an integrated presentation system for display of multimedia information.

4.2.1 Capabilities of the PT

The PT comprises an inheritance hierarchy of interaction mechanisms. The leaves of this hierarchy contain mechanisms capable of rendering the assets permitted in the HyperMART environment. Most of the functionality of the PT was developed as part of an Esprit research project MIPS where it serves as the front end. A detailed specification of the required API can be referenced in [MIPS 1993]. The PT currently renders the following asset types:

- text based - this includes encapsulations of the standard window text controls, ASCII text files with hotspot capability and RTF (Rich Text Format) files with hotspot capability.
- graphic based - this includes the BMP, PCX and GIF graphic formats. Specialisations of this type further allow graphically based check boxes, buttons and hotspots.
- MCI based - this renders time line assets (sound, video) via the Microsoft Windows Media Control Interface.

More complicated mechanisms can be constructed from these basic ones using inheritance and/or containership. These mechanisms may render many different formats. For example, choice of a European capital could be offered via a menu with the capitals' names or via a map with hotspots. A common underlying representation of the items for choice should exist regardless of the mechanism for rendition.

The PT provides an API for controlling the presentation of assets via these mechanisms. Many of these calls are common to all mechanisms (*show, hide,* etc.) while others will only have meaning for certain mechanisms (*play, stop,* etc. only have meaning for video and audio.)

4.3 Using the PT in other tools

Almost every other module in the system relies on rendition of assets. The development of the PT was a necessary starting point in the construction of the HyperMART suite. The original PT had capabilities only to render assets in a read only fashion or *render mode*. In order to fully accomplish the front end requirements the PT needed extending to have an *author mode* and a *mark up mode.*

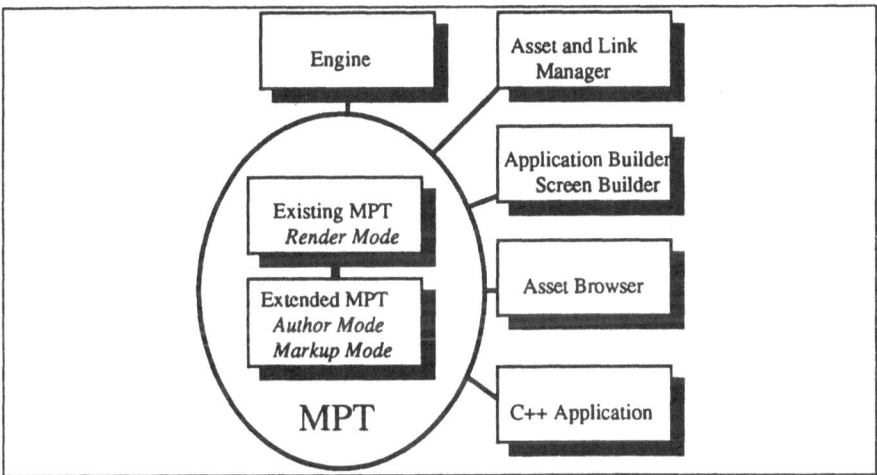

Figure 3 PT interface to the other modules.

4.3.1 Author mode

In author mode the assets can be moved, resized etc. on a screen for purposes of a presentation. This requires the PT to be extended so one can click and drag its interaction mechanisms and their contents, interrogate and change their properties, etc. This functionality is required by the Screen Builder.

4.3.2 Mark up mode

In markup mode, the author can directly interact with the assets, e.g. draw hotspots on a picture, etc. This requires the PT's interaction mechanisms to be extended to facilitate such interaction and have persistent storage methods. This functionality is required by the Hypermedia Object Manager.

5. Conclusions

The adoption of Object Oriented data models significantly enriches the possible data set for an open hypermedia system. In particular the OO paradigm extends the capability for including a range of data types and formats within an extensible open hypermedia system.

The implementation of an open hypermedia object model and link model would help fulfil the issues of adaptable environment of data tools and services, distributed and platform independent and facilitation of finding, updating, annotation, and exchange of information as identified by Malcolm et al [Malcolm 1991] as requirements for industrial strength hypermedia.

Many of the critical requirements in definitions of open hypermedia systems [Davis et al 1992] are also facilitated by adoption of the OO paradigm such as the lack of imposition of mark-up on the data, the ability to integrate with any tool, ease of adding new functionality and import or export to or from other hypertexts.

The display of such material in seamless windows with transparent access to different asset-types can reduce complexity for the user and benefits from the application of OO design and implementation.

A tool suite provides access to the information at a number of levels, fulfilling requirements of a number of users and applications.

The abstraction of the rendition platform (PC, UNIX, etc.) via the PT module allows portability of the system - it simply requires an implementation of PT for each platform accessed. At that most of the effort in porting would be for a small percentage of the PT - the basic rendering types only.

6. References

[Conklin 1987]   Jeff Conklin. *Hypertext -an introduction and survey*. IEEE Computer September 1987

[Davis et al 1992] Hugh Davis, Wendy Hall et al.. *Toward an Integrated Information Environment with Open Hypermedia Systems*. ECHT 1992

[Halasz 1991]   Frank Halasz. *Keynote Address*. Hypertext 91 -

[Landow 1987]   G.P. Landow. *Relationally encoded links and the rhetoric of hypertext*. Hypertext '87.

[Malcolm et al 1991] Katherine C Malcolm et al. *Industrial Strength Hypermedia: Requirements for a Large Engineering Enterprise*, Hypermedia 1991

[MIPS 1993]   SEMA Belgium, MIPS Consortium. *The definition of the*

MIPS system Volume 3 - The detailed functional specification of the HyTime Modules.

[Nelson 1967]   Ted Nelson. *Getting it out of our System. Information Retrieval: A Critical Review*, G Schechter ed., Thompson Books, Washington DC.

[Rogers 1994]   Dermot Rogers. *Anatomy of a Multimedia Project: Applying Multimedia to Public Transport and Tourist Information.* Proceedings ENTER 94.

[Van Dam 1987]   Andries Van Dam. *Keynote Address.* Hypertext 87

Actor Management in Documentary Applications

Amghar Youssef and Pinon Jean-Marie

LISI - INSA - Bat 502
20 Avenue A. Einstein
F-69621 VILLEURBANNE
email : amghar@if.insa-lyon.fr   Fax: +33 72 43 85 18

ABSTRACT. *In companies, documents are manipulated by different users who have different rights on them. Document management implies a clear definition of the roles played by the various users. These roles can be modelled trough a classification graph. The object paradigm which offers concepts such as class hierarchies seems to be an appropriate modelling context. However this model suffers of limitations which impede its use in some cases. The aim of this paper is to show how document management in organisation can be elegantly handled by an object oriented system although some extensions are needed. The emphazis is put on these new features. More precisely dynamic instance migration (from one class to another) and multi-instantiation of entities (the user is allowed to create several instances of the same entity, each of which is attached to a specific class) seem to be valuable concepts as modelling tools.*

KEY WORDS: *Document management, user role modelling, object oriented paradigm, multi-instantiation, dynamic class migration.*

1. Introduction

In an organisation, documents are accessed by number of users who can carry various actions on them. Each individual can be given specific rights on specific documents (or parts of documents). Similarly to data base systems for which views on data are tailored for users, this approach enforces document integrity, security and confidentiality. However the problem of view or right handling is more complex in the case of document than for data. More precisely, modelling the role of the user remains a major problem. In the context of object paradigm, an individual is represented as an object which can inherit several classes between which no inheritance links exist.

The aim of this paper is to show how object modelling can help to represent in a natural way the access rights on documents. We will see in paragraph 3 how a functional approach is useful to organise the various actors in a company under the form of an inheritance graph in which each class can reference a set of documents. We have used the concept of multi-instantiation as described by Van (Van de Riet, 1989) which appears as a valuable tool in our context to model the role played by an actor. This extention of the object paradigm makes it easy to represent an inheritance from two classes having no specialisation links. Before going into the details of this modelling, we will begin by showing how electronic documents can be represented in an information system.

2. Multimedia document modelling

Since the early 80's, there has been a growing interest in electronic document exchange and in some cases, in interactive document consultation (Vliet, 1988, André et al. 1989). This way made possible both by the extention of local or wide area networks (LAN, WAN) and by the development of computer based on tools for document production or document handling. In order to generalise the use of electronic documents, it was mandatory to define standards to have a common data representation. This is why an expert group was created within ISO to define these standards. A first standard proposal was made corresponding to what is called the SGML norm (ISO 8879, 1986), which was based on syntactic document modelling. The ODA standard (ISO 8613, 1987) which was created these last years uses the object paradigm. Each norm concern specific application domains and has its own supporters, even if the corresponding document architecturing are rather close. We will consider in this paper the ODA representation which suits better our approach (Pinon, 1989, Pinon, 1991).

ODA offers a set of concepts for document description and a set of processes for document handling. An exchange format (ODIF) is also defined. An ODA document can be seen from two different viewpoints: the logical view or the author's view corresponding to the various divisions of the document (sections, paragraphs, ...) and the physical view (pages, frames, blocs). In the current version of the norm, the content is decomposed into homogeneous parts which can be text, graphics, photos, ... Tables, mathematical or chemical formula, sounds or video sequences are extensions under study. For both views, ODA proposes a specific structure conform to a generic structure (a document model). This generic structure is instantiated wherever a specific document is needed, giving rise to specific structure. These structures can be modelled by an object paradigm, each object being described by attributes. The domain values of an attribute for an ODA specific object can be a list of numeric values, a string of characters, a reference to another object or a reference to a value. In the case of a generic object, an attribute can be a rule which computes values to the corresponding attributes in specific objects. In an object, an attribute may be mandatory or optional. When nothing is specified for an attribute, its value is derived according to deduction rules (inheritance, default values, ...). Beside theses four structures (logical, physical, generic, specific), formatting styles (for the document) and presentation styles (for the content) add further information when formatting or representing objects in the ODA model. ODA defines a universal document representation aimed at increasing productivity in office tasks and at making easier document interchange and interactive document querying (Amghar et al., 1989a, 1989b). A document may be in one of the three following forms:

Processable: the document is in its logical form an may be modified. However it cannot be displayed at once.
Formatted: the document is in its layout form and can be displayed, but no modification is allowed.
Processable and formatted: the document can be displayed. At the same time, the information on its logical structure have been saved allowing further modifications.

3. Actor's modelling

Very big and very complex documents are usually written by several persons, each of them taking in charge specific parts (Figure 1). Let us begin by defining the terminology used here after.

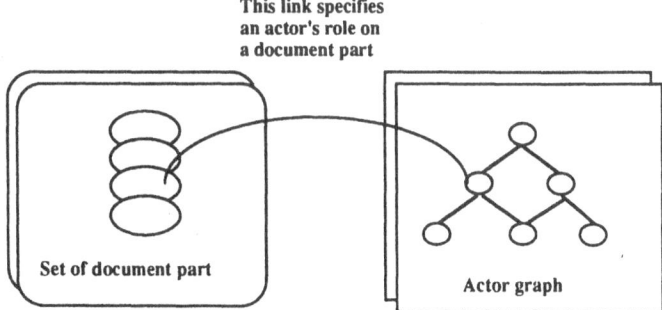

Figure 1 : Role definition. Documents and actors mapping.

Definition 1: An individual is a person working in the company.
Definition 2: An actor is an individual having access to a part of a document or to a whole document.
Definition 3: A role defines the operation type that may be done by an actor on a document part. It may be expressed by a mapping between the set of the parts of the documents belonging to the company and the set of the possible actors.

3.1. Actor and role presentation

The actor notion corresponds to user category. These actors operate on documents by given scripts. The actor organisation is hierarchical (Figure 2).

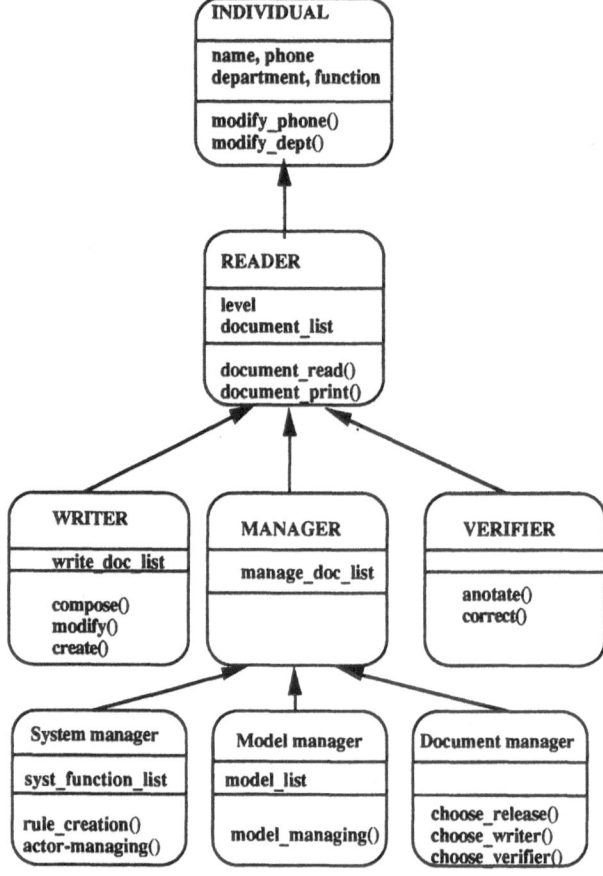

Figure 2 : Partial actor's hierarchy

Each node of the tree corresponds to a class describing a given actor set. The description concerns on the one hand, the attributes of the considered actor type, on the other hand, the possible methods. For example, the actor class *READER* describes the structural properties of readers such as *readAccessRights,* ...as also the methods *documentRead* and *documentPrint.* Then the methods implemented within classes allow to express constraints between actors and documents. Indeed, as the class *READER* implement only the methods *documentRead* and *documentPrint,* a reader will not be able to do anything except read or print a document. An attribute *documentSet* restricts (limits or defines) the set of documents that a person may read. Classifying users into categories allows a better checking of the document and so an increase of its security.

Each individual of the company is a person defined by a set of attributes such as the name, the function, the department, the telephone number, and so on. The class *INDIVIDUAL* has the following description:

```
class INDIVIDUAL (
attributes :
        name, phone,
        department, function;
methods :
        create ();
        modifyPhone();
        modifyDepartment();
        modifyFunction();
```

When an individual is provided with several roles, he becomes an actor. In order to build the actors' hierarchy, let us see what each actor may realise (Figure 3). The actors can be classified and the following classification is very common in companies:

The *READER* class: The actors of this class have only one role : the document consultation. The *READER* class may be itself sub-classified according to the documentary objet type which may be accessed (generic object used in models of documents, specific objects used in specific documents, scientific content, legislative content, and so on).

The *WRITER* class: The writers are in charge of offering the first draft of a document. When a document is very big complex, it is divided into several parts; each part is given to only one writer but a single writer can word several detached parts.

The *VERIFIER* class: verifiers read the documents in order to detect errors and propose modifications which he can possibly explain with written or vocal annotation (for this function, a system which manages sound and voice is interesting). A single verifier can check several sections or the whole document. Generally, a document subset is verified by several verifiers. Indeed conflicting modification can be proposed by the different verifiers (see editor's role).

The *EDITOR* class: the editor has the responsibility for the whole document. In particular, he must compare the writers' original version and the verifiers' modified versions. The editor, when resolving the conflicts has to accept or to refuse the proposed modifications in order that the document remains consistent. So the editor provide the new (or final) document version. This operation is called "document homogenisation" Generally speaking, this process is an iterative one. In other words, the new version is also verified, then corrected, next homogenised and so on. When all the conflicts are not solved to the first iteration.

The *MANAGER* class: Three types of *MANAGER* may be distinguished.

The role of the first (called *SYSTEM MANAGER* class) is to manage de *Document Data Base* and the *Document Data Base Management System*}. His must also manage the *ACTORS* (for example, he has to create new actors, to delete, or to modify the characteristics of some actors.

410

The second type (named "MODEL MANAGER" class) correspond to the "class document manager". He creates, modifies or deletes the generic documents (in other words the document models).

The third type (*DOCUMENT MANAGER* class) is the "specific document manager" whose work is to manage the life cycle of a specific document (production, indexation, mailing, storing, destroying, and so on). In other word, he checks that the rule which ensures the quality and the security of the document are systematically applied.

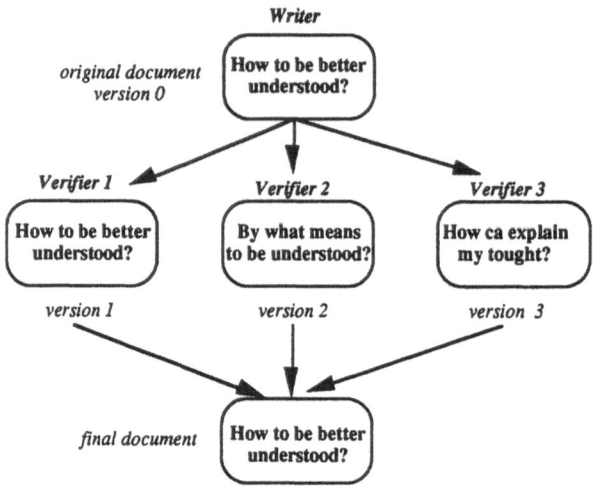

Figure 3 : Example of a multi-authored composition.

3.2. Modification Procedure

The modifications can be classified according to the type of the object on which they relate. Let us distinguish for example:

content modifications (insertion, deletion, or moving of a character string, or of a graphical primitive, or of a sonorous portion, and so on) which are located inside the content portion (a sequence of content portions linked to a same elementary logical object);

structure modification (insertion, deletion or moving of a logical object such as paragraph, section, chapter, figure, note, ...);

attribute modification of a logical object (modification of the user visible name or of the security level in a logical object) \item {\bf link modification}, that is to say the creation or the deletion of a link between two logical object such as a paragraph and a figure;

attribute modification of a link (type of the link, visibility level, icon or annotation associated, ...)

style modification such as modification of the size of a physical object (frame or page) in a layout style, colour modification in a presentation style (ISO 8613, 1986).

Some modifications concern only one object, for example content modification such as misspelling correction, ... These modification are called "local modifications".. However, some other modifications (such as structure modification or style modification, etc.) can have consequences on a subset or even on the whole document itself. As an example, the insertion or the deletion of a paragraph which can modify the number of the following paragraphs. Similarly, the replacement of a word by another one must be done everywhere in order that the document remains consistent. Consequently, to any modification, a range must be associated and it will be defined as the number of objects (paragraph, section, figure, ...) which are concerned by it. Not all modifications have the same importance for the verifier, some of them are mandatory (misspelling) or are only improvements. So let us distinguish several modifications categories such as "minor presentation modification", "major presentation modification", minor technical modification", "major technical modification", and so on ...

4. Object Oriented Actor Modelling

We can note for example that "VERIFIER" and "WRITER" classes inherit methods from the class "READER". Therefore, "VERIFIER" and "WRITER" are specialisations (or sub-class) of "READER". This latter which is itself a sub-class of "INDIVIDUAL" is described below.

```
class "READER" inherits from "INDIVIDUAL"
attributes:
        specificDocuments; /* allows to help to select
        a subset of documents */
methods:
        documentRead(); documentPrint();
```

Let us note that, usually, an actor cannot play all the possible roles (i.e. have all the rights) on a document. This consideration gives to the documentation management a feature of distributed application according to the actors of the company. In application of the proverb "To divide in order to govern (to reign)", the distribution of the rights between all the actors increases the document security (integrity and/or confidentiality). When the actors share the documents, they share the possible methods on these documents.

Let us study now how to represent the different roles of an individual towards the documents of the company. In an "Object Oriented Environment", the various actors are represented by instances of classes. Nevertheless, there is still an issue coming from the fact that the object oriented systems do not offer tools allowing to describe a role such as defined above, that is to say, to allow an actor to be an instance of several unknown classes before time (in advance, early, a priori, ...). Indeed, an individual can have several various roles according to the documents which he manipulates and according to his function in the organisation of the company. He can be at the same time "VERIFIER" and "MANAGER" of a same document (or of various documents). Therefore, he must be instance of several classes.

4.1 Using of the multi-instantiation concept for role modelling

In the kind of applications we deal with, it is important to have many different views of an object. For example, the person "Mike" can be manager or writer as well. In the object oriented context, the object representation of the entity "Mike" is an instance of many classes ("INDIVIDUAL", "MANAGER","WRITER") which are not necessarily linked in the specialisation graph (like "MANAGER" and "WRITER" classes). This concerns the multi-instantiation. Every actor of a company is first of all an individual. It is for this reason that the "Individual" class is the hierarchy root. A created instance at any level of the hierarchy inherits attributes and methods of the

"Individual" class. At every once an actor play a new role he is created like an instance of the class which implements the role in the form of a method (or method set). In this way, it becomes possible to apply to the instance all defined methods of the classes at which this instance is linked. It should be observed that the multi-instantiation calls into question the principle of object approach which wants the unicity of the instance-class pair.

In some way, the specialisation mechanism involves the multi-instantiation. Indeed an instance of a class may be considered as an instance of the super-class in a naturally way. Some ones speak about implicit or explicit multi-instantiation (Rieu et al., 1991).

The fundamental difference between specialisation and multi-instantiation concepts may be summarised as follows:

In the first case (specialisation), the inheritance of the super-class attributes and methods by the instance of the sub-class is systematic. In the second case every instantiation link may be explicitly specified. On another hand for the specialisation if we consider the class C2 as sub-class of the class C1, the object o1 can be:

> instance of C1 (uniquely)
> instance of C2 (this involves o1 inherits from C1 in systematic way).

In multi-instantiation case, if we consider two classes C1 and C2 with no direct link between them, the object o1 can be:

> an instance of C1 (uniquely);
> an instance of C2 (uniquely);
> an instance of both C1 and C2.

The instance deletion is another difference. For this purpose, in the multi-instantiation case the deletion consists in breaking the instantiation link between the object and one of the classes to which this object is attached. Whereas the instantiation link deletion involves the complete instance deletion. So, in the studied case the multi-instantiation allows to increase or decrease actor roles. This is translated into an instantiation links creation or deletion. The concept of multi-instantiation permits dynamic class migration of the instances.

4.2. Illustration

To illustrate the actor role management (Figure 4), let us consider the following situation. Let o1 be an entity represented by an instance of "Individual" class which values are given by the tuple {"Mike","78675645", "Financial", "Department manager"}. If "Mike" is a verifier on "Note 123" and "Report 2" documents, so the listOfDocuments attribute is at first instantiated to give the set ("Note 123", "Report 2"). Now, if "Mike" is manager on "Letter 23", "Note 98" and "Report 35" documents as well the listOfDocuments attribute will now be instantiated to the set ("Letter 23", "Note 98", "Report 35"). So this attribute is a reference list to the specific documents. In other respects, "Mike" is first of all created as an instance of the "Verifier" class and as instance of the "Manager" class.

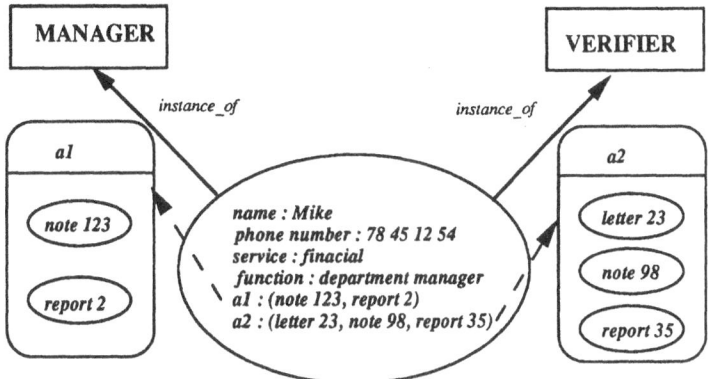

Figure 4 : Example of a person playing 2 roles on 2 document sets.}

4.3. Specific mechanisms

Object Oriented Data Base Management Systems (OODBMS) like O2 (Bancilhon et al., 1988), GEMSTONE (Maier, 1986), GBASE (Graphael, 1988), IRIS (Fishman, 1986), ... as currently marketed have no multi-instantiation mechanism and do not allow the instance migration. However, it is always possible to implement the multi-instantiation concept. For this purpose, it must be created sub-classes of all classes for which no specialisation links exist in the data base schema. For example, if we consider the actor model seen before, many sub-classes can be created. More particularly a sub-class "WRITER MANAGER" of "WRITER" and "MANAGER" classes may be created. So all instances of this sub-class will be a representation of individuals with both writer and manager roles. Then the multiple inheritance will express the multi-instantiation properties. However this method presents many drawbacks. Let us mention the schema complexity, the difficulty to develop applications and the lack of the modelling elegance. Making multi-instantiation possible in OODBMS induces a performance decrease of the developed system. To represent multiple inheritance without specialisation links in natural way, some mechanisms are necessary. When an instance is pointed it would be possible to attach it to another class (not its originate class). We outline the essential instructions to permit the instance evolution. Let us consider the example illustrated in the section 6. To realise this script one can imagine the following instructions:

1. "Mike" is an individual (entity of company)
- o1 = new(Individual)
/* initialise o1 with the tuple:
("Mike", "78675645", "Financial", "Department manager") */

2. now "Mike" has writing role:
o1 = addNew(Writer)
/* listOfDocuments" attribute is instantiated
a first time and has the value ("Note 123", "Report 2") */

3. now "Mike" has a new role (managing documents)
o1 = addNew(Manager)
/* listOfDocuments" attribute is instantiated a second time
with the value ("Letter 23", "Note 98", "Report 35") */

Giving the OODBSM an extention of instantiation mechanism to realise the multi instantiation supposes that the instance manipulation language is enriched accordingly. These technics of multi-instantiation present a big drawback. Indeed the decision to instantiate an object once again depends on application (user or program). The concept of active object is a good alternative to represent actor's role because such object can encapsulate any rules. Rules which are included in the schema description as components of objects, are given by the system manager. These rules are activated by events. A rule has the following form:

> rule rule_name
> on event if condition then action

Different coupling mode can be associated to event-condition and condition-action couples : immediate, deferred or detached. Therefore, this rule principle allows migration rule, versioning management and so on. In our context the multi-instantiation is coded by the action clause so permitting a correct control of roles. The action is triggered when the condition is satisfied and the event occurs. To define migration rules one must find both events which trigger theses rules and conditions to satisfy for action execution. If one considers the same example as above, one can define the following rule:

> event : on role change
> conditions : if individual role is not Writer
> action : add new role(Writer)

5. Conclusion

Documents' security of companies requires accurate management of the document access and a strict management of the users. The different roles of the actors have to be defined clearly for enhancing efficiency of the human resources organisation. As shown in this paper the object oriented approach and the multi-instantiation concept allow to organise the actors in a correctly and naturally way. The roles played by these actors are represented by methods in different classes. Each of them can be specialised to take advantage of other functionnalities. So each individual may be a reader, a manager or a verifier and so on. The concept of multi-instantiation enhances the power of object paradigm beside the specialisation concept. The inheritance becomes explicit when an instance is linked to two classes with no links between them. Finally the multi-instantiation offers a mean to consider an object according to multiple views.

References:

(Amghar et al 1989a): Amghar Y. and Pinon J.M., *Un éditeur de documents ODA: une application de l'approche objet*, congrès WOODMAN, Rennes, 29-31 June 1989.

(Amghar et al 1989b): Y. Amghar. *Base d'objets documentaires: mod\'elisation, manipulation et stockage de documents codés selon la norme ODA*, Thesis, Nbr: 89 ISAL 0070, Lyon 1989.

{André et al., 1989): J. Andre, R. Furuta and V. Quint. *Structured Documents*, Cambridge, Cambridge University Press, 1989, 229 pages.

(Bancilhon, 1988): P. Bancilhon. *The Design and Implementation of O2, an Object-Oriented Database System*, Proceedings of the Second international workshop on Object-Oriented database Systems, K. Dittrich Ed., bad-Munter, FRG, 1988, pp43-56.

(Fishman and al., 1986): D. Fishman al, *Iris: an object-oriented DBMS*, ACM TOIS, vol.5, nbr 1, January 1986, pp48-69.

Graphael, 1988): G-Base version 3, *Introductory guide*, Graphael 1988.

(ISO 8613, 1986): ISO TC97 SC18, *Information Processing - Text and Office Systems - Office Document Architecture (ODA) and Interchange Format (ODIF)*, Association Francaise de

NORmalisation (AFNOR), PAris, Draft International Standard 8613, 1987.for Standardisation.

(ISO 8879): ISO TC 97 SC18, *Information Processing System - Text and Office System Standard Generalised Markup Language (SGML)*, Association Francaise de NORmalisation (AFNOR), Paris, International Standard 8879, 1986.

(Maier et al., 1986): D. Maier and. al. *Development on an object-oriented DBMS*, Report CS/E-86-005, Oregon, Graduate Center, April 1986.

(Pinon, 1989): J.M. Pinon. *Multimedia Communication System*, Tutorial in Urban Data Management Symposium, Lisbon, 1989 61 pages or La documentation multimedia dans les organisations, Collection CTP Nbr 40, HERMES editor, Paris, 64 pages.

(Pinon, 1991): J.M. Pinon. *Base de documents hypermedia*, DB'91 Congress, Algiers, June 1991, CERIST Editor, pp 162-215.

(Rieu, 1991): D. Rieu and al. *Instantiation multiple et classification d'objets*, séminaire BD, Alger 15-17 Juin 1991, pp 26-44.

(Van de Riet, 1989): R.P. Van de Riet.. *Mokum: An Object-oriented active Knowledge base system*. Data and Knowledge Engineering, North Holland, Vol 4, No 1, July 1989.

(VanVliet, 1988): J.C. Van Vliet. "Document Manipulation and Typography", EP 88, The Cambridge Publishing, Ed. JC vanVliet.

Support System for Cooperative Edition of Multimedia Documents

Jean-Marie Pinon**, **Marc-Antoine Richez*** and **André Flory****

**EVER SA, 170 Bd Staligrad F-69006 Lyon FRANCE*
Fax: · 33 78 93 92 20
***LISI-INSA, Bat 502, 20 Av. Einstein F-69621 Villeurbanne FRANCE*
E-mail: pinon@if.insa-lyon.fr

ABSTRACT. *This paper describes a support system for cooperative edition of multimedia documents. This system concerns high level document's processing submitted to constraints of quality insurance. It uses a standard document representation (ODA, SGML) and an access path to the information system of the human organisation in order to maintain the global consistency. We present the first level prototype of our system, based on the integration of common softwares (MS-WINDOWS, UNIX, DORIS, ORACLE DBMS, etc.), and hardwares (PC, Unix servers). We present also DORIS which is an object oriented document management system developed by EVER.*

KEY WORDS: *Cooperative document processing - Object oriented document management system - Data and document consistency.*

1. Introduction

The Support System for Cooperative Edition of Multimedia Documents is conceived to help high level teams (executives, technicians,. ...) whose task consist of tools or complex applications design. For example, research and development teams in high technology companies (nuclear industry, aviation, car industry, public health, etc.), research laboratories , groups who write regulations, laws, safety procedures, etc. Their work is at first a thought and design work which is translated into "quality-document". A "quality- document" is a document submitted to constraints of quality insurance. These constraints, defined by rules, impose document models, procedures to respect during the document processing (choice of authors, method of reviewing, procedure of approval, time limits, etc.).

A "quality-document writing team" is composed by every people who cooperate to the document processing. This team will also have to use and to manage existing documents. Each member of a writing team needs a workstation to perform the various tasks related to his activity.

Most of these tasks need to use external resources. Access to these resources has to be performed simply from a workstation by applying rules of quality insurance in order to protect critical and private information. Moreover, relationships between the Support System for Cooperative Edition of Multimedia Documents and the company information system have to maintain consistency between both systems.

This article presents a prototype built by a French company EVER and LISI (Laboratoire d'Ingénierie des Systèmes d'Information), the Information System Engineering Laboratory of the INSA in Lyon. This prototype has been built in the context of the national program "Office of the Future" supported by the French Ministry of Industry. This prototype is built on personal computer, under the system MS-DOS, MS-WINDOWS, and uses softwares such as WINWORD from MICROSOFT and DORIS from EVER (EVER, 94).

We present in this paper three aspects of this work : functions and general architecture, representation of documentary information and descriptive data management performed by the software DORIS, and interfaces with the information system.

2. Function and architecture

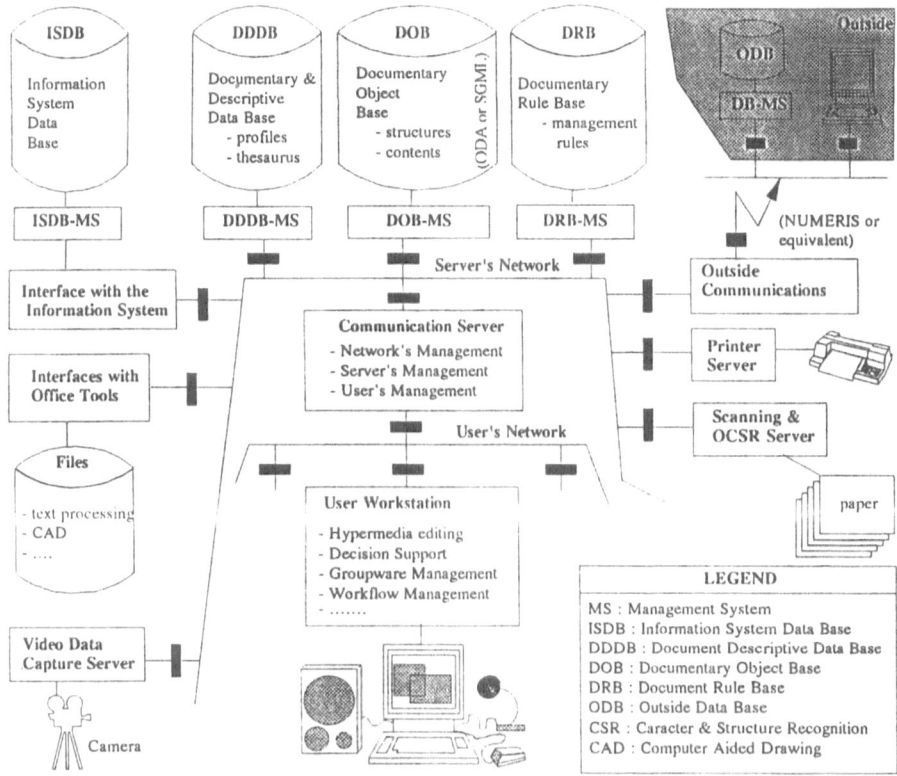

Figure 1 : Support System for Cooperative Edition of Multimedia Document

As figure 1 shows, the system architecture is distributed. The workstation is the central point of this system. The workstation is the entry point to the system for the user. It allows the following functions:
- Individual writing of multimedia document or part of multimedia document. A multimedia document mixes texts, geometrical drawings, photographs, worksheets, and sometimes video sequences and sounds ;
- Multi-criteria interrogation in the documentary bases which may be distant or local ;
- On-line consultation of documents, or document parts selected, by multi-criteria queries ;
- Extraction of documentary objects during consultation in order to insert them in an other document ;
- Consultation of safety insurance rules which must be applied to the current task ;
- Groupware management (reviewing, part of document merging) ;
- Access to the information system databases, and insertion of query results into logical object of the current document.

Workstations are connected together by a local area network or a wide area network . They access various resources through networks :

- Documentary database : it contains all descriptive information about documents (the profile according to ODA meaning) including titles, authors, keywords, owner, access rights, languages, lengths, coding (SGML, ODA, LATEX, WORD, R.T.F, ...), location (computer address or storage place of the paper document, ...), and the thesaurus (dictionary of words or keywords including relationship between these words) ;
- Base of documentary objects : we recommend standards preference SGML or ODA, but others representations will be possible (cf §2). Moreover this base contains models of document (generic structures for ODA or Typical Document Definition for SGML) ;
- Documentary rules base : it describes procedures and controls needed to be able to affirm that a document has the "quality" stamp ;
- Company information system database : it is accessed through an interface which allows at first to the exchange of data between information system and documentary system and also insure the coherence between both systems ;
- Different servers : they offer services such as the document printing, the scanerisation and character recognition, audio-visual sequences performing, etc. ;
- Files produced by common office systems such as interactive words processing, computer assisted drawing, chart editors, etc.

3. Electronic document representation : ODA OR SGML?

Two standards for document representation are currently recommended by the ISO : the Open Document Architecture standard (ISO 8613, 1988) and the "Switchboard Generalised Markup Language" standard (ISO 8879, 1986). A comparative description of both of these standards can be consulted in (PINON, 1989) or (PINON et al., 1990).

The "Standard Generalised Markup Language" defines a readable document representation based on the mixing of "text content" and "markups". Markups are character strings which structure a text document. Every documentary element is delimited by a "begin-tag" and a "end-tag". For example the title of this section would be so delimited:
<section-title> Electronic Document representation: ODA or SGML?</section-title>
The SGML Document Type Definition defines the logical structure of a document model. For example, our document model specifies the following possible structure: a paper is a sequence of a paper-header, paper-body and a paper-end. A paper header is a sequences of a paper-title, paper-authors-description.

The Open Document Architecture defines an Object Oriented representation for documents. An ODA document can have two hierarchical structures:

- A logical structure which divides the document into logical objects (composed or elementary) such as chapters, sections, paragraphs, ... ;
- A layout structure which divides the document into layout objects (composed or elementary) such as page-set, page, frame-set, frame, block.

Logical structure and layout structure are two views of a same multimedia content (text, geometric, raster) divided into content portion. Document model (or Document Class) is defined in ODA by the concepts of generic logical structure, generic layout structure and common contents. A specific document is an instanciation of a document class.

Should we choose ODA or SGML? The choice of SGML in the CALS project (MIL-HDB, 1990) (POWEL, 1993) (SANDOVAL, 1993) has influenced many organisations in their choice. Other organisations, generally associated with the telecommunication companies prefer ODA. We think that ODA and SGML are complementary. Indeed, SGML seems to be well adapted for closed application performed by a person group which Is able to agree on models and precise conventions. They are applications linked to the production of documents.

On the other hand, ODA seems to be well adapted for open applications, when document's readers have no connection with document authors. It Is the case of applications linked to remote consultation of large documentary bases. These bases are accessed by a great number of persons (national libraries, etc.). Moreover, ODA has been conceived at first to be integrated to the final model given by the standard ISO "Open System Interconnection".

4. Documentary database description

Our prototype is built upon an object oriented model which allows the document processing cycle. The different steps of this cycle are :
• Purpose definition ;
• Actors assignment ;
• Creation of various logical parts of the document, each part becomes a secondary document ;
• Parts integration ;
• Versions management, including all the reviewing mechanism ;
• Validation and approval ;
• Electronic document mailing and document access rights assignment.

We lead the domain analysis from real cases of document processing in office systems (memorandum, report, ...) and industrial field (specifications, analysis, design, ...). This domain analysis was based on an object oriented method (OOA). It defined five main topics :
• Document as a set of parts, and versions ;
• Document analysis as documentary analysis (key words, abstracts, ...) and normalised translation (based on SGML, ODA, HyTime) ;
• Actors, including writers, reviewers, readers, managers, and allowing access to the general information system of the company ;
• Projects, as context of the document processing ;
• Messages, which allows to preserve information about the document processing cycle.

Our prototype is built using common office tools (WINWORD 6, ...). It links this tools with a documentary object oriented database. Requests on this database are performed through the documentary database system manager DORIS (Documentary Object oriented Relational Information System).

DORIS is a DBMS merging database managing features and documentary features. DORIS uses a relational DBMS (like ORACLE, SYBASE, INFORMIX, ...) for physical data storage. Translation of object's features into the relational tables is implemented using the ASN standard (ISO 8824, 1990). Database managing features include creation, updating, removing, multi-users managing, calculated numerical fields, security managing. Documentary features include multi-values and multi-criteria requesting, comparative operators, step by step research, view editing, empty words list setting.

The user's action within the office tools updates in real time the documentary database. This function is implemented through the DORIS Application Programming Interface. This API is loaded as a dynamic linked library and called from the office tools in macro commands.

Meanwhile, DORIS allows to build a full documentary application as an external access to data. This application includes administrative utilities (as field control definition, view definition, ...), and a large set of documentary technics.

5. Information System Interface

Documents need to be filled with data which are given either by use or by database. The main problem is to generate the database calls and to execute them. Queries are directed to the DBMS, answers are obtained and transformed to the format accepted by the document or by an internal database (located on the workstation : for example in EXCEL format).

For this work we use a SQL-translator which generates SQL queries from the document's form definition. The user gives target attributes (which can be obtained using SQL's SELECT class). We assume we have something like an universal relation in a given universe. A universe is represented by a given part of the user's knowledge (for instance in a sales system, customer, invoice order represent the universe "sale"). Let us consider a document : "good customer" which contains attributes such as customer number, customer name, customer address, invoice #, amount, number of purchases, where a good customer is a customer whose number of purchases is greater than 30. The user must first indicate in which universe he works, gives the form and attributes of the document (see above) and choose the criteria (here : number of sales is greater than 30). The SQL translator then generates automatically the following SQL-query.
SELECT CUST #, NAME, NB_OF_PURCHASES, INVOICE #, AMONT
FROM CUSTOMER INVOICE
WHERE CUSTOMER_CUST # = INVOICE.CUST #
AND NB_OF_PUCHASES > 30

The SQL query is then linked to the document. This query is used every time we have to fill an instance of the document.

6. Conclusion

We showed in this paper the architecture for a support system for cooperative edition of multimedia document. This system allows to process (design, write and verify) high level documents submitted to constraints of quality insurance. Such system is based on integration of common softwares and hardwares. This integration needs standard document representation (SGML or ODA). Moreover, this system must be strongly linked with the information system of the human organisation. So a gateway have to be set up between both systems in order to control the consistency between data and documents. We built a first level prototype upon MS-WINDOWS environment for the workstation and UNIX for the servers. An important work about multi-authors document modelisation (releases of documentary object, annotation, etc.) is to be done. A base of multi-authors and multimedia documents is a kind of hyperdocument. So we plan to develop a model based on the HyTime or HyperODA Standards.

References

(EVER, 94): EVER S.A., *Manuel DORIS V2.1.6*, 1994
(ISO 8613, 1988): International standard. *Information Processing - Text and Office Systems - Open Document Architecture (ODA) and Interchange Format (ODIF)*, 1988.
(ISO 8879, 1986): International standard. *Information Processing - Text and Office Systems - Standard Generalised Markup Language (SGML)*, 1986.
(ISO 8824, 1990): International standard. *Information Technology - Open System Interconnection - Specification of Abstract Syntax Notation One (ASN.1)*, 1990.
(MIL-HDB, 1990): MIL-HDBK-59A. *Military Handbook, Computer-aided Acquisition and Logistic Support (CALS) Program Implementation Guide*, September, 1990

(PINON, 1989):   J.M. Pinon. *Multimedia communication Systems*, Tutorial of the 13th Urban Data Management Symposium, Lisbon, May 1989.

(PINON et al., 1990):   J.M Pinon - R. Laurini. *La documentation multimedia dans les organisations*, Collection CTP Hermès, Paris, 1990.

(POWEL, 1993):   R.G. Powell. *Introduction to CALS, First CALS Technical Seminar*, Proceedings, Tokyo, April 1993

(SANDOVAL, 1993):   V.Sandoval. *CALS: introduction et mise en oeuvre*, Hermès, Paris, 1993

OPERATING SYTEMS
AND
LANGUAGES

A Declarative Extension of IDL-based Type Definitions within Open Distributed Environments

Arno Puder

Department of Computer Science
University of Frankfurt
D-60054 Frankfurt
Germany
puder@informatik.uni-frankfurt.de

Abstract

An open distributed environment can be perceived as a service market where services are freely offered and requested. Any infrastructure which seeks to provide appropriate mechanisms for such an environment has to include some mediator functionality to bring together matching service requests and service offers. The matching algorithm that the mediator must perform commonly builds upon an IDL-based type definition for service specification. In order for the matching algorithm embedded in this mediator to succeed, the types of various services have to be standardized and distributed to all interested parties. We argue that those well defined "standards"[1] are too inflexible and even contradict the idea of an open service market. Therefore we propose a new way to augment an arbitrary IDL-based type definition by a semantic tag. Whereas several other authors have used pre- and post-conditions to add the notion of behavior description, we use the well established field of Horn clauses as a semantic extension. The advantage lies in the nature of the declarative semantic and it will be shown that the need for a well defined standard is abolished within so called type families.

Keywords: Open Systems, Trading, Subtyping, IDL, Declarative Semantics

1 Introduction

There have been several approaches to type theory, depending on which aspects of a problem are to be modeled. One common employment of type theory derives from the need to recognize programming errors in a high level language. Given the simple assignment statement $x:=a$ in a typed programming language, both entities, the variable x as well as the expression

---

[1]The term "standard" is not to be confused with ANSI- or ISO-like standards. For the context of this paper a standard is an agreement (or convention) between client and server implementors about what the services are going to be called and what the arguments will be.

2.1   Object based computations

The environment, which serves as a basis for this paper, builds upon the classical definition of an object (see [Booch91]): "An object has state, behavior and identity; the structure and behavior of similar objects are defined in their common class. The terms instance and object are interchangeable." Using this definition, a problem domain may be decomposed as a set of interacting and co-operating objects. A snapshot of such an object-based computation may be visualized as a directed graph, where nodes represent objects and arcs represent references. A reference (or arc) is therefore a referral of an object's identity. The direction of the arc determines whose identity is known to whom. For an object to hold a reference to another object means to know about the existence of this particular instance, allowing operation invocations (also commonly called method invocations). Thus a directed arc between two nodes (objects) represents the ability to invoke operations along the direction of this arc (i.e. the service provider is at the arc head, and the requester is at the tail). Service providers are also called server objects and service requesters are called client objects, respectively. The directed graph will be called an *object graph*.

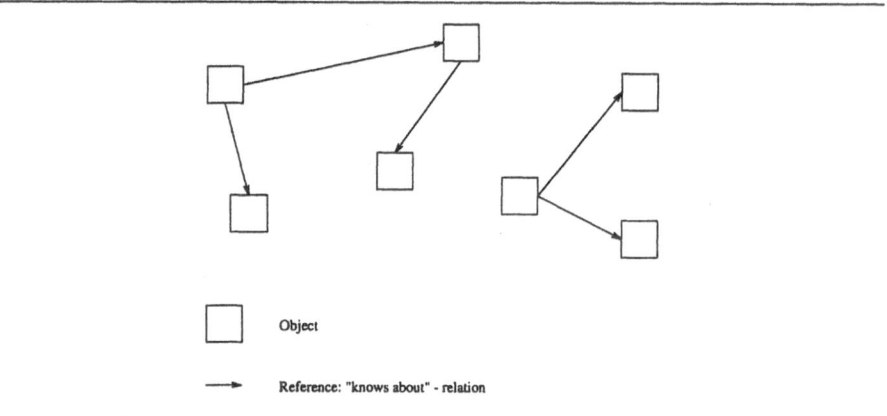

Figure 1: Directed graph as a snapshot of an object based computation

Both references and objects are typed and the definition of a type is assumed to be based upon some IDL. This view contributes to an elementary implication of the object model: the encapsulation of data and code. The definition of a type as an interface specification emphasises the decoupling of an object's implementation and the way it is accessed. Implementation details of a server object are irrelevant to a client. From a client object's perspective (the one holding the reference) a reference guarantees a treaty that the server object must fulfill (treaty is meant in terms of allowed method invocations). Polymorphism here occurs when the type of the reference is a super-type of the object to which it points. The server object therefore is a specialization to what the client expects, if it can fulfill the treaty[3].

---

[3]Polymorphism is often referred to as the "principle of substitutability" where an object of type A may be substituted by an object of type B without anything "bad" happening.

a are typed. The compiler can use the redundant type information to ensure that the type of *a* is compatible with the type of *x*. A type here resembles much a "suit of armor" [Card85], where it protects an underlying data item from invalid operations. The simplest requirement in the above example would be to check that the type of the left hand side of the assignment statement is identical to the type of the right hand side.

With the rise of the object paradigm, the definition of a type has changed due to the nature of the object model. One important feature of the object model is the encapsulation of data and code, which consequently decouples an object's interface from it's actual implementation[2]. The most general characteristics of any type definition are that a type denotes a set of objects with time-invariant, externally visible properties. *Time-invariant* means that the properties hold during the whole lifetime of an object and *externally visible* refers to the requirement of encapsulation, whereby implementation specific details are hidden within the object (see [Amer91]).

In order to define a type, the relevant properties have to be identified with respect to assumptions about the object model and the environment under consideration. This paper focuses on the implications of a type definition within open, distributed object-based environments which are characterized by an extensive network of independent vendors and customers. Service providers (vendors) and service requestors (customers) are modeled by objects (called server and client objects, respectively). As will be shown later, a type here is not only a basis for a "treaty" between a client and server object but also the only means for a client to find a suitable server in the first place. Therefore a type has the flavor of a standard which all participating parties have to agree upon *a priori*.

Within the context of this paper we assume that a type definition is based on some *interface definition language* (IDL for short) as the CORBA-IDL or DCE-IDL (see [OMG91] and [OSF92] respectively). The grammer defined by an IDL can be used for an interface specification for a set of objects. The main goal of this paper will be to extend an arbitrary IDL-based type definition by a declarative description which will weaken the need for an a priori, tight standard.

The rest of this paper is organized as follows: the next section defines the environment which serves both as a basis for this paper and as a motivation for the introduction of declarative types. Section 3 defines the notion of a type family which will be the starting point for a declarative extension to IDL-based type definitions. In section 4 an example is given which is followed by a formal definition of a declarative type. Section 6 presents an implementation for hierarchical programs (the proof of correctness is given in Appendix B). A summary and outlook conclude this paper.

2 Environment

In this section we present a basic model called the *object graph* to motivate some consequences on type definitions within open distributed systems. As the name implies, the framework builds upon the object model. The results given at the end of this section serve as a starting point for the so called *type families*, which will be discussed in detail in the following section.

---

[2]Languages like C++ do not make a distinct difference between type and class concept. Strictly speaking, a class is one possible implementation for a type.

In this paper we are not concerned with questions such as how the nodes of such an object graph are mapped onto a physical environment or how to implement an object's identity (i.e. whether objects (nodes) span machine boundaries; the programming language used to implement the object behavior; the problems with object identity and object migration, etc.). Our primary interest are the mechanisms by which the structure of the object graph may change over time. The following elementary operations can induce a change of the graph:

1. object creation,

2. object deletion,

3. passing of references as parameters of method invocations.

Operations 1 and 2 change the node set and possibly the arc set and operation 3 alters the arc set only. It is obvious that the client who invokes a method on another object may only pass those references that it has stored locally (i.e. "references do not come from nothing"). The only way to pass on another object's identity is by including a reference as a parameter of a method invocation.

2.2 Trading and the role of types

As has been motivated in the previous section, we impose no constraints as to how the object graph is actually mapped onto a physical environment but we do assume that the object graph is only loosely coupled. Client and server objects are not only decoupled in terms of locality, but also in terms of development domains. A client object may be implemented by one company, while a server object may be implemented by another. This scenario implies that a client object in general does not control the instantiation of a particular service, but rather has to browse the object graph for an appropriate service provider. These considerations have led to software components like the ODP Trader or CORBA's Request Broker (see [ISO93] and [OMG91] respectively), which serve as a mediator between service requesters and service providers.

The abstract functionality of such a mediator may be modeled within the object graph as a *lookup object* with a well known identity. Each newly created object is implicitly given a reference to this lookup object. The interface of the lookup object usually contains at least two methods: registration of a type and query for an instance of a particular type. Internally the lookup object maintains a database whose entries map from type descriptions to object identities. The parameter for a query therefore contains a type description of the desired service, which the lookup object must match against those stored in its database.

The implementation of the lookup object is based on numerous design decisions: caching of unsatisfiable queries; best match of two types according to some metric, etc. These issues are of no importance here. What is of importance is the matching algorithm itself, independent of any qualitative design decisions (i.e. according to the requirements of the subtype relation, this matching algorithm is simply supposed to return YES or NO).

It is important to think about the role of a type in such an environment. In order for the match algorithm within the lookup object to succeed, a type description must conform to a standard, which all participating parties have to agree upon *a priori*. This standard has to be

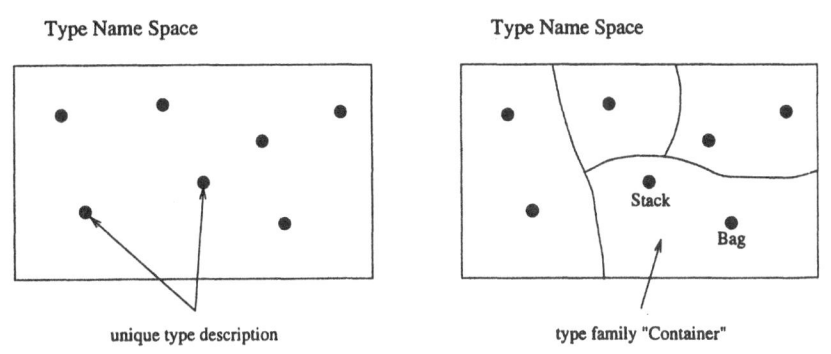

unique type description   type family "Container"

Figure 2: Partitioning of the type name space in type families

defined well enough to be matched unambiguously against other types. Current mediators, like the aforementioned ODP Trader, base their match algorithm mainly upon syntactic features of the IDL. The implication is that the exact syntactic structure of a particular service IDL must be communicated to all parties.

We propose a semantic extension to these purely syntactic based IDL's to allow for a certain "fuzziness" in type descriptions. Although the idea of introducing semantics to a type definition is not new (see for example [Amer91], [Lisk93] or [Larch93]), this paper develops a new method based upon the well known field of declarative semantics. The advantages, as will be seen in the following sections, are that the semantic extension is not based upon pre- and post-conditions. Therefore it won't be necessary to change the underlying IDL. Furthermore due to the nature of declarative semantics this will introduce the desired kind of flexibility of type specifications, which weakens the requirement for an a priori, well defined standard. In order to accomplish this task, the next section will introduce the notion of a type family.

3 Type Families

This section will establish the notion of a type family which serves as a basis for a declarative extension. In the following the term *type* is to denote a type definition based on some IDL. These IDL's (like DCE-IDL or CORBA-IDL) describe the interface of an object without explicit reference to their underlying semantics. The *semantics* associated with a type is implicit with respect to the behavior intended by the programmer. In order to distinguish between different types, there have to be very strict *syntactic* naming conventions. These conventions correspond to standards, which all participating parties have to agree upon *a priori*. Therefore the name space of all possible types consists of syntactically well distinguished type descriptions, as depicted on the left hand side of figure 2.

It is important to see that although some types denote different behavior they are similar in the way they are accessed by clients. For example consider these two type definitions based on the CORBA-IDL:

```
interface Bag {                        interface Stack
    Bag();                                 Stack();
    ~Bag();                                ~Stack();
    void GetChar( [out] char c );          void PopChar( [out] char c );
    void PutChar( [in] char c );           void PushChar( [in] char c );
    bool IsEmpty();                        bool IsEmpty();
}                                      }
```

From an abstract point of view these two types denote different containers, capable of storing and retrieving data items. The GetChar() method of a bag is non-deterministic in the sense that it is unknown in advance which data item GetChar() will return. In contrast the stack's PushChar() and PopChar() methods work according to the LIFO principle and therefore exhibit a deterministic behavior.

Although different in their actual behavior, these two types are used by client objects in a similar way (relative to the naming conventions like for example method names[4]). The informal definition of a type family is to partition the type name space according to these similar usage patterns. This grouping of types to a type family depends highly on those types currently defined in the type name space. Each type family has one *generic type*, representing the usage patterns of all it's members (a generic type for the bag and stack types for example would define a retrieval and deposit method). Note that although this generic type may be specified in terms of the underlying IDL, there is some loss of information. What is missing is some kind of "tag" to the generic type to denote the difference between the various members of a family. This tag will be defined in terms of a declarative Horn clause program.

A *declarative type* therefore identifies the family and the specific members of the family by means of a declarative description based on well known Horn clauses. The logic programming paradigm offers the advantage, that it describes *what* is particular about a type, not *how* this behavior is to be accomplished. Two parties may describe one member of a family differently; yet the lookup object is able to match these two descriptions. The need for a tight standard is reduced to a way to distinguish between different type families and a declarative description methodology to differentiate between various members of one family.

The syntax chosen here for a declarative description is derived from PROLOG, which itself stems from a subset of first order predicate calculus known as Horn clauses. Although the data structures found in PROLOG serve practical needs, we restrict the following example to the pure theory of Horn clauses.

4 Extended example

This section will present an extended example on how to use Horn clauses as a semantic tag for members of a type family. The example builds upon the aforementioned type family of containers. As has been explained in the previous section, there must be a generic type which serves as a general interface to any member of this type family. The following paragraphs will show how to use the declarative semantic to specify the difference between two members

---

[4]See [KONS93] for some hints on how to accomplish this mapping of various types.

of the type family Container, namely a stack and a bag. Note that the major difference between a stack and a bag is the non deterministic behavior of the retrieval method of a bag. The generic type for a type family of all containers is assumed to be defined as (using CORBA-IDL):

```
interface Container {
    Container();
    ~Container();
    void RetrieveChar( [out] char c );
    void DepositChar( [in] char c );
    bool IsEmpty();
}
```

It is important to note that the behavior description of various members of a type family is at an abstract level, sufficient for describing the *difference* in behavior and not a *complete* method by method specification (as done in [Lisk93] and [Larch93]). In the above example, the difference between a bag and a stack may be sufficiently described by choosing two arbitrarily distinct data items. Although the container will in general be able to store more than two kinds of elements, abstracting the behavior with only two elements will suffice for the declarative extension.

Two distinct elements, which can be placed and removed from a container, may be represented by different 1-ary function symbols. Let f and g be two such function symbols. A container with one f and three g's may be represented by the term $g(f(g(g(\epsilon))))$. Note that the constant symbol ϵ is used to terminate a term. The symbol ϵ by itself denotes an empty container. In order to provide a framework for a declarative description of the store and retrieval methods, the two predicate symbols *put* and *get*, both with three arguments, are introduced.

To see how a "semantic tag" to the generic type for a *bag* translates to a declarative program, consider the following six definite clauses, denoted by P_B (see Appendix A for the terminology):

$$P_B : get(f(x), x, f(\epsilon)) \leftarrow \qquad (1)$$
$$get(g(x), x, g(\epsilon)) \leftarrow \qquad (2)$$
$$get(f(x), f(y), z) \leftarrow get(x, y, z) \qquad (3)$$
$$get(g(x), g(y), z) \leftarrow get(x, y, z) \qquad (4)$$
$$put(x, f(x), f(\epsilon)) \leftarrow \qquad (5)$$
$$put(x, g(x), g(\epsilon)) \leftarrow \qquad (6)$$

Note that the predicate names *get* and *put* are chosen arbitrarily and have in particular no relation to the generic type method names or signatures. Furthermore the behavior of the additional method IsEmpty() defined for the generic type is not given, as it's semantic is assumed to be the same for all members of the type family container. This is the most distinguished difference to other approaches for semantic extensions to IDL-based type definitions: not the complete behavior of every method is given, rather only the part of the behavior sufficient for distinction between various members of one type family.

The informal semantics for *put* is that if an element (third argument of the predicate) is added to a container (first argument), the result is a new container with the added element (second argument). A legal ground instance from the Herbrand base B_L would be $put(f(g(f(\epsilon))), f(f(g(f(\epsilon)))), f(\epsilon))$. Here f is added to a container currently holding two f's and one g. An illegal ground instance would be $put(f(\epsilon), f(\epsilon), g(\epsilon))$. The informal semantics for *get* is analogous. The element to be removed is denoted by the third argument of the *get*-predicate. The element will be removed from a container (first argument) and resulting in a new container (second argument). In the following example, the legal ground instance $get(f(g(f(\epsilon))), f(f(\epsilon)), g(\epsilon))$ (which is an element for the least Herbrand model M_{P_B} of P_B) is derived in a bottom up technique from clauses in P_B:

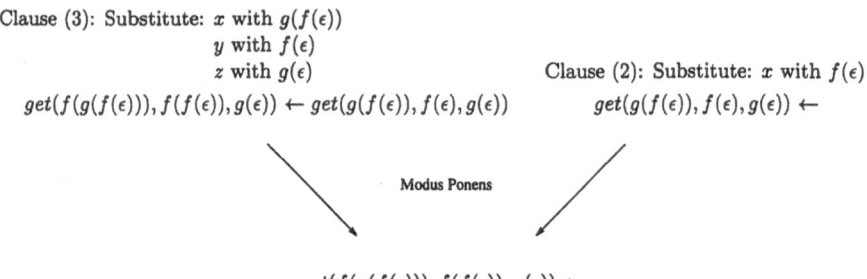

Clause (3): Substitute: x with $g(f(\epsilon))$
$\qquad\qquad\qquad\qquad y$ with $f(\epsilon)$
$\qquad\qquad\qquad\qquad z$ with $g(\epsilon)$
$\qquad get(f(g(f(\epsilon))), f(f(\epsilon)), g(\epsilon)) \leftarrow get(g(f(\epsilon)), f(\epsilon), g(\epsilon))$

Clause (2): Substitute: x with $f(\epsilon)$
$\qquad\qquad get(g(f(\epsilon)), f(\epsilon), g(\epsilon)) \leftarrow$

Modus Ponens

$$get(f(g(f(\epsilon))), f(f(\epsilon)), g(\epsilon)) \leftarrow$$

Substitutions of variables with terms are legal operations on clauses due to the universal closure. The last derivation step is allowed because of the Modus Ponens rule. All ground instances in M_{P_B} can be constructed in the same fashion. M_{P_B} now holds all "legal ground instances" (without proof), and thus divides B_L in two partitions. If the outermost function symbol in a term is to denote the last inserted element, then it can be seen that the above declarative program models a bag. Both ground atoms $get(f(g(\epsilon)), f(\epsilon), g(\epsilon))$ and $get(f(g(\epsilon)), g(\epsilon), f(\epsilon))$ are elements of M_{P_B}. The former atom would not represent a valid behavior for a stack. The fact that both ground atoms belong to M_P for P_B is the result of the non determinism of the *get*-operation.

The declarative program for a *stack*, denoted by P_S, is the same as for P_B, except that it lacks clauses 3 and 4. As can be seen, the least Herbrand model M_{P_S} for P_S lacks exactly those *get*-ground instances, which describe the non-deterministic behavior of a bag. Therefore we have the following set inclusion property: $M_{P_S} \subseteq M_{P_B} \subseteq B_L$. This gives a hint on how the subtype relation for declarative types will be defined in the next section.

To give an idea of the declarative nature of this type system, consider the following alternate program for a stack (denoted by $P_{S'}$):

$$
\begin{aligned}
P_{S'} : get(x, y, f(\epsilon)) \quad &\leftarrow \quad equal(x, f(y)) & (1) \\
get(x, y, g(\epsilon)) \quad &\leftarrow \quad equal(x, g(y)) & (2) \\
equal(x, x) \quad &\leftarrow & (3) \\
put(x, f(x), f(\epsilon)) \quad &\leftarrow & (4) \\
put(x, g(x), g(\epsilon)) \quad &\leftarrow & (5)
\end{aligned}
$$

Although the pure syntactic structure of P_S and $P_{S'}$ differ, it can easily be verified that the least Herbrand model of $P_{S'}$ contains exactly the same *get*-ground instances as those of P_S (without proof). What has happened here is that $P_{S'}$ contains a new predicate *equal* which denotes syntactical equivalence. The program $P_{S'}$ is used to describe the same type of object: a stack. This example shows the expressiveness of declarative types. Although the two programs P_S and $P_{S'}$ differ in their actual syntactical representation, they mean the same (except for the *equal*-ground instances).

The program $P_{S'}$ suggests that a programmer should be given the freedom to use as many predicates as necessary. These "helping"-predicates however are not subject to the subset relationship between the least Herbrand model of two programs. It is therefore inevitable to specify the relevant predicates, i.e. those predicates whose ground instances will be compared by a matching algorithm.

5 Formal definition of a declarative type

In this section a formal definition of a declarative type will be established. The term declarative type here is meant as a declarative extension to an IDL-based type notation. As has been mentioned earlier, the syntactic structure of the underlying IDL is not modified, rather the declarative extension is to be understood as an orthogonal augmentation (i.e. merely a semantic tag). For that reason, it is not necessary to tailor a declarative type for some specific IDL and the term IDL is meant to be treated as a generic expression for any IDL notation.

Def.: Declarative type DT: Let I be an IDL-based notation and L a first order language. A declarative type DT is a triple (S, P, R), where S is an interface specification based on I, P is a finite set of definite clauses based on L and R is a finite set of relevant predicate symbols based on L, such that for each predicate symbol in R exists a definition in P.

Def.: Subtype relation $\leq_{DT}$: Let $T_1 = (S_1, P_1, R_1)$ and $T_2 = (S_2, P_2, R_2)$ be two declarative types, where S_1 and S_2 are based on I. Let M_{P_1} be the least Herbrand model of P_1 and M_{P_2} the least Herbrand model of P_2 respectively. Let $\tilde{M}_{P_1} := \{p \in M_{P_1} \mid$ the predicate symbol of the ground instance p is an element of $R_1\}$. Definition of $\tilde{M}_{P_2}$ respectively. T_1 is a subtype of T_2 (denoted by $T_1 \leq_{DT} T_2$) iff

1. $S_1 =_{IDL} S_2$
2. $R_1 = R_2$
3. $\tilde{M}_{P_1} \subseteq \tilde{M}_{P_2}$

Note that the above two definitions can only be applied to positive atoms. The subtype relation still has to be extended for negation. The condition $S_1 =_{IDL} S_2$ of the subtype relation for declarative types represents the traditional interface matching algorithm found in common trader implementations. The equality relation $=_{IDL}$ may therefore be defined as syntactic equivalence. However the equality relation could be defined in terms of a more general equivalence relation which would match syntactically different types (like the stack and bag examples from a previous section). Work on object oriented interoperability (see [Kons93]) may serve as a basis for this equivalence relation.

6 Transformation Algorithm

Here, we will present an algorithm which checks the subtype relation $\leq_{DT}$ for a subset of the Horn clauses given two declarative types[5]. Unfortunately there exists no algorithm for $\leq_{DT}$ based on the complete Horn clause set. The (informal) reason for this is, that testing the subset property $\tilde{M}_{P_1} \subseteq \tilde{M}_{P_2}$ is equivalent to a logical implication (the conjunction of all clauses from P_1 implies the conjunction of all clauses from P_2). Thus allowing arbitrarily Horn clauses would be equivalent of testing satisfiability of first order expressions, which is undecidable. Therefore we have to restrict the set of all Horn clauses to obtain a decidable subset. The subset chosen here are the hierarchical programs (see Appendix A for a definition). The following algorithm transforms a hierarchical program to a set of unit clauses (i.e. facts), which are semantically equivalent:

Algorithm: Transformation of a hierarchical program to a set of unit clauses.
Input: P: a finite, hierarchical definite program with $T_P \uparrow \omega = T_P \downarrow \omega$.
Output: P_u: semantically equivalent program, containing only unit clauses.

1. $k := 0; P_0 := P$

2. If all clauses in P_k are unit clauses, goto 6.

3. Let $A \leftarrow B_1, \ldots, B_n$ be a non-unit clause in P_k, where the definition of each B_i consists only of unit clauses in P_k.

4. Let $\tilde{P} := \{A' \leftarrow |$ there exists a mgu σ, such that $A' = A\sigma$ and for each B_i there exists a unit clause $\{C \leftarrow\} \in P_k$ with $B_i\sigma = C\sigma\}$. Note that $\tilde{P}$ is finite.

5. Let $P_{k+1} := (P_k \setminus \{A \leftarrow B_1, \ldots, B_n\}) \cup \tilde{P}; k := k + 1;$ goto 2.

6. Let $P_u := P_k;$ stop.

Clearly the algorithm terminates as step 5 eliminates one non-unit clause per iteration. The application of steps 3-5 replace the non-unit clause by a finite set of semantically equivalent unit clauses. A formal proof of the correctness of these transformation steps is given in Appendix B. Once two hierarchical programs have been transformed according to the above algorithm, the set-inclusion property $\tilde{M}_{P_1} \subseteq \tilde{M}_{P_2}$ of the $\leq_{DT}$ relation can simply be verified via the subsumption principle on the transformed programs P_{1u} and P_{2u}.

7 Conclusion and future work

In this paper we have motivated and defined a declarative extension to IDL-based type definitions. Within open distributed environments a type resembles much a standard, by which a client object is able to locate a suitable server object via some mediator. So far this standard has to be very specific in the sense that the precise syntactic structure and semantics of a type have to be known by all programmers in advance. The purpose for a declarative extension is to weaken the need for an a priori tight standard, which is of

---

[5]The algorithm presented here has been implemented in C++ using LEX and YACC and is available via anonymous ftp at *diamant.vsb.cs.uni-frankfurt.de:/pub/dt/horn_clause/dt_imp.tar.Z*.

particular benefit for open, distributed environments to reduce communication overhead between implementors of various objects.

It has been shown that a declarative program can describe the difference in behavior within members of a type family. The benefits from using Horn clauses lie in the nature of declarative semantics which describes *what* constitutes a particular behavior, not *how* to implement it. For this reason the declarative extension to an IDL-based type notation weakens the need for an a priori standard (of course only with respect to members of one type family).

The future work will go in two directions: first of all, the grouping of type families other than containers will be investigated with respect to practical issues. For the other direction we will pursue the theory of declarative types to replace the transformation algorithm for stronger subsets of Horn clauses, which are more expressive than hierarchical programs.

Appendix A: Definitions

This appendix establishes well known definitions from the field of logic programming. A thorough introduction with more complete explanations may be found for example in [Lloyd87].

Def.: A *term* is defined inductively as follows:

- a variable is a term

- a constant is a term

- if f is an n-ary function symbol and $t_1, \ldots, t_n$ are terms, then $f(t_1, \ldots, t_n)$ is a term

Def.: If p is an n-ary predicate symbol and $t_1, \ldots, t_n$ are terms, then $p(t_1, \ldots, t_n)$ is called an *atomic formula* or, more simply, an *atom*.

Def.: A *substitution* θ is a finite set of the form $\{v_1/t_1, \ldots, v_n/t_n\}$, where each v_i is a variable, each t_i is a term distinct from v_i and the variables $v_1, \ldots, v_n$ are distinct. Each element v_i/t_i is called a binding for v_i.

Def.: Let $\theta = \{v_1/t_1, \ldots, v_n/t_n\}$ be a substitution and E an expression. Then $E\theta$, the *instance* of E by θ, is the expression obtained from E by simultaneously replacing each occurence of the variable v_i in E by the term t_i.

Def.: Let S be a finite set of simple expressions. A substitution θ is called a *unifier* for S if $S\theta$ is a singleton. A unifier for S is called a *most general unifier* (mgu) for S if, for each unifier σ of S, there exists a substitution γ such that $\sigma = \theta\gamma$.

Def.: A *definite program clause* is a formula of the form $\forall x_1 \ldots \forall x_s (A \leftarrow B_1 \wedge \ldots \wedge B_n)$ where $A, B_1, \ldots, B_n$ are atoms and $x_1, \ldots, x_s$ are all the variables occurring in the formula. Throughout this paper, a definite program clause will be denoted by $A \leftarrow B_1, \ldots, B_n$.

Def.: A *unit clause* is a definite program clause of the form $A \leftarrow$; i.e. clause with an empty body.

The informal semantics of $A \leftarrow B_1, \ldots, B_n$ is "for each assignment of each variable, if $B_1, \ldots, B_n$ are all true, then A is true."

Def.: A *definite program* is a finite set of definite program clauses.

Def.: In a definite program, the set of all program clauses with the same predicate symbol P in the head is called the *definition of P*.

Def.: A *level mapping* of a program is a mapping from its set of predicate symbols to the non-negative integers. We refer to the value of a predicate symbol under this mapping as the level of that predicate symbol.

Def.: A program is *hierarchical* if it has a level mapping such that, in every program statement $A \leftarrow B_1, \ldots, B_n$, the level of every predicate symbol B_i is less than the level of A.

Def.: Let L be a first order language. The *Herbrand universe U_L* for L is the set of all ground terms, which can be formed out of the constants and function symbols appearing in L.

Def.: Let L be a first order language. The *Herbrand base B_L* for L is the set of all ground atoms, which can be formed by using predicate symbols from L with ground terms from the Herbrand universe U_L as arguments.

Def.: A *pre-interpretation* of a first order language L consists of the following:

- a non-empty set D, called the domain of the interpretation,

- for each constant in L, the assignment of an element in D,

- for each n-ary function symbol in L, the assignment of a mapping from D^n to D.

Def.: Let L be a first order language. The *Herbrand interpretation* for L based on a pre-interpretation is given by the following:

- the domain of the pre-interpretation is the Herbrand universe U_L,

- constants in L are assigned themselves in U_L,

- if f is an n-ary function symbol in L, then the mapping from $(U_L)^n$ into U_L defined by $(t_1, \ldots, t_n) \rightarrow f(t_1, \ldots, t_n)$ is assigned to f.

Def.: Let P be a definite program and $\{M_i\}_{i \in I}$ be a non-empty set of all Herbrand models for P. Then $\bigcap_{i \in I} M_i$ is the *least Herbrand model* for P denoted by M_P.

As with every Herbrand interpretation, the least Herbrand model is a subset of the Herbrand base $(M_P \subseteq B_L)$. Although the programmer might have a different interpretation in mind, there is a strong reason to view M_P as the natural interpretation of the program: the atoms in M_P are precisely those that are logical consequences of the program.

Def.: Let P be a definite program. The mapping $T_P : Pot(B_P) \rightarrow Pot(B_P)$ is defined as follows: Let I be an Herbrand interpretation. Then $T_P(I) = \{A \in B_P \mid A \leftarrow B_1, \ldots, B_n$ is a ground instance of a clause in P and $\{B_1, \ldots, B_n\} \subseteq I\}$.

Def.: Let L be a complete lattice and $T : L \rightarrow L$ be a mapping. We say $a \in L$ is the *least fixpoint* (lfp) of T, if a is a fixpoint (that is, $T(a) = a$) and for all fixpoints b of T, we have $a \leq b$.

Theorem: *(Fixpoint Characterisation of the least Herbrand model)* Let P be a definite program. Then $M_P = lfp(T_P) = T_P \uparrow \omega$.

Appendix B: Proof

Let P be a hierarchical program, containing not only unit clauses. Let P' be constructed from P according to steps 3-5. Let this clause be $A \leftarrow A_1, \ldots, A_n$. Then $lfp(T_P) = lfp(T_{P'})$.

Proof: We have to show that $lfp(T_{P'}) \subseteq lfp(T_P)$ and $lfp(T_P) \subseteq lfp(T_{P'})$.

1.) $lfp(T_{P'}) \subseteq lfp(T_P)$

As P' lacks the clause $A \leftarrow A_1, \ldots, A_n$ contained in P, but on the contrary possesses more unit clauses as P, it suffices to show $T_{P'} \uparrow 1 \subseteq T_P \uparrow \omega$. Let $B \in T_{P'} \uparrow 1$.

Case 1: For some mgu σ and some unit clause $\{C \leftarrow\} \in P' \setminus \tilde{P}$ is $B = C\sigma \Longrightarrow \{C \leftarrow\} \in P \Longrightarrow B \in T_P \uparrow 1 \Longrightarrow B \in T_P \uparrow \omega$.

Case 2: For some mgu σ and some unit clause $\{C \leftarrow\} \in \tilde{P}$ is $B = C\sigma$. Since $\{C \leftarrow\} \in \tilde{P}$, according to the construction of $\tilde{P}$ in step 4, there is a mgu τ with $C = A\tau$. Furthermore all atoms in the body of $A\tau \leftarrow A_1\tau, \ldots, A_n\tau$ are unifiable with some unit clauses in P (according to step 4). All ground instances of these unit clauses are elements of $T_P \uparrow 1 \Longrightarrow$ all ground instances of $A\tau$ are elements of $T_P \uparrow 2$. Since $B = C\sigma$ and $C = A\tau \Longrightarrow B = (A\tau)\sigma \Longrightarrow B \in T_P \uparrow 2 \Longrightarrow B \in T_P \uparrow \omega$.

2.) $lfp(T_P) \subseteq lfp(T_{P'})$

Induction over n: $T_P \uparrow n \subseteq T_{P'} \uparrow \omega$

$n = 1$: All unit clauses in P are also in $P' \Longrightarrow T_P \uparrow 1 \subseteq T_{P'} \uparrow 1 \subseteq T_{P'} \uparrow \omega$

$n \rightsquigarrow n + 1$: I.H. $T_P \uparrow n \subseteq T_{P'} \uparrow \omega$
Let $B \in T_P \uparrow (n + 1)$. We have to show that $B \in T_{P'} \uparrow \omega$.
$B \in T_P \uparrow (n+1) \Longrightarrow$ there is a ground instance of a clause in P, $B \leftarrow B_1, \ldots, B_n$ with $\{B_1, \ldots, B_n\} \subseteq T_P \uparrow n \Longrightarrow \{B_1, \ldots, B_n\} \subseteq T_{P'} \uparrow \omega$.

Case 1: $B \leftarrow B_1, \ldots, B_n$ is a ground instance of some clause in $P' \Longrightarrow B \in T_{P'} \uparrow \omega$.

Case 2: $B \leftarrow B_1, \ldots, B_n$ is a ground instance of $A \leftarrow A_1, \ldots, A_n$ for some mgu σ. Therefore there is no ground instance of a clause in P'. According to the construction rule in step 4, $B_1, \ldots, B_n$ are all ground instances of some unit clauses in P (and therefore in P'). B is therefore a ground instance of some unit clause in $\tilde{P}$ (and therefore in P') $\Longrightarrow B \in T_{P'} \uparrow 1 \Longrightarrow B \in T_{P'} \uparrow \omega$.

q.e.d.

References

[Amer91] P. America. Designing an object oriented programming language with behavioral subtyping. In *REX School/Workshop, LNCS 489*. Springer, 1991.

[Booch91] G. Booch. *Object Oriented Design with Applications*. Benjamin/Cummings Publishing Company, Inc, Redwood City, California, 1991.

[Card85] L. Cardelli and P. Wegner. On understanding types, data abstraction and polymorphism. *Computing Surveys*, 17(4), December 1985.

[ISO93] ISO/IEC. *ODP-Trader, Document Title ISO/IEC JTC 1/SC 21 N 8192*. 1993.

[Kons93] D. Konstantas. Object oriented interoperability. In *ECOOP'93, LNCS 707*. Springer, 1993.

[Larch93] G. T. Leavens and Y. Cheon. Extending CORBA-IDL to specify behavior with Larch. Technical report, ftp.cs.iastate.edu:pub/techreports/TR93-20/larch-corba.txt, 1993.

[Lisk93] B. Liskov and J. Wing. A new definition of the subtype relation. In O. M. Nierstrasz, editor, *ECOOP'93: Object–Oriented Programming*. Springer, 1993.

[Lloyd87] J. W. Lloyd. *Foundations of Logic Programming, Second Edition*. Springer, 1987.

[OMG91] Object Management Group. *The Common Object Request Broker: Architecture and Specification Revision 1.1*. 1991.

[OSF92] Open Software Foundation. *Distributed Computing Environment, Version 1.0*. 1992.

Choosing Conceptual Objects — the Y^{++} Approach

Mike Brough

Department of Computer Science,
Keele University,
Keele, Staffordshire, ST5 5BG - UK
E-mail: mdb3@cs.keele.ac.uk   Fax: +44 782 713082

ABSTRACT: This paper describes a system modelling strategy, following the principles described in (Brough 1992) for the evolution of existing methods. It provides a taxonomy of objects, explaining why they are distinguished. Techniques for identifying conceptual objects are given, with a brief discussion of how implementation objects and 'layering' are used in design.

KEY WORDS: agent, architecture object, conceptual object, controller object, event thread, information object, object-oriented analysis, object-oriented design, subject-domain object.

1 Introduction

Like any system development approach, object-orientated methods require: modelling tools (to visualise different problem features); models (to aid decisions); heuristics (to guide model production and review); a balance between 'user-friendliness' and formality (to allow required policy to be captured, unambiguously stated, and delivered); support (training, software, industry standards). Sadly, few of these requirements have been met as yet. Most authors concentrate on the first of these requirements[1]. This paper attempts (in part) to meet some of the other objectives, by providing an object-modelling framework, and heuristics for identifying objects[2] and operations.

1.1 Why are frameworks and heuristics needed?

The main aims of 'object-orientation' are to separate units' services from their realisation (encapsulation) and aid their efficient development by abstraction (inheritance), facilitating reuse. But tools for specifying objects and visualising the relationship between them are not enough. If the 'wrong' objects are chosen, they are not generally useful and little reuse occurs. If the relationship between objects is not optimal (the specialisation network), inheritance does not give any pay-offs — each object is built separately (an 'object-based' solution). More subtly, system policy must be separated from subject-domain object capabilities for objects to be reusable in different systems (otherwise, they must be 'hacked' for each new application).

To obtain real benefits from O-O, we need guidelines for choosing objects. Many system developers still use ad-hoc methods of identifying objects, but the object-oriented paradigm should be more than just 'programming with classes'. Ideally, guidelines on how to identify the objects would be objective, in the sense that different analysts would identify the same objects. In reality, this may be too much to hope for.

An intuitive modelling framework is a key feature of all good system development methods. In spite of its other faults, 'top-down functional decomposition' described in (DeMarco 1978) was very good in this respect. The modeller easily understood 'where they were', what they were doing, and what to do next. Unfortunately, this is not always true of object-oriented methods; it is easy to get confused about exactly what one is doing at a particular time and what the goal of that activity is.

---

1 And there even problems in this respect. Most methods do not define the modelling semantics very well. Further, they sometimes use a single modelling perspective (and tool) to model everything.

2 This paper uses the term object to indicate the abstract role that can be instantiated in systems.

1.2 Reuse metrics and the 'event-driven' nature of systems

Developing system software components takes time and effort. Once developed, the more they are used, the better. We will make no serious attempt to quantify this, except to remark that the benefit obtained from a system component relates to the real-world event that it deals with. Each time the event occurs, the system collects information and takes decisions according to some defined specification[3], actions carried out, and outputs produced. The response to the event has some benefit to the enterprise (or it shouldn't be in the system!). In theory, this benefit could be calculated from the event frequency and the benefit of dealing with it.

Constructing appropriate quality system components that embody required policy costs money (in terms of time etc.). For a given system, we construct all components needed for the system behaviour that 'deals with' each event within the system's scope. The software cost for the system is the sum of their development (and integration and maintenance) costs. An efficient development strategy would choose units that allowed more reuse (and reduced development cost) considering *all* the events that the system deals with. This is a rather naïve; in reality, there will be several systems, developed at different times (and it is notoriously difficult to estimate the development cost in advance of the actual work). Nevertheless, it reminds us why systems exist — to deal with events, not satisfy lazy programmers! We should therefore look for counts like 'number of different events the code is used for' as a guide to reuse.

2 Conceptual and implementation objects

We will distinguish between objects that contain only enterprise policy and no implementation details (conceptual objects) and those that embody services provided by the implementation architecture in which the system runs (implementation objects). For example, a system in a company that ran courses for outside clients might include a Course object. In a system that controlled lifts, we might have a Lift (US: elevator) object. Both Course and Lift are conceptual objects, relating to the problem that the system deals with, rather than the technology used. They embody all the features (capabilities) of a specific concept that the system deals with.

On the other hand, the Table, Semaphore, ... objects correspond to a collection of services provided by an architecture. An application can make use of these — they do not embody system policy, but provide architectural support for different applications. The lowest layer of support can be imagined to be the hardware[4]. At run–time, these resources provide services (e.g., interrupts) for applications. In this paper, the layer containing hardware will be called the 'Processor layer' (it also includes inter-processor connections). We will also use a 'Run–time layer', containing services that can be used at run time by different applications. The application 'sits on top of' these layers.

Each layer provides services to the layer above (rather like the ISO OSI reference model). The idea of software in 'layers' has a long history (Dijkstra 1968), but we will organise services in each layer around 'objects'. For example, figure 1 shows part of the Keele telescope control system making use of a Timer object[5]. It could be used in any real-time application. We identify any object by the resource name (here Hardware), together with the object's name (here Timer). A resource is a collection of related objects, providing a coherent set of services.

All object-oriented analysis methods have a real-world orientation. There are many benefits to this. It helps to make the model understandable by organising around things that subject-matter experts can relate to — it also helps to avoid analyst bias (the tendency for analysts to impose their 'thought patterns' on a problem, rather than just eliciting and collating requirements). Hopefully, it may make the process more reproducible — the real world doesn't change arbitrarily over short periods of time. Finally, there is some hope that it eases the work required to modify the model when requirements change (the unit being taken out/replaced/upgraded probably corresponds to a cohesive real-world concept). [Of course, this argument is not new. Externally-oriented analysis

---

3 Usually. Some systems extemporise, though this is rare in synthetic systems at present.

4 The system can include people too, but we will only consider system policy allocated to digital processors.

5 Note that systems can include 'hardware objects' (as here), as well as software objects.

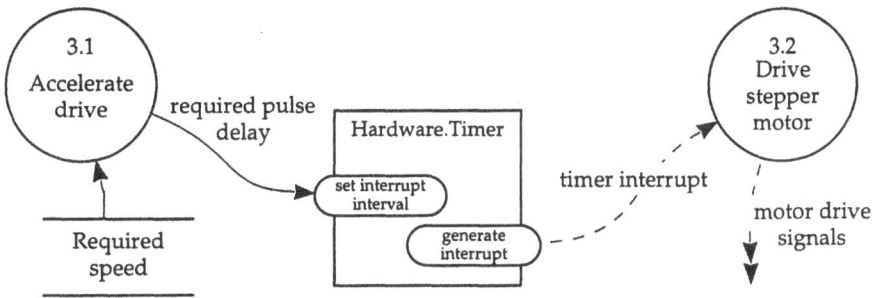

Figure 1: A hardware object

(based on entities and event) predates the extensive adoption of object-oriented techniques. (Chen 1976), (Flavin 1981), (McMenamin and Palmer, 1984), (Ward and Mellor, 1985).]

We will go further than this and advocate a complete separation of conceptual policy (in conceptual objects) and architecture (in implementation objects). A conceptual object can be hosted in different hardware and/or software architectures; this is of great benefit if exactly the same policy must be included on different platforms. By avoiding any application-specific features in implementation objects, we allow them to be reused to support different systems.

2.1 *Different types of conceptual objects*

We will further categorise conceptual objects into:

- □ **subject-domain objects:** the real-world things that the system will deal with;
- □ **controller objects:** containing the policy on how real-world things are controlled.

Subject-domain (or problem-domain) objects have operations that correspond to what the real-world things can do — their capabilities. They might, however, be dealt with in different ways by different systems. This is achieved by defining different controller objects for each system. The common properties and capabilities of the real-world thing (in the subject-domain object) will be the same in all cases. System policy (in the controller objects) on how they are used will be different.

To illustrate the differences between subject-domain objects and controller objects, consider a lift controller system (although a control system, these ideas readily extend to other types of system). It would have one instance of the Lift object to deal with each occurrence of the lift in the real world[6]. Each lift instance is capable of being moved, stopped, interrogated to find its current position, speed, etc. We might, however, construct several different lift systems, some dealing with only one lift; others with several. The scheduling and despatching algorithms might well be different. This would correspond to system-level control. We might also embody different policy on the way the lift was slowed down when approaching the floor (goods lift systems can be less 'stomach-friendly' than a passenger system). This would correspond to control at the individual lift level. The lift system would thus include a single-instance Lift system controller object and a Lift controller object with an instance for each lift (because one might be moving, while another is stationary).

2.2 *Structure of the Conceptual Model — the conceptual virtual machine*

The Conceptual Model (used in conceptual modelling) includes a subject-domain object for each real-world thing it deals with. It also contains one or more controller objects — one for the whole system; one for each event; or one to control each subject-domain object.

---

6 The distinction between object instances and object occurrences will be further discussed in §3.4.1.

System behaviour is defined by the collective behaviour of the operations that 'fire' when an event occurs. These operations are linked (and synchronised) by messages (data and/or event flows) between them. The behaviour of each operation must also be defined; each has a specification which defines exactly what it does when it receives a message. (As specifications can be inherited, there are generally less operation specifications than operations.)

To define system behaviour, we imagine a conceptual processor that supports several objects. Each can be single or multi-instance, with corresponding information (both instance and class) 'hidden' inside the object. Each object provides one or more operations, each acting at the instance or class level; an operation acting at the instance level operates in parallel with (and independently of) the same operation acting on other instances. When an operation is fired (by the arrival of the message; its stimulus), it carries out a function associated with it. The function can be owned by the object, or inherited from a more general one. Operations take zero time to complete[7].

The above outlines a virtual machine for an object–oriented Conceptual Model (Brough 1992)[8]. We did *not* define the model as 'consisting of a number of different types of diagram'. The approach is one where the diagrams are taken to be *derived* from some internal model; their generation (and control of updating of the internal model) is the responsibility of the CASE tool. This modelling paradigm is described in (Brough 1990a), (Baker et al., 1990), (Redmond-Pyle 1991).

3 Identifying subject-domain objects

We first identify subject-domain objects. We will then identify the operations they support and how they are controlled (by controller object operations). Finally, we will complete the model by organising the system-specific policy within controller objects.

All object-oriented analysis methods choose objects from the real world (the subject domain). Subject-domain objects are nothing more than entities, with their capabilities added as operations. The information modelling approach we will use is based on:

- **entity**: a class of real-world things with some property in common;
- **relationship**: a set of associations between instances of entities; each relationship has a relationship frame, e.g. <A> xxxx <B> yyy <C> involves the entities A, B, and C;
- **abstract data type**: a set of values used to represent similar categories of information;
- **attribute**: a mapping from an entity to an ADT;
- **subtyping**: a specialisation of an entity (the supertype) into one or more subtypes;
- **associative entity**: a relationship that is also treated as an entity.

Entities, relationships, and attributes are used by all information modellers and most modellers use subtyping. The use of ADTs is less widespread, but they provide a good abstraction. Associative entities were less frequently used until ERA modelling became an input to object-oriented design; it then becomes very useful concept[9]. Having constructed and reviewed the ERA model, the rule for identifying subject-domain objects is very simple:

each entity (including associative entities) becomes an object

The subtyping of one entity into one or more special subtypes lead quite naturally to one object being 'derived' from another. For example, we might consider a company that runs training courses for external clients. This might include the following pure entities: Customer, Company, Student, Course, Location, and Day[10]. There is one 'pure relationship': <Customer> represents <Company>, and two associative entities: Public course ::= <Course> scheduled to run at <Location>, starting on <Day>; and Booking ::= <Customer> reserves place for <Student> on <Scheduled

---

7 Actually, a simplification. Some operations are inherently time–continuous. For example, Lift.slow down.

8 (Baker el al., 1990) describe a 'process+data' virtual machine. We ignore common technical features such as MTBF.

9 We will call an entity that is not an associative entity a 'pure entity' (similarly, a 'pure relationship').

10 Day is a temporal entity. Different instances of it play the same role, but are distinguished. Treating Day as an entity (rather than using an attribute start date of Scheduled course) simplifies the modelling of 'schedules'.

course>. This leads to the identification of the following subject-domain objects:

Booking, Company, Course, Customer, Day, Location, Scheduled course, Student

We will not introduce an object for <Customer> represents <Company> in the Conceptual Model. We will allow the existence of relationships between objects. Some authors use special notations for these relationships. We will not. As, the correspondence between subject-domain objects and entities is 1-1, relationships can be identified by examining the corresponding ERD fragment. (Recall, we are using the 'internal model', rather than the 'model = set of diagrams' paradigm.)

Where there is a subtype in the ERD, there is a corresponding specialisation in the objects. For example, customers could not book places on all scheduled courses. Some are reserved for one company (inhouse courses); only those referred to as public courses can have places reserved on them. In the ERA model, Public course and Inhouse course are two subtypes of Scheduled course. The corresponding objects have the same relationship (<Course> scheduled to run at <Location>).

Note that inheritance that 'goes both ways'. When we create an instance of Public course, we automatically create an instance of Scheduled course at the same time (it is the *same* instance). On the other hand, if we deleted (as with any other instance operation) an instance of Scheduled course, there might be behaviour specific to Public course (or Inhouse course); this is automatically invoked if the instance of Scheduled course is an instance of Public course.

The transfer of properties of operations of one object to another via subtyping should be regarded as being 'transparent'. Certainly, there is no need to think of 'messages' between them. This is to be contrasted with some other forms of 'transferred' capabilities or behaviour (in a programming context, these are often casually all just referred to as 'inheritance').

3.1 Requirements for good information modelling

Because modelling the subject domain is so critical to the success of object-oriented analysis, great care must be taken. In particular, subtypings (which can be regarded as a set of 'ako' relationships) should not be confused with 'typing' ('isa' relationships). For example, if we ran a 'Space tours' company, we might need to deal with the relationship: <Passenger> is a <Species>. On the other hand, we might subtype Passenger into Paying passenger and Non-paying passenger. Note the differences. In an 'isa' relationship, many instances (at least potentially) of one entity can be *linked* to one instance of the other entity. On the other hand, in subtyping, every instance of the subtype *identically is* (transparently) an instance of the supertype at the same time.

As the ERA model of the subject-domain is the main source of subject-domain objects, it is very important that it is carefully reviewed. The semantics of the model components must be carefully examined. For example, does each attribute describe the entity that it is attributed to? Many information modellers are somewhat casual in this respect, sometimes worrying more about syntax than semantics. [But guidelines are available in, for example (Baker et al., 1990).]

3.2 Attributes and attribution

Each instance of an entity represents an occurrence of the entity in the real world. Attributes correspond to values associated with the instance of the entity. When we convert the entity to an object, the corresponding object will export operations that can be used to obtain (and set) this value for a corresponding instance of the object. [It is a moot point as to whether it helps to show such 'attribute operations' on object inter-connection diagrams. I usually suppress them.]

In conventional ERA modelling, criteria very similar to relational normalisation criteria are useful: can the value of the attribute for one instance of the entity vary independently of that for other instances of the same entity? If so, the attribution of the attribute to that entity is correct. But, it turns out, this is a little restrictive. It is based on a way of modelling information intended for use in a database. There is, in fact, a useful generalisation of the concept that can be made.

Conventionally, most modellers require that attribute values are stored (historically information modelling was aimed at an intended database); it is this that led to the definition and use of normalisation criteria. But we can also have non-stored attributes — for example, temporary attributes (seen in data flows) (Baker et al., 1990). More interestingly, an attribute can be *derived*. For example, a person's age can be derived from todays date and date of birth(a stored attribute). In any implementation of a system that included these attributes, it is unlikely that both would be stored in a database (but both might be data flow component; this was the reason for this concept in (Baker et al., 1990) — all data items were attributed).

When we convert the entity Student (for example) into the object Student, we, quite naturally regard date of birth as an attribute of the object. Without thinking, we might define it as 'instance data' (the conventional terminology). But what about age? It is certainly true that each student has an age; it describes the student. We thus expect the object Student to export it in the same way as it does date of birth. To a client there should be no difference. Indeed, it would be possible (but perverse!) to store age within Student and rederive date of birth every time it is used[11]. But whichever choice is made, the object Student exports date of birth *and* age. In the encapsulation spirit of 'O-O', a client should not be aware of any difference in how this is achieved within the object.

Derived attributes thus allow more possibilities than if we require all attributes to be stored. We will even allow a derived attribute to be 'owned' by another entity. For example (returning to the 'Space tours' example), each Passenger has an attribute normal body temperature; this is derived from the attribute <Species>.normal body temperature. In a system designed to monitor the comfort and safety of passengers, we could send a message to the Paying passenger object asking it to identify the temperature that their body should be maintained at (unfortunately, non-paying passenger get a rather 'down-market treatment'!). This would then be derived (transparently, as far as the client is concerned) by Passenger sending a message to the corresponding Species object. An object can thus export values of attributes owned by another entity.

This example used an isa (type) relationship. If one object's participation in a relationship has lower and upper limits [as described in (Baker et al., 1990)], of 1, it can be used to obtain values from the corresponding instance of one of the other participants in the relationship.

What about updating attributes? Certainly, if an attribute is owned by an entity, the corresponding object should include an operation to set the attribute. Inside the object, if the attribute is stored, the corresponding instance data will be modified. If the attribute is not stored (for example, an attempt to update age of Student, then it is likely that attempted updates would be ignored; on the other hand, in some cases, the items it is derived from might be changed. (The latter is not always possible, of course, particularly if the derived item depends on more than one other item.) The policy for each such attribute must depend on the situation; there are no absolute rules.

Note that we regard ADTs as a 'transparent' part of the conceptual architecture. Although we will *construct* them as objects, they will not be treated as objects in the Conceptual Model[12]. They certainly do not have time–continuous behaviour, for example. Conceptually, they are just value sets, with associated operations. They do not correspond to real-world objects, but to the *properties* of those objects. (At any instant of time, each attribute defines an instance of the ADT for each instance of the entity.)

3.3 *The different kinds of inheritance*

Many object-oriented modellers (certainly programmers!) 'lump all types of inheritance together'. As is now clear, type inheritance is *not* the same as subtyping (specialisation) inheritance. Meta-inheritance is one particular kind of type inheritance, where the isa relationship links two knowledge domains, one more abstract than the other. Thus any object (e.g., Student) inherits operations such as create from the meta-object Object.

There is also 'inheritance by aggregation'. An aircraft engine has an time–continuous attribute position. However, an engine generally has a particular position by virtue of the existence of an instance of the relationship: <Engine> is installed in <Aircraft>. Collecting the component parts of something into a group and using a 'placeholder' entity to hold information that refers to the group

---

11 We would have to increment age every day, which would be very inefficient; but not impossible. Indeed, this is exactly what is done with racehorses — on the 1st of January each year, every racehorse has its age incremented.

12 Some people refer to them as 'value' objects, or, rather strangely, as 'non-object objects'.

as a whole is an aggregation. In ERA modelling, this type of situation is relatively easy to recognise and model.

The subtle differences between specialisation (subtyping), type, and aggregation inheritance illustrates the importance of good semantic modelling of the subject domain. If an ERA model is carefully reviewed and then converted to an object model, a much better design is achieved. For example, we might have an Engine object, which exports its position. The client would not care how this is derived. Within Engine there would be a check to see if the engine is currently installed in an Aircraft (checking for a 'matching' relationship). If it is, a message would be sent to the corresponding Aircraft, requesting the position. This position is returned to the client, which is unaware of how this takes place. Without the preceding ERA modelling, it would be all too easy to define the Engine object as being *derived from* Aircraft(!). The correct model is to say that the Engine object *uses* the Aircraft object. [Of course, this can work the other way too; we can find the maximum thrust available to a given Aircraft (even if some engines have failed) using the objects Engine and Engine type]

3.4 Deriving conceptual objects from interaction views

Although ERA modelling provides the best insight into subject-domain concepts and thus is the main source of conceptual objects, it is not the only one. Another major source is investigating the interaction between a system and its environment. Systems exist to meet the needs of the agents (people, other systems, organisations, or hardware devices) in its environment. They are active units which interact with the system, generating information used by the system and/or using information produced by the system. The classic tool for visualising this interaction is a context diagram. For example, figure 2 is a partial context diagram for the training company system.

Subject-domain objects that are derived from examining the interaction of a system with its environment can be described as 'agent objects'. But they are not the only subject-domain objects. There are some things in the real world that the system is concerned with, yet does not interact directly with. For example, although the training system interacts directly with Customer and Student, it cannot interact with Company (which is certainly a subject-domain object!). All information about the company comes 'via' the customer that represents them.

Agent objects are necessarily 'active'; otherwise they could not interact with the system. It is unlikely that Company is ever active in this way. Some subject-domain object are clearly *never* active. In a system that dealt with drug prescriptions, the system would receive information about drug prescriptions from the doctor. Although Doctor is an agent object, neither Drug, or Prescribed

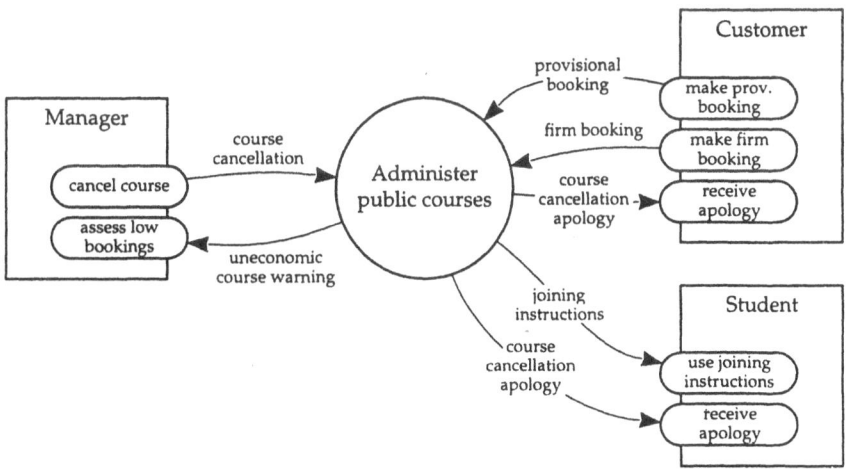

Figure 2: Interaction between the system and agent objects in its environment

treatment could *ever* be agents. The system will need, however, to create instances of them to hold information about the real world. Such conceptual objects are information objects.

3.4.1 Are external objects external?

We have distinguished between occurrences of objects (the real-world things) and instances of objects (the corresponding unit created and maintained by the system). The instance is used by the system to keep track of what the external object occurrence is doing and what messages should be sent to it. This means that there is, in fact, both an external and internal object for Customer (for example). The internal object provides a 'software wrap' around the corresponding real-world object occurrence. When another object within the system sends a message to a particular customer it sends the message to the 'software' Customer object that is within the system. Within this (and hidden to the rest of the system) is some way of ensuring that the message gets to the correct external occurrence of Person (a human being, not computer software!). This is how diagrams such as figure 2 should be interpreted. It is important to bear this distinction in mind. When one thinks about it, the distinction is obvious really. If an air traffic control system includes Runaway, or Aircraft objects, we do not actually expect to find these physical things within the system boundary!

Agent objects include a wrap of this type around the corresponding external agents that interact with the system. They include at least one 'active' operation that causes the occurrence of the external object to do something in response to a system output (or at least one operation that generates a system input). In addition, they will contain (probably many) operations that can be used to record information about the corresponding object occurrence. An information object is merely an object which only has this latter type of operation and *no active operations*. This means that the distinction between agent objects and information objects is not very significant. The only difference is that agent objects can appear on context diagrams.

3.5 Deriving objects from 'functional decompositions'

The main way of identifying conceptual objects is to start with an ERA model of the subject domain. Then, having identified subject-domain objects, individual events that the system needs to deal with are considered in sequence (as described below). The required system behaviour is then identified as operations and allocated to objects (some of which are controller objects).

For various reasons, this may not always be the only way objects are identified. There may be an existing model, organised in a traditional top-down (i.e. as a levelled set of DFDs) manner. It might also sometimes be convenient to think about the required system functions and then think about each in turn, eventually coming up with a detailed list of system functions. In such cases, the objects are typically fragmented and scattered around. The job of the analyst is to identify these fragments and join them back together again. Information modelling is then recommended, using the functions (and stores) as clues to the subject-matter of the system. Just occasionally, a lower-level DFD may correspond to a group of functions acting on one real-world concept. For example, we might have found: Note plan to develop new course,Note course available,Note change in course details, …, Note course retirement as a group of functions in a traditional system specification for a training centre system. The modeller has chosen to group all the functions which act on data related to the entity Course together. This is an obvious candidate for an object!

Of course, whether traditional (i.e. levelled sets of DFDs, together with minispecs) or an O-O approach is used to specify the system behaviour, it must be the *same* in both cases. The sum collection of system operations (and the way they respond to events) will be the same. What has happened is that the system functions have been allocated to operations in a different way and (more trivially), a grouping chosen for similar functions (or control) in the traditional P+D approach, whereas the grouping of functions is because they act on the same data in the O-O approach (Brough 1990b). But, it is not just a matter of 'renumbering bubbles'. Typically, in the traditional approach, there is one response for each event. In the object-oriented organisation, there will be several operations that need to fire for the occurrence of one event. One (usually) of these will be in a controller object; the others will be in subject-domain objects that must be accessed when the event occurs. One (the 'event recogniser') will often be in an agent object.

4 Identifying operations

We also need guidelines on how to identify object's operations. We can, of course, provide operations to obtain the values of attributes (and set them). If the object exhibits different states of behaviour over its life, we will also need to provide check state and change state operations too. But attributes and state operations are but one (and the most trivial aspect) of the problem. The more interesting operations are likely to correspond to quite specific behaviour. How can these operations be identified? Some are always required[13]. For example, create, delete (although this latter might not always be used). We will also assume a match operation, which takes any possible combination of items that make up the identifier of an object and returns a boolean value. For subject-domain objects, the identifier is (of course) the same as that for the entity. Controller objects will also (unless they are single-instance) need identifiers. We will also assume that subject-domain objects have 'attribute' operations. But other operations may be more difficult to identify.

4.1 Capabilities of subject-domain objects

An obvious technique is to look at subject-domain objects and ask 'What can this real-world thing *do*?'. This attribution of behaviour (as with attributes, state behaviour) needs to be carefully carried out, yet there are no mechanical checks that can be applied. (It is a semantic concept of attribution.) It is therefore rather subjective. In the absence of objective guidelines, this 'behaviour attribution' is quite reasonable (indeed, it is hard to see what guideline could be provided to avoid making it seem so 'open-ended'). Unfortunately, this is the approach that some modellers use for *all* objects! It then provides a 'hackers paradise'. Are there any guidelines? Yes, we *can* provide techniques for identifying operations. Furthermore, there is some hope that these guidelines are objective; i.e. two analysts could(!) come up with the same operations for the same objects in the same problem!.

4.2 The event-driven nature of systems; events and event–response threads

The main way of identifying operations is to examine what the system does when an event occurs. As is conventional, we demand that *all* conceptual system behaviour is in respond to some event (McMenamin and Palmer, 1984), (Ward and Mellor, 1985). Each time the event occurs, one or more fragments of system behaviour 'fire'; the system then returns to rest. The way system behaviour can be derived from events in 'P+D' approaches is well-known (Yourdon 1989), (Baker et al., 1990). This is an 'outside-in' approach to defining system behaviour; because of the event-driven nature of systems, a unit of behaviour is identified for each event. [See (Baker et al., 1990) for a further elaboration, including definitions of 'event–detection process' and 'event–response process'.]

In an object-oriented model, we organise the system's behaviour around objects. The operations in different objects (and also within the same object) communicate using messages. But we still require the same system behaviour: when the system detects the event, various object's operations fire, until all required processing has taken place; the system then returns to a quiescent state. We thus need an operation (in an object, of course) to detect that the event has occurred. By means of messages, other operations (in other objects) are then activated. We will choose, as in (Baker et al., 1990), to separate the detection of the event from the decision on what to do and the actual operations that need to be fired. In general, we have an 'event–detection operation', a 'controller operation' and one (or more) 'server operation's that need to be fired. The controller operation is the one that takes the decision on what needs to be done when the event occurs.

For example, consider the training centre company. We will consider two events:

1 Customer reserves place for student on course;

2 Time to send out joining instructions (to students who have reserved places on a given course).

The first is the simpler to deal with. We first must decide which object has the responsibility for detecting the event. As the event is 'generated' by the agent Customer, this is an easy decision. This

---

13 They are inherited (meta-inheritance) from the meta-object Object.

is one of the things a customer can do. We therefore need an operation reserve place in the Customer object. (See figure 2, where it is shown as Make prov. booking.) The decision on what to do about a booking is not the responsibility of the customer; it requires system policy. We will therefore create a controller operation Accept booking to deal with it. It will need to receive a message from Customer.reserve place (we use an obvious notation for indicating an object's operation). Determining what to do when such a reservation occurs is, of course, up to those defining the policy for the system. Nevertheless, the analyst shouldn't just sit back and wait for the policy to be defined.

One very important technique that can be applied to identify system behaviour in responding to the event is to think about which entities might need to be referenced when the event occurs. We will use entity state transition diagrams (eSTDs) to model this. The use of eSTDs to model the relationship between entities and events is not new of course. It can be used to identify events (as in SSADM); it can also be used to help clarify how a minispec should deal with each of the corresponding states of an entity (Baker et al., 1990). In this example, we might suppose that we have already considered what might happen to the Public course entity, as shown in figure 3. (The corresponding diagram for Booking is interesting in that the entity instance can be created in one of two states: provisional, or firm.)

So it looks as though we need to reference the corresponding objects Public course and Booking). The first-cut view of the system behaviour when the event occurs is thus as shown in figure 4. Public course receives a message, asking if it can take more bookings and sends a response back to Accept booking. This operation responds back to the customer and also creates a new instance of Booking. Note that we have left the operation Accept provisional booking 'un-allocated' — more of this later.

On closer examination, we find we also need to reference the Course object (to find out how many students can be accepted on a particular type of course). Where should this reference need to take place from? The immediately obvious conclusion is that each Public course ought to be able to deal with 'its fullness'; it is nothing to do with the controller logic. If this solution is adopted, then Scheduled course would send messages to/from Course about this. Public course would 'close' itself (change its state). (These messages would not be shown on this diagram, but would be 'hidden' inside the Public course object.) This might, however, be a rather poor strategy. If we needed to accept bookings from special privileged customers (even if the scheduled course is then

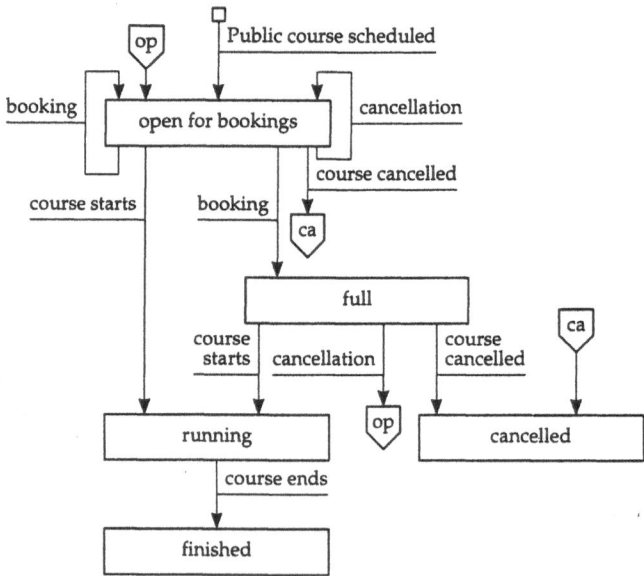

Figure 3: Entity state transition diagram for "Public course"

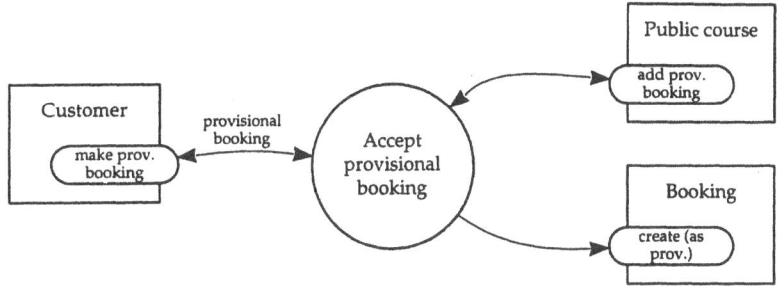

Figure 4: Event–response fragment for "Customer reserves place for student on course"

over-subscribed), we would need Accept booking to use the objects Customer and Course (as well as Scheduled course and Booking). [Modifications to the first-cut DFD in figure 4 (a DFD is 'message-passing diagram') is left as an exercise.]

4.2.1 Temporal events

The event Time to send out joining instructions does not have a stimulus (a system input used to 'flag the event') that can be used. The system must detect the event by monitoring the current time and some pre-scheduled time[14]. If we call this operation Detect time to send joining instructions (for example), where should this operation 'live'? The simplest solution is to place it in the object that has the information it needs. In this case, we would place it in the Scheduled course object. (More generally, these temporal event detectors might need to reference several other objects.)

Having detected the event, is the responsibility for sending the joining instructions the responsibility of the scheduled course? It could be, in which case, this operation would obtain the details about the course (from the Course object) and the location (from the Location object). The joining instructions would then be sent to the Customer and Student object (they would both want copies). A more flexible approach, however, is to have a separate operation that decides what to do when the event has been detected. If we call this operation Send joining instructions, we have identified another controller operation. (The event–response DFD fragment is left as an exercise.)

4.3 Choosing controller objects

We have two 'un-allocated' operations. When we consider other events, we will have more. What we do with them? One strategy is to create a 'system object' that embodies all these controller operations. It is served by all the subject-domain objects that acted as servers in each of the individual event–response threads. This is simple and also has a nice 'symmetry'. The enterprise, system, and an object are all very similar; each has functionality, events they deal with and 'internal data'. They only differ in scale.

For large systems, this is inconvenient. It is then probably better to use a high-level functional decomposition of the system's responsibilities and provide a controller object for each. For example, we might have one to deal with scheduled courses, one to deal with staff scheduling, one to deal with writing new courses, and so on. It also fails when the system needs to synchronise multiple instances of objects, as is often the case in real-time systems. Actually, it doesn't really fail, it just gets very complex. In those cases, it is often better to define a controller object for each subject-domain object, as well as the system as a whole.

For example, consider a system to control many lifts. It would not only require a subject-domain object Lift and controller object Lift controller, but also an overall Lift scheduler (a controller object)

---

[14] Temporal events can also be at 'fixed' times, as well as pre-scheduled ones.

(Brough and Sully, 1989). This is because of the '1:N' nature of the relationship between them. We might, additionally, have a Door controller object to control individual doors. This is because a Lift is an aggregate object, consisting of a lift cage, doors, ... An aggregate object can either have a controller object for the aggregation only, or it could have controller objects for each of the components too. The decision on which to choose is more a matter of the complexity of the controller. In this case, the state behaviour of the lift is easiest to understand if partitioned into behaviour for the door and behaviour (e.g. moving or not) of the lift as a whole[15].

Note that a system can now be regarded as an aggregate controller object. Any overall system policy is located in its operations. This leads to a 'homology' property. An aggregate object can coordinate other objects, using its own operations. The objects it controls and synchronises can themselves be aggregate objects, – objects 'all the way down' (like turtles).

4.4 *Summary of Conceptual Model organisation*

We organised the system's behaviour around objects, whose operation are responses to events. To be a *good* organisation, we must carefully consider where each operation 'lives'. If it contains *system policy* on how the subject-domain concepts are *used*, we place it in a controller object; if it corresponds to something an *entity can do*, we place it in a subject-domain object. Careful attribution is vital. It is here that the quality (separation) of the model is determined.

Object-oriented analysis must be intuitive. We also need a model structure that allows the elicited policy to be verified as a 'C^3' (complete, consistent and correct) statement of system requirements. We used the concept of an internal model, running in a virtual machine. A suitable CASE environment would support this, providing emulation and multiple views of the model.

5 Overview of OOD

An analysis strategy is of little use, unless it produces a model that can be transformed into a viable design, and thence into a system embodying the required conceptual policy and performance. As described in (Brough 1988) and (Baker et al., 1990), design consists of:

  □ processor allocation and processor interface design (including the HCI);
  □ allocation to the run–time architectures chosen;
  □ allocation to the code structures supported by the chosen programming language(s).

In conventional (process+data) treatments, this is a 'top-down' allocation of system functions to technology, as seen in a levelled set of DFDs. In the final model, the top-level DFD is a processor diagram; for each digital processor, a lower-level diagram (figures 1, 2, ...) shows run–time units (tasks, files, etc.) used in that processor; at the lowest level, each task (for example) has a diagram showing code units (procedures etc.) used within it; each code unit has a module specification.

Although we do not organise the model as a 'levelled set of DFDs' in OOD, we use the same logical sequence[16]. We take the Conceptual Model, consisting of conceptual objects and allocate it to processors, adding features to take account of processor architectures and inter-processor interfaces. This Processor Model is then mapped onto the Run–time Model, taking account of the run-time architectures (e.g., semaphores, tables, tasks, ...). Finally, we take account of the features (e.g., procedures, subroutines, functions, classes ...) supported by the programming languages. We can thus represent the design process by figure 5.

Each layer provides a virtual machine for the layer above it to run in (Brough 1990a, 1992). In each implementation layer, we define objects that export services to allow higher layers to be implemented. The Timer object is part of a 'hardware resource' in the processor layer. The hardware

---

15 Where instances of objects have state behaviour, we can use a controller operation containing a state machine (conventional in control systems). Alternatively (as for Booking), we can treat the state behaviour as a state variable (instance data). There is a whole spectrum of possible approaches between these two extremes.

16 Logical, rather than a strict temporal sequence (because of 'look-ahead', model revision, 'spiralling', ...).

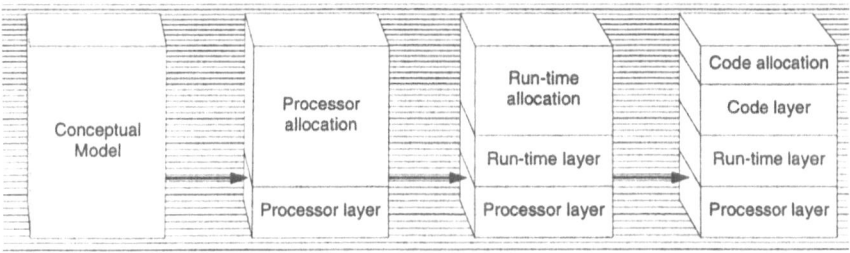

Figure 5: System design as successive allocation to architecture layers

resource is one of several in the Processor layer; others would include 'Windows' (for example), providing resources for constructing the HCI

5.1 Reasons for keeping layers separate

The alternative OOD strategy is to modify the objects in the Conceptual Model, so that they work in specific architectures. But using 'layering' to (largely) retain the same, unchanged policy in the highest layer has the following advantages:

- □ the system can be 'ported' to different hardware platforms and architectures with a minimum of disruption of the lower layers;
- □ we can ensure that the same policy implemented in different architectures — the *same* code is used in each case;
- □ class libraries for different architectures (for user interfaces, 'persistent objects', ...) can be built/bought in and used, with minimum disruption to the code defining system policy.

The architecture is made 'transparent' to the application. A 'wrap' is provided around any peculiarity of the hardware, run–time architecture ... so that it can be used more easily. For example, we might wish to use a specific DBMS on a specific machine. Rather than making the specifics of this DBMS visible in the policy code, we provide a wrap (possibly with more than one layer) around the collection of objects (or 'pseudo-objects') supported by the DBMS. The application then just sees a 'persistent object' storage class. The way this class depends on the DBMS would be 'transparent' to the application (so would any physical distribution of stored instance data). The final system might then look as in figure 6.

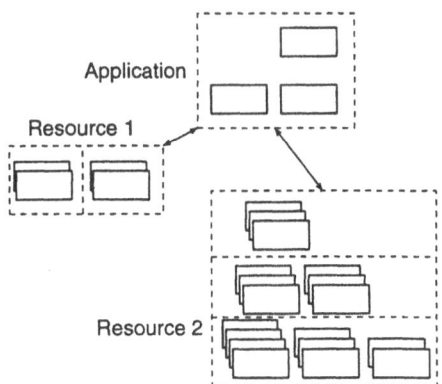

Figure 6: A delivered system, seen as an interaction with 'layered resources'.

Of course, we might need to 'collapse layers' because of performance requirements (a strategy that has been used for some time with comms. s/w). Even then, a 'layering strategy' provides a good starting point. It is certainly better than trying to do OOD 'in one go'.

5.2 Developing resources

Each resource can be modelled in the way that we have described conceptual system modelling for an application system. The only difference is that their subject-domain now becomes their client objects; events are requests from clients, etc. For example, if we were developing a comms resource, the subject domain (modelled by ERDs, etc.) would contain 'client program' channel, messages, and so on. Events would include non-temporal ones such as Client submits message for transmission, as well as temporal ones such as Destination fails to acknowledge receipt of message. In all respects, the approach described in the earlier part of this paper applies. The only difference is in the environment that the system operates in.

5.3 System allocation strategies

One interesting problem is how objects are allocated to processors, run–time units, and code units. In the literature, this is not usually dealt with very well. Analysts tend to assume perfect architecture (i.e., all these issues are transparent); designers tend to concentrate on reuse of code (e.g., by class taxonomies), with little modelling of the processor and run–time issues. We will only give a brief discussion here, to introduce some subtleties that can occur.

One issue is the 'horizontal' versus 'vertical' allocation of objects. The simplest situation is that an object is wholly and solely (both operations and data) allocated to a single processor[17]. Alternatively, we could have a horizontal allocation, where each processor implements all the operations, but each object instance has instance data on only one processor. In a vertical allocation, all object instances have their instance data on several processors, but each operation is only supported on some processors. (We will assume that no individual operation gets 'split', as described in (Ward and Mellor, 1985); in general, it could be.)

There are some immediate problems that must be addressed in either case. What happens to instance data (and operations) in horizontal allocation? How is instance data kept 'aligned' in vertical allocation? Some form of communication will need to be provided. But we will keep the 'transparency' objective in mind. Ideally, any client of the object should not be aware of these decisions, or how the problems have been overcome. It should only be aware of the operation and instance it deals with. The best approach seems to be to introduce 'transducer' objects, first described in (Meyer 1988). These are used transparently *within* an object to provide links to other instances or operations of the same object (transducers provide peer-peer links to services in the *same* layer, as contrasted with those like Timer, which provide links between *different* layers).

5.3.1 Run–time issues

There are parallel issues in allocation to the run–time architecture. The way 'threads' are implemented is particularly interesting. In the Conceptual Model (and conventionally, the Processor Model), we assume that an indefinite number of threads (processes) can be active at the same time. In real architectures this is not possible. Consider how operations are allocated to the threads that are allowed in the run–time architecture. Ideally, we would have a separate thread for each class operation of each object and each instance operation would have a separate thread for each instance of the object. Why is this desirable?

Consider the object Lift for example, with the operation slow down. (We will assume that the whole system is allocated to one digital processor; in reality, there are other interesting possibilities.) This operation must be time–continuous; further, there is a need to have current speed for each lift

---

17 We use allocation to processors as an example. There are similar issues in other allocations.

instance. The simplest design is to have a thread for each lift instance. The current speed and desired speed are then scoped within the thread (each thread contains the same policy as the others). Alternatively, we could have a single thread, with the current speeds (and statuses) of each lift held in a data structure. The thread would then 'pseudo-continuously' (in a polled loop) check the status of each lift; if it is slowing down, its current speed would be used to set its desired speed. This would be a suitable solution for architectures where many threads are not allowed (or have poor performance characteristics). The skill of the designer has always been in thinking about such options and identifying the trade-offs between simplicity and other desired properties, such as performance. Without going into the details, it is possible to 'hide' these issues in the same way as we hid the details of processor allocation. Ideally, any client object (e.g., the Lift scheduler) would not need to be aware of how the Lift object has been allocated.

The number of instances of Lift probably doesn't change dynamically over the system's life, but in an air traffic control system (for example), the numbers of instances *do* change dynamically. Any design must be able to accommodate this. And, importantly, the way the problem is solved should be transparent to clients; otherwise many of the benefits of the 'object' approach have been lost. This is not just how the source code constructs are used to provide abstraction and one instance of the object and operation. It also involves the instance-processor and instance-thread decisions.

5.4 Implementing a conceptual architecture for the application; logical architecture objects

We have discussed issues faced in dealing with real processor and run–time architectures. More subtly, there is the problem of implementing the architecture assumed in the Conceptual Model — we could to create new instances of objects, give attributes values, check for the existence of relationships, … Ideally, we should implement these with a minimum of disruption to policy already captured in the Conceptual Model.

This can be achieved by introducing logical architecture objects. These provide services that are logically equivalent to the idealised conceptual architecture (virtual machine), allowing an 'object model' to be run. By contrast, physical architecture objects are used to make a specific platform & environment usable. For example, if we implemented an 'enable' (to allow an operation to take place on a given object instance, possibly with a corresponding 'disable'), we could 'hack' the code of the client so that features of the run–time architecture are utilised. A better approach would be to construct a wrap around the real-time architecture, so that the client needing to use the 'enable' would have the peculiarities of the specific run–time architecture hidden. We might use a Process object, with operations such as enable and disable (messages to them would be 'prompts'). This would provide transparency and portability similar to that discussed above.

A Process object would probably only be useful in real-time systems, but all systems will need to implement ADTs as logical architecture objects. Any ADT object should be usable within many applications and run–time architectures. Value operations used (with attributes) in the Conceptual Model then reference operations owned by the specific ADT object.

Another interesting type of logical architecture object are those used to support the 'conceptual' relationships used in the Conceptual Model. Rather than 'hardcoding' pointers into the subject–domain objects that the relationship refers to, we create an object for each relationship. These objects inherit operations such as create, match, delete …) from the meta-object Relationship. The database community may consider this unnecessarily complex — can't we implement relationships using features of the DBMS? Possibly. But we are then limited by the 'semantic richness' of the DBMS. Relationships are usually much more complex than just 'instance links' and a Relationship object is easier to extend ('cleanly') to deal with this extra complexity.

In particular, consider 'relationship constraints'. Many types of constraint can be imposed on relationships. In existing DBMSs, some can be implemented at a 'structural level' (e.g., the '1:N'-ness of links can be guaranteed using foreign keys + referential integrity constraints); others need to be guaranteed using a variety of ad-hoc code (perhaps implemented using 'triggers'). Rather than scattering such constraint code around, it is a good idea to allow features of this type for *all* relationships, by defining a Relationship constraint meta-object. Instances of this can be used by different instances of the Relationship object. [See (Baker et al., 1990) for a discussion of the more general types of conceptual constraint required; they are there called 'rules of association'.]

6 Conclusions

This paper introduced the distinction between conceptual and implementation objects and strategies for identifying conceptual objects: from the subject domain and required system responses to events. System policy is captured in a Conceptual Model, organised in terms of subject-domain and controller objects. A Conceptual Model organised in this way is intuitive to understand, both in how it 'works' (the object-oriented virtual machine for the Conceptual Model) and how it is identified (from ERA and event modelling). It can be evolved into a viable design for a variety of platforms, with the policy kept separate from each of the different implementations.

References

(Baker et al., 1990): J. Baker, M. Brough and N. Matzke, *Yourdon Structured Method*, Yourdon Inc, 1990 (republished as *Yourdon System Modelling*, Prentice-Hall, 1993).

(Brough 1988): M. Brough, A Framework for Relating System Development Methods, *Structured Development Forum X*, San Francisco, 1988.

(Brough and Sully, 1989): M. Brough and P. Sully, Lift case study, Yourdon Internal document, 1989.

(Brough 1990a): M. Brough, Methods First, then Tools, *DECUS (Methods, Languages and Tools special interest group)*, 1990.

(Brough 1990b): M. Brough, *Adding OOD views to the standard YSM Models*, Yourdon internal technical paper, 1990.

(Brough 1992): M. Brough, Methods and Objects: Evolution of an Existing Method, *DECUS*, 1992.

(Chen 1976): P. Chen, "The Entity-Relationship Model - Towards a Unified View of Data", ACM transactions on Database Systems, Vol. 1, No. 1 (March 1976), pp. 9–36.

(DeMarco 1978): T. DeMarco, *Systems Analysis and Specification*, Yourdon Press, 1978.

(Dijkstra 1968): E. Dijkstra, "Structure of the THE – Multiprogramming System", *Communications of the ACM*, Vol. 11, No. 5 (May 1968), pp. 341–346.

(Flavin 1981): M. Flavin, Fundamental Concepts of Information Modeling, Yourdon Press, 1981.

(McMenamin 1984): S. McMenamin and J. Palmer, *Essential Systems Analysis*, Yourdon Press, 1984.

(Meyer 1988): B. Meyer, *Object-oriented Software Construction*, Prentice-Hall, 1988.

(Redmond-Pyle 1991): D. Redmond-Pyle, Can formal methods be user-friendly? *American Programmer*, May 1991.

(Ward and Mellor 1985): P. T. Ward and S. J. Mellor, *Structured Development for Real-Time Systems*, Yourdon Press, 1985 (volumes 1 and 2), 1986 (volume 3).

(Yourdon 1989): E. Yourdon, *Modern Structured Analysis*, Prentice-Hall, 1989.

NET/C: Toward the Fine Grained UNIX-like OS

Minoru Uehara*
Dept. of Information and Computer Sciences,
Toyo University

Short Paper

Abstract

NET/C is a concurrent object-based programming language which is suited to describe network applications. NET/C objects are running concurrently and communicate with each other via stream. The
syntax of NET/C is similar to C and its executing model is similar to UNIX process. However, NET/C
objects are better-grained than UNIX processes. In this paper, we propose the way that UNIX and its
compatible operating systems are restructured to be fine-grained by using NET/C.

1 Introduction

Massively parallel architecture is one of architectures for future computers. In such systems, applications
should be structured with fine-grained objects in order to draw the maximal performance of them. Then,
they are running on special operating systems dependent on individual architectures. However, it is hard
to develope such operating system for each system. Therefore, it is needed the way to port a conventional
operating system and its applications to other architectures. In this paper, we propose one of such ways.

The UNIX is an operating system used by many researchers and it has much software. However,
the design of UNIX is too traditional to be suited for multiprocessor architecture. Recently, several
UNIX-compatible operating systems, Mach, Apertos, etc. have been developed by using micro-kernel
and UNIX server[2]. In these systems, however, the granularity of a process is very coarse because of
binary level compatibility. Executing units could not be automatically changed from heavy process into
light weight process like thread even if all applications would be rewritten in sequential object-oriented
programming like C++. Only one correct solution of this problem is to use fine-grained concurrent
object-based programming languages like NET/C.

NET/C is a concurrent object-based programming language based on stream communication. A
NET/C object can communicate with external UNIX processes as same as other NET/C objects. NET/C
objects are executed by a virtual machine process. A group of NET/C objects seems a UNIX process.
In NET/C, an optimal granularity is decided by the number of objects in a virtual machine process and
it is realized at run time via object migration. In this way, a part of UNIX systems can be transparently
restructured with fine-grained objects by using NET/C. NET/C basically employs procedural semantics
but can write declarative program.

C-like concurrent object-oriented programming languages, ACT++, cooC[5] are not suited for such
purpose because they are based on message passing. The gap of comunication model increases software
maintenance cost because of inserting interface libraries to sources. C-unlike stream-based concurrent
programming languages, GHC, A'UM[7] increases educational cost.

This paper is organized as follows: In section 2, we describe the features of NET/C model/language.
In section 3, we introduce the language specification of NET/C. We show some examples in section 4.
Finally, contributions and conclusions are remarked.

---

*uehara@cs.toyo.ac.jp

2 Features of NET/C

In NET/C, the system is constructed as the network of concurrent objects, which we call actors, communicating with each other via stream. The linguistic features of NET/C is as follows:

- The syntax of NET/C is similar to C/C++ which are the standard programming language for UNIX users. Thus, beginners also learn NET/C easily.

- The creation and execution of an actor in NET/C is written like the function call in C.

- reply statement means "return a value then continue the following statements."

- NET/C compiler inserts duplicators automatically in order to represent same variable names to same data.

- NET/C programs can be visualized the data flow graph, which we call graphical representation of NET/C program. The translator from such graphical representations to text programs has been already developed.

3 Language

In this section, we describe the language specification of NET/C. One of the features of NET/C is that its syntax is similar to C. Thus, we explain the different point between NET/C and C.

3.1 Constant

The following C-like constants are allowed: 3, 2.5, 'a', ''abc''. In addition, the following special constants exist: nil, EOF, and so on. A constant is the outlet of infinite stream generating itself.

3.2 Variable

A variable designates either inlet or outlet of a stream and has a type, out(outlet of actor/inlet of stream) or in(inlet of actor/outlet of stream). If declared without data type signature, it is recognized as **any** which is matched to any data type.

There are two operations for the variables, assignment and concatenation. Assignment operation means alias. Concatenation operation means stream creation. These operations are written as follows:

```
in x = 3;       // assignment
in y <- out x; // concatenation
```

Of course, types of left and right values are checked in both operations.

3.3 Actor Creation

Actor creation in NET/C is represented as the function call in C. At the same time of actor creation, new one starts to run concurrently. However, the creator waits for a reply then it is blocked. An actor replies in the following cases: (1) when it is terminated, this is same as return nil. (2) when it executes return statement, it closes inlets of streams and connects outlets of streams to sink actor then it returns some value. (3) when to execute reply statement, it returns some value continues the next statement.

3.4 Actor Definition

An actor definition in NET/C represents function definnition in C. For examples, an actor f is described as follow:

```
in f(in x) {
    return x + x;
}
```

where actor + creates a buffer inside. This is important technique for the compatibility of C, for operators can smoothly connect each other. In C, both x are same value. In NET/C, however, both x are different value when not inserting duplicator.

3.5   Control Statement

In NET/C, all of control statements in C are allowed. As this result, however, the conditional statement, if, while, etc. is rather complex. The statement if has the following syntax:

> if (*condition*) *statement* [else *statment*]

where *condition* is the outlet of boolean stream, statement is any statement. Actors waits for *condition* when evaluating it.

3.6   Control Actor

Control actor is the abstraction of controls. For examples, assume that there is the following C program:

```
for(i=0;i<=9;i++) f(i);
```

This program means f(i=0,...,9). Then, the same NET/C program is represented by using control actors as follow:

```
f(interval(0,9,1))
```

where interval(s,e,d) generates series from s to e by d. Basically, NET/C programs can be written with control actor instead of control statement. There are the following control actors: cond(b,t,f) which is same as b?t:f in C, whileTrue(b,t) which passes data of t during b is true, etc.

4   Examples

In this section, we show several examples and evaluate the facility of NET/C.

4.1   Simple Example

First, we show a simple example.

```
in buffer(in x) {
    in xi <- out xo;
    reply xi;
    while(fifo(xo,only x));
}
```

where only modifier is disable to insert the duplicator. In this buffer actor, one stream is created between xi and xo. Buffer actor returns one-side xi then uses only another-side xo. This technique is frequently used for the purpose of pipeline processing. The actor fifo is primitive to transfer data from one stream to another.

4.2   UNIX Filter Command

When using UNIX, the following shell script are frequently used.

```
tail +$1 | head -1
```

The following NET/C program is equivalent to the above shell script:

```
void nth_line(in i, out o, out e, int in n) {
    in pi <- out po;
    tail(i, n, e, po);
    head(pi, o, e);
}
void main(int in argc, string in argv[]) {
    nth_line(cin, cout, cerr, atoi(argv[1]));
}
```

Like C, NET/C program starts main actor. In this case, main actor plays the role of interface between UNIX command line and NET/C actors. Both head and tail are UNIX-like NET/C actors which have at least three arguments, stdin, stdout, stderr. Here, head actor might call UNIX head command or might call other actors. However, users need not know its implementation. NET/C compiler translates above NET/C program text to the executive file(a.out). It is equivalent to above shell script.

5   Conclusions

NET/C is a stream-based concurrent programming language suitable for network description. It is easy for beginners to learn NET/C bacause of syntactical similarity of C. Its executing model is similar to UNIX but its granularity is different from UNIX. In this paper, we describe the overview of NET/C and suggest how to restructure UNIX by using fine-grained NET/C objects. NET/C contributes the following fields: visualization[1], fault torelant architecture[3, 4], neural networks, queuing networks, dynamic resource allocation in distributed systems[6], groupware, multimedia networks, and so on. Currently, the NET/C system is running on Sony NWS-1750,5000, Sun OS 4.1.x, Solaris 2.x, Omron Luna88K Mach2.5, DG/UX, SGI Onyx IRIS, etc.

References

[1] Ryuichi Iwata. *A Study on Graphical Representation of NET/C programs*. Graduation thesis, Toyo University, Dept. of Information and Computer Sciences, February 1994.

[2] M. Maekawa, M. Tokoro, and K. Shimizu. *Distributed Operating System - Next Generation*. Kyoritsu-shuppan, 1991. (in Japanese).

[3] Y. Michikawa. *Implementation of a Fault Tolerant Simulator*. Graduation thesis, Toyo University, Dept. of Information and Computer Sciences, February 1994.

[4] Hideki Mori and Minoru Uehara. Fault Tolerant Multicube Pipeline Processor. In *Proceedings of the International Conference on Wafer Scale Integration*, January 1994.

[5] R. Trehan, N. Sawashima, A. Morishita, I. Tomoda, and K. Maeda. Concurrent Object Oriented C(cooC). *ACM SIGPLAN NOTICES*, February 1993.

[6] Minoru Uehara and Mario Tokoro. An Adaptive Load Balancing Method in the Computational Field Model. In *Proceedings of the Workshop on Object-Based Concurrent Programming*, April 1991. OOPS MESSENGER, Vol.2, No.2.

[7] Kaoru Yoshida. *AUM: A Stream-Based Concurrent Programming Language*. PhD thesis, Keio University, January 1990.

METHODOLOGY
AND
DESIGN

Dynamic implementation of composite objects in ACSE project

Boulanger Danielle, Colloc Joël, Chahwan Pierre

Groupe Modeme
URA CNRS 1257 - I.A.E. Université Lyon III
15, Quai Claude Bernard - BP 0638
69239 Lyon Cedex 02, FRANCE   Fax : 33 - 72 72 45 45

ABSTRACT. *ACSE workshop is a generator of expert systems involving only object oriented concepts through a knowledge base, an application base, a user base and a kernel dealing with object interactions.*
We focus on object dynamic server and we explain our persistence needs to implement composite objects.
We finally justify our choices and present future extensions.

KEYWORDS : *Expert system, object oriented model, composite object, spontaneous evolution, persistence, dynamic object server*

1. Introduction

The ACSE project aims at building an expert system designing workshop (French acronym : Atelier de Conception de Système Expert).

ACSE supports object oriented model concepts. The model and its associated method were presented in previous works (Colloc, 1989) (Boulanger, 1993).

This tool includes three object bases (figure1): knowledge object base, application object base, user object base and a system module which deals with object interactions (figure 1).

The system module is composed of : a function editor, a function interpreter, a message processor, a temporal function update module and an object dynamic server.

In this paper, we will describe the object dynamic server implementation.
Most of existing OOL are compiled (generally compilers use an evoluted intermediate language). So, the designer must build the objects, compile and provide them to the user in libraries.

Each update needs to recompile the modified objects and to save them back to the library. This constraint impedes real time object prototyping, that is during the knowledge base design.

In the applications written in interpreted heap intensive languages like Smalltalk or Lisp, dynamically allocated objects tend to live a very short time. On the contratry, knowledge objects have to survive for a long time and should be stored in mass memory. However, some temporary objects should be deleted at the end of the working session.

Whereas expert system design often needs features to build complex composite objects whose structure (component sub-objects) and state (attribute values or constraints) must change spontaneously during object life time.

The object server of ACSE must conciliate this two paradoxical goals : persistence and the ability to specify and dynamically modify complex composite objects.

At first, we briefly summarize the concepts of our model and the architecture of the workshop.

The next section presents some persistence problems.
At last we describe ACSE's kernel, particularly its main module the dynamic object server.
In conclusion, we discuss our contribution and the perspectives of this research.

2. ACSE project environment

2.1. An object oriented model

The strong points of our model (Colloc, 1989)(Boulanger, 1992)(Colloc, 1993) are :

- Distinction between the internal environment and the external environment of object description.
  Objects are nested in each other. According to the application, a unit corresponding to a reference object type has to be defined. The unique object traces a boundary between two levels :
  - the internal structure represents the content of the object and its composing sub-objects which determine a partition of set of properties (at each level of the composition hierarchy).
  - the external environment expresses the relationships of an object with the others.
  Each sub-object can be seen, at any time, at level zero. Its proper sub-objects define its internal structure. We call zoom effect this adapted perception of objects.

- Two kinds of inheritance
  - the internal level includes aggregation relationships, which establish multiple ascending inheritance without conflicts. This level encapsulates attributes and functions which represent the static characteristics and the behaviour of the objects. Evaluation and dynamical functions provide means to access object-state and to model object evolution (even spontaneous evolution).
  - the external level includes generalization/specialization relationships between object types and sub-types. These relationships establish a simple descending inheritance.
  These two levels are linked by instantiation mechanism, interface functions (to respect encapsulation concept), message exchanges.

- Application object type
  It is a predefined system type to describe users' requirements.

  This O-O model offers semantic capability (Saltor, 1991); the application object type allows similarity algorithms implementation (Colloc, 1993) and then provides semantic relativism (Boulanger, 1992).
  Associated to this O.O. model, we developed a method to build expert systems (Boulanger, 1993).

2.2. Architecture of ACSE workshop

In this paragraph, we briefly describe the nature of important modules of ACSE (figure1).

- The object dynamic server
  The object server of ACSE allows to specify and modify objects dynamically according to knowledge expressed by the expert and formalized by the designer. Thus, the tool flexibility favours a quick design of expert system prototypes in complex domains like health and management.

- The Function editor
  In order to provide prototyping facilities, the designer must be able, during the session, to create, modify and delete object internal functions.
  This functions are expressed thanks to an interpreted language.

460

- The Function interpreter

The function interpreter translates and runs functions belonging to the internal environment of objects.

- The Application objects

Application objects contain internal instructions, triggered with the help of a metapointer, which carry out access to the object knowledge base like queries, object state evaluation... according to the expert system goals, states of knowledge objects, user queries and answers.

The generated expert system establishes a dialogue between the user represented by his "user object", "the application object" which stand for the reasoning modes expressed by the experts and the objects belonging to the knowledge base.

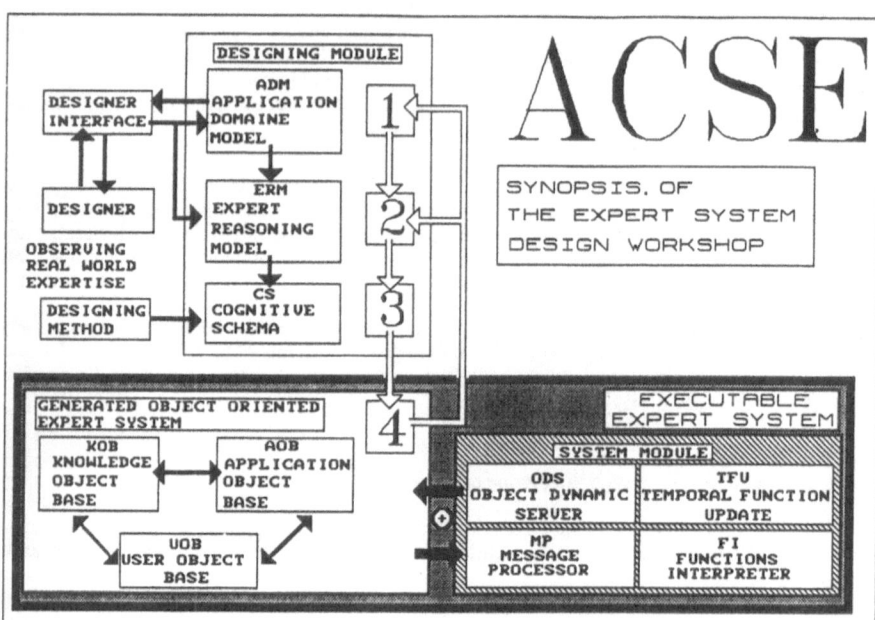

Figure 1 : ACSE workshop architecture.

3. Persistence features

We have to conciliate two opposite requirements : persistence with static storage and the necessity of to dynamically update composition links between objects.

3.1. Current persistence approaches

Traditionally DBMSs have assumed that all accessible data resides on magnetic disk, so persistence is respected. Recently several researchers have begun to consider the possibility that significant amounts of data will occupy space in a main cache memory; thus M. Stonebracker proposes an "object storage manager" to manage persistent objects in a multi-level store (Stonebracker, 1991).

OODBMS motivation would like to combine the advantages of DBMSs and OO systems; currently the major problem is how to implement persistence in an OO language (Amiel, 1993) (Bullat, 1993)(Khoshafian, 1989). In OODBMSs, we found two kinds of persistence implementation. In ONTOS persistence is implemented using inheritance by the means of class libraries. In O2 persistence is mentioned by syntax notation at the root creation and implicitly propagated to composing sub-objects (Amiel, 1993).

An other alternative is the proposition of a persistent data server like KALA (Simmel, 1992). Its objectives are to maintain the structure of data, to perform file system procedures and to offer database features. This server is not bound to a particular notion of object, because it can simultaneously support several types of objects.

3.2. Persistence needs to implement dynamic composite objects

Persistence needs concern the two OO model levels : the management of object composition hierarchy at the internel level, the management of type hierarchy at the external level (figure 2). So we have to deal with persistence from different points of view :

* Object type persistence
  Object type headers and linked descriptors of attributes and functions must be stored on mass memory. In main memory, the user must be able to modify types, instantiate objects according to defined constraints (figure 2).

* Object persistence
  In the composition hierarchy of complex object, object headers and linked values of attributes and functions have to be stored on secondary memory.

* Inheritance persistence
  Ascending inheritance : when a complex object should be stored in mass memory, all component sub-object links, values of attributes and functions must be handled.
  Descending inheritance : At the end of the work session, types and subtypes links, attribute and function descriptors have to be maintained.

* Persistence and spontaneous evolution of object structure and values
  Values returned by dynamic functions and updated by the refresh monitor are involved in the object header. Some of these values are relevant to dynamic attributes.

* Update transaction and persistence
  During a session, the user may update the values of specific attributes according to type constraints. The updated values should be stored to be available to the next session.

4. ACSE's kernel

In this paragraph, we describe object and type headers, function and attribute tables involved in ACSE's kernel. We propose means to implement internal and external inheritance and a monitor to deal with the spontaneous evolution of object structure and attribute values. To achieve late binding (Cox, 1986), ACSE's kernel must allow the user to change object and type structure and values during the session without compilation.

4.1. ACSE persistence : global description schema

A global description schema shows object and type headers, descriptor tables and value table. The schema exhibits relationships and constraints between headers and tables (figure2)

4.2. Object and type implementation

We have seen that the model makes a clear distinction between types and instances.
* An object is defined by its object components, attribute and function values available at any time. Thus, the object header contains references to sub_object headers, attribute and function

value tables,
- Object type describes instance composition and behaviour; thereby it includes a structure descriptor (allowed sub_object types) and some attribute and function descriptors. The object type header provides references to sub_object type headers, attribute and function descriptor tables.

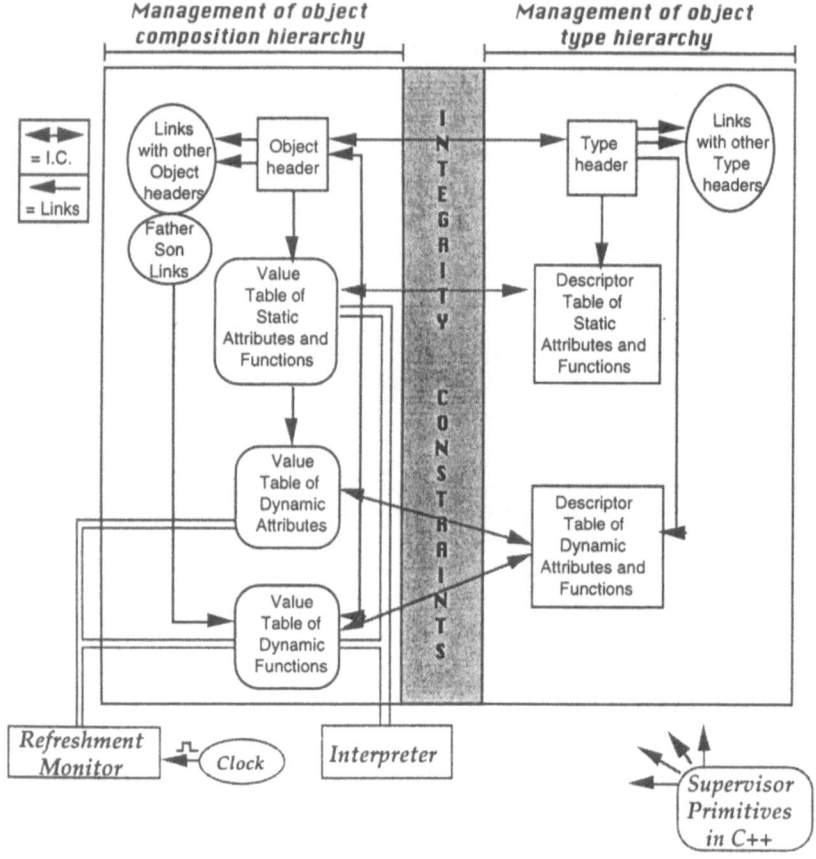

Figure 2 : Persistence implementation in ACSE project

4.2.1. The object header

The object header describes a unique object according to the model. It includes data : references to other header attribute and function values needed to represent the structure and the behaviour of the object during its lifetime. These references are encapsulated with their respective management functions.

The object header shows an object identifier (OID) provided by the system thanks to a hashcode function. Its OID comes with the object type identifier (TID), thereby providing a quick access to its descriptor.

A date field memorizes the time of the last object update.

A security field contains the owner identifier and expresses allowed access modes to different user categories.

The object header provides four composition links to implement the object composition hierarchy:
- father object link,
- left brother link,
- right brother link,
- first son link.

These links can have either a null value, either a main memory pointer or an OID on mass memory. The reference nature of each link is expressed by the value of a flag in the security field. The father object link can be moderated by the value (0 to 100 %) of a dynamic function whose identifier is provided in the object header. The dynamic function computed by the refresh monitor expresses the spontaneous variation of the composition link with the father object during the object life.

The object header contains references to the values of the static and dynamic attributes and to the values of static functions. All the values are stored in tables described later. Static function values express the behaviour of the object and its exchanges with the external environment. All the previous references are represented by bit fields according to the SOCRATE DBMS mechanism, (Abrial, 1971) excepted for dynamic functions whose identifier is directly provided by the object header.

4.2.2. The object type header

All references included in object type headers are linked to descriptors (other object types, attribute descriptors and function descriptors). Most of the object type header fields are similar to those of object header. This analogy with object header allows the use of the same code for management functions of the object type header fields. This feature enhances the system modularity.

Each object header is provided with a Type IDentifier (TID). Date and security fields have respectively the same format and use as in object headers.

The object type header provides four links to implement the generalization/specialization object type hierarchy:
- super_type (or father type) link,
- left brother type link,
- right brother type link,
- first sub type link.

NB: No dynamical function value is associated with the super_type link, because the object type has no spontaneous behaviour. They must be purposely updated by the type designer.

The object type header involves an instance count which shows how many objects belong to the associated class.

The object type header provides references to static and dynamic attribute and function descriptor tables which are presented in the next paragraph. References to attributes and functions are expressed by bit fields through the SOCRATE DBMS mechanism.

4.3. Implementing descriptors and values of static functions and attributes

Descriptors are referenced by object types whereas values are attached to instances.

Static attributes and functions should be explicitly and purposely modified or triggered by the user, whereas dynamic attributes and functions are automatically computed by the monitor, according to the instructions included in descriptors.

Since objects and types are persistent, related attributes and functions must be persistent too.

4.3.1. Value table of static functions and attributes

Static attributes and functions are considered similar because functions return a value. This table contains the returned value, the code is stored in function descriptors.

Each value of a static attribute or function is represented by an entry in the value table and identified by the ID field.

The value field represents the current available value of the attribute or the value returned by the function when triggered. The value is stored in a union to fit with different possible data types (Colloc, 1989)(Northrup, 1992).

A link count is an integer field used to find out the current number of objects which refer to this value entry thanks to the composition inheritance.

The native object OID identifies the object where the static attribute or function was explicitly created.

The last two fields are necessary to insure consistence where some objects, attributes or functions are deleted. For example: when the native object is to be deleted, the link count is set to zero, therefore no other object can inherit the value of the attribute. Moreover, if the deleted object has inherited the attribute, the link count is simply decremented.

The static attribute and function value table is a C++ object which comes with the necessary methods to store itself on mass memory.

4.3.2. Descriptor table of static functions and attributes

The descriptor table of static functions and attributes describes integrity constraints and insures the consistence of values. Several attribute or function value entries of the value tables may refer to the same entry of the descriptor table.

Each entry includes the following fields :
* the identifier of the entry,
* a symbol for the descriptor name exploited by the user,
* the measuring unit of the values,
* a coded character expresses the value type and whether they are continuous or they represent discrete states. This code allows to control the value types when the attribute values are changed or functions are computed,
* the minimum and the maximum values are also stored to insure the integrity control. Attribute and function values must fit between these limits,
* a function pointer establishes the link of a function with its corresponding code,
* the TID of the native object type is stored to indicate in which type the descriptor was created,
* a link count is used to find out the number of object types which refer to this descriptor thanks to type inheritance. The deletion of the native object type will set the count to zero. The deletion of an object type that inherits the descriptor will only decrement it.

4.3.3. Links between value table and descriptor table : integrity constraints

During the instantiation step, object type header, descriptor table of static attributes and functions are used as a guideline to build up the structure, the behaviour and the value constraints of the new object instance(grey arrows in figure 2).
* object type header deals with the structure,
* the descriptor table of static attributes and functions manages value constraints and their evolution,
* the descriptor table of dynamic attributes and functions supervises the spontaneous evolution of the structure and attribute values during the object life.

When building a valid complex object using composition operator, all expected sub-objects (according to the object type) must previously exist. This constraint evokes Date's referential integrity in the context of the relational model (Date, 1981).

In order to verify the complex object validity, a flag is set in the object header.

4.4. Dynamic features implementation

In our model the dynamic notion represents the spontaneous changes of attributes and functions as well as the structure of compound objects by means of a refresh monitor (described later). These dynamic attributes and functions are only updated by the monitor according to a refresh frequency, the user cannot purposely change the value of attributes nor trigger the dynamic functions himself. The persistence of this dynamic feature is realised by three tables :

4.4.1. Value table of dynamic attributes

The values of dynamic attributes are attached to objects by the bit field which exists in the object header. The main difference between dynamic and static attributes is the spontaneous change of dynamic attributes without any user intervention.

The first fields in this table are the same as those in the value table of the static attributes and functions previously described (4.3.1).

In order to insure the dynamic characteristic of these attributes, two fields are added to the table :
* period : represents the period of the elapsed time between two refreshments.
* time of the next update : after each refreshment of the dynamic attribute value, the monitor adds the period to the system time and stores it in this field. Thus, when the time of the next refreshment is less or equal to the system time, the dynamic attribute value will be automatically updated .

4.4.2. Value table of dynamic functions

As described in the object header, the dynamic function expresses the variation of the composition link during the object life. The value of this function is referenced by the object header.

This table contains the following fields : an identifier, a value, the identifier of the descriptor, a period for the time elapsed between two refreshments, the time of the next update and the identifier of the father object. This last field must be equal to the "father link field" in the sub-object header to moderate the link between the son and the father by the means of the dynamic function.

The refresh monitor will handle this table as well.

4.4.3. Descriptor table of dynamic functions and attributes

In this table, the descriptors of dynamic functions are treated in the same way as those of dynamic attributes. In fact, they are grouped together because they have the same fields :
* an identifier to each entry of the table,
* a symbol to identify the attribute or the function by its name,
* a measuring unit,
* a coded character to express the attribute or the function value type, in the same way as in the static descriptors (4.3.2.),
* a minimum and a maximum value for the integrity control,
* a link count for the number of the referring object types,
* the identifier of the native object type. For a function descriptor, this field represents the sub-object type,
* a period to express the time elapsed between two refreshments.

NB :   This table is attached to object types. Hence, a descriptor of a dynamic function, unlike its value, may be used by multiple sub-object types (by the link count). In fact, the value is a property of one and only one sub-object but the descriptor could be for more sub-object types. Consequently, descriptors of dynamic functions and attributes are grouped together.

4.4.4. Refresh monitor : temporal update of dynamic attributes and functions

The refresh monitor (TFU module in figure 1) guarantees the spontaneous updates of dynamic attributes and functions. Its job is to determine the time of the next update, it compares the update time to the system time. If the update time is less or equal, the monitor changes the value of the dynamic attribute or triggers the appropriate dynamic function. Then it adds the period to the system time and stores it in the "time of the next update" field of the corresponding attribute. The monitor itself is triggered within a certain cycle, and during its work it locks any access to the application.

The monitor must unlock the system as soon as possible, in order to let the user continue to run the application. In fact, the monitor stores the time that was employed in acheving the update procedure in the monitor_time attribute.

However, this monitor_time must be smaller than the time elapsed between two refreshments (the dead time of the cycle). And it is also used in the next update to insure that all periods are long enough, so the monitor will not monopolize the system.

For each instance 'i' of a dynamic attribute or function, we must have :

Monitor_Time << Period(i)

And if, for a certain instance 'i', the period is not long enough, the monitor must adjust it :

Period(i) = Monitor_Time + K (K is an adjustment constant)

4.5. Inheritance implementation

Inheritance is one of the most important features in an object oriented model. Thus, the inheritance implementation must be persistent in order to last for the entire life of an object, even when the application is turned off. Concurrently, inheritance should be implemented without any redundancy. Copying all inherited attributes in the new object leads to design huge database. In our ACSE's Kernel, we use a well known technique, applied in the SOCRATE DBMS, to deal with inheritance.

4.5.1. SOCRATE DBMS applied to inheritance in an object oriented context

As in SOCRATE DBMS (Abrial, 1971), a field of non-interpreted bits is used to attach attributes and functions to the object that owns them. Each bit represents an attribute or a function (an entry in the value table), and its position in the field corresponds to the entry record number (figure3). The entry will be attached to the object only when the appropriate bit is set to 1.

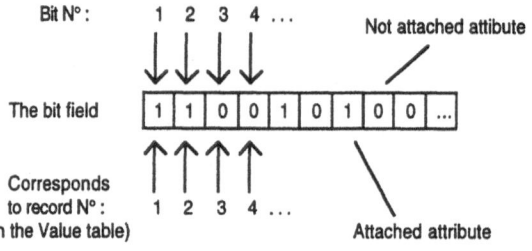

Figure 3 : Inheritance implementation

The use of C++ logical bit operators will help to set on or off the inherited attributes or functions during the working session without any compilation.

4.5.2. Multiple upward inheritance in object composition hierarchy

As we have seen at the internal level, the upward inheritance is applied. A father object inherits all the attributes and functions from all component sub-objects. A simple XOR logical operation will insure this procedure :

The bit field of the sub-object header	1 0 1 0 1 0 1 1 1 0 1 0
	XOR
The bit field of the father object header	0 0 0 1 0 1 0 0 0 0 0 1
The bit field of the new father header	1 0 1 1 1 1 1 1 1 0 1 1

In this way, the new father will be attached to all the inherited attributes. On the other hand, when a sub-object is to be released from a father, the father must give back the inherited attributes and functions. Another XOR will guarantee this operation :

The bit field of the sub-object header	1 0 1 0 1 0 1 1 1 0 1 0
	XOR
The bit field of the father object header	1 0 1 1 1 1 1 1 1 0 1 1
The bit field of the new father header	0 0 0 1 0 1 0 0 0 0 0 1

4.5.3. Simple descending inheritance in object type specialization hierarchy

At the external level, each new sub type inherits all the attribute and function descriptors from its super type. We use the same procedure as above to deal with descending inheritance:

The bit field of the super type header	0 0 1 1 1 1 0 1 0 0 0 0
	XOR
The bit field of the sub type header	0 1 0 0 0 0 0 0 0 1 0 1
The bit field of the new sub type header	0 1 1 1 1 1 0 1 0 1 0 1

As the internal level, another XOR logical operation will release, in the sub type, inherited attribute and function descriptors.

NB : The use of such a bitwise operator allows a compatible manipulation to set on or to set off internal upward inheritance in object headers and external descending inheritance in type headers. Thus, inheritance persistence is insured by storing object headers on mass memory.

4.5.4. Building classes of ACSE's kernel

C++ seems to be the most appropriate object oriented language to realize the implementation.
A C++ class hierarchy is built to implement our model features : object and type headers, descriptor tables and value tables previously described (figure2).

5. Conclusion

We justify the design of a specific object server because we do not found a tool provided with the necessary features to implement our model and to make objects and types persistent.
The upward inheritance have to propagate the properties of component objects to the composite object. The model expresses the evolution, even spontaneous, of the object structure (involved components). In the other hand, the user must have the ability to change object structures and types during the worksession without recompilation.
We have only found incremental compilation in some OODBMSs like O2.
At any time of a work session, we need to adapt the perception level of the objects according to expert's vision (zoom effect).
ACSE kernel is currently implemented with C++ on a SUN workstation. We developed a message manager (figure 1). Now we focus on the design of the command interpreter which will be able to trigger ACSE primitives during a transaction.

References :

(Abrial, 1971)   : JR. Abrial
                       Projet SOCRATE
                       Institut de Mathematiques Appliqués, rapport de recherche 1971
                       Grenoble, France

(Amiel, 1993)   : E. Amiel, M.J. Bellosta-Tourtier
                       "Etude de la persistance dans les SGBDOO"
                       Ingenierie des Systèmes d'Information
                       Volume1 n°1, 1993, pp.9-37.

(Boulanger, 1992)   : D. Boulanger, J. Colloc
                       "Detecting heterogeneity in a multidatabase environment through an
                       OO model"
                       IFIP DS 5 Conference Semantics of Interoperable Database Systems,
                       Lorne, Victoria, Australia.

468

(Boulanger, 1993)   : D. Boulanger, J. Colloc
"Une méthode orientée objet pour l'élaboration de systèmes experts."
Congrès VOLCAN-IA, Clermont Ferrand, Mars 1993.

(Bullat, 1993)   : F. Bullat
"SGBDOO répartis : problématique de l'intégration bases de données,
langage de programmation et distribution."
Congrès INFORSID, Lille, Mai 1993, pp 445-462.

(Colloc, 1989)   : J. Colloc, D. Boulanger
"Un modèle objet pour la représentation de connaissances empiriques."
Informatique Cognitive des Organisations ICO'89, Quebec, Canada,
Juin 1989, pp. 119-140.

(Colloc, 1993)   : J. Colloc, D. Boulanger
"Automatic Knowledge Acquisition for Object Oriented Expert Systems"
Thirteen International Conference : Artificial Intelligence, Expert
Systems,
Natural Language, Avignon, France, May 1993, pp. 99-108.

(Cox, 1986)   : B.J. Cox
"Object-Oriented Programming An Evolutionary Approach"- Mass. :
ADDISON-WESLEY, 986., 274 p. - ISBN 0-201-10393-1.

(Date, 1981)   : C.J. Date
"Referential Integrity"
in proceedings VLDB Cannes, France, 1981. pp 2-12.

(Khoshafian, 1989)   : S. Khoshafian
"A Persistent Complex Object Database Language."
Data & Knowledge Engineering, North Holland, Vol. 3, 1989,
pp. 225-243.

(Northrup, 1992)   : C.J. Northrup
"It's a multithreaded world, part 1"
Byte, May 1992, pp. 289-298.
"It's a multithreaded world, part 2"
Byte, June 1992, pp. 351-356.

(Saltor, 1991)   : F. Saltor, M. Castellanos, M. Garcia Solaco
"On Canonical Models for Federated DBs"
SIGMOD Record Vol. 20, n°4, December 1991.

(Simmel, 1992)   : S. S. Simmel, I. Godard
"Objects of substance"
Byte, December 1992, pp. 167-170

(Stonebracker, 1991)   : M. Stonebracker
"Managing persistent objects in a multi-level store"
in Proceedings of the 1991 ACM SIGMOD, International Conference on
Management of Data, Denver, Colorado, May 29-31, 1991, pp. 2-11.

An Algorithm for IS_A Hierarchy Derivation

Nadira Lammari, Régine Laleau, Mireille Jouve, Xavier Castellani

Laboratoire CEDRIC-IIE (CNAM)
18 allée Jean Rostand 91025 Evry - France
Fax: 33 1 69 36 73 05
Email: {lammari, laleau, jouve, castellani}@iie.cnam.fr

ABSTRACT. *This paper presents an algorithm that derives from a class an IS_A hierarchy. Each class of the obtained hierarchy represents a substructure of the initial class. We determine them by using existence dependencies. This algorithm can be used during the design of an object-oriented schema and can be integrated into an automated design process of normalized inheritance graphs.*

KEY WORDS: *Classes, Class substructures, IS_A hierarchy, Existence dependencies.*

1. Introduction

Many research projects are developed in the field of object-oriented system design. Generally the defined methods provide more or less precise rules that allow the seeking of objects and their gathering into classes. However, the designer who uses these methods is usually confronted with the problem of inheritance specification. In fact, to obtain high quality abstraction, most of the traditional methods (Booch, 1991), (Castellani, 1993), (Rambaugh et al., 1991) encourage, on one hand, the designer to define inheritances between model classes, if, of course, they share some characteristics. On the other hand, they advise him to avoid excessive inheritance refinements. However, no standards are fixed and no rules are stipulated thus avoiding arbitrary decisions. To overcome this lack of standards in the definition of inheritances, a standardized inheritance design method was proposed in (Laleau et al., 1992). Its aim was to advise the designer about decisions concerning the creation of inheritances. Validation rules for the decomposition of a class into subclasses and standardization rules of inheritances based on dynamic properties of the schema were proposed. However, this method acts on substructures previously proposed by the designer and does not therefore guarantee that all the possible inheritances are obtained. It is better to define a process that automatically determines all the substructures that can later be organized in an inheritance graph. In this paper we present a starting point for the realization of this aim.

A substructure is defined by a subset of the class attribute set. However, any subset of the set of the class attributes does not define substructures because no instance can be associated with. Indeed, this restriction is justified by the fact that in the class some optional attributes can exist for which the existence of a value in any class instance can be either exclusive with those of other attributes, and therefore impossible to describe a substructure, or conditioned by those of other attributes, and in this case they are not self-sufficient in defining a substructure. These constraints are captured by introducing three kinds of existence dependencies: *coexistence dependencies*, *conditional existence dependencies* and *exclusive existence dependencies*.

We have chosen a process in three steps that allows a progressive construction of the substructures according to the existence dependencies supplied by the designer. First, by means of the coexistence dependencies, we deduce the set of the closely linked attributes (those that coexist in class instances). By taking into account only those sets, we reduce our selection field. Then, from all the possible unions of the closely linked sets, we eliminate, by means of the exclusive existence dependencies, those that cannot generate substructures (because exclusive existence dependencies exist between some of their attributes). Finally, from all the selected unions we eliminate, by means of conditional existence dependencies, those that cannot be self-sufficient to build substructures.

The main restriction of this approach is that it does not take into account the definition of the class methods: future research is required in this area.

The remainder of the paper is organized as follows. Section 2 presents the state of the art. The example to which we refer all through the paper is mentioned in Section 3. Section 4 presents the different object concepts used in this paper. The three types of existence dependencies are formally defined in Section 5. The process for determining all the substructures of a class according to the existence dependencies is described in Section 6.

2. State of the art

This paper presents a process allowing the restructuration of a class into a set of classes related by IS_A relationships. The automatic deducing of IS_A relationships in relational models has been done by means of inclusion dependencies (Ling et al.,1991), (Pichat et al.,1990). The latter have also been used, by Andonnof (Andonnof, 1992), in object modeling, for deducing structural inheritances. Applied to object context, these dependencies constitute an interesting but limited mean for deducing inheritances because it can not allow all inheritances to be determined. In fact, classes in object modeling can have optional attributes (i.e. their values can be absent because they are inapplicable for some class instances) which express the gathering of entities that share common characteristics but which have their specific ones. Although these classes may not contain inclusion dependencies, they may, however, be restructured. For example let C be a class. Its structure is defined by the mandatory attributes *Name* and *First_Name* and the optional attribute *Maiden_Name*. Abviously this class doesn't contain inclusion dependencies, it can, however, be splited into two classes C1 and C2. The class C2 inherits from the class C1 the attributes *Name* and *First_Name*. It has as specific and mandatory attribute *Maiden_Name*. C2 represents the married women.

However, this situation can be captured by using existence dependencies which are a kind of null value constraints. So far, they have been mainly used as integrity constraints but never for restructuring classes or relations. We have divided them into three types: conditional existence dependencies, exclusive existence dependencies and coexistence dependencies. The conditional existence dependencies (widely known in the database literature as existence constraints) have been originally studied by Maier (Maier, 1980), (Maier, 1983) then by other authors such as Atzeni (Atzeni et al, 1983). They have formally defined them (formal definition and inference rules) and have also studied their interaction with functional dependencies. More precisely, conditional existence dependencies have mainly been used to control the presence of null values in the relation tuples and especially to extend the relational theory to relations with null values. Another use of existence dependencies is realized by Halpin (Hapin, 1991): in order to model conceptual constraints such as subset constraint in a relational implementation he has used existence dependencies as integrity constraints. Castellani (Castellani, 1993), has defined these three types of dependencies between types and has used them to describe the paradigms of the concepts of MCO methodology. However, only informal definitions have been presented. To our knowledge, no work defines formally the two other types of existence dependencies, which is presented in this paper.

3. The example

In this section, we present the example that illustrates the concepts used in the paper. It concerns the class *Person* of the model of a university personnel information system. Its attributes are: *Name, First_Name, Academic_Year, Academic_Cycle, Enrolment_Date, Function, Touch_Typing_Speed, Subjects_Taught*. The university personnel is composed of employees and students. Ph.D. students can teach. Only the attributes *Name* and *First_Name* are mandatory.

4. A brief summary of some object concepts

The process described in this paper can be applied to any object-oriented method. In this section, we present the definitions of the different concepts used. They correspond to those used in the object-oriented system design method MCO (Castellani, 1993).

A class regroups objects defined with the same characteristics: the same attributes and methods. The type of a class is defined by the *tuple* constructor applied to its attributes. All the objects belonging to the same class constitute the set of the instances of this class.

An attribute is defined by its name and its type. Its type describes the set of its possible values. It can be *atomic* or *complex* by using the tuple or the set constructor. If an attribute is a part of the tuple structure defining a class structure then it is a *first level attribute*.
Let I be the set of all the possible instances of a given class C, X be any attribute of C and i [X] the value of X for the instance i of I, then:

- X is optional $\Leftrightarrow \exists$ i $\in$ I, i[X] = null,

- X is mandatory $\Leftrightarrow \forall$ i $\in$ I, i[X] $\neq$ null.

The word "null" or "null value" have been widely used in the database literature. The ANSI/X3/SPARC (ANSI/X3/SPARC, 1975) report has quoted more than a dozen of interpretations. Codd (Codd, 1990) precises that the null value has two different semantics: the missing but applicable value and the missing and inapplicable value. Within the scope of our work, we use the word "null" to express the inapplicability of an attribute X in some instances. In the above mentioned example the attribute *Subjects_Taught* is optional because its value is missing and inapplicable for people of the university who are not teachers.
A complex attribute is optional if it is composed only of optional attributes. In the reverse case it is mandatory.

5. Existence dependencies

Generally, dependencies between values of attributes capture ways of binding data (Delobel et al., 1982). In this section, we present a type of dependencies that we consider worthwhile because it allows the determination of the different substructures in a class: the coexistence, the exclusive existence and the conditional existence dependencies.

Intuitively a coexistence dependency between two attributes X and Y of a class, denoted $X \leftrightarrow Y$, captures the simultaneous presence (or the simultaneous absence) of values for X and Y in the class instances. For example, in the class *Person*, the attributes *Academic_Year* and *Academic_Cycle* coexist (*Academic_Year↔Academic_Cycle*). Everybody who studies is in an academic cycle and in an academic year. In other words, each of the attributes *Academic_Year* and *Academic_Cycle* has necessarily a value in every instance describing a student. In the converse case both of them will be absent.

An exclusive existence dependency between two attributes X and Y, denoted $X \nleftrightarrow Y$, means that for any class instance where X is present, Y is imperatively absent and vice versa. For example, the existence of a value for the attribute *Touch_Typing_Speed* in a class instance excludes, for the same instance, the existence of a value for the attribute *Subjects_Taught* because that instance describes a secretary and a secretary cannot teach. Moreover, the existence of a value for the attribute *Subjects_Taught* in any instance of a class excludes, for the same instance, the existence of a value for the attribute *Touch_Typing_Speed* because this instance concerns a teacher. So, we say that there is an exclusive existence dependency between these two attributes or *Touch_Typing_Speed↮Subjects_Taught*.

A conditional existence dependency between two attributes X and Y, denoted $X \rightarrow Y$, means that for any class instance where X has a value Y must have also one. For example, the existence of a value for the attribute *Touch_Typing_Speed* in any instance of *Person* requires the existence of value for the attribute *Enrolment_Date*. The converse is not always true. As a matter of fact a secretary must be previously enrolled but not every employee is a secretary. Then we say that the existence of a value for the attribute *Touch_Typing_Speed* depends on the existence of a value for the attribute *Enrolment_Date* or *Touch_Typing_Speed→Enrolment_Date*.

Although presented between attributes, these dependencies can be also used to capture relationships between sets of attributes. We take this into account in the following formal definitions.

5.1. Formal definitions

Let C (U, I) be a class. U represents the set of the first level attributes of C. I represents the set of all possible instances of C. Let X and Y be two subsets of U composed respectively of $x_1, x_2, ..., x_k, ..., x_n$ and $y_1, y_2, ..., y_p, ..., y_m$. Then we say that:

- X *coexists with* Y or $X \leftrightarrow Y$, if and only if:

$$\forall\, x_k \in X, \forall\, y_p \in Y, \forall\, i \in I,\ i[x_k] \neq null \Leftrightarrow i[y_p] \neq null$$

- the existence of X *excludes the existence* of Y or $X \nleftrightarrow Y$, if and only if:

$$\forall\, x_k \in X, \forall\, y_p \in Y, \forall\, i \in I,\ i[x_k] = null \lor i[y_p] = null$$

- the existence of X *depends on the existence of* Y or $X \rightarrow Y$, if and only if:

$$\forall\, i \in I,\ i[x_1] \neq null \land ... \land i[x_n] \neq null \Rightarrow i[y_1] \neq null \land ... \land i[y_m] \neq null$$

5.2. Remarks

- Every coexistence dependency between two attribute subsets X and Y can be expressed by means of two conditional existence dependencies: $X \rightarrow Y$ and $Y \rightarrow X$. The converse is true if and only if X and Y are reduced to one attribute.
- We can define existence dependencies between attributes at every level of description. To preserve the structure of the class attributes in the obtained substructures, we only consider the dependencies between the first level attributes.
- The coexistence dependency is an equivalent relation. The equivalence classes represent the groups of attributes that coexist in the class instances.
- Some properties of the three dependency types can be expressed by inference rules as well as the interactions between them (for example: $X \leftrightarrow Y$ and $Z \leftrightarrow Y \Rightarrow Z \leftrightarrow X$). These properties are described in (Lammari et al., 1994). They allow the deduction of the closures and minimal covers of the three sets of dependencies. The definitions of the closure and the minimal cover of a functional dependency set (Delobel et al., 1982) can also be applied to the closure and minimal cover of any of the three dependency types.
- Starting from a set $F_{coexist}$ of coexistence dependencies (respectively from a set F_{cond_exist} of conditional existence dependencies or from a set F_{exclu_ex} of exclusive existence dependencies) ; by means of inference rules of this dependency type and inference rules that represent the interaction of this dependency type with the two other ones, we can obtain a new set $F^+_{coexist}$ of coexistence dependencies (respectively $F^+_{cond\_exist}$ or $F^+_{exclu\_ex}$) which represents the logical consequences of $F_{coexist}$ (respectively of F_{cond_exist} or of F_{exclu_ex}). $F^+_{coexist}$, $F^+_{cond\_exist}$ and $F^+_{exclu\_ex}$ represent respectively the closure of $F_{coexist}$, F_{cond_exist} and F_{exclu_ex}.
- By selecting among $F^+_{coexist}$ (respectively among $F^+_{cond\_exist}$ or among $F^+_{exclu\_ex}$) only the elementary and irredondant dependencies, we obtain the minimal cover of this set denoted $IRR(F^+_{coexist})$ (respectively $IRR(F^+_{cond\_exist})$ and $IRR(F^+_{exclu\_ex})$). For example, for the class *Person* we have:

$IRR(F^+_{coexist})$ = {*First_Name*↔*Name*; *Academic_Year*↔*Academic_Cycle*;
  Enrolment_Date↔*Function*}.

$IRR(F^+_{exclu\_ex})$ = {*Touch_Typing_Speed*↮*Subjects_Taught*;
  Touch_Typing_Speed↮*Academic_Cycle*}.

$IRR(F^+_{cond\_exist})$ = {*Subjects_Taught*→*Enrolment_Date*;
  Touch_Typing_Speed→*Enrolment_Date*;
  Academic_Cycle→*Name*; *Enrolment_Date*→*Name*;
  Academic_Cycle, *Enrolment_Date*→*Subjects_Taught*}.

- A set of elementary coexistence dependencies (or elementary exclusive existence dependencies) can be modelized by an undirected graph having as vertices the first level attributes of the class. A coexistence dependency (or an exclusive existence dependency) between two first level attributes is represented by an edge.

6. Mechanism for determining the class substructures

The fact that some attributes of a class are optional, inapplicable in some instances, indicates that there are, perhaps, concealed structures. It is worth exhibiting them to eventually create inheritances. Validation rules and standardization rules of a decomposition of a class into subclasses have been proposed in (Laleau et al., 1992). However, the described standardization mechanism takes into account only the substructures proposed by the designer. More significant is the definition of an automatic process allowing all the substructures concealed in a class to be discovered. They can, later, form subclasses, if, of course, they meet the decomposition conditions.

In this section, we present a formal definition of a class substructure. It is based on the existence dependencies binding the first level attributes of the class. Then, we describe the automatic process that allows all the substructures of a class to be found.

6.1. Definition of a substructure according to the existence dependencies

A substructure of a class is defined by the set of attributes describing it. It constitutes a subset of the class attributes. For instance, among substructures included in the class *Person*, we can mention: *Secretary, Student, Teacher, Employee, etc.* For example the attributes *Name, First_Name, Enrolment_Date, Function* and *Touch_Typing_Speed* describe the substructure *Secretary*. Among all the possible associations of the class attributes (the power set of the class attributes), only some of them describe substructures. The subsets of attributes qualified as substructures are those for which we can associate at least an instance of the class. For example the subset composed of the attributes *Name, First_Name* and *Enrolment_Date* is not a substructure included in *Person* because of the coexistence dependency *Enrolment_Date↔Function*. Indeed, an instance where the attribute *Enrolment_Date* has a value whereas the attribute *Function* has not cannot exist and vice versa.

So, if we denote $\wp(U)$ the power set of U (U represents the set of the first level attributes of a class C) and if we have a set of coexistence, conditional existence and exclusive existence dependencies then, the selection among $\wp(U)$ of the substructures is based on the three following rules:

i) if the existence of the attribute X depends on the existence of the attribute Y and if X appears among the elements of a part of U without Y, then this part cannot describe a substructure.

ii) if two attributes are linked by an exclusive existence dependency then every part of U where the two attributes appear, cannot describe a substructure.

iii) if two attributes are linked by a coexistence dependency then every part of U where only one of the two attributes appears, is unable to describe a substructure.

These three rules justify the following definition:

Definition

Let:

- C be a class.

- U be the set of the first level attributes of U: $U = \{x_1, x_2, \ldots, x_i, \ldots\}$.

- F_{cond_exist}, $F_{coexist}$ and F_{exclu_ex} be respectively the set of conditional existence, coexistence and exclusive existence dependencies linking the attributes of U.

- $F^+_{cond\_exist}$, $F^+_{coexist}$ and $F^+_{exclu\_ex}$ be respectively the closure of F_{cond_exist}, $F_{coexist}$ and F_{exclu_ex}.

- $T \in \wp(U)$.

We say that T is a substructure of C if and only if the following conditions are verified:

$$- \forall \, Y \subset T, \, Y \rightarrow X \in F^+_{cond\_exist} \Rightarrow X \subset T \tag{1}$$

$$- \forall \, x_i \in T, \, \forall \, x_j \in T, \, x_i \leftrightarrow x_j \notin F^+_{exclu\_ex} \tag{2}$$

$$- \forall \, x_i \in T, \, x_i \leftrightarrow X \in F^+_{coexist} \Rightarrow X \subset T \tag{3}$$

The conditions **1**, **2** and **3** of this definition respectively match the above rules i), ii) and iii). We can, now, reduce the number of conditions by reinforcing the hypotheses. By considering the coexistence dependencies of IRR($F^+_{coexist}$) we can decompose U into groups of coexisting attributes (those groups are denoted X_k). Then, the selection of substructures among the elements of the power set of U according to Conditions 1, 2 and 3 is equivalent to the selection of substructures among the elements of the power set of the coexisting groups. Thus Condition 3 being satisfied in advance, the selection is made exclusively according to Conditions 1 and 2. So, the condition **1**) is replaced by Hypothesis i) of the corollary below mentioned. Moreover, if we eliminate from these latter elements (elements of $\wp(\{X_1, \dots , X_k, \dots\})$) those that cannot coexist because there is at least an exclusive existence dependency linking two groups of coexisting attributes, we can, once more, reduce the number of conditions that must satisfy a substructure. So, Condition **2**) of the definition is replaced by Hypothesis ii) of the following corollary:

Corollary

Let:

- C be a class.

- U be the set of the first level attributes of U: $U = \{x_1, x_2, \dots , x_i, \dots\}$.

- F_{cond_exist}, $F_{coexist}$ and F_{exclu_ex} be respectively the set of conditional existence, coexistence and exclusive existence dependencies linking the attributes of U.

- $F^+_{cond\_exist}$, $F^+_{coexist}$ and $F^+_{exclu\_ex}$ be respectively the closure of F_{cond_exist}, $F_{coexist}$ and F_{exclu_ex}.

- IRR($F^+_{coexist}$) be the minimal cover of $F^+_{coexist}$

-$X_k = \overline{X}_k = \{x_i \in U, x_i \leftrightarrow x_k \in IRR(F^+_{coexist})\}$ i)

- $\{T_1, T_2, \dots , T_m, \dots \} \subset \wp(\{X_1, X_2, \dots , X_k, \dots\})$ such that:

      $\forall \, X_p \in T_m, \, \forall \, X_q \in T_m, \, X_p \leftrightarrow X_q \notin IRR(F^+_{exclu\_ex})$ ii)

We say that T_m is a substructure of C if and only if: $\forall \, Y \subset T_m, \, Y \rightarrow X \in F^+_{cond\_exist} \Rightarrow X \subset T_m$

Remark: This definition is still valid either for classes without optional attributes or for classes where optional attributes are not linked between them by any of the three dependency types.

6.2. The process

There are many ways of deducing all the substructures included in a class. The most intuitive consists in selecting among the elements of $\wp(U)$ those that verify the three conditions mentioned in the definition. This approach seems heavy and costly, (the number of selected elements is high) especially when the number of dependencies and the number of attributes is high. This led us to choose a progressive approach which is automatisable and can be integrated into a design tool. It relies on the above corollary. We propose a decomposition of the process into four phases (see Figure 1).

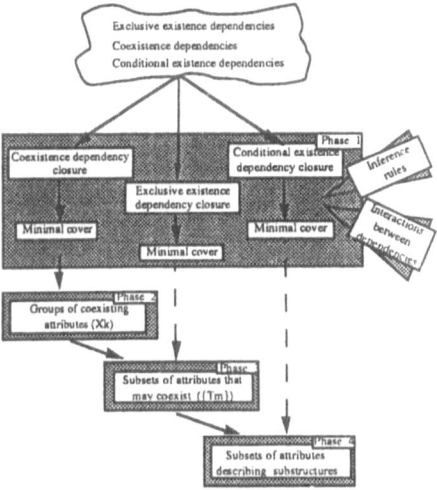

Fig 1 - Process for determining substructures of a class

The first phase is a preliminary phase. It computes the closure and the minimal cover of each set of coexistence, conditional existence and exclusive existence dependencies supplied by the designer.

The second phase corresponds to the decomposition of U into groups of coexisting attributes. These groups correspond to the X_k of the Corollary . This decomposition is equivalent to the definition of the equivalence classes of the coexistence relation or also to the determination of the strong components of the graph $G_{coexist}$ (U, Edges) with:

$$Edges = \{(X,Y) \in U^2, X \leftrightarrow Y \in IRR(F^+_{coexist})\}.$$

For example, the graph $G_{coexist}$ corresponding to the minimal cover of the coexistence dependencies linking the attributes of the class *Person* is represented in Figure 2. The set X of the strong components of $G_{coexist}$ is: {{*Name, First_Name*}; {*Academic_Cycle, Academic_Year*}; {*Enrolment_Date, Function*}; {*Subjects_Taught*}; {*Touch_Typing_Speed*}}.

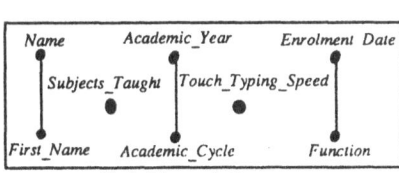

Fig 2 - The graph $G_{coexist}$

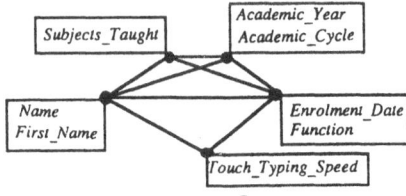

Fig 3 - The graph G_{exclu_ex}

The third phase is the construction of the possibly coexisting subsets T_m. We take into account the exclusive existence dependencies. The obtained subsets T_m, correspond to the different cliques[1] of the graph G_{exclu_ex} (X, Edges) where:

$$Edges = \{ (X_i, X_j) \in X^2, \forall x \in X_i, \forall y \in X_j, x \leftrightarrow y \notin IRR(F^+_{exclu\_ex}) \}$$

For our example, we must determine all the cliques of the graph represented in Figure 3. The number of cliques in this graph is important (≥ 15), we only mention two of them:
- {{*Name, First_Name*}; {*Touch_Typing_Speed*}; {*Enrolment_Date, Function*}},
- {{*Subjects_Taught*}; {*Enrolment_Date, Function*}}.

The last phase is the selection, among the T_m, of the subsets representing the substructures of C. By means of the conditional existence dependencies, among all the possible cliques we can select those that correspond to substructures. Every clique matching the condition mentioned in the previous Corollary determines a substructure. The distributed union of the components of the clique composes the attribute set of this substructure. Among the cliques deduced from the precedent graph only 6 are substructures. Figure 4 describes them.

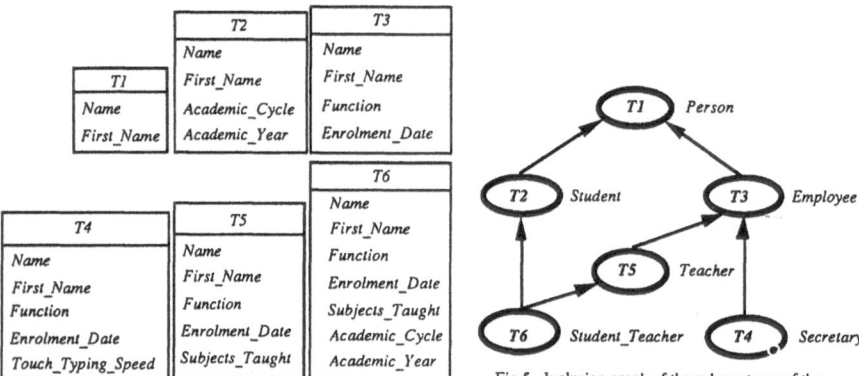

Fig 4 - Substructures of the class "Person"

Fig 5 - Inclusion graph of the subsructures of the class "Person"

Remark: The substructures obtained can then be organized in an inclusion graph. This graph is a starting point for the determination of a standardized inheritance graph (Laleau et al., 1992). For example, the inclusion graph corresponding to the substructures T1, T2,..., T6 is represented in Figure 5.

6.3. Algorithm

Here is the algorithm that implements the process described in the previous paragraph:

Inputs

- A class C and U the set of its first level attributes

- F_{cond_exist}, $F_{coexiste}$ and F_{exclu_ex} respectively the set of conditional existence, coexistence and exclusive existence dependencies linking the attributes of U.

---

[1] A clique represents the set of the vertices of a complete subgraph.

Output

- The set of the substructures included in class C

Body

Determine $F^+_{cond\_exist}$, $F^+_{coexist}$ and $F^+_{exclu\_ex}$; Determine $IRR(F^+_{coexist})$ and $IRR(F^+_{exclu\_ex})$;

Components = the strong components of $G_{coexiste}(U, Edges)$ with:

$\quad$ Edges = $\{(X, Y) \in U^2, X \leftrightarrow Y \in IRR(F^+_{coexist})\}$;

Cliques = the set of the possible cliques of G_{exclu_ex} (Components, Edges) with:

$\quad$ Edges = $\{ (X_i, X_j) \in Components^2, \forall\, x \in X_i, \forall\, y \in X_j, x \not\leftrightarrow y \in IRR(F^+_{exclu\_ex}) \}$;

Substructures = $\varnothing$;

For each clique $C_i \in$ Cliques *Do*

$\quad$ Is_Entity_Structure = True; T = the union of the components of C_i;

$\quad$ *For each* dependency d: $X \rightarrow Y$ *such that* $d \in IRR(F^+_{cond\_exist})$ *Do*

$\quad\quad$ *If* $X \subset T$ *then* Is_Entity_Structure = $Y \in T$ *Endif*;

$\quad$ *Endfor*;

$\quad$ *If* Is_Entity_Structure *Then* Substructures = Substructures $\cup$ T *Endif*;

Endfor.
---

7. Conclusion

In order to advise the designer during the specification of a conceptual schema our project aims at defining a mechanism to normalize inheritance graphs by taking into account both the dynamic and the static aspects of an object schema. In this paper, only the first step of the mechanism is described: the determination of substructures of a class that can, later, form subclasses. This process is based on the definition of dependencies between attributes that capture the simultaneous, exclusive, or conditional presence of attribute values in the same class instances.

In the same way as inclusion dependencies, the existence dependencies complete an already defined structuration of a class or a relation obtained by using functional and multivalued dependencies. More precisely, applying our process assumes that the relations or the classes have been already normalized. That is, in the relational context, the relations must be at least in 3NF and in the object context, any normalization mechanism such as this of OFM (Andonnof, 1992) has been used.

Comparatively to the obtained result (a substructures inclusion graph), the formal aspects developed in this paper can seem extensive. However, similar works have been realized in the relational context for normalization (Delobel et al., 1982), (Vardi, 1985). Moreover, if we want to prove the consistency of the process and then be able to integrate it into a CASE, this formal elaboration is worthwhile and necessary.

Furthermore, this process allows the determination of all substructures of a class and contrary to other methods that exhibit inheritances (OFM), it doesn't require a database expertise from the designer. We think that it is less difficult to extract, the coexistence, conditional existence and exclusive existence dependencies from the real world to model than to find the inclusion dependencies, especially when the studied field is large and complex.

The implementation of the described algorithm is, at the present time, in progress on a Sun station. It will be integrated into the MCO case. The described process concerns a schema optimisation. It will be used during the last step of the design of an application, just before the implementation step. However, we can forecast that it will give interesting results when applied to an object-oriented data base implementation.

In the first stage of this work we are only concerned by the structure of a class. The next step will take into account the class methods and a set of classes.

References:

(Andonnof, 1992):   E. Andonnof. *OFM: une méthode formelle pour la conception de base de données orientées objet*. Ph. D. thesis. University Toulouse III, France, september 1992.

(ANSI/X3/SPARC):   ANSI/X3/SPARC. *Study group on database management systems: interim report*. February 1975.

(Atzeni et al., 1983):   P. Atzeni and M. Morfuni. *Functional dependencies and existence constraints in databases relations with null values*. Information System Analysis Institute. Technical report n°R77, december 1983.

(Booch, 1991):   G. Booch. *Object oriented design with applications*. The Benjamin / Cummings Company, Inc., Redwood City, California, 1991.

(Castellani, 1993):   X. Castellani. *Méthodologie générale d'analyse et de conception des systèmes d'objets. Tome 1: L'ingénierie des besoins*. Masson, France, 1993.

(Codd, 1990):   E. F. Codd. *The relational model for database management. Version 2*. Addison-Wesley Publishing Company, Inc., 1990.

(Delobel et al., 1982):   C. Delobel and M. Adiba. *Bases de données et systèmes relationnels*. Dunod, France, 1982.

(Halpin, 1991):   T. Halpin. *A fact-oriented approach to schema transformation*. In the Proceedings of MFDBS'91, Springer-Verlag lecture notes in Computer Science. n°495, Rostock, 1991.

(Laleau et al.,1992):   R. Laleau, X. Castellani and M. Jouve. *Normalized design of the specialization inheritance*. Proceedings Indo-French Workshop on object-oriented systems. Goa, India, November 1992.

(Lammari et al., 1994):   N. Lammari, M. Jouve , R. Laleau and X. Castellani. *Dépendances d'existence: définitions formelles et utilisation pour déterminer des liens d'heritages entre classes*. CEDRIC-CNAM, Paris.Research report, may 1994, to be published.

(Ling et al., 1991):   T. W. Ling and C. H. Goh. *Logical database design with inclusion dependencies*. Department of information systems of the university of Singapore. Technical report n°TREA6, june 1991.

(Maier, 1983):   D. Maier. *Discarding the Universal Instance Assumption: Preliminary Results*. XP1 Workshop on relational database theory. Suny at Stony Brook, NY, June-July 1980.

(Maier, 1983):   D. Maier. *The theory of relational databases*. Computer Science Press, Inc., America, 1983.

(Pichat, 1990):   E. Pichat and R. Bodin. *Ingénierie des données*. Masson, Paris, 1990.

(Rambaugh et al., 1991):   J. Rambaugh, M. Blaha, W. Premerlani, F. Eddy and W. Lorensen. *Object-oriented modeling and design*. Prentice-Hall International Editions, 1991.

(Vardi, 1985):   M. Y. Vardi. *Fundamentals of dependency theory*. Technical report n°RJ4858. Computer Science, IBM Research Division, 1985.

Embedding Strategic Information into an Object-Oriented Analysis and Design Method

Christine Bonnet

LISI, INSA de Lyon
20, av. Albert Einstein
69621 Villeurbanne-France
E-mail: chris@lisiecrin.insa-lyon.fr   Fax: (33) 72 43 87 13

Abstract:
Most software systems are developed to provide information for decision making. Yet the decision maker is often neglected in current system analysis and design practice. As a result, many decisions that could be made by the help of computers are instead made from manual methods and/or from irrelevant information. This paper proposes an extension to the Object-Oriented Analysis (OOA)-Object-Oriented Design (OOD) method [Coad & al., 91] for building software systems to include piloting information. The approach presented is based on the use of strategic blackboards.

Key words: *object-oriented analysis and design method, blackboard, decision making, strategic information.*

I. Introduction

Systems are built to provide, in one way or another, input to a decision maker. However decision makers often cannot extract the information they need from the system. Enterprises (a) gather information but do not use it, (b) ask for more information but ignore it, (c) make decisions first and look at the information that could have been relevant afterwards, and (d) gather and process a great amount of information with little or no link with the decisions to make. The generality of such a phenomenon suggests the following idea: blaming our concept of the role taken by the information in enterprises rather than the decision makers [March, 91]. Therefore design teams have to attach a greater importance to the information required for decision making.

This paper proposes an extension to an existing object-oriented analysis and design method: the Object-Oriented Analysis (OOA)-Object-Oriented Design (OOD) method [Coad & al., 91] for building software systems to include this kind of information called strategic information. Strategic information can be defined [Bonnet, 91] as indicators about: activity (i.e.: the amount of production), cost (i.e.: manpower and equipment cost), efficiency (i.e.: quality, percentage of scrap), external data (i.e.: exchange rate), performance of the enterprise compared with the competitors, quantitative evaluation of the profits of future investments, etc. In short it concerns data or information, wheather from the enterprise or not, to help man in making a decision. The approach described herein integrates the processes of acquiring and modelling this strategic information into the stages of analysis and design of Information Systems (IS). The integration is done using strategic blackboards [Savall & al., 89].

The rest of this paper is organized as follows. Section 2 presents strategic blackboards. Section 3 discusses the choice of the object-oriented analysis and design method. Section 4 suggests an extension to the method for taking strategic information into account. Section 5 concludes the paper.

2. Strategic blackboards

Decision makers may have access to strategic information through various tools (fourth-generation languages, blackboard, spreadsheet tools, etc.). We have chosen strategic blackboards [Savall & al., 89] as they provide enough detailed information, in a straightforward and pedagogical frame and thereby enable a concrete piloting by decision makers. They are used in our approach to extract the strategic information needs (see section 4).

A strategic blackboard is a system made of qualitative, quantitative and financial indicators (strategic information). Its role is twofold: it helps to explain phenomena (permanent auto-diagnosis) and to take corrective actions (co-piloting). Different blackboards are designed according to the user's status within the enterprise. They are organized in a hierarchical way (Figure 1). Each blackboard contains local and global indicators. The latters are propagated along the hierarchy. The arrows of figure 1 symbolize this information sharing.

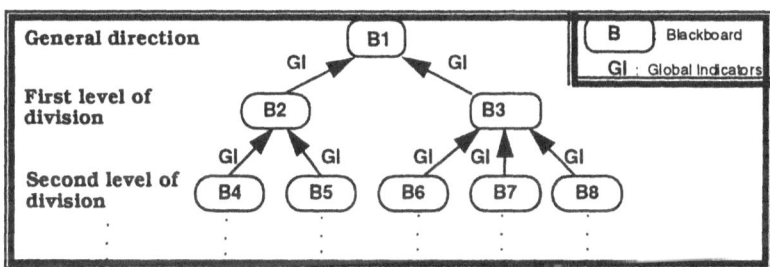

Figure 1: Articulation of blackboards.

3. Choice of an analysis and design method

Our analysis and design method, meant to take strategic information into account, is an object-oriented method. The object paradigm is well adapted for this integration. It allows the reuse of information at various levels of accuracy and at various times. Furthermore, the data and the processing models of these data are strongly linked in the framework of strategic management problems. The object model offers a number of significant benefits such as the expressive power, the reusability, the improvement of reliability and maintenance [Sutcliffe, 91]. Among the numerous analysis and design methods for the development of object-oriented systems [Mrdalj, 90], we have chosen the OOA analysis method and the OOD design method of Coad and Yourdon. This choice is based on the potentials of this method for representations and processes. It contains the components necessary for the problem domain analysis process, the solution domain design process, the object-oriented analysis and design representations, and for the treatment of complexity.

4. Taking strategic information into account

We propose to integrate stages into the OOA-OOD method to acquire and model the data of the enterprise's strategic information system. These data are extracted from the strategic blackboards.

The first step of the OOA-OOD methodology is concerned with extracting the information coming from the real-world to identify the classes and the objects necessary for the initialization of the information system. A class represents an abstraction. We may define it as a group marked by common attributes and common services (more commonly named methods), e.g., an order class, a customer class, etc. An object is an instance of a class.

This step is complemented by the identification of classes and objects meaningful for decision making (strategic classes and objects). The identification of strategic information should be done along with identification of management information. Actually some data are shared by the piloting and the management processes, others are linked. For instance, the "quantity of a given product in stock" could be an attribute of both a strategic and an operational class. The "number of orders per day" strategic attribute is linked to the "order" operational class. Furthermore the communication between the piloting and the management processes is essential (see below in this section). The identification of strategic classes and objects is made at two levels:
- Global view of the strategic information system: for each specific level of decision making, a class is created (e.g., general direction, consultants, executives, etc.).
- Detailed view: the retained classes group information devoted to the piloting. For instance, in a bank agency, one can distinguish two classes that correspond to:
  - Internal strategic information: delay for obtaining a loan, number of bank accounts opened each month, number of shares and titles invested, etc.
  - External strategic information: exchange rate, new bank products, markets of investment (call for bids), etc.

Once the entities of the real and strategic environment of the enterprise have been identified, they must be organized according to the generalization/specialization structure. Such a structure between two classes C1 and C2 is used to make explicit the link between these two classes (if C1 generalizes C2, C2 specializes C1). C2 inherits the structure and the behavior defined by C1. Among other things, this structure allows the optimizing of the code of methods defined in classes and the diminution of the errors' sources during the implementation, due to the inheritance mechanism. The structures corresponding to the managerial classes are established (traditional object analysis). The structures of the strategic classes are organized according to the strategic indicators of the enterprise. In the articulation of the enterprise's blackboards (see figure 1), the link between the various levels of the hierarchy is expressed by the global indicators. For instance, blackboard class B1 corresponding to the general direction is a sub-class of classes B2 and B3 associated with the first level of division. Therefore the global indicators are inherited from classes B2 and B3. In case of multiple inheritance the mechanisms of conflict resolution are used. However, B2 and B3's local indicators must not be inherited by B1. A partial inheritance mechanism is then needed.

The classes extracted from the first step are described by a set of attributes. The strategic classes' attributes represent the abstractions of the local and global indicators. They are classified in two categories:
*Attributes describing qualitative information (e.g., the personalization of the contacts between a bank agency and the customers). These attributes are not deductible from the

traditional IS. The range of values that this particular kind of attributes could take have to be set by designers.

*Attributes describing quantitative information (e.g., the number of customer's complaints) or financial information (e.g., the cost of employees' training). Unlike the first category, the values taken by these attributes may be the result of processing on the traditional IS or directly extracted from the IS.

The inter-object communications in the OOA-OOD method are carried out through "services". They may be simple (e.g., connect/disconnect an object from another, create a new object, etc.) or complex (e.g., process a result from attributes' values, etc.). These communications are established after identifying the messages' connections (services needed by a given object that belong to other objects, etc.). For instance, the querying of the "number of bank accounts opened" indicator triggers a message that is passed to the class abstracting the internal strategic information. This last class propagates the request (if necessary completed) to the customer's class of the traditional IS. Communications between strategic and operational classes are established whenever data are shared or linked by these two kinds of classes.

The bridge between the blackboards and the traditional IS thus created plays several roles:
• Visualization of the results about the indicators,
• Features allowing to modify the communications' modes in output,
• Easy evolution of blackboards,
• Optimization of exchanges (the temporary results are saved).

5. Conclusion

Throughout this paper we have shown the significance of taking the enterprise's strategic information into account and integrating it into the processes of analysis and design of the enterprise's IS.

We have extended an object-oriented analysis and design method to include strategic information. The mechanisms provided by the object paradigm (inheritance, generalization / specialization, message passing) make the identification, the modelling and the integration of strategic information into a traditional IS easier.

References:

[Bonnet, 91]: C. Bonnet, "Pilotage d'un système de gestion," rapport interne n°1091,LISI, INSA de Lyon, 1991.
[Coad & al. 91]: Coad P., Yourdon E., "Object Oriented Analysis," 2nd Edition, Yourdon Press computing Series, 1991.
[March, 91]: March J.G., "How decisions happen in organizations," Human-Computer Interaction, 1991, Volume 6, pp. 95-117.
[Mrdalj, 90]: Mrdalj S.,"Bibliography of object oriented system development," ACM Sigsoft Softw. Eng. Not., 15,5,1990, pp. 60-63.
[Savall & al., 89]: Savall H., Zardet V., "Maîtriser les coûts et les performances cachés," Economica Paris, 1989.
[Sutcliffe, 91]: Sutcliffe A.G., "Object oriented system analysis: the abstract question," proceedings of the IFIP Conference, Elsevier Science Publishers B.V., 1991, pp.23-37.

OBJECT-ORIENTED

DATABASES

AND

APPLICATIONS

Design of an Academic Personal Information Manager Using An Object Oriented Database Approach

Hu Li*, Ritchie C**, & Cole R J.***

* Departments of Computer Studies and Mathematics,
**Department of Computer Studies
***Software Measurement Laboratory,Department of Mathematics,
all at Glasgow Caledonian University, Glasgow G4 OBA, UK

ABSTRACT. *This paper presents a design of an Academic Personal Information Management Tool, whose purpose is to improve information management in an academic environment. The APIM model integrates hierarchical file system, hypertext system, and object-oriented database techniques. OODB techniques are used as the basis for structured data modelling and physical data storage of APIM.*

KEY WORDS: *Object Oriented Database, Peraonal Information Management, Data Modelling*

1. Introduction

Information production and storage management are important aspects of work in an academic environment. Tasks include:
- producing teaching and research materials with software tools,
- grouping a set of relevant materials for teaching and research tasks, and
- storing information using a variety of specific structuring facilities.

This paper describes the design of an information management tool called the **Academic Personal Information Manager** or **APIM** which is intended to assist academic staff in managing their personal information space.

There are many high-level user interfaces for information production and management, a current popular example being the Microsoft Windows system. Two common characteristics of these interfaces are that they offer a set of software tools to create application data and a set of functional facilities. In particular, they would provide a functional facility for managing a data store, which implements a data organisation model. Our proposed system, APIM, acting as an information production and management environment, provides support in the following areas:
- integrating a set of popular software tools,
- static data modelling for higher-level application aggregation concepts;
- rich semantic organisation of information store .

APIM can be visualised as a layer that carries information about data and data relationships and is built on a normal file system. Figure 1 shows the context of APIM :

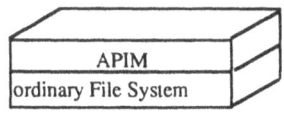

Figure 1. APIM context

The rest of this paper is organised as follows. In section 2, the problems being addressed by APIM are described; in section 3, an informal description of the structural OO model and the semantic data organisation facilities in APIM is provided; section 4 presents a short summary and conclusion.

2. Data management problem analysis

2.1. Tasks and features of data use in an academic environment

The main tasks in an academic environment can be classified as *teaching* and *research*, or more abstractly, *knowledge delivery* and *knowledge accumulation*. Each of these tasks is composed of a series of more basic activities. Of principal interest to us are the activities that are concerned with producing and structuring information in an academic environment. These activities include:
- technical reading and taking notes,
- maintaining a bibliography of research material,
- research paper preparation,
- routinely producing course materials such as teaching notes, assignment specifications and examination papers.

The most outstanding aspect of these activities is personalised information management with various complex data structures. Following Malone's study [Malone 1983], we can identify the following key features:
- Personalised content of information.
  Since an academic organisation is, primarily, a human expert organisation, each person's information interest is quite distinct. Information content is personalised and possibly confidential, in contrast to a conventional commercial office environment where information generally pertains to company activities.
- Personalised organisation of information space
  Most teaching activities can be characterised as *knowledge delivery*. This implies that information sharing among staff normally occurs at a quite high level, and some activities in gathering, structuring and filtering source data will be done by individuals.
- Complex structure of information
  Knowledge is represented by information structures, most of which, in an academic environment, are not simple. It is important, therefore, that the structure of complex information remains understandable. In the absence of suitable tools, users tend to organise informationn in an ad hoc fashion, mentally managing the higher levels of information organisation. However, this is always successful.
- Fixed and variable data structure
  Complex information objects could have a (relatively) fixed or variable data structure.

Other aspects in these activities are :
- A set of software tools
- Information capturing
- production planning

2.2. Requirements for personal information management in an academic environment

Based on the discussion above, we can summarise the requirements for an APIM:
- accessible integration with various software tools,
  In principle, external software tools, for example tools in Windows, can be accessed as data types to produce data instances.
- richer semantic facilities to manage dynamic relationships between information units.
  A key requirement is facilities for modelling a data organisation dynamically, implemented by a set of built-in domain-specific semantic facilities. These facilities includes the structures *direct assertion links, sets, lists, webs* and *versions* .
  A direct assertion link can be used to facilitate navigational queries between two data objects. A label attached to a link explains the relationship between two participant data objects; for example, an examination paper could be linked to a report with a label "results". An ordinary set can be defined on homogeneous or heterogeneous objects; queries against objects' attributes or labels of assertion links should be allowed. Set-theoretic operations are required on sets to help to produce query results. For file management, some special sets are needed, namely, a *list*, which presents a fixed sequence and hierarchy semantics of a composed file, a semantic *web*, which functions both as a context-based view over objects and complex links between objects, and a *version*, which

provides objects' parent-child relationships (indicating the difference between versions) and a default version.

- support for the process of making an information production plan,
- facilities for user-defined application data types and application data model,
  The type constructor should allow a natural structural object oriented diagram. Primitive data types for building these include: collection types used also in dynamic data organisation, atomic types such as text string and date, as well as software tool types for fully-formatted information production. There is a limited data exchange mechanism between these component data types.
  An application data model is described in a structural object oriented schema, which, based on the types, defines application concepts and extension of the concepts. Over a schema, some typical database facilities are available.
- mechanisms to help users manage large information space,
  These mechanisms include automatically classifying information, activating information at a given time and capturing incidental information, as well as supporting queries on universal attributes of information

2.3. User interface techniques in information management relevant to the APIM

User interface techniques of data management relevant to the APIM are: file system, conventional database, and hypertext. These techniques are quite different in principle and together provide a wide range of data management facilities. These characteristics are summarised below.

2.3.1. File system

A file system is the most commonly-used data management interface, enhanced frequently by a graphical front-end, such as File Manager in Microsoft Windows. It is easy to use in managing files in a hierarchy and many software tools are developed based on it.

In terms of its ability to express semantic associations, a conventional file system is somewhat limited; having a single simple tree/web structure the system only supports a one-directional *containing* relationship between directories and sub-directories or files. The directory structure is often used to classify files, usually supplemented at some level by the use of filenames that contain additional classification information. However, a filename long enough to contain useful information is rather unwieldy for other purposes and no facilities generally exist in the file system to utilise the information embedded in the filename.

2.3.2. Database techniques

Although user interfaces of conventional relational databases are simple to use, it does not readily enable non-professional users to represent and query against complicated data structures. High-level semantic data models, such as EER and SDM, have better expressive ability to model data structures and relationships between data than the record-based relational model. User interfaces based on semantic data models are, for example, ISIS [Goldman 1985] and those reviewed in [Kappel 1992]. Limitations in general-purpose database user interfaces as a general data modelling facility for non-professional users still exist. Generally they supply users with data types as building blocks that are too primitive relative to the structural requirements and operational requirements of application domains. Using query facilities needs some expertise in database techniques, especially for complicated queries. Another inflexibility of this technique is generally in the dynamic modelling of data organisation.

2.3.3. Hypertext

The hypertext data model represents various involuted relationships between general multimedia objects and is very powerful in dynamically constructing associations between objects. According to [Conklin 1987], typical applications are *macro literary, problem exploration, structured browsing* and *general hypertext technique.* The problems with the technique are "disorientation" and "cognitive overhead" [Conklin 1987]. These problems are amplified in a shared application and changeable environment, because of the existence of different mental models between developers and users. Some solutions to "disorientation" include "history stack" [Nielsen 1990], "fisheye view" [FairChild 1988] and hierarchical search support [Girill 1992]. Conklin's suggested solution is the use of database query and view facilities. General hypertext systems do not provide database facilities that support the definition of new application data types, attribute-based queries or set-based operations such as intersection, union and difference operations.

In summary, file systems, general database and hypertext interfaces have their own strength and weakness. Our proposed APIM system combines the three into a more effective integrated environment.

3. The Academic Personal Information Manager

3.1. Conceptual overview of APIM

The general features of APIM are illustrated in Figure 2. APIM provides a set of inter-object relationships having special structure and allowable operations. Some hypertext systems have similar facilities, such as DNP [Sommerville 1990], which is a design-aid tool. APIM has also other facilities to enhance its usability.

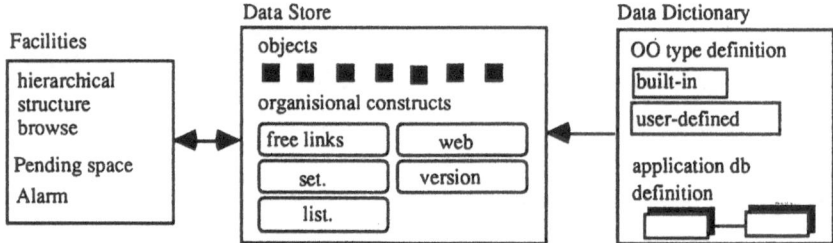

Figure 2. Conceptual diagram of APIM

3.2. Design & Development Tool

The data-intensive nature of APIM requires that the design be based on an underlying object-oriented database. The OODB data model has been studied in both research and application areas for several years. Some pioneering research and development [Oxborrow 1991, Brown 1991] suggests that OODB might be more effective than conventional databases in constructing a complex information environment. Though the technique is still far from maturity and has many inadequacies [Ling, 1993], it is seen as better suited to our problem domain. Several commercial OODBs have appeared in the market such as ONTOS, Versant and O^2. For our purposes, we have chosen **ObjectStore** from Object Design, since it appears to have the features necessary for our APIM project, including object persistence orthogonal to type and semantic facilities such as *collection* and *version*. The data model of ObjectStore is based on the OO programming language C++. It is representative of the first-wave of OODB products and has been widely discussed in the literature and used in application projects.

3.3. Data types

In APIM, the type system consists of built-in types and application types built with an OO type constructor. The whole type hierarchy in APIM is shown in Figure 3.

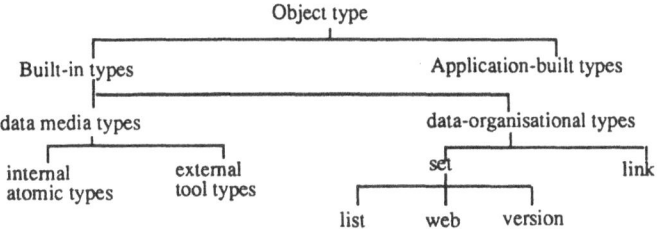

Figure 3. APIM types

In this type system, we define the models of each type as follows:

- Object type:
  All data types derive from this type. A data object of this type is a pair *(oid, value)*. The *oid* is
  an **object identifier**, consisting of two components, an internal *oid* and an external *comment*.
  The internal *oid* is unique and is used as an internal reference between objects; the external
  comment can be optionally defined by users to explain itself. Where users frequently use a
  browsing tool in queries, such textual external *comments* are necessary. However, unlike
  overloaded filenames in a file system, external *comments* are optional and are mainly about the
  content of objects in APIM. The *value* of an object is an instance of a domain, which is formed
  by a type definition. Hence a *value* of an object has at least a type or several compatible types.
  The Object type has a set of attributes for forming universal queries.
- application-built types:
  Any application type is a derived type of the *object* type and is built using a type constructor.
- built-in type:
  These types realise certain facilities for semantic management of information. They are used by
  means of an operational interface. Except for the *link* type, they can also be used as attributes'
  types in defining application-built types.
- data-organisation type:
  We define the model of each data-organisation type as follows :
  set
  Each member of the set consists of an index having a string label and a pointer to a data object.
  Set-theory relationships between sets are supported based on *oids* of included objects. Given
  sets : Δ, A, B,..., users can use *operators* », -, «, and *punctuators* (,) to form *set
  expressions*, then use ∫, Õ, π to form *set relationship expressions*. All individual *set
  relationship expressions* with implicit *AND* logic form the system *classification schema*. Any
  operation on the sets must not violate the classification schema otherwise the operation is not
  performed.
  list
  This is essentially a set, with the addition of an ordering and an indent level indicator to each
  of the list members.
  link
  A link is any bi-directional connection between two objects and models a directed assertion
  between them, illustrated in Figure 4. Since a link is between two objects, if one of the two
  ends is deleted, the link object is also deleted. To simplify the model, a link is not treated as a
  qualified object for further linking.

Figure 4. A link diagram

version
The model of *version* is illustrated in Figure 5. A versioned object records evolutionary
relationships between objects in a set, capturing reasons for the evolution as well as defining a
default version. Two-level views are supported: viewing from other objects via a pointer, a

490

version set equals its default version; for more details, users can open the version set to see the whole evolutionary graph.

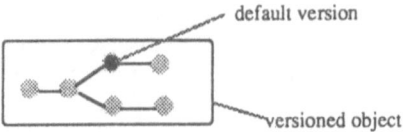

Figure 5. A versioned object

semantic web

A semantic web, illustrated in Figure 6, comprises a set of selected objects together with links between the objects. The existence of these objects and links may be either independent of or dependent on the web.

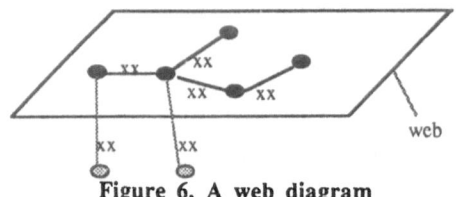

Figure 6. A web diagram

To illustrate the use of these facilities, we use a task as an example to show how it is to be solved in the APIM system. The task is the reading-sourcing-writing process.

To support the reading-sourcing-writing process, suppose that a data model has the following features:

- a group of reference cards, holding data about bibliographic references
- a reference card is related to a group of reading notes,
- links between reference cards or reading notes to record facts, e.g. "A presents a good example of B",
- one or multiple keyword systems to classify both reference cards and reading notes,
- a draft page used to plan aggregation of relevant information and representation logic of the paper.

Figure 7 shows how this would be represented and managed in APIM:

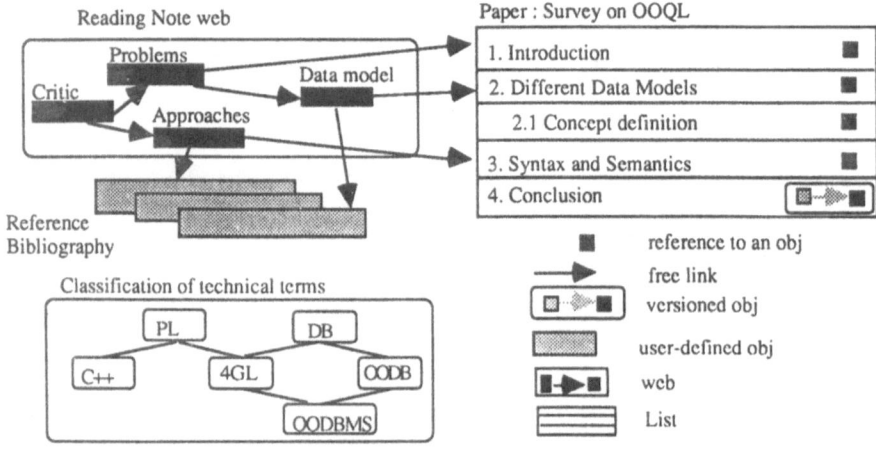

Figure 7. Reading-sourcing-writing: an application example in APIM

With this organisational model, the working process would be:
- in reading & sourcing processes:
  1. create a reference entry, a structured object, for a new reference,
  2. read and make notes,
  3. link reference entries and reading notes as indicated by the relationships between the items,
  4. put reference entries and reading notes under appropriate keyword sets,
  5. graphically present relationships among reading notes using a presentation web
- in drafting & writing processes:
  1. draft a paper framework,
  2. for each section, search references under keyword combinations and select related reading notes,
  3. make version changes of sections or the whole design of the paper framework.

3.4. Structural OO data model

ObjectStore is used as the underlying data system for the APIM data model. A brief comparison of the OO data model in ObjectStore with the relational data model reveals two points that help in understanding data modelling in APIM.

Firstly, in a relational model, entity tables are important as physical sets of data records. In ObjectStore by contrast, an object's physical position is not important and a type is not automatically a collection of all its data objects. To use and retrieve objects, ObjectStore gives objects system-defined *oids* and offers *roots*, that is navigational entry points, *collections* and *attributes* to hold these *oids*. The difference is that in using a record-based model, users must have knowledge about logical positions of the objects, whilst in ObjectStore, objects are located in terms appropriate to applications. Object location is illustrated in Figure 8.

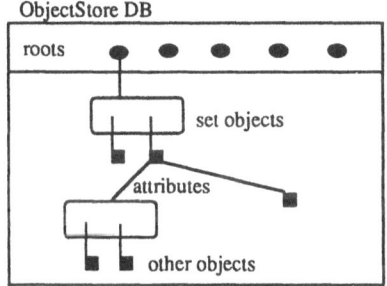

Figure 8. Object location in ObjectStore

From this difference, we can say that in OO data modelling, conceptual modelling does not directly means generation of a database schema, while latter is more dependent on the requirement of applications.

Secondly, a relational model uses relationship tables as collections of associations of data entity ids. For example, a table of a binary n:m relationship (ignoring possible other relationship attributes) has two columns holding the ids of records of two participant entity tables, and is essential in linking records in these tables. In an OO data model, such relationship types are not necessary, since the OO model can embed inter-object links inside objects using reference attributes, as shown in Figure 9.

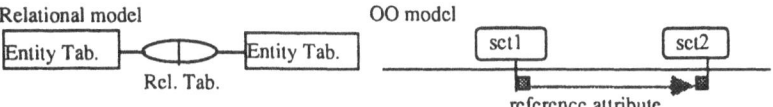

Figure 9. Comparison of ER model and OO model

This makes it possible to model relationships between relationships by static structure modelling. However, in some applications, relationship tables also serve to physically classify entities further. This kind of classification is absent in OO modelling. If a user application requires this kind of classification, we should able to give static designation of virtual or physical collection objects to objects' reference attributes.

In view of this discussion, in APIM, we introduce two stages in data modelling, viz. *type modelling* and *database schema generation*, and define facilities for each.

3.4.1. Type modelling in APIM

Users define types using relationship attributes in an OO diagram corresponding to relationships in an ER diagram. Additional integrity constraints and relationships between relationship attributes can be defined by this structure modelling. Some transformation methods from an ER to an OO model have appeared in the literature, [Hughes 1990, Cattell 1991]. These methods can serve as a guide using the OO model, but they do not refer to additional constraints used at the structure level. In a high-level user interface such as APIM, it is significant that the interface is able to assist users to maintain data integrity by capturing more constraints from users during the static structure modelling stage.

In APIM, a structure definition defines a set of types used in special tasks. Users can employ inheritance both to reduce repetition and to provide an automatic mechanism for classification. As a result, objects can be classified invariably by their *types* instead of their *value*. Types are only types for data generation. They have no meaning as sets as in a conventional database. Because users can define some special application types from a set of supertypes for many unrelated tasks, forcing all instances of a type into a set is not required. In APIM, an object, after generation, is accessed along paths starting from a database entry (root).

Constraints which can be introduced into the schema definition stage of APIM are:
- *Subtype* relationships: specify whether two subtypes of a supertype are able to intersect,
- *Dependent-on* attributes: specify attributes, whose existence is dependent on other attributes. This constraint is simply an AND/OR logical expression,
- *Exclusive* attributes: specify mutually exclusive attributes. This constraint is simply an AND/OR logical expression,
- *Not-null* attributes: specify attributes, which must have a value; for a set attribute, it should have at least one member,
- PART_OF attributes: specify attributes, whose component objects are dependent on the aggregated object,
- *Default* value: specifies a default-value for an attribute.

The Subtype, Dependent-on and Exclusive constraints have higher priority than the Not-null constraint.

Adding Dependent-on and Exclusive constraints on attributes is natural to a structural OO diagram, since relationships between entities have been merged into entities as referenced attributes.

3.4.2 Database schema generation in APIM

Path-dependent access to individual objects is sometimes too restrictive in applications that need to place objects into sets automatically by their types or roles. For this kind of application, a group of sets can be designated to types and attributes in a structure schema to represent respectively "type extension" and "attribute extension" in data modelling. We call the group of sets "set-configuration" for a local database application. A set-configuration can support:
- an automatic mechanism in APIM, which enables the oids of component objects in a structured object to be stored in proper sets in the set-configuration,
- "inclusive dependency" semantics in database applications in APIM. For example, within a set-configuration, there are *Lecturers* and *Departments* sets. If users wish to link a lecturer in the *Lecturer set* to a department, the system first recommends objects in *Departments* set.

The constraints with set-configuration definition are:
- unique attributes in a set: the system checks this attribute to keep its uniqueness in a set. In implementation an index table must be set for the attribute.
- additional default values for attributes in a set.

3.4.3. An example to illustrate static data modelling in APIM

Let us take an example of building a database schema for a document reference database. There are two stages in this process.

Stage 1: Type modelling

Suppose the user wishes to construct his own reference type instead of using what is offered by the system. Using an ER diagram the reference schema could appear as shown in Figure 10:

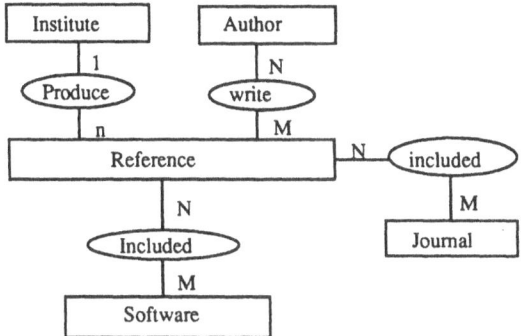

Figure 10.   ER diagram of the static data modelling example

For this diagram, typical constraints are :
- All software manuals should be produced by an Institution,
- No software manual is treated as a published research paper,
- Each published reference must be related to human authors.

At this stage, users might like to have all objects of *Reference* classified, for example, into mutually exclusive *Internal* and *External* sets, and add *Contract* type related to *internal* reference. The transformed OO diagram is shown as Figure 11:

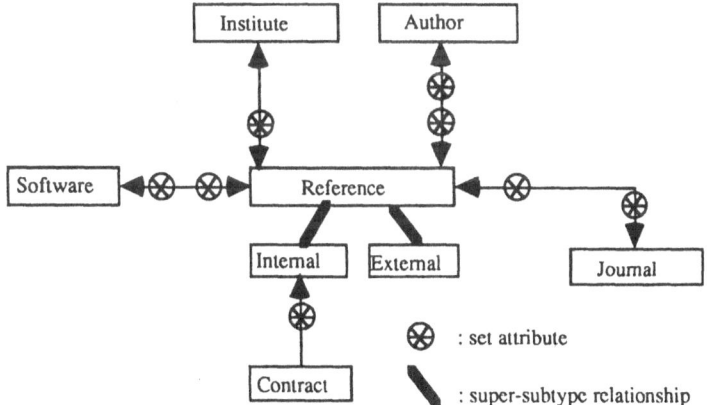

Figure 11.   OO diagram of the static data modelling example

Using Figure 11, the type definitions can be produced. Constraints are written in bold below. An object, under a type, can break constraints, but then the system will always show it as an incomplete object.

494

Type Reference **covered by** Internal, External
[Attributes:
   Authors : set (Author) ;
   Author_Institution : Institution ;
   In_Journal : set (Journal) ; **Dependent_On Authors**   ...
   Software_Document : set (Software) ; ¯**Dependent_On Author_Institution,**
                                          Exclusive In_Journal
...
]
Type Internal **from** Reference, **exclusive** External
[Attributes :
   Funded_by : set (Contract);
]
Type External **from** Reference

Stage 2: Set configuration for the schema

For this schema, users can specify a set configuration, which enables the system to put the relevant ids of objects in the relevant sets. The set-configuration, My_DB, is defined as follows :
   My_DB : {**set** *References* **for type** *Reference*;
            set *Internal_reference* **for type** *Internal*;
            set *Contracts* **for type** *Contract*;
            set *Software_reference* **along with attribute** *Reference.Software_Document*;
       }
The OO diagram of My_DB is shown in Figure 12:

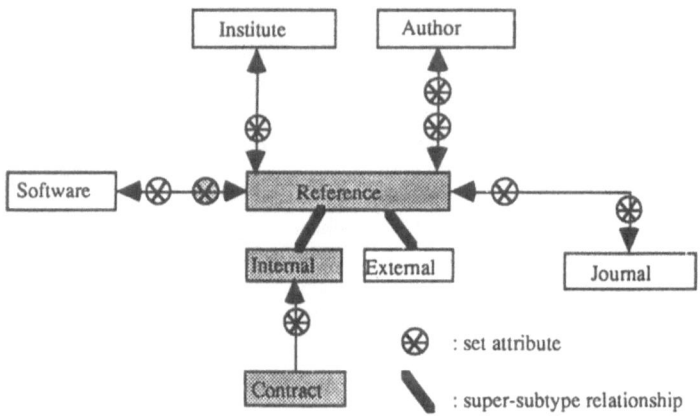

Figure 12. My_DB diagram

So in My_DB, four sets of oids are always maintained, the first three being defined on types, and the last one defined on an attribute. At run-time, when users insert an object into set *Reference*, automatic insertion into the *Internal_reference* and *Software_reference* sets is decided by its type and value. Hence the *Software_reference* set does not have to be generated by queries along attribute paths every time. Contracts linked to internal references are inserted into set *Contract*. Sets in a set-configuration can be used in set-operations. For example, from above My_DB, following results can be obtained :
   External_reference = Reference - Internal_reference

4. Conclusion

In this paper the requirements of information management in an academic environment were set out, and a model (APIM) presented to meet these requirements. The APIM uses both a structural OO data model to model application data types and a dynamic hypertext model with a set of special organisation facilities to build the information space. From a static modelling viewpoint, users can define structural OO application structures to form a global DB schema, and particularly, use set-configuration to maintain local "type extension" and "attribute extension". From the dynamic viewpoint, users can set links between objects with different semantic organisational facilities.
A prototype demonstrator is under development to investigate this comprehensive model's potential and usability in managing personal information space.

References:

[Brown 1991]   Brown, A, *Object-Oriented Databases applications in Software Engineering*, McGRAW-HILL, England, 1991.

[Cattell 1991]   R.G.G. Cattell, *Object-Oriented and Extended Relational Database systems*, Addison-Wesley, Reading, Mass., 1991.

[Conklin 1987]   Conklin, J. "Hypertext: An Introduction and Survey", COMPUTER, September, 1987, 17-41.

[FairChild 1988]   Fairchild, K.M., Poltrock, S.E. & Furnas, G.W."SemNet : three-dimensional graphic representation of large knowledge bases" In R. McAleese, Ed. Hypertext: Theory into Practice, 105-125. Oxford: Intellect Limited

[Girill 1992]   Girill, T.R. and Luk, C.H., "Hierarchical search support for hypertext on-line documentation", Int. J. Man-Machine Studies 1992, **36**, 571-585

[Goldman 1985]   Goldman,K J, Glodman, S A, Kanellakis, P C and Zdonik, S, "ISIS: interface for a semantic information system", Proc. ACM SIGMOD Int. Conf. Manage. Data 1985, 328-342.

[Hughes 1991]   Hughes, J G, *Object-Oriented Database*, Prentice Hall, Hertforshire, England, 1991.

[Kappel 1992]   Kappel, G and Tjoa, A M, "State of art and open issues on graphical user interfaces for object-oriented database systems" Information and Software Technology, Vol **34** No. 11, November 1992, 721-730.

[Ling 1993]   T W Ling and P K Teo,"Toward resolving inadequacies in object-oriented data model"   Information and Software technology vol 35 No 5 May 1993, 267-276.

[Malone 1983]   Malone, T W. "How do people organise their desks ?", ACM Trans Office Info Systems, 1, 99-112, 1983

[Nielsen 1990]   Neilsen, J. "The art of navigating through hypertext" Communications of the ACM, **33**, 296-310, 1990

[OD 1992]   Object Design, "ObjectStore User Guide", 1992

[Oxborrow 1991]   Oxborrow, E, Davy, M, Kemp, Z, Linington, P and Thearle, R, "Object-oriented data management in specialized environments", Information and Software technology, vol **33**, No 1, January/February1991, 22-30.

[Sommerville 1990] Sommerville, Ian, Haddley, Neil, Mariani, John A, Thomson, Ronnie, "The designer's notepad - a hypertext system tailored for design", In *Hypertext state of the art,* Ray Mcaleese & Catherine Green (eds), 260 - 266, Ablex, Norwood, NJ, 1990

Towards Object-Oriented Textual Databases

Jacques Le Maitre

Laboratoire d'Informatique de Marseille
Faculté des Sciences de Luminy - Case 901
163, Av. de Luminy - 13288 Marseille CEDEX 9
E-mail: jlm@lim.univ-mrs.fr

ABSTRACT. *This paper studies the advantages and the drawbacks of object-oriented database systems for the management of textual databases. In order to reduce the drawbacks it proposes to introduce new datatypes and to extend existing object-oriented query languages with operators for traversing and modifying tree structured texts.*

KEY WORDS: Textual Databases, SGML, Object-Oriented Databases, Query Languages.

1. Introduction

The objective of this short paper is twofold: (1) it brings to the fore the advantages but also the drawbacks of existing object-oriented database management systems (OODBMS) for the management of textual databases and (2) it proposes new functionalities to limit these drawbacks.

This work is in progress within the context of the MULTEXT LRE european project whose aim is to develop a set of software tools for analysing, tagging and querying multilingual texts. Databases management systems and their high level query languages seem particularly suited to do these tasks. Due to the complexity of text structures, OODBMS particularly seem attractive because their two first "mandatories features" (Atkinson et al. 90) are to support complex objects and object identity which allows object sharing and object updates.

This paper is organized as follows: section 2 summarizes the main characteristics of textual structures, section 3 is devoted to the object-oriented modelization of a text, section 4 is devoted to text manipulation by means of object-oriented query languages and section 5 concludes.

2. Textual structures

Several visions of a text are possible: an external vision which concerns its appearance on a paper or on a screen, a semantical vision which concerns its meaning, a conceptual vision which concerns its structure, etc. This paper focuses on the conceptual vision.

We can consider two parts in a text structure:

- A *hierarchical structure*: a text is composed of elements (title, chapters, sections, bibliography), hierarchically organized.

- A *network structure*: an element can contain cross-references to some others elements (footnotes, upward or forward elements, bibliographical references).

A particularity of textual structures is that certain elements as, for example, cross-references, annotations or underlining are embedded in text and can occur at any point.

Several specialized languages have been developped for textual structures. Their common characteristic is to modelize texts by the grammar which generates them (Gonnet et al. 87). Usually this grammar is a regular definition (Aho et al. 1986). Among these languages the most popular certainly is SGML (Goldfarb 90) which allows to structure texts in a sophisticated way. Figure 1 gives an example of SGML Document Type Definition (DTD) and a document of this type.

A SGML Document Type Definition	An instance of this type

`<!DOCTYPE ScientificBook [`
`  <!ELEMENT Book`
`    (Title, Author+, Chapter+, Biblio)>`
`  <!ELEMENT Title (#PCDATA)>`
`  <!ELEMENT Author (#PCDATA)>`
`  <!ELEMENT Chapter`
`    (Title, P*, Section+)>`
`  <!ELEMENT Section (Title, P+)>`
`  <!ELEMENT P`
`    (#PCDATA) +Underline +Refbib>`
`  <!ELEMENT Underline (#PCDATA)>`
`  <!ELEMENT Refbib (#EMPTY)>`
`  <!ELEMENT Biblio (Reference+)>`
`  <!ELEMENT Reference (#PCDATA)>`
`  ...`
`  <!ATTLIST Reference id ID #REQUIRED>`
`  <!ATTLIST Refbib`
`    ref IDREF #REQUIRED>`
`]>`
	`<ScientificBook>`
	`  <Book>`
	`    <Title>Bases de données et systèmes relationnels</Title>`
	`    <Author>Claude Delobel</Author>`
	`    <Author>Michel Adiba</Author>`
	`    ...`
	`    <Chapter>`
	`      <Title>Les problèmes d'intégrité</Title>`
	`      <P>`
	`      ... un état <Underline>cohérent</Underline> et ...`
	`      </P>`
	`      ...`
	`      <Section>`
	`        <Title>Notes bibliographiques</Title>`
	`        <P>Le problème de ...</P>`
	`        <P>`
	`          <Refbib ref=Date [1977]> dresse dans son ...`
	`        </P>`
	`      </Section>`
	`    </Chapter>`
	`    ...`
	`    <Biblio>`
	`      ...`
	`      <Reference id=Date [1977]>`
	`      DATE, C. J., [1977], An introduction to ...`
	`      </Reference>`
	`      ...`
	`    </Biblio>`
	`  </Book>`
	`</ScientificBook>`

Figure 1

Let us remark, in this DTD, the element *P* (paragraph) whose content is a text in which elements of type *Underline* or *Refbib* can be embedded. In the following we shall call *mixed elements*, elements as *P* and *mixed texts* their content. Let us remark also the use of attributes *id* and *ref* for describing cross-references between elements.

3. Object-oriented modelization of texts

To illustrate object-oriented modelization of texts, we study how an SGML DTD can be translated in a typical OODBMS : the O_2 system (Deux et al. 90).

In (Le Maitre et al. 94) we have given a procedure to transform a regular definition in an O_2 schema. With the exception of mixed elements, the translation of the hierarchical structure of a text is easy. For example the SGML DTD of Figure 1 can be translated into the O_2 schema of Figure 2.

```
class Book       type tuple(title: Title, authors: list(Author), chapters: list(Chapter), biblio: Biblio)
class Title      type string
class Author     type string
class Chapter    type tuple(title: Title, paragraphs: list(P), sections: list(Chapter))
class Section    type tuple(title: Title, paragraphs: list(P))
class Biblio     type list(Reference)
class Reference  type string
```

Figure 2

Let us observe on this schema that a class is associated with each element type, that compound elements are represented by tuples and that repeated elements are grouped in lists. The main problem raised by this translation is, in most cases, a loss of expressiveness. The reason is that SGML allows various kinds of element composition (ordered or not, alternates, repeated, optionals) whereas most OODBMS offers a unique way to compose objects : the tuple constructor.

Due to object sharing the network structure of a text is represented in a natural way. A reference is an object identifier because, as we said above, each element of a text is an object.

The representation of mixed texts is more problematic. Let e be a text mixed with elements of type $T_1, ..., T_n$. One solution is to declare e as having the type $union(string, T_1, ..., T_n)$. Unfortunately most OODBMS do not offer disjunctive types. These can be simulated by inheritance but this is a complex and expansive solution.

Our opinion is that a specific predefined type is needed, whose objects are strings with embedded elements identifiers. We propose to call "MixedText" such a type. It must be parameterized by types of embedded elements. For example the O_2 schema of Figure 1 can be completed by the following declarations:

class P	**type** MixedText(Reference, Underline)
class Underline	**type** string

This type must be equipped with a comprehensive set of methods, among others: pattern-matching, linguistic tools, etc.

4. Object-oriented manipulation of texts

We consider here high-level manipulation by means of a query language. Many query languages exist today for object-oriented databases. The question is: "are they suitable for text manipulation?".

Schematically we can distinguish between two kinds of manipulation: either *extracting* or *modifying* elements which verify certain conditions. These elements can be specified in two differents ways:

1) By giving the path allowing to reach the elements from the root of the document. For example: "Find titles of chapters containing a section containing a paragraph containing the word 'database'?".

2) By giving the types of the elements (chapter, section, title, etc.) without specifying the path. For example: (Q1) "Find the paragraphs containing the word 'database'?".

The second way is most frequently used because it allows the user not to be aware of all details of text structures which generally are complex (Kilpelaïnen et al. 93). Unfortunately existing object-oriented query languages are not suitable to "access by type" because they do not provide operators which, in a tree, select nodes whose type is given (Le Maitre et al. 94).

Another kind of operation difficult to take in account, is the modification of certain elements in a text. For example: (Q2) "Project all sections of a book on their title" (i. e. suppress all paragraphs of each section). The only possibility is to reconstruct the whole element.

Therefore, new operators are needed. For elaborating these new operators, we can draw our inspiration from (Gonnet et al. 87). Consider, for example, the two following operators:

every T **descendant_from** x

which returns the set of all elements of type T descending from x, and:

replace T y **of** x **by** f(y)

which modify element x by replacing every element y of type T descending from x by $f(y)$. If we extend the O_2Query language (Bancilhon et al. 89) with the above operators, queries Q1 and Q2 are easily expressed. Q1 can be expressed by:

select p **from** p **in every** P **descendant_from** myBook **where** p = "*databases*"

and Q2 by:

replace Section s **of** myBook **by** s.title.

Another interessant technique is the use of path expressions to simplify queries (Van den Bussche et al. 93), (Christophides et al. 94).

5. Conclusion

In this paper we have exhibited the interest and the drawbacks of OODBMS in the field of textual data. To limit these drawbacks we have proposed to extend OODBMS with new functionalities: a larger set of composition constructors, a predefined type to take into account mixed texts and a set of operators for manipulating tree structured texts.

We are now experimenting our propositions. We have defined and implemented a first version of a language, named SgmlQL, to query SGML files. SgmlQL is an extension of O_2Query cited above. We are also developping a prototype of an object-oriented textual DBMS on top of O_2.

References:

(Aho et al. 86):   A. Aho, R. Sethi, J. Ullman, *Compilers*, Addison-Wesley, 1986.

(Atkinson et al. 90):   M. Atkinson et al., "The Object-oriented Database Manifesto", *Proceedings of the First International Conference on Deductive and Object-Oriented Databases*, Kyoto, 1989, pp. 223-240.

(Bancilhon et al. 89):   F. Bancilhon, S. Cluet, C. Delobel, "Query languages for object-oriented database systems : the O_2 proposal", *Proceedings of the International Conference on Database Programming Languages*, Salishan Lodge, Oregon, 1989.

(Christophides et al. 94):   V. Christophides, S. Abiteboul, M. Scholl, "From structured documents to novel query facilities", *Proceedings of ACM SIGMOD*, Minneapolis, 1994.

(Deux et al. 90):   O. Deux et al., "The Story of O_2", *Transactions on Knowledge and Data Engineering*, 2(1), 1990, pp. 91-108.

(Goldfarb 90):   C. F. Goldfarb, *The SGML Handbook*, Oxford University Press, 1990.

(Gonnet et al. 87):   G. Gonnet, F. W. Tompa, "Mind your grammar: a new approach to modelling text", *Proceedings of 13th Conference on Very Large Data Bases*, Brighton, 1987, pp. 339-346.

(Kilpeläinen et al. 93):   P. Kilpeläinen, H. Mannila, "Retrieval from hierarchical texts by partial patterns", *Proceedings of ACM-SIGIR'93*, Pittsburgh 1993.

(Le Maitre et al. 94):   J. Le Maitre, N. Ide, J. Véronis, "Modélisation et interrogation de bases de données lexicales", *Ingénierie des Systèmes d'Information*, Hermès, 2(1), pp. 57-82.

(Van den Bussche et al. 93):   J. Van den Bussche, G. Vossen, "An extension of Path Expressions to Simplify Navigation in Object-Oriented Queries", *Proceedings of the Third International Conference on Deductive and Object-Oriented Databases*, Phoenix, 1993.

Application–Specific Benchmarks for Object Databases: A Multiple–Case Study Approach

Akmal B. Chaudhri[1] and Norman Revell

Department of Business Computing
The City University
Northampton Square, London EC1V 0HB – UK
E–mail: {a.b.chaudhri, n.revell}@city.ac.uk   Fax: +44 71 477 8586

ABSTRACT. *Object database benchmarks have tended to focus on raw performance and the manipulation of in–memory graph structures with small objects, suggestive of engineering applications. However, the increasing use of object databases for multimedia, financial modelling, healthcare applications, etc. requires new performance metrics to be developed. This paper proposes a multiple–case study approach to developing application–specific benchmarks.*

KEY WORDS: *object database performance, database benchmarks, case study research.*

---

1. Introduction

The development of performance metrics for database systems is useful for several reasons.

Firstly, benchmarks provide a "level playing field", and give users some sense of DBMS performance on a standard collection of commands (Stonebraker, 1988). The alternative is to implement a complete application on different DBMSs and compare the results. This is usually too expensive (Anderson et al., 1990).

Secondly, performance is one of the major factors that determine the success and measure of competitiveness of different database products (Inmon, 1989). For object databases, performance is typically more important than functionality (Cattell, 1991), and is probably among the top three selection criteria for users when deciding which object database to purchase (Rotzell & Loomis, 1991).

Finally, for users, standard benchmarks can alleviate the cost of designing and implementing their own benchmarks. For example, it is possible to spend $100,000 implementing a benchmark on several object databases (Barry, 1994a).

It is clear then that good performance metrics are indeed useful for object databases. How these can be developed will be the subject of the remainder of this paper. Section 2 will briefly describe related work. Section 3 discusses issues currently faced by benchmark designers. Section 4 will propose a multiple–case study approach to developing application–specific benchmarks as a possible solution to some of these issues. The main conclusions will be presented in section 5.

2. Related work

OO1 (Cattell & Skeen, 1992), HyperModel (Anderson et al., 1990) and OO7 (Carey et al., 1993) are perhaps the most well–known object database benchmarks, and certainly the most often–cited in object database performance literature. The major emphasis of these benchmarks has been for engineering applications with small objects, manipulation of in–memory graph structures, and very

---

[1] Supported by a research grant from the United Kingdom Engineering & Physical Sciences Research Council.

small database sizes. Table 1 (adapted from Khoshafian et al., 1992) summarises the major features of these three benchmarks.

	OO1	HyperModel	OO7
Database Generation	Synthetic, uniform distribution	Synthetic, uniform distribution	Synthetic, uniform distribution
Industry Acceptance	Wide, ODBMS vendors	No	Too early to tell
Mixed Workload	Yes	Yes	Yes
Number of Users	Single	Single	Single/Multi
Orientation	Engineering	Engineering	Engineering
Performance Metric	Response times of individual queries	Response times of individual queries	Response times of individual queries
Specification	Detailed	Limited	Detailed
System Size	Scalable	Scalable	Scalable
Utility Operations	No	No	No
Benchmark Source Code	Morgan Kaufmann ($)	Very hard to find now	Readily available

Table 1 – Comparison of OO1, HyperModel, OO7.

These three benchmarks, however, have not been based on any performance studies. In some cases, therefore, benchmark design decisions are questionable. For example, the OO7 Benchmark uses an inheritance hierarchy of depth seven, but without appropriate justification. Similarly, the OO7 developers used code to simulate what a query executor *would* do to evaluate a test query. However, you can't test what isn't there (Anderson et al., 1990). Clearly, a better approach is needed to developing performance metrics for object databases. A more thorough discussion and critiques of these benchmarks, together with a survey of other object database benchmarks, can be found in (Chaudhri & Revell, 1994).

3. Issues in object database benchmark design

Major issues currently facing all object database benchmark designers include the following:
- Excluding engineering applications, where measuring multi–user performance may not be relevant, most commercial applications *are* typically multi–user. Although there is a multi–user version of OO7 (6–12 users) under development, this can only test a few scenarios from many possibilities.
- Current benchmarks focus on low–level read/write operations. It is difficult to extrapolate from these to application performance, which may consist of combinations of many such operations.
- Unlike SQL for relational databases, there is no standard interface for object databases at the present time, although the Object Database Management Group (ODMG) is working towards the specification of a database language for object databases.
- Object databases are being increasingly used for many non–engineering applications. This has been confirmed by survey results reported by (Everest & Hanna, 1992). Furthermore, (Wade, 1994) has briefly discussed the use of object databases in corporate computing. These applications have different data manipulation requirements from engineering applications.
- Object database architectures vary considerably, with each having particular strengths and weaknesses. This makes it extremely difficult to develop benchmarks that can fairly represent each architecture.
- There are many possible feature interactions that can influence performance. For example, (Barry, 1994b) has discussed how the interaction of just two features (lock granularity and method execution location) can have a significant impact on performance.

- Logical and physical tuning can also provide additional performance improvements. This is particularly applicable to the development of actual applications, which may be specifically designed around the optimisations provided by a particular product.
- Current benchmarks do not test utility operations. The work by (Lakey, 1989), for example, showed that the time to load and "wire" objects together in an object database can be significant. For some commercial applications, utility operations may be extremely important.

The corollary is that the task of developing a single generic benchmark that can address all these issues is non–trivial. Additionally, treating performance and its measurement generically is wrong, and can lead to incorrect conclusions (Inmon, 1989).

4. A possible solution

One possible solution to these issues is to develop application–specific benchmarks. These involve a great deal of work, but when they become available, would be better than existing benchmarks, and a good thing for the object database industry (Cattell, 1994).

Using a pragmatic approach, application–specific benchmarks are being developed by collaborating with users in industry. Furthermore, a more rigorous and scientific approach to developing object database benchmarks is being used, by applying a variety of recognised research techniques. Such an approach has already been successfully used in the development of an OLTP benchmark for relational databases (the CITY Benchmark).

Considering the alternative research techniques discussed by (Galliers, 1991), the case study approach would seem to be the most appropriate, as the overall aim is to see *how* object databases are being used in reality, and *how* benchmarks can be developed based on these observations. Furthermore, (Benbasat et al., 1987; Yin, 1989) discuss various characteristics of case study research that agree with the aims of this work.

An initial case study is being used for exploratory purposes and to help select the most appropriate research techniques (e.g. analysis of system documentation, data collection, interviews, etc.) for subsequent studies. Furthermore, the use of a number of alternative techniques will provide triangulation and external validity.

Whilst a single–case study would be very useful to confirm or challenge that existing benchmarks such as OO1, HyperModel or OO7 are representative of engineering applications, a multiple–case study approach would be preferable, since one of the aims of this work is to try and develop a more comprehensive theory of object database performance. Additionally, there is the opportunity to use cross–case analysis, which would be very useful for situations where similar applications were found at different organisations.

From the case studies (as with experiments) deriving analytical generalisations will be more appropriate than statistical generalisations, which are more suitable for surveys (Yin, 1989). These generalisations will provide the basis for models, upon which the benchmarks can be based.

When deciding what is to be measured, (Stein, 1992) has suggested a number of factors that provide a useful starting point. Additional factors that are being studied include examining database and application schemas for interesting patterns and common features, such as object sizes, depth of inheritance, types and numbers of methods per class, indexes, clustering, etc. Additionally, transaction behaviour is being analysed, including complete operations at the application level, types of processing (I/O or CPU–bound), and query results.

5. Conclusions

This paper has suggested that performance metrics for object databases are useful, but extremely difficult to design for a variety of reasons. A multiple–case study approach has been discussed as a way to develop performance metrics based on studying actual applications and transaction profiles.

From previous experience using this approach, an OLTP benchmark for relational databases has been successfully developed at City University, conclusively showing the inadequacies of industry–standard benchmarks in this area. Similar results are expected from the work on object databases.

References:

(Anderson et al., 1990): T.L. Anderson, A.J. Berre, M. Mallison, H.H. Porter and B. Schneider. *The HyperModel Benchmark*. In the Proceedings of the 2nd International Conference on Extending Database Technology, pages 317–331, Venice, Italy, 1990.

(Barry, 1994a): D. Barry. *Should you take the plunge?* Object Magazine. 3 (6):24–27, 1994.

(Barry, 1994b): D. Barry. *The importance of understanding ODBMS features*. Object Magazine. 4 (2):76–77, 1994.

(Benbasat et al., 1987): I. Benbasat, D.K. Goldstein and M. Mead. *The Case Research Strategy in Studies of Information Systems*. MIS Quarterly. 11 (3):369–386, 1987.

(Carey et al., 1993): M.J. Carey, D.J. DeWitt and J.F. Naughton. *The OO7 Benchmark*. SIGMOD Record. 22 (2):12–21, 1993.

(Cattell & Skeen, 1992): R.G.G. Cattell and J. Skeen. *Object Operations Benchmark*. ACM Transactions on Database Systems. 17 (1):1–31, 1992.

(Cattell, 1991): R.G.G. Cattell. *Object Data Management: Object–Oriented and Extended Relational Database Systems*, Addison–Wesley, Reading, Massachusetts, 1991.

(Cattell, 1994): R.G.G. Cattell. *Private communication*. 14 March 1994.

(Chaudhri & Revell, 1994): A.B. Chaudhri and N. Revell. *Benchmarking Object Databases: Past, Present & Future*. In the Proceedings of Object–Oriented Databases: Realising their Potential and Interoperability with RDBMS, London, UK, 1994.

(Everest & Hanna, 1992): G.C. Everest and M.S. Hanna. *Survey of Object–Oriented Database Management Systems*. Technical Report, Carlson School of Management, University of Minnesota, 1992.

(Galliers, 1991): R.D. Galliers. *Choosing Appropriate Information Systems Research Approaches: A Revised Taxonomy*. In Information Systems Research: Contemporary Approaches and Emergent Traditions, H.–E. Nissen, H.K. Klein & R. Hirschheim (Eds.), North–Holland, Amsterdam, 1991.

(Inmon, 1989): W.H. Inmon. *Benchmarking the Benchmarks*. Database Programming & Design. 2 (8):54–59, 1989.

(Khoshafian et al., 1992): S. Khoshafian, A. Chan, A. Wong and H.K.T. Wong. *A Guide to Developing Client/Server SQL Applications*, Morgan Kaufmann, San Mateo, California, 1992.

(Lakey, 1989): B. Lakey. *Developing Benchmarks for Comparing Relational and Object–Oriented Database Systems*. MS Thesis, Oregon Graduate Center, Beaverton, Oregon, 31 July 1989.

(Rotzell & Loomis, 1991): K. Rotzell and M.E.S. Loomis. *Benchmarking an ODBMS*. Journal of Object–Oriented Programming. 4 (1):66–72, 1991.

(Stein, 1992): J. Stein. *Evaluating object database management systems*. Journal of Object–Oriented Programming. 5 (6):71–73, 1992.

(Stonebraker, 1988): M. Stonebraker. *Performance and Database Machines*. In Readings in Database Systems, M. Stonebraker (Ed.), Morgan Kaufmann, San Mateo, California, 1988.

(Wade, 1994): A.E. Wade. *ODBMSs...in corporate computing?* Journal of Object–Oriented Programming. 7 (1):6,53, 1994.

(Yin, 1989): R.K. Yin. *Case Study Research: Design and Methods*, Sage Publications, Newbury Park, California, 1989.

Author Index